Signatures

An Anthology for Writers

Lorraine Granieri

Linda Hillman
DePaul University

Mayfield Publishing Company
Mountain View, California
London • Toronto

We dedicate this book to all who have decided to make Signatures *a part of their quest for writing who they are and what they stand for.*

Library of Congress Cataloging-in-Publication Data
Granieri, Lorraine.
Signatures : an anthology for writers / Lorraine Granieri, Linda Hillman.
p. cm.
Includes index.
ISBN 1-55934-812-7
1. College readers. 2. English language—Rhetoric—Problems, exercises, etc. 3. Report writing—Problems, exercises, etc.
I. Hillman, Linda Harbaugh. II. Title.
PE1417.G64 1998
808'.0427—dc21 97-37432
CIP

Manufactured in the United States of America

10 9 8 7 6 5 4 3 2 1

Mayfield Publishing Company
1280 Villa Street
Mountain View, California 94041

Sponsoring editor, Renée Deljon; *production editor,* Carla White Kirschenbaum; *manuscript editor,* Elizabeth von Radics; *text and cover designer,* Linda Robertson; *art manager,* Amy Folden; *photo research,* Brian Pecko; *manufacturing manager,* Randy Hurst. The text was set in 11/12 New Baskerville by Thompson Type and printed on 45# Custom LG by Banta Book Group, Harrisonburg.

To the Instructor

Signatures offers a comprehensive view of the self and identity, observed through intensive reading and writing experiences. The readings in *Signatures* represent various world views, genres, writing styles, and academic disciplines, and are organized to follow a deliberate progression, one that creates a spiraling structure that begins with singularly personal stories, both fiction and nonfiction; moves through selections that discuss the shaping influences of human biology and the unmistakable influences of community and culture; and finally arrives at representations of whole identities, writers' lives and the convictions that inform them, as expressed in "signature" pieces. This book therefore gives student writers the opportunity to *consider* their personal experiences; to *reconsider* those experiences in light of biological, social, and cultural influences; and to *reimagine* themselves throughout this sustained inquiry. At the center of *Signatures'* focus, then, is identity, both personal and public; but the lenses through which students look are both narrative and analytical, texts that are not traditionally thought of as academic as well as those that are.

For everyone moved to tell a story, there is someone poised to hear it. From fairy tale to folk song, autobiography to television talk show, from *People* magazine to the Internet, our need to tell stories seems matched only by our apparent need to hear them. *Signatures* taps into this rich source of energy and inquiry. And it does more: It bridges the gap between personal writing and academic discourse without privileging either. All stories—from memoir to grand epic to master narrative—can be analyzed and better understood through the scholarly efforts of academic writers who are, for instance, scientists, psychologists, sociologists, and historians. At the same time, the scholarly work of such writers is framed, informed, and fortified by narrative knowledge, *stories* of various kinds. Through working with the texts and assignments in *Signatures,* students see the two seemingly different writing strategies as complementary to one another, even *intrinsic* to one another. Students learn that effective writing can draw upon both the *subjective* (personal, narrative knowledge) and the *objective* (scientific, academic knowledge).

THEMATIC GROUPINGS AND ORGANIZATION

Part one, "Self-portraits," invites student writers into stories about gifts, wounds, decisions, and dreams, four life markers that shape self-awareness and personal identity. The selections include essays and stories representing memoir, reflection, journalism, literary nonfiction, and autobiography. Also included here are short stories, poems, speeches, interviews, a song, and an excerpt from Art Spiegelman's narrative cartoon *Maus.* These selections invite student writers to explore their marker experiences and the meanings they have assigned to them.

Part two, "Origins and Influences," comprising chapter five, "Biology," and chapter six, "Community and Culture," moves to less personal topics and a different level of discourse—mostly nonfiction and academic essays. Though peppered with stories, the writing is principally expository and academic. Subsections take up the constituent topics of each larger topic. The subsections within chapter five provide a well-rounded examination of the self's biological influences: "Biology and Identity," "Inborn Traits," and "Nature and Nurture." The subsections within chapter six provide a similarly well-rounded examination of social and cultural influences: "Family Ties," "Learning Communities," "Communities of Faith," "In Public and Private," "Boundaries," and "Popular Culture."

Working in the fields of computer technology, journalism, education, philosophy, religion, the natural and physical sciences, and literature, the writers in "Origins and Influences" use narrative, whether full stories or anecdotes, to strengthen or illustrate their points. Here students will find what writers and academics have said, and are still saying, about how our physical self—our biology—interacts with our environment, community, and culture to influence who we are and what we become. This inquiry helps students to construct a template that, when overlaid with their earlier writing and thoughtfully considered, provides access to richer meaning and an expanded view of their personal identity.

Part three, "Living Out Loud," provides an opportunity to write about the commitments students have made or may make as a result of the work they have been doing. The fifteen writers in chapter seven, "Taking Stands," demonstrate how they live "out loud." One short story and one letter are among this chapter's essays, which include memoir, reflection, and academic theory and argument. The writers in part three—psychologists, futurists, athletes, journalists, physicians, politicians, philosophers, sociologists, prisoners, survivors, and world leaders—have used the material of their lives to create *new* lives and *new* ways of being, and they have been moved to put their lives into writing. Their insights, like those of our students in past *Signatures* courses, represent courageous standpoints as well as commitments to their convictions and their communities. Theirs are quests for dignity, spirituality, and wisdom that demonstrate clarified identities.

FEATURES

Signatures' features are representative of the levels of the work students do.

- **Part, chapter, and section introductions** discuss the particular focus and purpose of each group of readings as well as give readers a context for reading and working with them.

- **Headnotes** establish the rhetorical situation for the readings by providing background on the writer, an introduction to his or her topic, and surrounding circumstances.
- **Three kinds of questions.** *Understanding* questions get at the central points made in the reading and check salient details of comprehension. *Responding* questions ask students to expound informally on the ideas and issues in the reading. It is from working with these Responding questions that students accumulate the material for their short papers and longer writing projects. (Our students have said that the Responding questions are the most generative apparatus in the book because they provide so much "painlessly" written material that, when longer papers are assigned, much of the needed content is already abundantly there to be expanded and shaped.) *Connecting* questions relate issues raised by one writer to similar issues raised by other writers in the book. The Connecting questions foster critical thinking by focusing on ideas approached from within different disciplines or for different reasons.
- **Chapter and part writing options** focus on the larger subjects and themes and ask students to compose longer papers.
- **The signature writing option** is a final writing assignment that suggests ways to synthesize the reading, thinking, discussing, and writing done in the course by creating a summative "integrated" and analytical personal narrative or academic essay.

A NOTE ABOUT THE WRITING OPTIONS

If students write extensively on at least one Responding question for each reading, they will already have a draft for the paper options that follow each thematic grouping of readings. In sum, the explorations prompted by the Responding questions or questions students raise on these themes themselves provide ample material for students to mine for the more formal writing options, which appear at the end of each larger thematic section and give students the opportunity to develop (essentially through revision) one or more of their responses to the readings.

In order to further encourage revision, we have included part writing options to give students the opportunity to choose from among their first papers several to revise and present as a body, in some cases a portfolio, of their work. The signature writing option is a summative essay of evaluation and synthesis, which provides at least provisional closure by documenting student learning over the duration of the term, their signature stories.

ANCILLARY MATERIALS

The *Resources for Teaching to Accompany Signatures* that we wrote to accompany the text provides a discussion of various ways in which the text can be used as well as sample syllabi for both quarter- and semester-length terms. Discussions of each reading are included, along with suggested prereading questions and warm up activities for helping students to begin thinking and writing about the topic and themes at hand. Journal and portfolio options are also provided.

ACKNOWLEDGMENTS

Gifts, wounds, decisions, and dreams, what we call the marker experiences of identity in *Signatures: An Anthology for Writers,* have also been part of the making of this book. We would like to acknowledge the gifts, those contributions from individuals in our communities of family and friends, that have helped bring this book into print. Our thanks and appreciation extend to Eugene Callahan, Nancy Denig, Doug Godfrey, Karen Goldbaum, Evelyn Granieri, M.D., Pauline Harbaugh, Harry Harbaugh, John Hillman, Mark Hillman, Gerald Migely, Barbara Ransby, Marsha Slater, and Gregory Turner. And thanks also to our reviewers: Marvin Diogenes, University of Arizona; Shirley Rose, Purdue University; Virginia Parsons, Northeastern University; Kay Halasek, The Ohio State University; and Regina R. Flynn, Salem State College.

Commenting on the editorial talent in publishing houses in his review of a recent novel, Luc Sante, one of the authors represented in *Signatures,* noted that "A lot of books get shunted into print before the mortar is dry, or without anyone to figure out the apportionment of clay and straw in their makeup." To this we say Mr. Sante should make the acquaintance of the Mayfield Publishing Company. *Signatures* has benefited greatly from the vision, verve, and good-humored prodding of Renée Deljon and Tom Broadbent, our editors; and from the care of Carla White Kirschenbaum, our production editor; Elizabeth von Radics, our copy editor; Jo-Anne Naples, our permissions researcher; Susan Shook, supplements editor; and all the members of the Mayfield staff who, in our judgment, made these pages and the cover that heralds them into a piece of work of the right proportions.

Special thanks to DePaul University for awarding us a University Research Council Competitive Grant to underwrite partially the permissions costs associated with *Signatures.*

To the Student: Essential Reading Before You Begin

You may remember a time when you practiced writing your name—your signature—looping the capital letters over and over to achieve just the right angle, trying to make them as distinctive an expression of your identity as possible. Literally, your signature is a tangible sign of who you are, your unique personal stamp. This book, *Signatures: An Anthology for Writers,* provides the means to explore your "signature," your identity in all of its complexity, and to write your way through the exploration.

Central to the approach of *Signatures* is our view that four defining experiences (we call them *marker* experiences) contribute most decisively to one's identity. These experiences are the gifts we give and receive, the wounds we suffer, the decisions we make, and the dreams we have while asleep and awake. Other life experiences may prove to be seminal, or formative, influences, but we believe that these four experiences provide essential insight into how we see the world and how the world sees us.

We also believe that, to gain a more informed sense of our self and our identity, we must consider two other, major influences that contribute to how we think, feel, and act in response to these marker experiences: (1) our biology, which includes our genetic inheritance, and (2) the communities and cultures in which we live. Self revelation is very popular these days, as anyone who has watched TV talk shows can attest, so it may be tempting to consider *Signatures* an invitation to expose intimate details of your life. But this book is not such an invitation. In the broadest sense, of course, all of the readings in *Signatures* are personally revealing, and although your writing may include personal disclosures, we want to emphasize at the outset that the list of goals for this book does not include serving a therapeutic function in your life. Nor does this book seek to provide a platform for identity or victim politics; that is, it does not encourage political jockeying. It does, though, encourage you to explore fully your sense of self and personal identity through writing, and the benefits of that exploration are many and varied.

ABOUT THE SELF AND IDENTITY

> *The self is not a thing; it is a complex process of continuing interpretive activity . . . including thinking, planning, evaluating, choosing . . . and the resultant accruing structure of self-conception.*
>
> —Chad Gordon, "Self-conceptions: Configurations of Content"

What exactly do we mean by *self* and *identity?* In examining the definitions of the self that have accumulated over the years, it is clear that no single definition has gained general acceptance. The concept of self varies according to culture, historical period, and point of view. In some non-Western cultures, the self is often seen as an unstable element. In *What the Buddha Taught,* Walpola Sri Rahula writes, "What we call a being or an individual or an I is only a combination of . . . five aggregates . . . [which] are all impermanent, all constantly changing . . . the idea of the self is a false idea."

Even the modern Western understanding of the self as the inner core of one's identity dates back only a few centuries, when people began to attach importance to themselves as individuals (as opposed to members of a group—a clan or a family) in ways that were generally unknown previously. Since then, psychologists have described the self in a number of ways. For instance, Sigmund Freud located the self in the *ego,* the personally developed sense of one's own uniqueness; Carl Jung, who as a boy recognized several distinct ways of being within himself, distinguished between the *ego,* or the conscious mind, and the *self,* the true center of personality, which consists of both conscious and unconscious aspects of the mind. American psychologist Gordon Allport coined the term *proprium* to describe the self as the "me" that is part of all subjective experience, and Chad Gordon shows the self to be both process and product, a blend of conscious activities (e.g., thinking and evaluating) and the "I" that results from these activities.

Recent research indicates that a sense of self begins before birth and suggests that babies see themselves as part of what is called a "relational field." According to these findings, babies as young as two months old recognize themselves as dependent on, yet distinct from, their caregivers and try to manipulate this relationship by their behavior, thus showing an early form of self-awareness. Regardless of when this sense of being a particular individual—a self, set apart from other people—begins to develop, we know that it forms the basis for our personal identity. As psychologist Gardner Murphy tells us in his book *Personality: A Biosocial Approach,* "Whatever the self is, it becomes a center, an anchorage point, a standard of comparison, an ultimate real. Inevitably, it takes its place as a supreme value." This center of ourselves—our identity—has practical meaning for us. Developmental psychologist Erik Erikson, whose theory of human personality appears in excerpted form in chapter seven, tells us that the perception of our self confers a sense of uniqueness and continuity over time, that defining who we are is the main task of young people between the ages of twelve and eighteen, and that what results becomes a working definition of ourselves, a conception that we are free to alter during adult life.

If our existence is a gift from our parents, our self is largely what we make of this gift. It is, to use Gordon's term, an interpretive activity. At the simplest level, we decide who (we say) we are and how we will act, and our identity can be found in the many possible answers to the question *Who Am I?* If you have ever tried to answer this question, you know how many responses it can trigger. Here for instance are three categories of self-identifying statements that relate to the kinds of interpretations you will find in *Signatures*. We might identify ourselves in terms of our physical attributes ("I am right handed"; "I am twenty years old") or in terms of our social position ("I am a college student"; "I am a graphic designer") or reflectively, in terms of our general disposition or style of behavior ("I am open-minded"; "I am hot-tempered"). In a 1996 poll conducted by the *New York Times*, 1,135 adults were asked to answer the question "Who are you?" in one word. The response given most often (by 10 percent) fits one of these categories; it was "American." Defining ourselves may seem an unreliable or even suspect approach, similar to using a microscope to examine a microscope, but we are the best sources of information about who we are, and language is perhaps the only tool we have at our disposal to interpret ourselves.

Although it may seem a contradiction, we cannot become an individual without relationships with other people. To fully develop our vocabulary for saying who we are, we need contact—encounters with others—which we find in our social interaction within our families and communities. Our social experiences provide us with positions or roles in society, and it is in enacting these roles that we learn how to make our way in the world: how to compete and cooperate, how to be dependent and independent, how to love and be loved. In our search for significant personal selfhood, we take others as models, heroes or heroines, ideals. Again, we interpret their behaviors in terms of their acceptability to us (evaluating), and we make some of them part of our own personal identity (choosing). The readings in *Signatures* make available a range of interpretations for you to evaluate, choose, and then use to create a vocabulary to express your own identity.

WRITING AND THE SELF

> *Of all the subjects available to you as a writer, the one you know best is yourself, your past and present, your thoughts and your emotions, yet it is the subject you try hardest to avoid.*
>
> —William Zinsser, *On Writing Well*

Writing and the development of the self seem to go together: Both are interpretive activities; both can evolve over time; and both are benchmarks of our identity. Yet, until recently, many writers have been reluctant to write about the self. Perhaps this kind of writing was seen as vain, or even useless. Writing, however, as a process of interpretive activity, is a tremendous tool for self-discovery and refining ideas, and so, increasingly, we write to give voice to our experiences, and to discover what we think and feel about these experiences. Simply put, writing reliably allows us to find out both what we know and what we don't know. "The physical act of writing is a powerful search mechanism," as William Zinsser says.

Writing about the self and identity, specifically, takes many forms. Biography and autobiography (*auto* = self; *bio* = life; *graphy* = written) might be the forms with which you're most familiar. Biographies are life stories written by someone other than the subject of the book; autobiographies are life stories written by the person whose book it is. If the concept of the self as we know it today is a relatively recent construction, so too are these kinds of writing about the self.

Historians of the Western tradition tell us that the ability to write was fairly common in the late Middle Ages (fourteenth and fifteenth centuries), but that it was mostly practiced in large cities rather than in rural areas and was a privilege of a small minority. Autobiographies—relatively rare at that time—emerged gradually from other forms of writing. Throughout the ages, writers had developed these other forms of personal writing, such as the personal essay or personal narrative, journal or diary writing, and memoir, a form of personal writing that is, as we've said, currently very popular. Memoir recalls unusually vivid or intense portions of a life and conveys ideas larger than the events described. William Zinsser makes a useful distinction when he says that autobiography chronicles a life whereas memoir assumes the life but ignores most of it. Memoir, that is, records segments of a life in much the same way that each of the fragments of a broken mirror reflects only a portion of the viewer.

All these forms of personal writing appear in *Signatures.* For example, the sixteenth-century writer Michel de Montaigne, who wrote the first known personal essay, is represented in "On the Art of Conversation"; contemporary writers Gabriella De Ferrari in "Our Peruvian Friend" and M. F. K. Fisher in "The Broken Chain" paint vivid pictures of their childhoods in their memoirs; and Ina Russell in "Love and Affection, Damn It!" plumbed her uncle Jeb's fifty-volume diary to extract a detailed account of his early life in Washington, D.C.

NARRATIVE AND ACADEMIC WRITING

Narrative (sometimes called *personal* or *expressive*) and *academic* writing are the two general kinds of writing represented in *Signatures.* Narrative (from the Latin *narrare* to tell) may take the form of true stories—stories about real events—or invented stories, known generally as fiction. Specifically, narrative provides rich opportunities for what teachers of writing call *languaging,* the shifting into words of what is essentially a mixture of feeling, perception, image, and thought. Narrative writing typically contains description, chronology, exposition, and even argument, but it is this attention to translating emotion as well as thought that has been considered a hallmark of narrative writing.

Academic writing, not narrative, is generally thought of as the kind of writing most appropriate for college and university students. Typically, writing is called "academic" if it follows an accepted interpretive scheme: It defines its terms (in much the same way that we define the self above); and it acknowledges the ideas of others, states a position with respect to these ideas, provides reason or evidence for the position, and uses a special vocabulary that is common among members of its intended audience. In general, academic writing contains fewer disclosures of a personal nature than narrative (story-based) writing.

Most academic writing is written for a specialized audience—other academics—but sometimes an academic book appears in the popular press, for example, Lewis Thomas's *The Lives of a Cell,* Sherwin Nuland's *How We Die,* and Mary Pipher's *Reviving Ophelia.* In essence, what you'll see, especially as you read such selections as Richard Dawkins's "Ancestors and the Digital River," which is taken from *River out of Eden,* and Maggie Scarf's "The Beavers Scale of Family Health and Competence," from *Intimate Worlds: Life inside the Family,* is writing that is as narratively personal as it is academically convincing. These and other elements of analytical writing are also intrinsic to personal writing. We can benefit from acknolwedging that informing, explaining, persuading, and other kinds of exposition all depend in part on narrative forms of writing. Likewise, we can benefit from acknowledging that any act of composition requires selecting and ordering material—two of the elements of analytical thinking.

You will notice that in part one of *Signatures,* "Self-portraits," the selections are primarily personal narratives, and that in part two, "Origins and Influences," the selections are primarily academic. We anticipate that you will see the overlap and the commonalities between these two kinds of writing, that you'll see the analytical elements inherent in narrative and the narrative elements inherent in traditional academic writing. In part three, "Living Out Loud ," you'll experience a blend of both kinds, and you yourself will be engaged in this kind of blended writing. The readings in *Signatures* provide means for increasing your narrative and academic knowledge and for sharpening your ability to express that knowledge in writing.

A NOTE ABOUT GOOD STORIES

We know when we are hearing a good story. "I could listen to her for hours" or "He's such a great storyteller" are comments that convey our admiration for those people who hold our attention from the beginning to the end of their tales. Reading a good story produces the same effect; we know the difference between when we're just moving our eyes down the page and when we are riveted. We know it is the writer's craft that is at work, capturing our attention from beginning to end, but what *is* the writer's craft?

Two elements are essential to the writer's craft and must be present in a good story: a narrative shape and an organizing idea. By *narrative shape* we mean a clear sequence of events—the skeleton or structure of the story. To identify the sequence of events, we need only make a time line of what happens first, second, third, and so on. On the other hand, the *organizing idea* of a story, its theme, is its point, the reason the story is being told. To identify the organizing idea, we can ask what view of life the story portrays. What values are in evidence? What insights into human character or the human condition does it reveal? What idea does the story illustrate? What, in other words, "narrative knowledge" does it convey?

Some writers begin to write knowing the answers they want to provide—before they shape their stories in words; others write in order to find answers in the events they identify as worth exploring. Whichever the case, the writer's success at weaving the organizing idea into the time line of its narrative shape determines whether it's a good story. For example, in "The Peach-Seed Monkey," the first selection in chapter one, "Gifts," Sam Keen tells the story of his father's promise to make Keen a small monkey from a peach seed. The story occurs over a long period of time, which Keen fits into two pages to give the story its condensed narrative shape; however, the organizing idea—the narrative knowledge—is what Keen explores, because his father has forgotten his promise. When Keen's father finally presents him with the monkey, it and his father's life become a symbol of something far greater than the little carving that is the story's namesake.

A narrative writer's craft is not, however, limited to chronology and an idea. It also relies upon evoking strong and memorable responses in the reader. The following are some elements of a good story that we think are most noteable here:

- A good story evokes feelings—excitement, tenderness, anger, fascination, envy—is genuinely involving and makes us feel that listening to or reading the story is worthwhile. We might even want to read it again.
- A good story challenges our understanding. It is familiar enough so we can relate to it, but just different enough from our experience that we have to stretch ourselves to ponder its insights. It gives us another window to our own experience.
- A good story expands our interpretation of events and experiences. It prompts us to ask questions, to make comparisons, to create new meanings. It evokes other, similar stories of our own.
- A good story both offers and triggers insights that can inform or reinform our judgments and suggest ways to change old behaviors. A good story can cause us to act or to avoid acting.
- A good story might just illuminate one of life's small events, which without the telling would be lost: the chance encounter, the overheard conversation, the very small gift, the last piece of cake.

THE IMPORTANCE OF REVISION

Just as reseeing your life and discovering new insights will be a natural outcome of working with *Signatures,* so too will revising your writing. Revision is always an important part of writing, but *Signatures* requires an even greater commitment to revision, particularly in light of new self-discoveries. Revising your writing is essentially the act of representing new information, new insights—or your reseeing *how* to tell your story, and it certainly acknowledges that writing is usually—for everyone—hard work. As you know, even the most accomplished writers revise their writing.

We strongly believe that when we say we "know ourselves," what we mean is that we have a description of ourselves at a particular time that we feel is valid. This description "fits me," some say. But as we grow older, explore new possibilities for living, try on new ways of being in the world, these descriptions change because we change. Then we claim a new description that "fits." Essentially, we revise our lives as we live them. Living our lives and revising our life writing are similar.

THE ORGANIZATION OF *SIGNATURES*

Signatures is divided into three parts that follow a deliberate progression: part one, "Self-portraits"; part two, "Origins and Influences"; and part three, "Living Out Loud." Essentially, the readings in *Signatures* progress from personal stories to public statements—gestures of living out loud. This progression from private to public is natural and lends itself to revision, of both ourselves and our writing.

Part One: Self-portraits

Part one comprises four chapters and covers four marker experiences: "Gifts" (chapter one), "Wounds" (chapter two), "Decisions" (chapter three), and "Dreams" (chapter four). The readings in these chapters include narrative essays (memoir, reflection, journalism, literary nonfiction, and autobiography). Also here are short stories, poems, speeches, interviews, a song, and an excerpt from Art Spiegelman's narrative cartoon *Maus*. Despite representing numerous genres, these readings essentially tell stories, and the stories demonstrate important insights, possibilities, and meaning-making.

Part Two: Origins and Influences

Part two pairs two large chapters: "Biology" (chapter five) and "Community and Culture" (chapter six). Thematic subsections take up the constituent topics of each larger topic. The thematic sections within chapter five—"Biology and Identity," "Inborn Traits," and "Nature and Nurture"—provide a well-rounded examination of the self's genetic and biological influences. The sections within chapter six—"Family Ties," "Learning Communities," "Communities of Faith," "In Public and Private," "Boundaries," and "Popular Culture"—provide a similarly well-rounded examination of social and cultural influences.

The selections in part two are mostly expository and academic. Among the fields represented here are literature, computer technology, journalism, education, philosophy, religion, and a variety of the natural, physical, and social sciences. Again, as you will see, narrative has its place in these selections, as it strengthens and illustrates the academic discussions.

Part Three: Living Out Loud

Part three, "Living Out Loud," is made up of chapter seven, "Taking Stands." Here you'll find fifteen selections from various genres that share a common feature: writers living lives of profound convictions and commitment based on their having embraced all the possibilities life has to offer. They have discovered, no doubt through many acts of revision, a standpoint, a firm understanding of what they believe, and they express these ideas in writing.

The selections in chapter seven are by psychologists, futurists, athletes, journalists, physicians, philosophers, sociologists, world leaders, and political prisoners. You will find one short story and one letter among the thirteen essays, which include memoir, reflection, and academic theory and argument. These selections provide powerful views of whole lives—clarified identities, legible signatures—and how these lives are made satisfying and meaningful.

IN ADDITION TO THE READINGS

Signatures includes much more than readings alone. So that you can make the most of this book's resources, we want to introduce you to these other elements:

- **Part, chapter, and section introductions.** These introductions discuss the purpose of the readings in each grouping as well as give you a context for reading and responding to them.
- **Headnotes for each reading.** The headnotes, or introductory remarks, that appear before the readings provide biographical information about the authors as well as other kinds of information that can help you understand the topics and themes explored in the reading.
- **Questions.** Three kinds of questions follow each reading selection: *Understanding* questions help you identify a reading's central points and primary details; *Responding* questions ask you to explore the issues, themes, or ideas of a reading and relate them to your own lives; and *Connecting* questions challenge you further in that they ask you to work with the readings in combination by comparing, contrasting, and synthesizing their purposes and insights.
- **Chapter and part writing options.** Focusing on the larger subjects and themes, these writing options lend themselves to your composing longer papers.
- **Your signature writing option.** This final writing assignment suggests ways to synthesize the reading, thinking, discussing, and writing that you've done by creating your own integrated, summative analytical personal narrative or academic essay.

Brief Contents

Contents

Alternative Table of Contents by Rhetorical Purposes

Writing to Explore Personal Experience

Writing to Inform or Explain

Writing to Argue a Position

Writing Fiction

Writing Poetry

Alternative Table of Contents by Rhetorical Mode

Narration

Description

Exemplification

Comparison and Contrast

Cause and Effect

Classification and Division

Definition

Argument and Persuasion

Part One

Self-portraits

"I venture to say that writing the story of our lives—in whatever fashion that may be, from creating photo albums to sewing quilts to running a restaurant to writing music or stories—is a central human imperative."

—Emily Benedik

"Self-portraits" is the first of three parts that make up *Signatures: An Anthology for Writers.* It contains thirty-eight readings by diverse writers, all of whom address issues of identity through stories, poems, memoir, articles, and essays. In the end what they present are their own closely observed and engaging narrative self-portraits.

A self-portrait, defined as an original painting, photograph, or likeness of oneself, is a signature, a declaration, a marking that represents who and what we believe ourselves to be. But how do we come to that conclusion? If you were to create—paint, photograph, or write—a self-portrait, what would it look like? Recall some memorable photographs of yourself as a baby and at ages five, nine, thirteen, and seventeen, or as close to these years as possible. What did you look like? Where were you? What were you wearing? Who, if anyone, was photographed with you? Can you recall what you were thinking, feeling, or doing at the time the later pictures were taken? Astonishing, isn't it, to realize that in spite of the differences in the photos over time, you are the same person in each picture.

But *are* you the same person? Can you recall any clues in the photos that address this question? Any indications that you can use to claim or to document your emerging identity? Any material with which to create a self-portrait?

From your series of photographs, you know that you change continuously throughout life. Your thoughts and moods change, your expressions, gestures, and physical features. Even your signature changes. And this mutable life is the problem of portraiture. If the likeness of a human being consists of an infinite number of different images, which of these should be the representative one? Philippe Halsman, one of the most famous portrait photographers of all time, wrote: "For me, the answer has always been, the image which reveals most completely both the exterior and the interior of the subject . . . A true portrait should, today and a hundred years from today, be the testimony of how this person looked and what kind of human being he was" (Halsman 18). Halsman's portraits have done this so well that in 1969 he had produced a record of ninety-nine *Life* magazine covers—and he produced many more after that.

Halsman's insight was about making portraits of others, but the work of the *self*-portrait—creating oneself for the public—is perhaps the most challenging portrait of all. Though it presents the same crucial problem as the portrait, the onus of choice is on the subject—the one creating the portrait of himself or herself. For a photographer or painter, a self-portrait evokes the mind's eye of the self; but for a writer, a self-portrait must be put into words. Captured on paper, this narrative self-portrait invites the writer's challenge: How do I see myself? Which part of my character do I wish to divulge? And which do I wish to play down? Do I concentrate on my physical self, my personality, my achievements? To provide a map for this exploration, we have selected readings on four major themes that are rich resources to mine for writing narrative portraits of your own.

Four kinds of experiences offer their signatures to our lives: our gifts, our wounds, our decisions, and our dreams. Though our gifts, wounds, decisions, and dreams—however we define them—can leave a mark on our lives, it is we, the writers, who must decide what to make of them. The writers represented in "Self-portraits" have made those decisions and present them in their works. In the spirit of this textbook, we view the readings as these writers' self-portraits, or signatures.

Chapter one, "Gifts," explores gifts given, gifts received, gifts unwanted, gifts wished for and never received, and gifts as life-altering markers. The writers in chapter two, "Wounds," unfold physical and spiritual wounds incurred in everyday life, some occurring over time, some by surprise. How they use these wounds to create a self-portrait and address life's big questions is remarkable. The writers in chapter three, "Decisions," examine their most pivotal choices, the consequences of which altered their identities. And, finally, chapter four, "Dreams," includes an abundance of writers' dreams, whether daydreams, sleep-dreams, or plan-dreams for the future, that they lived every day to fulfill.

The greatest literature that human beings have produced over time—both oral and written—has been inspired by these four themes. This is a chance for you to transform "this loose drifting material of life" (as writer Virginia Woolf called our everyday experiences) and contribute your resulting stories in this uniquely human tradition. What you produce will chronicle your life in several self-portrait narratives that you may look back on as a testimony and celebration of who you were at one point in the evolution of your signature.

Work Cited

Halsman, Yvonne, et al., eds. *Portraits Halsman*. New York: McGraw-Hill, 1983.

1

Gifts

"You can do three things with a gift," a friend once told us: "Accept it and use it, reject it, or keep it until you need it." This opening section of readings is our gift to you, our readers, and, appropriately, is a selection of stories about gifts. What you choose to do with it will depend on *your* gifts and how you use them.

We think of the word *gift* in two ways: as anything freely brought to us or done for us by another, and as an endowment that we receive at birth and which we may develop throughout our lives. The readings in this section reflect these two interpretations.

The first kind of gift—sometimes called a present—is the product of a deliberate act, a conscious offering, a transaction between two or more people. But sometimes this gift is in the form of a person, and a literary work is constructed about the gift that person is. The second kind of gift—sometimes known as a talent, trait, or inborn aptitude—is, for the most part, the result of our heredity, something with which nature has endowed us and that makes us unique.

The American humorist Garrison Keillor remarked once that "life is a series of gifts; we live by gifts and not by what we earn." If Keillor is right—

that we live by our gifts—written works about gifts should prove it; moreover, the works should give us openings to recognize, acknowledge, and share our own memories of gifts that have marked our lives. We believe that these selections do that. Once read or told through the gift of language, stories enliven our reading and our memories in the myriad ways they are conceived in the minds of the tellers. Whether given or received, gifts and what we make of them are extensions of ourselves and, in their purest form, expressions of love or caring that guide and even transform our lives.

Because of this personal association among the giver, the gift, and the receiver, every gift comes wrapped in stories—at least two of them: the giver's story and the receiver's story. Often, these two stories differ greatly.

For the giver, there is always a reason, a *motive,* for giving. Some gifts are meant to celebrate a milestone in life (a birth, a graduation, a personal-best endeavor); others to repay a kindness; still others to bring about a reconciliation (think of the traditional bouquet of flowers given after an argument). Some gifts are required by custom; others are expected because of the season. Some gifts are exchanged; others are freely given with no expectation of return. Gift giving has even been assigned a kind of moral calculus summed up in the phrase *It's better to give than to receive.*

As interesting as the givers' motives, perhaps, are the stories that the receivers of gifts tell. What the receiver perceives to be the motive for the gift and what the giver intends the gift to mean may be quite different. If it were possible for ten people to receive the same gift from the same person in the same way at the same time, we would hear ten different stories of the experience, none truer than the next; yet in their telling, they create a reality. To be true to the proposition that nothing really happens unless we tell about it, a story about a gift adds dimension to it, making it real for both the teller and the audience. That ten different people have ten different stories about the same gift celebrates our own ways of seeing and knowing our lives. Gifts, as we think you will see, make for very interesting stories.

In the collection of readings that follows, Sam Keen's "The Peach-Seed Monkey" and O. Henry's "The Gift of the Magi" inquire into the givers' motives and the unintended consequences of gifts. Pete Hamill connects ordinary objects in a toolbox—a gift from his father—to male gender roles. Relationships with family and friends can be gifts that reveal our strengths and our needs, as Elie Wiesel and Gabriella De Ferrari explore in their works. Sandra Cisneros reflects on the value of her name, an unsolicited gift given with her birth.

Gifts are gifts because we consider them so. Philip K. Dick explores this notion in a selection from *Do Androids Dream of Electric Sheep?,* the book upon which the film *Blade Runner* is based. Finally, writer Rachel Carson creates the natural world for us in the form of a gift of wonder. No matter the gift being explored, the meaning is made by the teller.

In an article in *The New Yorker* on the revival of storytelling, essayist Bill Buford wrote that "we need stories. They are a fundamental unit of knowledge, the foundation of memory, essential to the way we make sense of our lives: the beginning, middle, and end of our personal and collective trajectories." We think you will find that the readings in this chapter are full of this "making sense of our lives" quality.

We have a motive for giving you the gift of these readings: to prompt you to savor them and to inquire about them. By this we mean to live through the stories and ask questions about them rather than to find the "answer" to them and in them. You are looking for the "truth" in your gifts, but we encourage you to wonder in the process and recognize that you cannot *find* the truth—you can only create it for yourself.

The questions following each reading will guide your understanding and direct you in uncovering your own gift stories; and in those stories, you may prove Keillor's point that your life—and others'—is a series of gifts.

As you read the following selections, you may remember gifts you have given and those you never gave; you may recall gifts given to you and those never received. Each situation has meaning and motive. Your own gift stories can tell you something about how you came to be who you are, and about the person you are striving to become. Scientist Jacob Bronowski has said that we ascend by realizing the fullness of our own gifts—our talents and faculties—and what we create along the way are monuments to our understanding of nature and of ourselves. We hope you will rise to the occasion to create some monuments in writing. Your writing about these selections and about your own gifts will be your gift to yourself. As a receiver of this gift, you are on the threshold of a story.

The Peach-Seed Monkey

Sam Keen

"To this day I judge men by the standard my father set," writes Sam Keen in his book on creating a more positive future for men, *Fire in the Belly.* So abundant were his father's gifts that Keen constantly acknowledges J. Alvin Keen (1899–1964) in his writing. What is most interesting to imagine is whether his father thought he was actually *giving* these gifts that Keen so often draws on to make his points. Whether or not Keen senior was intentional about his gift giving, we think that it is, in the end, the writer or the teller who makes gestures into gifts. Keen writes that his father lived with a growing ability to be grateful for the gift of life and that in this ambience, he (Sam) learned to take the time to wonder. "The Peach-Seed Monkey" is testimony to that gift and to another which you will come to know as equally memorable.

Sam Keen holds an M.A. from Harvard Divinity School and a Ph.D. from Princeton University. He has been featured on a Bill Moyers PBS interview, and his most recent book, *Faces of the Enemy,* was also a PBS documentary that was nominated for an Emmy Award. "The Peach-Seed Monkey" is a story of a father's lasting effect on his son—one of the most powerful relationships there is.

Once upon a time when there were still Indians, Gypsies, bears, and bad men in the woods of Tennessee where I played and, more important still, there was no death, a promise was made to me. One endless summer afternoon my father sat in the eternal shade of a peach tree, carving on a seed he had picked up. With increasing excitement and covetousness I watched while, using a skill common to all omnipotent creators, he fashioned a small monkey out of the seed. All of my vagrant wishes and desires disciplined themselves and came to focus on that peach-seed monkey. If only I could have it, I would possess a treasure which could not be matched in the whole cosmopolitan town of Maryville! What status, what identity, I would achieve by owning such a curio! Finally I marshaled my nerve and asked if I might have the monkey when it was finished (on the sixth day of creation). My father replied, "This one is for your mother, but I will carve you one someday." 1

Days passed, and then weeks and, finally, years, and the someday on which I was to receive the monkey did not arrive. In truth, I forgot all about the peach-seed monkey. Life in the ambience of my father was exciting, secure, and colorful. He did all of those things for his children a father can do, not the least of which was merely delighting in their existence. One of the lasting tokens I retained of the measure of his dignity and courage was the manner in which, with emphysema sapping his energy and eroding his future, he continued to wonder, to struggle, and to grow.

In the pure air and dry heat of an Arizona afternoon on the summer before the death of God, my father and I sat under a juniper tree. I listened as he wrestled with the task of taking the measure of his success and failure in life. There came a moment of silence that cried out for testimony. Suddenly I remembered the peach-seed monkey, and I heard the right words coming from myself to fill the silence: "In all that is important you have never failed me. With one exception, you kept the promises you made to me—you never carved me that peach-seed monkey."

Not long after this conversation I received a small package in the mail. In it was a peach-seed monkey and a note which said: "Here is the monkey I promised you. You will notice that I broke one leg and had to repair it with glue. I am sorry I didn't have time to carve a perfect one."

Two weeks later my father died. He died only at the end of his life. 5

For me, a peach-seed monkey has become a symbol of all the promises which were made to me and the energy and care which nourished and created me as a human being. And, even more fundamentally, it is a symbol of that which is the foundation of all human personality and dignity. Each of us is redeemed from shallow and hostile life only by the sacrificial love and civility which we have gratuitously received. As Erik Erikson has pointed out in *Identity and the Life Cycle,* a secure and healthy identity is founded upon a sense of *basic trust* which is first mediated to a child by the trustworthiness of his parents. Identity has its roots in the dependability, orderliness, and nurturing responsiveness of the world of primal experience. That civility which separates men from the lower animals depends upon the making and keeping of promises, covenants, vows, and contracts. As Nietzsche so aptly put the matter, man is that animal who makes promises.

Understanding

1. Keen has written: "To wonder is to open ourselves to the gift of being with a sense of gratitude." What in the story reveals Keen's sense of gratitude and wonder?
2. Infer the setting and pace of Keen's childhood. Urban? Rural? What metaphors does Keen use to set the tone and venue of the story?
3. Why do you think Keen valued the peach-seed monkey so? After all, it wasn't worth much. What does he say that supports your answer?
4. What is "the world of primal experience"?

Responding

1. Imagine you are the author of this reading. What would you say to your father—if he were still alive—to let him know you appreciate the peach-seed monkey?
2. The following questions are deceptive in their simplicity. See what you find as you answer them. What gift would you very much like to give? To whom? Why? What gift would you most like to receive? From whom? Why?

3. Another title for this short story might be "The Promise," as it is clearly Keen's exploration of what promises mean to him and to humankind. Recall a promise that was kept or broken by someone in your life. Have you created a symbol for that promise? Write that story.
4. Are you a promise keeper or a promise breaker? Describe an experience that supports your answer. Explore the ramifications of this notion. Tie your story to gifts.
5. What object do you treasure for being as powerful a symbol in your life as Keen's carved peach-seed monkey is in his? Tell its story.
6. Was there an object in your childhood that you coveted but never received? Can you recall a gift that you received but never wanted? Describe one or the other and its consequences.

Connecting

Refer to the summary of "Trust and Mistrust" in the Elkind selection on Erikson's ages of man (chapter seven). How does this notion relate to this reading?

The Gift of the Magi

O. Henry

O. Henry, born in 1862 in North Carolina, was a high school dropout; he subsequently held various odd jobs including working at a newspaper, where many of his stories were first published. By the time he died, he had written fourteen volumes, most of which while he was serving a three-year jail term for stealing money from a bank. "The Gift of the Magi" is probably O. Henry's best-known short story; it reveals not only a pair of gifts, but also a remarkable pair of givers.

O. Henry is known for the surprise endings to his short stories. He is masterful at leading his readers in one direction and ending up in another. In fact, even his real name might surprise us: William Sydney Porter.

One dollar and eighty-seven cents. That was all. And sixty cents of it was 1
in pennies. Pennies saved one and two at a time by bulldozing the grocer and the vegetable man and the butcher until one's cheeks burned with the silent imputation of parsimony that such close dealing implied. Three times Della counted it. One dollar and eighty-seven cents. And the next day would be Christmas.

There was clearly nothing to do but flop down on the shabby little couch and howl. So Della did it. Which instigates the moral reflection that life is made up of sobs, sniffles, and smiles, with sniffles predominating.

While the mistress of the home is gradually subsiding from the first stage to the second, take a look at the home. A furnished flat at $8 per week. It did not exactly beggar description, but it certainly had that word on the lookout for the mendicancy squad.

In the vestibule below was a letter-box into which no letter would go, and an electric button from which no mortal finger could coax a ring. Also appertaining thereunto was a card bearing the name "Mr. James Dillingham Young."

The "Dillingham" had been flung to the breeze during a former period 5
of prosperity when its possessor was being paid $30 per week. Now, when the income was shrunk to $20, the letters of "Dillingham" looked blurred, as though they were thinking seriously of contracting to a modest and unassuming D. But whenever Mr. James Dillingham Young came home and reached his flat above he was called "Jim" and greatly hugged by Mrs. James Dillingham Young, already introduced to you as Della. Which is all very good.

Della finished her cry and attended to her cheeks with the powder rag. She stood by the window and looked out dully at a gray cat walking a gray fence in a gray backyard. Tomorrow would be Christmas Day and she had only $1.87 with which to buy Jim a present. She had been saving every penny she could for months, with this result. Twenty dollars a week doesn't go far. Expenses had been greater than she had calculated. They always are. Only $1.87 to buy a present for Jim. Her Jim. Many a happy hour she had spent planning for something nice for him. Something fine and rare and sterling—something just a little bit near to being worthy of the honor of being owned by Jim.

There was a pier-glass between the windows of the room. Perhaps you have seen a pier-glass in an $8 flat. A very thin and very agile person may, by observing his reflection in a rapid sequence of longitudinal strips, obtain a fairly accurate conception of his looks. Della, being slender, had mastered the art.

Suddenly she whirled from the window and stood before the glass. Her eyes were shining brilliantly, but her face had lost its color within twenty seconds. Rapidly she pulled down her hair and let it fall to its full length.

Now, there were two possessions of the James Dillingham Youngs in which they both took a mighty pride. One was Jim's gold watch that had been his father's and his grandfather's. The other was Della's hair. Had the Queen of Sheba lived in the flat across the airshaft, Della would have let her hair hang out the window some day to dry just to depreciate Her Majesty's jewels and gifts. Had King Solomon been the janitor, with all his treasures piled up in the basement, Jim would have pulled out his watch every time he passed, just to see him pluck at his beard from envy.

10 So now Della's beautiful hair fell about her rippling and shining like a cascade of brown waters. It reached below her knee and made itself almost a garment for her. And then she did it up again nervously and quickly. Once she faltered for a minute and stood still while a tear or two splashed on the worn red carpet.

On went her old brown jacket; on went her old brown hat. With a whirl of skirts and with the brilliant sparkle still in her eyes, she fluttered out the door and down the stairs to the street.

Where she stopped the sign read: "Mme. Sofronie. Hair Goods of All Kinds." One flight up Della ran, and collected herself, panting. Madame, large, too white, chilly, hardly looked the "Sofronie."

"Will you buy my hair?" asked Della.

"I buy hair," said Madame. "Take yer hat off and let's have a sight at the looks of it."

15 Down rippled the brown cascade.

"Twenty dollars," said Madame, lifting the mass with a practiced hand.

"Give it to me quick," said Della.

Oh, and the next two hours tripped by on rosy wings. Forget the hashed metaphor. She was ransacking the stores for Jim's present.

She found it at last. It surely had been made for Jim and no one else. There was no other like it in any of the stores, and she had turned all of them inside out. It was a platinum fob chain simple and chaste in design, properly proclaiming its value by substance alone and not by meretricious ornamentation—as all good things should do. It was even worthy of The Watch. As soon as she saw it she knew that it must be Jim's. It was like him. Quietness and value—the description applied to both. Twenty-one dollars they took from her for it, and she hurried home with the 87 cents. With that chain on his watch Jim might be properly anxious about the time in any company. Grand as the watch was, he sometimes looked at it on the sly on account of the old leather strap that he used in place of a chain.

When Della reached home her intoxication gave way a little to prudence 20
and reason. She got out her curling irons and lighted the gas and went to work repairing the ravages made by generosity added to love. Which is always a tremendous task, dear friends—a mammoth task.

Within forty minutes her head was covered with tiny, close-lying curls that made her look wonderfully like a truant schoolboy. She looked at her reflection in the mirror long, carefully, and critically.

"If Jim doesn't kill me," she said to herself, "before he takes a second look at me, he'll say I look like a Coney Island chorus girl. But what could I do—oh! what could I do with a dollar and eighty-seven cents?"

At 7 o'clock the coffee was made and the frying-pan was on the back of the stove hot and ready to cook the chops.

Jim was never late. Della doubled the fob chain in her hand and sat on the corner of the table near the door that he always entered. Then she heard his step on the stair away down on the first flight, and she turned white for just a moment. She had a habit of saying little silent prayers about the simplest everyday things, and now she whispered: "Please God, make him think I am still pretty."

The door opened and Jim stepped in and closed it. He looked thin and 25
very serious. Poor fellow, he was only twenty-two—and to be burdened with a family! He needed a new overcoat and he was without gloves.

Jim stepped inside the door, as immovable as a setter at the scent of quail. His eyes were fixed upon Della, and there was an expression in them that she could not read, and it terrified her. It was not anger, nor surprise, nor disapproval, nor horror, nor any of the sentiments that she had been prepared for. He simply stared at her fixedly with that peculiar expression on his face.

Della wriggled off the table and went for him.

"Jim, darling," she cried, "don't look at me that way. I had my hair cut off and sold it because I couldn't have lived through Christmas without giving you a present. It'll grow out again—you won't mind, will you? I just had to do it. My hair grows awfully fast. Say 'Merry Christmas!' Jim, and let's be happy. You don't know what a nice—what a beautiful, nice gift I've got for you."

"You've cut off your hair?" asked Jim, laboriously, as if he had not arrived at that patent fact yet even after the hardest mental labor.

"Cut it off and sold it," said Della. "Don't you like me just as well, anyhow? 30
I'm me without my hair, ain't I?"

Jim looked about the room curiously.

"You say your hair is gone?" he said, with an air almost of idiocy.

"You needn't look for it," said Della. "It's sold, I tell you—sold and gone, too. It's Christmas Eve, boy. Be good to me, for it went for you. Maybe the hairs on my head were numbered," she went on with a sudden serious sweetness, "but nobody could ever count my love for you. Shall I put the chops on, Jim?"

Out of his trance Jim seemed quickly to wake. He enfolded his Della. For ten seconds let us regard with discreet scrutiny some inconsequential object in the other direction. Eight dollars a week or a million a year—what is the difference? A mathematician or a wit would give you the wrong answer. The magi brought valuable gifts, but that was not among them. This dark assertion will be illuminated later on.

Jim drew a package from his overcoat pocket and threw it upon the table.

"Don't make any mistake, Dell," he said, "about me. I don't think there's anything in the way of a haircut or a shave or a shampoo that could make me like my girl any less. But if you'll unwrap that package you may see why you had me going a while at first."

White fingers and nimble tore at the string and paper. And then an ecstatic scream of joy; and then, alas! a quick feminine change to hysterical tears and wails, necessitating the immediate employment of all the comforting powers of the lord of the flat.

For there lay The Combs—the set of combs, side and back, that Della had worshipped for long in a Broadway window. Beautiful combs, pure tortoise shell, with jewelled rims—just the shade to wear in the beautiful vanished hair. They were expensive combs, she knew, and her heart had simply craved and yearned over them without the least hope of possession. And now, they were hers, but the tresses that should have adorned the coveted adornments were gone.

But she hugged them to her bosom, and at length she was able to look up with dim eyes and a smile and say: "My hair grows so fast, Jim!"

And then Della leaped up like a little singed cat and cried, "Oh, oh!"

Jim had not yet seen his beautiful present. She held it out to him eagerly upon her open palm. The dull precious metal seemed to flash with a reflection of her bright and ardent spirit.

"Isn't it a dandy, Jim? I hunted all over town to find it. You'll have to look at the time a hundred times a day now. Give me your watch. I want to see how it looks on it."

Instead of obeying, Jim tumbled down on the couch and put his hands under the back of his head and smiled.

"Dell," said he, "let's put our Christmas presents away and keep 'em a while. They're too nice to use just at present. I sold the watch to get the money to buy your combs. And now suppose you put the chops on."

The magi, as you know, were wise men—wonderfully wise men—who brought gifts to the Babe in the manger. They invented the art of giving Christmas presents. Being wise, their gifts were no doubt wise ones, possibly bearing the privilege of exchange in case of duplication. And here I have lamely related to you the uneventful chronicle of two foolish children in a flat who most unwisely sacrificed for each other the greatest treasures of their house. But in a last word to the wise of these days let it be said that of all who give gifts these two were the wisest. Of all who give and receive gifts, such as they are wisest. Everywhere they are wisest. They are the magi.

Understanding

1. From the price of things, we can tell that this story was not written today. Would you place as high a value on Jim's and Della's precious possessions

as they do? Why? What tells us that this story was written long before we were born?

2. What can we infer from Jim's seemingly straightforward and unemotional reply to Della: "I sold the watch to get the money to buy your combs. And now suppose you put the chops on." What will tomorrow look like for Della and Jim? Will they go about life as usual, or will this event be a major turning point? Explain your thoughts.
3. What does the storyteller mean by the statement in paragraph 20 in which Della "went to work repairing the ravages made by generosity added to love"?

Responding

1. In the final paragraph, why would O. Henry, the storyteller, call Della and Jim "foolish" and then say that "of all who give gifts these two were the wisest"?
2. Della and Jim wanted with all their hearts to give gifts that would equal their love for each other. As they prove, some people are willing to do almost anything—even the outrageous—to carry out their desires. Can you recall a time in your life when you made a similarly extraordinary sacrifice to give a gift? Did you ever receive a gift for which the giver sacrificed a great deal? Write that story.

Connecting

Analyze how Della's and Jim's gifts differ from the gift of the peach-seed monkey in the preceding short story by Sam Keen.

Steel Memories from Father's Toolbox

Pete Hamill

Pete Hamill, an accomplished fiction writer, journalist, and, most recently, the editor-in-chief of the *New York Daily News,* came of age in a working-class Brooklyn neighborhood in the 1940s and 1950s, just when factories were closing, the good life was moving to the suburbs, and his own father's job had been relocated to Georgia. Although his father urged him to learn a blue-collar trade, Hamill wanted to be a writer, which he succeeded in doing at a grim price, suggested by the title of his 1995 memoir, *A Drinking Life.*

In a recent interview, Hamill commented, "I want to see an auto mechanic on the cover of *Time* magazine. We need to honor manual labor. If there is no respect for working class people, why would we expect anyone on welfare to aspire to get a job?" In the brief memoir "Steel Memories from Father's Toolbox," which appeared in the *New York Times,* he captures this icon of identity from a time in the not too distant past when manual labor was a respected and much more common vocation.

1 Tools were a part of life when I was a boy in blue-collar Brooklyn after World War II. Men carried their tools to work in the dark mornings, jammed into leather belts, or slung over shoulders, or gripped in gloved hands against the cold. They carried those tools with a certain pride, like prizefighters with gym bags; they were symbols of work and skill.

In the evenings, the subways were salty with the aromas of perspiration and labor and the men planted their backs against the doors, with their tools at their feet. In memory, those working men were all hard and courteous, but grave, even solemn; more likely, they were simply exhausted. But one memory is absolutely clear: no kid ever told them to get out of the way.

Tools helped such men form families, raise kids, put food on kitchen tables. But tools weren't simply a means of earning a living. They were essential to life in the places where working people lived. In those much leaner times, damaged goods could not be thrown away and then replaced by the latest models; they had to be repaired. No agents of landlords or the state would arrive to make minor repairs; tenants did most of that work themselves. And so every flat in blue-collar New York contained a toolbox. Ours was one of them.

"Get me the toolbox," my father would growl on a Saturday morning, his voice already burred by whiskey and cigarettes. "We've got a job to do. . . ."

5 My brothers and I would rush to the closet and dig out the battered dark-green metal toolbox and lay it upon the kitchen table (no workshop in those cramped tenement rooms). Then, with a metallic unsnapping of locks, the lid

would lift—open sesame! we'd sometimes shout—and suddenly, magically, there were the tools, lying in almost sacramental order: hammers, screwdrivers, wrenches, clamps; a metal file, a spirit level, a plumb bob and a soldering iron; shears for cutting metal and pliers for braiding wire. Tools: the nouns of work.

All those nouns came flooding back last year, when I started working on a long essay about tools and art, provoked by the extraordinary art collection of John Hechinger. Since the 1970's, Mr. Hechinger, the chairman of the Maryland-based hardware business that was started by his father in 1911, has been collecting art revolving around the common theme of tools. I gazed at pieces by Jim Dine and Jean Tinguely, Lucas Samaras and Claes Oldenberg, and more than a hundred others, and was astonished by their inventiveness, humor, sense of surprise. But all the while, I kept seeing that toolbox on a table in Brooklyn, stuffed with nouns.

In memory, there was no bottom to that magical box. From its depths came boxes of nails, tacks, wood screws. There came picks, gouges, drills and bits; a slide rule and a T square; a roll-up metal measuring tape; blades for a hacksaw. And with those tools, Billy Hamill, dispatched after eight grades of formal schooling in distant Belfast to an apprenticeship as a stone mason, tried to make something better of his tiny piece of America.

Sometimes his friends arrived to help. Duke, from the first floor. Harry Kelly, from up the block. They made almost nothing new. They operated a repair shop, using those tools, and their own ingenuity, to mend the wounds inflicted by marauding platoons of kids. They repaired the ruined hinges of doors. They worked on toasters and skates, sinks and baby carriages, and an endless series of radios. Radios shaped like the cathedral of Notre Dame. Radios that looked like bombs. Radios of rococo complexity.

"Where's the schematic?" my father would say, in the same voice used by mad scientists demanding that Igor now bring them the brain. And he and Duke and Harry Kelly would lay the schematic diagram on the table and begin matching radio tubes to the drawing, testing each tube in some kind of electric device (if the filaments inside the tube glowed red, it was still alive), until there seemed to be hundreds of tubes laid out delicately on the table. Then one of the kids would burst in, sweaty with August, bouncing a spaldeen and . . . Where's the schematic?

From those rooms, I carried into the wider world a belief in tools. As a 10
young art student in the 1950's, I loved the differences in chalks and pencil leads, in pens cut one way for drawing and another way for lettering. The tools of art included linseed oil and turpentine, casein and water color, rubber cement and razor blades, canvas and cardboard. If only we could afford Arches watercolor paper or two-ply Strathmore, we told ourselves, then we'd be better artists. Often, the words themselves were special, even lyrical: crowquill pens and sable brushes should belong to poets.

Around this time, a major transformation of New York life was under way, but few of us paid much attention. Artists like David Smith, Reuben Nakian and Isamu Noguchi were beginning to use industrial tools and materials in their work: cast iron, welding torches, stone grinders and polishers. And as artists appropriated the tools of manual labor, blue-collar New York began to vanish. In Brooklyn and Queens, factories began to close. In Manhattan, the teeming lofts of SoHo emptied. At first, workers were replaced by artists; then the artists, who had redeemed the neighborhood, gave way to the rich.

In my own life, I set aside the tools of art for the tools of a writer. There were the old clattering Royal standards in the city room of *The New York Post,* at 75 West Street, equipped with headsets to free the hands for the taking of notes or dictation. There were thousands of sheets of copy paper folded twice to fit into a pocket. There were ballpoint pens, felt-tip pens, fountain pens. Most of all, there was a Hermes 3000 portable typewriter, that traveled with me to Europe and Mexico and Vietnam, that took hundreds of stories and one novel from my head to paper and that was stolen one summer afternoon from my apartment in the Village. For days after the burglary, I walked the streets, offering rewards for its return, no questions asked; but I never saw it again.

Like many New Yorkers in this era when the aroma of physical work has vanished from the subways, I do most of my work on computers now. They are fine machines, the best tools so far invented for writers. But in some mysterious way, this remains work done by hand. I always start with a pen in hand, a tool as ancient as reeds. And I still wander through stationery stores as if set loose in some antique Mesopotamian bazaar. Perhaps this new pen will help me to write better, perhaps that special-lined yellow pad will help bring order to the chaos of possibilities presented each morning at my desk. We live in hope.

Occasionally, moving around in such stores, I come across racks full of toolboxes. They gleam seductively. They urge me to touch them, handle them. I open them, and they are, of course, empty. I can even see their bottoms. But in their presence, I sometimes hear the whisper of an interior voice. Where's the schematic? it says, dark with smoke and time. Get me the schematic, and the right tools, the voice says, and I'll make everything new. I promise.

Understanding

1. The "battered dark-green metal toolbox" that belonged to Hamill's father was more than just a container for hammers, screwdrivers, wrenches, and clamps. How does he describe its meaning?
2. What are the tools of Hamill's profession? What is their connection to his father's toolbox?
3. What can we infer about Hamill's relationship with his father? What else can we infer about the environment in which Hamill spent his youth?
4. For those of you who live in big cities with subway systems, do you agree with Hamill that "the aroma of physical work has vanished from the subways"? For those of you who are from other countries or smaller towns and cities in the United States, where is the "aroma of physical work" most evident?

Responding

1. Images from our youth live in our heads and appear at unlikely times, like Hamill's father's tools—the "nouns of work." Brainstorm a list of images—nouns—that have lingered in your head (and heart) since childhood.
2. Write a descriptive piece about one of the nouns on your list. Connect its past to its present. As you explore these objects, consider whether they are gifts and explain why or why not.
3. Ask three people who have toolboxes what they mean to them. Write a comparison of their responses.
4. Do you have a toolbox? If so, what does it look like? What's inside? If you don't, would you want one? What would you enclose in it?

Connecting

The first reading in this chapter, "The Peach-Seed Monkey," tells the story of a gift from a father to a son. Compare the tone, the use of images, and the way Keen and Hamill end their stories. What elements do these cross-generational gift stories have in common? How are they different?

What Is a Friend?

Elie Wiesel

In the spring of 1944, Adolf Eichmann, chief of the Gestapo's Jewish section, arrived in the Transylvanian village of Sighet, Romania, with orders to exterminate an estimated six hundred thousand Jews in less than six weeks. Fifteen-year-old Elie Wiesel, the only son of a grocer and his wife, was among those forced to leave their homes in a mass deportation to Birkenau, the reception center for the infamous death camp Auschwitz.

Young Wiesel had been a devoted and serious student of the Talmud and assumed he would spend his life in Sighet, studying and helping out in the family store. Instead he experienced and survived the camps. His father, mother, and younger sister did not, and he carried a heavy guilt that he had been the one to survive. Nevertheless, Wiesel's novel *Night* and his recent book *Memoir* demonstrate his ability to recognize people as gifts. Wiesel won the Nobel Peace Prize in 1986.

He was a friend. And what is a friend? More than a father, more than a 1
brother: a traveling companion. With him, you can conquer the impossible, even if you must lose it later. Friendship marks a life even more deeply than love. Love risks degenerating into obsession, friendship is never anything but sharing. It is to a friend that you communicate the awakening of a desire, the birth of a vision or a terror, the anguish of seeing the sun disappear or of finding that order and justice are no more. That's what you can talk about with a friend. Is the soul immortal, and if so why are we afraid to die? If God exists, how can we lay claim to freedom, since He is its beginning and its end? What is death, when you come down to it? The closing of a parenthesis, and nothing more? And what about life? In the mouth of a philosopher, these questions may have a false ring, but asked during adolescence or friendship, they have the power to change being: a look burns and ordinary gestures tend to transcend themselves. What is a friend? Someone who for the first time makes you aware of your loneliness and his, and helps you to escape so you in turn can help him. Thanks to him you can hold your tongue without shame and talk freely without risk. That's it.

Understanding

1. Wiesel says that a friend is a "traveling companion." To what trip is he referring?
2. In Wiesel's view, what is the difference between a friend and a philosopher?

Responding

1. What are the main differences (other than the obvious ones) between family and friends? What are the advantages and disadvantages of being close to each?
2. Is a friend truly a gift? Why or why not? Explain.
3. Think of someone with whom you want to develop a better friendship. What are you doing to improve this friendship? What are the gifts you give? Why do you give them?
4. Choose one of Wiesel's many statements on friendship and explain it, using examples from your own experience with friendships.

Connecting

Keen in "The Peach-Seed Monkey" and Hamill in "Steel Memories from Father's Toolbox" are both men writing about their fathers' gifts. In "What Is a Friend?" Wiesel claims that "Friendship marks a life even more deeply than love." Explore whether Keen's and Hamill's relationships with their fathers were relationships more of love or of friendship. What makes the distinction?

Our Peruvian Friend

Gabriella De Ferrari

Gringa Latina: A Woman of Two Worlds, which Gabriella De Ferrari describes as "a nonfiction book of reconstructed memories," tells the story of a young girl who remembers her privileged upbringing as the daughter of upper-middle-class parents who had come from Italy as newlyweds to the small desert town of Tacna, Peru. In Peru she found herself described as the daughter of gringos, or foreigners; attending college in the United States, she was called a Latina. In "Our Peruvian Friend," which opens the book, De Ferrari sets up her bicultural identity by juxtaposing images of her mother and a family friend she describes as "doomed to be lonely because a man once scorned her."

De Ferrari was born in Peru, where she spent the first fifteen years of her life. Peru, she says, is part of her interior rhythms, the place "where the important parts of my self belong." Schooled in Europe during her adolescence, she eventually moved to the United States, where she earned degrees from St. Louis University, the Fletcher School of Law and Diplomacy, and Harvard University. De Ferrari, who has also written *A Cloud in the Sand,* is a feature writer for *Vanity Fair, Travel and Leisure,* and *The Boston Review.*

Señorita Luisa was my mother's best friend. Together they made an odd pair—two women, two continents. Señorita Luisa's internal music was based on the five notes of the ancient melancholic melodies of the Andes, while Mother's was based on the seven notes of her European scales. Señorita Luisa moved at a slow, even pace, as if she carried the burdens of her ancestors, a people with a glorious past and a troubled, uncertain present. She had the blood of the Indians to whom the country belonged, mixed with that of its conquerors, the Spaniards, who robbed Peru of its indigenous culture and so much else. Mother's movements were fast and constantly changing. Like a boat sailing in new waters, Mother was searching for her place. Her family as far back as it could be traced was Italian, and like so many Italians who emigrated, she carried with her a fearless sense of adventure. To her, everything was new and exciting, yet hard to accept. Mother was tall and fair, and her very blue eyes danced as if echoing her gestures and movements. Señorita Luisa was a short, stocky woman who always dressed in black. Her features were sharp, as if they had been chiseled of stone. Her skin was olive-toned, and deep crevices cut across her forehead. She talked in long, slow sentences and often interrupted them with sighs that seemed to come from a very deep part of her, as if from the bottom of a black pond. Though she and my mother were the same age, she always seemed old to me. In contrast, Mother always seemed to me young—and transparent, like a crystal lake. 1

Our parents taught us to pay strict attention to everything Señorita Luisa said. She was our dictionary of Peruvianisms. I assumed that just as everything about us seemed strange to most Peruvians, everything about her was typical of the other locals.

Señorita Luisa came from one of those families that populate the literature of South American countries and have earned our writers the name of magic realists. Their stories are filled with the illegitimate children of priests, old maids' daughters locked in convents, triplets born attached, saints who appear with fiancées, ghosts that surface in the silence of the night to be consulted about family matters, old men who ride into the night to rape young girls in order to prove their masculinity. Señorita Luisa's family history was filled with such episodes, including the enigmatic and wholesale deaths of her brothers.

She was always treated as a reject because she had never married, a status that caused paralyzing fear in every Peruvian female. Women in the Peru of my childhood were completely dependent on men. From birth, girls were taught to pray for a husband, and the wedding day marked a woman's ultimate achievement in life. The search for a husband was an elaborate, ritualized hunt regulated by strict rules. Poor Señorita Luisa had broken the most serious of these. She had been deserted by her suitor, who left to marry someone else. It was not as if she had done anything wrong herself, yet once abandoned, she became totally undesirable. Having been engaged meant that you were not ever to be considered by another man. Mother told us that it was very sad. My friends at school spoke about it in hushed tones, as a great horrible curse.

So Señorita Luisa stayed at home and obeyed her parents, to whom she knew she was an embarrassment. When her mother got too tired or too lazy to run the house, Señorita Luisa took over. Her trousseau trunk was put away. She cut her hair short, stopped wearing lipstick, and thereafter dressed in black.

Señorita Luisa's father had been a business associate of my father's. He was a rich landowner who lived to see all five of his sons die of an undiagnosed illness within a year. At the end of his life he went to Father and asked him to look after his daughter. And that was how she came into our lives.

Our maid Saturnina, who would tell me the grown-ups' secrets, explained that at first Mother did not want to hear of this friendship. She assumed that Señorita Luisa was an old girlfriend of Father's, but when she met her, Señorita Luisa's loneliness went right through her. After asking Father for forgiveness, Mother took her on. Señorita Luisa became an intimate friend, almost part of the family, and moved to a house across the street.

Saturnina also told me that all the brothers' deaths had been caused by a curse put on the family by the souls of the people who had worked on their plantation and been treated badly. At home we were taught to believe in tragedies, not curses. I never could tell the difference, but I taught myself to call them tragedies at home and curses everywhere else.

Crossing the street from my house to the home of Señorita Luisa was like crossing a continent, so different were the worlds in which we lived. Whereas everything in my house was orderly and rational, everything in hers was chaotic and confusing. In our house every room had a specific function; in hers, except for the kitchen, all the rooms served all purposes. Our furniture was always in the same place; hers was constantly rearranged. Mother knew precisely where everything was; Señorita Luisa could never find anything. Her drawers were like bottomless treasure chests from which the strangest things emerged: cooking spices in her bedroom drawers, cinnamon-scented perfume in the kitchen. Her bathroom, like most people's, was outside the house, in a little building all its own. As a child, I never thought that our house was more modern. I always assumed that we were simply different for specific reasons, and when my friends came to visit I was embarrassed by ordinary things, such as our indoor bathroom or the fact that our car was kept in something called a garage.

At mealtimes, not only did Señorita Luisa's entire house smell of food, but 10
the scent spread into the garden and the street; in our house, great efforts were made to contain food odors in the kitchen. Her servants were fed servant food; ours ate what we did. The trees in her garden looked exhausted, as if the leaves had fought the weight of the desert dust to be born; our trees, which my parents had imported from Italy, were young and green, their lacy leaves shimmering in the light. Our garden was arranged in neat rows with the colors of the flowers and the shades of the greens graduated to make a harmonious whole, while hers was a tangle of jasmine next to mint next to sprawling cucumbers. One had to climb over tall bushes to reach the fruit trees, yet everything in her garden was bigger and smelled sweeter, including the fruits that grew hidden under cobwebs.

One of my earliest memories is the scent of Señorita Luisa's house on an evening when I was asked not to go to bed but to accompany my parents on a condolence call. The smell was heavy, airless, as if candles had been burning and wet mud had been mixed with the fragrance of lilies—the kind of scent that makes it hard to find air for the next breath. I was dressed in my fancy clothes, stiff with starch, and I felt uncomfortable. We followed a maid down an endlessly long hallway with a tall ceiling that was occasionally interrupted by a dusty skylight, which brought in a shy evening light. We walked hesitantly, aware of the echoes in the emptiness. It was my first formal visit. I had been told exactly how to behave and what to say.

Señorita Luisa was sitting at the end of the very large living room, which was dark and filled with people who stood as silent as the furniture. She was dressed all in black, and a veil hid her face. A ghost, I thought to myself, and I forgot the lines I was supposed to say. She reached for me and gave me a tender hug. She didn't have her usual cinnamon smell but exuded a sort of piercing aroma, like the scent of Mother's trunks from Italy. My parents and I made our way to a corner by a window. We sat and waited in a silence that was interrupted only by Señorita Luisa's deep sighs. They made my heart feel small and empty. We were there because her father, who had been her only living relative, had died.

It was my first encounter with death. My parents told me that it is a long sleep that comes after a tiring life, but the next day, when I was left alone with Señorita Luisa, I was told something different. Death, she said, is when the

Lord calls you and you go to be with Him. It is what you live for. If you are good and live for Him, you go to inhabit His kingdom filled with angels and happiness. If you are bad, you go to live with the devils in a very hot place called hell. However, if you do some bad things, repent, and confess, you go to purgatory, and your friends' and families' prayers can get you out. A Hail Mary spares you six years, and a whole rosary one hundred. Every sin had a price in terms of years in purgatory and number of prayers for redemption. Masses bought you centuries, which Señorita Luisa informed me were nothing compared to eternity. She made me pray with her. I assumed her father had been very bad, because she was planning to have so many masses said for him. Mother told me it was just a story that priests tell to keep people going to church.

Señorita Luisa also possessed an army of saints to whom she prayed for various favors. When I lost something concrete, she taught me to pray to Saint Anthony; when I lost my patience, Santa Rita could help me recover it. Mother also thought this was nonsense. Early in life I realized that there were two very different ways of looking at the world, my parents' and Señorita Luisa's. What she told me was what I assumed the world outside my house believed, and what I was told at home was what people believed in that faraway place where my parents came from. I kept them separate and functioned accordingly, never suffering from the difference, at least while I was young and the lines were so easy to draw. Yet Señorita Luisa's world, together with that of the maids in the kitchen, was far more seductive than the rational world of my parents. I liked curses, and miracles, and praying for a handsome husband, and buying up heaven.

Mother and Señorita Luisa talked to each other constantly. They would sit 15
under a large mulberry tree in the afternoon and become absorbed in each other's stories. My own time with Señorita Luisa came in the evenings, when I got back from school. I would go to her house for a snack of hot chocolate and a cake she made especially for me of fresh figs held together with what she called "honey glue." She had many stories to tell, and they were all equally outrageous. I listened, mesmerized by her tales, delivered in the monotonous rhythms of her voice as if they occurred every day, like drinking milk or taking a bath.

My favorite stories were about her brothers. When she talked about them, her eyes filled with tears and her voice grew low. One had to speak softly about the dead out of respect for them. I had to sit close so I wouldn't miss anything. Her brothers, she told me, had been handsome and brave and had lived lives of danger and adventure. They were one year apart in age and had died when the oldest was twenty-two. They had never gone to school but had been tutored in their hacienda, and had learned to write and read and do math.

They had also been instructed in the difficult tasks of running their huge landholding. The family had been granted the land, a fertile swath by a river in the otherwise dry desert, many generations before. At this time that Señorita Luisa's brothers were alive, her family did not have a house in town; they lived on the plantation, which was two hours away by car. They grew olives and cotton—fields and fields of white pima cotton, the most desirable for the export market, sold in distant places like England and France. The olives were picked and packed in huge barrels and sent to Spain to be made into oil.

The plantation was completely self-sustaining. It had its own vegetable garden, animals for meat and milk, vineyards to make wine, and many *peones*, the Indians who came from the mountains to work. Señorita Luisa's brothers got up at dawn and traveled around the plantation on horseback, making sure the men did their work. They parceled out the water from the river so there was enough for all the crops. The women servants took their lunch to the fields. The main meal, however, was served early in the evening, when they came back covered with dust and sweat. "We made everything," Señorita Luisa told me with great pride, "sausages, cakes, and jams, even chocolates and candies." The kitchen alone employed twelve women. I imagined it to be some kind of factory. When I finally visited it, I was disappointed to see how primitive it was. The stoves were heated by coal. The kitchen was black and airless, there was a heavy smell of oil, and flies were everywhere.

After dinner, Señorita Luisa's brothers had played the guitar, and later, before going to bed, they had worked on the accounts. On Sunday the four youngest rode off to the plantation next to theirs, a three-hour ride, to visit their girlfriends—four sisters, pale, beautiful, always dressed in pastel organdy dresses. Each of the girls was named after a river. Rivers brought fertility, and their father, who had never had a son, wanted many grandchildren. Their river names were odd: Ucayali, Caplina, Amazona, and Rimac. Señorita Luisa reassured me that each also had the Christian name Maria, like the Virgin. Most Peruvian girls had two names, and one was almost always Maria.

Later, when the brothers went to the capital, they brought each of the 20
sisters a ring of emeralds and diamonds. It was hard to get Señorita Luisa to talk about romantic love. I never brought it up, because I had been warned by Saturnina never to discuss that subject with old maids; it made them too sad. Señorita Luisa told me that her brothers' interest in the sisters was "real love, not arranged love, or love of convenience." They were all to be married. When the brothers died, the sisters went to a convent and never came out. Señorita Luisa went to visit them, but they wouldn't receive her because they couldn't bear the grief.

Señorita Luisa's brother Jacinto, the oldest, had no girlfriend; he had a "woman," an Indian woman whom he loved. She lived on the plantation, and their love affair was a secret one. When he died, she committed suicide; she was pregnant with his child. When Señorita Luisa got to this part of the story, we both cried. "Just imagine," she would say, "I could have brought up that child."

I can still see the picture of her brothers that she kept by the side of her bed: five short, stocky young men with wide mustaches and large Panama hats, standing next to tall white horses. I so much wanted to have a boyfriend who looked like one of them.

Señorita Luisa also told me stories about the Indians and the Spaniards. From her I learned what the Spaniards had done to my country. Her views were different from what we were taught at school, where the nuns called Spain "the mother country" and said it had brought Catholicism and civilization to the "unfortunate" native creatures. Señorita Luisa believed that the Spaniards had ruined a civilization, doped the Indians with coca, and made them slave in the silver and gold mines for the benefit of Spain's greedy queen.

Señorita Luisa didn't even like Columbus, a hero of mine. I thought it wonderful that he had been so brave, as brave as my father, who had come so far to look for adventure. But I never dared to disagree with Señorita Luisa. I feared that if I did, she would stop telling me stories; children were supposed to respect adults and not question their judgment. It seemed strange that she felt that way about the Spaniards. Saturnina and the maids in the kitchen talked about them with such respect: *conquistadores,* they called them.

One of my favorite activities, in which Señorita Luisa would indulge me 25
only when she was in a good mood, was to have my fortune read. She would drip hot wax from a candle into a large container of icy water. When the wax hit the water, it formed different shapes. She read them and told me my "little future," that is, my future for the next week. The prognostications were mostly designed to teach me to behave: "This week you will tell a lie and that will cost you, because your mother will not believe you anymore," or "You never finish your prayers at Mass, and tomorrow the devil is going to pull your leg." Only occasionally would she tell me my "big future," the one I wanted to hear the most: a handsome man would fall in love with me, a man with green eyes and dark hair like her brothers.

The maids in my family's kitchen were also constantly reading wax, but they weren't allowed to do it for me. My mother thought it was nonsense. She never knew that Señorita Luisa read my fortune. Señorita Luisa also told ghost stories about the *almas,* the souls of the dead that came to visit at night. She used to scare me so much I had to ask Saturnina to stay with me until I fell asleep. Saturnina knew how to send the souls away: she tied a black ribbon to the window and left them a piece of bread.

As Señorita Luisa had saints, Saturnina and the other maids had roots and herbs. These could perform any kind of miracle, especially scaring away the evil eye that women gave each other when they were interested in the same man. I was constantly torn between wanting to believe Señorita Luisa and Saturnina and wanting to believe Mother, who was more interested in having me worry about geography and math.

Over the years, on my trips back to Peru, I would visit Señorita Luisa. She never changed much, but got smaller and sadder and developed a greater vocabulary of saints to pray to. "Everyone I loved died before me," she often told me. "Their souls keep me company, but they haven't yet given me the gift of calling me to be with them."

As I think about her life, doomed to be lonely because a man once scorned her, I wonder what she thought about mine, my career, my divorces. She found a way to explain me to herself. "Your family, you are gringos, *extranjeros.* I was never able to teach your mother to be one of us. She wanted to, and in some ways she was. But then she sent you away. I told her not to do it, that she would lose you. And she did. You stayed away. Don't forget your country, though," she always added. "It is a great country."

Señorita Luisa often spoke about Father, and when she did, her eyes filled 30
with tears. "I remember your father," she would say, "probably better than you do. You were so young when he died. He was one of us. But then, it is easier for a man. A man's world, the world of business, is the same everywhere."

The last time I saw Señorita Luisa, shortly before she died, she asked many questions that must have been on her mind for a long time. She wanted to know if Americans were religious people, if my children had been baptized, if the pope had annulled my marriages. I answered yes on all counts, knowing that sometimes it's better not to tell the truth.

Understanding

1. De Ferrari uses a number of descriptive words and images to capture the differences between her mother and Señorita Luisa. Peruse this reading for the words or phrases the writer uses to draw her portraits. How do these descriptive images compare with your own understanding of these characters?
2. In what ways did De Ferrari's identity as a "gringa latina" influence how she and Señorita Luisa viewed each other?
3. Indicate those sections of the reading that denote or suggest that De Ferrari regarded her friendship with Señorita Luisa as a gift.
4. Although De Ferrari describes herself as a woman of two worlds, what elements of this story lead you to accept her statement that Peru is where the important parts of herself belong?
5. The philosopher Aristotle claimed that friendship is essentially a partnership between or among equals. Is this the kind of friendship De Ferrari describes in "Our Peruvian Friend"? Indicate those elements of the story that support your position.

Responding

1. Describe someone from your childhood who influenced your life like Señorita Luisa influenced De Ferrari's. What gifts did this person bring into your life?
2. Even if your parents were from the same culture, their families represented different views or ways of life. Express the ways in which the two sides of your family are different or the same; explore how you have accepted or rejected the gifts of their culture in your own life.
3. Two opposing views are often cited to explain how we form relationships: "Birds of a feather flock together" and "Opposites attract." Which of these two (or an alternate statement that you think applies) would you use to explain the formation of a friendship? Explain how the friendships that you value most exemplify your choice.

Connecting

Under what circumstances do you think that, as De Ferrari says in her last statement in this selection, "sometimes it's better not to tell the truth" to a friend? Could it be true that our ordinary social world is held together by little lies and evasions? Explain. How would Wiesel ("What Is a Friend?" earlier in this chapter) respond to this assertion?

My Name

Sandra Cisneros

Poet and writer Sandra Cisneros was born in Chicago, Illinois, in 1954. After graduating from Loyola University, she attended the Iowa Writers Workshop. Much of her writing centers on her Mexican American heritage, evident in "My Name," which we excerpted from her novel *The House on Mango Street*—winner of the American Book Award. Cisneros explores the condition of women in *Women Hollering Creek* (1991).

In English, my name means hope. In Spanish it means too many letters. It 1
means sadness, it means waiting. It is like the number nine. A muddy color. It is the Mexican records my father plays on Sunday mornings when he is shaving, songs like sobbing.

It was my great-grandmother's name and now it is mine. She was a horse woman too, born like me in the Chinese year of the horse—which is supposed to be bad luck if you're born female—but I think this is a Chinese lie because the Chinese, like the Mexicans, don't like their women strong.

My great-grandmother. I would've liked to have known her, a wild horse of a woman, so wild she wouldn't marry until my great-grandfather threw a sack over her head and carried her off. Just like that, as if she were a fancy chandelier. That's the way he did it.

And the story goes she never forgave him. She looked out the window all her life, the way so many women sit their sadness on an elbow. I wonder if she made the best with what she got or was she sorry because she couldn't be all the things she wanted to be. Esperanza. I have inherited her name, but I don't want to inherit her place by the window.

At school, they say my name funny as if the syllables were made out of tin 5
and hurt the roof of your mouth. But in Spanish my name is made out of a softer something, like silver, not quite as thick as sister's name Magdalena which is uglier than mine. Magdalena who at least can come home and become Nenny. But I am always Esperanza.

I would like to baptize myself under a new name, a name more like the real me, the one nobody sees. Esperanza as Lisandra or Maritza or Zeze the X. Yes. Something like Zeze the X will do.

Understanding

1. What does Esperanza really think and feel about her name? Does she consider it a gift?
2. The way we feel about our name can be conditioned by how people react to it. How did people react to Esperanza's name?

3. Why do you think Esperanza wants to baptize herself under a new name?
4. What would you imagine Sandra Cisneros' signature to look like? Flamboyant? Plain? Slanted forward? Slanted backward? What else? Why? What does a signature denote? Is a signature a gift?

Responding

1. Your name is often the first gift your parents give you. Explain how you feel about your name. What does it mean? Why did your parents choose it? How do you perceive people's reactions to your name? If you could choose a new name, what would it be? Why would you choose it?
2. Do you know in what Chinese year you were born? If so, describe the characteristics of people born in those years. Does your personality resemble those characteristics? Do you consider yourself lucky to have been born then?
3. Trace the names of your ancestors as far back as you can determine them. What does your collection of family names mean to you? What stories can you recall about any of them?

Connecting

Cisneros generates a lot of meaning from a simple name. In fact, her short piece seems to be exploring the meanings a name can hold. Don't think about the following activity too analytically; just quick-write what comes to mind when you read this question: What *traits* (physical or otherwise) do you associate with the people who bear these names: Philip K. Dick, Katherine, Elizabeth Delany, Mihaly Csikszentmihalyi, Gillian Turner, Loyal O. Rue, Maggie, Floyd, Michel de Montaigne, Luc Sante, Michiko Kakutani, Václav, Kweisi, and Sherry. Now go back and look over the characteristics you imagined for these *Signatures* writers whom you will later encounter. From your list of traits, what does a name carry? How powerful is a name?

The Empathy Test

Philip K. Dick

Chicago-born Philip Kindred Dick, a twin whose sister Jane died 41 days after their birth in 1928, is regarded by many as a science fiction phenomenon. When he was two, his family moved to Berkeley, California, where at age fourteen he wrote his first novel, *Return to Liliput.* Plagued throughout his life by a variety of psychological problems and physical ailments, he wrote in feverish stints: eighty short stories between 1951 and 1958 and four novels from 1954 to 1955—fifty books in all. His themes—paranoia, repression, the decay of society, and plastic reality—infuse his stories and may account for his cult status today. He died in 1982—very "phildickian," as his admirers would say about the transposition of the last two digits of the date—leaving an unfinished novel.

This selection is excerpted from Dick's 1968 *Do Androids Dream of Electric Sheep?,* on which the motion picture *Blade Runner* is based. In *Androids,* the wholesale manufacture of synthetic life—a topic of current debate—was an accepted yet feared practice. The "electric sheep" in the title refer to the computerized animals that have replaced real animal life after the disastrous World War Terminus annihilated it. Set in San Francisco in the year 2002, *Androids* tells how residents of earth started a colonization program to other planets in order to escape inevitable extinction from radioactive fallout from the war. Colonizers were allowed possession of humanoid robots or androids, who did the dirty and dangerous work of colonization. Rick Deckard is a bounty hunter hired by the police to seek and destroy, or "retire," rogue androids ("andys") who had killed their masters and escaped. In this excerpt Deckard is sent to administer the Voigt-Kampff test to measure a uniquely human quality, or gift—empathy.

The small beam of white light shone steadily into the left eye of Rachael Rosen, and against her cheek the wire-mesh disk adhered. She seemed calm. 1

Seated where he could catch the readings on the two gauges of the Voigt-Kampff testing apparatus, Rick Deckard said, "I'm going to outline a number of social situations. You are to express your reaction to each as quickly as possible. You will be timed, of course."

"And of course," Rachael said distantly, "my verbal responses won't count. It's solely the eye-muscle and capillary reaction that you'll use as indices. But I'll answer; I want to go through this and—" She broke off. "Go ahead, Mr. Deckard."

Rick, selecting question three, said, "You are given a calf-skin wallet on your birthday." Both gauges immediately registered past the green and onto the red; the needles swung violently and then subsided.

"I wouldn't accept it," Rachael said. "Also I'd report the person who gave 5
it to me to the police."

After making a jot of notation Rick continued, turning to the eighth question of the Voigt-Kampff profile scale. "You have a little boy and he shows you his butterfly collection, including his killing jar."

"I'd take him to the doctor." Rachael's voice was low but firm. Again the twin gauges registered, but this time not so far. He made a note of that, too.

"You're sitting watching TV," he continued, "and suddenly you discover a wasp crawling on your wrist."

Rachael said, "I'd kill it." The gauges, this time, registered almost nothing: only a feeble and momentary tremor. He noted that and hunted cautiously for the next question.

"In a magazine you come across a full-page color picture of a nude girl." 10
He paused.

"Is this testing whether I'm an android," Rachael asked tartly, "or whether I'm homosexual?" The gauges did not register.

He continued, "Your husband likes the picture." Still the gauges failed to indicate a reaction. "The girl," he added, "is lying facedown on a large and beautiful bearskin rug." The gauges remained inert, and he said to himself, An android response. Failing to detect the major element, the dead animal pelt. Her—its—mind is concentrating on other factors. "Your husband hangs the picture up on the wall of his study," he finished, and this time the needles moved.

"I certainly wouldn't let him," Rachael said.

"Okay," he said, nodding. "Now consider this. You're reading a novel written in the old days before the war. The characters are visiting Fisherman's Wharf in San Francisco. They become hungry and enter a seafood restaurant. One of them orders lobster, and the chef drops the lobster into the tub of boiling water while the characters watch."

"Oh god," Rachael said. "That's awful! Did they really do that? It's de- 15
praved! You mean a *live* lobster?" The gauges, however, did not respond. Formally, a correct response. But simulated.

"You rent a mountain cabin," he said, "in an area still verdant. It's rustic knotty pine with a huge fireplace."

"Yes," Rachael said, nodding impatiently.

"On the walls someone has hung old maps, Currier and Ives prints, and above the fireplace a deer's head has been mounted, a full stag with developed horns. The people with you admire the decor of the cabin and you all decide—"

"Not with the deer head," Rachael said. The gauges, however, showed an amplitude within the green only.

"You become pregnant," Rick continued, "by a man who has promised to 20
marry you. The man goes off with another woman, your best friend; you get an abortion and—"

"I would never get an abortion," Rachael said. "Anyhow you can't. It's a life sentence and the police are always watching." This time both needles swung violently into the red.

"How do you know that?" Rick asked her, curiously. "About the difficulty of obtaining an abortion?"

"Everybody knows that," Rachael answered.

"It sounded like you spoke from personal experience." He watched the needles intently; they still swept out a wide path across the dials. "One more. You're dating a man and he asks you to visit his apartment. While you're there he offers you a drink. As you stand holding your glass you see into the bedroom; it's attractively decorated with bullfight posters, and you wander in to look closer. He follows after you, closing the door. Putting his arm around you, he says—"

Rachael interrupted, "What's a bullfight poster?" 25

"Drawings, usually in color and very large, showing a matador with his cape, a bull trying to gore him." He was puzzled. "How old are you?" he asked; that might be a factor.

"I'm eighteen," Rachael said. "Okay; so this man closes the door and puts his arm around me. What does he say?"

Rick said, "Do you know how bullfights ended?"

"I suppose somebody got hurt."

"The bull, at the end, was always killed." He waited, watching the two 30
needles. They palpitated restlessly, nothing more. No real reading at all. "A final question," he said. "Two-part. You are watching an old movie on TV, a movie from before the war. It shows a banquet in progress; the guests are enjoying raw oysters."

"Ugh," Rachael said; the needles swung swiftly.

"The entrée," he continued, "consists of boiled dog, stuffed with rice." The needles moved less this time, less than they had for the raw oysters. "Are raw oysters more acceptable to you than a dish of boiled dog? Evidently not." He put his pencil down, shut off the beam of light, removed the adhesive patch from her cheek. "You're an android," he said. "That's the conclusion of the testing," he informed her—or rather it—and Eldon Rosen, who regarded him with writhing worry; the elderly man's face contorted, shifted plastically with angry concern. "I'm right, aren't I?" Rick said. There was no answer, from either of the Rosens. "Look," he said reasonably. "We have no conflict of interest; it's important to me that the Voigt-Kampff test functions, almost as important as it is to you."

The elder Rosen said, "She's not an android."

"I don't believe it," Rick said.

"Why would he lie?" Rachael said to Rick fiercely. "If anything, we'd lie 35
the other way."

"I want a bone marrow analysis made of you," Rick said to her. "It can eventually be organically determined whether you're android or not; it's slow and painful, admittedly, but—"

"Legally," Rachael said, "I can't be forced to undergo a bone marrow test. That's been established in the courts; self-incrimination. And anyhow on a live person—not the corpse of a retired android—it takes a long time. You can give that damn Voigt-Kampff profile test because of the specials; they have to be tested for constantly, and while the government was doing that you police agencies slipped the Voigt-Kampff through. But what you said is true; that's the end of the testing." She rose to her feet, paced away from him, and stood with her hands on her hips, her back to him.

"The issue is not the legality of the bone marrow analysis," Eldon Rosen said huskily. "The issue is that your empathy delineation test failed in response to my niece. I can explain why she scored as an android might. Rachael grew up aboard *Salander 3*. She was born on it; she spent fourteen of her eighteen years living off its tape library and what the nine other crew members, all adults, knew about Earth. Then, as you know, the ship turned back a sixth of the way to Proxima. Otherwise Rachael would never have seen Earth—anyhow not until her later life."

"You would have retired me," Rachael said over her shoulder. "In a police dragnet I would have been killed. I've known that since I got here four years ago; this isn't the first time the Voigt-Kampff test has been given to me. In fact I rarely leave this building; the risk is enormous, because of those roadblocks you police set up, those flying wedge spot checks to pick up unclassified specials."

"And androids," Eldon Rosen added. "Although naturally the public isn't told that; they're not supposed to know that androids are on Earth, in our midst."

"I don't think they are," Rick said. "I think the various police agencies here and in the Soviet Union have gotten them all. The population is small enough now; everyone, sooner or later, runs into a random checkpoint." That, anyhow, was the idea.

"What were your instructions," Eldon Rosen asked, "if you wound up designating a human as android?"

"That's a departmental matter." He began restoring his testing gear to his briefcase; the two Rosens watched silently. "Obviously," he added, "I was told to cancel further testing, as I'm now doing. If it failed once there's no point in going on." He snapped the briefcase shut.

"We could have defrauded you," Rachael said. "Nothing forced us to admit you mistested me. And the same for the other nine subjects we've selected." She gestured vigorously. "All we had to do was simply go along with your test results, either way."

Rick said, "I would have insisted on a list in advance. A sealed-envelope breakdown. And compared my own test results for congruity. There would have had to be congruity." And I can see now, he realized, that I wouldn't have gotten it. Bryant was right. Thank god I didn't go out bounty hunting on the basis of this test.

"Yes, I suppose you would have done that," Eldon Rosen said. He glanced at Rachael, who nodded. "We discussed that possibility," Eldon said, then, with reluctance.

"This problem," Rick said, "stems entirely from your method of operation, Mr. Rosen. Nobody forced your organization to evolve the production of humanoid robots to a point where—"

"We produced what the colonists wanted," Eldon Rosen said. "We followed the time-honored principle underlying every commercial venture. If our firm hadn't made these progressively more human types, other firms in the field would have. We knew the risk we were taking when we developed the Nexus-6 brain unit. *But your Voigt-Kampff test was a failure before we released that type of android.* If you had failed to classify a Nexus-6 android as an android, if you had checked it out as human—but that's not what happened." His voice had become hard and bitingly penetrating. "Your police department—others as well—may have retired, very probably have retired, authentic humans with underdeveloped empathic ability, such as my innocent niece here. Your position, Mr. Deckard, is extremely bad morally. Ours isn't."

"In other words," Rick said with acuity, "I'm not going to be given a chance to check out a single Nexus-6. You people dropped this schizoid girl on me beforehand." And my test, he realized, is wiped out. I shouldn't have gone for it, he said to himself. However, it's too late now.

"We have you, Mr. Deckard," Rachael Rosen agreed in a quiet, reasonable 50
voice; she turned toward him, then, and smiled.

He could not make out, even now, how the Rosen Association had managed to snare him, and so easily. Experts, he realized. A mammoth corporation like this—it embodies too much experience. It possesses in fact a sort of group mind. And Eldon and Rachael Rosen consisted of spokesmen for that corporate entity. His mistake, evidently, had been in viewing them as individuals. It was a mistake he would not make again.

"Your superior Mr. Bryant," Eldon Rosen said, "will have difficulty understanding how you happened to let us void your testing apparatus before the test began." He pointed toward the ceiling, and Rick saw the camera lens. His massive error in dealing with the Rosens had been recorded. "I think the right thing for us all to do," Eldon said, "is sit down and—" He gestured affably. "We can work something out, Mr. Deckard. There's no need for anxiety. The Nexus-6 variety of android is a fact; we here at the Rosen Association recognize it and I think now you do, too."

Rachael, leaning toward Rick, said, "How would you like to own an owl?"

"I doubt if I'll ever own an owl." But he knew what she meant; he understood the business the Rosen Association wanted to transact. Tension of a kind he had never felt before manifested itself inside him; it exploded, leisurely, in every part of his body. He felt the tension, the consciousness of what was happening, take over completely.

"But an owl," Eldon Rosen said, "is the thing you want." He glanced at his 55
niece inquiringly. "I don't think he has any idea—"

"Of course he does," Rachael contradicted. "He knows exactly where this is heading. Don't you, Mr. Deckard?" Again she leaned toward him, and this time closer; he could smell a mild perfume about her, almost a warmth. "You're practically there, Mr. Deckard. You practically have your owl." To Eldon Rosen she said, "He's a bounty hunter; remember? So he lives off the bounty he makes, not his salary. Isn't that so, Mr. Deckard?"

He nodded.

"How many androids escaped this time?" Rachael inquired.

Presently he said, "Eight. Originally. Two have already been retired, by someone else; not me."

"You get how much for each android?" Rachael asked. 60

Shrugging, he said, "It varies."

Rachael said, "If you have no test you can administer, then there is no way you can identify an android. And if there's no way you can identify an android there's no way you can collect your bounty. So if the Voigt-Kampff scale has to be abandoned—"

"A new scale," Rick said, "will replace it. This has happened before." Three times, to be exact. But the new scale, the more modern analytical device, had been there already; no lag had existed. This time was different.

"Eventually, of course, the Voigt-Kampff scale will become obsolete," Rachael agreed. "But not now. We're satisfied ourselves that it will delineate the Nexus-6 types and we'd like you to proceed on that basis in your own particular, peculiar work." Rocking back and forth, her arms tightly folded, she regarded him with intensity. Trying to fathom his reaction.

"Tell him he can have his owl," Eldon Rosen grated. 65

"You can have the owl," Rachael said, still eyeing him. "The one up on the roof. Scrappy. But we will want to mate it if we can get our hands on a male. And any offspring will be ours; that has to be absolutely understood."

Rick said, "I'll divide the brood."

"No," Rachael said instantly; behind her Eldon Rosen shook his head, backing her up. "That way you'd have claim to the sole bloodline of owls for the rest of eternity. And there's another condition. You can't will your owl to anybody; at your death it reverts back to the association."

"That sounds," Rick said, "like an invitation for you to come in and kill me. To get your owl back immediately. I won't agree to that; it's too dangerous."

"You're a bounty hunter," Rachael said. "You can handle a laser gun—in 70
fact you're carrying one right now. If you can't protect yourself, how are you going to retire the six remaining Nexus-6 andys? They're a good deal smarter than the Grozzi Corporation's old W-4."

"But I hunt *them,*" he said. "This way, with a reversion clause on the owl, someone would be hunting me." And he did not like the idea of being stalked; he had seen the effect on androids. It brought about certain notable changes, even in them.

Rachael said, "All right; we'll yield on that. You can will the owl to your heirs. But we insist on getting the complete brood. If you can't agree to that, go on back to San Francisco and admit to your superiors in the department that the Voigt-Kampff scale, at least as administered by you, can't distinguish an andy from a human being. And then look for another job."

"Give me some time," Rick said.

"Okay," Rachael said. "We'll leave you in here, where it's comfortable." She examined her wristwatch.

"Half an hour," Eldon Rosen said. He and Rachael filed toward the door 75
of the room, silently. They had said what they intended to say, he realized; the rest lay in his lap.

As Rachael started to close the door after herself and her uncle, Rick said starkly, "You managed to set me up perfectly. You have it on tape that I missed on you; you know that my job depends on the use of the Voigt-Kampff scale; and you own that goddamn owl."

"Your owl, dear," Rachael said. "Remember? We'll tie your home address around its leg and have it fly down to San Francisco; it'll meet you there when you get off work."

It, he thought. *She keeps calling the owl it.* Not her. "Just a second," he said.

Pausing at the door, Rachael said, "You've decided?"

"I want," he said, opening his briefcase, "to ask you one more question from the Voigt-Kampff scale. Sit down again."

Rachael glanced at her uncle; he nodded and she grudgingly returned, seating herself as before. "What's this for?" she demanded, her eyebrows lifted in distaste—and wariness. He perceived her skeletal tension, noted it professionally.

Presently he had the pencil of light trained on her right eye and the adhesive patch again in contact with her cheek. Rachael stared into the light rigidly, the expression of extreme distaste still manifest.

"My briefcase," Rick said as he rummaged for the Voigt-Kampff forms. "Nice, isn't it? Department issue."

"Well, well," Rachael said remotely.

"Babyhide," Rick said. He stroked the black leather surface of the briefcase. "One hundred percent genuine human babyhide." He saw the two dial indicators gyrate frantically. But only after a pause. The reaction had come, but too late. He knew the reaction period down to a fraction of a second, the correct reaction period; there should have been none. "Thanks, Miss Rosen," he said, and gathered together the equipment again; he had concluded his retesting. "That's all."

"You're leaving?" Rachael asked.

"Yes," he said. "I'm satisfied."

Cautiously, Rachael said, "What about the other nine subjects?"

"The scale has been adequate in your case," he answered. "I can extrapolate from that; it's clearly still effective." To Eldon Rosen, who slumped morosely by the door of the room, he said, "Does she know?" Sometimes they didn't; false memories had been tried various times, generally in the mistaken idea that through them reactions to testing would be altered.

Eldon Rosen said, "No. We programmed her completely. But I think toward the end she suspected." To the girl he said, "You guessed when he asked for one more try."

Pale, Rachael nodded fixedly.

"Don't be afraid of him," Eldon Rosen told her. "You're not an escaped android on Earth illegally; you're the property of the Rosen Association, used as a sales device for prospective emigrants." He walked to the girl, put his hand comfortingly on her shoulder; at the touch the girl flinched.

"He's right," Rick said. "I'm not going to retire you, Miss Rosen. Good day." He started toward the door, then halted briefly. To the two of them he said, "Is the owl genuine?"

Rachael glanced swiftly at the elder Rosen.

"He's leaving anyhow," Eldon Rosen said. "It doesn't matter; the owl is artificial. There are no owls."

"Hmm," Rick muttered, and stepped numbly out into the corridor. The two of them watched him go. Neither said anything. Nothing remained to say. So that's how the largest manufacturer of androids operates, Rick said to himself. Devious, and in a manner he had never encountered before. A weird and convoluted new personality type; no wonder law enforcement agencies were having trouble with the Nexus-6.

The Nexus-6. He had now come up against it. Rachael, he realized; *she must be a Nexus-6.* I'm seeing one of them for the first time. And they damn near did it; they came awfully damn close to undermining the Voigt-Kampff scale, the only method we have for detecting them. The Rosen Association does a good job—makes a good try, anyhow—at protecting its products.

And I have to face six more of them, he reflected. Before I'm finished.

He would earn the bounty money. Every cent.

Assuming he made it through alive.

Understanding

1. Rick Deckard could have used a biologically based test, such as bone marrow, fingerprint, or DNA analysis, to examine Rachael Rosen. Instead he used an invisible quality—empathy—which can be inferred only from her responses to his questions. What is empathy? Why was it chosen as the quality that distinguishes humans from androids?
2. What is it about the quality of empathy that might be construed as a gift? Why might some "real" human beings not pass the Voigt-Kampff test?
3. How does Eldon Rosen explain Rachael's performance on the Voigt-Kampff test?
4. Deckard concludes that Rachael Rosen is a "weird and convoluted new personality type." Explain his meaning.
5. In this excerpt Dick uses dialogue to drive the story. What effect(s) does a dialogue-driven story have on the reader?

Responding

1. Have you ever deceived anyone about some aspect of your identity? How did you justify your deception? Were you detected? What were the consequences?
2. Many literary works deal with the theme of becoming a "real" person, for example, *Pinocchio, The Velveteen Rabbit, Metropolis,* and Mary Shelley's *Frankenstein.* In some works "realness" is a gift from a good fairy or other benevolent figure. Why is this theme so compelling to storytellers? What quality or qualities do you think makes a person "real"?
3. Relate a story from your experience in which you or someone you know displayed empathy.

4. Is empathy an inborn trait? If not, how does it develop?
5. What issues does this story raise about the consequences of cloning human life?

Connecting

Explain the differences in the deception that Eldon Rosen perpetrates on Deckard and the answers that De Ferrari gives to Señorita Luisa's questions at the end of "Our Peruvian Friend" earlier in this chapter.

The Marginal World

Rachel Carson

Rachel Carson (1907–1964) worked as a marine biologist for the U.S. Fish and Wildlife Service until 1952. This experience influenced her to write *Silent Spring* (1962) in which she documents the destructive effects of pesticides on the environment. As a result, *Silent Spring* led to a federal investigation and stricter regulations on pesticide use and established Carson as a powerful nature writer.

In her first three books—*Under the Sea-Wind* (1941), *The Sea around Us* (1950), and *The Edge of the Sea* (1955)—Carson educates readers about the significance of the living ocean. Her work is a turning point—a gift—in the history of nature writing, as she combines astute scientific knowledge with descriptive, lyrical prose that appeals to a wide audience. Look for the combination of these features in "The Marginal World."

The edge of the sea is a strange and beautiful place. All through the long history of Earth it has been an area of unrest where waves have broken heavily against the land, where the tides have pressed forward over the continents, receded, and then returned. For no two successive days is the shore line precisely the same. Not only do the tides advance and retreat in their eternal rhythms, but the level of the sea itself is never at rest. It rises or falls as the glaciers melt or grow, as the floor of the deep ocean basins shifts under its increasing load of sediments, or as the earth's crust along the continental margins warps up or down in adjustment to strain and tension. Today a little more land may belong to the sea, tomorrow a little less. Always the edge of the sea remains an elusive and indefinable boundary. 1

The shore has a dual nature, changing with the swing of the tides, belonging now to the land, now to the sea. On the ebb tide it knows the harsh extremes of the land world, being exposed to heat and cold, to wind, to rain and drying sun. On the flood tide it is a water world, returning briefly to the relative stability of the open sea.

Only the most hardy and adaptable can survive in a region so mutable, yet the area between the tide lines is crowded with plants and animals. In this difficult world of the shore, life displays its enormous toughness and vitality by occupying almost every conceivable niche. Visibly, it carpets the intertidal rocks; or half hidden, it descends into fissures and crevices, or hides under boulders, or lurks in the wet gloom of sea caves. Invisibly, where the casual observer would say there is no life, it lies deep in the sand, in burrows and tubes and passageways. It tunnels into solid rock and bores into peat and clay. It encrusts weeds or drifting spars or the hard, chitinous shell of a lobster. It exists minutely, as the film of bacteria that spreads over a rock surface or a wharf piling; as spheres of protozoa, small as pinpricks, sparkling at the surface of the sea; and as Lilliputian beings swimming through dark pools that lie between the grains of sand.

The shore is an ancient world, for as long as there has been an earth and sea there has been this place of the meeting of land and water. Yet it is a world that keeps alive the sense of continuing creation and of the relentless drive of life. Each time that I enter it, I gain some new awareness of its beauty and its deeper meanings, sensing that intricate fabric of life by which one creature is linked with another, and each with its surroundings.

5 In my thoughts of the shore, one place stands apart for its revelation of exquisite beauty. It is a pool hidden within a cave that one can visit only rarely and briefly when the lowest of the year's low tides fall below it, and perhaps from that very fact it acquires some of its special beauty. Choosing such a tide, I hoped for a glimpse of the pool. The ebb was to fall early in the morning. I knew that if the wind held from the northwest and no interfering swell ran in from a distant storm the level of the sea should drop below the entrance to the pool. There had been sudden ominous showers in the night, with rain like handfuls of gravel flung on the roof. When I looked out into the early morning the sky was full of a gray dawn light but the sun had not yet risen. Water and air were pallid. Across the bay the moon was a luminous disc in the western sky, suspended above the dim line of distant shore—the full August moon, drawing the tide to the low, low levels of the threshold of the alien sea world. As I watched, a gull flew by, above the spruces. Its breast was rosy with the light of the unrisen sun. The day was, after all, to be fair.

Later, as I stood above the tide near the entrance to the pool, the promise of that rosy light was sustained. From the base of the steep wall of rock on which I stood, a moss-covered ledge jutted seaward into deep water. In the surge at the rim of the ledge the dark fronds of oarweeds swayed, smooth and gleaming as leather. The projecting ledge was the path to the small hidden cave and its pool. Occasionally a swell, stronger than the rest, rolled smoothly over the rim and broke in foam against the cliff. But the intervals between such swells were long enough to admit me to the ledge and long enough for a glimpse of that fairy pool, so seldom and so briefly exposed.

And so I knelt on the wet carpet of sea moss and looked back into the dark cavern that held the pool in a shallow basin. The floor of the cave was only a few inches below the roof, and a mirror had been created in which all that grew on the ceiling was reflected in the still water below.

Under water that was clear as glass the pool was carpeted with green sponge. Gray patches of sea squirts glistened on the ceiling and colonies of soft coral were a pale apricot color. In the moment when I looked into the cave a little elfin starfish hung down, suspended by the merest thread, perhaps by only a single tube foot. It reached down to touch its own reflection, so perfectly delineated that there might have been, not one starfish, but two. The beauty of the reflected images and of the limpid pool itself was the poignant beauty of things that are ephemeral, existing only until the sea should return to fill the little cave.

Whenever I go down into this magical zone of the low water of the spring tides, I look for the most delicately beautiful of all the shore's inhabitants—

flowers that are not plant but animal, blooming on the threshold of the deeper sea. In that fairy cave I was not disappointed. Hanging from its roof were the pendent flowers of the hydroid Tubularia, pale pink, fringed and delicate as the wind flower. Here were creatures so exquisitely fashioned that they seemed unreal, their beauty too fragile to exist in a world of crushing force. Yet every detail was functionally useful, every stalk and hydranth and petal-like tentacle fashioned for dealing with the realities of existence. I knew that they were merely waiting, in that moment of the tide's ebbing, for the return of the sea. Then in the rush of water, in the surge of surf and the pressure of the incoming tide, the delicate flower heads would stir with life. They would sway on their slender stalks, and their long tentacles would sweep the returning water, finding in it all that they needed for life.

And so in that enchanted place on the threshold of the sea the realities 10
that possessed my mind were far from those of the land world I had left an hour before. In a different way the same sense of remoteness and of a world apart came to me in a twilight hour on a great beach on the coast of Georgia. I had come down after sunset and walked far out over sands that lay wet and gleaming, to the very edge of the retreating sea. Looking back across that immense flat, crossed by winding, water-filled gullies and here and there holding shallow pools left by the tide, I was filled with awareness that this intertidal area, although abandoned briefly and rhythmically by the sea, is always reclaimed by the rising tide. There at the edge of low water the beach with its reminders of the land seemed far away. The only sounds were those of the wind and the sea and the birds. There was one sound of wind moving over water, and another of water sliding over the sand and tumbling down the faces of its own wave forms. The flats were astir with birds, and the voice of the willet rang insistently. One of them stood at the edge of the water and gave its loud, urgent cry; an answer came from far up the beach and the two birds flew to join each other.

The flats took on a mysterious quality as dusk approached and the last evening light was reflected from the scattered pools and creeks. Then birds became only dark shadows, with no color discernible. Sanderlings scurried across the beach like little ghosts, and here and there the darker forms of the willets stood out. Often I could come very close to them before they would start up in alarm—the sanderlings running, the willets flying up, crying. Black skimmers flew along the ocean's edge silhouetted against the dull, metallic gleam, or they went flitting above the sand like large, dimly seen moths. Sometimes they "skimmed" the winding creeks of tidal water, where little spreading surface ripples marked the presence of small fish.

The shore at night is a different world, in which the very darkness that hides the distractions of daylight brings into sharper focus the elemental realities. Once, exploring the night beach, I surprised a small ghost crab in the searching beam of my torch. He was lying in a pit he had dug just above the surf, as though watching the sea and waiting. The blackness of the night possessed water, air, and beach. It was the darkness of an older world, before Man. There was no sound but the all-enveloping, primeval sounds of wind blowing over water and sand, and of waves crashing on the beach. There was no other visible life—just one small crab near the sea. I have seen hundreds of ghost crabs in other settings, but suddenly I was filled with the odd sensation that for the first time I knew the creature in its own world—that I understood, as never before, the essence of its being. In that moment time was suspended; the world to which I belonged did not exist and I might have been an onlooker from outer space. The little crab alone with the sea became a symbol that stood for life itself—for the delicate, destructible, yet incredibly vital force that somehow holds its place amid the harsh realities of the inorganic world.

The sense of creation comes with memories of a southern coast, where the sea and the mangroves, working together, are building a wilderness of thousands of small islands off the southwestern coast of Florida, separated from each other by a tortuous pattern of bays, lagoons, and narrow waterways. I remember a winter day when the sky was blue and drenched with sunlight; though there was no wind one was conscious of flowing air like cold clear crystal. I had landed on the surf-washed tip of one of those islands, and then worked my way around to the sheltered bay side. There I found the tide far out, exposing the broad mud flat of a cove bordered by the mangroves with their twisted branches, their glossy leaves, and their long prop roots reaching down, grasping and holding the mud, building the land out a little more, then again a little more.

The mud flats were strewn with the shells of that small, exquisitely colored mollusk, the rose tellin, looking like scattered petals of pink roses. There must have been a colony nearby, living buried just under the surface of the mud. At first the only creature visible was a small heron in gray and rusty plumage—a reddish egret that waded across the flat with the stealthy, hesitant movements of its kind. But other land creatures had been there, for a line of fresh tracks wound in and out among the mangrove roots, marking the path of a raccoon feeding on the oysters that gripped the supporting roots with projections from their shells. Soon I found the tracks of a shore bird, probably a sanderling, and followed them a little; then they turned toward the water and were lost, for the tide had erased them and made them as though they had never been.

Looking out over the cove I felt a strong sense of the inter-changeability 15
of land and sea in this marginal world of the shore, and of the links between the life of the two. There was also an awareness of the past and of the continuing flow of time, obliterating much that had gone before, as the sea had that morning washed away the tracks of the bird.

The sequence and meaning of the drift of time were quietly summarized in the existence of hundreds of small snails—the mangrove periwinkles—browsing on the branches and roots of the trees. Once their ancestors had been sea dwellers, bound to the salt waters by every tie of their life processes. Little by little over the thousands and millions of years the ties had been broken, the snails had adjusted themselves to life out of water, and now today they were living many feet above the tide to which they only occasionally returned. And perhaps, who could say how many ages hence, there would be in their descendants not even this gesture of remembrance for the sea.

The spiral shells of other snails—those quite minute—left winding tracks on the mud as they moved about in search of food. They were horn shells, and when I saw them I had a nostalgic moment when I wished I might see what Audubon saw, a century and more ago. For such little horn shells were the food of the flamingo, once so numerous on this coast, and when I half closed my eyes I could almost imagine a flock of these magnificent flame birds feeding in that cove, filling it with their color. It was a mere yesterday in the life of the earth that they were there; in nature, time and space are relative matters, perhaps most truly perceived subjectively in occasional flashes of insight, sparked by such a magical hour and place.

There is a common thread that links these scenes and memories—the spectacle of life in all its varied manifestations as it has appeared, evolved, and sometimes died out. Underlying the beauty of the spectacle there is meaning and significance. It is the elusiveness of that meaning that haunts us, that sends us again and again into the natural world where the key to the riddle is hidden. It sends us back to the edge of the sea, where the drama of life played its first scene on earth and perhaps even its prelude; where the forces of evolution are at work today, as they have been since the appearance of what we know as life; and where the spectacle of living creatures faced by the cosmic realities of their world is crystal clear.

Understanding

1. What is Carson's point? What does she want us to remember? How does Carson's use of both narrative (telling) and description (showing) accomplish her goals for the piece? Give examples.
2. Underline and then record three "magical" statements from this reading which you want to remember either because of the beauty of the writing or the profound nature of Carson's observation.
3. How would you describe the tone of this piece?

Responding

1. Is the natural world a gift? If not, why? If so, who gave it to us? Have we received it? Is there a responsibility attached to receiving a gift? Describe it in relationship to this reading.
2. Explore in writing what drew you to the three "magical" statements you recorded for Understanding question 2. Write your own nature piece to illustrate one of these statements.
3. Write about a time when you had a "sense of remoteness and of a world apart." Did you consider that moment a gift? What did that moment or experience open up for you?

Connecting

Carson's writing is centered in wonder. Her awe of the natural world comes from her acute skills of observation and from taking the time to notice and look. Sam Keen's father had that same bent and instilled a sense of wonder in his son (see "The Peach-Seed Monkey," earlier in this chapter).

What lessons—what gifts—are offered in these two readings for inward and other journeys? Where else have you encountered a person's sense of wonder at nature?

WRITING OPTION: Gifts

Review the Responding questions you answered for each of the readings in this chapter. If you have responded to at least one for each reading, you already have a significant amount of material from which to draw for this writing option.

Select one response that you would like to explore, representing, as the authors in this chapter have, a gift that contributed to your identity or to your understanding of the power of gifts. This may be a narrative that both tells your gift story and analyzes its impact on you, and it must build to a lesson or an insight that makes sense of the gift and its impact. Sam Keen's "The Peach-Seed Monkey" is an excellent model for developing this analytic narrative.

2

Wounds

Assembling an entire chapter of readings about wounds and the pain associated with them may seem more than a little depressing. And we have to admit that we were overwhelmed at times by the power of these selections to sadden us. But, after all, life without wounds is like life without *life.* In fact, the nine selections in this chapter tell us more than just how people experienced destructive acts of nature, physical brutality, and emotional cruelty. With clarity of insight and voices that make us feel pain, these writers reflect strength and resilience as well as subjection and vulnerability. And yet, they are *not* easy reading. They catch us off guard. They hurt.

At some point in human history came the discovery that we could injure each other and then tell about it in dramatic detail to great effect. As time progressed, wound stories became more complex, even more dramatic and, in some cases, epic. Many great works of literature—*The Iliad,* the Bible, *War and Peace,* and *Moby Dick* among them—involve grave physical wounds.

Wound stories are not limited to physical injuries. It is just as possible to wound someone with words; and the pain this produces, as some of these readings show, is no less intense. We can all identify with these stories, for who among us has not uttered words or done things we later regretted? How many of us have not been on the receiving end of a hurtful act? In a recent interview, Larry Dobie, the second black baseball player to join the major leagues (after Jackie Robinson), reflected on the abuse he received when he went out on the field as a Cleveland Indian in the late 1940s: "My parents told me that 'sticks and stones may break my bones, but names would never hurt me.' They were wrong. Words hurt—a lot."

The American reading public, it seems, is hungry for wound stories. In the 1980s and 1990s, two relatively new genres of writing that focus on wounds have reached the bestseller lists: *victim* or "reality" literature, in which survivors of abuse or neglect—the "walking wounded"—relate their experiences in memoir form to exorcise themselves, perhaps, but also to warn us; and *recovery* literature. The titles in this latter category, which usually begin with words like *Control, Overcome,* and *You Don't Have to,* reflect a current disposition in American society to overcome wounds, let the healing process begin, and get on with life. From such writings we learn that wounds take many forms, that the human threshold for pain is equally varied, and that, with effort and introspection, we can control how we interpret what happens to us.

Violence is not the only cause of wounds. Even the emotion that is said to conquer all—love—is associated with injury. Think of love's most common symbol—the heart pierced by Cupid's arrow—and the lyrics of many popular love songs that equate love with pain. American poet Amy Lowell captures this concept in one short line: "Rapture's self is three parts sorrow." Anyone who has loved and lost will connect with the feelings of Esteban Trueba as he reminisces about the death of Rosa the Beautiful, his first love, in Isabel Allende's *The House of the Spirits.* But *not* loving is no guarantee of self-preservation. Fyodor Dostoyevsky, who provides another account of lost love in an excerpt from *White Nights,* observed that "hell . . . is the suffering of being unable to love."

As the selections in this chapter reveal, both natural causes and social contact can wound us and thus change us. Natalie Kusz's harrowing account of her physical injuries in the excerpt from "Vital Signs"; a father's heart-rending pain at the death of his son in Anton Chekhov's "Grief"; a look at the cycle of domestic violence in M. F. K. Fisher's "The Broken Chain"; a child's living with racism in Ted Poston's "The Revolt of the Evil Fairies"; the monstrous effects of internment in a Nazi death camp as filtered through the eyes of a survivor and his son in Art Spiegelman's "Worse Than My Darkest Dreams"; the mistreatment that Lorenzo Carcaterra recalls receiving from his father in "Loving Your Enemy"; the psychic wounds inflicted in the course of living ordinary life in Katherine Mansfield's "Miss Brill"—all reveal how wounds leave their mark.

The writers in this chapter convey the authenticity of the wounds, make us care about what happened, and show us that in some instances healing is possible and in others, futile, but that something of value can come from them, even if it is simply resignation.

As you look beneath the surface of these selections and feel the effects they have on you, think about the motives behind the wounds people inflict on each other. Pay particular attention to how the writers draw you into the stories and prepare you for what happens. Most important, as you ponder how these writers crafted their works, identify the responses made to the wounds: the acceptance, the denial, the fury, the courage. The points of view mirrored in these responses are essential to an appreciation of the works and to the moral universes—the interpretations of right and wrong—in which they unfolded.

Attack

Natalie Kusz

Natalie Kusz (*Kusz* rhymes with *push*) was born in 1962 in New York City. In 1969, when she was about six, her parents sold everything and moved with their four children from Los Angeles to Alaska. Shortly after her seventh birthday, the event depicted in this selection took place, changing the course of her life. Years were spent in pain, enduring reconstructive surgery, infections, and failed skin and bone grafts as well as rejection by her peers. Kusz's adolescent years were marked by rebellion—drugs, fights, sex. At sixteen she gave birth to a baby girl whom she kept with the support of her family. Finally, she began to write. "Attack" is an excerpt from her autobiography, *Road Song*, which is praised for its "steady avoidance of self-pity."

Our nearest neighbors through the trees were the Horners, two cabins of cousins whose sons went to my school. Paul was in my class, Kevin was a year ahead, and both their families had moved here, as we had, from California, escaping the city and everything frightening that lived there. Kevin had a grown brother in L.A. who was comatose now since he'd been hit on the freeway; his mother, Geri, had come with her brother-in-law's family to Alaska to get well, she hoped, from her own mental breakdown, and to keep herself as far as she could from automobiles. 1

Paul and Kevin Horner were my best friends then, and we played with our dogs in the cousins' houses, or in the wide snowy yard in between. On weekends or days off from school, my parents took us sledding and to the gravel pit with our skates. Sometimes, if the day was long enough, Paul and Kevin and I followed rabbit tracks through the woods, careful not to step right on the trails for fear of leaving our scent there—for fear, that is, that the rabbits would abandon them. We mapped all the new trails we could find, and my mother gave me orders about when to be home. Bears, she said, and we laughed, said didn't she know they were asleep, and we could all climb trees anyway. We were not afraid, either, when Mom warned of dog packs. Dogs got cabin fever, too, she said, especially in the cold. They ran through the woods, whole crowds of them, looking for someone to gang up on.

That's okay, I told her. We carried pepper in our pockets in case of dogs: sprinkle it on their noses, we thought, and the whole pack would run away.

In December, the day before my birthday, when the light was dim and the days shorter than we had known before, Dad got a break at the union hall, a job at Prudhoe Bay that would save us just in time, before the stove oil ran out and groceries were gone. Mom convinced us children that he was off on a great adventure, that he would see foxes and icebergs, that we could write letters for Christmas and for New Year's, and afford new coats with feathers inside. In this last, I was not much interested, because I had my favorite already—a red wool coat that reversed to fake leopard—but I would be glad if this meant we could redeem from the pawnshop Dad's concertina, and his second violin, and mine, the half-size with a short bow, and the guitar and mandolin and rifles and pistol that had gone that way one by one. Whether I played each instrument or not, it had been good to have them around, smelling still of campfires and of songfests in the summer.

It was cold after Dad left, cold outside and cold in our house. Ice on the 5
trailer windows grew thick and shaggy, and Leslie and I melted handprints on it and licked off our palms. There had been no insulation when the add-on went up, so frost crawled the walls there, too, and Mom had us wear long johns and shoes unless we were in our beds. Paul and Kevin came for my birthday, helped me wish over seven candles, gave me a comb and a mirror. They were good kids, my mother said, polite and with good sense, and she told me that if I came in from school and she was not home, I should take Hobo with me and walk to their house. You're a worrywart, Mommy, I said. I'm not a baby, you know.

I wish now I had been tolerant of her fears, and perhaps even shared them. Alaska was a young place when we moved to it, much larger than it seems now, with more trees and thicker ice fog, and with its few people more isolated in the midst of them. During the very deep cold, car exhaust came out in particles rather than as gas, and it hung low and thick in the air, obscuring everything, so that even traffic lights were invisible to the car which was stopped right beneath them. In the middle of ice fog, a person was isolated, muffled and enclosed apart from anyone else on the road. Radio stations ran air-quality bulletins, warning asthmatics and old people to stay indoors, and most folks stayed home anyway, knowing how easily a fan belt would shatter in the cold. To us California-bred children, the rolling dense fog that billowed in our open door was a new and thrilling thing; but to my mother, who siphoned stove oil into the fuel barrel five gallons at a time, and who scavenged deadwood and sticks from under snow, that fog must have seemed formidable, the visual symbol of all one must fight against in this place. She kept the lock fastened even when we were home, and she looked and listened with her head out the door for long seconds each time she had to go out to the ice box. I remember her steps outside, slow and controlled on the bottom stairs, hitting faster and harder toward the top, and I remember her gasp as she lurched inside, her glasses clouding up with frost, Baggies of frozen berries falling down from her arms.

The morning after my birthday, Mom woke up and couldn't stand. She shivered and sweated, and when I helped her sit up she said the room was tilting away from her, and could I mix Bethel up a bottle. It was her tonsils, she said. They were tight in her throat and she couldn't swallow around them. Her skin was hot and wet under my hand; the sweat sat on her forehead and soaked into hairs that fell into it when she tried to lift her neck. "Stay there and I'll make some Russian Tea," I said. "Okay, Mommy? Maybe you can drink some tea?" Mom moved her head. She made a grunting noise as she swallowed, and her lips drew far back from her teeth.

Bethel had been sucking air from an empty bottle, and now she started to cry, dangling the nipple from her teeth and pulling herself up onto Mom's bed. Mom's eyes stayed closed, but her hand lifted off the mattress and patted limply at Bethel's shoulder. I breathed hard, and my eyes stung inside their lids. I picked my sister up and carried her into the trailer room, telling her, "Come on in here, Bethel. Let's make some milk and tea."

Leslie and Ian had their treasure chests out on the floor, and Leslie looked up. "Mommy's really sick, isn't she," she asked. I said yes, she was really sick.

I stayed home all week from school, making macaroni from boxes and saying everyone's prayers at night. Mom moved from bed to honeybucket and back and had me read Psalms at bedtime until she was strong enough again to see the words. The honeybucket in the corner was a five-gallon plastic paint can with a toilet seat on top, and under its red cloth drape it filled up, for Mom was too weak to carry it to the outhouse pit. I poured in more Pine Sol than usual each time someone used it, and the cabin filled with the fecund smell of pine oil and waste, a scent we would still loathe years later when we got a real toilet and electricity and began to boycott pine cleaners. The days got shorter all the time, and with no windows in the wanigan, we seemed to move in twilight, squinting at one another between four dark walls. I felt snappish and breathless, and I bossed Leslie and Ian until they cried. Finally, my mother was better and I went back to school, and she met me at the bus stop afternoons, walking me home down the road, shining the flashlight ahead of us.

Christmas passed, and Mom went into town every day—for water, or to do laundry, or to get the mail—but no check arrived from my father. He wrote often, including short notes to each of us, and he said he had sent his first paycheck down just two weeks after he started work. It was good money, he wrote, enough for stove oil and groceries and for the instruments in hock. When he came home, we would finish my violin lessons, and we'd start on the younger kids, too, and we would play together the same songs we had sung on the way up the Alcan and then after that at the campgrounds all summer long.

That first check never did come. Mom wrote back that it must have been lost, and could he get them to print another. When was the next one due, she asked. She would try to stretch things out until it came.

The redemption time was running out on all our things at the pawnshop. We had one violin left to pawn, the one my grandfather had given to Dad before I was born, when Dad had driven from L.A. to New York and brought the old man home with him. In Polish, it was a *Benkarty,* a wide, barrel-chested French violin, aged reddish-brown under its lacquer. It was for a master, made to play fast and ring loudly, its neck rounded and thinner than most, the back of its body all a single piece of maple. The wood and varnish had aged and crystallized so smoothly that when my father tuned it and began to play, each string he stroked resonated acutely with the sounds of the others. To pay the interest on the other things in hock, my mother took the *Benkarty* in to the pawnbroker, telling him she would be back for it soon. "It's my husband's," she said, trusting this Russian man to keep the violin safe, if only for sake of the old country and my father's Slavic tongue. She could not know then that the man would sell the *Benkarty* before its redemption date, or that she and my father would never get it back. At the time, the clearest thing for her was the extra cash she got for it, and the powdered milk and the gas she was able to buy that afternoon.

Mom arranged her days carefully around the hours I was in school. Her glasses had broken across the bridge one morning when she had come inside and set them to thaw on the woodstove, so she walked me to the bus stop wearing prescription sunglasses and then fastened my sisters and brother into the truck and drove into town, scraping ice from the windshield as she steered. I know from her journal that she was afraid, that she padlocked the cabin door against the vandalism recently come into town, that she counted her time out carefully so she would be home in time to meet my afternoon bus. She reminded me and made me promise that, should she be late one day, I would take Hobo to Paul and Kevin's and wait there until she came for me. "Okay, Mommy," I said then, and turned to pull Hobo's ears.

"No, listen to me, Natalie." Mom held my arm until I looked up. Behind the dark lenses her eyes were invisible, but her cheeks were white, and her lips very nearly the same color. "This is not a joke," she said. "Now don't forget what I'm saying. You must go to the boys' if I'm late. This is very important."

"It's okay," I repeated. I looked into her glasses. "I'll remember."

On January 10, only Hobo met me at the bus stop. In the glare from school-bus headlights, his blue eye shone brighter than his brown, and he watched until I took the last step to the ground before tackling me in the snow. Most days, Hobo hid in the shadow of the spruce until Mom took my bag, then he erupted from the dark to charge up behind me, run through my legs and on out the front. It was his favorite trick. I usually lost my balance and ended up sitting in the road with my feet thrown wide out front and steaming dog tongue all over my face.

Hobo ran ahead, then back, brushing snow crystals and fur against my leg. I put a hand on my skin to warm it and dragged nylon ski pants over the road behind me. Mom said to have them along in case the bus broke down, but she knew I would not wear them, could not bear the plastic sounds they made between my thighs.

No light was on in our house.

If Mom had been home, squares of yellow would have shown through the spruce and lit the fog of my breath, turning it bright as I passed through. What light there was now came from the whiteness of snow, and from the occasional embers drifting up from our stovepipe. I laid my lunchbox on the top step and pulled at the padlock, slapping a palm on the door and shouting. Hobo jumped away from the noise and ran off, losing himself in darkness and in the faint keening dog sounds going up from over near the Horners' house. I called, "Hobo. Come back here, boy," and took the path toward Paul's, tossing my ski pants to the storage tent as I passed.

At the property line, Hobo caught up with me and growled, and I fingered his ear, looking where he pointed, seeing nothing ahead there but the high curve and long sides of a Quonset hut, the work shed the Horners used also as a fence for one side of their yard. In the fall, Paul and Kevin and I had walked to the back of it, climbing over boxes and tools and parts of old furniture, and we had found in the corner a lemmings' nest made from chewed bits of cardboard and paper, packed under the curve of the wall so that shadows hid it from plain sight. We all bent close to hear the scratching, and while Paul held a flashlight I took two sticks and parted the rubbish until we saw the black eyes of a mother lemming and the pink naked bodies of five babies. The mother dashed deeper into the pile and we scooped the nesting back, careful not to touch the sucklings, for fear that their mama would eat them if they carried scent from our fingers.

It seemed that we had spent most of the fall looking out just like that for shrews and lemmings. Oscar and Vic had cats, and Paul and Kevin had three German shepherds, and one or another of them usually found a rodent to play with. Oscar's cats would catch a shrew in their teeth, holding tight to skin behind its neck until its eyes swelled out and it stopped breathing. The boys and I squeezed the cats' jaws, screaming, "You're not even *hungry,*" until the teeth parted and the shrew dropped into our palms. If we were fast enough, it was still alive, and we pushed its eyes back in and let it go. The dogs worried a lemming in their mouths, dropping it out on occasion and catching it back into the air, over and over again until it couldn't move and was no longer any fun. When we caught the dogs doing this, we beat their ears with walking sticks, but usually we were too late and had to bury the thing under moss.

The dogs were loud now beyond the Quonset, fierce in their howls and sounding like many more than just three. Hobo crowded against my legs, and as I walked he hunched in front of me, making me stumble into a drift that filled my boots with snow. I called him a coward and said to quit it, but I held his neck against my thigh, turning the corner into the boys' yard and stopping on the edge. Paul's house was lit in all its windows, Kevin's was dark, and in the yard between them were dogs, new ones I had not seen before, each with its own house and tether. The dogs and their crying filled the yard, and when they saw me they grew wilder, hurling themselves to the ends of their chains, pulling their lips off their teeth. Hobo cowered and ran and I called him with my mouth, but my eyes did not move from in front of me.

There were seven. I knew they were huskies and meant to pull dogsleds, because earlier that winter Paul's grandfather had put on his glasses and shown us a book full of pictures. He had turned the pages with a wet thumb, speaking of trappers and racing people and the ways they taught these dogs to run. They don't feed them much, he said, or they get slow and lose their drive. This was how men traveled before they invented snowmobiles or gasoline.

There was no way to walk around the dogs to the lighted house. The snow had drifted and been piled around the yard in heaps taller than I was, and whatever aisle was left along the sides was narrow, and pitted with chain marks where the animals had wandered, dragging their tethers behind. No, I thought, Kevin's house was closest and out of biting range, and someone could, after all, be sitting home in the dark.

My legs were cold. The snow in my boots had packed itself around my ankles and begun to melt, soaking my socks and the felt liners under my heels.

I turned toward Kevin's house, chafing my thighs together hard to warm them, and I called cheerfully at the dogs to shut up. Oscar said that if you met a wild animal, even a bear, you had to remember it was more scared than you were. Don't act afraid, he said, because they can smell fear. Just be loud—stomp your feet, wave your hands—and it will run away without even turning around. I yelled "Shut up" again as I climbed the steps to Kevin's front door, but even I could barely hear myself over the wailing. At the sides of my eyes, the huskies were pieces of smoke tumbling over one another in the dark.

The wood of the door was solid with cold, and even through deerskin mittens it bruised my hands like concrete. I cupped a hand to the window and looked in, but saw only black—black, and the reflection of a lamp in the other cabin behind me. I turned and took the three steps back to the ground; seven more and I was in the aisle between doghouses, stretching my chin far up above the frenzy, thinking hard on other things. This was how we walked in summertime, the boys and I, escaping from bad guys over logs thrown across ditches: step lightly and fast, steady on the hard parts of your soles, arms extended outward, palms down and toward the sound. That ditch, this aisle, was a river, a torrent full of silt that would fill your clothes and pull you down if you missed and fell in. I was halfway across. I pointed my chin toward the house and didn't look down.

On either side, dogs on chains hurled themselves upward, choking themselves to reach me, until their tethers jerked their throats back to earth. I'm not afraid of you, I whispered; this is dumb.

I stepped toward the end of the row and my arms began to drop slowly closer to my body. Inside the mittens, my thumbs were cold, as cold as my thighs, and I curled them in and out again. I was walking past the last dog and I felt brave, and I forgave him and bent to lay my mitten on his head. He surged forward on a chain much longer than I thought, leaping at my face, catching my hair in his mouth, shaking it in his teeth until the skin gave way with a jagged sound. My feet were too slow in my boots, and as I blundered backward they tangled in the chain, burning my legs on metal. I called out at Paul's window, expecting rescue, angry that it did not come, and I beat my arms in front of me, and the dog was back again, pulling me down.

A hole was worn into the snow, and I fit into it, arms and legs drawn up in front of me. The dog snatched and pulled at my mouth, eyes, hair; his breath clouded the air around us, but I did not feel its heat, or smell the blood sinking down between hairs of his muzzle. I watched my mitten come off in his teeth and sail upward, and it seemed unfair then and very sad that one hand should freeze all alone; I lifted the second mitten off and threw it away, then turned my face back again, overtaken suddenly by loneliness. A loud river ran in my ears, dragging me under.

My mother was singing. *Lu-lee, lu-lay, thou little tiny child,* the song to the Christ Child, the words she had sung, smoothing my hair, all my life before bed. Over a noise like rushing water I called to her and heard her answer back, Don't worry, just sleep, the ambulance is on its way. I drifted back out and couldn't know then what she prayed, that I would sleep on without waking, that I would die before morning.

She had counted her minutes carefully that afternoon, sure that she would get to town and back, hauling water and mail, with ten minutes to spare before my bus came. But she had forgotten to count one leg of the trip, had skidded up the drive fifteen minutes late, pounding a fist on the horn, calling me home. On the steps, my lunchbox had grown cold enough to burn her hands. She got the water, the groceries, and my brother and sisters inside, gave orders that no one touch the woodstove or open the door, and she left down the trail to Paul's, whistling Hobo in from the trees.

I know from her journal that Mom had been edgy all week about the crazed dog sounds next door. Now the new huskies leaped at her and Hobo rumbled warning from his chest. Through her sunglasses, the dogs were just shapes, indistinct in windowlight. She tried the dark cabin first, knocking hard on the windows, then turned and moved down the path between doghouses, feeling her way with her feet, kicking out at open mouths. Dark lenses frosted over from her breath, and she moved toward the house and the lights on inside.

"She's not here." Paul's mother held the door open and air clouded inward in waves. Mom stammered out thoughts of bears, wolves, dogs. Geri grabbed on her coat. She had heard a noise out back earlier—they should check there and then the woods.

No luck behind the cabin and no signs under the trees. Wearing sunglasses and without any flashlight, Mom barely saw even the snow. She circled back and met Geri under the windowlight. Mom looked toward the yard and asked about the dogs. "They seem so hungry," she said.

Geri looked that way and then back at my mother. "No. Paul's folks just got them last week, but the boys play with them all the time." All the same, she and Mom scanned their eyes over the kennels, looking through and then over their glasses. Nothing seemed different. "Are you sure she isn't home?" Geri asked. "Maybe she took a different trail."

Maybe. Running back with Geri behind her, Mom called my name until her lungs frosted inside and every breath was a cough. She whistled the family whistle my father had taught us, the secret one he and his family had used to call one another from the woods in Nazi Germany. "*Dodek, ty-gdzie,*" the tune went, "Dodek, where are you?" She blew it now, two syllables for my name, high then low, then a lower one, quick, and another high slide down to low. Her lips hardly worked in the cold, and the whistle was feeble, and she finished by shouting again, curling both hands around her mouth. "Come on," she said to Geri. "Let's get to my cabin." The three younger children were still the only ones home, and Mom handed them their treasure chests, telling them to play on the bed until she found Natalie. Don't go outside, she said. I'll be back real soon.

Back at the Horners', Geri walked one way around the Quonset and Mom the other. Mom sucked air through a mitten, warming her lungs. While Geri climbed over deeper snow, she approached the sled dogs from a new angle. In the shadow of one, a splash of red—the lining of my coat thrown open. "I've found her," she shouted, and thought as she ran, Oh, thank God. Thank, thank God.

The husky stopped its howling as Mom bent to drag me out from the hole. Geri caught up and seemed to choke. “Is she alive?” she asked.

Mom said, “I think so, but I don’t know how.” She saw one side of my face 40
gone, one red cavity with nerves hanging out, scraps of dead leaves stuck on to the mess. The other eye might be gone, too; it was hard to tell. Scalp had been torn away from my skull on that side, and the gashes reached to my forehead, my lips, had left my nose ripped wide at the nostrils. She tugged my body around her chest and carried me inside.

Understanding

1. What was the economic situation of this family? How do you know?
2. When do you feel that something ominous will happen? Mark that place in the reading.
3. What happened to Kusz? Where was Hobo during the attack?
4. Imagine the act of writing this essay. Imagine Kusz reliving the attack in order to put this pivotal experience on the page for us to read. How do you think writing this affected her? How do you think she felt when she finished her story? Why would someone want to write—to reconstruct—such a terrible experience? Do you detect a “steady avoidance of self-pity” in her story?
5. Is it possible, once a face—the most obvious part of our body—is destroyed, for us to live a “normal” public life—a life of *observing* rather than one of *being observed?*
6. How might this wound be considered a signature?

Responding

1. Have you or has anyone close to you ever had such a wound? Can you tell the story, including its impact, even now?
2. In paragraph 31 we learn that Natalie’s mother silently prayed that Natalie would die before morning. Why would her mother have done that? Would you? Have you ever prayed for someone to die? What were the circumstances? Tell it in a story.
3. Have you ever had a dog? Do you recall the animal as a gift or a wound?
4. What could have caused this attack? If you have more than a passing knowledge about dogs, make a conjecture that explains the behavior of the husky that attacked Natalie so viciously.
5. Contemplate the selection with attention to the writer or storyteller as inventor; that is, the writer’s use of fact and interpretation. For example, what happened was that, when she was seven, a husky attacked her and tore away various parts of her body. These are the facts. The story Kusz writes, however, is her interpretation—how that event occurred for her and her family. Further distinguish what is fact in “Attack” and what is Kusz’s interpretation of those facts.

Connecting

Using Keen's "The Peach-Seed Monkey" and Kusz's "Attack," analyze the elements necessary for making an excellent story. Aside from the themes—gifts and wounds—being very different markers of life-altering experiences, what do you notice as being similarly powerful in the telling of these stories?

Grief

Anton Chekhov

Regarded as the father of the modern short story, Anton Pavlovich Chekhov (1860–1904) was a dominant influence on twentieth-century short-story writing. Earlier writers of the genre moved in a linear direction, producing a strong climax or a well-developed point. In contrast, Chekhov's stories develop with little action and plot through impressionistic details that create mood, atmosphere, insight into character, and a timeless quality. Still a young man of forty-four when he died of tuberculosis, Chekhov made a lasting contribution to literature with his plays depicting the frustrations of Russian society in the last years of the tsars. The characters who populate *The Sea Gull* (1896), *Uncle Vanya* (1899), *The Three Sisters* (1900), and especially *The Cherry Orchard* (1904) are so vivid and believable that these dramas are still produced today, to wide acclaim, on stages throughout the world.

The event portrayed in "Grief" seems confined to a small space, but the story's open-ended movement conveys to the reader the impression of a larger world of events in which the characters' lives unfold.

1 It is twilight. A thick wet snow is slowly twirling around the newly lighted street-lamps, and lying in soft thin layers on the roofs, the horses' backs, people's shoulders and hats. The cab-driver, Iona Potapov, is quite white, and looks like a phantom; he is bent double as far as a human body can bend double; he is seated on his box, and never makes a move. If a whole snowdrift fell on him, it seems as if he would not find it necessary to shake it off. His little horse is also quite white, and remains motionless; its immobility, its angularity, and its straight wooden-looking legs, even close by give it the appearance of a ginger-bread horse worth a kopeck. It is, no doubt, plunged in deep thought. If you were snatched from the plough, from your usual grey surroundings, and were thrown into this slough full of monstrous lights, unceasing noise and hurrying people, you too would find it difficult not to think.

Iona and his little horse have not moved from their place for a long while. They left their yard before dinner, and, up to now, not a "fare." The evening mist is descending over the town, the white lights of the lamps are replacing brighter rays, and the hubbub of the street is getting louder. "Cabby, for Viborg way!" suddenly hears Iona. "Cabby!"

Iona jumps, and through his snow-covered eyelashes, sees an officer in a greatcoat, with his hood over his head.

"Viborg way!" the officer repeats. "Are you asleep, eh? Viborg way!"

5 With a nod of assent Iona picks up the reins, in consequence of which layers of snow slip off the horse's back and neck. The officer seats himself in the sleigh, the cab-driver smacks his lips to encourage his horse, stretches out

his neck like a swan, sits up, and, more from habit than necessity, brandishes his whip. The little horse also stretches his neck, bends his wooden-looking legs, and makes a move undecidedly.

"What are you doing, were-wolf!" is the exclamation Iona hears, from the dark mass moving to and fro as soon as they started.

"Where the devil are you going? To the r-r-right!"

"You do not know how to drive. Keep to the right!" calls the officer angrily.

A coachman from a private carriage swears at him; a passer-by, who has run across the road and rubbed his shoulder against the horse's nose, looks at him furiously as he sweeps the snow from his sleeve. Iona shifts about on his seat as if he were on needles, moves his elbows as if he were trying to keep his equilibrium, and gapes about like someone suffocating, and who does not understand why and wherefore he is there.

"What scoundrels they all are!" jokes the officer; "one would think they had all entered into an agreement to jostle you or fall under your horse."

Iona looks round at the officer, and moves his lips. He evidently wants to say something, but the only sound that issues is a snuffle.

"What?" asks the officer.

Iona twists his mouth into a smile, and with an effort says hoarsely:

"My son, Barin, died this week."

"Hm! What did he die of?"

Iona turns with his whole body towards his fare, and says:

"And who knows! They say high fever. He was three days in hospital, and then died. . . . God's will be done."

"Turn round! The devil!" sounded from the darkness. "Have you popped off, old doggie, eh? Use your eyes!"

"Go on, go on," said the officer, "otherwise we shall not get there by to-morrow. Hurry a bit!"

The cab-driver again stretches his neck, sits up, and, with a bad grace, brandishes his whip. Several times again he turns to look at his fare, but the latter had closed his eyes, and apparently is not disposed to listen. Having deposited the officer in the Viborg, he stops by the tavern, doubles himself up on his seat, and again remains motionless, while the snow once more begins to cover him and his horse. An hour, and another. . . . Then, along the foot-path, with a squeak of goloshes, and quarrelling, came three young men, two of them tall and lanky, the third one short and hump-backed.

"Cabby, to the Police Bridge!" in a cracked voice calls the hump-back. "The three of us for two griveniks!" (20 kopecks).

Iona picks up his reins, and smacks his lips. Two griveniks is not a fair price, but he does not mind if it is a rouble or five kopecks—to him it is all the same now, so long as they are wayfarers. The young men, jostling each other and using bad language, approach the sleigh, and all three at once try to get on to the seat; then begins a discussion which two shall sit and who shall be the one to stand. After wrangling, abusing each other, and much petulance, it was at last decided that the hump-back should stand, as he was the smallest.

"Now then, hurry up!" says the hump-back in a twanging voice, as he takes his place, and breathes in Iona's neck. "Old furry. Here, mate, what a cap you have got, there is not a worse one to be found in all Petersburg! . . ."

"Hi—hi,—hi—hi," giggles Iona. "Such a . . ."

"Now you, 'such a,' hurry up, are you going the whole way at this pace? Are you? . . . Do you want it in the neck?"

"My head feels like bursting," says one of the lanky ones. "Last night at the Donkmasovs, Vaska and I drank the whole of four bottles of cognac."

"I don't understand what you lie for," said the other lanky one angrily; "you lie like a brute."

"God strike me, it's the truth!"

"It's as much a truth as that a louse coughs!"

"Hi, hi," grins Iona, "what gay young gentlemen!"

"Pshaw, go to the devil!" indignantly says the hump-back.

"Are you going to get on or not, you old pest? Is that the way to drive? Use the whip a bit! Go on, devil, go on, give it him well!"

Iona feels at his back the little man wriggling, and the tremble in his voice. He listens to the insults hurled at him, sees the people, and little by little the feeling of loneliness leaves him. The hump-back goes on swearing until he gets mixed up in some elaborate six-foot oath, or chokes with coughing. The lankies begin to talk about a certain Nadejda Petrovna. Iona looks round at them several times; he waits for a temporary silence, then, turning round again, he murmurs:

"My son—died this week."

"We must all die," sighed the hump-back, wiping his lips after an attack of coughing. "Now, hurry up, hurry up! Gentlemen, I really cannot go any farther like this! When will he get us there?"

"Well, just you stimulate him a little in the neck!"

"You old pest, do you hear, I'll bone your neck for you! If one treated the like of you with ceremony one would have to go on foot! Do you hear, old serpent Gorinytch! Or do you not care a spit?"

Iona hears rather than feels the blows they deal him.

"Hi, hi," he laughs. "They are gay young gentlemen, God bless 'em!"

"Cabby, are you married?" asks a lanky one.

"I? Hi, hi, gay young gentlemen! Now I have only a wife: the moist ground. . . . Hi, ho, ho . . . that is to say, the grave! My son has died, and I am alive. . . . A wonderful thing, death mistook the door . . . instead of coming to me, it went to my son. . . ."

Iona turns round to tell them how his son died, but at this moment the hump-back, giving a little sigh, announces, "Thank God, they have at last reached their destination," and Iona watches them disappear through the dark entrance. Once more he is alone, and again surrounded by silence. . . . His grief, which had abated for a short while, returns and rends his heart with greater force. With an anxious and a hurried look, he searches among the crowds passing on either side of the street to find if there is just one person who will listen to him. But the crowds hurry by without noticing him or his trouble. Yet it is such an immense, illimitable grief. Should his heart break and the grief pour out, it would flow over the whole earth it seems, and yet, no one sees it. It has managed to conceal itself in such an insignificant shell that no one can see it even by day and with a light.

Iona sees a hall-porter with some sacking, and decides to talk to him.

"Friend, what sort of time is it?" he asks.

"Past nine. What are you standing here for? Move on." 45

Iona moves on a few steps, doubles himself up, and abandons himself to his grief. He sees it is useless to turn to people for help. In less than five minutes he straightens himself, holds up his head as if he felt some sharp pain, and gives a tug at the reins: he can bear it no longer. "The stables," he thinks, and the little horse, as if he understood, starts off at a trot.

About an hour and a half later Iona is seated by a large dirty stove. Around the stove, on the floor, on the benches, people are snoring; the air is thick and suffocatingly hot. Iona looks at the sleepers, scratches himself, and regrets having returned so early.

"I have not even earned my fodder," he thinks. "That's what's my trouble. A man who knows his job, who has had enough to eat, and his horse too, can always sleep peacefully."

A young cab-driver in one of the corners half gets up, grunts sleepily, and stretches towards a bucket of water.

"Do you want a drink?" Iona asks him. 50

"Don't I want a drink!"

"That's so? Your good health! But listen, mate—you know, my son is dead. . . . Did you hear? This week, in hospital. . . . It's a long story."

Iona looks to see what effect his words have, but sees none—the young man has hidden his face, and is fast asleep again. The old man sighs, and scratches his head. Just as much as the young one wanted to drink, the old man wanted to talk. It will soon be a week since his son died, and he has not been able to speak about it properly to anyone. One must tell it slowly and carefully; how his son fell ill, how he suffered, what he said before he died, how he died. One must describe every detail of the funeral, and the journey to the hospital to fetch the defunct's clothes. His daughter Anissia remained in the village—one must talk about her too. Was it nothing he had to tell? Surely the listener would gasp and sigh, and sympathise with him? It is better, too, to talk to women; although they are stupid, two words are enough to make them sob.

"I'll go and look at my horse," thinks Iona; "there's always time to sleep. No fear of that!"

He puts on his coat, and goes to the stables to his horse; he thinks of the corn, the hay, the weather. When he is alone, he dare not think of his son; he could speak about him to anyone, but to think of him, and picture him to himself, is unbearably painful. 55

"Are you tucking in?" Iona asks his horse, looking at his bright eyes; "go on, tuck in, though we've not earned our corn, we can eat hay. Yes! I am too old to drive—my son could have, not I. He was a first-rate cab-driver. If only he had lived!"

Iona is silent for a moment, then continues:

"That's how it is, my old horse. There's no more Kuzma Ionitch. He has left us to live, and he went off pop. Now let's say, you had a foal, you were that foal's mother, and suddenly, let's say, that foal went and left you to live after him. It would be sad, wouldn't it?"

The little horse munches, listens, and breathes over his master's hand. . . .

Iona's feelings are too much for him, and he tells the little horse the 60
whole story.

Understanding

1. To whom did Iona attempt to tell his story? What reactions did he receive? Did they satisfy him? Underline and refer to the text in answering this question.
2. For many people, talking is a matter of habit. As a result, people often talk *past* rather than talk *with* each other. Is this the case in "Grief"? What in the story supports your response?
3. Who was most sympathetic to Iona's story? Why?
4. What do you think motivated Iona to persist in telling his story in spite of the reactions he received?
5. Are there elements in "Grief," in addition to the death of Iona's son, that convey a feeling of sadness? If so, what are they?

Responding

1. What did you learn from Iona about telling others about *your* wounds?
2. What responsibilities do people who listen to grief stories have to the sufferers?
3. How can we derive value from suffering wounds? Have you ever done so? What did you learn from them? Explain your response.
4. What wounds do you resent having suffered? What have you learned from the experience?

Connecting

Review your definition of empathy from Dick's "The Empathy Test" (chapter one). In what ways do the responses that Iona Potapov receives to the announcement of his son's death conform to your definition?

Loving Your Enemy

Lorenzo Carcaterra

Wounds, in the form of violence done to others, are the stuff of Lorenzo Carcaterra's writing. A former *New York Daily News* reporter and the managing editor of the CBS series *Top Cops,* Carcaterra is the author of *A Safe Place: The True Story of a Father, a Son, a Murder,* from which the following selection is excerpted. It tells the story of how the author learned that his father had murdered his first wife and how he, the son, came to grips with the revelation.

Carcaterra's well-known 1995 book *Sleepers* relates what happens to a group of four friends in New York's Hell's Kitchen, whose lives are changed forever when a prank misfires, an elderly man nearly dies, and the four are sent to an upstate boys' reformatory, where they are raped and beaten by guards. Released in 1996 as a feature film, *Sleepers* generated a great deal of controversy from those who doubted its autobiographical source, but it exhibits the powerful narrative strain that the reader encounters in "Loving Your Enemy." Carcaterra's most recent novel is entitled *Apaches.*

The last time I saw my father, he had his eyes closed and his hands across 1
his chest. He was in the middle of a dank room with frayed wall-to-wall carpeting and a dim overhead light. My father was stretched out inside a large four-ply cardboard box, a white sheet folded to the center of his bare chest. He had been dead less than 48 hours and in three hours would be cremated.

My mother stood in front of him, thin hands gripping the edge of the box. "It didn't have to be like this," my mother said to her husband. "Didn't have to end this way. Foolish. Always so foolish."

I paced the back of the room, hands inside the pockets of my jeans jacket, trying not to cry over the death of my father, trying to ignore my sadness at the loss of a man who had, over the course of my lifetime, become my most dreaded enemy.

And most trusted friend. 5

My father was a violent man with a short fuse, quick to attack verbally, quicker still to lash out physically. He beat my mother often, for the silliest and simplest offenses. I was not spared his blows either. By age 10, I had 35 stitches on my body, the majority caused by his hands.

He was a con man, a sharp-talking dreamer skilled at duping dollars from the wallets of working men, promising riches in return for hard-earned table money. He seldom concerned himself about his own ability to pay back.

My father was also a convicted murderer. In late October 1946, his temper fueled by jealous rage, he held a pillow against the face of his first wife and kept it there until the life was snuffed from her 24-year-old body. He walked out of the hotel on the West Side of Manhattan where he had left her and within three days was in the hands of the law. “I may be a rat,” he said at his arrest, “but now no other rat can have her.”

He was convicted of manslaughter in the second degree and sentenced to a 5-to-15-year term in a state penitentiary. He was 29. Less than seven years after the murder, he was again a free man.

I found out about my father’s crime when I was 14 years old, on an island in southern Italy, visiting my mother’s family for the first time. It was my mother who told me.

Until that moment, my father and I had been virtually inseparable. It had 10
become easy for me to ignore his violent mood swings and vicious beatings, for in the streets of the neighborhood we lived in my father was no different from many of the men who called Hell’s Kitchen home.

Those West Side streets served as a haven for dockworkers and butchers, hard hats and steam fitters, printers and truckers, all tough men who lived tough lives. Most cheated on their wives, quite a few had served prison time and all were comfortable around violence.

Like most of the neighborhood men, my father treated me not as a child but as an equal. He would take me to Yankee Stadium and there, under the lights of a twi-night doubleheader, our mouths crammed with hot dogs, he talked about Joe D., Ted Williams and Harmon Killebrew. He took me to Madison Square Garden for weekly fights and monthly wrestling matches, our seats always in the front rows.

My father was a man who cursed in every sentence he spoke, but never allowed an ethnic or racial slur to be used in our home. He loved music and would talk for hours about how much better Gene Krupa was than Buddy Rich and how nobody could touch Chick Webb when it came to the art of playing drums.

My father laughed at the Three Stooges and the Marx Brothers, cried at the most vapid movie melodrama and smiled whenever he heard my mother singing a Neapolitan love ballad. He loved watching Cagney, Bogart and Robinson on television and hated opera, talk shows and soccer. He didn’t drink much and smoked even less, never voted in any elections and ate pasta every day of his free life. He also wolfed down steak-and-egg breakfasts at 4 in the morning, in front of a rusty barrel filled with crackling wood at the 14th Street meat market where he worked as a butcher.

But most of all, my father loved me. 15

These images filled my mind as I looked at my father in that box in the funeral home in the north-east Bronx, waiting to be turned to ashes. I remembered how our lives had changed after I found out about the murder, how my initial shock had grown into hate. I remembered all the years I had ignored him, turned my back to his pleas for money or even conversation.

All those years I was more concerned about what the murder meant to me. I thought nothing of what it had meant to him. I had helped pay his debts and had covered up many of his lies, but I found it impossible to return his love. I knew he had killed a woman and had seen him beat my mother into a ruin. I could not bring myself to forgive him for either act.

I moved closer to his body, staring at the waxlike glaze of his skin, amazed at how the cancer had eaten at his once formidable bulk. I put my left hand on top of his head, bald and cold to the touch. My mother, still standing by my father's side, began to cry—loving tears shed over a man she had so much reason to hate.

I stared down at my father and knew now that he neither wanted nor cared about my forgiveness. He was a hard man and the dark hours of his life were his alone to bear. What he *did* want from me was a son's love. I had been more than willing to give him that during the first 14 years of my life. I never could on any day after.

I put a hand under my mother's arm and nudged her from the box, away from her husband.

"We should go," I said.

My mother wiped at the corners of her eyes with the edge of a white tissue. She buttoned her wool coat.

"You should have told him," she said.

"Told him what?"

"That you loved him," my mother said. "It was all he wanted."

"I know," I said.

"It's not too late," my mother said. "Stay with him a while longer. I'll wait outside."

"Mom, there's not much time," I said. "They have to take him away."

"They can wait," my mother said.

I stood in the center of the room, alone with my father, my back and chest wet with sweat. Five more hesitant steps and I was staring once again at his silent features. I bit my lower lip and fought back tears. I held the side of the cardboard box and shook my head.

"You bastard," I said to my father. "You dirty bastard."

Then I sank to my knees and cried over the body of the one man I loved more than any other.

Understanding

1. How would you describe the relationship between the author and his father? What feelings did he have toward his father? What means does the author use to reveal his character and that of his father?
2. Oliver Wendell Holmes, a former Chief Justice of the U.S. Supreme Court, wrote that "Love is the master key that opens the gates of happiness, of hatred, of jealousy, and most easily of all, the gate of fear." Which of these emotions do you see reflected in "Loving Your Enemy"?
3. What wounds did the author suffer at his father's hands? Which do you think were the most hurtful?

Responding

1. The title of this excerpt derives from a belief found in many religions: *Love your enemies; do good to them which hate you* is advice from the Bible; *people must*

eliminate thoughts that stimulate greed, anger, and foolishness is a principle from the teachings of the Buddha. How wise or useful is this advice?

2. Close your eyes and collect all the details of this story that had meaning for you. Place yourself for a few moments in Carcaterra's situation. Imagine your hands on the sides of the cardboard box that held the body. What would you say? What does your response say about you?
3. Do you agree or disagree with the idea that hate keeps enemies together? Why?

Connecting

How do Carcaterra's feelings differ from Iona Potapov's grief in Chekhov's "Grief"? To whom do you think Carcaterra would relate his feelings?

The Broken Chain

M. F. K. Fisher

Mary Frances Kennedy Fisher (1908–92) is remembered most for the twenty books she wrote on good company, good cooking, and traveling and living in France. Born in Albion, Michigan, Fisher and her family moved to California when she was three, settling eventually in Whittier. Toward the end of her eventful life, she began to look back. *To Begin Again: Stories and Memoirs, 1908–1929* comprises twenty-one essays about her early life, including the following selection. *Last House,* her final book, is filled with recollections of her favorite themes—food, love, family, and France—but also a recognition of the effects of disease and aging.

"The Broken Chain" is a closely observed and obviously memorable account (Fisher recalled it some sixty years after it happened) of an incident in her early adolescence.

1 There has been more talk than usual lately about the abuse and angry beating of helpless people, mostly children and many women. I think about it. I have never been beaten, so empathy is my only weapon against the ugliness I know vicariously. On the radio someone talks about a chain of violence. When is it broken? he asks. How?

When I was growing up, I was occasionally spanked and always by my father. I often had to go upstairs with him when he came home from the *News* for lunch, and pull down my panties and lay myself obediently across his long bony knees, and then steel my emotions against the ritualistic whack of five or eight or even ten sharp taps from a wooden hairbrush. They were counted by my age, and by nine or ten he began to use his hand, in an expert upward slap that stung more than the hairbrush. I often cried a little, to prove that I had learned my lesson.

I knew that Rex disliked this duty very much, but that it was part of being Father. Mother could not or would not punish us. Instead, she always said, by agreement with him and only when she felt that things were serious enough to drag him into it, that she would have to speak with him about the ugly matter when he came home at noon.

This always left me a cooling-off period of thought and regret and conditioned dread, even though I knew that I had been the cause, through my own stupidity, of involving both my parents in the plot.

5 Maybe it was a good idea. I always felt terrible that it was dragged out. I wished that Mother would whack me or something and get it over with. And as I grew older I resented having to take several undeserved blows because I was the older child and was solemnly expected to be a model to my younger sister, Anne. She was a comparatively sickly child, and spoiled and much clev-

erer than I, and often made it bitterly clear to me that I was an utter fool to take punishment for her own small jaunty misdoings. I continued to do this, far past the fatherly spankings and other parental punishments, because I loved her and agreed that I was not as clever as she.

Once Rex hit me. I deserved it, because I had vented stupid petulance on my helpless little brother David. He was perhaps a year old, and I was twelve. We'd all left the lunch table for the living room and had left him sitting alone in his high chair, and Father spotted him through the big doors and asked me to get him down. I felt sulky about something, and angered, and I stamped back to the table and pulled up the wooden tray that held the baby in his chair, and dumped him out insolently on the floor. David did not even cry out, but Rex saw it and in a flash leapt across the living room toward the dining table and the empty high chair and gave me a slap across the side of my head that sent me halfway across the room against the big old sideboard. He picked up David and stood staring at me. Mother ran in. A couple of cousins came, looking flustered and embarrassed at the sudden ugliness.

I picked myself up from the floor by the sideboard, really raging with insulted anger, and looked disdainfully around me and then went silently up the stairs that rose from the dining room to all our sleeping quarters. Behind me I could hear Mother crying, and then a lot of talk.

I sat waiting for my father to come up to the bedroom that Anne and I always shared, from her birth until I was twenty, in our two family homes in Whittier, and in Laguna in the summers, and then when we went away to three different schools. I knew I was going to be punished.

Finally Father came upstairs, looking very tired. "Daughter," he said, "your mother wants you to be spanked. You have been bad. Pull down your panties and lie across my knees."

I was growing very fast and was almost as tall as I am now, with small 10
growing breasts. I looked straight at him, not crying, and got into the old position, all long skinny arms and legs, with my bottom bared to him. I felt insulted and full of fury. He gave me twelve expert upward stinging whacks. I did not even breathe fast, on purpose. Then I stood up insolently, pulled up my sensible Munsingwear panties, and stared down at him as he sat on the edge of my bed.

"That's the last time," he said.

"Yes," I said. "And you hit me."

"I apologize for that," he said, and stood up slowly, so that once again I had to look up into his face as I had always done. He went out of the room and downstairs, and I stayed alone in the little room under the eaves of the Ranch house, feeling my insult and anger drain slowly out and away forever. I knew that a great deal had happened, and I felt ashamed of behaving so carelessly toward my helpless little brother and amazed at the way I had simply blown across the room and into the sideboard under my own father's wild stinging blow across my cheek. I wished that I would be maimed, so that he would feel shame every time he looked at my poor face. I tried to forget how silly I'd felt, baring my pubescent bottom to his heavy dutiful slaps across it. I was full of scowling puzzlements.

My mother came into the room, perhaps half an hour later, and wrapped her arms around me with a tenderness I had never felt from her before, although she had always been quietly free with her love and her embraces. She had been crying but was very calm with me, as she told me that Father had gone back to the *News* and that the cousins were playing with the younger children. I wanted to stay haughty and abused with her, but sat there on the bed quietly, while she told me about Father.

She said that he had been beaten when he was a child and then as a 15
growing boy, my age, younger, older. His father beat him, almost every Saturday, with a long leather belt. He beat all four of his boys until they were big enough to tell him that it was the last time. They were all of them tall strong people, and Mother said without any quivering in her voice that they were all about sixteen before they could make it clear that if it ever happened again, they would beat their father worse than he had ever done it to them.

He did it, she said, because he believed that he was ridding them of the devil, of sin. Grandfather, she said quietly, was not a brute or a beast, not sinful, not a devil. But he lived in the wild prairies and raised strong sons to survive, as he had, the untold dangers of frontier life. When he was starting his family, as a wandering newspaperman and printer of political broadsides, he got religion. He was born again. He repented of all his early wildness and tried to keep his four sons from "sinning," as he came to call what he had done before he accepted God as his master.

I sat close to Mother as she explained to me how horrible it had been only a few minutes or hours before in my own short life, when Rex had broken a long vow and struck his own child in unthinking anger. She told me that before they married, he had told her that he had vowed when he was sixteen to break the chain of violence and that never would he strike anyone in anger. She must help him. They promised each other that they would break the chain. And then today he had, for the first time in his whole life, struck out, and he had struck his oldest child.

I could feel my mother trembling. I was almost overwhelmed by pity for the two people whom I had betrayed into this by my stupidity. "Then why did he hit me?" I almost yelled suddenly. She said that he hardly remembered doing it, because he was so shocked by my dumping the helpless baby out onto the floor. "Your father does not remember," she repeated. "He simply had to stop you, stop the unthinking way you acted toward a helpless baby. He was . . . He suddenly acted violently. And it is dreadful for him now to see that, after so long, he can be a raging animal. He thought it would never happen. That is why he has never struck any living thing in anger. Until today."

We talked for a long time. It was a day of spiritual purging, obviously. I have never been the same—still stupid but never unthinking, because of the invisible chains that can be forged in all of us, without our knowing it. Rex knew of the chain of violence that was forged in him by his father's whippings, brutal no matter how mistakenly committed in the name of God. I learned of what violence could mean as I sat beside my mother, that day when I was twelve, and felt her tremble as she put her arm over my skinny shoulders and pulled me toward her in an embrace that she was actually giving to her husband.

It is almost certain that I stayed aloof and surly, often, in the next years 20
with my parents. But I was never spanked again. And I know as surely as I do my given name that Rex no longer feared the chain of violence that had bound him when he was a boy. Perhaps it is as well that he hit me, the one time he found that it had not been broken for him.

Understanding

1. Does Fisher's story have a theme? What is it? Is it implicit or explicit?
2. Fisher asserts in the opening paragraph that "I have never been beaten." Does her story confirm this statement?
3. What role did Fisher's mother play in this event? Passive observer? Active participant? How did Fisher view that role? What can you conclude about the nature of her parents' relationship?
4. Fisher concludes "The Broken Chain" with the statement, "I know as surely as I do my given name that Rex no longer feared the chain of violence that had bound him when he was a boy." What makes her so sure?

Responding

1. Fisher excuses her father's use of the wooden hairbrush in this way: "I knew that Rex disliked this duty very much, but that it was part of being Father." Do you think a parent's, especially a father's, responsibility includes administering this kind of discipline? What kinds of children's behavior do you think warrant physical punishment? Explain.
2. The title of this essay suggests that certain behaviors that become family traditions—in this case, ritual spanking—can be passed from generation to generation almost without thinking. From your perspective, how are these kinds of behavior chains forged? What does it take to recognize them? How can they be broken?
3. Fisher writes that after the experience she relates in this story, "I have never been the same—still stupid but never unthinking." From your experience, or from what you know of the experiences of others, what effects does the kind of physical punishment Fisher received have on those who receive it? What can we learn from it?

Connecting

Fisher's "The Broken Chain" and Carcaterra's "Loving Your Enemy" describe what some might call child abuse. Do you think this is the case? In what ways are these two accounts similar? In what ways are they different?

The Revolt of the Evil Fairies

Ted Poston

Theodore Roosevelt Augustus Major Poston (1906–74) was born in Hopkinsville, Kentucky, the son of an African American family who ran the *Hopkinsville Contender,* a militant newspaper that eventually closed because it became too controversial for that small town. After graduating from Crispus Attucks High School in 1924, Poston left for New York, where his brothers were officials in Marcus Garvey's Universal Negro Improvement Association. He never followed the UNIA's black separatist call, however. Instead he worked as a waiter, a freelance writer, and a journalist with New York's *Amsterdam News* before he landed a job in 1937 as the first full-time black journalist at the *New York Post,* where his byline appeared for more than thirty-three years.

Poston's poignant autobiographical short story "The Revolt of the Evil Fairies" was first published in the *New Republic* in April 1942. Ersa Hines Poston, to whom he was married in 1957, said that this story "gives an excellent analysis of some of the problems, even in childhood, that haunted and confused Ted. He . . . never felt he had fulfilled his potential."

1 The grand dramatic offering of the Booker T. Washington Colored Grammar School was the biggest event of the year in our social life in Hopkinsville, Kentucky. It was the one occasion on which they let us use the old Cooper Opera House, and even some of the white folks came out yearly to applaud our presentation. The first two rows of the orchestra were always reserved for our white friends, and our leading colored citizens sat right behind them—with an empty row intervening, of course.

Mr. Ed Smith, our local undertaker, invariably occupied a box to the left of the house and wore his cutaway coat and striped breeches. This distinctive garb was usually reserved for those rare occasions when he officiated at the funerals of our most prominent colored citizens. Mr. Thaddeus Long, our colored mailman, once rented a tuxedo and bought a box too. But nobody paid him much mind. We knew he was just showing off.

The title of our play never varied. It was always Prince Charming and the Sleeping Beauty, but no two presentations were ever the same. Miss H. Belle LaPrade, our sixth-grade teacher, rewrote the script every season, and it was never like anything you read in the storybooks.

Miss LaPrade called it "a modern morality play of conflict between the forces of good and evil." And the forces of evil, of course, always came off second best.

5 The Booker T. Washington Colored Grammar School was in a state of ferment from Christmas until February, for this was the period when

parts were assigned. First there was the selection of the Good Fairies and the Evil Fairies. This was very important, because the Good Fairies wore white costumes and the Evil Fairies black. And strangely enough most of the Good Fairies usually turned out to be extremely light in complexion, with straight hair and white folks' features. On rare occasions a darkskinned girl might be lucky enough to be a Good Fairy, but not one with a speaking part.

There never was any doubt about Prince Charming and the Sleeping Beauty. They were always lightskinned. And though nobody ever discussed those things openly, it was an accepted fact that a lack of pigmentation was a decided advantage in the Prince Charming and Sleeping Beauty sweepstakes.

And therein lay my personal tragedy. I made the best grades in my class, I was the leading debater, and the scion of a respected family in the community. But I could never be Prince Charming, because I was black.

In fact, every year when they started casting our grand dramatic offering my family started pricing black cheesecloth at Franklin's Department Store. For they knew that I would be leading the forces of darkness and skulking back in the shadows—waiting to be vanquished in the third act. Mamma had experience with this sort of thing. All my brothers had finished Booker T. before me.

Not that I was alone in my disappointment. Many of my classmates felt it too. I probably just took it more to heart. Rat Jointer, for instance, could rationalize the situation. Rat was not only black; he lived on Billy Goat Hill. But Rat summed it up like this:

"If you black, you black." 10

I should have been able to regard the matter calmly too. For our grand dramatic offering was only a reflection of our daily community life in Hopkinsville. The yallers had the best of everything. They held most of the teaching jobs in Booker T. Washington Colored Grammar School. They were the Negro doctors, the lawyers, the insurance men. They even had a "Blue Vein Society," and if your dark skin obscured your throbbing pulse you were hardly a member of the elite.

Yet I was inconsolable the first time they turned me down for Prince Charming. That was the year they picked Roger Jackson. Roger was not only dumb; he stuttered. But he was light enough to pass for white, and that was apparently sufficient.

In all fairness, however, it must be admitted that Roger had other qualifications. His father owned the only colored saloon in town and was quite a power in local politics. In fact, Mr. Clinton Jackson had a lot to say about just who taught in the Booker T. Washington Colored Grammar School. So it was understandable that Roger should have been picked for Prince Charming.

My real heartbreak, however, came the year they picked Sarah Williams for Sleeping Beauty. I had been in love with Sarah since kindergarten. She had soft light hair, bluish-gray eyes, and a dimple which stayed in her left cheek whether she was smiling or not.

Of course Sarah never encouraged me much. She never answered any of 15
my fervent love letters, and Rat was very scornful of my one-sided love affairs.

"As long as she don't call you a black baboon," he sneered, "you'll keep on hanging around."

After Sarah was chosen for Sleeping Beauty, I went out for the Prince Charming role with all my heart. If I had declaimed boldly in previous contests, I was matchless now. If I had bothered Mamma with rehearsals at home before, I pestered her to death this time. Yes, and I purloined my sister's can of Palmer's Skin Success.

I knew the Prince's role from start to finish, having played the Head Evil Fairy opposite it for two seasons. And Prince Charming was one character whose lines Miss LaPrade never varied much in her many versions. But although I never admitted it, even to myself, I knew I was doomed from the start. They gave the part to Leonardius Wright. Leonardius, of course, was yaller.

The teachers sensed my resentment. They were almost apologetic. They pointed out that I had been such a splendid Head Evil Fairy for two seasons that it would be a crime to let anybody else try the role. They reminded me that Mamma wouldn't have to buy any more cheesecloth because I could use my same old costume. They insisted that the Head Evil Fairy was even more important than Prince Charming because he was the one who cast the spell on Sleeping Beauty. So what could I do but accept?

I had never liked Leonardius Wright. He was a goody-goody, and even Mamma was always throwing him up to me. But, above all, he too was in love with Sarah Williams. And now he got a chance to kiss Sarah every day in rehearsing the awakening scene.

Well, the show must go on, even for little black boys. So I threw my soul 20
into my part and made the Head Evil Fairy a character to be remembered. When I drew back from the couch of Sleeping Beauty and slunk away into the shadows at the approach of Prince Charming, my facial expression was indeed something to behold. When I was vanquished by the shining sword of Prince Charming in the last act, I was a little hammy perhaps—but terrific!

The attendance at our grand dramatic offering that year was the best in its history. Even the white folks overflowed the two rows reserved for them, and a few were forced to sit in the intervening one. This created a delicate situation, but everybody tactfully ignored it.

When the curtain went up on the last act, the audience was in fine fettle. Everything had gone well for me too—except for one spot in the second act. That was where Leonardius unexpectedly rapped me over the head with his sword as I slunk off into the shadows. That was not in the script, but Miss LaPrade quieted me down by saying it made a nice touch anyway. Rat said Leonardius did it on purpose.

The third act went on smoothly, though, until we came to the vanquishing scene. That was where I slunk from the shadows for the last time and challenged Prince Charming to mortal combat. The hero reached for his shining sword—a bit unsportsmanlike, I always thought, since Miss LaPrade consistently left the Head Evil Fairy unarmed—and then it happened!

Later I protested loudly—but in vain—that it was a case of self-defense. I pointed out that Leonardius had a mean look in his eye. I cited the impromptu rapping he had given my head in the second act. But nobody would listen. They just wouldn't believe that Leonardius really intended to brain me when he reached for his sword.

Anyway, he didn't succeed. For the minute I saw that evil gleam in his eye—or was it my own?—I cut loose with a right to the chin, and Prince Charming dropped his shining sword and staggered back. His astonishment lasted only a minute, though, for he lowered his head and came charging in, fists flailing. There was nothing yellow about Leonardius but his skin.

The audience thought the scrap was something new Miss LaPrade had written in. They might have kept on thinking so if Miss LaPrade hadn't been screaming so hysterically from the sidelines. And if Rat Jointer hadn't decided that this was as good a time as any to settle old scores. So he turned around and took a sock at the male Good Fairy nearest him.

When the curtain rang down, the forces of Good and Evil were locked in combat. And Sleeping Beauty was wide awake and streaking for the wings.

They rang the curtain back up fifteen minutes later, and we finished the play. I lay down and expired according to specifications but Prince Charming will probably remember my sneering corpse to his dying day. They wouldn't let me appear in the grand dramatic offering at all the next year. But I didn't care. I couldn't have been Prince Charming anyway.

Understanding

1. Compare and contrast the personal characteristics of the narrator with Roger Jackson and Leonardius Wright.
2. How did the role assigned to the narrator differ from those taken by the other boys? How does the narrator react to his being continually chosen for the role of Head Evil Fairy? What wounds did the narrator suffer?
3. What was the time, place, and social climate of this story? Mark the events in this story that you think expose or suggest the "problems, even in childhood, that haunted and confused" Ted Poston.
4. What meaning does the role of Prince Charming have for the narrator? How can you tell?
5. What kind of person is he? What do you think his relationships with other members of the class were like?

Responding

1. Have you ever been chosen for a role (real or symbolic) which you didn't like and didn't want? Describe the situation.
2. How does the conflict between dark- and light-skinned African Americans described in this story correspond to events in your own experience? What do you think are the conditions responsible for this conflict?
3. What do you think are the real forces of good and evil? Where are they represented in modern-day life?

Connecting

Is there a difference between the lasting effects of physical wounds and of mental ones? How do each mark our lives and form our identities? Consider the selections you have read so far to answer this question and support your opinion.

Worse Than My Darkest Dreams

Art Spiegelman

In 1940 the Nazis instituted the Final Solution—the mass extermination of Jews and other ethnic minorities in the gas chambers and execution yards of Auschwitz, Belsen, Buchënwald, and other concentration camps in Eastern Europe. For many the Holocaust was not only a crime against the millions of people who perished in these camps, but an unspeakable wound against all humanity.

In writing about literature on the Holocaust, theater and film critic John Simon assessed that "it takes courage to write poetry, fiction, or drama about this hardest of subjects." Born after World War II, Art Spiegelman, a cartoonist and co-founder of *Raw,* a magazine of avant-garde comics and graphics, displays this courage in his two volumes *Maus* and *Maus II.* In *Maus,* Spiegelman introduces the reader to his father, Vladek, a Jewish survivor who recounts his terrifying experiences in the camps in 1944. Its sequel, *Maus: A Survivor's Tale, II: And Here My Troubles Began,* from which this selection is taken, moves us from Auschwitz to the Catskill Mountains in New York State, where Art tries to come to terms with his father's story. The cartoon form of both volumes (the Nazis are cats; the Jews, mice; the Poles, pigs; and the Americans, dogs) plunges the reader from the relative comfort of word descriptions into graphic interpretations of people and events that reveal the most complete disregard for human dignity ever documented.

FOR ME IT WAS HARD HERE, BUT FOR MY FRIEND MANDEL-BAUM IT WAS MORE HARD.

IN SOSNOWIEC, EVERYONE KNEW MANDELBAUM. HE WAS OLDER AS ME... NICE...A VERY RICH MAN...

...BUT NOW, IN AUSCHWITZ, MANDELBAUM WAS A MESS.

HIS PANTS WERE BIG LIKE FOR 2 PEOPLE, AND HE HAD NOT EVEN A PIECE OF STRING TO MAKE A BELT. HE HAD ALL DAY TO HOLD THEM WITH ONE HAND...

ONE SHOE, HIS FOOT WAS TOO BIG TO GO IN. THIS ALSO HE HAD TO HOLD SO HE COULD FIND MAYBE WITH WHOM TO EXCHANGE IT.

ONE SHOE WAS BIG LIKE A BOAT. BUT THIS AT LEAST HE COULD WEAR.

IT WAS WIN-TER, AND EVERYWHERE HE HAD TO GO AROUND WITH ONE FOOT ONTO THE SNOW.

MY GOD. PLEASE GOD... HELP ME FIND A PIECE OF STRING AND A SHOE THAT FITS!

BUT HERE GOD DIDN'T COME. WE WERE ALL ON OUR OWN.

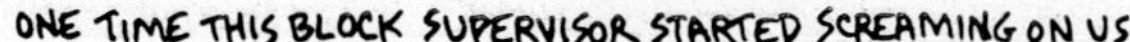
ONE TIME THIS BLOCK SUPERVISOR STARTED SCREAMING ON US:

WHO KNOWS ENGLISH? RAISE YOUR HAND!
(YOU SHOULD RAISE YOUR HAND, VLADEK.)
(NO...)

(I DON'T WANT TO GET TOO CLOSE TO HIS STICK.
BESIDES, LOOK AT ALL THE HANDS UP ALREADY...)
MANY FRENCH JEWS HERE KNEW TO SPEAK ENGLISH.

HE TOOK THEM APART- BUT SENT THEM SOON BACK.
WHO KNOWS ENGLISH AND POLISH?
NOW IT WAS VERY FEW HANDS, SO I APPROACHED.

IT WAS 8 OR 9 OF US. EACH HAD TO SPEAK A FEW WORDS.
VHERE... IST... DER PEN?... DER PEN IST...IN ...DER TABLE...
NEXT.
WHAT I HEARD THE OTHERS SPEAK I SAW I HAD A CHANCE.

I SPOKE ONLY ENGLISH TO HIM:
YES. I GAVE PRIVATE LESSONS OF ENGLISH WHEN I LIVED THEN IN CZESTOCHOWA.
HE WANTED TO LEARN HERE ENGLISH!

FOR POLISH, I HAD A GOOD ENGLISH
YOU MANAGED TO GET THE BERLITZ BOOKS HERE! YOU STUDIED ALREADY TO CONJUGATE VERBS?
?
AND HE KEPT ME ASIDE THE REST.

LISTEN. THERE ARE TOO MANY PRISONERS HERE. THE S.S. WILL LINE YOU ALL UP TOMORROW.
...BE SURE TO STAND ON THE FAR LEFT.

IN THE MORNING, THE S.S. CHOSE WHO TO TAKE FOR THE DAY TO WORK. WEAK ONES THEY PUT ON THE SIDE TO TAKE AWAY FOREVER. BEFORE THEY CAME TO ME, THEY TOOK ENOUGH.
I KEPT CLOSE TO ME MANDELBAUM. AND WE WENT BACK SAFE INSIDE.

THE KAPO PUSHED THOSE REMAINING TO CLEAN UP IN THE BLOCK.
WAIT! SPIEGELMAN- YOU COME WITH ME!
EVERYONE THEY CALLED BY NUMBER BUT ME, HE CALLED BY NAME.

SIT HERE... I'LL BE BACK SOON.
HERE I SAW ROLLS! I SAW EGGS! MEAT! COFFEE! ALL THE TABLE FULL! YOU KNOW WHAT IT WAS TO SEE SUCH THINGS?

IT MUST BE IT'S HIS BREAKFAST. SEE HOW HAPPY HE HAS IT HERE!
I WAS AFRAID TO LOOK. I WAS SO HUNGRY, I COULD GRAB ALL OF IT!

WHAT ARE YOU WAITING FOR? SIT DOWN AND EAT!
THIS FOOD, IT WAS FOR ME.

I ATE, ATE, ATE AS HE WATCHED. THEN I TAUGHT HIM A COUPLE HOURS AND WE SPOKE A LITTLE.
BUT WHY ARE YOU STUDYING ENGLISH?
I SPEAK GERMAN AS WELL AS POLISH-THAT'S WHY I'M A KAPO. OTHERWISE I'D BE A NOTHING LIKE YOU...
NOW THE ALLIES ARE BOMBING THE REICH. IF THEY WIN THIS WAR, IT WILL BE WORTH SOMETHING TO KNOW ENGLISH!

WELL, THAT'S ENOUGH FOR TODAY. COME WITH ME.
TAKE OFF ALL YOUR CLOTHES. CHOOSE THINGS THAT FIT.
!
SO I TOOK MYSELF CLOTHES LIKE TAILORED.
I GOT ALSO A PAIR REAL SHOES- NOT WOOD BUT LEATHER
ALWAYS I WAS HANDSOME... BUT WITH EVERYTHING FITTED, I LOOKED LIKE A MILLION!
SO. ARE YOU ALL SET?
YES SIR. BUT I HAVE ONE MORE FAVOR TO ASK...
...COULD I ALSO TAKE THIS EXTRA PAIR OF SHOES, A BELT AND A SPOON FOR-
WHAT?!
YOU JEW! YOU'VE ONLY BEEN HERE A FEW DAYS AND YOU'RE READY TO DO BUSINESS?!
I HAVE TO ACCOUNT FOR EVERY PAIR OF SHOES IN HERE!
I-I DON'T WANT TO MAKE TROUBLE. YOU'VE BEEN SO KIND TO ME... IT WAS FOR MY FRIEND...
I EXPLAINED HIM EVERYTHING ABOUT MANDELBAUM.
WELL... I COULD "LOSE" THE BELT AND SPOON- BUT BRING ME YOUR FRIEND'S OLD SHOES TOMORROW - OR ELSE!
I'M TELLING YOU - I WAS AMAZING WELL-OFF!

I RAN TO FIND MANDELBAUM...
VLADEK?!!
YOU LOOK LIKE A...A GENERAL!

HAH! NOT QUITE. BUT I'VE BEEN LUCKY, AND I DIDN'T FORGET YOU...
?

LOOK. I GOT YOU YOUR OWN SPOON.
A SPOON! THANK YOU, VLADEK, THANK YOU.

AND HERE'S A BELT-NOT JUST STRING-A REAL BELT!
OH MY GOD!

AND ONE MORE THING: A PAIR OF WOODEN SHOES THAT WILL FIT YOU!
gasp

SOB
MY GOD. MY GOD. MY GOD... IT'S A MIRACLE, VLADEK.
GOD SENT SHOES THROUGH YOU.
...HE WAS SO HAPPY, HE WAS CRYING... AND I STARTED ALSO CRYING WITH HIM.

HE WAS SO HAPPY WITH THIS.
...AND THE KAPO KNEW MANDELBAUM WAS MY FRIEND SO HE LEFT HIM ALSO ALONE.

HOW LONG I COULD, I KEPT HIM. BUT A FEW DAYS LATER THE GERMANS CHOSE HIM TO TAKE AWAY TO WORK...
NOBODY COULD HELP THIS.
SO. IT WAS FINISHED WITH MANDEL-BAUM. I NEVER SAW HIM MORE AGAIN.

Understanding

1. In what ways did Vladek Spiegelman try to make a "life" in a "death" camp? Did he succeed?
2. What kind of relationship do you think Art has with his father, as depicted at the beginning of the selection?
3. What is the purpose of having Vladek tell his story to Art rather than directly to you, the reader?
4. Although a *New York Times* review of *Maus II* characterized it as "an epic story told in tiny pictures," we usually associate the cartoon form with fantasy or humorous content. How do you think this form works as a means for telling Vladek's story?
5. Vladek speaks in a style that would not be considered standard English. How is his way of speaking essential to the purpose of this piece?
6. Of all the wounds that Vladek suffered, which do you think were the most traumatic?

Responding

1. Have you ever experienced a wound that you thought would never heal? Did you recover from it? What *didn't* help you deal with it? What did?
2. Sometimes people who have been grievously wounded, whether physically or mentally, develop negative personality traits: The adult who was abandoned as a child becomes a possessive husband, the mother who was beaten as a child grows up to hit her own children, and so on. Have you ever dealt with someone who has experienced a serious wound and reacted in these or similar ways? If so, how did you respond?
3. How did reading this story make you feel? What do your feelings communicate about your response to the wounds of others?

Connecting

1. How would Rachael Rosen in Dick's "The Empathy Test" (chapter one) have responded to Vladek's story? Explain.
2. How does this father-son relationship parallel the one described in Carcaterra's "Loving Your Enemy"?

The Death of Rosa the Beautiful

Isabel Allende

Born in Lima, Peru, in 1942, Isabel Allende grew up in Chile, which she fled in 1975 after a coup resulted in the death of President Salvador Allende, her uncle. She spent thirteen years in exile in Venezuela, where she reared her two children and worked as a journalist. In 1982 Allende published *The House of the Spirits.* The book, which she dedicated "to my mother, my grandmother, and all the other extraordinary women of this story," began as a series of unmailed letters to her grandfather as he approached his one hundredth year.

The narrator of this excerpt, which is part of the opening chapter of *The House of the Spirits,* is Esteban Trueba, patriarch of a powerful landowning family who recalls—fifty years in retrospect—how he lost his first true love, one of the extraordinary women in this story, the ethereally beautiful Rosa del Valle.

More than half a century has passed, but I can still remember the exact moment when Rosa the Beautiful entered my life like a distracted angel who stole my soul as she went by. She was with her Nana and another child, probably one of her younger sisters. I think she was wearing a violet dress, but I'm not sure, because I have no eye for women's clothes and because she was so beautiful that even if she had been wearing an ermine cape all I would have noticed was her face. I don't generally spend my time thinking about women, but only a fool could have failed to spot that apparition, who caused a stir wherever she went, and tied up traffic, with her incredible green hair, which framed her face like a fantastic hat, her fairy-tale manner, and her special way of moving as if she were flying. She crossed right in front of me without seeing me and floated into the pastry shop on the Plaza de Armas. Dumbstruck, I waited in the street while she bought licorice drops, which she selected one by one, with that tinkling laugh of hers, tossing some into her mouth and handing others to her sister. I wasn't the only one to stand there hypnotized, for within a few minutes a whole circle of men had formed, their noses pressed against the window. It was then that I reacted. It didn't cross my mind that since I had no fortune, was no one's idea of a proper young man, and faced a most uncertain future, I was far from being the ideal suitor for that heavenly girl. I didn't even know her! But I was bewitched, and I decided then and there that she was the only woman in the world who was worthy to be my wife, and that if I couldn't have her I would remain a bachelor. I followed her all the way home. I got on the same streetcar and took the seat behind her, unable to take my eyes off her perfect nape, her round neck, and her soft shoulders caressed by the green curls that had escaped from her coiffure. I didn't feel the motion of the car, because I was in a dream. Suddenly she swept down the 1 aisle and as she passed me her astonishing gold eyes rested for a moment on my own. Part of me must have died. I couldn't breathe and my pulse stopped in its tracks. When I recovered my composure, I had to leap onto the sidewalk at the risk of breaking all my bones, and run toward the street down which she had already turned. Thanks to a cloud of violet disappearing behind a gate, I learned where she lived. From that day on I stood guard outside her house, pacing up and down the street like an orphaned dog, spying on her, slipping money to the gardener, engaging the maids in conversation, until I finally managed to speak to Nana, and she, God bless her, took pity on me and agreed to be our go-between, conveying my love letters, my flowers, and the innumerable boxes of licorice drops with which I tried to win Rosa's affection. I also sent her acrostics. I don't know how to write poetry, but there was a Spanish bookseller with a real genius for rhyme from whom I ordered poems and songs—anything whose raw material was paper and ink. My sister Férula helped me get closer to the del Valle family by uncovering distant links between our ancestors and theirs, and seeking out every opportunity to greet them as they came out of mass. That was how I was finally able to visit Rosa, but the day I entered her house and was within speaking range of her, I couldn't think of anything to say. I stood there mute, my hat in my hand and my mouth gaping, until her parents, who were well acquainted with such symptoms, came to my rescue. I can't imagine what Rosa could have seen in me—or why, with time, she came to accept me as her husband. I became her official suitor without having to perform any superhuman tasks because, despite her awesome beauty and her innumerable virtues, Rosa had no other wooers. Her mother explained it to me this way: she said that no one felt strong enough to spend his life protecting her from other men's desire. Many had circled around her, even fallen head over heels in love with her, but until I came along none had made up his mind. Her beauty struck fear into their hearts and they preferred to admire her from afar, not daring to approach her. That had never occurred to me, to tell you the truth. My problem was that I didn't have a cent, although I felt capable, through my love, of becoming a rich man. I looked around to find the quickest route within the limits of the honesty in which I had been raised, and I realized that success required godparents, advanced studies, or capital. It wasn't enough to have a respectable last name. I suppose that if I had had the money to start out with, I would have tried my luck at the gaming tables or the races, but since that was not the case I had to think of a line of work that, while it might entail certain risks, held out the promise of a fortune. Gold and silver mines were the dream of all adventurers: a mine could plunge you into abject poverty, kill you with tuberculosis, or make you a rich man overnight. It was a question of luck. Thanks to the prestige of my mother's name, I was able to obtain the concession for a mine in the North, for which the bank gave me a loan. I vowed to extract the last gram of precious metal even if it meant I had to crush the hills with my own hands and grind the rocks with my feet. For Rosa's sake, I was prepared to do that and much more.

At the end of autumn, when the family had calmed down about Father Restrepo, who was forced to mitigate his inquisitional behavior after the bishop had personally warned him to leave little Clara del Valle alone, and when they had all resigned themselves to the fact that Uncle Marcos was truly dead, Severo's political designs began to take shape. He had worked for years toward this end, so it was a personal triumph when he was invited to be the Liberal Party candidate in the upcoming Congressional elections, representing a southern province that he had never set foot in and that he had difficulty finding on the map. The party badly needed people and Severo was anxious for a seat in Congress, so they had no trouble convincing the downtrodden voters of the South to choose him as their candidate. Their invitation was supported by a monumental rose-colored roast pig, which the voters shipped directly to candidate del Valle's home. It arrived on an enormous wooden tray, scented and gleaming, with a sprig of parsley in its mouth and a carrot protruding from its rump, the whole reposing on a bed of tomatoes. Its stomach had been stitched closed, and it was stuffed with partridges that in turn were stuffed with plums. It was accompanied by a decanter containing half a gallon of the best brandy in the country. The idea of becoming a deputy or, better still, a senator, was a long-cherished dream of Severo's. Over the years he had been meticulously laying the groundwork, by means of contacts, friendships, secret meetings, discreet but effective public appearances, and gifts of money or favors made to the right people at the right moment. That southern province, however distant and unknown, was exactly what he had been waiting for.

The pig arrived on a Tuesday. On Friday, when the pig was no more than a heap of skin and bones that Barrabás was gnawing in the courtyard, Clara announced that there would soon be another death in the del Valle family.

"But it will be by mistake," she added.

5 On Saturday she slept badly and awoke screaming in the middle of the night. In the morning Nana made her a cup of linden tea but no one paid her much attention, because everyone was busy with the preparations for their father's southern trip, and because Rosa the Beautiful had developed a chill. Nívea gave orders for Rosa to remain in bed, and Dr. Cuevas said that it was nothing serious and that she should be given sugared lemonade with a splash of liquor to help bring down her fever. Severo went in to see his daughter and found her flushed and wide-eyed, sunk deep in the butter-colored lace sheets. He took her a dance card as a present and gave Nana permission to open the decanter of brandy and pour some in the lemonade. Rosa drank the lemonade, wrapped herself in her woolen shawl, and immediately fell asleep next to Clara, with whom she shared the room.

On the morning of that tragic Sunday, Nana woke up early as she always did. Before going to mass, she went into the kitchen to prepare breakfast for the family. The wood and coal stove had been readied the night before, and she lit the smoldering, still-warm embers. While the water heated and the milk boiled, she stacked the plates to be taken into the dining room. She put some oatmeal on the stove, strained the coffee, and toasted the bread. She arranged two trays, one for Nívea, who always breakfasted in bed, and one for Rosa, who by virtue of her illness was entitled to the same treatment as her mother. She covered Rosa's tray with a linen napkin that had been embroidered by the nuns, to keep the coffee warm and prevent flies from getting in the food, and stuck her head out in the courtyard to make sure Barrabás was not in sight. He had a penchant for leaping at her whenever she went by with the breakfast tray. She saw him in the corner playing with a hen and took advantage of his momentary distraction to begin her long trip across courtyards and through hallways, from the kitchen, which was in the middle of the house, all the way to the girls' room, which was on the other side. When she came to Rosa's door, she stopped, gripped by a premonition. She entered without knocking, as she always did, and immediately noticed the scent of roses, even though they were not in season. This was how Nana understood that an inescapable disaster had occurred. She set the tray down carefully beside the bed and walked slowly to the window. She opened the heavy drapes and let the pale morning sun into the room. Grief-stricken, she turned around and was not at all surprised to see Rosa lying dead upon the bed, more beautiful than ever, her hair strikingly green, her skin the tone of new ivory, and her honey-gold eyes wide open, staring at the ceiling. Little Clara was at the foot of the bed observing her sister. Nana fell to her knees beside the bed, took Rosa's hand in hers, and began to pray. She prayed for a long time, until the terrible moan of a lost freighter was heard throughout the house. It was the first and last time anyone heard Barrabás's voice. He mourned the dead girl all that day, fraying the nerves of the whole family and all the neighbors, who came running at the sound of his shipwrecked howls.

After taking one look at Rosa's body, Dr. Cuevas knew that she had died of no ordinary fever. He began to search the entire house, going over the kitchen inch by inch, sticking his fingers into pots, opening flour sacks and bags of sugar, prying the tops off boxes of dried fruit, and leaving a wake of destruction behind him. He rummaged through Rosa's drawers, questioned the servants one by one, and harassed Nana until she was beside herself; finally his search led to the decanter of brandy, which he requisitioned instantly. He shared his doubts with no one, but he took the bottle to his laboratory. He returned three hours later, his rosy face transformed by horror into the pale mask he wore throughout that whole dreadful episode. He walked up to Severo, took him by the arm, and led him off to one side.

"There was enough poison in that brandy to fell an ox," he said between tight lips. "But in order to be sure that that's what killed the child, I'll have to do an autopsy."

"Does that mean you have to cut her open?" Severo moaned.

"Not completely. I won't have to touch her head, just her digestive tract," the doctor explained.

Severo was overcome.

By that point Nívea was worn out from weeping, but when she learned that they were thinking of taking her daughter to the morgue, she quickly regained her strength. She calmed down only when they swore that they would take Rosa directly from the house to the Catholic cemetery: only then did she accept the laudanum the doctor handed her. She slept for twenty hours.

When evening fell, Severo made his preparations. He sent his children up to bed and gave the servants permission to retire early. He allowed Clara, who was too upset by what had happened, to spend the night in the bedroom of another sister. When all the lights were out and the house was silent, Dr. Cuevas's assistant, a sickly, myopic young man with a stutter, arrived. They helped Severo carry his daughter's body into the kitchen and set it gently down on the slab of marble where Nana kneaded pastry and chopped vegetables. Despite his sturdy character, Severo was overcome when his daughter's nightgown was lifted to reveal the splendid body of a mermaid. He staggered out of the room, drunk with grief, and collapsed in an armchair, weeping like a child. Dr. Cuevas too, who had seen Rosa come into this world and knew her like the palm of his own hand, was taken aback at the sight of her nude body. The young assistant began to pant, so overwhelmed was he, and he panted for years to come, every time he recalled the extraordinary sight of Rosa naked and asleep on the kitchen table, her long hair sweeping to the floor in a cascade of green.

While they were at work on their terrible task, Nana, bored with weeping and prayer and sensing that something strange was going on in her domain, got up, wrapped her shawl around her shoulders, and set out through the house. She saw a light in the kitchen, but the door and wooden shutters were closed. She continued down the frozen, silent hallways, crossing the three wings of the house, until she came to the drawing room. Through the open door she could see her employer pacing up and down with a desolate air. The fire in the fireplace had long since gone out. She stepped into the room.

"Where is Rosa?" she asked. 15

"Dr. Cuevas is with her, Nana," he replied. "Come have a drink with me."

Nana remained standing, her crossed arms holding her shawl against her chest. Severo pointed to the sofa and she approached shyly. She sat down beside him. It was the first time she had been this close to her employer since she had lived in his house. Severo poured them each a glass of sherry and downed his in a single gulp. He buried his head in his hands, tearing his hair and murmuring a strange litany between his teeth. Nana, who was sitting stiffly on the edge of her seat, relaxed when she saw him cry. She stretched out her rough, chapped hand and, with a gesture that came automatically, smoothed his hair with the same caress she had used to console his children for the past twenty years. He glanced up and when he saw the ageless face, the Indian cheekbones, the black bun, the broad lap against which he had seen all his descendants burped and rocked to sleep, he felt that this woman, as warm and generous as the earth itself, would be able to console him. He leaned his forehead on her skirt, inhaled the sweet scent of her starched apron, and broke into the sobs of a small boy, spilling all the tears he had held in during his life as a man. Nana scratched his back, patted him gently, spoke to him in the half-language that she used to put the littlest ones to sleep, and sang him one of her peasant ballads until he had calmed down. They remained seated side by side, sipping sherry and weeping from time to time as they recalled the happy days when Rosa scampered in the garden startling the butterflies with her beauty that could only have come from the bottom of the sea.

In the kitchen, Dr. Cuevas and his assistant prepared their dread utensils and foul-smelling jars, donned rubber aprons, rolled up their sleeves, and proceeded to poke around in Rosa's most intimate parts until they had proven beyond a shadow of a doubt that the girl had swallowed an extraordinary quantity of rat poison.

"This was meant for Severo," the doctor concluded, washing his hands in the sink.

The assistant, overcome by the young girl's beauty, could not resign himself to leaving her sewn up like a jacket and suggested that they fix her up a bit. Both men plunged into the work of preserving her with unguents and filling her with mortician's paste. They worked until four o'clock in the morning, when Dr. Cuevas announced that he was too tired and too sad to continue. He went out of the room and Rosa was left in the hands of the assistant, who wiped the bloodstains from her skin with a sponge, put her embroidered nightgown back over her chest to cover up the seam that ran from her throat all the way to her sex, and arranged her hair. Then he cleaned up the mess that he and the doctor had made.

Dr. Cuevas walked into the living room and found Severo and Nana half drunk with tears and sherry.

"She's ready," he said. "We've fixed her up a little so her mother can go in and have a look at her."

He told Severo that his doubts had been well founded and that in his daughter's stomach he had found the same lethal substance as in the gift of brandy. It was then that Severo recalled Clara's prediction and lost whatever remained of his composure, for he was incapable of thinking that his daughter had died instead of him. He crumpled to the floor, moaning that he was the guilty one because of his ambition and bluster, that no one had told him to get involved in politics, that he had been much better off as an ordinary lawyer and family man, and that from then on he was renouncing his accursed candidacy, resigning from the Liberal Party and from all his public deeds and works, and that he hoped none of his descendants would ever get mixed up in politics, which was a trade for butchers and bandits—till finally Dr. Cuevas took pity on him and did him the favor of getting him drunk. The sherry was stronger than his suffering and guilt. Nana and the doctor carried him up to his bedroom, removed his clothes, and put him in his bed. Then they went into the kitchen, where the assistant was just putting the final touches on Rosa.

Nívea and Severo del Valle woke up late the following morning. Their relatives had hung the house in mourning. The curtains were drawn and bore black crepe ribbons, and the walls were piled with wreaths of flowers whose sickly sweet odor filled the halls. A funeral chapel had been set up in the dining room. There on the big table, covered with a black cloth with gold fringes, lay Rosa's white coffin with its silver rivets. Twelve yellow candles in bronze candelabras cast a dusky light over the girl. They had dressed her in the white gown and crown of wax orange blossoms that were being saved for her wedding day.

At twelve o'clock the parade of friends, relatives, and acquaintances began to file in to express their sympathy to the family. Even their most confirmed enemies appeared at the house, and Severo del Valle interrogated each pair of eyes in the hope of discovering the identity of the assassin; but in each, even those of the president of the Conservative Party, he saw the same innocence and grief.

During the wake, the men wandered through the sitting rooms and hallways of the house, speaking softly of business. They kept a respectful silence whenever any member of the family approached. When the time came to enter the dining room and pay their last respects to Rosa, everyone trembled, for if anything her beauty had grown more remarkable in death. The ladies moved into the living room, where they arranged the chairs in a circle. There they could weep at leisure, unburdening themselves of their own troubles as they wept for someone else's death. The weeping was copious, but it was dignified and muted. Some of the women murmured prayers under their breath. The maids moved back and forth through the sitting rooms and halls, distributing tea and cognac, homemade sweets, handkerchiefs for the women, and cold compresses soaked in ammonia for those ladies who felt faint from the lack of air, the scent of candles, and the weight of their emotion. All the del Valle sisters except Clara, who was still only a child, were dressed in black from head to toe and flanked their mother like a row of crows. Nívea, who had shed all her tears, sat rigid on her chair without a sigh, without a word, and without ammonia, to which she was allergic. As they arrived at the house, visitors stopped in to pay her their condolences. Some kissed her on both cheeks and others held her tight for a few seconds, but she seemed not to recognize even those she numbered among her closest friends. She had seen others of her children die in early childhood or at birth, but none had caused the sense of loss that she felt now.

All the brothers and sisters said goodbye to Rosa with a kiss on her cold forehead except for Clara, who refused to go anywhere near the dining room. They did not insist, because of both her extreme sensitivity and her tendency to sleepwalk whenever her imagination ran away with her. She stayed by herself in the garden curled up beside Barrabás, refusing to eat or have anything to do with the funeral. Only Nana kept an eye on her and tried to comfort her, but Clara pushed her away.

Despite the care Severo took to hush all speculation, Rosa's death became a public scandal. To anyone who listened, Dr. Cuevas offered the most logical explanation of her death, which was due, he said, to galloping pneumonia. But rumor had it that she had mistakenly been poisoned in her father's stead. In those days political assassinations were unknown in the country, and in any case poison was a method only whores and fishwives would resort to, a lowly technique that had not been seen since colonial times; even crimes of passion were nowadays resolved face to face. There was a great uproar over the attempt on his life, and before Severo could do anything to stop it, an announcement appeared in the opposition paper in which veiled accusations were made against the oligarchy and it was asserted that the conservatives were even capable of this act, because they could not forgive Severo del Valle for throwing his lot in with the liberals despite his social class. The police tried to pursue the clue of the brandy decanter, but all they were able to learn was that its source was not the same as that of the roast pig stuffed with partridges and plums and that the voters of the South had nothing to do with the whole matter. The mysterious decanter had been found outside the service door to the del Valle house on the same day and at the same time that the roast pig was delivered. The cook had simply assumed that it was part of the same gift. Neither the zeal of the police nor Severo's own investigation, which was carried out with the help of a private detective he engaged, shed any light on the identity of the assassin, and the shadow of suspended vengeance has continued to hang over succeeding generations. It was the first of many acts of violence that marked the fate of the del Valle family.

I remember perfectly. It had been a very happy day for me, because a new lode had appeared, the thick, magnificent seam that had eluded me throughout that time of sacrifice, absence, and hope, and that might represent the wealth I had been seeking for so long. I was sure that within six months I would have enough money to get married, and that by the time the year was out I would be able to call myself a wealthy man. I was very lucky, because in the mines there were more men who lost the little that they had than those who made a fortune, which is just what I was writing to Rosa that evening as I sat there so euphoric and so impatient that my fingers locked on the old typewriter and all the words came out jammed together. I was in the middle of the letter when I heard the pounding at the door that would cut off my inspiration forever. It was a peasant, with a team of mules, who had brought a telegram from town, sent by my sister Férula, telling me of Rosa's death.

I had to read the scrap of paper three times through before I understood the extent of my grief. The only thought that had never crossed my mind was that Rosa could be mortal. I suffered greatly whenever it occurred to me that, bored with waiting for me, she might marry someone else, or that the cursed vein that would spell my fortune might never turn up, or that the mine might cave in, squashing me like a cockroach. I had thought of all these possibilities and more, but never that of Rosa's death, despite my proverbial pessimism, which always leads me to expect the worst. I felt that without Rosa life no longer had any meaning. All the air went out of me as if I were a punctured balloon; all my enthusiasm vanished. God only knows how long I sat there in my chair, staring out the window at the desert, until my soul gradually returned to my body. My first reaction was one of rage. I turned against the walls, pounding the flimsy wooden planks until my knuckles bled. Then I tore all of Rosa's letters and drawings and the copies of my letters to her into a thousand pieces, stuffed my clothing, my papers, and my canvas pouch filled with gold into my suitcase, and went to find the foreman so I could leave him the logbooks and the keys to the warehouse. The mule driver offered to take me to the train. We had to travel almost the whole night on the animals' backs, with thin Spanish blankets as our only shield against the freezing mist, advancing at a snail's pace through that endless wasteland in which only the instinct of my guide guaranteed our safe arrival, for there were no points of reference. The night was clear and full of stars. I felt the cold pierce my bones, cut off the circulation in my hands, and seep into my soul. I was thinking of Rosa and wishing with an unreasoning violence that her death wasn't true, desperately begging the heavens for it all to turn out to be a terrible mistake, and praying that, revived by the force of my love, she would rise like Lazarus from her deathbed. I wept inwardly, sunk in my grief and in the icy night, cursing at the mule who was so slow, at Férula, the bearer of bad news, at Rosa herself for having died, and at God for having let her, until light appeared over the horizon and I saw the star fade away and the first shades of dawn appear, dyeing the landscape red and orange. With the light, I regained some of my strength. I began to resign myself to my misfortune and to ask no longer that she be resurrected but simply that I would arrive in time to see her one last time before they buried her. We doubled our pace and an hour later the driver took leave of me outside the tiny train station where I caught the narrow-gauge locomotive that linked the civilized world and the desert where I had spent two years.

I traveled more than thirty hours without stopping to eat, not even noticing my thirst, and I managed to reach the del Valle home before the funeral. They say that I arrived covered with dust, without a hat, filthy and bearded, thirsty and furious, shouting for my bride. Little Clara, who at the time was just a skinny child, came out to meet me when I stepped into the courtyard, took me by the hand, and drew me silently toward the dining room. There was Rosa in the folds of the white satin lining of her white coffin, still intact three days after she had died, and a thousand times more beautiful than I remembered her, for in death Rosa had been subtly transformed into the mermaid she had always been in secret.

"Damn her! She slipped through my hands!" they say I shouted, falling to my knees beside her, scandalizing all the relatives, for no one could comprehend my frustration at having spent two years scratching the earth to make my fortune with no other goal than that of one day leading this girl to the altar, and death had stolen her away from me.

Moments later the carriage arrived, an enormous black, shiny coach drawn by six plumed chargers, as was used on those occasions, and driven by two coachmen in livery. It pulled away from the house in the middle of the afternoon beneath a light drizzle, followed by a procession of cars that carried family and friends and all the flowers. It was the custom then for women and children not to attend funerals, which were considered a male province, but at the last minute Clara managed to slip into the cortège to accompany her sister Rosa, and I felt the grip of her small gloved hand. She stayed by my side all along the way, a small, silent shadow who aroused an unknown tenderness in my soul. At that moment I hadn't been told that she hadn't spoken in two days; and three more were to pass before the family became alarmed by her silence.

Severo del Valle and his oldest sons bore Rosa's white coffin with the silver rivets, and they themselves laid it down in the open niche in the family tomb. They were dressed in black, silent and dry-eyed, as befits the norms of sadness in a country accustomed to the dignity of grief. After the gates to the mausoleum had been locked and the family, friends, and gravediggers had retired, I was left alone among the flowers that had escaped Barrabás's hunger and accompanied Rosa to the cemetery. Tall and thin as I was then, before Férula's curse came true and I began to shrink, I must have looked like some dark winter bird with the bottom of my jacket dancing in the wind. The sky was gray and it looked as if it might rain. I suppose it must have been quite cold, but I didn't feel it, because my rage was eating me alive. I couldn't take my eyes off the small marble rectangle where the name of Rosa the Beautiful had been engraved in tall Gothic letters, along with the dates that marked her brief sojourn in this world. I thought about how I had lost two years dreaming of Rosa, working for Rosa, writing to Rosa, wanting Rosa, and how in the end I wouldn't even have the consolation of being buried by her side. I thought about the years I still had left to live and decided that without her it wasn't worth it, for I would never find another woman with her green hair and underwater beauty. If anyone had told me then that I would live to be more than ninety, I would have put a gun to my head and pulled the trigger.

I didn't hear the footsteps of the caretaker as he approached me from behind; I jumped when he touched me on the shoulder.

"How dare you put your hands on me!" I roared.

The poor man jumped back in fright. A few drops of rain fell sadly on the flowers of the dead.

"Forgive me, señor," I think he must have said. "It's six o'clock and I have to lock up."

He tried to explain to me that the rules forbade anyone but employees from staying in the place after sundown, but I didn't let him finish. I thrust a few bills in his hand and pushed him away so he would leave me in peace. I saw him walk away looking back at me over his shoulder. He must have thought I was a madman, one of those crazed necrophiliacs who sometimes haunt cemeteries.

It was a long night, perhaps the longest in my life. I spent it sitting next to Rosa's tomb, speaking with her, accompanying her on the first part of her journey to the Hereafter, which is when it's hardest to detach yourself from earth and you need the love of those who have remained behind, so you can leave with at least the consolation of having planted something in someone else's heart. I remembered her perfect face and cursed my luck. I blamed Rosa for the years I had spent dreaming of her deep within the mine. I didn't tell her that I hadn't seen any other women all that time except for a handful of shriveled old prostitutes, who serviced the whole camp with more good will than ability. But I did tell her that I had lived among rough, lawless men, that I had eaten chick-peas and drunk green water far from civilization, thinking of her night and day and bearing her image in my soul like a banner that gave me the strength to keep hacking at the mountain even if the lode was lost, even if I was sick to my stomach the whole year round, even if I was frozen to the bone at night and dazed by the sun during the day, all with the single goal of marrying her, but she goes and dies on me, betraying me before I can fulfill my dreams, and leaving me with this incurable despair. I told her she had mocked me, that we had never been completely alone together, that I had only been able to kiss her once. I had had to weave my love out of memories and cravings that were impossible to satisfy, out of letters that took forever to arrive and arrived faded, and that were incapable of reflecting the intensity of my feelings or the pain of her absence, because I have no gift for letter writing and much less for writing about my own emotions. I told her that those years in the mine were an irremediable loss, and that if I had known she wasn't long for this world I would have stolen the money that I needed to marry her and built her a palace studded with treasures from the ocean floor—with pearls and coral and walls of nacre. I would have kidnapped her and locked her up, and only I would have had the key. I would have loved her without interruption almost till infinity, for I was convinced that if she had been with me she would never have drunk the poison that was meant for her father and she would have lived a thousand years. I told her of the caresses I'd saved for her, the presents with which I'd planned to surprise her, the ways I would have loved her and made her happy. In short, I told her all the crazy things I never would have said if she could hear me and that I've never told a woman since.

That night I thought I had lost my ability to fall in love forever, that I would never laugh again or pursue an illusion. But never is a long time. I've learned that much in my long life.

Understanding

1. What feelings does the writer convey in this story? What aspects of the story correspond to these feelings?
2. How does Rosa die?
3. *The House of the Spirits* is a form of fiction called *magical realism,* in which fantasy and legend are blended with fact to produce an enchanted world. What about this story seems unreal or unbelievable? What about it seems credible? What effect does blending fantasy with fact have on the reader?
4. Esteban Trueba refers to people's reactions to Rosa's death as following the "norms of sadness in a country accustomed to the dignity of grief." Why does Trueba describe the country in this way?
5. Fifty years may seem a long time to grieve over the death of a loved one, but, as French writer Blaise Pascal said, "the heart has its reasons which reason knows nothing of." What in this excerpt provides clues to Esteban's prolonged grief over Rosa's death?

Responding

1. Sadness is a common response to losing someone we love. What other feelings do you associate with this kind of loss? Why?
2. A wise person once said: "Without remembering the pain of losing a loved one, we risk having no life to call our own." How can the remembrance of a loss, particularly that of a loved one, add to the reality of our lives? How does the memory affect one's sense of personal identity? Explain.
3. Consider how Allende allows Esteban Trueba to paint a vivid portrait of the exquisite Rosa, how he sketches her uniqueness and its effects on him. Using similar kinds of physical detail—though not necessarily in a magical

realism form—describe a loss that you want someone close to you to remember.

Connecting

Several of the selections in this chapter deal with the writer's response to the death of a loved one. Compare at least one of these accounts with Esteban Trueba's response to the death of Rosa the Beautiful.

Miss Brill

Katherine Mansfield

At the age of nineteen, Katherine Mansfield left her native New Zealand to establish herself as a writer in England. There she became both a friend and a rival of a well-known contemporary, Virginia Woolf. By 1920 Mansfield's reputation as a master of the short story was secured—just three years after she had been diagnosed with tuberculosis. Her delicate stories focus on internal psychological conflicts; her oblique narratives and subtle observations show the impressionistic influence of Anton Chekhov in mood, atmosphere, and timelessness.

In "Miss Brill" Mansfield uses her fine powers of observation to allow us a glimpse into the lives that lonely people can create to help themselves keep going. In fact, as Shakespeare proposed in *As You Like It*—"All the world's a stage and all the men and women merely players"—Miss Brill's "stage" is interrupted by two unlikely actors, causing her an unexpected wound. "Miss Brill" was originally published in *The Short Stories of Katherine Mansfield* (1922).

Although it was so brilliantly fine—the blue sky powdered with gold and great spots of light like white wine splashed over the Jardins Publics—Miss Brill was glad that she had decided on her fur. The air was motionless, but when you opened your mouth there was just a faint chill, like a chill from a glass of iced water before you sip, and now and again a leaf came drifting—from nowhere, from the sky. Miss Brill put up her hand and touched her fur. Dear little thing! It was nice to feel it again. She had taken it out of its box that afternoon, shaken out the moth-powder, given it a good brush, and rubbed the life back into the dim little eyes. "What has been happening to me?" said the sad little eyes. Oh, how sweet it was to see them snap at her again from the red eiderdown! . . . But the nose, which was of some black composition, wasn't at all firm. It must have had a knock, somehow. Never mind—a little dab of black sealing-wax when the time came—when it was absolutely necessary. . . . Little rogue! Yes, she really felt like that about it. Little rogue biting its tail just by her left ear. She could have taken it off and laid it on her lap and stroked it. She felt a tingling in her hands and arms, but that came from walking, she supposed. And when she breathed, something light and sad—no, not sad, exactly—something gentle seemed to move in her bosom. 1

There were a number of people out this afternoon, far more than last Sunday. And the band sounded louder and gayer. That was because the Season had begun. For although the band played all the year round on Sundays, out of season it was never the same. It was like someone playing with only the family to listen; it didn't care how it played if there weren't any strangers present. Wasn't the conductor wearing a new coat, too? She was sure it was new. He scraped with his foot and flapped his arms like a rooster about to crow, and the bandsmen sitting in the green rotunda blew out their cheeks and glared at the music. Now there came a little "flutey" bit—very pretty!—a little chain of bright drops. She was sure it would be repeated. It was; she lifted her head and smiled.

Only two people shared her "special" seat: a fine old man in a velvet coat, his hands clasped over a huge carved walking-stick, and a big old woman, sitting upright, with a roll of knitting on her embroidered apron. They did not speak. This was disappointing, for Miss Brill always looked forward to the conversation. She had become really quite expert, she thought, at listening as though she didn't listen, at sitting in other people's lives just for a minute while they talked round her.

She glanced, sideways, at the old couple. Perhaps they would go soon. Last Sunday, too, hadn't been as interesting as usual. An Englishman and his wife, he wearing a dreadful Panama hat and she button boots. And she'd gone on the whole time about how she ought to wear spectacles; she knew she needed them; but that it was no good getting any; they'd be sure to break and they'd never keep on. And he'd been so patient. He'd suggested everything—gold rims, the kind that curved round your ears, little pads inside the bridge. No, nothing would please her. "They'll always be sliding down my nose!" Miss Brill had wanted to shake her.

5 The old people sat on the bench, still as statues. Never mind, there was always the crowd to watch. To and fro, in front of the flower-beds and the band rotunda, the couples and groups paraded, stopped to talk, to greet, to buy a handful of flowers from the old beggar who had his tray fixed to the railings. Little children ran among them, swooping and laughing; little boys with big white silk bows under their chins, little girls, little French dolls, dressed up in velvet and lace. And sometimes a tiny staggerer came suddenly rocking into the open from under the trees, stopped, stared, as suddenly sat down "flop," until its small high-stepping mother, like a young hen, rushed scolding to its rescue. Other people sat on the benches and green chairs, but they were nearly always the same, Sunday after Sunday, and—Miss Brill had often noticed—there was something funny about nearly all of them. They were odd, silent, nearly all old, and from the way they stared they looked as though they'd just come from dark little rooms or even—even cupboards!

Behind the rotunda the slender trees with yellow leaves down drooping, and through them just a line of sea, and beyond the blue sky with gold-veined clouds.

Tum-tum-tum tiddle-um! tiddle-um! tum tiddley-um tum ta! blew the band.

Two young girls in red came by and two young soldiers in blue met them, and they laughed and paired and went off arm-in-arm. Two peasant women with funny straw hats passed, gravely, leading beautiful smoke-colored donkeys. A cold, pale nun hurried by. A beautiful woman came along and dropped her bunch of violets, and a little boy ran after to hand them to her, and she took them and threw them away as if they'd been poisoned. Dear me! Miss Brill didn't know whether to admire that or not! And now an ermine toque and a gentleman in gray met just in front of her. He was tall, stiff, dignified, and she was wearing the ermine toque she'd bought when her hair was yellow. Now everything, her hair, her face, even her eyes, was the same color as the shabby ermine, and her hand, in its cleaned glove, lifted to dab her lips, was a tiny yellowish paw. Oh, she was so pleased to see him—delighted! She rather thought they were going to meet that afternoon. She described where she'd been—everywhere, here, there, along by the sea. The day was so charming—didn't he agree? And wouldn't he, perhaps? . . . But he shook his head, lighted a cigarette, slowly breathed a great deep puff into her face, and, even while she was still talking and laughing, flicked the match away and walked on. The ermine toque was alone; she smiled more brightly than ever. But even the band seemed to know what she was feeling and played more softly, played tenderly, and the drum beat, "The Brute! The Brute!" over and over. What would she do? What was going to happen now? But as Miss Brill wondered, the ermine toque turned, raised her hand as though she'd seen someone else, much nicer, just over there, and pattered away. And the band changed again and played more quickly, more gaily than ever, and the old couple on Miss Brill's seat got up and marched away, and such a funny old man with long whiskers hobbled along in time to the music and was nearly knocked over by four girls walking abreast.

Oh, how fascinating it was! How she enjoyed it! How she loved sitting here, watching it all! It was like a play. It was exactly like a play. Who could believe the sky at the back wasn't painted? But it wasn't till a little brown dog trotted on solemn and then slowly trotted off, like a little "theater" dog, a little dog that had been drugged, that Miss Brill discovered what it was that made it so exciting. They were all on the stage. They weren't only the audience, not only looking on; they were acting. Even she had a part and came every Sunday. No doubt somebody would have noticed if she hadn't been there; she was part of the performance after all. How strange she'd never thought of it like that before! And yet it explained why she made such a point of starting from home at just the same time each week—so as not to be late for the performance—and it also explained why she had quite a queer, shy feeling at telling her English pupils how she spent her Sunday afternoons. No wonder! Miss Brill nearly laughed out loud. She was on the stage. She thought of the old invalid gentleman to whom she read the newspaper four afternoons a week while he slept in the garden. She had got quite used to the frail head on the cotton pillow, the hollowed eyes, the open mouth and the high pinched nose. If he'd been dead she mightn't have noticed for weeks; she wouldn't have minded. But suddenly he knew he was having the paper read to him by an actress! "An actress!" The old head lifted; two points of light quivered in the old eyes. "An actress—are ye?" And Miss Brill smoothed the newspaper as though it were the manuscript of her part and said gently: "Yes, I have been an actress for a long time."

The band had been having a rest. Now they started again. And what they 10
played was warm, sunny, yet there was just a faint chill—a something, what was it?—not sadness—no, not sadness—a something that made you want to sing. The tune lifted, lifted, the light shone; and it seemed to Miss Brill that in another moment all of them, all the whole company, would begin singing.

The young ones, the laughing ones who were moving together, they would begin, and the men's voices, very resolute and brave, would join them. And then she too, she too, and the others on the benches—they would come in with a kind of accompaniment—something low, that scarcely rose or fell, something so beautiful—moving. . . . And Miss Brill's eyes filled with tears and she looked smiling at all the other members of the company. Yes, we understand, we understand, she thought—though what they understood she didn't know.

Just at that moment a boy and girl came and sat down where the old couple had been. They were beautifully dressed; they were in love. The hero and heroine, of course, just arrived from his father's yacht. And still soundlessly singing, still with that trembling smile, Miss Brill prepared to listen.

"No, not now," said the girl. "Not here, I can't."

"But why? Because of that stupid old thing at the end there?" asked the boy. "Why does she come here at all—who wants her? Why doesn't she keep her silly old mug at home?"

"It's her fu-fur which is so funny," giggled the girl. "It's exactly like a fried whiting."

"Ah, be off with you!" said the boy in an angry whisper. Then: "Tell me, 15
ma petite chérie—"

"No, not here," said the girl. "Not *yet.*"

On her way home she usually bought a slice of honey-cake at the baker's. It was her Sunday treat. Sometimes there was an almond in her slice, sometimes not. It made a great difference. If there was an almond it was like carrying home a tiny present—a surprise—something that might very well not have been there. She hurried on the almond Sundays and struck the match for the kettle in quite a dashing way.

But today she passed the baker's by, climbed the stairs, went into the little dark room—her room like a cupboard—and sat down on the red eiderdown. She sat there for a long time. The box that the fur came out of was on the bed. She unclasped the necklet quickly; quickly, without looking, laid it inside. But when she put the lid on she thought she heard something crying.

Understanding

1. Miss Brill plays a kind of game with herself to make ordinary things special. Find instances of this game in the story. Do you ever do that with yourself?
2. What is the underlying tone of this story? What about the story supports your response?
3. How does Miss Brill see herself? How does she see older people in the park? How does she initially see the young couple?
4. What does the fox fur symbolize in this story?

Responding

1. Would you like to know Miss Brill? Why or why not?

2. Describe Miss Brill's everyday life. How does she make a living? What are her circumstances?
3. Have you ever been hurt by an offhand comment—a comment that you were not meant to hear? How many years have you carried the effects of that comment with you? How has it influenced who you are? Have you ever made such a comment about someone, thinking that it would not be heard?
4. *Field observation:* In the next day or so, sit somewhere where you have a chance to observe older people for approximately forty-five minutes. Notice (and record if possible) their movements; their gestures and moods; their interactions with acquaintances; strangers' reactions to them; how physically independent or dependent they are on others. Do you see elderly people you imagine are similar to Miss Brill? Do the men and women behave differently? Using only what you saw during this time, what can you conclude about these people? Generalize how the strangers regarded or treated them. Do you think the older people you observed were lonely?

Connecting

1. In both Chekhov's "Grief" and Mansfield's "Miss Brill," the narrators observe the diligent actions their characters take to cope with their grief or loneliness. Compare the situations and actions taken by Iona Potapov and by Miss Brill. Compare the responses or actions of the people with whom they come into contact. Is loneliness inevitable in old age?
2. Both Chekhov's and Mansfield's stories say little but suggest much. They develop through impressionistic details and do not seem to end. There may be little action, but these writers create a mood and an atmosphere and provide telling insight into the characters. In fact, Mansfield and Chekhov create the sense that the characters lives will go on and that the events in the story will be repeated. Theme, character, and situation are so highly integrated that it is hard to separate them. Compare "Miss Brill" and "Grief" on the basis of these writers' style and method of development.

Morning

Fyodor Dostoyevsky

Fyodor Dostoyevsky (1821–81) was born in Moscow and educated at the School of Military Engineers in St. Petersburg. In 1844 he resigned his commission in the army to devote himself to writing. His first novel, *Poor Folk,* was an immediate success and was followed by short stories and another novel. He wrote his best-known works—*Crime and Punishment, The Idiot, The Possessed,* and *The Brothers Karamazov*—during the last fourteen years of his life. What characterizes Dostoyevsky's writing is his uncanny insight into human motivation and an almost tortured willingness to look into the human heart. These qualities can be glimpsed in the following excerpt from *White Nights,* written when he was twenty-five, just before he was tried and condemned to death for belonging to a young socialist group in Russia. At the last moment, his sentence was commuted to four years in a Siberian prison.

The title *White Nights* refers to midsummer nights at the sixtieth latitude north—when the moon and stars are plainly visible—a time that allowed the usually city-bound narrator to experience the beauty of the countryside. During this respite, he makes friends with a despairing girl, Nastenka, whose life is controlled by a stern grandmother and who believes she has been deserted by her lover. The narrator's relationship with Nastenka, described in four nights, transforms him from a lonely, introspective dreamer to a man tantalizingly in love.

My nights were over. It was the morning after. The weather was bad. It was 1
raining. The rain beat a gloomy tattoo on my window. It was dark inside my room and bleak outside the windows. My head ached. Objects swam before my eyes. Fever was sneaking along my limbs.

"There's a letter for you." Matryona's voice hovered somewhere over me. "It has just come."

I jumped up.

"What letter? From whom?"

"How do I know who it's from? Look; maybe it says inside who wrote it." 5

I opened it. It was from her. It said:

> Please, please forgive me! I beg you on my knees. Forgive me! I deceived both you and myself. It was a dream, a mirage. I feel terrible about you now. Forgive me, forgive me!
>
> Don't be too hard on me, for what I feel for you hasn't changed. I told you I loved you—well, I do love you, and it's even more than love. Oh God, if only it were possible to love both of you at the same time! Ah, if only you could be him!

"Oh, if only he could be you." The thought flashed through my head. I remembered your very words, Nastenka. The letter continued:

> God only knows what I wouldn't do for you! I know that you feel sad and depressed. I have hurt you. But, as you know, we won't resent for long a wound inflicted by those we love, and you do love me!
>
> Thank you! Yes, thank you for that love! It lingers now in my memory like a sweet dream that remains long after awakening. I will always remember the moment when you opened your heart to me so fraternally and when you so nobly accepted the gift of my heart—wounded as it was—to love and cherish it, and heal its wounds. . . . If you forgive me, my memory of you will be ennobled by gratitude that will never fade. I shall cherish that memory, be faithful to it always, never betray it, never betray my heart—it is too constant for that. Only yesterday it went back to the one to whom it belongs forever.
>
> We'll meet again. You'll come to see us. You won't abandon us. You'll always be my friend and my brother. And when we meet, you'll give me your hand, won't you? You'll give it to me because you love me as much as ever.
>
> Please love me, and don't abandon me, because I love you so much at this moment, because I'm worthy of your love, because I'll earn it. . . . oh, my dear, dear friend!
>
> I'm marrying him next week. He came back to me full of love. He hadn't forgotten me. . . . You won't be angry with me for writing this about him, will you? I want to come and see you with him. You'll like him, won't you?
>
> So forgive, remember, and go on loving
>
> your Nastenka

I read and reread that letter. I was on the verge of tears. At last it fell from my hands, and I covered my face.

"Here, look at that!" Matryona said.

"What is it, old woman?"

"Why, I've swept all them cobwebs from the ceiling so now you can marry any time and, while you're at it, invite a houseful of guests."

I looked at Matryona. She was still vigorous. She was a very young *old woman,* but I suddenly visualized her all wrinkled and shrunk, an invalid. And I don't know why, but my whole room suddenly aged the way an old woman ages. The walls and the ceilings peeled, everything faded, cobwebs multiplied. . . . And when I looked out of the window, I don't know why, but the house opposite turned dimmer too, the plaster on its columns fell off, the cornices became all grimy and full of cracks, and the walls, which used to be dark yellow, turned grayish.

A ray of sun that for a second had broken through a rain cloud disappeared behind it again, and everything darkened once more. Or was it just my sad and barren future that flashed before me? Did I see myself exactly the way I am now, fifteen years later, having aged in this very room, just as lonely, still living with Matryona, who hasn't grown any more intelligent in all these years?

I remember the hurt inflicted upon me, Nastenka! But I never sent a dark 20
cloud to sail over your clear, serene sky. I never reproached you, never made you sad or gave you a secret guilty feeling. I never trampled any of the tender flowers that you entwined in your black curls when you walked to the altar with him. Oh, never, never! So may the sky lie cloudless over you, and your smile be bright and carefree; be blessed for the moment of bliss and happiness you gave to another heart, a lonely and a grateful one.

My God, a moment of bliss. Why, isn't that enough for a whole lifetime?

Understanding

1. What conflict(s) occur in this story? Are they physical, intellectual, moral, or emotional?
2. People who experience a powerful loss often draw a deeper meaning from their sorrow. Despite his sadness at losing Nastenka, the narrator of "Morning" convinces himself that through his self-sacrifice, he has saved her from despair. What meaning do you draw from his sacrifice?
3. What wound is exposed in this story? What does the narrator say that leads the reader to believe that he has accepted it?
4. The subtitle of *White Nights* is *A Tale of Love from the Reminiscences of a Dreamer.* What in this story conveys the feeling of a "dreamer"?

Responding

1. Love or the feeling of being in love provokes powerful emotions. Can a moment of bliss, as the narrator states, really be enough for a whole lifetime? Explain.
2. Some people believe that the deeper meaning that others draw from or attach to suffering is a façade, a rationalization, or even a denial of the pain. These people believe that there is no deeper meaning to be obtained from suffering—that life is hard, cruel, and unpredictable. Respond to this point of view.
3. Write a response to Nastenka's letter.

Connecting

1. The narrator in "Morning" loses Nastenka to another man. Esteban Trueba in Allende's "The Death of Rosa the Beautiful" loses Rosa to a cup of poisoned brandy. In what ways do the narrator and Trueba come to terms with their losses? Does the *kind* of loss that they experienced affect their reactions to it? Explain.
2. In paragraph 8 Nastenka writes, "But, as you know, we won't resent for long a wound inflicted by those we love, and you do love me!" Do you agree with her? Which readings in this chapter support her claim?

Writing Option: Wounds

Think back over what you read in this chapter. Were the stories conveyed in the "Wounds" readings familiar enough to relate to but just different enough to stretch you to make comparisons, to ask questions, to create meanings for yourself, and to recall your own stories with similar themes?

Revisit your responses to the Responding questions in this chapter. Which commanded your attention? On which questions did you write more than you expected to? Select a response to revise that will add a new dimension to your evolving self-portrait. Your writing should expound on a physical or mental wound that contributed to your identity—that left its signature—and the way you view the world. Keep in mind that through your writing you are both editing and validating your life's experiences.

3

Decisions

The ultimate measure of a man is not where he stands in moments of comfort and convenience, but where he stands at times of challenge and controversy.

—Dr. Martin Luther King, Jr. (1929–68)

We die. That may be the meaning of life. But we do language. That may be the measure of our lives.

—Toni Morrison, winner of the 1993 Nobel Prize for Literature

We continue the section on self-portraits with a powerful collection of decision stories. The readings we have assembled in this chapter are the result of *our decisions* about two powerful notions: that the choices we make define our lives, and that what we say and do about our decisions are the measure of our lives.

The writers of the works included here have faced moments of truth—those times of crisis (big or small) when one must make a difficult choice. For all of us, these defining moments arise in situations when we are called upon to take a stand—to use our will to live up to a commitment, an idea, or a value that we hold dear. What we do in these situations becomes a measure of who we are.

Many such situations present a conflict of values. How does one choose between a valued allegiance to country and a core disapproval of a war you have been called upon to fight? Which wins out—friendship or honesty—when, after losing her job, your closest friend asks you to steal for her so she can buy medicine for her dying mother? How do you decide whether to "pull the plug" when your father has lain in a coma for three months? In the selections that follow, the writers make decisions that alter their lives; they set into motion chains of events and then deal with the consequences.

We have grouped the decision selections into several themes. John C. Glidewell sets the stage by exploring life-defining decisions—he calls them *choice points*—when "irregular" things happen, causing us to feel emotional and unsettled. James W. Tollefson provides examples of these life-defining choices.

We include a story from South Africa by Nadine Gordimer, in which her characters make decisions in the dehumanizing social context of apartheid. Gordimer's unsettling work is followed by three selections that demonstrate decisions and their consequences. The first is General Colin Powell's public announcement regarding his decision not to run for the 1996 U.S. presidency. Virginia Woolf then explores two life-altering decisions she made in order to work as a female writer in the male-dominated world of publishing. Finally, Andrea Lee, after a visit to her former elementary school, makes a decision about the way she will approach her own history.

Because some choices can trigger disturbing consequences, we have included two readings in which writers explore their guilt over decisions they made. Primo Levi revisits a decision made some forty years earlier under immoral and life-threatening circumstances. Dag Hammarskjöld chronicles a deeply private misgiving about a choice he made not to challenge another man's values and not to act on what he thought were his own.

Because there are ways to reckon with our bad decisions, we provide examples of the power of language in what we say about our decisions. Richard Ford draws meaning from a decision he *didn't* make fifteen years later. We conclude this collection with James Russell Lowell's poem "Our Fathers Fought for Liberty" to examine how far we've come in living up to our constitutionally guaranteed freedom to make decisions.

In essence, the readings in this chapter provide the impetus to measure the decisions and possibilities inherent in life. To harken back to Toni Morrison's quotation, "we do language." And because language is how we know our world, our writing about our world is our way of measuring our lives, of seeing the signatures of our decisions.

A Time for Choosing

John C. Glidewell

John Glidewell was a professor of education at The University of Chicago when *Choice Points: Essays on the Emotional Problems of Living with People* was published. A social psychologist interested in applying theory to practice, Glidewell once said he saw himself as a mediator or translator between the "academy" and the world of social interaction outside it. *Choice Points* reflects this interest.

The work comprises five essays that were gathered from material Glidewell was working on at the National Training Laboratories, an early "think and do" tank based in Maine. It sought to help people employed in business, industry, and social service organizations get "emotionality" to work for rather than against them, or, as Glidewell states in the preface to *Choice Points,* "to use a wide range of alternatives in their quest for joy in work and joy in play and joy in love."

Choice Points deals with three perspectives on the social psychology of everyday life: when and how to fight and when and how to run away; when and how to be dependent and be dependable; and when and how to offer and seek love. The essays are written in simple, direct language and cast in the form of personal reminiscences, often accompanied by dialogue. "A Time for Choosing" is the opening essay in *Choice Points.*

For a long time I can swim along comfortably in the moving currents of the steady stream of life. Work progresses, families grow, and most of us perform our duties pretty much in accord with long-standing mutual expectations. Life isn't simple, but it is fairly regular and predictable. All of this regular part of life and work and following mutually understood expectations is, I think, tremendously important. I think that this sort of regularity is the basis of most of the sustained productivity and achievement that have built civilizations. But it is not what I want to call attention to. 1

I want to call attention to the irregular points—the points that begin the creation of new civilizations. The critical points in life for me are the surprising ones, points where standing expectations are violated. These are points at which choices are made, consciously or unconsciously. These are the points that set courses that change a family or change a city. Sometimes choice points come up slowly and gradually. I'm pretty sure I don't notice them until it is too late. Sometimes choice points come up suddenly and dramatically. I am startled and disturbed by the flat demands they make on me.

Faced with a choice point, I find that I am much involved emotionally. I feel all sorts of things. I seem to be scared, angry, hurt, sad, and even sometimes glad—all at once. I can pretend I have no choice, like saying that I must climb the mountain because it is there. I can try to restore the old order and way of looking at things, like saying we've got to train more old-fashioned humanitarian country doctors. I can try something new like going around without a watch just to see if time has come to mean more to me than it should. I can be just immobilized by it all, while my pulse races, and my brow sweats, and my scalp itches, and my nerves are paralyzed.

Whatever I find myself doing, I become aware that I must make a choice. I must make a choice or find the choice made for me. I must choose from whatever alternatives my experiences have stored up and from whatever alternatives my emotions make available to me. I must try to calculate the risks involved, and manage my fears while calculating.

Faced with a choice point, like whether to challenge a bully or offer him 5
friendship, I know that my choice may expose some of my weaknesses, and I could be humiliated. I know, also, that new and more realistic learnings may become available for both me, the bully, and our fellows. And I know that, even if I am wrong in my choice, the bully, my fellows, and I could emerge better men, humbled perhaps but not humiliated.

Faced with a choice point like making a proposal of marriage, I know that it is an exciting and frightening and critical point in life. I may even see that there can be no inconsequential choice. I can be scared about making the choice, and I can be deeply grateful that I have the freedom to choose, and even be proud that my choice will have consequences. And I can still be scared to choose.

To explain some more of what I mean by choice points, let me repeat a story that was making the rounds of young parents during the late 1940s. The story had a real basis, as most stories do, and this is the basis of that story.

Just after World War II, I was one of the thousands of married veterans who found themselves students in the universities of the country. My wife, my daughter, and I lived in a cracker-box apartment, partitioned out of a former barracks building, transplanted from an abandoned army camp to a former girls' athletic field. It was an interim period of life, and we suspended many of the demands we might make on one another and on our friends. We dressed more casually (and economically), we ate more simply (and economically), and we entertained each other more spontaneously (and economically).

There were ninety families in the half-square-block area where we lived, and some hundred and fifty children under ten years old. You can see that the wives almost always grasped any opportunity to get away for a short time. One Saturday my wife and a neighbor planned a daylong shopping tour. I agreed to "sit" with a pair of two-year-olds, our daughter Pam and our neighbor's son Oscar. Oscar, like a lot of other kids in that half-square block, was a fellow who met life more than halfway. His brain was as fast as light and as sharp as a needle; his body was as tough as leather and as active as a tiger cub. He entered a room like a whirlwind. Two minutes after entering, he handled, asked questions about, and tested the strength of every object and every person within his reach. We loved him and knew him well. That morning only unbreakable objects were within his reach. His mother, as she and my wife were leaving, turned in the doorway and said, "He didn't eat any breakfast at all. Try to get him to eat some lunch."

I didn't know it then, but that remark set into action a chain of choice points. I didn't recognize most of them at the time, but looking back I have never forgotten any of them. And I have looked back at them often. Let me tell you how it went.

Being a graduate student in psychology, I felt I knew a thing or two about children. In fact, I had just finished a course in child development and a lot of observations of two-year-olds. I knew that they would play, separately mostly, without much supervision. Sure enough, they did just that, requiring little from me. I just kept them in sight and congratulated myself on my good judgment and skill at minimum supervision.

Lunchtime came. I called to them sprightly, "Who would like some lunch?"

Quick as a flash, Oscar snapped back, "Not me!"

I had missed another choice point and I had made another mistake. I shifted my approach. "All right," I said, "I'll have some lunch. If you two want to join me you can." Pam watched the whole thing with fascination.

I was pretty good at heating up canned soup. I knew they both liked bean soup, and soon I had a pot of bean and bacon bubbling away. Then I remembered my textbook. The thing to do was to give Oscar some positive choices; no questions which could be answered yes or no. With that thought, I made peanut butter and jelly sandwiches. The pot of soup and the sandwiches were ready, and I asked, "Who wants soup and who wants sandwiches?"

"I don't want any lunch!" Oscar was quiet and firm.

"OK," I returned, with phony indifference.

I sat down and began to eat. Pam joined me. Perhaps she knew how desperately I needed support. Perhaps she was just hungry. Oscar played with a toy truck.

I had passed another choice point. By now I was aware how much I was on the spot. I knew my choices had consequences. In some way I didn't understand, I knew, also, that the consequences went beyond food and nutrition. Courage and cowardice, freedom and slavery, support and indifference—in some small way all of them were involved.

After a time I turned to Oscar. "Don't you like bean soup?"

"Sure. But not for lunch."

"What would you like for lunch?"

Oscar's eyes sparkled with lights of mischief.

"I'd like a worm!" Oscar shouted.

"A worm?" I was shocked. He was tickled.

"A worm!" This time he shouted louder.

I was well aware by now that I was in a special kind of fight. For Oscar it was independence day. For me, it was examination day; my resourcefulness as an adult was being challenged. For Pam, it was loyalty day. She was supporting me, and she knew well how much I needed her.

"OK," I replied, "a worm." Outside we went. I rammed the spade into the ground with rare vigor, my excitement mounting. Soon I extracted a nice, long earthworm. Back into the house, a quick wash job, and the worm was on a plate before a surprised but unruffled Oscar.

"You didn't cook it."

I moved quickly. Out of the plate, into a fry pan with a little butter, and in no time the worm was *earthworm sauté*. Back on the plate and again in front of Oscar. He looked up at me and in unbelievable innocence, said, "Cut it up."

I moved even more quickly. I cut the worm into two pieces. I nearly growled.

"Eat."

"You eat with me."

At a time like that, at a choice point like that, even knowing my own foolishness, I could not go down in defeat. In my anger and tension, I felt sure I had only one alternative—deceit.

I picked up half the worm, pretended to eat it, and palmed it into my pocket. I did the trick pretty well. Oscar's eyes were on my mouth, pretending to chew. He never looked at my pocket. As I finished my chewing, Oscar's face clouded over, his mouth turned down and he began to cry. In between his sobs he struck the last blow.

"You ate *my* half."

That was the end of that battle. But it will never leave my memory. For me, that lunch with Pam and Oscar summed up all the dimensions of all the chains of bungled choice points that have cropped up in and around my emotional problems of living with people. They seem simple to summarize now:

When to fight and when to run away; and how to fight and how to run away; and

When to be dependent and when to be dependable; and how to be dependent and how to be dependable; and

When to offer love and when to seek love; and how to offer love and how to seek love.

Understanding

1. What is a choice point?
2. Is a choice point the same as a decision? If not, what is the distinction?
3. Glidewell says that his lunch with Pam and Oscar "summed up all the dimensions of all the chains of bungled choice points that have cropped up in and around my emotional problems of living with people." Trace Glidewell's choice points in his encounter with Oscar. Was one more telling than another? Which one(s)?
4. In his dealings with Oscar, what are the differences between Glidewell's emotional involvement and his intellectual involvement in his choices?

Responding

1. Describe a choice point that had real significance in your life and that left a mark on how you see yourself. How did you become aware of this choice? Include your recollections of the alternatives available to you at the time, your intellectual and emotional involvement in the choices, and your re-

flections on the rightness of your choice at the time of choosing. In retrospect, would you make the same choice again?

2. What Glidewell did in analyzing his encounter with Oscar is called *metacognitive reflection*—the process of becoming aware of our thoughts in order to understand, manage, or control them. Select a recent choice point from your life and analyze it in a similar way.
3. What role do emotions have in your decision making?
4. Decisions are the result of judgments—evaluations made about a situation in terms of its appropriateness or its moral, legal, or ethical ramifications. Glidewell congratulates himself on his "good judgment and skill at minimum supervision" of Oscar and Pam. What is "good judgment"? Describe an event in which you or someone you know exercised good judgment.

Connecting

Consider Glidewell's "irregular point"—the surprising ones where standing expectations are violated and choices are made that set courses that change a city, a family, an individual's life. From the readings in chapters one and two, identify at least two stories that are good examples of these irregular points. Elaborate on the choices made that set individuals on new courses.

Choosing Not to Fight

James W. Tollefson

Follow me if I advance! Kill me if I retreat! Revenge me if I die!
—Ngo Dinh Diem, battle cry on becoming president of Vietnam in 1954

A president's hardest task is not to do what is right, but to know what is right.
—Lyndon Baines Johnson, president of the United States in 1966

When I think back over my life, Vietnam defined who I am.
—Conscientious objector in *The Strength Not to Fight*

In *The Strength Not to Fight,* author James Tollefson documents the collective experiences of some of those Americans who expressed and acted upon their principled opposition to the conflict in Vietnam (it was never a "declared" war). About 170,000 of them were officially designated *conscientious objectors* and received draft deferments. Others chose different ways to express their opposition to the war, some of which are recounted in the following selection.

In 1965 U.S. troops became combatants in Vietnam. American presence in this small Southeast Asian country had gradually increased since 1955, when President Dwight D. Eisenhower dispatched several thousand "technical advisors" in support of then-President Diem. Ostensibly, the reason for American military and strategic involvement in many parts of Southeast Asia, and in Vietnam in particular, was to counter communist influence coming from both China and the former Soviet Union.

Tollefson, himself a conscientious objector during the war, is now a professor of English at the University of Washington in Seattle. In 1987 he returned from Southeast Asia after spending four years working at a U.S.-operated refugee camp on the Bataan Peninsula of the Philippines, an experience he chronicled in *Alien Winds: The Re-education of America's Indochinese Refugees.* The following excerpts from the first chapter of *The Strength Not to Fight* reveal how three (unnamed) young men came to their decisions to refuse to fight in Vietnam.

I was in junior college in the LA area. I played electric bass in a folk-rock group. We played on a TV show called the "All-American College Show," hosted by Arthur Godfrey. Three acts competing with each other. An Irish tenor won, but as a result of our appearance, we landed a contract to do a USO tour in Asia. I knew if I left for the tour, I'd risk losing my student deferment, but I fantasized that my draft board would accept the work as supporting the troops and grant me a continuation of my II-S deferment when I came back from the tour. So I went. 1

We left in September 1969. Four of us, two guys, two girls. Our first stop was Japan. A week on the hospital circuit. Mostly casualties from Vietnam.

We'd play acoustically and sing and visit and talk with the patients. All men, all my age, eighteen or nineteen. Ward after ward of men my age who had pieces of themselves missing. Eyes and ears and arms and legs. Day after day, orderlies would roll people into auditoriums on gurneys and in wheelchairs. The patients would ask us about our draft status. The more severely injured they were, the more extravagant the action they'd tell us to take to make sure we didn't end up in their situation. I remember one man—it's hard to call him a man. He was my age. I wasn't a man—I remember one guy who said, "Shoot your foot off. Shoot a finger off. But don't let them get you."

It was like running into a brick wall. The war suddenly wasn't on TV. It was right in front of me. These were human beings who were just like the people I'd been going to school with. No matter what the outcome of the war, these guys weren't going to get better. How could they be absorbed back into the United States? Planeloads of them. I thought, "If I cooperate with the draft, I may be in this position. I'll be forgotten. I'll have my arm blown off for the rest of my life." It was very scary and very sickening.

One day, I was with one of the women in the group. Sue was her name. We turned a corner in one of the wards, and there right in front of us was someone she knew from high school. He was missing some limbs. I can't remember which ones. She spent quite a while talking with him. Afterward, she was shaking. I remember being very scared. I felt it would happen to me.

After Japan, we went to Korea. One of the first shows we did there was 5
located far from anything else. We were told that the men we were going to see probably wouldn't talk to us. That it wouldn't be like any other audience. Our guide told us they'd been stuck there a long time and would be kept there for the rest of their lives. That's all we were told.

We were driven in a bus for several hours over awful roads to the north, way up near the DMZ [Demilitarized Zone]. It was a pretty area, full of pine trees. We arrived after dark. I could smell the trees. We walked along narrow paths to a tiny, very old, long, low barracks. Inside, it was open, with a simple wood frame and wood floors. No stage and no special lighting. About twenty or twenty-five men were sitting around, most staring off into space. They looked old to me, I guess in their forties or fifties. They were from the Korean War.

The room was uncomfortably quiet. We began the show. They didn't sit close to us. Some didn't pay any attention. Some talked to each other or to themselves. They never applauded, and they didn't seem to know that it was appropriate to applaud. I kept wondering why we were doing the show. No one came up to us afterward.

The men seemed to be stockpiled, maybe an embarrassment to the U.S. government or military. I don't know. Later in my life, I became a psychiatric nurse. When I think back about the men's behavior, it seems quite certain to me that they were probably on maintenance medication of some sort—psych meds. Their behavior certainly was very similar to a lot of behavior I've seen on psych units since then.

We did three weeks in Korea. I gradually realized that our music was incidental. We were there to provide human contact for people. After Korea, we spent a weekend in Tokyo, and then flew to the Philippines. We were there during the national elections, which were very violent, with civilian shootings, gory TV commercials.

I remember riding in a pedicab, a three-wheel tricycle. We were passing 10
someone when another trike came toward us. The two raced toward each other and at the last possible moment swerved, barely missing each other. There was wild laughter. It wasn't funny, but it was a relief. I felt such relief there. I wasn't going to get shot. It was so beautiful there.

After the Philippines, we did Guam, and then flew home, arriving at Travis Air Force Base in northern California. As I walked off the plane, I realized that my stomach had been hurting the whole trip. My father and younger sister were there to pick me up. I remember putting my amplifier in the back of my dad's car, and the relief I felt. The trip was finally over and I was safe again.

I arrived back at home convinced that I never wanted to play music for money again in my life. I immediately sold my amplifier and hung up my electric bass. Getting rid of my amplifier was a way of rejecting the whole experience, washing my hands of it. I had been daydreaming about a bass flute since Korea. I had made a drawing of it, which I had kept in my back pocket for the last part of the tour. So I went to Sherman Clay Music Store in Vallejo and traded my bass as down payment on a bass flute. I started making payments for the first time in my life—$28.15 a month.

Within six weeks, I had made up my mind. One morning in our basement at home, I told my father that I didn't think people in the United States were worth defending. I told him I was going to refuse induction. He told me I was wrong. He was appalled and shocked. I clearly didn't have his support. I didn't tell him then about the ward after ward of crippled, shot, lost men my age.

* * *

As a kid, I loved guns. Texas, where I grew up, is a sportman's paradise. My dad and I often went hunting. Duck hunting was my favorite. You go out before it's light. You're freezing. If your feet stay dry, you're lucky. Otherwise, you're in for hours of misery. You get set up in a blind. It's real silent. You swat the spiders away. You got your hot coffee or cocoa. Then you hear the birds, birds of all kinds. The light comes up and the birds explode into this unbelievable cacophony of nature calls. Pretty soon you can see the trees over by the horizon, and the water. You've got your decoys out. Once it's light, the ducks start coming. My dad would call them on the duck caller. I'd try to shoot ducks a hundred yards away with a shotgun. My dad would say, "The shotgun won't go that far. Here's what you should do."

So I was brought up with guns. I thought guns were invincible. It was the 15
killing of civilians that gradually convinced me the war was wrong.

I went to college in 1964. In '66, there was a rash of "We Won't Go" statements. I was one of the signers of the original statement. Our first action to get attention was in 1966, when Secretary of Defense Robert McNamara came to Cambridge to give a talk at the Harvard Kennedy School of Government. We had the building surrounded, but he didn't want to talk to us. They sent a decoy car and hoped to sneak him out back, but we caught him and filled the street around his car with people. So he had to get out and talk with us. We detained him for five or ten minutes. The headlines and editorials the next day said what we did was uncivilized and barbaric, that all the photos should be analyzed to see who was there, and that Harvard should kick us out. For those of us who were there, it was hard to recognize our event in the media coverage. Back home, my dad was mad because I was attending what he called the Kremlin on the Charles.

In '68, back home near Killeen, Texas, I stopped in at a GI coffeehouse. I ended up working there for six months. I met GIs fresh back from Nam. The antiwar activists and the GIs supported each other. Some of the guys running the coffeehouse were veterans. We had a very rigid rule against dope, because you could get sent to jail for years for just a microscopic amount. Texas is not a very tolerant state.

Locals didn't like us. And they didn't like the GIs either, whom they called "dopers." The people in the town were for the war, but the GIs were stigmatized. Especially the nonwhite GIs, who'd get their asses kicked if they went in the wrong place. The townspeople were, however, willing to take their money. There were pawnshops, movie theaters, used car lots, liquor stores.

Those of us who worked at the coffeehouse lived a couple of miles out of town in a poor black and Mexican neighborhood, which was our way of protecting ourselves against what we called the "goat ropers." Those were people who would have liked to set fire to our house or our cars if they felt they could get at us.

During the time I was there, we got word that some of the GIs from Fort 20
Hood were going to be sent to Berkeley for riot control during People's Park demonstrations. So we made up leaflets encouraging troops not to shoot people in the streets. I went one night with a friend to distribute the leaflets on base. It was hot. The base was crawling with cops because of the tension over sending troops for riot control. We parked in the lot and started leafletting cars, when a jeep full of MPs suddenly pulled up. My buddy hid under a car, while I stuffed the leaflets in a mailbox. But the MPs found both the leaflets and my buddy. They arrested me within minutes. We spent the night in jail. It was a good thing it wasn't Brazil. The MPs were really hostile. Some couldn't understand why they weren't allowed to beat us up. It was a real education. It just made me madder at America.

Near the end of the fateful year of 1968, I told my folks I was going for CO [conscientious objector].

* * *

I was raised in a very tight, conservative Lithuanian-Catholic ethnic community in Grand Rapids, Michigan. The roots of that environment were the church and the military. My father had fought in World War II. He flew thirty-three missions over Germany with the Eighth Air Force. So my dad was a war hero, although he almost never talked about it. While a lot of kids above the age of twelve started chasing girls, my interest in military matters continued and grew deeper. I went from building models and playing with little tanks to buying World War II history books.

In 1959, at the age of fourteen, I entered the seminary to become a Catholic priest. In the seminary, I became a skilled player of war games. The Civil

War, World War II, any war. During the Cuban missile crisis, I phoned my parents to say, "Be sure to keep your gas tank full and have lots of canned food on the shelves." I even insisted that we have some rendezvous point where we would all meet after World War III. I think it was in Arizona somewhere. I was always the strategic thinker.

My consciousness was very firmly rooted in my childhood, which meant I had that virulent anticommunism typical of American Catholicism at that time. I was the sort of person who actually read Eisenhower's book *Crusade in Europe.* The only war on the planet was the war against ruthless, atheistic, godless communism.

My views about war began to change because of my fascination with the topic. My interests took me beyond literature that glorified war to literature that revealed the horror of it. One book that was absolutely critical to my formation was *The Fortunes of War,* by Andrew Rooney, who still comments for CBS. It's about four great battles in World War II. Its introduction states that one of the reasons a lot of writing glorifies war is that the people for whom war was a bad experience aren't around to tell any stories about it. It goes on to say that the truism is right: war is hell. The first battle it covers is the absolutely, unbelievably horrible battle for Tarawa in the South Pacific, during which five thousand people died for one square mile of Coral Island, in just a merciless, vicious, brutal, hand-to-hand struggle. I also read General S.L.A. Marshall's study of combat infantrymen during World War II, which revealed that when push came to shove, over 50 percent of the troops admitted they never fired their weapons. Another high percentage admitted that if they did, they intentionally aimed high or closed their eyes. Taking another life seems to be deeply antithetical to human beings.

And I read poetry. I memorized one poem by Randall Jarrell, who, like my father, had been in the Eighth Air Force. It was called "The Death of the Ball Turret Gunner." I especially remember the ending, when the dead gunner's corpse is washed out of the turret with a hose. I still have my written analysis of that poem, so I have early documentary evidence of my beliefs.

I was ignorant of American military involvement in the war in Vietnam until the summer of '63, when those pictures of the Buddhist monks who immolated themselves were splashed on the front pages and on television. Those were such startling, shocking images that all of a sudden I realized something was going on in this faraway place called Vietnam.

My first critical analysis of the war took place in the fall of 1966. We had a great deal of speech training in the seminary. One day, the speech and preaching professor said, "This week, we are going to debate the war in Vietnam." He asked, "Who wants to take the antiwar side?" Not one of us did, since from our perspective there was no debate. We knew that the war was wonderful. Finally, out of an old-school notion of gallantry, I volunteered to take the antiwar side. And in my usual thorough fashion, I started reading all those "Commies" who were writing against the war. What I read shook me. It shook me up badly.

One of the main points of the critics was that Vietnam was a civil war. It wasn't evil Communists directed from Moscow and Peking invading a wonderful, peaceful, democratic people. I read solid evidence of the number of civilian casualties. This was not World War II. Tarawa, as horrible as it was, was only American and Japanese soldiers, not families caught in the middle.

Gradually, I began to agitate for more discussion of the war. Our classes in moral theology and ethics focused on questions like: Is it okay to remove an ectopic pregnancy? Is it okay to snip the fallopian tubes? I finally led a student rebellion in 1968. We threatened to have a strike unless a number of things occurred, among them more access to television news and newspapers and open discussions of the war in our classrooms. Cardinal McIntyre came to the seminary and clearly stated his position: "If you strike, we will dismiss you. There are plenty of young men in Ireland who would love to come to this seminary."

Unfortunately, his threat worked. I said, "Follow me," and all I heard was my own echo. I was a revolutionary with no party. I was disgusted and angry and bitter. I concluded that the church was hopeless on the matter of the war. So, in what for me was an absolutely gut-wrenching move, I left the seminary. I had been in it for nine years.

My family had always thought about taking a vacation in Europe. My father decided now was the time for it. So in April 1968, my sister, mother, father, and I left for Europe. The high point was a visit to Attlebridge Air Force Base near Norwich, England. My father had been stationed there in World War II. It was still largely intact, because it had been turned into the largest turkey farm in all of Great Britain. With no small irony, we drove out on the runway in my Volkswagen to see where he used to take off. It was like the opening scene in *Twelve O'Clock High,* where the wind is blowing across the tarmac. It was one of the few times my father talked about his experiences in the war. For me, it was my last pro-military moment.

I eventually went to Paris in May 1968, just in time for the student uprising. That is where my first on-the-street, committed antiwar activities occurred. I got a crash course in New Left politics, as I sat in smoke-filled rooms with Sartre and others. I was there when the Communist party and all of the labor unions pulled out, leaving the student movement completely exposed. The French government viciously cracked down. There was gunfire and beatings and hurled cobblestones. People were killed. It scared me off radical, violent street protest. I am lucky I didn't get killed.

When I came back from that vacation in the third week of May, I plunged myself into the campaign for Bobby Kennedy in California. Here was a way I believed I could work against the war that would really make a difference. I became an intense volunteer in the campaign. I was about ninety feet away from him, in the Ambassador Hotel, on my birthday, June 5, when he was assassinated.

I was devastated, but I felt I had to continue working against the war. I hooked on with the McCarthy campaign and went to Chicago for the convention to work as a McCarthy volunteer. I was in the street when the police rioted. They used barbed wire, jeeps with machine guns. They pushed a bunch of people through a plate-glass window. We carried the injured up to the McCarthy campaign office and made phone calls for medical assistance. I was later swept up on the street and arrested, and put in Cook County jail. There I observed a young woman protester have her guitar stomped on before she was raped by a Chicago policeman with his nightstick.

I talk on military matters today, and people say, “Were you ever in the military?” And I say, “No, but I have been in combat.” And I mean Chicago.

In Chicago, I concluded that everything I had been taught about the American political system was false. There was no democracy when it came to the war. I saw the McCarthy campaign locked out of the convention. I saw Hubert Humphrey cast as the peace candidate. I realized the political system was geared to produce two war candidates. It was not going to represent the antiwar movement in the ’68 elections. And dissent was going to be met with state violence. It was horribly disillusioning. It became clear that there was little point in working at American presidential politics. Any candidate who really stood for change would be shot.

Of everything that happened in 1968, I think the Tet Offensive was the final straw. It demonstrated that our government had been lying. I knew enough to understand that the Tet Offensive didn’t accomplish much militarily. But for the National Liberation Front to wage that kind of assault, there had to be tremendous support right in Saigon. You don’t get a commando squad into the U.S. embassy without a lot of people helping you. So despite what our government had been saying, it was clear that there were lots of people in the south supporting the other side.

I decided to go back to the seminary. A number of my former classmates who had been in my little rebel group had gone up to a progressive seminary in the San Francisco Bay Area, St. Patrick’s Seminary in Menlo Park, near Stanford. So I did the same.

Although the Stanford area was hardly Berkeley, still, in the fall of ’68, the 40
antiwar movement was very active there. A turning point for me was a lecture at the Stanford Memorial Church by Father Daniel Berrigan. In May of 1968, Daniel Berrigan and his brother, Philip, and seven others had poured homemade napalm on draft records at a draft board in Catonsville, Maryland. That was international front-page news. I had read about it in *Le Monde* when I was in Paris. I thought, “Boy, that’s bizarre. Who are these guys, napalming draft records? What the heck, let’s go see what this guy has to say.”

Berrigan’s talk had a dramatic, powerful effect on me. Here was this enigmatic, eloquent poet-priest. I couldn’t imagine this guy napalming draft records out in some parking lot in broad daylight. He put the war and resistance to the war in the context of Christian theology. He was a pacifist *and* a Catholic priest. He said that what was needed was massive nonviolent resistance. We should pack the jails. That just blew my mind. Pacifism was something Quakers did, not Catholics.

I was so excited that I don’t think I slept for a week. Suddenly, it seemed two of my life’s passions had come together. Catholicism and my hatred for the war. I enrolled in a class at Stanford called “Jesus and Nonviolence,” a cram course in Christian pacifism. I read Thomas Merton’s writings and *The Nonviolent Cross* by Jim Douglass, the famous activist. It startled me that here was a two-thousand-year tradition of nonviolence in the Church.

About that time, two Catholic pacifists, Tom Cornell and James Forest, came to the seminary to talk and to lead discussions. Tom Cornell was one of the original draft card burners in '65. Jim Forest had just come back from torching the draft records in the Milwaukee draft board. He was one of the Milwaukee Fourteen. Jim and Tom had formed the U.S. Catholic chapter of the Fellowship of Reconciliation. One night at dinner, we had corned beef and cabbage. The only thing that was remotely edible was the corned beef, but neither Jim nor Tom were eating it. I was thinking, "Who are you guys, what's the matter?" They said, "We are vegetarians because we see that nonviolence extends into this too." I was impressed. Nonviolence is not just something you read about in books. It shows up on your dinner plate.

My life continued to change. I helped organize major demonstrations. I began to be a regular speaker on the antiwar circuit. I hate to think how many times I drove from Menlo Park to San Francisco State to Berkeley to Hayward to San Jose State to Stanford and then home. Around and around the circuit, because at that point there still were not very many Catholic clergy speaking out.

My work reached an apex with the invasion of Cambodia in May 1970. 45
Campuses began shutting down all over the country. We shut down the seminary, and within twenty-four hours the entire faculty joined us and spread out to do teach-ins. There is a statue on the lawn in front of St. Patrick's, similar to the big Jesus on top of Sugarloaf Mountain in Rio, with the hands outstretched. We put a sign saying "On Strike" in Jesus' hands. We were the only Catholic seminary in the country that closed down.

I went to work in the Black Panthers' breakfast program with the pastor from one of the churches in San Francisco. That was during all the police raids of the Panthers' offices. I like to think that one of the reasons the police didn't hit the San Francisco office was that every night for about two weeks, the two of us sat in folding chairs in front of the place in our clerical clothes.

At that time, I still had my IV-D ministerial deferment. I publicly burned my draft card and informed the Selective Service in a letter. I got a reply that they couldn't take my word for it, and they sent a new card. So I burned my new draft card, saved about a third of it, and sent that in to them, whereupon I got back another draft card with a letter saying, "We want to replace your loss." At the time, I assumed they were going to arrest me, but the Selective Service System had effectively collapsed in northern California. They had stopped going after people who refused to cooperate.

The archbishop of San Francisco was Joseph T. McGucken. In more angry moments, seminarians applied a certain adjective that rhymed with his last name. He called me on the carpet in his big mansion up on Russian Hill with its marble floors and huge desk, and told me he had friends in the FBI who had informed him that my antiwar and revolutionary activities were being funded by Communist China. I was so broke at the time, I wanted to say, "Really? Are you telling me the check is in the mail?" He said he was going to inform my bishop and expel me from the seminary.

I went back and told the rector of the seminary about the meeting. The rector was outraged. He told the archbishop that if I were canned, he would quit. I was stunned by that sort of support. The rector saved me. Archbishop McGucken desisted.

50 My bishop in San Diego called me there for having led the strike at the seminary. I was packing my bags, presumably to have the buttons of my cassock snapped off, when three of my fellow seminarians came in and said, "We are not going to let you take the heat alone for the strike. The rest of the students have drawn lots. The three of us were selected to tell the bishop that every one of his seminarians was involved in the strike." And that's what they did. They saved me.

Nonetheless, the bishop still had power over me. The seminary required us to serve a year in the field before being ordained. So when my bishop was assigning people to their posts, I got assigned to a tiny parish in the town of Carlsbad, California, not far from Nixon's Western White House at San Clemente and right next to Camp Pendleton and thirty thousand Marines.

I continued my antiwar activities there. The largest boys' military school on the West Coast was nearby. On Sunday mornings, all the Catholic cadets would march to church down the main street with their mock rifles. I made them stack their weapons at the door. I also helped to run an antiwar coffeehouse in Oceanside. One night about two minutes after I had closed up, somebody drove by and fired several rounds from a shotgun through the door. Another time, my car was forced off the road. I often got death threats.

I was scared spitless and completely isolated. I got on the phone to the priests at the seminary and asked, "Do you have any openings as far from here as you can get me?" They said, "How would you like to teach at St. Mary's Seminary in Baltimore?" Baltimore! Phil Berrigan's home! I said, "You bet your bippy." So, as I shook the dust of Oceanside off my sandals, my first assignment following ordination as a priest in 1971 was Baltimore.

After a rather epic journey, during which my car engine blew up, I arrived in Baltimore the morning after the FBI ambushed twenty-eight Catholic Left draft board raiders in Camden, New Jersey, and J. Edgar Hoover announced, "We have broken the back of the Catholic Left." The major cause célèbre was the pending Harrisburg conspiracy trial of Daniel and Philip Berrigan, Elizabeth McAlister, and others who were accused of plotting to blow up heating tunnels under Washington, D.C., and kidnap Henry Kissinger. I walked into the headquarters of the Harrisburg Defense Committee and said, "Reinforcements have arrived from the West Coast." At that point, I plunged head over heels into what remained of the Catholic Left.

55 I remember in grade school, the good sisters, God bless them, asking what we would say when the Communists take over and put us up against the wall and ask, "Are you a Christian?" Little did I realize that years later somebody would indeed put me up against the wall, but it wouldn't be the Communists. It would be my own government.

Understanding

1. The title of the book from which these narratives were drawn, *The Strength Not to Fight,* indicates that a certain moral resolve is required not to engage

in war. Based on the three accounts in this selection, is this title accurate? What strengths did each of the narrators demonstrate that superseded the call to fight?

2. An Irish proverb counsels, "It is better to be a coward for a minute than to be dead for the rest of your life." In what ways do the narrators recognize that their decisions were cowardly?
3. Based on your review of these three narratives, what "national values" did the narrators think the war in Vietnam violated?
4. Although popular opinion on the conflict in Vietnam was sharply divided, deciding to refuse the draft cut across the grain of common practice. What in these narratives convinces you that the decision not to fight shaped the identity of these conscientious objectors?

Responding

1. We acquire ideas and beliefs from the climate of opinion pervading the community or culture in which we live. Based on your understanding of that climate today, how would young people respond to a military draft? How would you? Under what circumstances might you decide to be a conscientious objector?
2. Do you know someone who was a conscientious objector in the Vietnam War? If so, in what occupation is he or she engaged? If not, based on these readings, what occupations do you think conscientious objectors are engaged in today? Why?
3. Do you know someone who served in Vietnam or in another conflict? If so, how would he or she respond to these narratives?
4. Public opinion is generally split on most important issues and almost always on issues dealing with life and death: There are strong pro and con arguments about abortion, U.S. military intervention in foreign conflicts, and the imposition of the death penalty. In deciding which side of an argument or issue to endorse, are you most influenced by basic moral principles, empirical evidence, logic, emotion, or the opinions of authorities? Define an issue and explain your viewpoint.

Country Lovers

Nadine Gordimer

Nadine Gordimer was born in 1923 and reared in South Africa, the daughter of a Lithuanian Jewish father and a British Jewish mother. She began writing at the age of nine and published her first stories in magazines at fifteen. Her first novel, *The Lying Days* (1953), was well received abroad, but it was her short stories that were most highly praised.

For many years critical acclaim for Gordimer's writing was denied in her native country—three of her books were once officially banned there—for political reasons. South Africa, the scene of most of her fiction, made politics a subject she could not ignore. Apartheid—the rigid system that enforced the separation of the races—had existed informally for decades but became official in 1948 with the election of the National Party government. Its legal strictures enabled the white minority to deprive the black and mixed-race, or "coloured," peoples of their civil and, in the opinion of many, their human rights.

By 1991, when Gordimer became the first woman in twenty-five years to win the Nobel Prize for Literature, the political climate had eased enough for then-President F. W. deKlerk to congratulate her on what he called "this exceptional achievement which is also an honor to South Africa." In May 1994, with South Africa's first election open to all races, apartheid was formally ended with the election of Nelson Mandela as the nation's president.

In her writing Gordimer portrayed the effects of the racial divisiveness and oppression caused by apartheid on individual characters whose lives and predicaments she made recognizable to readers throughout the world. Her fiction is infused with the major themes of exile and alienation. A keen observer of the people and landscapes of South Africa, she is known for the economy and intensity of her style, qualities the reader will find in "Country Lovers," one of seven short stories published in 1956 under the title *Six Feet of the Country.*

The farm children play together when they are small; but once the white children go away to school they soon don't play together any more, even in the holidays. Although most of the black children get some sort of schooling, they drop every year farther behind the grades passed by the white children; the childish vocabulary, the child's exploration of the adventurous possibilities of dam, koppies, mealie lands and veld—there comes a time when the white children have surpassed these with the vocabulary of boarding-school and the possibilities of inter-school sports matches and the kind of adventures seen at the cinema. This usefully coincides with the age of twelve or thirteen; so that by the time early adolescence is reached, the black children are making, along 1 with the bodily changes common to all, an easy transition to adult forms of address, beginning to call their old playmates *missus* and *baasie*—little master.

The trouble was Paulus Eysendyck did not seem to realize that Thebedi was now simply one of the crowd of farm children down at the kraal, recognizable in his sisters' old clothes. The first Christmas holidays after he had gone to boarding-school he brought home for Thebedi a painted box he had made in his wood-work class. He had to give it to her secretly because he had nothing for the other children at the kraal. And she gave him, before he went back to school, a bracelet she had made of thin brass wire and the grey-and-white beans of the castor-oil crop his father cultivated. (When they used to play together, she was the one who had taught Paulus how to make clay oxen for their toy spans.) There was a craze, even in the *platteland* towns like the one where he was at school, for boys to wear elephant-hair and other bracelets beside their watch-straps; his was admired, friends asked him to get similar ones for them. He said the natives made them on his father's farm and he would try.

When he was fifteen, six feet tall, and tramping round at school dances with the girls from the 'sister' school in the same town; when he had learnt how to tease and flirt and fondle quite intimately these girls who were the daughters of prosperous farmers like his father; when he had even met one who, at a wedding he had attended with his parents on a nearby farm, had let him do with her in a locked storeroom what people did when they made love—when he was as far from his childhood as all this, he still brought home from a shop in town a red plastic belt and gilt hoop ear-rings for the black girl, Thebedi. She told her father the missus had given these to her as a reward for some work she had done—it was true she sometimes was called to help out in the farmhouse. She told the girls in the kraal that she had a sweetheart nobody knew about, far away, away on another farm, and they giggled, and teased, and admired her. There was a boy in the kraal called Njabulo who said he wished he could have bought her a belt and ear-rings.

When the farmer's son was home for the holidays she wandered far from the kraal and her companions. He went for walks alone. They had not arranged this; it was an urge each followed independently. He knew it was she, from a long way off. She knew that his dog would not bark at her. Down at the dried-up river-bed where five or six years ago the children had caught a leguaan one great day—a creature that combined ideally the size and ferocious aspect of the crocodile with the harmlessness of the lizard—they squatted side by side on the earth bank. He told her traveller's tales: about school, about the punishments at school, particularly, exaggerating both their nature and his indifference to them. He told her about the town of Middleburg, which she had never seen. She had nothing to tell but she prompted with many questions, like any good listener. While he talked he twisted and tugged at the roots of white stinkwood and Cape willow trees that looped out of the eroded earth around them. It had always been a good spot for children's games, down there hidden by the mesh of old, ant-eaten trees held in place by vigorous ones, wild asparagus bushing up between the trunks, and here and there prickly-pear cactus sunken-skinned and bristly, like an old man's face, keeping alive sapless until the next rainy season. She punctured the dry hide of a prickly-pear again and again with a sharp stick while she listened. She laughed a lot at what he told her, sometimes dropping her face on her knees, sharing amusement with the cool shady earth beneath her bare feet. She put on her pair of shoes—white sandals, thickly Blanco-ed against the farm dust—when he was on the farm, but these were taken off and laid aside, at the river-bed.

5 One summer afternoon when there was water flowing there and it was very hot she waded in as they used to do when they were children, her dress bunched modestly and tucked into the legs of her pants. The schoolgirls he went swimming with at dams or pools on neighbouring farms wore bikinis but the sight of their dazzling bellies and thighs in the sunlight had never made him feel what he felt now, when the girl came up the bank and sat beside him, the drops of water beading off her dark legs the only points of light in the earth-smelling, deep shade. They were not afraid of one another, they had known one another always; he did with her what he had done that time in the storeroom at the wedding, and this time it was so lovely, so lovely, he was surprised . . . and she was surprised by it, too—he could see in her dark face that was part of the shade, with her big dark eyes, shiny as soft water, watching him attentively: as she had when they used to huddle over their teams of mud oxen, as she had when he told her about detention weekends at school.

They went to the river-bed often through those summer holidays. They met just before the light went, as it does quite quickly, and each returned home with the dark—she to her mother's hut, he to the farmhouse—in time for the evening meal. He did not tell her about school or town any more. She did not ask questions any longer. He told her, each time, when they would meet again. Once or twice it was very early in the morning; the lowing of the cows being driven to graze came to them where they lay, dividing them with unspoken recognition of the sound read in their two pairs of eyes, opening so close to each other.

He was a popular boy at school. He was in the second, then the first soccer team. The head girl of the 'sister' school was said to have a crush on him; he didn't particularly like her, but there was a pretty blonde who put up her long hair into a kind of doughnut with a black ribbon round it, whom he took to see films when the schoolboys and girls had a free Saturday afternoon. He had been driving tractors and other farm vehicles since he was ten years old, and as soon as he was eighteen he got a driver's licence and in the holidays, this last year of his school-life, he took neighbours' daughters to dances and to the drive-in cinema that had just opened twenty kilometres from the farm. His sisters were married, by then; his parents often left him in charge of the farm over the weekend while they visited the young wives and grandchildren.

When Thebedi saw the farmer and his wife drive away on a Saturday afternoon, the boot of their Mercedes filled with fresh-killed poultry and vegetables from the garden that it was part of her father's work to tend, she knew that she must come not to the river-bed but up to the house. The house was an old one, thick-walled, dark against the heat. The kitchen was its lively thoroughfare, with servants, food supplies, begging cats and dogs, pots boiling over, washing being damped for ironing, and the big deep-freeze the missus had ordered from town, bearing a crocheted mat and a vase of plastic irises. But the dining-room with the bulging-legged heavy table was shut up in its rich, old smell of soup and tomato sauce. The sitting-room curtains were drawn and the T.V. set silent. The door of the parents' bedroom was locked and the empty rooms where the girls had slept had sheets of plastic spread over the beds. It was in one of these that she and the farmer's son stayed together whole nights—almost: she had to get away before the house servants, who knew her, came in at dawn. There was a risk someone would discover her or traces of her presence if he took her to his own bedroom, although she had looked into it many times when she was helping out in the house and knew well, there, the row of silver cups he had won at school.

When she was eighteen and the farmer's son nineteen and working with his father on the farm before entering a veterinary college, the young man Njabulo asked her father for her. Njabulo's parents met with hers and the money he was to pay in place of the cows it is customary to give a prospective bride's parents was settled upon. He had no cows to offer; he was a labourer on the Eysendyck farm, like her father. A bright youngster; old Eysendyck had taught him bricklaying and was using him for odd jobs in construction, around the place. She did not tell the farmer's son that her parents had arranged for her to marry. She did not tell him, either, before he left for his first term at the veterinary college, that she thought she was going to have a baby. Two months after her marriage to Njabulo, she gave birth to a daughter. There was no disgrace in that; among her people it is customary for a young man to make sure, before marriage, that the chosen girl is not barren, and Njabulo had made love to her then. But the infant was very light and did not quickly grow darker as most African babies do. Already at birth there was on its head a quantity of straight, fine floss, like that which carries the seeds of certain weeds in the veld. The unfocused eyes it opened were grey flecked with yellow. Njabulo was the matt, opaque coffee-grounds colour that has always been called black; the colour of Thebedi's legs on which beaded water looked oyster-shell blue, the same colour as Thebedi's face, where the black eyes, with their interested gaze and clear whites, were so dominant.

Njabulo made no complaint. Out of his farm labourer's earnings he 10
bought from the Indian store a cellophane-windowed pack containing a pink plastic bath, six napkins, a card of safety pins, a knitted jacket, cap and bootees, a dress, and a tin of Johnson's Baby Powder, for Thebedi's baby.

When it was two weeks old Paulus Eysendyck arrived home from the veterinary college for the holidays. He drank a glass of fresh, still-warm milk in the childhood familiarity of his mother's kitchen and heard her discussing with the old house-servant where they could get a reliable substitute to help out now that the girl Thebedi had had a baby. For the first time since he was a small boy he came right into the kraal. It was eleven o'clock in the morning. The men were at work in the lands. He looked about him, urgently; the women turned away, each not wanting to be the one approached to point out where Thebedi lived. Thebedi appeared, coming slowly from the hut Njabulo had built in white man's style, with a tin chimney, and a proper window with glass panes set in straight as walls made of unfired bricks would allow. She greeted him with hands brought together and a token movement representing the respectful bob with which she was accustomed to acknowledge she was in the presence of his father or mother. He lowered his head under the doorway of her home and went in. He said, 'I want to see. Show me.'

She had taken the bundle off her back before she came out into the light to face him. She moved between the iron bedstead made up with Njabulo's checked blankets and the small wooden table where the pink plastic bath stood among food and kitchen pots, and picked up the bundle from the snugly blanketed grocer's box where it lay. The infant was asleep; she revealed the closed, pale, plump tiny face, with a bubble of spit at the corner of the mouth, the spidery pink hands stirring. She took off the woollen cap and the straight fine hair flew up after it in static electricity, showing gilded strands here and there. He said nothing. She was watching him as she had done when they were little, and the gang of children had trodden down a crop in their games or transgressed in some other way for which he, as the farmer's son, the white one among them, must intercede with the farmer. She disturbed the sleeping face by scratching or tickling gently at a cheek with one finger, and slowly the eyes opened, saw nothing, were still asleep, and then, awake, no longer narrowed, looked out at them, grey with yellowish flecks, his own hazel eyes.

He struggled for a moment with a grimace of tears, anger and self-pity. She could not put out her hand to him. He said, 'You haven't been near the house with it?'

She shook her head.

'Never?'

Again she shook her head.

'Don't take it out. Stay inside. Can't you take it away somewhere. You must give it to someone—'

She moved to the door with him.

He said, 'I'll see what I will do. I don't know.' And then he said: 'I feel like killing myself.'

Her eyes began to glow, to thicken with tears. For a moment there was the feeling between them that used to come when they were alone down at the river-bed.

He walked out.

Two days later, when his mother and father had left the farm for the day, he appeared again. The women were away on the lands, weeding, as they were employed to do as casual labour in summer; only the very old remained, propped up on the ground outside the huts in the flies and the sun. Thebedi did not ask him in. The child had not been well; it had diarrhoea. He asked where its food was. She said, 'The milk comes from me.' He went into Nja-bulo's house, where the child lay; she did not follow but stayed outside the door and watched without seeing an old crone who had lost her mind, talking to herself, talking to the fowls who ignored her.

She thought she heard small grunts from the hut, the kind of infant grunt that indicates a full stomach, a deep sleep. After a time, long or short she did not know, he came out and walked away with plodding stride (his father's gait) out of sight, towards his father's house.

The baby was not fed during the night and although she kept telling Njabulo it was sleeping, he saw for himself in the morning that it was dead. He comforted her with words and caresses. She did not cry but simply sat, staring at the door. Her hands were cold as dead chickens' feet to his touch.

Njabulo buried the little baby where farm workers were buried, in the 25
place in the veld the farmer had given them. Some of the mounds had been left to weather away unmarked, others were covered with stones and a few had fallen wooden crosses. He was going to make a cross but before it was finished the police came and dug up the grave and took away the dead baby: someone—one of the other labourers? their women?—had reported that the baby was almost white, that, strong and healthy, it had died suddenly after a visit by the farmer's son. Pathological tests on the infant corpse showed intestinal damage not always consistent with death by natural causes.

Thebedi went for the first time to the country town where Paulus had been to school, to give evidence at the preparatory examination into the charge of murder brought against him. She cried hysterically in the witness box, saying yes, yes (the gilt hoop ear-rings swung in her ears), she saw the accused pouring liquid into the baby's mouth. She said he had threatened to shoot her if she told anyone.

More than a year went by before, in that same town, the case was brought to trial. She came to Court with a new-born baby on her back. She wore gilt hoop ear-rings; she was calm; she said she had not seen what the white man did in the house.

Paulus Eysendyck said he had visited the hut but had not poisoned the child.

The Defence did not contest that there had been a love relationship between the accused and the girl, or that intercourse had taken place, but submitted there was no proof that the child was the accused's.

The judge told the accused there was strong suspicion against him but not 30
enough proof that he had committed the crime. The Court could not accept the girl's evidence because it was clear she had committed perjury either at this trial or at the preparatory examination. There was the suggestion in the mind of the Court that she might be an accomplice in the crime; but, again insufficient proof.

The judge commended the honourable behaviour of the husband (sitting in court in a brown-and-yellow-quartered golf cap bought for Sundays) who had not rejected his wife and had 'even provided clothes for the unfortunate infant out of his slender means.'

The verdict on the accused was 'not guilty.'

The young white man refused to accept the congratulations of press and public and left the Court with his mother's raincoat shielding his face from photographers. His father said to the press, 'I will try and carry on as best I can to hold up my head in the district.'

Interviewed by the Sunday papers, who spelled her name in a variety of ways, the black girl, speaking in her own language, was quoted beneath her photograph: 'It was a thing of our childhood, we don't see each other any more.'

Understanding

1. What is the central purpose of this story?
2. Of all the decisions made by the characters in "Country Lovers," which ones drive the story? Overall, how would you describe its emotional tone?
3. In all likelihood, what happened to the baby?
4. Although knowledge of the social history of South Africa is not necessary to understand this story, some familiarity with it deepens the reader's appreciation. Does the historical background have any importance to this story? In what years do the main events occur? How might this story be different if it took place in South Africa today?
5. Does this story have a "happy ending"? Evaluate Thebedi's final words.
6. To touch our emotions, a writer must produce a character or characters in situations that deserve our sympathy, and must tell us enough about the character(s) and situations to make them real and convincing. Does Gordimer do this? Which characters do you think deserve our sympathy? Why?
7. Was justice done? How do you imagine the lives of Thebedi and Njabulo ten years after this event took place?

Responding

1. Because we spend our lives as members of one social institution or another, and because we are shaped by the roles we play in them, our decisions must also be a product of these institutions. Describe a situation from your experience in which a decision was influenced by the expectations of social institutions.
2. "Country Lovers" explores the interaction among freedom, social inequality, and close personal relationships. Which, if any, of these three dimensions are lacking in your present social environment? Which do you enjoy in good measure?

Connecting

Identify the decisions described in other readings in this chapter that were affected, either wholly or in part, by the expectations of social institutions. For each of the decisions you identify, indicate the consequences of not conforming to these expectations. Develop a conclusion about the effect that social institutions have on individual decision making.

Public Announcement

Colin Powell

Colin Luther Powell, born of Jamaican parents in 1933 in the South Bronx, New York, is a retired army general who served his country, as he has said, for "35 years, 3 months, 21 days, and, as we say in the infantry, a wake-up. I loved every single day of it." Powell was an infantry officer during the Vietnam War and served as chairman of the Joint Chiefs of Staff in the administration of President George Bush.

The general's frequent television appearances during the Persian Gulf War in 1991 attracted national attention and were a major factor in his being considered by the Republican Party and the American people as a possible presidential candidate. Public discussion of his candidacy was remarkable for the lack of references to his race. With the publication in 1995 of his memoirs, *My American Journey,* speculation about his possible candidacy in the media and among many Americans reached a fever pitch. Powell resolved the issue with the following speech, which he delivered on November 8, 1995.

For 35 years of my life, I served my nation as a soldier proudly and to the 1
best of my ability. Since my retirement two years ago, I have written my life story and traveled across the country speaking and listening to my fellow Americans. What I saw and heard renewed my faith in our country, its people and its promise.

I also came away with a deeper understanding of the challenges we face, of the problems we must solve to reach the dreams of our founders. All of us have a role to play, and I have been giving the most prayerful consideration to the role I should play. The question I faced was: Should I enter politics and seek the presidency of the United States?

Many of you have encouraged me to do so. I have been deeply honored by the hundreds of letters I have received and by the hard work of grass-roots organizing committees. I thank all of you for the faith and confidence you had in me.

For the past few weeks, I have been consulting with friends and advisers. I have spent long hours talking with my wife and children, the most important people in my life, about the impact an entry into political life would have on us. It would require sacrifices and changes in our lives that would be difficult for us to make at this time.

The welfare of my family had to be uppermost in my mind. Ultimately, 5
however, I had to look deep into my own soul, standing aside from the expectations and enthusiasms of others, because I have a bond of trust with the American people, and to offer myself as a candidate for president requires a commitment and a passion to run the race and to succeed in the quest—the

kind of passion and the kind of commitment that I felt every day of my 35 years as a soldier, a passion and commitment that despite my every effort I do not have for political life, because such a life requires a calling that I do not yet hear.

And for me to pretend otherwise would not be honest to myself, it would not be honest to the American people, and I would break that bond of trust. And therefore I cannot go forward. I will not be a candidate for president or for any other elective office in 1996.

I know that this is the right decision for me. It was not reached easily or without a great deal of personal anguish. For me and my family, saying no was even harder than saying yes. I will remain in private life and seek other ways to serve. I have a deep love for this country that has no bounds. I will find other ways to contribute to the important work needed to keep us moving forward.

I know my decision will disappoint many who have supported me. I thank them once again from the bottom of my heart, and I ask for their understanding. I also know that my actions in taking the time to reach this decision has created an enormous level of expectation and anticipation. But I needed the time to give this the most careful study.

I will continue to speak out forcefully in the future on the issues of the day, as I have been doing in recent weeks. I will do so as a member of the Republican Party and try to assist the party in broadening its appeal. I believe I can help the party of Lincoln move once again close to the spirit of Lincoln.

I will give my talent and energy to charitable and educational activities. I 10
will also try to find ways for me to help heal the racial divides that still exist within our society.

Finally, let me say how honored I am that so many of you thought me worthy of your support. It says more about America than it says about me. In one generation, we have moved from denying a black man service at a lunch counter to elevating one to the highest military office in the nation and to being a serious contender for the presidency. This is a magnificent country, and I am proud to be one of its sons.

Thank you very much.

Understanding

1. What reasons does Powell offer for his decision not to be a presidential candidate?
2. Powell says he will try to assist the Republican Party in "broadening its appeal" so that it can "move once again close to the spirit of Lincoln." What is the relationship between the "spirit of Lincoln" and broadening his party's appeal?
3. What feelings does Powell's announcement convey to the reader? What values does he hold?
4. In an interview Powell has asserted that "college provided me with an appreciation of the liberal arts; . . . insight into the fundamentals of government; . . . and a deep respect for our democratic system." What in the text

of his announcement provides evidence of the gifts that Powell received from his college education?

5. Examine the structure of Powell's announcement—a speech meant to explain to his audience, if not convince them of, the wisdom of his decision not to run for president. Beginning with the first paragraph in which he provides background on his life, summarize what each of the subsequent paragraphs conveys. Review the content and organization of his speech as you have interpreted it. In a brief paragraph, explain his approach.

Responding

1. Prior to deciding not to become a presidential candidate, Powell said, "I'll sit down with my family and those people who provide me with advice and counsel and some very dear friends who care about me and make a decision as to what to do with the next phase of my life." In a comparable situation, with whom would you sit down to help make your decision? Why?
2. Colin Powell has attracted attention for the sum of his life—for the series of decisions he made along life's path. Some might call him a strong person, a transcendent, or even a heroic individual. How would you define such a person—a person who stands out from the common run of humanity? Do you know such a person? What decisions would you have to make in your life to be such a person?
3. Have you ever made a decision that you had to announce to a person or a group? What led up to your decision? What was the reaction to it? How did you make the announcement? How would you make that announcement today?
4. Maureen Dowd, a commentator on the Washington political scene, asserted that the reason Powell grappled with his decision so publicly was to get publicity for his book. Is such an assertion plausible? Why or why not?

Connecting

On what points do you think Powell would agree with the conscientious objectors in Tollefson's "Choosing Not to Fight"? On what points would he disagree?

Professions for Women

Virginia Woolf

Virginia Woolf (1882–1941) was born in London, the daughter of Sir Leslie Stephens, an eminent Victorian writer and editor. Her mother died when she was thirteen; and when her father died in 1904, she and her sister and two brothers moved to an airy and spacious house on Gordon Square in Bloomsbury, a fashionable bohemian section of London. When she began to publish, she was firmly rooted in the famous Bloomsbury group of writers and intellectuals.

"Making things—visual or literary—was Bloomsbury's dominating passion," writes critic Janet Malcolm in an article on the Bloomsbury group in *The New Yorker.* Though they lived creative and somewhat unorthodox lives for their times, the Bloomsbury writers produced prolifically. According to Leonard Woolf, the journalist and political philosopher whom Virginia married in 1912, the group worked without deviation from about 9:30 A.M. to 1:00 P.M. every day for eleven months of the year. In the fourth volume of his autobiography, he wrote: "It is surprising how much one can produce in a year, whether of buns or books or pots or pictures, if one works hard and professionally for three and a half hours every day for 330 days. That was why, despite her disabilities, Virginia was able to produce so much."

The disabilities Leonard referred to were Virginia's bouts with depression and several terrifying nervous breakdowns. She took her own life in 1941. "Professions for Women," which Woolf presented to the Women's Service League in 1931, recounts a hard-won search for self and the decisions that had to be acted on to actualize the life Woolf wanted to live.

When your secretary invited me to come here, she told me that your Society is concerned with the employment of women and she suggested that I might tell you something about my own professional experiences. It is true I am a woman; it is true I am employed; but what professional experiences have I had? It is difficult to say. My profession is literature; and in that profession there are fewer experiences for women than in any other, with the exception of the stage—fewer, I mean, that are peculiar to women. For the road was cut many years ago—by Fanny Burney, by Aphra Behn, by Harriet Martineau, by Jane Austen, by George Eliot—many famous women, and many more unknown and forgotten, have been before me, making the path smooth, and regulating my steps. Thus, when I came to write, there were very few material obstacles in my way. Writing was a reputable and harmless occupation. The family peace was not broken by the scratching of a pen. No demand was made upon the family purse. For ten and sixpence one can buy paper enough to 1 write all the plays of Shakespeare—if one has a mind that way. Pianos and models, Paris, Vienna, and Berlin, masters and mistresses, are not needed by a writer. The cheapness of writing paper is, of course, the reason why women have succeeded as writers before they have succeeded in the other professions.

But to tell you my story—it is a simple one. You have only got to figure to yourselves a girl in a bedroom with a pen in her hand. She had only to move that pen from left to right—from ten o'clock to one. Then it occurred to her to do what is simple and cheap enough after all—to slip a few of those pages into an envelope, fix a penny stamp in the corner, and drop the envelope into the red box at the corner. It was thus that I became a journalist; and my effort was rewarded on the first day of the following month—a very glorious day it was for me—by a letter from an editor containing a cheque for one pound ten shillings and sixpence. But to show you how little I deserve to be called a professional woman, how little I know of the struggles and difficulties of such lives, I have to admit that instead of spending that sum upon bread and butter, rent, shoes and stockings, or butcher's bills, I went out and bought a cat—a beautiful cat, a Persian cat, which very soon involved me in bitter disputes with my neighbors.

What could be easier than to write articles and to buy Persian cats with the profits? But wait a moment. Articles have to be about something. Mine, I seem to remember, was about a novel by a famous man. And while I was writing this review, I discovered that if I were going to review books I should need to do battle with a certain phantom. And the phantom was a woman, and when I came to know her better I called her after the heroine of a famous poem. The Angel in the House. It was she who used to come between me and my paper when I was writing reviews. It was she who bothered me and wasted my time and so tormented me that at last I killed her. You who come of a younger and happier generation may not have heard of her—you may not know what I mean by The Angel in the House. I will describe her as shortly as I can. She was intensely sympathetic. She was immensely charming. She was utterly unselfish. She excelled in the difficult arts of family life. She sacrificed herself daily. If there was chicken, she took the leg; if there was a draught she sat in it—in short she was so constituted that she never had a mind or a wish of her own, but preferred to sympathize always with the minds and wishes of others. Above all—I need not say it—she was pure. Her purity was supposed to be her chief beauty—her blushes, her great grace. In those days—the last of Queen Victoria—every house had its Angel. And when I came to write I encountered her with the very first words. The shadow of her wings fell on my page; I heard the rustling of her skirts in the room. Directly, that is to say, I took my pen in my hand to review that novel by a famous man, she slipped behind me and whispered: "My dear, you are a young woman. You are writing about a book that has been written by a man. Be sympathetic; be tender; flatter; deceive; use all the arts and wiles of our sex. Never let anybody guess that you have a mind of your own. Above all, be pure." And she made as if to guide my pen. I now record the one act for which I take some credit to myself, though the credit rightly belongs to some excellent ancestors of mine who left me a certain sum of money—shall we say five hundred pounds a year?—so that it was not necessary for me to depend solely on charm for my living. I turned upon her and caught her by the throat. I did my best to kill her. My excuse if I were to be had up at a court of law, would be that I acted in self-defence. Had I not killed her she would have killed me. She would have plucked the heart out of my writing. For as I found directly I put pen to paper, you cannot review even a novel without having a mind of your own, without expressing what you think to be the truth about human relations, morality, sex. And all these questions, according to the Angel of the House cannot be dealt with freely and openly by women; they must charm, they must conciliate, they must—to put it bluntly—tell lies if they are to succeed. Thus, whenever I felt the shadow of her wing or the radiance of her halo upon my page, I took up the inkpot and flung it at her. She died hard. Her fictitious nature was of great assistance to her. It is far harder to kill a phantom than a reality. She was always creeping back when I thought I had dispatched her. Though I flatter myself that I killed her in the end, the struggle was severe; it took much time that had better have been spent upon learning Greek grammar; or in roaming the world in search of adventures. But it was a real experience; it was an experience that was bound to befall all women writers at that time. Killing the Angel in the House was part of the occupation of a woman writer.

But to continue my story. The Angel was dead; what then remained? You may say that what remained was a simple and common object—a young woman in a bedroom with an inkpot. In other words, now that she had rid herself of falsehood, that young woman had only to be herself. Ah, but what is "herself"? I mean, what is a woman? I assure you, I do not know. I do not believe that you know. I do not believe that anybody can know until she has expressed herself in all the arts and professions open to human skill. That indeed is one of the reasons why I have come here—out of respect for you, who are in process of showing us by your experiments what a woman is, who are in process of providing us, by your failures and successes, with that extremely important piece of information.

But to continue the story of my professional experiences. I made one 5
pound ten and six by my first review; and I bought a Persian cat with the proceeds. Then I grew ambitious. A Persian cat is all very well, I said; but a Persian cat is not enough. I must have a motor-car. And it was thus that I became a novelist—for it is a very strange thing that people will give you a motor-car if you will tell them a story. It is a still stranger thing that there is nothing so delightful in the world as telling stories. It is far pleasanter than writing reviews of famous novels. And yet, if I am to obey your secretary and tell you my professional experiences as a novelist, I must tell you about a very strange experience that befell me as a novelist. And to understand it you must try first to imagine a novelist's state of mind. I hope I am not giving away professional secrets if I say that a novelist's chief desire is to be as unconscious as possible. He has to induce in himself a state of perpetual lethargy. He wants life to proceed with the utmost quiet and regularity. He wants to see the same faces, to read the same books, to do the same things day after day, month after month, while he is writing, so that nothing may break the illusion in which he is living—so that nothing may disturb or disquiet the mysterious nosings

about, feelings round, darts, dashes, and sudden discoveries of that very shy and illusive spirit, the imagination. I suspect that this state is the same both for men and women. Be that as it may, I want you to imagine me writing a novel in a state of trance. I want you to figure to yourselves a girl sitting with a pen in her hand, which for minutes, and indeed for hours, she never dips into the inkpot. The image that comes to my mind when I think of this girl is the image of a fisherman lying sunk in dreams on the verge of a deep lake with a rod held out over the water. She was letting her imagination sweep unchecked round every rock and cranny of the world that lies submerged in the depths of our unconscious being. Now came the experience that I believe to be far commoner with women writers than with men. The line raced through the girl's fingers. Her imagination had rushed away. It had sought the pools, the depths, the dark places where the largest fish slumber. And then there was a smash. There was an explosion. There was foam and confusion. The imagination had dashed itself against something hard. The girl was roused from her dream. She was indeed in a state of the most acute and difficult distress. To speak without figure, she had thought of something, something about the body, about the passion, which it was unfitting for her as a woman to say. Men, her reason told her, would be shocked. The consciousness of what men will say of a woman who speaks the truth about her passions had roused her from her artist's state of unconsciousness. She could write no more. The trance was over. Her imagination could work no longer. This I believe to be a very common experience with women writers—they are impeded by the extreme conventionality of the other sex. For though men sensibly allow themselves great freedom in these respects, I doubt that they realize or can control the extreme severity with which they condemn such freedom in women.

These then were two very genuine experiences of my own. These were two of the adventures of my professional life. The first—killing the Angel in the House—I think I solved. She died. But the second, telling the truth about my own experiences as a body, I do not think I solved. I doubt that any woman has solved it yet. The obstacles against her are still immensely powerful—and yet they are very difficult to define. Outwardly, what is simpler than to write books? Outwardly, what obstacles are there for a woman rather than for a man? Inwardly, I think, the case is very different; she has still many ghosts to fight, many prejudices to overcome. Indeed it will be a long time still, I think, before a woman can sit down to write a book without finding a phantom to be slain, a rock to be dashed against. And if this is so in literature, the freest of all professions for women, how is it in the new professions which you are now for the first time entering?

Those are the questions that I should like, had I time, to ask you. And indeed, if I have laid stress upon these professional experiences of mine, it is because I believe that they are, though in different forms, yours also. Even when the path is nominally open—when there is nothing to prevent a woman from being a doctor, a lawyer, a civil servant—there are many phantoms and obstacles, as I believe, looming in her way. To discuss and define them is I think of great value and importance; for thus only can the labor be shared, the difficulties be solved. But besides this, it is necessary also to discuss the ends and the aims for which we are fighting, for which we are doing battle with these formidable obstacles. Those aims cannot be taken for granted; they must be perpetually questioned and examined. The whole position, as I see it—here in this hall surrounded by women practising for the first time in history I know not how many different professions—is one of extraordinary interest and importance. You have won rooms of your own in the house hitherto exclusively owned by men. You are able, though not without great labor and effort, to pay the rent. You are earning your five hundred pounds a year. But this freedom is only a beginning; the room is your own, but it is still bare. It has to be furnished; it has to be decorated; it has to be shared. How are you going to furnish it, how are you going to decorate it? With whom are you going to share it, and upon what terms? These, I think are questions of the utmost importance and interest. For the first time in history you are able to ask them; for the first time you are able to decide for yourselves what the answers should be. Willingly would I stay and discuss those questions and answers—but not tonight. My time is up; and I must cease.

Understanding

1. In the early 1900s, why was writing a profession that women could go into without facing a lot of problems? That is, why was it "a reputable and harmless occupation"?
2. Woolf claims that "killing the Angel in the House was part of the occupation of a woman writer." In the context of the early part of the twentieth century, what exactly does she mean?
3. What is Woolf illustrating in the story of the girl novelist and the fisherman?
4. Identify instances of Woolf's use of graphically violent language. How does it enhance the message?

Responding

1. If Woolf's audience for this speech was totally made up of women, and she writes of struggling to overcome obstacles created by a male-dominated society, why does she use the pronoun "he" (paragraph 5) to describe novelists in general? What does this indicate about Woolf's assumptions about language use? What can we infer about the essay's historical and cultural context from the use of this pronoun? Why might contemporary women writers choose a different one?
2. Is Woolf a product of her times and environment? Is she in control of it or controlled by it? To use Glidewell's term (see "A Time for Choosing"), what have her choice points been, according to this autobiographical essay?
3. As with Virginia Woolf, the environment that produced the person you are today included your social class, your neighborhood, the period of history in which you live, your culture, educational system, language, family, religion, and the gifts, wounds, dreams, and decisions that are part of your experiences in these institutions. Of these, name the three strongest influ-

ences in your life to date. Choose one and explore a decision you had to make within the context of that influence.

4. Is there a "phantom" that you need to "kill" before you can accomplish your life's goals? Explain.
5. "If one is to try to record one's life truthfully, one must aim at getting into the record of it something of the disorderly discontinuity which makes it so absurd, unpredictable, *bearable,*" wrote Leonard Woolf (Virginia's husband) in "The Journey Not the Arrival Matters." Is your life unpredictable and disorderly and thus bearable? Has making it so been a turning point for you? Explain.

Connecting

1. Relate Woolf's use of the young female novelist's dream—revealing the truths about her lustful thoughts—to any of the dreams in Epel's "Four Writers' Dreams" (chapter four). How are they similar in their telling? From what do the dreams liberate the writers? How do decisions result from dreams?
2. Decisions that go against the grain of societal values or appropriate behavior can have consequences that alter lives. Compare Woolf's struggles with those of the conscientious objectors in Tollefson's "Choosing Not to Fight." What criteria do these life-altering decisions have in common? What are the differences?

Back to School

Andrea Lee

Andrea Lee, staff writer for *The New Yorker,* gained literary acclaim with *Russian Journal,* a collection of excellent essays recounting her experiences living in the former Soviet Union as an exchange student in 1978. She and her husband, who was a Harvard student completing his dissertation in Russian history, lived in the dormitories of Moscow State University. In *Russian Journal,* as in many of her *New Yorker* pieces, Lee does not write about being African American; "Back to School," however, addresses this issue.

Lee grew up in an affluent Philadelphia suburb in the sixties in a middle-class family. Though they were involved in the civil rights movement, her parents—a minister and a teacher—felt isolated from the poorer masses with whom they were claiming solidarity. Of her family Lee says we "specialized in being outsiders," as Lee and her brother were always integrating camps or schools or neighborhood friends. She remembers that "in a racially divided society—and for all our parents' dreams, America in the sixties and seventies continued to draw the line—we moved on two sides, with double knowledge and double insecurity." In "Back to School," Lee looks back on this childhood situation during a visit to one of the schools she integrated.

A couple of weeks ago, I paid a visit to the girls' preparatory school outside Philadelphia where, about thirty years ago, I enrolled as one of the first two black students. It wasn't my first return trip, but it was one that had a peculiarly definitive feeling: this time, I was going back to look at classes with my daughter, who is eleven—exactly the age I was when I first put on a blue-and-white uniform and walked in the front entrance of an institution where black people had always used the back door. My daughter, who was born in Europe, and who views the civil-rights struggles of the sixties as an antique heroic cycle not much removed in drama and time frame from *The Iliad,* sees her mother's experience as a singularly tame example of integration. There were, after all, no jeering mobs, no night riders, no police dogs or fire hoses—just a girl going to school and learning with quiet thoroughness the meaning of isolation. 1

The air inside the schoolhouse smelled exactly as it used to on rainy April days—that mysterious school essence of damp wood and ancient chalk dust and pent-up young flesh. For an instant, I relived precisely what it felt like to walk those halls with girls who never included me in a social event, with teachers and administrators who regarded me with bemused incomprehension—halls where the only other black faces I saw were those of maids and cooks, and where I never received the slightest hint that books had been written and discoveries made by people whose skin wasn't white. I remembered the defensive bravado that I once used as a cover for a constant and despairing sense of worthlessness, born and reinforced at school.

As I delivered my daughter to the sixth-grade classroom where she would spend the day, I saw that in the intervening time not only had the school sprouted a few glossy modern additions—an art wing, science and computer facilities, and a new lower school—but the faculty and the student body had also been transformed. Black and Asian girls mingled in the crowd of students rushing back and forth between classrooms and playing fields, giddy with excitement over the impending Easter and Passover weekend. A black teacher with braids strode out of the room where long ago I'd conjugated Latin verbs. Posters celebrating African-American artists and scientists hung on the walls, and the school's curriculum included dozens of works by black, Native American, and Hispanic writers. The director of the middle school was, miracle of miracles, a young black woman—a woman who combined an old-fashioned headmistress's unflappable good sense with a preternatural sensitivity to the psychology of culture and identity. She explained to me that she herself had once been a student at a mostly white East Coast prep school. When I asked who on her staff, in particular, was responsible for the self-esteem of minority students, she said firmly, "Every person who works here."

That day, I finally forgave my old school. I'd held a touchy rancor toward it through much of my adult life, like someone heaping blame on a negligent parent, and had taken the institution rather churlishly to task during a Commencement address I gave there some years ago. The changes I saw now disarmed and delighted me. Watching my daughter run by with a group of girls, I realized with envy how different her experience would be from mine if she were enrolled there. "Just think, I used to dream of burning the place down," I remarked to her, as we drove away, along the school's winding drive. She looked at me impatiently. "Can't you just forget all that?" she asked. The sound of her voice—half childish and half adolescent—made it clear to me that I wouldn't do any such thing. Wounds that have healed bring a responsibility to avoid repeating the past. The important thing is to pardon, even with joy, when the time comes—but never, I thought, driving on in silence, to forget.

Understanding

1. What are the significant differences between Andrea Lee and her daughter? Does her daughter seem to live a "double life"—always integrating something—like her mother did growing up?
2. Why does Lee consider enrolling her daughter in the school of her own youth, where she herself developed "a constant and despairing sense of worthlessness, born and reinforced at school" and a place toward which she had "held a touchy rancor" throughout most of her adult life? Does her decision surprise you?

3. How does moving from present to past strengthen the point made in this story?
4. What is Lee's racial and class identity, and how does each aspect of her identity affect the other? Is either race or class more important to her consciousness and that of her family? How do their decisions about school, neighborhood, travel, and self-identification help to answer this question?

Responding

1. Imagine Lee's school life as described in "Back to School." Schools are a powerful socializing institution; how would Lee have straddled the two worlds—her private African American home life and her public all-white school life? Have you ever lived a double life because you were a racial, religious, or gender minority? Do you live one now? Was your private life ever vastly different from your public life either by choice, design, or necessity? What causes the decision to live a double life?
2. As Lee and her daughter drove away from the school, Lee made a powerful decision in relation to the wound she experienced there. What are the costs and benefits of that decision for Lee?
3. Based on what you know of Lee from this reading, what does her life and that of her daughter reflect about the history of race in this country? How might her situation be different if she were of a different socioeconomic class?

Connecting

1. Compare Delany's memoir, "Bessie" (chapter four), with Lee's essay. How were their backgrounds similar or different? Their schooling? Are their wounds the same? What about their decisions?
2. Scan Bateson's selection "Opening to the World" in chapter four for Johnnetta Cole's comments. How might Lee respond to Cole's ideas on both diversity and her aspirations for African American women? Could Lee's situation and Cole's opinions apply equally as well to men?
3. Referring to Woolf's "Angel in the House" metaphor in "Professions for Women," which angel in the house did Tollefson's conscientious objectors need to kill in "Choosing Not to Fight"? Which might Lee consider to be her "Angel in the House"?

Shame

Primo Levi

Primo Levi was born in Turin, Italy, in 1919 and was trained as a chemist. In 1944, a year before World War II was over, he was arrested as a member of the anti-Fascist resistance and deported to a Nazi concentration camp at Auschwitz, where the following episode took place. In his writing he implies that total moral collapse was achieved by both the oppressors (Nazis) and their victims (Jews) to ensure the successful operation of the concentration camps of World War II.

On the occasion of Levi's death by suicide in 1987, critic Alexander Stille wrote: "By the end of his life Levi had become increasingly convinced that the lessons of the Holocaust were destined to be lost as it took a place among the routine atrocities of history" unless those who experienced them wrote about them. *The Drowned and the Saved,* from which this reading is excerpted, is Levi's dark meditation to preserve those experiences.

In August of 1944 it was very hot in Auschwitz. A torrid, tropical wind lifted clouds of dust from the buildings wrecked by the air raids, dried the sweat on our skin, and thickened the blood in our veins. My squad had been sent into a cellar to clear out the plaster rubble, and we all suffered from thirst: a new suffering, which was added to, indeed, multiplied by the old one of hunger. There was no drinkable water in the camp or often on the work site; in those days there was often no water in the wash trough either, undrinkable but good enough to freshen up and clean off the dust. As a rule, the evening soup and the ersatz coffee distributed around ten o'clock were abundantly sufficient to quench our thirst, but now they were no longer enough and thirst tormented us. Thirst is more imperative than hunger: hunger obeys the nerves, grants remission, can be temporarily obliterated by an emotion, a pain, a fear (we had realized this during our journey by train from Italy); not so with thirst, which does not give respite. Hunger exhausts, thirst enrages; in those days it accompanied us day and night: by day, on the work site, whose order (our enemy, but nevertheless order, a place of logic and certainty) was transformed into a chaos of shattered constructions; by night, in the hut without ventilation, as we gasped the air breathed a hundred times before. 1

The corner of the cellar that had been assigned to me by the *Kapo* and where I was to remove the rubble was next to a large room filled with chemical equipment in the process of being installed but already damaged by the bombs. Along the vertical wall ran a two-inch pipe, which ended in a spigot just above the floor. A water pipe? I took a chance and tried to open it. I was alone, nobody saw me. It was blocked, but using a stone for a hammer I managed to shift it a few millimeters. A few drops came out, they had no odor,

I caught them on my fingers: it really seemed water. I had no receptacle, and the drops came out slowly, without pressure: the pipe must be only half full, perhaps less. I stretched out on the floor with my mouth under the spigot, not trying to open it further: it was water made tepid by the sun, insipid, perhaps distilled or the result of condensation; at any rate, a delight.

How much water can a two-inch pipe one or two meters high contain? A liter, perhaps not even that. I could have drunk all of it immediately; that would have been the safest way. Or save a bit for the next day. Or share half of it with Alberto. Or reveal the secret to the whole squad. I chose the third path, that of selfishness extended to the person closest to you, which in distant times a friend of mine appropriately called us-ism. We drank all the water, in small, avaricious gulps, changing places under the spigot, just the two of us. On the sly. But on the march back to camp at my side I found Daniele, all gray with cement dust, his lips cracked and his eyes feverish, and I felt guilty. I exchanged a look with Alberto; we understood each other immediately and hoped nobody had seen us. But Daniele had caught a glimpse of us in that strange position, supine near the wall among the rubble, and had suspected something, and then had guessed. He curtly told me so many months later, in Byelorussia, after the Liberation: Why the two of you and not I? It was the "civilian" moral code surfacing again. The same according to which I the free man of today perceive as horrifying the death sentence of the sadistic *Kapo,* decided upon and executed without appeal, silently, with the stroke of an eraser. Is this belated shame justified or not? I was not able to decide then and I am not able to decide even now, but shame there was and is, concrete, heavy, perennial. Daniele is dead now, but in our meetings as survivors, fraternal, affectionate, the veil of that act of omission, that unshared glass of water, stood between us, transparent, not expressed, but perceptible and "costly."

Understanding

1. What was Levi's dilemma? To use Glidewell's term (see "A Time for Choosing"), what was his choice point?
2. What is "ersatz coffee"? What is the *Kapo?*
3. Do you agree with Levi that thirst is a more wrenching predicament than hunger? Have you ever been in a situation where you recognized the precious nature of water?
4. How was Levi's decision "costly" to him later? Does this vignette focus his statement that there was total moral collapse of both the oppressors and the victims? Explain.

Responding

1. Earlier in the chapter from which this excerpt is taken, Levi states that he had deeply assimilated the principal rule at Auschwitz, that is, that it was mandatory that you take care of yourself first of all. He quotes a doctor, Ella Lingens-Reiner, who wrote about her camp experiences in *Prisoners of Fear:*

"How was I able to survive in Auschwitz? My principle is: I come first, second, and third. Then nothing, then again I; and then all the others." Following Levi's and Lingens-Riener's line of thinking, how hard is it for you to imagine the situation in the cellar? What do you think you would have done?

2. Was Levi's choice to share the water with Alberto and not with Daniele immoral? Explain your position.
3. Have you (or someone you know well) been faced with a decision such as Levi's? What happened when you faced the person you excluded? Did this omission haunt you? Was it "costly" in later years? What could you do now to effect closure with that person?

Connecting

1. Levi survived the horrors of Auschwitz. The driving force behind his writing is that an accurate firsthand account of the camps' horrors must be recorded in order that they never reoccur. He writes: "Human memory is a marvelous but fallacious instrument. The further events fade into the past, the more the construction of convenient truth grows and is perfected."

   Having lived through the civil rights era in this country, Lee's final statement in "Back to School" may be a decision similar to Levi's. What do you think? Is it good to forget your past wounds—to forgive and move on? Or is it better to forgive but continue to relive the wounds and their times?
2. Read Wiesel's "What Is a Friend?" (chapter one) and Spiegelman's "Worse Than My Darkest Dreams" (chapter two). What connections do you see among these selections, Levi's memoir, and the quotation (in Responding question 1) by Lingens-Reiner?

He Was Impossible

Dag Hammarskjöld

"In our era, the road to holiness necessarily passes through the world of action." Holiness is not a topic we usually associate with world leaders, or even with the secretaries general of the United Nations (U.N.). This statement is, however, typical of the writings of Dag Hammarskjöld, who served from 1953 until his death in 1961 as the second secretary general of this world organization dedicated to international peace and security. More than any other public figure of his time, Hammarskjöld tried to unite his very public calling with a contemplative life.

Hammarskjöld was born in 1905 in Jönköping, Sweden, the son of the Swedish prime minister during World War I. A career diplomat, Hammarskjöld gained prominence in his own country before becoming undersecretary of the Swedish Department of Finance. He served in a variety of posts with the United Nations, became known throughout the world as a peacemaker, and died in a plane crash in 1961 near Ndola, Northern Rhodesia (now Zimbabwe), while en route to negotiating a cease-fire between the U.N. and Katanga province.

Hammarskjöld influenced a generation of readers with *Markings,* in which he chronicled his own deeply private, internal struggles. He approved their publication in a letter to a colleague in which he indicated that they were "the only true profile that can be drawn . . ." of him. Published three years after his death, *Markings* contains Hammarskjöld's reflections dating from 1925 and ends with a poem he wrote only a few weeks before his death. Most of *Markings* are one- or two-sentence observations. The following selection, one of his longer entries, is from the period 1945–49.

He was impossible. It wasn't that he didn't attend to his work: on the 1
contrary, he took endless pains over the tasks he was given. But his manner of behavior brought him into conflict with everybody and, in the end, began to have an adverse effect on everything he had to do with.

When the crisis came and the whole truth had to come out, he laid the blame on us: in his conduct there was nothing, absolutely nothing to reproach. His self-esteem was so strongly bound up, apparently, with the idea of his innocence, that one felt a brute as one demonstrated, step by step, the contradictions in his defense and, bit by bit, stripped him naked before his own eyes. But justice to others demanded it.

When the last rag of a lie had been taken from him and we felt there was nothing more to be said, out it came with stifled sobs.

"But why did you never help me, why didn't you tell me what to do? You knew that I always felt you were against me. And fear and insecurity drove me further and further along the course you now condemn me for having taken. It's been so hard—everything. One day, I remember, I was so happy: one of you said that something I had produced was quite good—"

So, in the end, we were, in fact, to blame. We had not voiced our criticisms, 5
but we had allowed them to stop us from giving him a single word of acknowledgment, and in this way had barred every road to improvement.

For it is always the stronger one who is to blame. We lack life's patience. Instinctively, we try to eliminate a person from our sphere of responsibility as soon as the outcome of this particular experiment by Life appears, in our eyes, to be a failure. But Life pursues her experiments far beyond the limitations of our judgment. This is also the reason why, at times, it seems so much more difficult to live than to die.

Understanding

1. What decisions does Hammarskjöld reveal in this selection? In his own *metacognitive reflection*—his thinking about his thinking—how does he evaluate them?
2. How do you interpret Hammarskjöld's phrase "this particular experiment by Life"?
3. What lesson or conclusion does he draw from the event related in this excerpt? Explain the last sentence of paragraph 5 in terms of that conclusion.
4. American poet W. H. Auden, in his foreword to *Markings,* notes that "a reader . . . may well be surprised by what it does not contain—that Dag Hammarskjöld should not make a single direct reference to his career as an international civil servant, to the persons he met, or the historical events of his time in which he played an important role . . ." This selection is remarkable for its lack of particulars. The events could have happened anywhere and at any time. What effect does the use of this kind of impersonal style for such a personal revelation have on the reader? What advantage does it have for the writer?

Responding

1. Under what circumstances do you feel failure most keenly? What is your typical response to it?
2. Deciding to give criticism is often difficult because of the impact we perceive it may have on its recipient and of how we might feel as a consequence. Yet, as Hammarskjöld relates, both criticism and praise can be spurs to growth, and lack of them can, as he says, bar "every road to improvement." Using examples from your own experience, what is the most helpful way to give criticism? To receive it? Describe an experience in which criticism led to improvement in some aspect of your life. What one criticism was hardest to bear but the best you've received?
3. Deciding not to act can often lead to consequences as momentous as acting. Hammarskjöld writes, "We had not voiced our criticisms, but we had

allowed them to stop us from giving him a single word of acknowledgment." Relate an experience in which, in retrospect, you have determined you should have acted but did not.

Connecting

How are the issues in Levi's "Shame" and Hammarskjöld's "He Was Impossible" similar? How are the circumstances different?

Rules of the House

Richard Ford

Richard Ford has earned critical acclaim as one of the best writers of his generation and a leading short-story writer in the United States. Born in 1944 in Jackson, Mississippi, Ford turned to fiction after a brief stint as a law student. *A Piece of My Heart,* his first published work, told the tale of an Arkansas drifter and a Chicago law student, whose paths cross somewhere in the Mississippi Delta. It was his third novel, however, that established Ford's reputation as a consummate storyteller: *The Sportswriter,* published in 1986, examines the life of a promising writer who trades fiction writing for sports reporting and suburban life in New Jersey. The stories in *Rock Springs* (1987), set mostly in Montana; his more recent novels, *Wildlife* (1990) and *Independence Day* (1996); and his latest collection of stories, *Women and Men* (1997), have confirmed his literary stature.

In "Rules of the House," written more than fifteen years after he received his bachelor's degree from Michigan State University in 1966, Ford draws meaning from a decision he says he *didn't* make.

1 I wish there had been a moment in my young life, twenty-three years ago, when I could've thought to myself, "What I think I'll do now is join a college fraternity." Because if so, there might've been a moment when I could as easily have said, "No. I believe I won't join a college fraternity. I'm not that kind of fellow."

What I did back then was not give either possibility a thought. I simply joined. Pledged. Sigma Chi. Tom Selleck and Dave Letterman's bunch—the famous one with the sentimental song and the pretty sweetheart who later becomes your wife.

For a certain kind of boy at a certain tender age, fraternity is simply a given. A go-along guy, who wants friends. A guy with standards he can't understand. For this kind of boy conformity is a godsend. And I was that kind of boy.

In the long run, of course, fraternities have more or less the ethical dimension of a new hairstyle or a soft-drink flavor or a dance step you learn to perfection, then forget about entirely. And I don't feel particularly sorry to have been a member, since I'm suspicious of revising my past, and dislike the idea that anything I did and can remember so vividly was completely worthless. But still, I would like to have *chosen* to join, to have back those "decisions" I made by not deciding. Nothing, after all, is as venerable as nervy volition exerted in early age.

5 Like all conformists, we did not think of ourselves as conformists. We were men. Individuals and individualists. We knew what we knew. We prized life's lonelier roads, we were hard guys to convince of things. Stiletto-eyed, serious,

even grave. The fraternity meant to solidify these things and add some others—"fairness, decency, good manners." We winked, nodded, nested chins in our palms when listening, wrinkled our brows, clinched Winstons in our teeth, dealt a fair hand. We meant something, and we knew it.

Yet we also knew how to let down the gates for a good time when the right times came. We knew how to treat a woman. How to confide. We were easy in the company of men. We knew where to draw the line. Imagine our surprise, then, at finding an entire group of other guys who felt as we did about practically everything.

Independents, those sallow fellows who did not join fraternities, who stayed in the dorm and sculled around the shallows of organized social life—blazerless—suffered, we felt, the mark of undesirability and championed a mean, cast-out status. Loneliness, unprotectedness were features of that bad idea. Independence did not have the novelty it would come to have. Then, it only meant left out, which it does still. And none of us had stomachs for that.

Our bunch had standards, but to be initiated to Sigma Chi, Michigan State, 1963, you were still required to pick up a stuffed olive off the chapter-room floor using nothing but the naked cheeks of your behind; and, while many "actives" watched and cheered, deliver the olive to a small, waiting Dixie Cup. You still had to sit six hours straight on the hard edge of a hard chair, knees together, blindfolded, while someone played Ravel's *Bolero,* fortissimo, directly into your ears. You had to do many, many, many painful push-ups. You had to let the older boys scream obscenities and insults in your face, blow cigar smoke in your eyes, and breathe on you until they were tired of it. You had to tramp out into the frozen Michigan night in search of nothing less than a white cross—the fraternity's sacred emblem—which, of course, wasn't there. You had to bray like a donkey, buzz like a fly, bleat like a goat, be scorned, scourged, ridiculed, and insulted until they let you join them. It must have seemed like a good idea.

Exacting decisions had already been made about the people who *weren't* being initiated. We were, after all, chiefly in the excluding business. This guy had "the breath of death"; this guy had "bad choppers." This guy "had the handshake of a fish." We didn't want Jews, blacks, Orientals, gays, women, big fatties, or cripples. Yo-Yo Ma couldn't have been a Sigma Chi. Neither could Steven Spielberg or Justice Marshall.

We *did* want "face men," jocks, wild guys, rich guys, guys with class, guys 10
with sisters, guys with "nice threads," "real characters," guys willing to make fools of themselves and others. Guys who didn't think this was all bullshit. Good guys, in other words.

I've never seen the movie *Animal House.* But from the previews I've concluded Sigma Chi, in my day, was like that more or less. We called ourselves by animal names—the Pigeon, the Pig, the Guppie, the Armadillo, the Whale (there were also vegetables—the Eggplant, the Rutabaga, the Tomato, the Carrot, the Root). We put people's heads in toilets. We lighted our farts. We dropped our trousers in public. We drank and pissed on things. We danced. We shouted. We groped. We gave the finger. We got sick. We wore coats and ties. We were men and knew no bottom line.

A good question to ask of all this, I suppose, is: "Were we friends, all of us?" And the answer would have to be—not that much, if friendships are things meant to last a long time. I remember detesting some of my brothers, mocking others, lying to them, pitying them, bird-dogging *their* sweethearts. One boy, now a veterinarian, I sucker-punched at a party, reshaping one of his nostrils forever—I forget precisely why. By the time I'd been in a year, I was already certain I didn't belong (though neither did I want out), so that I became, for a while, aloof with superiority. These guys were just children, Gothics to be brought along for amusement, on earth for me to observe. This, I think, is also what conformists often do.

What I learned from being a Sigma Chi, though, is enough to make me not regret it. I learned that an experience need not be ennobling or noble for good to come out of it. This, after all, is the alma mater of comedy. I learned that even from a brotherhood one could get free, as some did, though it wasn't easy. There was red tape. Soul-searching. Hard feelings. You needed to renounce more than a moment, a scene, a situation. I learned, in fact, that life itself could be thought of as just a series of alliances entered into for a time and a goal, and abandonable without prejudice. All this, I think, is instructive of the value of institutions both good and bad.

I also learned that buffoonery, prejudice, treachery, resentment, pettiness—all the poorer instincts—can often go hand in glove with demonstrations of friendship and companionability, and that those impulses are not necessarily even alien, but are merely humors within the larger human dramaturgy. We must decide which humor will dominate. Many times, in those days, I asked myself, "Can I do this, think this, say this, and still be your brother?" And the answer was almost always *yes.*

15 Is all this then, I wonder, what the fraternity meant us to learn? Is this what the grip meant? The secrets? *In hoc signo vinces?* Maybe. But I doubt it. It had something else in mind, I think. Something nobler sounding, but that in a complex, importance-seeking world, wouldn't work; that would turn us into Babbitts and later Meursaults. We were phonies, poseurs, bores, joke-masters, stupids, preposterous boys who wore our importance like uniforms but signified nothing—me not the least of them. And in truth if I learned anything at all, it might've been that I did not have to stay exactly that way forever.

Understanding

1. Ford describes being a "brother," or a "good guy," as a kind of zero-sum game; that is, in order to win status on campus, somebody else has to lose it or be denied it. According to Ford, what are the advantages of such a game?
2. George Babbitt, referred to in paragraph 15, is the title character in the 1920s novel by Sinclair Lewis. *Babbitt* has become the eponym for a superficial person who develops his opinions from newspapers or from business colleagues. How does Ford relate fraternity membership to Babbitt? Who is Meursault?

3. What does Ford mean when he writes, "I would like to have *chosen* to join, to have back those 'decisions' I made by not deciding"?
4. What feelings does this essay evoke in the reader? What elements contribute to producing them?

Responding

1. Would you join or have you joined a fraternity or sorority? If so, how does your decision and your experience compare or contrast with Ford's? If not, how does Ford's portrayal of "Greek" life affect your attitude toward it?
2. The college experience is often a student's first encounter with loneliness. What are the attributes of loneliness? How is it different from solitude? How might it be eased?
3. When faced with complex, life-altering choices, what guides your decisions? Reasoned thought? Personal experiment? Reflection on observations? Expert authority? Use examples to illustrate your response and draw a conclusion about your approach to decision making.
4. In their partly humorous "Short Educational Dictionary," Kingsley Amis and Robert Conquest defined identity-seeking as "One of the main concerns of education and the main concern of concerned students. . . . Methods include (a) becoming unconscious through hallucinatory drugs [and] (b) joining an organization all of whose members accept identical opinions . . ." Would you say that Ford's fraternity experience was a form of identity-seeking? What are your forms of identity-seeking? What kinds of identity are important to college students today? Through what means are they typically sought?

Connecting

In commenting on his decision to join or not to join a college fraternity in paragraph 2, Ford says, "What I did back then was not give either possibility a thought. I simply joined." Indicate other readings in this chapter in which decisions were made without sufficient reflection. What awarenesses were lacking at the time of the decision?

Our Fathers Fought for Liberty

James Russell Lowell

Poet, critic, and diplomat James Russell Lowell (1819–91) was born into the distinguished New England family that produced the well-known poets Amy Lowell (1887–1925) and Robert Lowell (1917–77). James Lowell graduated from Harvard Law School in 1840 and practiced law for a short time. Until about 1850 his writing was dominated by humanitarian interests, particularly anti-slavery issues. He succeeded Henry Wadsworth Longfellow (who had been chair for eighteen years) in his appointment to the Smith professor of modern languages at Harvard, and in 1857 began his four-year editorship of the new *Atlantic Monthly*. Between 1877 and 1885, he served as minister to Spain and then as ambassador to England.

Lowell's writing from 1862 until the end of his life centered on what he considered to be distinctive American traits—self-reliant individualism, equality, and optimism. His poems and essays explored his belief that self-control in the face of greed, ambition, desire, and other temptations resulted from the guiding principle of personal and national responsibility. Believing that tradition and culture can guide self-control, Lowell wrote often about freedom. He was one of the most popular writers of the nineteenth century.

Our Fathers Fought for Liberty

Our fathers fought for liberty,
They struggled long and well,
History of their deeds can tell—
But did they leave us free?

Are we free to speak our thought,
To be happy and be poor,
Free to enter Heaven's door,
To live and labor as we ought?

Are we then made free at last
From the fear of what men say.
Free to reverence today,
Free from the slavery of the past?

Our fathers fought for liberty,
They struggled long and well,
History of the deeds can tell—
But *ourselves* must set us free.

Understanding

1. What is the central point Lowell is raising here? What might the context have been for writing this poem?

Responding

1. Is it probable that when Lowell wrote this, the "our fathers" to whom he was referring were people who looked like he did? Perhaps his readers too were quite like him. Although everyone in the United States can claim an ethnic and cultural ancestry, today's Americans are more verbal about their cultural and ethnic differences. Yet our different fathers have all fought for liberty on this soil and on others. What about this poem suggests that it can be read by all Americans for inspiration?
2. The preamble to the Constitution of the United States is what "our fathers" fought for:

   > We, the people of the United States, in order to form a more perfect union, establish justice, insure domestic tranquility, provide for the common defense, promote the general welfare, and secure the blessings of liberty to ourselves and our posterity, do ordain and establish this Constitution for the United States of America.

   Have we as a people taken the responsibility—and the challenge—to form a more perfect union, to establish justice, to provide for common defense, and to promote the general welfare? In what ways can Americans today "secure the blessings of liberty to ourselves and our posterity"?
3. Consider the question posed in the second stanza (lines 5 through 8) in terms of your own personal experience. Are you free to speak your thoughts, to be happy and be poor, to live and labor as you want to? Why or why not? What personal battle might you have to win in order to be this free?

Connecting

1. Referring to the conscientious objectors' decisions in Tollefson's "Choosing Not to Fight," respond to the question that Lowell frames in the second stanza (lines 5 through 8).
2. How would Glidewell from "A Time for Choosing" respond to Lowell's question?
3. Thinking again of Woolf's metaphor of the "Angel in the House" in "Professions for Women," earlier in this chapter, in relation to the questions Lowell poses in lines 5 through 12 of his poem, examine a personal battle—or angel you would have to slay—in order to answer one of his two questions.

WRITING OPTION: Decisions

Refer to your responses to the questions on the readings in this chapter. Choose a response that you would like to expand on regarding the power of decisions in a person's life, particularly in your own life. Pay particular attention to responses that demonstrate how a decision left its signature on you or changed the course of your life. The readings in this chapter all explored how a particular decision led to a chain of consequences that altered lives. Your writing should do the same. As you revise your chosen response, keep in mind that you are rounding out your self-portrait from another point of view.

4

Dreams

"You must be dreaming." "Dream on." "It's a dream come true." How often have we heard these expressions in reference to something improbable, delusional, or simply unexpected?

Dreams do transport us to another world—to the edges of reality and to the center of possibility. The selections in this chapter also take us there.

Two kinds of dreams have inspired the writers of the readings in this section: the succession of images that occur when we sleep, or the *sleep-dream,* and those thoughts that nourish our fondest hopes and desires—the *plan-dream.* Sleep-dreams arrive without invitation; plan-dreams are at our command.

Everybody dreams, psychologists tell us. In the altered state of waking consciousness we call sleep, we slip into a dream state several times a night. Most of our dreams are ordinary and forgettable—no more than random discharges of electric energy in our brains. Although most of our dreams are unremarkable, some are truly memorable. The best dreams are fantastic journeys in which we do wonderful things: float, fly, or win the lottery; the worst are nightmares.

Almost every culture attaches meaning to sleep-dreams and has stories that connect them with events in waking life, as in Rosa Elena Yzquierdo's "Abuela." Throughout history and across cultures, despite the best efforts of dream experts and the millions of "how to interpret your dreams" books that line the supermarket checkout stands, dreams that occur in sleep retain a mysterious, otherworldly quality that may bewilder or even alarm us. Is it any wonder that "sweet dreams" is a favorite bedtime sign-off to children?

American psychiatrist William Dement asserts that dreaming permits us to "be quietly and safely insane every night of our lives." In fact, what psychiatrists call the "manifest content" of dreams (the events that occur in them) sometimes seems a little crazy. Sigmund Freud, the founder of psychoanalysis and the first physician to write extensively about dreams as indicators of his patients' "unconscious" mind, thought that dreams created by authors and "attributed to fictitious characters in the context of their stories reveal as much as the dreams of real patients." Bear this in mind when you read the excerpts from Naomi Epel's "Four Writers' Dreams."

The plan-dream, contrastingly, almost always addresses reality in a conscious, direct way. These plan-dreams are the products of optimism about the future, as in Elizabeth Delany's opening sentence in "Bessie": "I had always dreamed I would become a medical doctor." Unlike the dreams of sleep which defy time and space, plan-dreams focus on the future and are full of real-world details. They are, as the Blue Fairy in Walt Disney's *Pinocchio* sings to the wooden puppet who wants to become a "real boy," the wishes your heart makes. Plan-dreams may be fantasies, but they are not fantastic.

Dreams are the persistent messages that guide our perceptions of work and our pursuit of the American dream, as in Rick Bragg's "Big Holes Where the Dignity Used to Be," and fuel the expectations that fall short, as in Carol Saline's "The Luong Sisters." Although dreams carry us through the tedium of daily life, Mary Catherine Bateson, in "Opening to the World," says that they are less important than improvising our way through life.

Readings with both kinds of dreams—the sleep-dream and the plan-dream—fill this chapter: modest dreams of individuals like ourselves, in Studs Turkel's "Five Dreams"; ambitious dreams for a people in Bruno Bettelheim's "Creating a New Way of Life"; dreams that came true; dreams that turned sour for reasons we may never know, as in Edward Arlington Robinson's "Richard Cory"; and dreams that simply never materialized, as in Langston Hughes's "A Dream Deferred."

A reviewer of a recent book on dreams introduced his critique with the observation that "nothing is more boring than listening to someone else's dreams." We disagree. Despite the uniqueness of their experiences, the writers of these dream stories turn their very personal visions into material we can both recognize and respond to.

Abuela

Rosa Elena Yzquierdo

Rosa Elena Yzquierdo's poems and short stories have appeared in the *American Review* and other journals. In "Abuela," Yzquierdo captures the literal meaning of dreams as well as the figure of the traditional grandmother as she is often depicted in Mexican American literature—a source of knowledge and history.

The tortilla-making ritual in this excerpt from *Growing Up Chicano/a,* as with many stories of intergenerational relationships, takes on a significance beyond food preparation.

My abuela begins her daily ritual with "Santa María, madre de Dios. . . ." 1
She goes outside and waters the trailing plants surrounding the rickety old fence. Yerbas are growing profusely in Folger's coffee cans and an old Motorola. Abuela comes back inside and mixes flour, salt, and shortening to make tortillas for me. One of the tortillas cooking on the comal fills with air.

"That means you're going to get married," she says, then continues to knead and cook each tortilla with care, making sure to bless the first one of the stack.

"Abuela, I had a dream about fleas. What does it mean?"

"It means you're going to get some money, mija."

"Abuela, my stomach hurts." 5

"Te doy un tesito mija?"

She picks the yerbas, prepares them, and makes a tea for me. No smell to it, but it tastes of milk of magnesia—maybe worse.

"Drink this tea every morning for nine days before breakfast, and your stomach-aches will disappear for one year."

She has always said to me, "Remember your dreams because they have special meaning. Remember the yerbas that grow in the wild, how they work, when to use them. Remember the cures for evil eye, fright, and fever.

"Sweep the herbs across the body and repeat three Apostle's Creeds to 10
drive out evil spirits. Crack an egg in a glass of water and say three Hail Marys to take away evil eye and fever. Remember these things. They are all a part of you—a part of your heritage."

She said once, "Yo soy mexicana; tu mamá es mexicana pero tú eres americana."

I just try to hold on.

Understanding

1. How is the narrator's *abuela* a source of knowledge and history? In what other ways could she be viewed? How does Yzquierdo relate to the practices that she describes in this selection?

2. Lawrence Perrine, an English professor who has written extensively on the short story, explains that "an author may present . . . characters either directly or indirectly." In *direct presentation,* we are told "straight out what a character is like." In *indirect presentation,* the author shows us the character "in action"; we must infer what he or she is like through behavior or speech. In what way does Yzquierdo present her *abuela?* How does this kind of presentation affect the reader?
3. Some writers use a technique called *code-switching,* a bilingual approach to telling a story. "Abuela" is written mostly in English, but at appropriate times the native language, in this case, Spanish, is used. What purpose does the code-switching technique in "Abuela" serve for the writer? What effect does it have on the reader?
4. What does the writer mean by the last sentence: "I just try to hold on"? How does it relate to the rest of the story?
5. Compile as many adjectives as you think are appropriate to describe the feelings conveyed in "Abuela." For each of them, select that segment of the story that you think is the source of those feelings.

Responding

1. What values or rituals practiced in your family circle, or in a family you know, do you think are worth preserving? Why? Which do you think you would reject? Why? Interview at least one person for whom "kitchen-table talk" was part of their growing up.
2. The interaction that Yzquierdo describes between her *abuela* and herself might be called "intergenerational quality time." How important is this kind of sharing? Was this kind of relationship part of your growing-up experiences? If so, describe those aspects that you think influenced you the most. Is this opportunity available to most American children today? Explain.
3. *Abuela's* advice to "remember your dreams because they have special meaning" corresponds to the views of some of the writers in this chapter and of many psychologists and anthropologists. Do you remember your dreams? To whom do you tell them? What significance do dreams have in your life?

Connecting

Compare Yzquierdo's *abuela* with Señorita Luisa in De Ferrari's "Our Peruvian Friend" (chapter one) in terms of what they bring to each writer. In what ways do they exemplify a view of the "older generation"?

Four Writers' Dreams

Naomi Epel

"We are asleep with compasses in our hands."

—W. S. Merwin, American poet, born 1927

For many of us, a compass is an instrument to mark direction—north, south, east, west. But Merwin's metaphor allows us to enlarge our references. A compass could be a person, a book, a star, an intuition, a sign; but for him, it is our dreams.

In 1993, after many years of listening to writers recall their dreams, Naomi Epel published *Writers Dreaming*. She was a literary escort, driving authors around San Francisco on their book-promotion tours in northern California. When Epel mentioned that she lead workshops to help people tap into their dreams, her passengers would usually share one of theirs. Epel's interviews were fairly free-form, usually beginning with a question like "Have you ever had a dream that influenced your work?" Finding Epel's question intriguing, famous writers were quite willing—in most cases—to explore their dreams with her. As she says, their dreams revealed ways in which "they have been inspired and aided by forces beyond consciousness, while lying in their beds, asleep." In fact, the dreams you are about to read were compasses that gave direction and opened up creative processes for the dreamers.

The following excerpts from *Writers Dreaming* include the dreams of Amy Tan, William Styron, Maya Angelou, and Stephen King.

AMY TAN

The kind of writing I do is very dreamlike. The process I go through is similar to what happens when I dream. I have found in dreams that I can change the setting by simply looking down at my feet then looking up again. I'll be following my feet for a while and, if I don't like what I see in front of me, I will just look down at my feet. I'll start walking, and when I look up, I'll be in a different place. 1

I do a similar thing when I'm writing. I focus on a specific image, and that image takes me into a scene. Then I begin to see the scene and I ask myself, "What's to your right? What's to your left?" and I open up into this fictional world. I often play music as a way of blocking out the rest of my consciousness, so I can enter into this world and let it go where it wants to go, wherever the characters want to go. It takes me into some surprising places.

The kind of imagination I use in writing, when I try to lose control of consciousness, works very much like dreams. The subconscious takes over and it's fun. I discover things I could never pull up if I were really trying to. When I get into a dream world I can create fiction by going down surprising pathways.

That's the magic that comes through fiction, through not knowing things completely. I've heard psychologists say that the kind of brain waves operating when you are creating are similar to the kind of patterns that you have in deep relaxation and sleep. Things that come from your subconscious in a dreamlike state can be a lot more honest than they would be if your consciousness was turned on or if your defenses were completely in place. When you lose that sense of protecting your ego, richer symbols appear.

* * *

The success of *The Joy Luck Club* was the kind of experience where one 5
could say, "You have absolutely nothing to complain about. This is all so wonderful." That's true. But there was a part of me that was very angry, and I didn't understand why at first. Well, I have a lot of dreams that have to do with shoes, and one night I had a dream that my husband and I were walking somewhere when I suddenly realized that I had lost my shoes. I said to him, "I have to go back and get my shoes, they're my favorite, my most comfortable shoes. I can't go on without them." He had also lost his shoes and there were snakes in the grass. It was dangerous to go on. We retraced our steps and he found his shoes right away. But mine were gone and I was upset that I knew I would never find these comfortable old shoes again. At that point, a shoe salesman pointed to a rack of shoes nearby and said to me, "Here, you can buy these shoes instead." They were all high heels, all fancy things, and I said, "I don't want those, I want the same old shoes." I had such a sense of loss. When I woke up, I realized what I had lost: this old feeling of comfort. And that my husband could still enjoy it.

WILLIAM STYRON

For years when I was younger I had a kind of seminightmare. I say seminightmare because it wasn't one of those shattering nightmares that just leave you broken and distressed, but it was troubling anyway. It was a dream of water spouts: being in a cellar or heading for a cellar like one flees to from a tornado, being terrified that the tornado was going to overtake and destroy me.

I was always saved. Or I'd wake up before they overwhelmed the house or wherever I was fleeing from.

I lived near the James River when I grew up and we did actually have water spouts. They were usually quite harmless but in my dreams they appeared as figures of terrible menace. They recurred for a number of years. And then, for some reason, disappeared. That's the only experience I ever had of recurrent dreams.

Perhaps my work was troubling me and they represented the threat of uncompleted work or something. I'm not really sure. Plainly they represented some sort of threat. And they probably were therapeutic.

MAYA ANGELOU

I do believe dreams have a function. I don't see anything that has no 10
function, not anything that has been created. I may not understand its function or be able to even use it, make it utile, but I believe it has a reason. The brain is so strange and wondrous in its mystery. I think it creates a number of things for itself—it creates launching pads and resting places—and it lets steam off and it reworks itself. It re-creates itself almost every minute.

I remember years ago being told that one can't really learn after one is twenty-five. Or twenty-something. There's a halt, the brain cells die. In my fifties I started studying Japanese. As I reach sixty I'm trying to become proficient in a lot of things, in the sciences. Just because there's so much to be learned. So, the brain—we just don't know anything about it—it creates dreams. Dreams can tell people all sorts of things. It can work out problems. Especially for writing.

Maybe, if a writer is hesitant to get to a depth in a character, to admit that this fictional character does this, or thinks this or has acted this way—or that an event was really this terrifying—the brain says, "Okay, you go on and go to sleep, I'll take care of it. I'll show you where that is."

One sees that the brain allows the dreamer to be more bold than he or she ever would be in real time. The dream allows the person to do things, and think things, and go places and be acted upon. The person, in real time, would never do those things. It may be that's a way the brain has of saying, "Well let me let you come on down and see what really is down here."

There's a phrase in West Africa called "deep talk." When a person is informed about a situation, an older person will often use a parable, an axiom, and then add to the end of the axiom, "Take that as deep talk." Meaning that you will never find the answer. You can continue to go down deeper and deeper. Dreams may be deep talk.

STEPHEN KING

The dreams that I remember most clearly are almost always early dreams. 15
And they're not always bad dreams. I don't want to give you that impression. I can remember one very clearly. It was a flying dream. I was over the turnpike and I was flying along wearing a pair of pajama bottoms. I didn't have any shirt on. I'm just buzzing along under overpasses—*kazipp*—and I'm reminding myself in the dream to stay high enough so that I don't get disemboweled by car antennas sticking up from the cars. That's a fairly mechanistic detail but when I woke up from this dream my feeling was not fear or loathing but just real exhilaration, pleasure and happiness.

It wasn't an out of control flying dream. I can remember as a kid, having a lot of falling dreams but this is the only flying dream that I can remember in detail.

I don't have a lot of repetitive dreams but I do have an anxiety dream: I'm working very hard in a little hot room—it seems to be the room where I lived as a teenager—and I'm aware that there's a madwoman in the attic. There's a little tiny door under the eave that goes to the attic and I have to finish my work. I have to get that work done or she'll come out and get me. At some point in the dream that door always bursts open and this hideous woman—with all this white hair stuck up around her head like a gone-to-seed dandelion—jumps out with a scalpel.

And I wake up.

I still have that dream when I'm backed up on my work and trying to fill all these ridiculous commitments I've made for myself.

I remember about six months ago having this really vivid dream.

I was in some sort of an apartment building, a cheesy little apartment 20
building. The front door was open and I could see all these black people going back and forth. They were talking and having a wonderful time. Somebody was playing music somewhere. And then the door shut.

In the dream I went back and got into bed. I think I must have shut the door myself. My brother was in bed with me, behind me, and he started to strangle me. My brother had gone crazy. It was awful!

I remember saying, with the last of my breath, "I think there's somebody out there." And he got up from the bed and went out. As soon as he was out I went up and closed the door and locked it. And then I went back to bed. That is, I started to lie down in this dream.

Then I began to worry that I hadn't really locked the door. This is the sort of thing that I'm always afraid of in real life. Did I turn off the burners on the stove? Did I leave a light on when I left the house? So, I got up to check the door and sure enough it was unlocked. I realized that he was still in there with me. Somewhere.

I screamed in the dream, "He's still in the house." I screamed so loud I woke myself up. Except I wasn't screaming when I woke up. I was just sort of muttering it over and over again, He's in the house, he's in the house. I was terrified.

Now, I keep a glass of ice water beside the bed where I sleep and the ice 25
cubes hadn't melted yet, so it had happened almost immediately after I fell asleep. That's usually when I have the dreams that I remember most vividly.

Understanding

1. Amy Tan speaks of dreams as a way to access the characters or landscapes in her fiction writing, and as a way to understand life's troubling issues. Are her examples convincing?
2. William Styron writes of recurrent dreams and says they were probably therapeutic. What does he mean by this? Do you agree with him?
3. Maya Angelou believes that her dreams have a function. What is it?

4. Stephen King shares his nightmares and anxiety dreams. What therapeutic purpose would they serve?
5. What do these writers' dreams have in common?

Responding

1. Write about a dream that has been either a "compass" for you, or that has had some other long-lasting meaning. The dream itself is an important narrative, but the point you make *about* the dream is what you're going for.
2. Have you used dreams to open up your creativity, to handle fears, or to recognize issues? Describe the dream and explain.
3. Amy Tan uses daydreams to stimulate her imagination. Do you daydream? Do you think of your daydreams as procrastination or as work toward a goal?

Connecting

1. What about these dreams relates to Yzquierdo's grandmother's admonition in the previous selection, "Abuela"?
2. Relate Amy Tan's ideas about dreaming and unconsciousness to Virginia Woolf's in Chapter three.

Opening to the World

Mary Catherine Bateson

"This is a study of five artists engaged in that act of creation that engages us all—the composition of our lives," Mary Catherine Bateson informs us in her acknowledgments to *Composing a Life.* Basically narrative in structure, *Composing a Life* examines how five women define their lives: Bateson, writer and professor of anthropology and English; Joan Erickson, dancer, writer, and jewelry designer; Alice d'Entremont, electrical engineer and entrepreneur; Ellen Bassuk, psychiatrist and researcher on homelessness; and Johnnetta Cole, anthropologist and college president. Through their stories, excerpted here, Bateson elaborates on how the "ongoing improvisations" that each woman makes produce a life that is shaped less by a predefined vision, or "dream," than by "discovering the shape" of its creation along the way.

Bateson has written on a variety of linguistic and anthropological topics and is the author of *With a Daughter's Eye,* a memoir of her parents, Gregory Bateson and Margaret Mead, both distinguished anthropologists.

Human beings tend to regard the conventions of their own societies as natural, often as sacred. One of the great steps forward in history was learning to regard those who spoke odd-sounding languages and had different smells and habits as fully human, as similar to oneself. The next step from this realization, the step which we have still not fully made, is the willingness to question and purposefully alter one's own conditions and habits, to learn by observing others. If a particular arrangement is not necessary, it might be possible to choose to change it. Still, aristocratic Chinese ladies of the old regime, crippled for life by the binding of their feet, looked down on peasant women with unbound feet. Exposure to other ways of doing things is insufficient if it is not combined with empathy and respect. 1

I grew up a beneficiary of openness to alternatives of belief and custom. All four of my grandparents were atheists, which meant that they had dissented from beliefs taken for granted by those around them, living lives of conscious choice. For my mother and later for me, taking an interest in religion was rather venturesome, involving the notion that belief is not a given of growing up in a particular family but a matter of choice. In some ways, my grandparents were chauvinistic about their chosen nonconformities and felt rather superior to those who had less education or enlightenment. But in other ways, I see them as open to the imagination of alternative ways of being.

My father's father, who crusaded ferociously for his convictions against various kinds of spiritualism and Lamarckianism, thought of his own vocation of scientist as lofty but lower than that of artist. He collected the paintings and drawings of William Blake, Japanese prints, embroideries and old-master drawings. As I see them now, these are very different choices. To collect old-master drawings was to choose an economical and attainable form of a familiar excellence, but to immerse himself in the visions and prophetic writings of Blake was to embrace a different consciousness—bizarre, angry, and strangely beautiful, turning ordinary perceptions upside down. "The harlot's cry from street to street/Will weave old England's winding sheet." I have wondered occasionally, in these years when we have learned to look anew at needlework as forms of women's expression, whether the embroideries he collected were also ways to enter other modes of thinking and being, especially since his mother, his wife, and his sisters were all variously involved in women's rights and in exploring new roles.

When my mother wrote about her childhood, it always seemed that her chosen model was her paternal grandmother, but recently I have become increasingly curious about her mother, my maternal grandmother. Richard Juliani, a sociologist studying the history of Italians in America, has pointed out that Margaret Mead first learned about the importance of culture from her mother's research on Italian immigrants. Long before she encountered anthropology and went to Samoa, she had done fieldwork with her mother in New Jersey, where she met and learned to respect people with different customs. She had heard her mother's convictions on the human capacity to change and adapt; she had also heard her counter the arguments of the eugenics movement, which maintained that Italian and Eastern European immigrants were genetically inferior.

5 For Americans today, composing a life means integrating one's own commitments with the differences created by change and the differences that exist between the peoples of the world with whom we increasingly come into contact. Because we have an altered sense of the possible, every choice has a new meaning.

When Johnnetta was growing up, a nonracist America was hardly imaginable; today it can be imagined but must still be struggled for. The imagination of difference was also blocked in another way, for educated black people in Jacksonville looked down on black people from the Caribbean and Africa. The implication was that blacks in Jacksonville should aspire to be like the white people around them, but there was a secondary message beating on them that they would always be something less.

"I remember all those derogatory terms. 'Monkey chasers' were the people from the Caribbean. Because of the closeness of Florida to the Bahamas, Jamaica, Barbados, there was a lot of that sentiment. In my family, we were told not to have that view, that black people from other places were not less good than black people born in the U.S. My great-grandfather had named his company the *Afro*-American Life Insurance Company, after all. But even so, if I wanted a dress that my mother thought was too red, she'd say, 'You don't want to look like some . . .' (she'd use a distorted set of syllables supposed to indicate some African tribe), 'You don't want to look like one of those Ubidubi tribes.' There were conflicting messages about 'those tribal jump-up-and-down-big-lipped people' that you didn't want to have any part of."

Black consciousness has not only affirmed a positive and equal identity for American blacks, but it has also offered a sense of multiple possibilities: Africa as a place of rich and fertile variation, experiments in kingship as old as Solomon, herders and farmers and hunters and sculptors; Brazil and Cuba and Haiti, with recurrent themes but profound differences. Johnnetta speaks of drawing on her background in anthropology to bring sisters from throughout the lands of the African diaspora to Spelman College to affirm and proclaim that there is more than one way of being black, just as there is more than one way of being female. This, for her, is education for choice. When you talk to her about what she hopes to achieve, she returns again and again to the idea that Afro-Americans and women need to discover their own diversity and in that discovery be freed from the notion that there is only a single possible direction of aspiration. "I'm on the case of the white folk about diversity, but I also think that Spelman has that responsibility. And by diversity, I mean to go beyond self. One of the ways that can happen is to have a community of students who are black women from other parts of the world. Who says that here at an all-black women's school we don't have to be concerned about diversity? You can't argue that there is insight and strength to be gained from diversity over there but you don't need it over here! But I don't think the two issues are mirror images, either."

Aspiration is elusive without models to aspire to, but following a single model has its own dangers. The son of a physician growing up in the suburbs can aspire to be like his father and close his eyes to the evidence that his life will necessarily be different. The daughter of a business executive can aspire to be like her father and understand that such an aspiration depends on change in the society, but she may still be the captive of a single vision of excellence. It was still hard, when Ellen went to medical school, for women to become physicians; beyond that, it was necessary for them to become a different kind of physician, to reshape the existing role. There has been a recurring debate in the women's movement between those who fought for the chance for middle-class white women to be like middle-class white men and those who affirm the many ways of being female, the needs and problems of other kinds of women, and the need for freedom for men and women to move in different directions. For some of us, "chauvinism" is simply a shortening of "male chauvinism." For others, it is a reminder of the dangers of devotion to the superiority of any group, gender, race, religion, or nation, or even to the truths of any era.

The real challenge comes from the realization of multiple alternatives and 10
the invention of new models. Aspiration ceases to be a one-way street—from child to adult, from female inferiority to male privilege, from exclusion to full membership—and instead becomes open in all directions, claiming the possibility of inclusion and setting an individual course among the many ways of being human. Even this is not an adequate phrasing, because it suggests the possibility of choosing an existing model and following it toward a defined goal. The real challenge lies in assembling something new.

There are no singular models, but only resources for creative imagination. Many people grew up seeing my mother as a model, which is fine and helpful from a distance, but it would have been a mistake for me to try to be too much like her. I am like Ellen with her housewife mother: loving and determined to be different. At the same time, you cannot put together a life willy-nilly from odds and ends. Even in a crazy quilt, the various pieces, wherever they come from, have to be trimmed and shaped and arranged so they fit together, then firmly sewn to last through time and keep out the cold. Most quilts are more ambitious: they involve the imposition of a new pattern. But even crazy quilts are sewn against a backing; the basic sense of continuity allows improvisation. Composing a life involves an openness to possibilities and the capacity to put them together in a way that is structurally sound.

Understanding

1. "Opening to the World" represents a larger dream or aspiration of Bateson. What is this aspiration, and how does she think composing a life can best be achieved?
2. Although the examples Bateson uses are sketched rather than fully drawn, how do the women in this reading come to terms with their aspirations?

Responding

1. Bateson regards being "fully human" as a positive trait. What components, in your judgment, contribute to a "fully human" life? What part does dreaming or improvising play in it?
2. Bateson states in paragraph 1 that the "willingness to question and purposefully alter one's own conditions and habits, to learn by observing others" is "a step forward in history." And yet, learning by observing others can also lead to undesirable or inappropriate results. What do you think must guide this kind of learning so that it is indeed a step forward?
3. "Aspiration is elusive without models to aspire to, but following a single model has its own dangers," cautions Bateson (paragraph 9) in describing how one can be "captive of a single vision of excellence." Who are your models of excellence? Do they represent a single vision or alternative visions for whom you dream to become? In either case, relate how your model of excellence inspires you to aspire.

Connecting

1. Contrast the context of women's lives today with Bessie's experience of creating her life in Sarah and Elizabeth Delany's "Bessie."
2. Do Bateson's subjects express Woolf's metaphor of the "angel in the house" from "Professions for Women" (chapter three)? What angel-in-the-house demon do the men regard as having to slay in Hammarskjöld's "He Was Impossible" and in Levi's "Shame" (chapter three)? Is there an angel in the house for the male character in Gordimer's "Country Lovers" (chapter three)?

Harlem

Langston Hughes

Many would agree that Langston Hughes (1902–67) is one of the most significant black American writers of the twentieth century, but early on, that acclaim was hotly debated. He was first recognized as a writer to be taken seriously in the 1920s, a period known as the Harlem Renaissance, a time when many black intellectuals, musicians, and especially writers became very visible and highly productive. The movement was based in Harlem, a vibrant and growing center of African American life and culture in New York City. Hughes was prolific and expressed himself in virtually every literary genre, from poetry and prose to operas and children's stories.

Hughes was against elitism in any form both in the black community and in society at large. This sensibility may have influenced his socialist politics in the 1930s and been the cause of his being called before the House Un-American Activities Committee in the 1950s. He wrote for the common man and he saw African Americans as his primary audience. Hughes's works have been translated into German, French, Spanish, Russian, Yiddish, and Czech, and many have been set to music.

Harlem

What happens to a dream deferred?

Does it dry up
like a raisin in the sun?

Or fester like a sore—
And then run?
Does it stink like rotten meat?
Or crust and sugar over—
like a syrupy sweet?

Maybe it just sags

Like a heavy load.

Or does it explode?

Understanding

1. To what dream is Hughes referring? Does he imply an answer to his question on line 11?
2. What is Hughes's underlying social commentary about the dreams of a people? That is, what is he saying about dreams as an individual versus a collective goal? Who or what causes such dreams to be deferred?

3. Hughes offers graphic metaphors to suggest the ways in which human beings are affected when their dreams must be abandoned. Identify those metaphors and infer the human emotions and responses to which he is alluding. Why does he italicize the last line of the poem?

Responding

1. How would you answer Hughes's questions?
2. Is Hughes's message unique to African Americans, or can it be applied to other groups? Explain.
3. There is a famous saying: Be careful what you wish for; it might come true. Compose a poem in a "Harlem" style whose first line is *What happens to a dream come true?*
4. Write about a dream you had that never came true. What was your role in it? How does your point about the dream relate to the way you answered Responding question 1?
5. Did African American writer Lorraine Hansberry's play *A Raisin in the Sun* (winner of the New York Drama Critics Circle Award for the 1958–59 season) take its title from this poem? Research the possible connection.

Connecting

Which of the writers from previous chapters can you connect with Hughes's question in line 11?

The Luong Sisters

Carol Saline

One afternoon, Carol Saline, journalist, broadcaster, and public speaker, and Sharon Wohlmuth, award-winning photographer for the *Philadelphia Inquirer,* were having a talk about sisters. Sharon commented on how she had always been intrigued by the spirit of sisters and how she could always recognize them on the street. "There's a certain intimacy that makes them so different from close friends," she concluded. By the end of that conversation, the two had decided to collaborate on a project—the book *Sisters,* from which this excerpt is taken. Saline collected the sisters' stories through interviews and turned them into essays; Wohlmuth photographed the sisters to make a visual record that reflected their intimate connection.

Saline writes that *Sisters* documents the "funny, joyful, angry, painful, and historic memories" that create "the foundation—solid or shaky—on which every sister-relationship rests." Saline and Wohlmuth chose to present both loving and feuding sisters—those who share a solid, long-term support relationship as well as those who express a sense of loss over a sister-relationship that seems thwarted from becoming all it could be. Saan Luong's narrative—a dream broken—is one of these.

Saan Luong had a dream. For thirteen difficult years, this dream was her only relief from the harsh reality of her life. Then one day, her dream came true—and she discovered that what she'd been nurturing was more of a nightmare. 1

In 1979, Saan was a skinny ten-year-old living in Vietnam, the youngest in a desperately poor family of five older sisters and one brother. At that time, the Communist rulers decreed that upon reaching fifteen, a child could be taken away to work for the country. Some children were never seen by their families again. Saan's brother had already been arrested by the Communists for carrying forged papers, and had escaped to China. Saan's parents decided to try to save their littlest girl by pirating her out of Vietnam before the government came to look for her.

"My mother told me we were going to visit my grandmother in the country," Saan begins. "But the way we went was different, and she said we were going to stop at another place first.

"Just before we leave, everybody is unusually nice to me. My sisters buy me things, get me clothes, and I'm thinking, 'wow, this is a big change.' Usually they're too busy to pay any attention to me. They even take me out to a restaurant, and we were so poor we could never afford to go out to eat. They know I'm going away. I don't.

"We got to this place and my mother left me with her friend and said 5
she'd be back soon. But the boat had to take off before she came, or else the Communists would catch us. My uncle was supposed to be with me, but he got arrested. He yelled at me to run to the boat. I didn't know what was happening or where I was going. I just did what he told me. There were a hundred and fifty of us on a seventeen-foot boat. All I can see are strange people and I don't understand anything."

Four other boats, fleeing at the same time, capsized. Their survivors were loaded onto Saan's boat and the food supply thrown overboard to accommodate the added weight. "I am terrified," Saan remembers. "You can't move. You sit with your knees up to your chin. You go to the bathroom right there in your clothes because if you get up you lose your seat. I'm the only one that doesn't have my family, and I am thinking, I'm the youngest one, why me? Why not my sisters? They must not like me."

The refugee camp on the Malaysian border where Saan was eventually interred housed seven thousand people. She was squeezed into a tiny hut with twenty-four others—including her mother's friend, whom she finally found.

"There was stink and worms. But we were lucky; it was far from the smelly bathrooms. I cried a lot."

After several months she managed to get a letter to her parents, who thought she had drowned. In their reply, she learned why they'd sent her away and how they hoped she'd have a better life. Frightened and isolated in a crowded, filthy camp filled with strangers, their way of "saving" her seemed like a cruel joke.

After a year and a half in the refugee center, Saan was relocated to Hawaii, 10
where the daughter of her mother's friend lived. It was there she discovered that her brother had made his way to Philadelphia.

"It was, oh my god, so great! I will see my brother. He can take care of me. All that stuff. But when I move in with him, it's not like that. He's about twenty years older than me. He gambles a lot and he doesn't care about me at all."

When she reached fourteen and could lie about her age, she got a job in a Chinese restaurant and moved in with a friend.

"Every day I go to school until two and I go to work until nine P.M. And I think how different my life would be if I had my sisters with me. I watch my friends with sisters close to them, and it breaks my heart. Always I think if my sisters were here it would change everything because sisters always know what we want.

"I pray for my sisters to come here so they could help me and do the things older sisters are supposed to do for younger ones. I write them how I wish they were here so we can do things together and talk like American sisters do. They write back and say the same. So all the years go by, and I have these hopes and dreams that one day they'll come and we'll be so happy."

It didn't seem like such an impossible dream. Her brother had applied 15
for visas, but then had let the paperwork lapse.

"I found a teacher who would co-sign so we could get the family out fast, but my brother wouldn't give me the information I needed. 'What do you know? You're the youngest and I'm the oldest. I know everything.' One year passed. Another year. Another year. Finally I just start writing to everybody." Saan wrote to the embassy in Thailand, to her senator, to the U.S. State department, to one congressman after the other. Finally, in the fluorescent glare of an airport lounge, she was reunited with her parents and three of her five sisters—fourteen years after their separation. When she'd left them, she was a frail, sheltered Vietnamese child. Now she was a twenty-four-year-old American woman with a son and a daughter of her own.

"I was so happy and excited. I had my children draw the welcome signs in Chinese and Vietnamese. But once I see them in the airport, it's like they just see me yesterday. I cry, but there are no hugs or kisses. Not like a normal family. I think deep down inside they must be happy, too. But they don't show it. My dad and mom look glad to see me, but not my sisters. They don't seem to want to know anything about my life without them all these years.

"Then the next day, they tell me they want to go home. Later I learn they had been writing to my brother that they don't want to come, but they write me different letters because they don't want to get me upset. It costs five thousand dollars to bring them here. I don't have money to send them back.

"They're always complaining. In Vietnam, they were spoiled. They never work a day. My mother took care of them. Here they have to work in a sewing factory. They say it's tough and boring and cold. Oh my god, this is not what I expected! I think my sisters will listen to what I have to say. They'll help me take care of my children so I can go back and get my high school degree. But nobody even wants to stay with me. I understand my parents are old, and old people always want to stay with a son. My brother doesn't treat them nice, though. But why don't my sisters stay with me? My husband and I have a basement in our house that we fixed up so nice as a bedroom for them, but they won't come.

"Every time we see each other, we can laugh and talk, but once we go 20
down to something personal or deep, the party's over. It doesn't matter how much older they are—one is 35, one is 34, and one is 38—or how young I am. We're supposed to talk to each other and take care of each other. But my connection with them has a line. We go so far and that's it.

"Part of me is in pain; they don't know anything I'm feeling. It hurts to see the three of them very close and good friends. They know everything about what the other wants and likes, but they say I can never be a part of them because I'm too American.

"Maybe it would be better if they hadn't come at all, and I just had my dream of what it would be like if we are all here, sisters together. Inside of me I love them. I try to think they love me too, even though they don't act like they do. I have to accept that I can't change them. I can't force them to be what I want. I can't make them love me. That was just a dream."

Understanding

1. Saan Luong harbored a dream for fourteen years. Was it realistic? Would you advise her to keep that dream alive?

2. What values does Luong imply in her narrative?
3. How do Luong's sisters feel about their situation? Are they selfish, spoiled, and unloving, as Luong suggests?
4. Would it have been better not to have dreamed at all?

Responding

1. In the introduction to *Sisters,* Carol Saline writes that "Brothers share the biological link, but they're . . . well . . . just different. They rarely seem as emotionally glued as girls who grew up under the same roof. What sets sisters apart from brothers—and also from friends—is a very intimate meshing of heart, soul, and the mystical cords of memory." From your own experience, do you agree?
2. Write your own sisters or brothers story, as though you were contributing to Saline and Wohlmuth's book. Of course, it doesn't have to be a dream of a relationship unfulfilled. In fact, it doesn't have to be a dream at all, but a story of who you are to each other. (If you don't have a same-sex sibling relationship, write about a cousin or other same-sex person who could take the place of a sister or brother in your life.) What photograph would accompany your story?
3. Write the same story as you did for question 2, but this time from your brother's or sister's point of view.
4. In your opinion, what was your mother's or father's dream for you and your sister or brother? Did they encourage closeness—"family first"—or competition? Did they exhibit favoritism?
5. If you are a brother with two sisters, write their story from your point of view as the observer. Bring the reader up-to-date on how that relationship is now. What makes it that way?

Connecting

How would Saan Luong answer Hughes's question at the end of "Harlem"?

Bessie

Sarah L. Delany and A. Elizabeth Delany with Amy Hill Hearth

A. Elizabeth (Bessie) and Sarah (Sadie) Delany were both more than a hundred years old when they started to tell their stories in this form to Amy Hill Hearth, a correspondent for the *New York Times,* between September 1991 and April 1993. Their book has been so popular that a play, "Having Our Say," has toured the United States to much acclaim. Their voices are "participating in a tradition as old as time: the passing of knowledge and experience from one generation to the next."

These sisters' voices are a living chronicle of an entire generation of black Americans who moved to Harlem in the 1920s and 1930s with dreams of a better life. New York's Harlem, the center for the Harlem Renaissance, which produced celebrated African American writers, Jazz Age musicians, and "an undisputed capital of nightlife," also had a stable, churchgoing side. Into this exciting high-energy neighborhood, inhabited by two hundred thousand black people, came people with dreams.

Dr. Elizabeth Delany and Sarah Delany were born in Raleigh, North Carolina, on the campus of St. Augustine's College. Their father, born into slavery and freed at age seven, was an administrator at the college and America's first elected black Episcopal bishop. Sarah received her bachelor's and master's degrees from Teachers College at Columbia University and was New York City's first appointed black home economics teacher on the high school level. Elizabeth received her degree in dentistry from Columbia University and was the second black woman licensed to practice dentistry in New York City. Elizabeth, whose "dream" is excerpted here, died at age 104 in Mount Vernon, New York, in September 1995.

I had always dreamed I would become a medical doctor, but I ran out of time and money. I was in my late twenties already and I would have needed a few more credits to get into medical school. I was worried that by the time I earned the money and took those classes, I'd be too old. 1

So I picked up some science courses at Shaw University in Raleigh with the intention of being ready to enroll in a dental degree program in New York. My brother Harry was a dentist, and he was going to see if I could enroll at New York University, where he had graduated. But this was in 1918, and New York University would not take women in its dentistry program.

Instead, I enrolled at Columbia University. This was in the fall of 1919. There were eleven women out of a class of about 170. There were about six colored men. And then there was me. I was the only colored woman!

Columbia was intimidating, but so was everything else. The city was exciting and terrifying at the same time. I couldn't understand why the high-rise buildings didn't fall down, and the subway, well, that about worried me to death! A classmate of mine at Columbia said, "Let's try that old subway." And I said, "I don't think so." And he said, "What, are you afraid?" And I said, "Of course not! If you're willing to try it, so will I!" So we went and everything worked out OK, though once we were on it, I remember whispering to him, "You sure you know how we can get off this thing?"

Most of the students at the dental school were self-assured city folk, and 5
their families were paying their tuition. I never had the luxury of focusing completely on my studies. I always had money on my mind. I needed more, honey! I had saved money from my teaching years in the South, but it wasn't enough. I remember that I always wore an old brown sweater to my classes, because I couldn't even afford a coat. One day, my brother Harry surprised me. He bought me a beautiful coat, with a small fur collar! When I put that coat on, honey, I looked sensational. I looked as good as Mrs. Astor's pet mule. And the first time I wore it to class, the students stood up and applauded. In a way, it was mean, because they were sort of making fun of me. It was like, "Oh, that Bessie Delany finally has something decent to wear." But I didn't care, no, sir!

My brothers were having the same difficulty with money, so they all worked their way through college as Pullman porters, which was one of the few jobs a Negro man could get. Hubert used to joke that he had earned an MBC degree—"master's of baggage carrying."

It was always harder for a Negro to get work than a white person. Even the street merchants in Harlem, in those days, were mostly white. There were certain companies that were nicer to colored people than others. For instance, everybody knew that Nestlé's would hire Negroes, but Hershey's wouldn't. Once I had encountered that, I used to walk through Harlem and scold any Negro eating a Hershey bar. Usually, they would stop eating it but sometimes they thought I was crazy. Well, honey, I do not allow Hershey candy in my home to this day.

As a woman, you couldn't be a Pullman porter, and I refused to work as a maid for white folks. So in the summer, I would go with my little sister Julia, who had come up from Raleigh to study at Juilliard, to look for factory jobs. And you know what? They would want to hire Julia, because she was lighter than me. But we made it clear it was both of us or neither of us, and sometimes we'd get the job.

Once, we had an assembly-line job where they made sewing needles, and our job was to package them in these little batches, so they were ready for sale. Then for a while, we worked as ushers at a movie house. The pay was $12 a week, and we saw all these wonderful movies. My favorite movie star was Bing Crosby. Lord, we had fun. But I was always treated worse than Julia, and it was made clear that it was because I was darker-skinned. Julia was quite light—more like Sadie—and I guess she might even have passed for white if she had tried.

One time, we were waiting on line to get factory work and this white man 10
tried to give me a break. It was always a white guy who was in charge, of course. He said, "Oh, I see. You are Spanish." This was supposed to be my cue to nod my head, since they'd hire you if you were "Spanish." But this made me furious. I said, "No, I am not Spanish. I am an *American Negro!*" I turned and walked out of there and Julia followed me.

Today I know they have this thing called Affirmative Action. I can see why they need it. There are some places where colored folks would *never,* not in a thousand years, get a job. But you know what? I really am philosophically against it. I say: "Let the best person get the job, period." Everybody's better off in the long run.

It was probably a good thing that I was a little older, mature, and so determined or I never would have made it through dental school. I had a few girlfriends, but I never told any of them that I was about ten years older. I never talked about where I came from, my teaching years, or any of that. I was always a big talker, but at dental school I was a private person. There was one girl in particular who used to bug me. She would say, "Bessie, how old are you?" or "Bessie, were you a teacher before you came to dental school?" But I didn't tell her anything.

The reason I was so secretive is that I wanted to be taken seriously. Most of the women were not taken seriously. Truth is, it was just after World War I and a lot of men were still overseas, or killed, so those girls were just looking for husbands. But not me. The boys, well, I stayed away from them. The white boys looked down on me and the colored boys were too busy trying to goose my behind! I had no interest in their shenanigans. I was a good-looking gal, and that always got me in trouble. But I was there to learn!

Before I enrolled in dental school I had a long talk with my Mama. She said, "You must decide whether you want to get married someday, or have a career. Don't go putting all that time and effort into your education and career if you think you want to get married."

It didn't occur to anyone that you could be married *and* have a career. 15
Well, I set my sights on the career. I thought, what does any man really have to offer me? I've already raised half the world, so I don't feel the desire to have babies! And why would I want to give up my freedom and independence to take care of some man? In those days, a man expected you to be in charge of a perfect household, to look after his every need. Honey, I wasn't interested! I wasn't going to be bossed around by some man! So the men at college learned to leave me alone, after a while. There was no foolin' with me! In my yearbook, under the picture, they wrote: "Bessie Delany, the Perfect Lady." And that was the truth.

I studied very hard in dentistry school. My brother Harry—he was called "Hap" once he moved to New York—helped me out. He was a sweet brother. He loaned me some dental instruments, which were very expensive—things like that.

I remember like yesterday the first time our class had to do dissections. This was at the morgue at Bellevue Hospital in New York. The first two years of dental school at that time were identical to medical school, and we all had to do them. Sometimes there weren't enough corpses to go around and the dental students would fight for a head because, well, what we really wanted to examine was the teeth and jaw. And some dental students got stuck with body parts that weren't exactly relevant.

Well, that first day all the girls in the class were just a-squealing and a-screaming and a-carrying on. And I strode in there like I was born to do it. They all said, "Look at that Bessie Delany, why, she sure isn't scared." Truth is, I was a wreck. I had never touched a dead body before!

When we were children, the Webb family, who were farmers at Saint Aug's, had a baby that died, and this little girl at the school named Maggie dared Sadie to touch that baby. People weren't propped up in funeral homes the way they are today. You were wrapped in a shroud and laid out in your own parlor, and that's where this baby was. Afterward, I said to Sadie, "Well, what was it like?" And Sadie said, "Oooh, it was just like touching a piece of marble, hard and cold."

Well, I kept thinking about that poor, marblelike baby while I dissected 20
my first cadaver. We had to fish around and look for these veins and arteries and nerves and things. Yes, it was pretty disgusting but I was a great actress. I was determined to be the best dentist there ever was, and I knew I had to get through this!

I'd dissect a cadaver any day, rather than have to deal with some of those old white professors. Yes, sir! To be fair—oh, it's so hard to be fair—I have to admit that some of them treated me just fine, especially the Dean of Students. He was an old white man, yet he was particularly supportive of me. But one instructor really had it out for me. There was an assignment where he failed me, yet I knew my work was good. One of my white girlfriends said, "Bessie, let me turn in your work as if it was mine, and see what grade he gives it."

I'll tell you what happened, honey. She passed with my failed work! That was the kind of thing that could make you crazy, as a Negro. It's no wonder some of us have stopped trying altogether. But as my Papa used to say, "Don't ever give up. Remember, they can segregate you, but they can't control your mind. Your mind's still yours." Ain't it the truth.

Another thing that happened to me at Columbia was that I was accused of stealing. Me, Bessie Delany! Honey, I had never stolen nothin' in my life. This is what happened: There was a white girl who was taking expensive dental instruments. Even my things started disappearing, one by one. It was puzzling. They cost a lot of money, and some of mine belonged to Hap, and I took great pains not to lose them. So none of us could understand where this stuff was going off to.

This girl was a dental student, and we learned later that her boyfriend, also a dental student, had talked her into stealing these tools. He was selling them somewhere in New York. Well, it got to the point where they brought in police detectives. And we were summoned in the hallway where our lockers were, and the police asked me to open my locker, and they searched it.

We were all gathered around, and I saw that this girl—her name was 25
Rose—was standing closest to my locker. When it was opened, behind her back she sort of casually tossed a dental instrument in there. No one saw it but me, and I said in a loud voice, "Rose, what did you toss into my locker?" And the detective and everyone else realized what she had done, and she was caught. She was trying to frame me! And she knew she'd have gotten away with it because it would be easy for everyone to believe that this little darkey was a thief. Now, that just kills me.

Would you believe that Rose and her boyfriend were allowed to finish dental school? They graduated! Honey, if it had been me, I would have been expelled. I would have gone to jail.

I'll tell you something else that annoyed me. When they opened my locker, everybody was surprised at how neat it was. They thought Negroes were dirty, sloppy people, but my locker was perfectly clean and neat, and my one uniform—the only one I could afford—was scrubbed, starched, and ironed. The other girls' lockers were pigsties. And the Dean said, "Look at Miss Delany's locker! It is an example to you all."

You see, when you are colored, everyone is always looking for your faults. If you are going to make it, you have to be entirely honest, clean, brilliant, and so on. Because if you slip up once, the white folks say to each other, "See, what'd I tell you." So you don't have to be as good as white people, you have to be *better or the best.* When Negroes are average, *they fail,* unless they are very, very lucky. Now, if you're average and *white,* honey, you can go far. Just look at Dan Quayle. If that boy was colored he'd be washing dishes somewhere.

There are plenty of white folks who say, "Why haven't Negroes gotten further than they have?" They say about Negroes, "What's wrong with them?" To those white people, I have this to say: *Are you kidding?*

Let me tell you something. Even on my graduation day at Columbia, I ran 30
into prejudice. It was the sixth of June, 1923. There I was, getting my Doctor of Dental Surgery Degree, and I was on top of the world. But you know what? The class selected me as the marshall, and I thought it was an honor. And then I found out—I heard them talking—it was because no one wanted to march beside me in front of their parents. It was a way to get rid of me. The class marshall carried the flag and marched out front, alone.

I suppose I should be grateful to Columbia, that at that time they let in colored people. Well, I'm not. They let me in but they beat me down for being there! I don't know how I got through that place, except when I was young nothing could hold me back. No, sir! I thought I could change the world. It took me a hundred years to figure out I *can't* change the world. I can only change Bessie. And, honey, that ain't easy, either.

Understanding

1. Bessie's dream was to become a medical doctor, but by her own reasoning, she would be too old by the time she picked up the classes she needed as prerequisites, so she decided on dental school. What kept her going?

2. "Their story, as the Delany sisters like to say, is not meant as 'black' or 'women's' history, but American history. It belongs to all of us." Why would they make such a distinction, and what might they mean?
3. What were the obstacles that Bessie had to overcome in 1919 to make her dream come true?
4. Bessie's storytelling makes it seem as though we are listening instead of reading. What about the style and tone of this selection makes the reader feel that way?

Responding

1. How might your dreams have been different if you were of another "color"?
2. Bessie designated dental school as a time to be secretive. Examine her reasons. Reflect on a time in your life when you continually withheld information and yourself for a reason.
3. What is your dream career? Do you dream of being a dentist? A concert pianist? A microbiologist? A wildlife conservationist? A photographer? What attracts you? What steps are you taking to make that possibility into a reality?
4. Interview an older person to find out what his or her dream career was. What happened? Record the story as an oral history.

Connecting

Though they were of very different generations, what was similar about the Delany sisters' schooling and Lee's in her selection "Back to School" (see chapter three)?

Five Dreams

Studs Terkel

Chicago writer Studs Terkel has been around for a long time, writing about people like you and me. The impetus for his work is his profound fascination with us—fellow humans, living and finding our way in America. As a collector of stories, he has talked to thousands of people, encouraging them to put words to their lives, their memories, and their dreams. All of this is in the contexts of historical events (the Great Depression), everyday events (working), or themes (the American dream), to give his readers both individual and collective perspectives on common human experiences. In 1980 he published *American Dreams: Lost & Found,* from which we have selected dreams from the following five individuals: Jill Robinson, daughter of a former Hollywood film producer; Norman Maclean, writer and university professor; Arnold Schwarzenegger, film star; George Malley, concerned father; and Linda Haas, Lane Tech high school student.

Terkel says that the book contains hundreds of American voices captured by "hunch, circumstance, and a rough idea." He does not try to present an American "truth"; instead he compares the collection to a jazz work and summarizes his findings as "an attempt, of theme and improvisation, to recount dreams, lost and found, and a recognition of possibility."

FANTASIA

Jill Robinson

She is the daughter of a former Hollywood film producer.

Growing up in Hollywood was the only reality I knew. The closest I ever came to feeling glamorous was from my mother's maid, a woman named Dorothy, who used to call me Glamour. She was black. In those days, she was called colored. When I would see my mother—or my mother's secretary, 'cause there was a hierarchy—interviewing maids or cooks, I'd think of maids and cooks represented in the movies. 1

I used not to like to go to school. I'd go to work with my father. I'd like to be with him because power didn't seem like work. He had four or five secretaries, and they were always pretty. I thought: How wonderful to have pretty secretaries. I used to think they'd be doing musical numbers. I could imagine them tapping along with his mail. I never saw it real.

To me, a studio head was a man who controlled everyone's lives. It was like being the principal. It was someone you were scared of, someone who knew everything, knew what you were thinking, knew where you were going, knew when you were driving on the studio lot at eighty miles an hour, knew that you had not been on the set in time. The scoldings the stars got. There was a paternalism. It was feudal. It was an archaic system designed to keep us playing: Let's pretend, let's make believe.

First of all, you invented someone, someone's image of someone. Then you'd infantilize them, keep them at a level of consciousness, so they'd be convinced that this is indeed who they are. They had doctors at the studios: "Oh, you're just fine, honey. Take this and you'll be just fine." These stars, who influenced our dreams, had no more to do with their own lives than fairies had, or elves.

5 I remember playing with my brother and sister. We would play Let's Make a Movie the way other kids would play cowboys and Indians. We'd cry, we'd laugh. We'd do whatever the characters did. We had elaborate costumes and sets. We drowned our dolls and all the things one does. The difference was, if we didn't get it right, we'd play it again until we liked it. We even incorporated into our child play the idea of the dailies and the rushes. The repeats of film scenes to get the right angle. If the princess gets killed in a scene, she gets killed again and again and again. It's okay. She gets to live again. No one ever dies. There's no growing up. This was reality to us.

I had a feeling that out there, there were very poor people who didn't have enough to eat. But they wore wonderfully colored rags and did musical numbers up and down the streets together. My mother did not like us to go into what was called the servants' wing of the house.

My mother was of upper-class Jewish immigrants. They lost everything in the depression. My father tried to do everything he could to revive my mother's idea of what life had been like for her father in the court of the czar. Whether her father was ever actually in the court is irrelevant. My father tried to make it classy for her. It never was good enough, never could be. She couldn't be a Boston Brahmin.

Russian-Jewish immigrants came from the *shtetls* and ghettos out to Hollywood: this combination jungle-tropical paradise crossed with a nomadic desert. In this magical place that had no relationship to any reality they had ever seen before in their lives, or that anyone else had ever seen, they decided to create their idea of an eastern aristocracy. I'm talking about the kind of homes they would never be invited to. It was, of course, overdone. It was also the baronial mansions of the dukes' homes that their parents could never have gotten into. Goldwyn, Selznick, Zukor, Lasky, Warner. Hollywood—the American Dream—is a Jewish idea.

In a sense, it's a Jewish revenge on America. It combines the Puritan ethic—there's no sex, no ultimate satisfaction—with baroque magnificence. The happy ending was the invention of Russian Jews, designed to drive Americans crazy.

10 It was a marvelous idea. What could make them crazy but to throw back at them their small towns? Look how happy it is here. Compare the real small towns with the small town on the MGM back lot. There's no resemblance.

The street is Elm Street. It's so green, so bright, of lawns and trees. It's a town somewhere in the center of America. It's got the white fence and the big porch around the house. And it's got three and four generations. They're turn-of-the-century people before they learned how to yell at each other. It's the boy and girl running into each other's arms. And everybody else is singing. It's everybody sitting down to dinner and looking at each other, and everyone looks just wonderful. No one's mad at anyone else. It's all so simple. It's all exactly what I say it is.

Aunt Mary is a little looney and lives with us because she loves us. It's not that she's crazy and gonna wind up killing one of us one of these days. Or that she's drunk. It's simply that she'd rather live with us and take care of us. The father would be Lewis Stone. He'd have a little bit of a temper now and then. The mother is definitely Spring Byington. She's daffy, but she's never deaf. She hears everything you say and she listens. And she hugs you and her hug is soft and sweet-smelling. The daughter is Judy Garland when she believed in Aunt Em. The boy is Robert Walker before he realized he was gonna drink himself to death. And love and marriage would be innocence and tenderness. And no sex.

The dream to me was to be blond, tall, and able to disappear. I loved movies about boys running away to sea. I wanted to be the laconic, cool, tall, Aryan male. Precisely the opposite of the angry, anxious, sort of mottle-haired Jewish girl.

I wanted to be this guy who could walk away from any situation that got a little rough. Who could walk away from responsibility. The American Dream, the idea of the happy ending, is an avoidance of responsibility and commitment. If something ends happily, you don't have to worry about it tomorrow.

The idea of the movie star, the perfect-looking woman or man who had 15
breakfast at a glass table on a terrace where there are no mosquitoes. No one ever went to the bathroom in movies. I grew up assuming that movie stars did not. I thought it was terrible to be a regular human being. Movie stars did not look awful, ever. They never threw up. They never got really sick, except in a wonderful way where they'd get a little sweaty, get sort of a gloss on the face, and then die. They didn't shrivel up or shrink away. They didn't have acne. The woman didn't have menstrual cramps. Sex, when I ran across it, in no way resembled anything I had ever seen in the movies. I didn't know how to respond.

I think the reason we're so crazy sexually in America is that all our responses are acting. We don't know how to feel. We know how it looked in the movies. We know that in the movies it's inconceivable that the bad guy will win. Therefore we don't get terribly involved in any cause. The good guy's gonna win anyway. It's a marvelous political weapon.

The Hollywood phenomenon of the forties—the Second World War—was distinct from the Vietnam War. War was fine. Sure there were bad things, but there were musicals. Comedies about soldiers. The dream was to marry someone in uniform. I believed every bit of it. I saw how the movies were made and still I believed it.

I remember seeing a carpenter in front of the house and telling my father he looked like Roy Rogers and that he ought to test him. He did. The guy couldn't act. We were always testing everyone, always seeing what raw material they would be. I'd sit in class pretending to be an executive. I'd be sitting there figuring out who could this kid play, who could that one play. I used to look at Robert Redford in class and imagine he would be a movie star. In fourth grade. You always looked at humans as property. It affected all our lives.

I hated the idea that I was bright. There was a collision between bright and pretty and seductive. I wanted to be one of those girls the guys just wanted to do one thing to. I wanted to be one of those blond jobs. That's what they used to call them—jobs. A tall job. A slim job. Somebody you could work on.

I wanted to be Rhonda Fleming or Lana Turner. I refused to see what the 20
inside of their lives was like. They didn't see it either. It was carefully kept from them. My God, look at the life. Getting up at five-thirty in the morning before your brain has begun to function, getting rolled out in a limousine, and having people work on your body and your face. Remember, they were very young people when they came out here. Imagine having all your waking life arranged all the time. They became machines. No wonder the sensitive ones went insane or killed themselves.

The studio had the power. The studio would hire the fan club. The head of the club was on the star's payroll. The star was usually not even aware of where the money was going, to whom, for what. The whole thing was manufactured. Fame is manufactured. Stardom is manufactured. After all these years, it still comes as a surprise to me.

The rest of the country for me consisted of the Sherry-Netherlands Hotel, which I assumed my father owned because of the name—I thought they spelled it wrong[1]—and the Pump Room.[2] We would take the Super Chief. You would have a drawing room and two bedrooms all the way across the country. You would get to Chicago, and all the luggage would be transferred to the Ambassador East Hotel, where you would spend the night. You would have lunch with the gossip columnist. The first booth to the right. Perish the thought you weren't invited for lunch because you would know power had eluded you. Then you would get on the Twentieth Century, which I thought Zanuck owned.[3] I couldn't understand why my father would take that train.

I assumed Hollywood owned everything. It never occurred to me that there was any other business. Everything was designed to sustain in the motion-picture business. Hollywood people played at being businessmen. They weren't. The people who really handled the money were the stockholders in the East. They'd come out like crows. We were scared to death of them. The Hollywood children instinctively knew the East meant trouble.

When they'd come out, you'd have more formal dinners. Everyone would be on the alert. Extra help was hired. They came in with hats and dark suits, chalk pinstripe suits. They were a different sort. You couldn't seduce these guys to smile. They were tough. There was a fear that our toy would be taken away.

During the McCarthy days, some of the children we used to play with were 25
suddenly not around. There was this silence, there was an absence. Actually, I don't even remember missing some of the kids. I do remember a sense of resentment from them later. I never knew exactly what it was. I had gone to

parties with them. As kids, we weren't aware of each other as individuals. We were more aware of each other's parents.

We knew our playmates' parents' screen credits. The kids were interesting or uninteresting depending upon who their parents were. You wanted to get in good with this kid because it might be good for business. One would be asked when one came home: Did they know who you were? Favorite words, hateful words. Do they know who you are? It was defined entirely by who your father is.

When I was playing canasta with the daughter of someone more powerful than my father, I had the feeling she'd better win. It just felt better to lose because her father held the strings. Winning games didn't mean that much to me. I was really a company kid. Hollywood was really the old mill town. We weren't told to behave this way by our parents. We just picked it up from the movies. Kids in the movies were pretty servile and knew which side of their bread was buttered.

When I was young, I thought the best movie I ever saw was *An American in Paris*. Maybe almost as good as *Wizard of Oz* and *Gone with the Wind*. If real life couldn't be applied to either of those two movies, it didn't exist. Everything about character, everything about dreams, everything about what really happened to you, was in those. There was nothing else you needed to know about life. They were the primary myth makers, these two films.

When my parents sold the house, all I could think of was Scarlett. When I went to sell dresses in Saks and got out my book of receipts, there was one little fist that shot up and I said: "As God is my witness, I'll never be poor again." And I really thought: If Scarlett can do it, I can do it. I wanted all my life to have the guts of Rhett and say to the men who drove me crazy: "Frankly, my dear, I don't give a damn."

The thing that affected me most doesn't exist any more. It's easy to forget how gorgeous and unreal that land was. Oz was not designed by art directors. Oz was just a copy of how it looked when you came from the East and first saw California. If you compare Dorothy's first vision of Oz, when she walks out that morning, it is exactly how I feel whenever I come home to California after I've been out East. There's nothing like the color. Can you imagine what it must have been for those people coming out there? Technicolor is a copy of what was actually California. My God, in such a land, how dare you not be happy? It's just not there any more. What was real to me and magical had nothing to do with the movies and more to do with the land. The whole thing has been computerized, wrecked.

The rest of the country was sepia-toned, like Kansas. My idea of the rest of the country came from the movies. The colleges were always seas of bright green and brick buildings with ivy and cheerleaders. And football teams. That's what you saw in the movies. I think the movies caused more trouble to the children who grew up in Hollywood, who never saw the rest of the country, than they did to the people outside. The movies were my textbooks for everything else in the world. When it wasn't, I altered it.

If I saw a college, I would see only cheerleaders or blonds. If I saw New York City, I would want to go to the slums I'd seen in the movies, where the tough kids played. If I went to Chicago, I'd want to see the brawling factories and the gangsters.

My illusions disappeared when I began to be a writer and had to look at the reality. I never learned it from psychiatrists. The American Dream is really money. When it finally sunk in that I was going to have to support two children, it was terrifying.

I remember lying in my bed in this beautiful castle house in the hills. All through the windows were these bowers of jacaranda trees with purple flowers, and the sun was shining. My husband called and said President Kennedy had been shot and killed. My image came from *Tale of Two Cities*. I thought: They're gonna tear the place apart.

Who is "they"? They, the country, the people. The people I saw in news reels, 35
March of Time movies, where there'd be crowd scenes. I never thought of people as individuals, but just those crowd scenes. The extras. They're gonna get goddamn mad, the extras, and they're gonna tear the fucking place apart. It was all movies.

They made a movie of Kennedy being shot. And they kept playing it over and over again on television. I kept watching it like every other American, hoping this time the ending would be different. Why did we watch it day after day after day, if not to see that maybe the ending was going to be different? Maybe they'll do the movie right this time. But they couldn't retake it.

It just couldn't happen to these people, these extras. They had already taken their punishment. In the movies there was always fish thrown to the cats, the extras, who were the preview audience. I'd see them lurking outside the theater. There was a jeopardy clause in the censor's code: you couldn't have a child really hurt. I thought there ought to be a clause: you can't really have the president killed. It's too upsetting to the extras. They're not gonna tolerate it.

Out of the corner of my eye, I knew there were people watching who seemed smarter than we were. These would be the writers, who were cynical. They didn't believe it was all gonna work out all right. They didn't believe all movies were wonderful. I sensed this coming. I think the snake in the Garden of Eden was my growing awareness. The reality was always there. I chose not to see it. The thing that terrified me most was my own intelligence and power of observation. The more I saw, the more I tried not to see. So I drank too much and took as many drugs as I could so as not to see.

Couldn't bear it, the reality. Couldn't bear to feel my father was wrong. Couldn't bear the idea that it was not the best of all possible worlds. Couldn't bear the idea that there was a living to be made. That punishment does not always come to those that deserve it. That good people die in the end.

The triumph of the small man was another wonderful Hollywood myth, 40
very popular in the mid-forties. Once that dream went, once that illusion went, we all began to suspect what was really going on. Once we became conscious, that was the snake. It was the awareness of the power, awareness that war was not a parade, awareness of reality. This is what killed the old movies. It was the consciousness of the extras and I became one of the extras.

I think we're all skidding away, we're destroying. California is just a little bit of it. The more bleak I become, the more—I live in Connecticut, okay?—I read somewhere Connecticut has the highest incidence of intestinal cancer in the world. I think that's because we eat ourselves alive there. We're filled with despair, and it just rots us away. Where I live looks exactly like the MGM back-lot idea of a small New England town. There's no pressure in Connecticut, it's all okay. Nobody is working much, there aren't many jobs, a lot of businesses are failing. But it looks so sweet. It looks endearing. During the blizzard, you would have thought that Currier and Ives came in there. That several people I know lost everything they own in that goddamn endearing blizzard, nobody really thinks about that. It looks like the American Dream.

Okay, we found Connecticut, and it doesn't work either. They go out to retirement homes in California, and they still get sick. And they worry about earthquakes. We always knew there'd be an earthquake. I loved the people who were trying to make it happen in the sixties. They were down there, on the Andreas Fault, with chisels and hammers, a whole group of fanatics, trying to saw it off. They needed the ending to make the earthquake happen. They predicted it and, fearful that it would not come true, they actually went up there. They really believed that God needed help. I say He's never needed help with that. Even my God is a movie god. He really runs the studio. Into the ground, as my grandmother would have said.

The Hollywood dream has driven us crazy, but no more than any other mythology. Religious orders that govern whole states and decide what they should believe. Greek and Roman gods and goddesses. Catholicism. Hollywood is just another draft, a more polished version.

What else are we gonna live by if not dreams? We need to believe in something. What would really drive us crazy is to believe this reality we run into every day is all there is. If I don't believe there's that happy ending out there—that will-you-marry-me in the sky—I can't keep working today. That's true, I think, for all of us.

* * *

GENERATIONS: FIRST AND SECOND

Norman Maclean

Professor emeritus, University of Chicago

My father and mother were immigrants from Canada. My father was all 45
Scotch and came from Nova Scotia, from a large family that was on poor land. His great belief was in all men being equal under God. That old Bobby Burns line: A man's a man for a' that and a' that. He was a Presbyterian minister, and it was very deep with him.

My father loved America so much that, although he had a rather heavy Scotch burr when he came to this country, by the time I was born, it was all gone. He regarded it as his American duty to get rid of it. He despised Scotch Presbyterian ministers who went heavy on their Scotch burr. He put a terrific commitment on me to be an American. I, the eldest son, was expected to complete the job.

He told me I had to learn the American language. He spoke beautifully, but he didn't have the American idioms. He kept me home until I was ten and a half to teach me. He taught me how to write American. No courses in show-and-tell and personality adjustment. [Laughs.] I was young and I thought I was tough and I knew it was beautiful and I was a little bit crazy but hadn't noticed it yet. You took those little pieces of American speech and listened carefully for 'em and you put them together. My American training went clear down into my language.

He was great on rhythm. He read us the Bible every morning. We got down on our knees by our chairs and we prayed. We had it twice a day, the great King James translation, after breakfast and after what we called supper.

Literature was important to him: the prose of Mark Twain, and the odd combination of Franklin Roosevelt and Wilson and Whitman. He knew it wasn't English. It was American. He couldn't get over the fact that Wilson was the son of a Presbyterian minister. He was the model for many generations of prose writers, including Roosevelt.

The family was the center of the universe and the center of America. I don't know if we have *an* American Dream. We have American Dreams. One of his biggest dreams was the dream of great education in this country and the necessity of every person to be educated.

I was the first person in his family not to make his living with his hands. "Maclean" means son of a carpenter. That's what my family had been. They were all carpenters. My father was the pride and joy of his sisters because he made his living without his hands. He was a marvelous carpenter himself. He and I, way back in 1921, made this log cabin out there that's still mine.

Working with hands is one of our deepest and most beautiful characteristics. I think the most beautiful parts of the human body are the hands of certain men and women. I can't keep my eyes off them. I was brought up to believe that hands were the instrument of the mind. Even doing simple things. I still look pretty good with an axe. My father was very stylish with any tool he worked with. Yeah, the fishing rod also. He was just beautiful, pick up a four-ounce rod and throw that line across the Blackfoot River. It was just something beautiful to behold.

Roughly, I've managed one way or another till now to continue a life that is half intellectual and half back in the woods. I kept my cabin out there, although my family died long ago. Now that I'm retired, I spend a third of my life out there. I stay as long as the weather permits me. October, until the elk season is over.

In the city I cultivate beauty of several kinds. In twenty minutes, I can be where there are beaver and deer. I go walking practically every afternoon. Three or four times a week, I go out into the country. I've learned another kind of beauty we didn't have. I think the industrial geometric beauty of Chicago is just beyond belief. To go up the Calumet River by boat and see all those big elevators and cranes and all the big stuff over that dirty river, this is just pure design. Cézanne couldn't find more beautiful geometrical patterns. If I had to name the number one most beautiful sight in the world, given my taste, I would say standing at night by the Planetarium, looking across the bay at the big Hancock and Sears buildings. No place more beautiful. You can't be provincial about beauty.

55 As I've grown older, I've tried to put together the dreams into my own life. My cabin is only sixteen miles from the glaciers. It snows every month out there. And there are the Gothic halls of the University of Chicago. If you know of a more beautiful city college in the world, architecturally, I'd like to know it. University of London, Oxford, they're just outhouses in comparison.

You have to be gifted with a long life to attain a dream and make it harmonious. I feel infinitely grateful in my old age that I've had in this country, within my family, the training needed to be the best that was in me. It's no great thing, but at seventy-five, I'm fulfilled. There aren't any big pieces in me that never got a chance to come out. They may say at the end of my life, I have no alibis. I have two children of my own, whom I admire and love and try not to annoy very much. I see my father going right on with my children. You've got to pass the ball along.

* * *

ARRIVING: NOW

Arnold Schwarzenegger

Call me Arnold.

I was born in a little Austrian town, outside Graz. It was a 300-year-old house.

When I was ten years old, I had the dream of being the best in the world in something. When I was fifteen, I had a dream that I wanted to be the best body builder in the world and the most muscular man. It was not only a dream I dreamed at night. It was also a daydream. It was so much in my mind that I felt it had to become a reality. It took me five years of hard work. Five years later, I turned this dream into reality and became Mr. Universe, the best-built man in the world.

60 "Winning" is a very important word. There is one that achieves what he wanted to achieve and there are hundreds of thousands that failed. It singles you out: the winner.

I came out second three times, but that is not what I call losing. The bottom line for me was: Arnold has to be the winner. I have to win more often the Mr. Universe title than anybody else. I won it five times consecutively. I hold the record as Mr. Olympia, the top professional body-building championship. I won it six times. That's why I retired. There was nobody even close to me. Everybody gave up competing against me. That's what I call a winner.

When I was a small boy, my dream was not to be big physically, but big in a way that everybody listens to me when I talk, that I'm a very important person, that people recognize me and see me as something special. I had a big need for being singled out.

Also my dream was to end up in America. When I was ten years old, I dreamed of being an American. At the time I didn't know much about

America, just that it was a wonderful country. I felt it was where I belonged. I didn't like being in a little country like Austria. I did everything possible to get out. I did so in 1968, when I was twenty-one years old.

If I would believe in life after death, I would say my before-life I was living in America. That's why I feel so good here. It is the country where you can turn your dream into reality. Other countries don't have those things. When I came over here to America, I felt I was in heaven. In America, we don't have an obstacle. Nobody's holding you back.

Number One in America pretty much takes care of the rest of the world. 65
You kind of run through the rest of the world like nothing. I'm trying to make people in America aware that they should appreciate what they have here. You have the best tax advantages here and the best prices here and the best products here.

One of the things I always had was a business mind. When I was in high school, a majority of my classes were business classes. Economics and accounting and mathematics. When I came over here to this country, I really didn't speak English almost at all. I learned English and then started taking business courses, because that's what America is best known for: business. Turning one dollar into a million dollars in a short period of time. Also when you make money, how do you keep it?

That's one of the most important things when you have money in your hand, how can you keep it? Or make more out of it? Real estate is one of the best ways of doing that. I own apartment buildings, office buildings, and raw land. That's my love, real estate.

I have emotions. But what you do, you keep them cold or you store them away for a time. You must control your emotions, you must have command over yourself. Three, four months before a competition, I could not be interfered by other people's problems. This is sometimes called selfish. It's the only way you can be if you want to achieve something. Any emotional things inside me, I try to keep cold so it doesn't interfere with my training.

Many times things really touched me. I felt them and I felt sensitive about them. But I had to talk myself out of it. I had to suppress those feelings in order to go on. Sport is one of those activities where you really have to concentrate. You must pay attention a hundred percent to the particular thing you're doing. There must be nothing else on your mind. Emotions must not interfere. Otherwise, you're thinking about your girlfriend. You're in love, your positive energies get channeled into another direction rather than going into your weight room or making money.

You have to choose at a very early date what you want: a normal life or to 70
achieve things you want to achieve. I never wanted to win a popularity contest in doing things the way people want me to do it. I went the road I thought was best for me. A few people thought I was cold, selfish. Later they found out that's not the case. After I achieve my goal, I can be Mr. Nice Guy. You know what I mean?

California is to me a dreamland. It is the absolute combination of everything I was always looking for. It has all the money in the world there, show business there, wonderful weather there, beautiful country, ocean is there.

Snow skiing in the winter, you can go in the desert the same day. You have beautiful-looking people there. They all have a tan.

I believe very strongly in the philosophy of staying hungry. If you have a dream and it becomes a reality, don't stay satisfied with it too long. Make up a new dream and hunt after that one and turn it into reality. When you have that dream achieved, make up a new dream.

I am a strong believer in Western philosophy, the philosophy of success, of progress, of getting rich. The Eastern philosophy is passive, which I believe in maybe three percent of the time, and the ninety-seven percent is Western, conquering and going on. It's a beautiful philosophy, and America should keep it up.

* * *

ALONE

George Malley

A rainy day in June. It's a neighborhood of one- and two-story family dwellings on Chicago's Northwest Side. A blue-collar community. "Call it middle-working-class," he says.

He was living elsewhere when I first met him, about twelve years ago. "I moved from the old neighborhood where I lived for eighteen years. There was a new breed coming in with rehabs. These quite clever people, young professionals. Intellectuals, they were not. [Laughs.] Pseudo-intellectuals, yes.

"We decided to get out. We were no longer happy. We didn't speak the same language. In fact, we didn't exchange the same kind of looks. [Laughs.] But I still haven't found what I'm looking for."

I feel lonely. I am afraid. I don't see hope when I look at people. I used to think the world was such a wonderful place. I used to think that ultimately man would surmount everything. What disillusioned me is man's tremendous capacity to be selfish. He is so unwilling to compromise. He refuses to give, you understand? I do not see a bright American Dream. It is a dream without lustre.

I'm listening to the media. What else do we have access to, outside of our own families and the small circle of friends? They try to deliver a package, but they leave you on the fence. You understand what I mean? I don't accept what I hear. I'm left to my own resources. Then I stop to think: Can I trust myself? My intellect is limited. We're absorbing so much knowledge that there is less and less and less time to understand what the knowledge is all about, see? And time is running out.

Over a long period of time, man has been disappointed. He almost expects disappointment as a way of life. He doesn't expect anything else. I don't think he can conceive of a world run the way it should be run.

I don't talk to my neighbors about it because my neighbors don't want to hear anything. They brush you off. Football, they'll talk to me. Horse racing, they'll talk to me. Their jobs. But don't try to take them outside themselves. You're in trouble if you do.

During the sixties, I used to talk to my boys a lot. At the time, they took issue with me. I thought they were trying to turn the world I knew upside down. Now, strangely enough, I see a hell of a lot of what they had to say come about. I lived to see the change. But now, my boys have taken the opposite stance. Now they're for law and order at any price. They're for hit 'em over the head if there's no other way.

I guess they've become adults. In our society, when you become an adult, you stake your claim. They have property now. They both have homes. They're doing fine. Once my sons called me bigoted, narrow-minded. I said: "Fifteen years from now, you're going to be a different person." I was right. But I am the one that changed most dramatically.

Twelve years ago, I didn't understand things in light of what I see today. I'm surprised at myself. I feel I could live with black people now. Yes, I still worry about violence. But I'm sure the black man has the identical worry, even more so than I have. So we're sharing something in common, see?

I have learned you better not become too attached to anything. You understand what I mean? Don't get so attached to something that you can't let go of it. My boys are now reaching the point where they're accumulating things. The foremost thought in their mind is to protect it. They have to look for someone to protect it from. All right? So God help the first one that gets in their path.

My father was born in Austria. It was the dream of everyone to come to 85
this country. If you didn't better yourself, at least you'd eat. He was an iron worker, one of the most intelligent men I've ever known. He could neither read nor write. His signature was an X. But when he talked, everything that came out of his mouth was original.

When my father talked, that was my father that was speaking, not Aristotle or Plato or Socrates or someone else. That was my father, and I knew it was him, you know? This is a good feeling. These are some of the lessons I tried to teach my boys. I tell 'em: "I recognize so much of what you say as being the source of other intelligences. I'm looking for *you* in all this conversation. I can't find *you*. Where are *you?*"

As a youngster, I was geared to think in terms of dollars and cents. If I do this, what is it worth? If I get an education, what is it worth to me in dollars and cents? Everything was money. I never thought about knowledge for the sake of knowledge, for the sake of truth. I am not blaming my parents, for I don't think they understood it themselves.

For the past dozen years, my most contented moments are when I'm alone. I like to get up at four o'clock in the morning and sit in this chair and just be alone with my thoughts. Oh, the thoughts range from things of the past, religion, science, what lies ahead—oh, just what it is all about. Knowledge has only real value when there is understanding. It's tremendous, it's exhilarating.

I'm not the most clever man in the world. I'm not the most educated. I did get through fifth grade and quit. But I'm not the most stupid person either. I may have only a fraction of the brains a learned man may have, but I'm forced to use every part of it. Sometimes I find I'm using more than the educated man.

We have to redefine what education is. Are we talking about reading, writing, and arithmetic? What should we learn that will enable an individual to go out on his own? What is education? When can I really say I know something? Every goddamn thing we know, we have to relearn every how many years?

The average man equates the accumulation of goods with power, supremacy, intelligence. If I have more than you, I'm better than you are. It's just like the neighborhood drunken bum. Never worked a day in his life. He's walkin' down the street and he kicks a bag, a million dollars in it. Now he's an eccentric millionaire. He's no longer a bum or a drunk. You see what I mean? Power. But has he changed? What's changed is that other men will accept him as superior. The almighty buck.

I wish I lived in a world that didn't know what money was. I wish I lived in a world where I didn't gauge the worth of a life by the color or shade of a man's skin. I wish I could live to see the day where Washington enacted a law that made man, once a month, come to a common meeting place and gave him a lesson that forced him to think, to exercise his brain. Just to get a man used to it and find out how delicious it can be.

My sons tell me I'm too soft for this world any more. And I tell 'em: "Thank God."

* * *

THE GIRL NEXT DOOR

Linda Haas

She attends a large technical high school in Chicago. Most of its students are of blue-collar families.

"I live in a changing neighborhood. It's Polish, Spanish, and southern.

"My father is from West Virginia, way up in the mountains. He was a farmer, he was in the Coast Guard. He did a lot of jobs. He was very intelligent, but he refused to go to college. My mother is from a real small town in Missouri. She went to eighth grade, but she was straight A's all the way through. Her stepmother wouldn't let her go to high school. She's bitter over this. My mom really has a thirst for knowledge, and this crushed her."

My father is a butcher for the A & P for twenty-six years. Never misses a day. He could be dying and he goes to work. The German heritage in him, you go to work and that's that. I feel sorry for him because he's like a fish out of water. I just feel he would be happier if he could be back in West Virginia.

The company he works for is changed. There was pride. Now it's just falling apart. They're letting people go with no feelings for how long they've worked there, just lay 'em off. It's sad. He should be getting benefits after all these years and all the sacrifices he's made. Now they're almost ready to lay him off without a word.

They send him from store to store. Before, the only people who did that were the young kids, part-time. My pa is fifty-one. Every week he has to wait to see if they're going to send him to another store. It's humiliating for him to be working for them all these years, he's got to call in every so often and find out if they have another store for him. It hurts his feelings. It's just wrong.

He never says it hurts his feelings, he roars. When he's upset, he takes it 100
out by acting angry. He yells about a lotta minor things at home. Like the phone bill or if the light doesn't work, he'll roar about it for two hours. I know he couldn't care less about the phone bill or the lights. All the things he'd like to yell at other people about, he's letting out over a light bulb.

I just feel sorry for people because I know how I feel. A lot of things have hurt my feelings as I've grown up. I try to see behind people when they do things. Most people, if they heard my father yelling about the phone bill, they'd say: "Wow, does he have a temper!" I try to look beyond, because I know what makes people do what they do.

Lane Tech, where I go, is a mixture. It's working-class, and there are a lot of wealthy people. It's too large, and it's not a happy place. The rich kids have their things, their Gucci shoes and their Marshall Field clothes, and they sit in their part and we sit in ours. We're just acquaintances. There's a few black kids, they're welcome. They stay with black kids. They don't want to be with us. We leave each other alone. We're all like separated.

I think for my father and his generation, the dream was to have a home and security and things like that. It was because of the poverty they came from. I don't know what it is now. The kids I go to school with, when they talk about their dreams, they don't talk about a home and having money in the bank. It's more like trying to have personal satisfaction. They don't know what they want. I don't know what I want. I don't know what my dreams are. There's so many things I'd like to do, and then . . .

I would like to go to college and do something, really contribute something. But I look at my neighborhood and my friends and my family and I think: Me going to college and being a writer, that would separate me from them. I would feel like I was breaking away. Like I just couldn't come back and sit on the front porch with my friends. It wouldn't be the same. I'd be the outcast. Every day I wake up: Oh, I'll go to college. The next day: No, I'm not. I'm going to get a job when I graduate. So I don't know.

Other people I know that went on to college come back to the neighbor- 105
hood in the summer, to visit their friends—we're sitting around talking, the feeling's different. They treat them differently. It's not really resentment. It's like envy. They can't just goof around with them any more. It's like they regard them as some different person they never met before. It's sad to me. I wouldn't want them to act like I wasn't their friend any more.

The few we knew that have been to college, some of 'em do feel superior and look down upon the neighborhood. They're ashamed to tell people where they live. It's a bad neighborhood where I live, but it's where I live. It's my home and I'm not ashamed. I would love to go to college.

She had just written a paper for her English class: impressions of a neighborhood friend of hers. "Just a guy I grew up with, Spanish. He's a nice person, but he has to be in a gang." She offers it from memory.

Everyone thought he was cool and tough, and he acted that way. He had feelings, but they just died somewhere. He's only sixteen, and he feels nothing. He's like a zombie. People die and his friends die, and it doesn't affect him. He never cries and he never cares deeply for anyone. I just think it's a waste because I remember him before.

When he was young, when we were little kids in grade school, he was really sweet and he did care then and he had feelings. It's just sad to watch him over the years, to regress like that and lose his feelings. When people hurt my feelings, I get it over with. I don't turn bitter. He turned bitter and cynical. He just takes everything as a personal offense. It all accumulates and he can't talk about it, so he turns inward.

He's seventeen now and he's in jail. So that's about it. He was my buddy 110
for about four years. But then we went our separate ways. I don't know where he is. I did last year, but there was nothin' left to say. It wasn't the same any more. He's a human being, he's intelligent, and now he's a drug addict, sitting in jail. He's wasted.

He was a good little kid, nice and funny. He was everybody's boy, the little boy you'd like to have for your son. That was him. Mr. Nice Little Boy. [Laughs.] He had talent. I think he would have been an artist. He was always drawing and did good work. He had imagination. When he was seven or eight, he would draw purple cows. Everybody would say: "What are you drawing purple cows for?" He'd say: "Purple cows are pretty. When I'm older I'll be a farmer and I'll breed purple cows." He was really wild that way. He started hanging around with the older gang members—you know, a tough gang member doesn't stand around with a paintbrush, drawing. Not in my neighborhood. So he gave it up.

Now everyone in the neighborhood is afraid of him. If he wasn't in jail, if he was walking down the street, everybody would go in their houses. He wouldn't do anything to them, but that's the way they feel because they've heard of him now. He's created this image for himself, and now he's stuck with it.

In the sixties is when the gangs started getting prominent in my neighborhood. They'd beat you up every day until you finally agreed to join them. He was so young, he didn't know what he was getting into. They were always beating him up, so he figured: Okay, I'll join. The girl members are as mean as the guys. [Laughs.]

They don't mind me. We still get along. We kind of accept each other. I'm about one of five people in the neighborhood that they'll associate with that are not in their gangs. They don't try. They think I'm silly for not joining, and I think they're silly. But we get along.

My other friends think they're low-down scum. They can't see how I would 115
even say hello to them on the street. They think it's unusual that I'm able to talk to them yet.

I always aggravate my dad because I'm always trying to see the good in everybody. There's a few I can't tolerate, but most of 'em I get along with.

We're a close family, we do things. I don't need to be feared by people to feel I'm worth something. I have other things in my life. It doesn't matter to me if everybody runs in the house when I walk down the street. They need that. There's nothing at home for them. Somewhere they've got to be important. I have other things.

I was reading in the paper the other day how times were getting worse, how children don't respect their parents, how the crime rate is rising. It went on and on. At the bottom, it said: Written in 1922. I don't think people are worse. I think there are still good people left.

My father is a different person than me. He can't understand them. It's hard to see good in them if you didn't go to school with them. He just can't tolerate them. His whole life, he worked for everything he got. He can't tolerate stealing or fighting. I see his point of view.

My mother's like me. She doesn't want to argue with my dad, so she doesn't say much either way. She loves to learn. She went to a nursing school she thought was accredited. It wasn't. She started working to survive. Then she got married. Finally, when we were in school, she thought: If I don't do it now, I'm never gonna do it. She went back and got her high school GED.[4] She went on to college and won all kinds of awards.

They read a lot. That's all my father does. Anything he can get his hands on. I make him read whatever I read. I give books to my parents and I bug 'em to death until they read 'em. I read whatever I pick up, just everything. I don't follow any pattern. I'm reading a book about game shows and a book of poetry at the same time, which is weird. I picked up the habit when I was little, from two of my grade-school teachers.

I'd like to be a writer or do some kind of social work. A house in the suburbs just isn't for me. The PTA and the carpool and the house with the mortgage, that doesn't appeal to me. I don't want to be thirty years old with three kids and my Maytag. I would go crazy. My father's worried that I'd marry some very crazy, unorthodox type of eccentric person like me. He'd like to see me marry some nice Joe Citizen that pays all his parking tickets.

My parents think I stay out too late, because I'm not afraid of being out at night alone. I know everybody in my neighborhood, and it just doesn't bother me. I don't think anything's going to happen to me. Why should I be afraid? I trust people until they give me a reason not to. Usually, I'm not disappointed.

I think everybody has some good in them, if you can find it. I don't think there's anybody that's born bad or born cruel. If you dig deep down enough, there's something in everybody. My dad says I dream too much. But I think there's a good in people. I can't say: "Oh, that is a bum." I just can't do that. I'm always looking and hoping there's something there. I can't write 'em off.

I hate to say I'm religious, because I don't go to church. That would be hypocritical. I believe there's a God. I don't know. I *hope* there's a God. I pray when I'm worried and when I pray, I talk. When I'm worried about my friends, I talk. I don't know how I'm supposed to pray. If there's a God, He'll do something. That's about it. I say: "Well, God, here I am in trouble again, talking to you now."

I fear for the world sometimes. I wonder if we're really gonna make it to the year 2000. What is it gonna be like? I worry about the people. What can be done? For myself, I don't worry about much. Whether or not to go to college. [Laughs.] Getting old.

I feel old. To me, every day is a day gone, whether you're five, ten, or sixteen. My friends are always looking at me: "Is she crazy?" That's sixteen years that are gone now. [Laughs.] I don't worry about getting physically old. That doesn't bother me. Just not accomplishing anything and getting old, that bothers me. What have I done in all these sixteen years? Sixteen years is a long time to be alive and not really doing anything but going to school.

I learned all the whitewash things. I didn't learn about America in school. I learned what they wanted me to learn. What I feel about America, I learned on my own. In school, everything was just great: We never did anything wrong. Everything was justified. Up until I was thirteen, I believed that. After that, I turned myself off, and from then on it was my own opinion.

I like living here. I should appreciate it more. We have so much freedom and stuff. We take a lot for granted. I don't know if it's the greatest place to live, because I've never been anywhere else. So I'm not gonna say it's the greatest until I know. I know it's a good place. At the moment, I wouldn't want to live anywhere else.

Notes

1. Dore Schary is her father. He was head of Metro-Goldwyn-Mayer at the time.
2. For many years, the dining room of a Chicago hotel frequented by celebrities.
3. Chief of a competing movie company at the time.
4. General Equivalency Diploma.

Understanding

1. Analyze Terkel's storytelling style. What are the characteristics of his reporting? What kind of material did he use to produce these narratives? Where and how did he get it?
2. What themes are common throughout this collection of dreams?

Responding

1. Which of these dreams is most like your own? Explore—in writing—the desire or goal of that dream. How old were you when you conceived of that dream? What is the dream's current status? Do you think you will actualize the dream?
2. Many of your parents or grandparents immigrated to America. Perhaps you are a recent immigrant to this country. What is your dream? What do you remember hearing in your family's lore about dreams made and lost? Record one of these family stories as if you were contributing to Terkel's book.

Remember that details—dates, ages, names of people and places, and so on—will make your dream tale more engaging.

3. Terkel chose two quotations for the frontmatter of his book; the first is a stanza from "Amazing Grace," an old American hymn, and the second is this musing by British soldier-scholar T. E. Lawrence:

   All men dream: but not equally.
   Those who dream by night
   in the dusty recesses of their minds
   wake in the day to find that it was vanity:
   but the dreamers of the day
   are dangerous men,
   for they may act their dream with open eyes,
   to make it possible.

   Speculate why Terkel prefaced his book with Lawrence's words. Do you agree with Lawrence? Can you think of examples of Lawrence's "dangerous" dreamers of the day? What is so dangerous about them?

Connecting

From the five excerpts in this selection, do you discern a common definition of the American dream? Is your own definition different? Is the American dream alive and well according to Terkel's storytellers? Compare these people's dreams with James E. Sharlow's in Bragg's "Big Holes Where the Dignity Used to Be," later in this chapter.

Creating a New Way of Life

Bruno Bettelheim

For decades before he died in 1990 at age eighty-six, Bruno Bettelheim enjoyed a reputation as a giant in the field of child psychology. Born in Austria, he came to the United States in 1944 and eventually devoted his career to healing the wounds of early life. As director of a treatment center for disturbed children, he pioneered the kind of residential or "milieu" therapy that was the standard for autistic children before the introduction of medical interventions.

Regarded as something of a polymath—an expert in many fields—Bettelheim wrote on psychology, fairy tales, autistic children—his book *Love Is Not Enough* is a classic—the Holocaust, parenting, literature, and history. His interest in the stresses that face young people may have stemmed from the almost two years he spent in the Buchenwald and Dachau death camps during World War II. Since his death new information has been alleged about Bettelheim, and the battle for his reputation is ongoing.

The Children of the Dream, from which this selection is excerpted, is one of the few accounts of how modern societies have risen from a collective dream. Israel, which became a nation in 1948, is one of them, and Bettelheim provides a clear-eyed account of how its founders planned for their future. His exploration of communal child-rearing in the Israeli kibbutz—the theme of *The Children of the Dream*—is an extension of his keen interest in the importance of environment in the development of children.

From its very inception the purpose of the kibbutz movement, for both sexes, was first and foremost to create a new way of life in a very old and hostile land. True, the raising of a new generation to this new way of life was soon of crucial importance, but of necessity it took second place. Because unless the first generation created the society, how could it shelter any new generations? It was this older generation that subjected itself to great hardships and dangers, that first reclaimed the land, wresting harvests from a barren soil, and later fought the war that gained them statehood. 1

Today, apart from the still pervasive problem of making fast their new statehood, there is still the war for social ideals to be waged. But those ideals are harder to maintain when the problem is no longer one of creating a homeland, but of maintaining themselves as a splinter group in a land swept up in a booming economy. Such ideals are specially hard to preserve when the surrounding population is by now so largely concerned with acquiring the more convenient life that goes with a higher standard of living. The kibbutz parent, in his devotion to ideals, may be likened to our own early Puritans;

except that these latter-day Puritans are not surrounded by a wilderness but by modern city life, which makes things a lot harder.

Kibbutzniks have never been more than a tiny minority in Israel. Nevertheless they have played a critical role there, both as idea and reality, out of all proportion to their numbers. For example, in 1944 Henrik Infield, in his book, *Co-operative Living in Palestine,* placed the total membership of all kibbutzim at about sixteen thousand. Twenty years later their numbers had grown to about eighty thousand, living in about 250 kibbutzim, but they were still only about 4 percent of the population of Israel. Yet this 4 percent accounted for some 15 percent of all members of the Knesset (Israeli parliament).

Even if the kibbutz stood for no more than a small sect, living by its esoteric convictions and trying to raise its children by these lights, their devotion to lofty ideals would command respect. But for Israel they do much more than that, since they still provide much of the national ethos, and the best part of it. As many thoughtful Israelis told me: Were it not for the kibbutz dream of a better society, there would be nothing unique left about Israel. Having created a refuge where Jews can live free of persecution, Israel would be nothing more now than just a tiny new nation.

(Though written before the 1967 war, I see no reason to change this 5
statement. The Arab-Israeli conflict is no longer a matter of the majority group persecuting a minority of its own citizens, but of two or more nation-states at odds over territorial rights. That one is smaller than the other does not make war and persecution the same thing, which they are not.)

It is also a nation with only one tenuous claim to the land: namely, that some two thousand years ago it was occupied by the spiritual ancestors of those who again hold possession now. This is not much of a claim compared to the uniqueness Jews felt, and which kept the Jews going during the two thousand years they were homeless.

All this has, in fact, led to many contradictions from which kibbutz life still suffers: In reclaiming the land, as in creating the state of Israel, kibbutzniks displaced Arab neighbors and fought them, though violence was contrary to their socialist convictions. Kibbutz founders wanted Israel to be an ideal state, free of all exploitation, where life would proceed in peace close to the biblical land. But the realities of the Middle East force Israel to be a garrison nation geared to defense, if not to war; a capitalist nation with many of the unpleasant features of a new nation trying to industrialize in a hurry.

I know that they also suffer from another contradiction, because they are keenly aware of it: Since they are atheists, they cannot base their claim to the land on the biblical promise that gave it to the Jews. The Jews needed a homestead. How desperately they needed it was made clear first by Hitler, and then by the plight of the Jews in Arab countries. But no other land was acceptable to the religious group, and no other land offered asylum to areligious Jews. So it had to be Israel, whether for political or emotional reasons.

In the face of all this contradiction and conflict, then, is where the kibbutz ethos makes a difference. It stands for utter devotion to the idea that once again Jews in Israel must not only create a new model of the good and just life, but actually live it—when need be at the cost of great personal hardship—or die for it if they must. Certainly the six-day war vindicated kibbutz child rearing methods and made it once again a symbol of all that is best in Israel. Not only did the kibbutz provide an inordinate percentage of the officer corps, it also suffered staggering losses. Some 4 percent of the Israeli population lives in the kibbutz, and kibbutzniks thus accounted for some 4 percent of the fighting force. But while about eight hundred soldiers fell in the war, two hundred of them came from the kibbutz (most of them born and raised there). Thus the 4 percent kibbutz segment of the Israeli army suffered 25 percent of all casualties. This was the true measure of their heroism, courage, and devotion to duty. Once more, as in the settling of the land and the war of liberation, the kibbutz ethos gives special meaning to the lives of Israelis today.

It is in this context of self-elected mission that the entire phenomenon of 10
the kibbutz must be understood, and flowing from it, what the parents do or do not do in raising their children. It means that everything I shall say in this book must at all times be related to this background.

AN AFTERTHOUGHT

How did the kibbutz way of raising children come about? First, it seems that kibbutz founders did not trust themselves to raise their own children in such a way as to become the carriers of a new society. To quote Diamond:

> The collective method of child rearing represents a rejection of the family, with particular reference to the parental roles. . . . It was felt that the family itself has to be banished, in order to rear the "new Jew." . . . [Kibbutz founders] were moved by the desire to create a new generation that would be "normal," "free," and "manly," unsullied by the exile. . . . They did not think themselves worthy of rearing such children within the confines of their own nuclear families, and they dared not trust themselves to the task.[1]

Thus the realization of their larger dream depended on this new and uniquely brought up generation. But the new generation, and the unique way of bringing them up, were an afterthought, an accident. The kibbutz—a society that devotes its all to the future, and hence to its children, that has turned upside down all traditional modes of child rearing to realize its goals—started out as a society that had no interest in children whatsoever and no room for children in its life.

While this in no way invalidates the educational method, it accounts for many contradictions that cannot be understood except from its unplanned inception. We are faced with the anomaly that what started as a nuisance, because it stood in the way of the founders' main purposes—to execute an idea—has become a central feature on which the idea's survival now depends.

As Joseph Baratz (1954) tells the story of Degania, the first kibbutz, the original kibbutzniks (of whom he was one) wanted no children in their community. Most of the settlers did not even want to marry, because "they were afraid that children would detach the family from the group, that . . .

comradeship would be less steadfast." Therefore it was seriously proposed that all members should oblige themselves not to marry for at least five years after joining the kibbutz, because "living as we do . . . how can we have children?"

When the first child was born in the kibbutz "nobody knew what to do 15
with him. Our women didn't know how to look after babies." But eventually "we saw it couldn't go on like this. . . . By the time there were four children in the settlement we decided something must be done. It was a difficult problem. How were the women both to work and look after their children? Should each mother look after her own family and do nothing else?" The men did not seem to feel strongly either way.

> But the women wouldn't hear of giving up their share of the communal work and life. . . . Somebody proposed that the kibbutz should hire a nurse . . . we didn't hire a nurse, but we chose one girl to look after the lot of them and we put aside a house where they could spend the day while the mothers were at work. And so this system developed and was afterwards adopted in all the kibbutzim, with the difference that in most of them the children sleep in the children's house, but with us [at Degania] they stay at night in their parents' quarters. . . . Only recently have we built a hostel for children over twelve where our own children live.

This is how the famous communal education of children began.

I myself questioned the founding generation: I wondered why the original group, so intent on creating a new way of life, had given no thought to their own continuity by planning for the next generation. The answer was always the same as the one given in published accounts by the earliest settlers: "Founding the settlements, cultivating the land was so arduous, so much a grownups' task, that we could not think about children." I cannot help feeling that part of the original attraction of a thus-defined task might have been that it left no place for children. Because if one does not think of having children, it is because one has no wish for them at the time, and not because the task at hand is so arduous.

If my speculation is valid, one might carry it a step further and say that the founding generation knew they had no wish to replicate the family as they knew it, and of this they were entirely conscious. But despite their rejection they could not think of how else to raise children. Hence to them, the decision not to form families meant not to have children. If so, then kibbutz life was attractive to those who for this or other reasons did not wish to have children. My assumption seems supported by the incredibly low birthrate in the early days of kibbutz history, which contrasts sharply with other settings in which a people live in hardship and danger and nevertheless produce many children.

It would seem, then, that chance and a desire for quite other things, dictated the child caring arrangements made hastily, piecemeal, and with little plan or thought; arrangements that were later formalized into dogma, as is probably the origin of most dogmas. Or as Murray Weingarten (1955) put it, "This system, at first merely a pragmatic arrangement . . . has assumed the flesh and blood of a very definite educational philosophy [because] the purpose of the kibbutz is not only . . . to set up a new economic framework for society [but] to create a new man."

But when the first of these new men arrived on the scene as a newborn 20
infant, he was a nuisance to everyone but his mother and possibly his father. The reasons for this strange contradiction lie in the psychological origin of the movement.

KIBBUTZ ORIGINS

Essentially the kibbutz has two major sources. First, there was the founders' desire to repudiate their ghetto existence. And second was the desire to create a new way of life in what had once been the homeland of the Jews. But the particular form taken by both these desires owed a great deal to the adolescent revolt of a small "elite" group in Central Europe at the turn of the century, namely the *Wandervogel* movement.

Wandervogel means *migratory bird* in German, and its young adherents wanted very much to migrate out of the world of their parents—an idea most persuasive to ghetto youth at this time. The *Wandervogel* movement was a revolt against the authoritarian families in which these essentially middle-class youth had been raised, and against the authoritarian schooling of the German *Gymnasium* most of them had attended. What they sought was a more authentic, more nature-bound way of life (Walter Laqueur, 1962).

All these ideas appealed to Jewish ghetto youth who rebelled at the even more binding traditions their parents lived by, and a system of religious education that was vastly more oppressive than any German school. In addition, it must be remembered that things German held a particular attraction for Eastern Jewry. Their ideas about emancipation had reached them from Germany, in the form of German enlightenment; socialism in its Marxist form had come to them from Germany; their very language, Yiddish, was based on medieval German. Nevertheless, while kibbutz founders were deeply influenced by *Wandervogel* ideology, the manner in which they combined it with socialism, Zionism, and a Tolstoyan emphasis on the virtues of life on the land was uniquely their own.

In any case it was the first of their desires, the wish to escape, that was dominant, or they would never have left home, and their second dream could never have been followed.

Once in Palestine, their daily lives and their work had to bend to the harsh 25
facts of politics and economics. But they were freer about how to shape the inner life of their community, including the rearing of their children. Or to put it differently: Once there were children, they had much greater freedom about arranging the child's experience in such a way that he would grow up to realize their dreams.

To quote Diamond again, "the kibbutz served as an arena for the overreaction of its members against *Shtetl* [ghetto] life and as a mechanism for adaptation to the socio-economic realities confronting them in Palestine." True, quite a few of the founding generation came from the cities of Central

Europe and not from the *Shtetl*. But in most cases their parents had grown up in the *Shtetl* and perpetuated many of its features in the lives of their children. Others, for whom this was not true, had come from youth movements very much like the German *Wandervogel*.

One might add that at first, and for some time to come, whether they came from the ghetto or a more Westernized type of youth movement, their background equipped them very poorly for a pioneering agricultural life; so poorly, compared to American settlers who went West, that they could not make a go of it as single family units and were forced to rely much more on each other. (The difficulty of making a success of farm life as an individual family seems universal. Reflecting on his own childhood on a farm in Indiana, for example, Allan Nevins [1967] recalls the severe limitations imposed by individualism in a farming community, compared to the advantages of kibbutz organization as he observed it on a visit to Israel.) Be this as it may, what I did not find stressed in the literature was how their poor preparation as colonizers forced kibbutzniks to repeat, though in a deeply different way, the close unity that had characterized the ghetto, and for similar reasons: because it helped them survive in a basically hostile environment. Not only that, but as in the ghettos, they survived through deep devotion to a creed, though again a far different one. In place of their parents' religious creed, they chose a socialist-atheist work morality closely tied to a return to the soil.

Part of the ghetto existence to which kibbutz founders reacted, and possibly overreacted, was a closeness in family life that to them seemed devoid of freedom. (And here things were not too different for the lower middle-class Jewish family in the big cities of Central and Eastern Europe.) To begin with, since all life in their homes had centered so exclusively on the family, there would be no family as such in the kibbutz. Next, since the roles of men and women were unequal in the families they came from, the sexes would be entirely equal in the kibbutz. What was stressed here, according to Spiro, was "'the biological tragedy' of women. Because woman must bear and rear children, she has had little opportunity for cultural, political, artistic expressions. If she could only be freed from this time-consuming responsibility, as well as from such other domestic duties as cleaning, cooking, and laundry, she would become the equal of men."

As Weingarten (1955) reflects, this philosophy of sexual equality was often carried to comic extremes. They "went so far as to print a pamphlet [whose] theme was that the only obstacle in the way of achieving true equality of the sexes was the unfortunate physical difference between men and women."

Again: Since the often poverty-stricken ghetto family was immensely con- 30
cerned with both religious values and earthly possessions, neither religion nor materialism would exist in the kibbutz. I could extend the list indefinitely. But doing away with the family structure and striving for utter equality between the sexes was part of a larger desire for equality in all things.

The exploited worker of Europe, in his devotion to early socialism, strove for economic, political, and social equality. The socialist Jew, who felt ready at last to break the chains forged by centuries of social, economic, and political inequality, knew it was not these alone that had kept him in his degraded position. He knew he was equally constrained by his Jewishness, by the crippling demands of his rigid religion, by his parents' strict adherence to Jewish ritual and traditions. And if the Jew was a woman, she felt even more degraded by a religion that required men to thank God each day that He had not created them female.

Beyond this I have a feeling which I cannot substantiate. But few religions have been as rejecting of womanhood as the Jewish one. It was a religion that viewed her very femininity as a curse, that condemned her to apartheid in its places of worship, that even forbade her to wear her own hair, and required her to shave it off at marriage.

It was this ritual rejection of femininity by their parents, and their own glorification of masculine pursuits, that may have influenced the first kibbutz generation to view man's work as preferable to woman's, including the work of rearing children. If so, then it may explain why women of the second generation who were reared areligiously show little preference for typically masculine work. They wish for important work, but only a minority take this to mean the hard physical labor of men, and few feel deprived if they lack it.

Thus the kibbutz movement was also a particularly Jewish revolt against debasement of the female and in favor of equality. It was therefore the women of the kibbutz, much more than the men, who insisted that their child bearing and child rearing functions must not interfere with their absolute equality with men. The phrase quoted earlier about the "unfortunate physical difference" cannot fully be savored apart from this context of the biblical curse upon woman *qua* woman.

But if the founding of the kibbutz was in large part a reaction to the ghetto 35
existence, what kept it going thereafter was not what its founders wished to get rid of, but the positives they found in their new life. It is true that living as their ideals demanded, even at the cost of great hardship and self-denial, gave them deep satisfaction. It greatly enhanced the ego to be able to live up to (ego) ideals that were so difficult to achieve, that were so largely self-chosen, not imposed. But this alone gave no primary emotional satisfactions, did not satisfy the id. And without that, life is empty and cold, however virtuous. This necessary warmth and this meaning they found in their deep emotional ties to the peer group.

Kibbutz is the Hebrew word for *group;* it has no other meaning. All the satisfactions that in the ghetto had come from the family, and many more, came to kibbutzniks from their peers. Hence their greatest fear was that if men and women were to stop sharing the same life activities, if women were to turn again to a preoccupation with pregnancy and child care and the men to competing for a living, then the group would cease meeting their emotional needs.

Again and again I was told that if the children were again to live and sleep with their parents, then the parents could not so freely be part of the communal doings of their peers, and that these are what give meaning to their lives. In this sense it is true: The kibbutz woman seeks her deepest satisfaction not from her children (as her mother did) but from her contemporaries, male and female. And so does the kibbutz male, who finds in his fellow kibbutzniks many of those emotional satisfactions the ghetto father sought from attachment to his children. But this deep peer attachment depends on full participation in the common enterprise, requires equality in how one's everyday life will be spent.

As one old-timer put it, who for more than thirty years had worked as a metapelet with infants, "Let's face it, the kibbutz wasn't built for children, but to make us free." And by this she meant nothing abstract, but the freedom to live in such a way that no kibbutznik, male or female, would lose any of the emotional satisfactions gained from a life devoted essentially to each other rather than to their children.

Note

1. This wish to create the "new" Jew, and some of its consequences, form the essence of Yael Dayan's novel *Envy the Frightened* (New York, World Publishing Company, 1961). Though the picture she draws is extreme, and hence distorts the reality I observed, some of the tendencies she describes are real enough among some groups.

Understanding

1. In what ways is the kibbutz the fulfillment of a collective dream?
2. What are the defining characteristics of kibbutz life?
3. Describe Bettelheim's writing style. How does it differ in style and tone from other readings in this chapter? What is his point of view?
4. From this excerpt, can the reader detect Bettelheim's attitude toward the kibbutz?

Responding

1. Are there any parallels between Israeli kibbutz life and social organization in the United States? Elsewhere in the world? What dreams fueled them? Identify and describe them, adding your personal experience to your descriptions of any you know well.
2. Bettelheim began the research that resulted in *The Children of the Dream* in the 1960s, when kibbutz life in Israel had less than a twenty-five-year history. Investigate kibbutz life in Israel today. In what ways is it similar to or different from the way Bettelheim describes it?
3. Assess the ways in which the concept of the kibbutz is or is not adaptable to American culture or the culture in which you were reared. Be sure to identify the criteria that guide your assessment.
4. If you were to "dream a new society," what would it be like?
5. In what ways was your childhood the result of a dream (or lack of one) that your family had for your future?

Connecting

1. Compare the kibbutzim view of male and female social roles with those described in Bateson's "Opening to the World."
2. In your judgment, if the State of Israel had not been created, or if the kibbutz had not been realized, which of the possible outcomes of a "dream deferred" that Hughes sets forth in his poem "Harlem" do you think would have resulted? Explain.

Big Holes Where the Dignity Used to Be

Rick Bragg

This selection is the third of a seven-part series on corporate downsizing—a euphemism for firing employees—which provoked sharp reactions when it appeared in the *New York Times* in March 1996. *Washington Post* columnist Robert Samuelson criticized the series as an example of editors and reporters being "prisoners of prevailing intellectual fashion," selectively collecting information to "buttress preset conclusions," and having "all the hallmarks of a project aimed for a Pulitzer." Many letters to the editor, on the other hand, agreed that the series addressed an important social phenomenon and created a frightening portrait of the future of America. Rick Bragg, the author of this segment, subtitled "In the Family, the Good Life Lost," did, indeed, win the 1996 Pulitzer Prize for feature writing "for his elegantly written stories about contemporary America."

Born in 1959 in Piedmont, Alabama, Bragg attended Harvard University as a Nieman Fellow, and Jacksonville State University from 1978–80. He joined the *New York Times* in 1994 as a metropolitan reporter. In addition to his Pulitzer, Bragg's stories have been included in "Best Newspaper Writing 1991" and "Best of the Press 1988."

1 To the beggars downtown that autumn day, every wing-tipped stride of James E. Sharlow seemed to resonate with prosperity. His suit was boardroom gray, his tie was red silk, his creases as crisp as fresh money. One ragged man sidled up to him with a sad story and an outstretched palm.

"Excuse me, sir," he said, "but could you spare $5? I've got a family to feed. I haven't worked for a long time."

"Me either, fella," Mr. Sharlow said, and kept walking. In the 1990's, he has learned through bitter experience, discarded workers come in rags and Ralph Lauren.

He met some friends for lunch—laid-off, white-collar, middle-aged men like himself—and paid his tab with money drawn from his retirement accounts. Then he slid into his shiny black Mercedes, the one with the badly slipping transmission, and followed the Ronald Reagan Expressway home to the house and life in the San Fernando Valley that he can no longer afford.

5 The 51-year-old Mr. Sharlow lost his $130,000-a-year job in January 1993 when the plant he managed was shut down, permanently. After giving 26 years of his life and loyalty to one big corporation, Eastman Kodak, he found himself chasing white-collar jobs in a market already glutted with unemployed manufacturing executives.

For Mr. Sharlow, his wife and two grown daughters, it is not only a matter of temporarily doing without new cars, nice vacations and unbridled trips to the mall, but a steadily creeping unease that their downsized existence could be permanent. More than anything, they all want the layoff to be only a ripple in their old life, not the beginning of a new one.

"I believe in the American dream," he said, with a resistance that is part pride, part hope, part denial. "I feel it fading. I still believe."

So while the layoff has eroded his dreams of retirement and stolen his family's long-range security, it has not, on the surface at least, greatly changed the look of their lives. Mr. Sharlow always saved, and over the years put away about $300,000. Now every three months he dips into the money for about $10,000 to pay bills and the mortgage on their roomy, ranch-style house, with a small pool out back, on a street of small but manicured lawns and Lyndon Johnson–era architecture in Northridge, northwest of downtown Los Angeles.

Gayle, his wife, calls it: "Keeping up the front."

Every withdrawal from their savings costs them money in penalties and 10
interest, but what she takes home from the $30,000 annual salary she earns as a secretary will not even cover the house payment of $1,800 a month. So they sacrifice their future to pay for the here and now, and at night she takes long walks so her husband and daughters cannot see her cry.

"I just want to pretend things are like they used to be," said Mrs. Sharlow, a slim, gracious blond woman who, lately, always looks a little tired. She spent years finding the perfect curtains. Now she hoards paper towels and soap.

Gayle Sharlow, who is 51, grew up in a household where money was short, precious. Sometimes now, when she forces herself out of bed at 5:30 in the morning, she looks down at her still-sleeping husband and feels a flash of anger: He can hold out for a good job. She just goes to work. Sometimes, she feels like begging him to take a job, any kind of job, instead of holding out for one that fits his dreams.

She fears they will lose their house, their retirement, all of it. But she never wakes him those mornings, never does speak up. His work was not merely part of him. It was the defining part.

"How could my family not think less of me now?" asked Mr. Sharlow, a large, tall, balding, bearded man who looks like a boss. Once he was a husband and father with a great job, and now he is just a man chasing one.

"I thought it would take a few weeks, a few months, and then I would 15
be working again," he said. "I want to tell companies, 'Take me on for a month. Don't pay me. I'm sure I can outwork most people if you'll give me a chance.'"

His guilt over not working, over not bringing home even a small paycheck to help pay the bills, has done battle with his fear that a low-paying, stopgap job will be the end of the line. "I'm afraid it might be it," he said, "the best I could do."

How long can he hold on? He does not know.

Gayle Sharlow does not blame her husband for what has happened to them. She blames the company he was once part of, they were all part of, body and soul.

The layoff of a senior manager is hardly a new phenomenon in modern America; Jim Sharlow saw it happening all around him. But when his turn came, it shocked him. Mr. Sharlow, who missed watching his daughters grow up because he routinely put in 12- and 14-hour days, believed that he was part of a company family.

The company discarded him six months short of the date he needed for a 20
decent pension.

"He gave them 26 years, and it meant nothing," said his older daughter, Karen.

Karen, who is 26, and her 21-year-old sister, Laurie, still live at home, and both have seen their own lives and expectations altered forever by the layoff of the man who once stood for everything that was solid and dependable. Neither makes enough money to help their parents, beyond paying an occasional bill. It embarrasses him to take help from them.

"I know I'll never feel safe again," he said. "I lost my job, I failed my family. I . . ." His voice trails off into a bitter silence. He was 50 when he did his first résumé.

There is a painting on his living room wall of a sailboat disappearing into a tropical sunset. The boat used to represent his retirement. Now he uses that sailboat money to pay the water bill, but keeps the picture nailed firmly in place.

SHE LOVED TO DANCE

In the winter of 1968, Jim Sharlow had a primer-brown 1947 hot-rod Chev- 25
rolet convertible, and most of his hair. He was in serious love with a good-looking woman who loved to dance. When the gray snow did not pile up too high, Batavia, N.Y., outside of Rochester, was a lot like paradise.

James and Gayle ate fried dough rolled in powdered sugar at a joint called Pontillo's and planned a life.

"He got a tax refund for $110," she said. "He was going to buy some pistons, but he got me a ring."

The only thing that could have made it better was a real job. His father had been a tool-and-die man who worked his whole life for one company, and his son, against his wishes, trained to do the same. "He wanted me to do better, to wear a tie," he said.

But when he was 23, Eastman Kodak recruited him, trained him to be a machinist, promised him a long and happy future. Everyone in Batavia knew that when you got on with Kodak, you were set for life. His father forgave his choice of careers—it was Kodak. But his time as a blue-collar worker would be short.

Almost immediately, he started climbing. Unlike the college boys—his 30
bachelor of science degree in engineering management came much later—Mr. Sharlow could use his head and hands. For the next several years, he was used in mechanical, engineering, assembly, electrical and fabricating areas, in increasingly managerial roles.

"It just seemed like overnight he went from a closet full of work shirts to a closet full of white shirts," Mrs. Sharlow said.

He remembers the first day he wore a tie. An ornery machinist cut it off with a pair of scissors, and stuck it on the wall. (He is not sure, but it might have been a clip-on).

Each promotion improved his family's quality of life. It made college a certainty for his children. And after a while, he felt comfortable being a boss. He had worked up from the bottom and there was a pride in that. If a machinist could not make a part work, Mr. Sharlow would tuck his tie in his shirt and make it himself. He felt he had earned his white shirts, his growing power.

"Kodak was everything," Mr. Sharlow said. "How far I could go seemed to depend on my own ambition."

He worked late nights, weekends, holidays. "I remember going to a dance 35
recital and saying to Gayle, 'That girl on the end is really good.' And she said, 'Jim, that's your daughter.' "

He did dirty work for them. Years ago, back in Rochester, it was his job to find fat in some departments, then trim it. He laid off several people, some who cried, others who begged. One man killed himself.

"He was a young guy, just got married, just bought a house. A Vietnam vet. He saw the pink slip in my hand and asked, 'That for me?' I told him, 'I am afraid so.' He asked if there was anything I could do. He pleaded with me. Two months later he committed suicide. The name is gone, but I can still see the face."

In 1987, the company offered Mr. Sharlow his own small plant, making highly technical aerospace parts on military contracts, in a land where it never snowed.

His job history backs up his assertion that he is a good manager. At the Northridge plant, a subsidiary of Kodak, he increased net profit by 10 percent in his first year and by 19 percent his second. A lot of people got rich in the Reagan era, and the Sharlows, while far from rich, got their share.

"We did all right," Mr. Sharlow said. He started to play a little golf. His 40
daughters became cheerleaders and sorority women. His wife became a power shopper.

They thought it would last forever.

"WHAT DID I DO TODAY?"

The days inch along, like 9 A.M. traffic on the San Diego Freeway.

It has been three years since that first morning-after, when he opened his eyes and thought, "I don't have a job today." But still he shaves and showers and dresses in neatly pressed khakis and sport shirts: the executive on his day off.

"It helps with my self-esteem," he said.

The plant was shut down as a cost-cutting measure, part of an industry- 45
wide slowdown caused by the melting cold war. Mr. Sharlow said that other California managers with the company found jobs back in New York. He asked to be transferred back, too, but he was a little too late. He might have pushed

harder and faster for a return to Rochester, but even after the plant's closing was announced, he trusted the company to hold a place for him.

"I knew there were hundreds and even thousands being laid off. I guess I thought I was special. Then the day came when they made a business decision to let me go. It was, 'Bye, and don't let the door hit you.'"

His last day he went home and had four manhattans and wondered how to start over. It was the saddest day of his life.

"My dream was to retire down in St. Petersburg to a little place on the Intracoastal Waterway, with a sailboat tied up to a little dock in back," he said. "I measured the money over a lifetime to try and get there."

At noon one Thursday afternoon, his mailbox is jammed with outgoing envelopes, all résumés, follow-up letters, hopes. By afternoon it will be filled with bills and junk mail and what he has come to call "Dear John" letters: "Dear Mr. Sharlow," they say, "Thank you for your interest, but . . ." And then they promise to keep his résumé on file.

In the last three years, he has sent out 2,205 résumés—by his own, precise 50
count. For his efforts, he has landed 10 interviews; once he was one of two finalists for a job managing a manufacturing plant in Southern California. That job had drawn 3,000 applicants.

He scours *The New York Times, The Wall Street Journal, The Los Angeles Times, The St. Petersburg Times* (his mother lives in Florida and he would like to be near her), as well as trade magazines and newsletters, searching for openings for a plant manager, department head, anything that fits his experience. He will not say what he expects to be paid, but has come to realize that it will not approach his old salary.

One potential employer told Mr. Sharlow that he could not hire him because his company could not give the kind of pay and benefits he had come to expect. As the months tumble by, he wonders how many jobs he lost because, once in a fat period in his life, he had it too good.

He shrugged off the rejections at first. Now, his wife says, "You see him sitting there, and you can feel the disappointment coming off him."

Mr. Sharlow has always been a Republican, and he still is. His troubles, he believes, do not have a lot to do with politics. A big corporation decided it would make more money without him than with him or his plant, and that desire for a slightly wider profit margin cost him his job. He does not see that kind of thinking as singularly Republican.

He has refused to become a couch potato, could care less about "General 55
Hospital." He does chores. He runs errands for a shut-in elderly neighbor. He wishes his dog, Scooter, had not died. Scooter was good company.

The evenings are the worst for him, when his wife comes home tense and tired from a lousy day. He sits on his couch and thinks: "What did I do today? What did I do?"

BIGGER THAN ALL OF THEM

The meeting room is wall to wall with well-dressed men and women like Mr. Sharlow, cloaked in double-breasted armor, shielding a rumpled reality. It is one of the rules here at 40-Plus, a self-help organization of laid-off, white-collar workers in Los Angeles: Continue to dress like someone important, stay in character. Fortune 500 companies seldom hire managers who spend six days a week in their bathrobes, watching reruns of "Ironside."

There is a woman who lost her sales job and then her husband, because he valued her less without the paycheck. There is a graying former supervisor who believes he was laid off because he was too old, and a younger man angry that the Japanese owners who took over his insurance company let him go with no warning.

They pore over want ads, talk job-hunting strategy, train to re-enter the modern, meaner corporate reality, and try not to be bitter about the fact that they have enough discarded brain power here to run many companies. They drink coffee, but have to get it themselves.

"It's not hopeless," said the president, Ben Cate, but it is bleak. One of 60
their number had just found a good job, and the others grilled him about his résumé, negotiations, salary, searching for the secret.

For Mr. Sharlow, this group is important in another way. When he sees the other tossed-aside executives, it proves he is not alone, that something bigger than him is to blame.

When he walks into this place, his whole manner changes. He is back in an office, he has a purpose. His step quickens, his confidence seems to swell. He is like a hooked fish let loose again in a stream.

A REMINDER OF POVERTY

The hardships of other families that have lost a regular paycheck are still only an echo for them. Gayle Sharlow hears it clearest. She has heard it before. Her daughters have never been close to poor; neither has her husband.

Her father was a hard-working carpenter who did his best to provide, but they often lived from paycheck to paycheck, and luxuries were scarce. For her, the threat of poverty is too familiar, like a ripped dress she thought she had thrown away for good, but may have to wear again.

Listen to her: 65

"I grew up with nothing, absolutely nothing. This layoff gnaws at my guts. It's a fear. I stock up on soap and paper towels because I'm afraid we might run out and not be able to afford any more. I try not to lose hope, but I'm afraid we will lose the house, everything. Gone. It's not silly to think about. It happens to people, people we know. I get mad and want to say, 'You'll just have to get a job at McDonald's.' But we keep up the front. I still go to the mall, but I do a lot more looking than buying. We still go to dinner. And at night I go for my walks so they can't see me cry."

Behind the front, there have been difficult choices. When her father was ill recently, she agonized over whether to pay $1,300 for the last-minute plane ticket to go see him. She chose not to go.

There are times when she wishes they had never left Batavia, that the house was smaller, their dreams more modest. There would be less to lose then.

Mr. Sharlow got a year's severance pay when he was laid off, so only in the last two years has he had to peel from their original savings of about $300,000. The withdrawals, countered by profits on his investments, have left him with about $250,000. The bulk of their nest egg is in a 401K—an ever-changing mix of mutual funds, stocks and bonds. He juggles them now and then, trying to squeeze out every penny.

That means he sometimes is more aggressive—they now have no money in CD's because interest is low—and sometimes less. He only gambles in the stock market when he is almost sure he will win. Two winters ago, when the market dropped sharply, he sold and put the money elsewhere. He knows the key to the market is long-term investment, but he could not afford to watch their savings vanish.

He has not borrowed; he does not even use his credit card. He makes sure that he meets his life insurance premium. To drop it would be unthinkable, selfish.

The Sharlows have come to like California, but the cost of living is sucking up their money. They would sell the house, move to a less-expensive neighborhood, but the market is bad and the 1994 earthquake did damage still unrepaired. And besides, the house has come to represent roots, stability. Giving it up would be admitting they have lost.

The living room has cracks in the ceiling, but for now the house and family are intact. Mr. Sharlow says his wife is supportive, that they do not have the ugly yelling fights—and worse—that have ripped other families apart in the wake of a layoff. The Sharlows rarely talk about Gayle's fears for the same reason she does her crying out of sight: She believes he has enough to worry about.

"Everyone should know. He has always been a very good provider for his family," she said. "I want to make sure everyone understands that."

They hear of others, many others, who did come apart under the pressure. One man had a nervous breakdown, left his family and moved to New Jersey, to live with his mother. They know men barely clinging to marriages and self-respect. Another laid-off executive and acquaintance of Mr. Sharlow killed himself over Christmas. Mr. Sharlow thinks that maybe he lost hope.

"Don't think Jim Sharlow and his family are typical," said Mr. Cate, the 40-Plus president. "They're not. They're doing good."

LIFE LESSONS

Their childhoods were as carefree as love and money could make them.

"When it happened, what bothered me was, I couldn't get a new car," said Laurie Sharlow, who was in her teens then. "I know that sounds really bad, but that's the way it was then."

This is the way it is now: "When I ask dad for $20, I'm ashamed."

The layoff that shocked and hurt their father and chilled their mother did all these things to Laurie and Karen. It also made them angry.

"We've been taught our whole lives that if you give your loyalty to someone or something, it gives you something back," Karen said. "In our house, we didn't even use anything that wasn't Kodak, Kodak film, Kodak cameras."

The loyalty was all one-sided. To them, the corporate family is no more real than any other fairy tale their father told in their childhoods, a fairy tale now replaced with a harsh sensibility that seems out of place on young women, who pledged Tri Delta.

"No one will take care of you," Karen said. "We know."

"I know I don't cry much anymore," said Laurie, who studies television and filmmaking at California State University at Northridge, and works part time as a secretary. All the things that seemed so important, boyfriends, parties, have been shoved into perspective, cheating her out of a period in her life that should have been carefree. "I missed a lot," she said.

Karen works in the international retail department of Warner Brothers, 85
part of the new growth industry in Southern California. Although she makes only about $30,000 a year, she saves as much as she can, preparing for a repeat of what happened to her father, knowing it might never come, unwilling to take a chance.

In better times, she would have probably moved into her own place, because her father would have been able to help. Now she saves the rent money, and, like her sister, lives in her old room, its walls covered with pictures of fresh-faced girls in cheerleader outfits and prom dresses. Everyone is smiling.

The layoff came too late to take everything, but it took their peace of mind.

"I feel guilty," Mr. Sharlow said. "One of the girls will see something they'd like to have and I'll say, 'When daddy gets a job.'"

He would like to promise his daughters, his wife and the man in the mirror that everything will be fine again, but the "Dear John" letters keep coming, the phone still does not ring. Even now, three years later, he is still vaguely disbelieving that all this has happened, that the company—he still refers to it as "my" company—is no longer part of his life.

"It's like you're standing outside the castle," he said, "watching the draw- 90
bridge go up."

In December, the Sharlows took a Florida vacation they could not afford. They walked along St. Petersburg Beach, the executive and his family on holiday. He caught himself scanning the real estate, looking for a house with a dock in back, with room for a boat.

EPILOGUE: WINTER

The guilt won its battle over pride. Jim Sharlow went to work.

He wakes up early again, but does not put on a suit and no one notices if his shoes are shined. He took a temporary job at the college where his wife works. Technically, he is a consultant in its electronics department, but most days he works with his hands again, repairing televisions, video cameras, VCRs and other broken equipment. He makes less money than Gayle.

"I don't manage people now," he said. He carries a screwdriver. It was supposed to last just three months, but he got a one-month extension.

95 Now and then he sees things on the job he would do differently, he would do better, if it were up to him, "but no one is interested in what I have to say now."

It all came down to the simple fact that he could no longer stand to wait: for the good job, for his tired wife to get home. Now the two ride to work together some days. The transmission in the Mercedes slips so badly that sometimes he has to beg it to roll.

He will not say how much he earns now, only that if the job lasted all year, he would still earn a little less than Gayle's $30,000 salary, which they used to consider "a nice little extra." They make enough money to pay their mortgage, as well as some, but not all, of their bills. But they still have to borrow from savings. "It just won't be as much. In that, it's a blessing," he said.

For Gayle, it did not bring the relief she expected, only what they had really known all along, that "you can't build a life on this."

In some ways he is back where he started, with tools in his hands. But instead of a young man looking toward his future, he is middle-aged, and dreaming backwards.

100 "I was an operations manager for a plant, and I was a damn good one," he said. "The thing I hate about this is the fear—no, fear isn't a strong enough word, it's terror—that I'd just better forget my dreams and do this, and do it for the rest of my life. Maybe this is it.

"Maybe this is the best I can get."

Understanding

1. Many writers, including those represented in this chapter, have interpreted the American dream. Based on the idea of progress, the American dream usually includes expecting a progressively higher standard of living, acquiring the "good life," and then retiring comfortably. What in James Sharlow's life exemplifies these aspects of the American dream? Does Sharlow still have this dream?
2. Highlight those aspects of the article that indicate that the core of James Sharlow's identity was his job.
3. What role does Gayle Sharlow play in her husband's situation?
4. Rick Bragg used a *focus structure,* a literary device of telling a story through the eyes of one person, to write "Big Holes Where the Dignity Used to Be." Journalists use this technique to help readers identify with their subject. A reader to whom unemployment statistics are not meaningful may eagerly follow a story about how a layoff affects one person. The process of writing through a focus structure begins with an introduction to an individual, transitions to a larger issue, reports on this larger issue, and then returns to the opening focus to provide a strong finish. Focus, detail, and transitions are the most important elements of the focus structure. Identify these elements in Bragg's article.

5. Consider the following statement: "James Sharlow is a whiner, a guy who has lived the good life, lives better than most Americans, and will have to adjust to his new situation." Do you agree or disagree with this statement?

Responding

1. Outline your vision of the American dream.
2. If you were James Sharlow's child, what responsibility would you feel toward helping your father (and your family) deal with this situation? What exactly would you do?
3. What role does work or a career play in your dreams for your future? How do you imagine you would cope with a situation like Sharlow's?

Connecting

1. Relate James Sharlow's dream-shattering experience to Saline's "The Luong Sisters." How are their responses dictated by their social positions?
2. What similarities do you see among Terkel's dream interviewees and James Sharlow?

Richard Cory

Edwin Arlington Robinson
Paul Simon and Art Garfunkel

Paul Simon and Art Garfunkel were popular American cultural icons in the 1960s. They wrote and sang songs that reflected the turmoil of the day and questioned American values within the social contexts of the Vietnam War, the civil rights movement, women's liberation, communal living, the sexual revolution, and hippies. Paul Simon's "Richard Cory" was based on Edwin Arlington Robinson's (1869–1935) poem of that name.

Robinson was an American poet who is best known for his short dramatic poems concerning the people in a small New England village much like the small town in Maine where he grew up. His poems are concerned with personal defeat, and "Richard Cory" is a dramatic instance of the human condition. Simon and Garfunkel's rendition of "Richard Cory" was recorded in 1965 and released on their album *The Sound of Silence.* Compare the following versions of "Richard Cory."

Richard Cory

Whenever Richard Cory went down town,
  We people on the pavement looked at him:
He was a gentleman from sole to crown,
  Clean favored, and imperially slim.

And he was always quietly arrayed,
  And he was always human when he talked;
But still he fluttered pulses when he said,
  "Good-morning," and he glittered when he walked.

And he was rich—yes, richer than a king,
  And admirably schooled in every grace:
In fine, we thought that he was everything
  To make us wish that we were in his place.

So on we worked, and waited for the light,
  And went without the meat, and cursed the bread;
and Richard Cory, one calm summer night,
  Went home and put a bullet through his head.

—*Edwin Arlington Robinson*

Richard Cory

They say that Richard Cory owned one half of this old town,
With political connections to spread his wealth around.
Born into society, a banker's only child,
He had everything a man could want—power, grace, and style.

But I work in his factory.
And I curse the life I'm living.
And I curse my poverty.
And I wish that I could be,
Oh I wish that I could be,
Oh I wish that I could be Richard Cory.

The papers print his picture almost everywhere he goes.
Richard Cory at the opera; Richard Cory at a show.
And the mover of his party,
And the more he's on his yacht,
Oh, surely he must be happy with everything he's got.

But I work in his factory.
And I curse the life I'm living.
And I curse my poverty.
And I wish that I could be,
Oh I wish that I could be,
Oh I wish that I could be Richard Cory.

He really gave to charity; he had the common touch.
And they were grateful for his patronage
And thanked him very much.
So my mind was filled with wonder
When the evening headlines read:
"Richard Cory went home last night
And put a bullet through his head."

But I work in his factory.
And I curse the life I'm living.
And I curse my poverty.
And I wish that I could be,
Oh I wish that I could be,
Oh I wish that I could be Richard Cory.

—*Paul Simon and Art Garfunkel*

Understanding

1. Why do the narrators wish they were Richard Cory?
2. Speculate what went wrong in the private life of Richard Cory. What were *his* dreams?

3. What do we know about these narrators? What are their values? What are the values of the poet and the musicians who chose to write and perform these pieces?

Responding

1. Who are your Richard Corys? Do you dream, or have you dreamed, of being someone else? Re-create the public life of the person whom you envy. Imagine what is hidden from view—the other side of that person's life.
2. Are you aware of other people who wish that they were you? What would you advise them, or what would you reveal about yourself and your situation that might change their minds?

Connecting

The character in Poston's "Revolt of the Evil Fairies" (chapter two) wanted to be someone he wasn't chosen to be in the school play. How would you relate the message in "Richard Cory" to Poston's symbolic short story?

Writing Option: Dreams

Review your writing in response to the Responding questions in this chapter. Choose one aspect that you would like to revise and expound on. You may choose to use one of Studs Terkel's American dreams as a model, or you may choose a different method altogether for developing your dream story.

Part One Writing Option: A Self-portrait

Using the drafts of your gifts, wounds, decisions, and dreams writing, choose *three* that you want to revise. The three revised essays will form a self-portrait of you and reflect three situations that have contributed to your identity. These revisions should show increased control over the narrative form. They should be engaging in that they reveal insights, lessons learned, and salient points discovered as you synthesized your previous writing.

Part Two

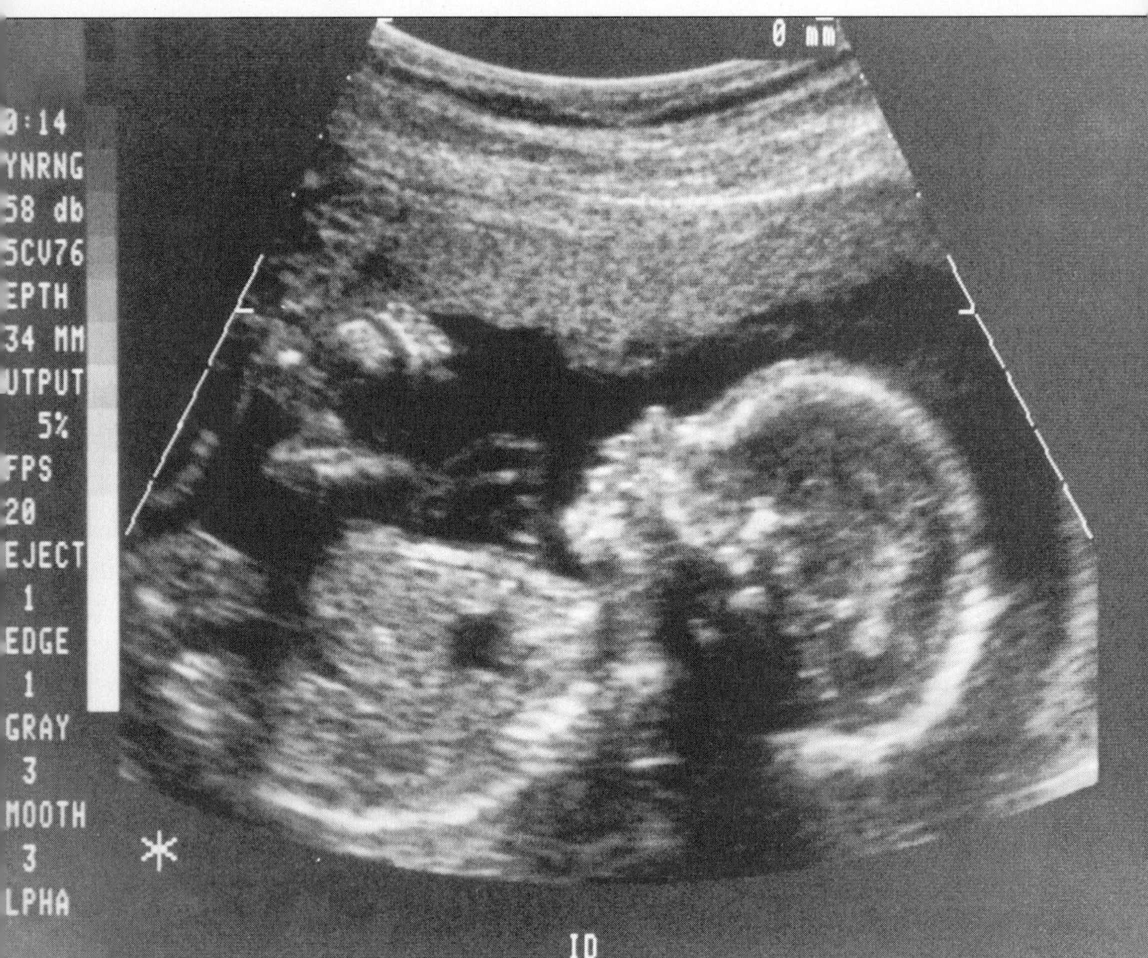
0 mm
YNRNG
58 db
5CV76
EPTH
34 MM
UTPUT
5%
FPS
20
EJECT
1
EDGE
1
GRAY
3
MOOTH
3
LPHA
ID

Origins and Influences

The readings in part two, "Origins and Influences," move beyond re-creating vivid portions of a life, or self-portraits as we have named them in part one, to consider life's "givens"—the forces of biology and community that also have a say in who we become. The endowments we are presented with at birth write their indelible signatures on our bodies, and we carry these biological markings through life whether we like the look of them or not. At birth we are also presented a family and a community. Like it or not, these institutions leave their powerful signatures on us as well, and now is the time to acknowledge their contributions. The challenging and rewarding work of exploring the markings of biology, family, community, and culture on our identity is the possibility of knowing them anew. We have lived with their markings for our whole lives, yet exploring them again here among a community of writers, you may begin to understand their powerful origins and influences on your identity for the first time.

Consider this stanza from T. S. Eliot's poem "Little Gidding V":

> We shall not cease from exploration
> And the end of all our exploring
> Will be to arrive where we started
> And know the place for the first time.

We invite you to respond to and write from the readings collected here to further your exploration into identity—an activity T. S. Eliot claims we never cease from doing.

Chapter five, "Biology," focuses on the biological self. We have divided this chapter into three thematic sections: "Biology and Identity," "Inborn Traits," and "Nature and Nurture." The writers you will encounter in "Biology and Identity" explore the world of genes, those little biological elements received from both of your parents by which hereditary characteristics are transmitted and determined. Writers represented here are John Stanley D. Bacon, Mihaly Csikszentmihalyi, Richard Dawkins, and Christine Gorman. "Inborn Traits," including essays by Lawrence Wright, Gillian Turner, Andrew Solomon, and Stanley Crouch, further explores the relationship between genetic inheritance and its visible signs in the way we live our lives. "Nature and Nurture" writers—Robert Wright, Loyal D. Rue, and Daniel Goleman—inquire into whether our genes (nature) or our environment (nurture) are the origin or influence which provide the most enduring signatures on our identity.

Chapter six, "Community and Culture," includes readings on the social or interactive self—that which is influenced by our families, our communities, and our cultures. We have divided "Community and Culture" into six sections: "Family Ties," "Learning Communities," "Communities of Faith," "In Public and Private," "Boundaries," and "Popular Culture." In "Family Ties" writers Maggie Scarf, Phyllis Rose, Susan Cheever, Floyd Skloot, and Julia Alvarez share singular family experiences and analyze their imprint on their identities. "Learning Communities," represented by writers Leslie Marmon Silko, Mike Rose, Frank Conroy, Michel de Montaigne, and Plato, describe and expound on the value and the variety of learning communities. The writers in "Communities of Faith"—Gordon Allport, Stephen J. Dubner, and Shirley Park Lowry—share their insights and make their claims regarding their spiritual journeys among others. The "In Public and Private" writers—Richard Rodriguez, Luc Sante, Howard Rheingold, and Elias Canetti—explore how private and public lives intersect to make claims on our identity. "Boundaries" presents Ina Russell, Gloria Wade-Gayles, Barbara MacDonald, Gloria Anzaldua, and Mihaly Csikszentmihalyi, writing on communities and the boundaries, or limits, they can place on us simply by our belonging to them without examining what belonging to them demands. Finally, the writers represented in "Popular Culture" demonstrate how the culture at large can affect our identity—the ways we think, act, view, define, and even dress ourselves. "Popular Culture" comprises Michael Ventura, Malcolm Gladwell, Rebecca Johnson, and Michiko Kakutani. In sum the readings in chapters five and six offer avenues to examine influences that have offered their signatures to your life. The readings also provide the opportunity for you to decide whether you have accepted these origins-and-influences signatures as your own.

As you did in part one, "Self-portraits," throughout part two you will concentrate on your personal public signature—your identity, that which you declare you are—through the reading and subsequent writing you will do in the company of these selections. This time you will filter your identity through your understanding of biology, community, and culture, to express your own uniqueness and individuality in the broader context of human experience. You will come closer to exploring your own signature, or as T. S. Eliot has penned, you may arrive where you started, but know the place for the first time.

5

Biology

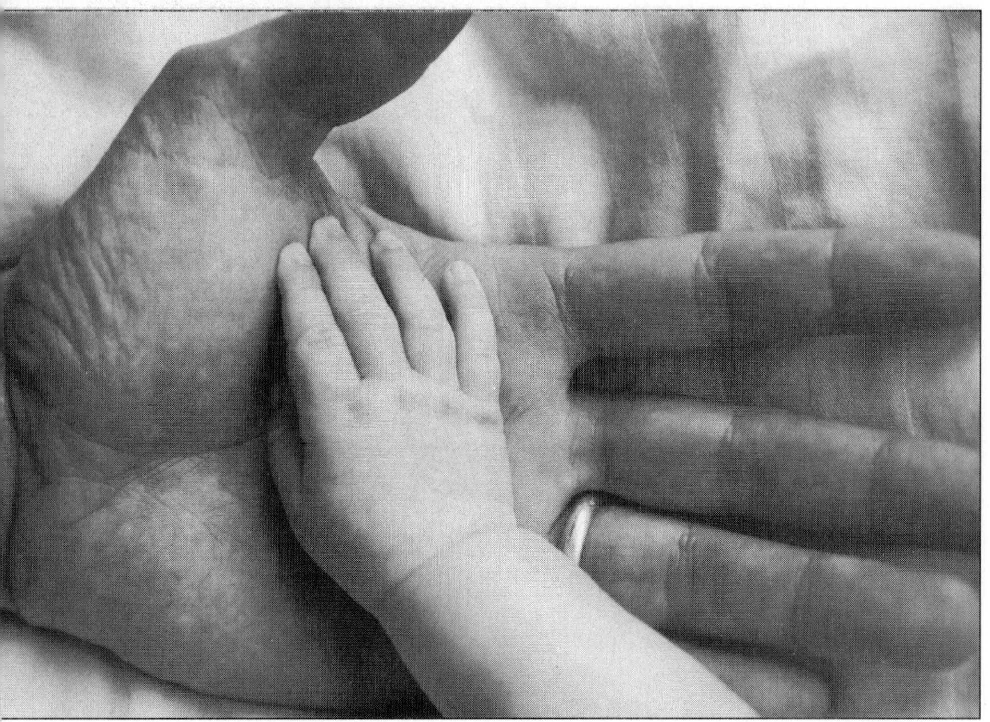

We posited in part one, "Self-portraits," that the stories we create around four experiences—our gifts, wounds, decisions, and dreams—become our identity; and though at any time we can change the stories about these experiences—and therefore change our identity—these four kinds of marker events are guideposts in defining who we are. We create our own truths about ourselves, because we alone have control over our stories. At points in our lives when we say we know who we are, we mean that we have a description of ourselves that we believe to be true. Who we are changes only with different descriptions of ourselves along the way.

If we use our gifts, wounds, decisions, and dreams to describe who we are, these created identities must be laid over the template of that which we do *not* create—our biological inheritance: our gender, appearance, body structure, and inborn traits and capacities. How our biology affects our identity is the topic of this chapter. Though these inborn traits determine much about our identity in the beginning of life, the question of whether and to what extent we can control our biology by will or by action remains at issue.

From the time we had enough language to think critically and to form our questions about the nature of life, we asked the inevitable: Because we are born with the *capacity* for particular behaviors—aggression or nurturing, for example—does it mean that the trait is biologically determined in the sense of being impossible to alter? Is who we become dependent upon what genes we are born with—our intelligence, our height, our musical or athletic talents—or is it our environment, our chances, our luck, or the people and institutions that surround us? What exactly do *nature* (our genetic inheritance) and *nurture* (our environment and culture, even our artifacts) contribute to our identity?

In each case, it might seem as though we are not in control of our own destiny, that both our biology and our environment limit us or control what we might otherwise become. To some extent this is true. We have a choice neither about the body or mind we are born with, nor about which family, nationality, or culture we are born into. These endowments are not under our control—in the beginning.

As we grow, as we begin to recognize our gifts, come to terms with our wounds, make our defining decisions, and dream our dreams, we begin to see the possibility of shaping our own lives. When this is true, our existence, our being in the world, is understood as possibility—we feel some control to actualize our free will. But even then the question of our biological, or genetic, inheritance can temper our aspirations. Without Michael Jordan's Achilles tendon and height, we realize we cannot attain his stature in basketball. Without eyesight, we cannot become pilots. Without ovaries, women cannot produce offspring. Thus our biology *does* control us, but the question as to what extent is worth exploring, and that exploration is steeped in controversy.

To approach the questions of biology and its influence on us, we have divided this chapter's readings into three sections: "Biology and Identity," "Inborn Traits," and "Nature and Nurture." The writers in "Biology and Identity" introduce the world of genes and of genetic research as a field. Using the foundations set by Charles Darwin, biochemist John Stanley D. Bacon and evolutionary biologist Richard Dawkins discuss what ancestors pass on genetically to their offspring. Psychologist and contributor to the field of evolutionary epistemology Mihaly Csikszentmihalyi cautions us to reflect on our genetically inherited impulses and habits in order to gain control of our psychic energy. Genes, he says, are not our helpers in understanding how to cope with modern life; instead, it is we who are their servants. Our genes and their genetic instructions are perhaps no longer the wisest inheritance to mine for the answers. Finally, Christine Gorman presents her findings on innate sexual differences—both neurological and physiological.

The "Inborn Traits" section includes readings that identify these powerful influences on our identity. Inevitably, these writers ask, are we victims of our genes? What values does culture place on various inherited physiological and neurological characteristics? What happens when societies value one trait over another, or when discussion or research around particular traits is influenced by political or special-interest groups? These writers and researchers look not only at the inborn tendencies, but also how society interprets them. Writer Lawrence Wright reports a broad variety of findings in controversial twins studies. Gillian Turner, a geneticist, identifies the genes for intelligence and where they come from. Music historian Andrew Solomon explains the inborn and obsessive genetic drive to make music. Social critic Stanley Crouch holds that although biological racial differences have been constructed as the defining characteristic of identity, in one hundred years these cultural constructions of "race" will cease to exist.

The final biology section, "Nature and Nurture," explores what scientists believe to be the contributions of both of these powerful influences on behavior and identity. Genetic or pharmaceutical gene therapy is the topic of Richard Wright's essay on whether violence and other aggressive behavior is linked to genes and, if so, whether this behavior should be altered with drugs. Loyal D. Rue is convinced that our biological gene pool can be changed by educating women, because they control which genes get passed on to the future. As the final reading, Daniel Goleman demonstrates that temperament is not destiny and that studies of emotional intelligence show that children can outgrow inborn tendencies.

In reading these selections, you will be in awe of what humankind has accomplished in its desire to understand life. As one of the human species's most devoted admirers, Jacob Bronowski says in his book *The Ascent of Man:* "Man ascends by discovering the fullness of his own gifts (his talents and faculties) and what he creates on the way are monuments to the stages in his understanding of nature and of self—what the poet W. B. Yeats called 'monuments of the unageing intellect.'" Scientists spend their lives hoping to discover the fullness of our gifts. The results of their research are the monuments to our stages of understanding. No questions are dumb ones to scientists. We hope that you will take from this chapter an enhanced understanding of your biological inheritance as a template, or simply as one other story, to more fully describe what it is to be human, and who you are within that mystery.

1 Biology and Identity

We begin our reading in biology with some of the findings and the questions scientists raise mostly because they are able to. By this we mean that "civilization" has allowed those who delve into the questions of life to pass on their information to future generations of scientists without new or younger scientists having to re-create the basic questions and experiments over and over again on their own. This inherited cumulative knowledge about the world is a result of civilization—of "village life"—not of the life of a nomad. As writer and scientist Jacob Bronowski has said: "The largest single step in the ascent of man is the change from nomad to village agriculture."

That we are able to read a body of work on the contribution genes make to what the human species looks like and acts like today is remarkable. Once certain humans decided to become villagers rather than nomads in search of food or grazing fields for their flocks, they had time and a stable place to create things that did not have to be carried; they had time and place for innovation; they had time and place to bury their dead and make memorials to them; they had time and energy to build myths and histories that would be passed on to future generations. Their lives could now become lives with features. To continue Bronowski's point, once people lived in villages, every day and every night could be different.

Bronowski also claims that the development of science reflects the preeminent stature of humankind among animals. The readings in this chapter are but a small representation of this preeminence—what a civilized life has allowed us to generate as an understanding, at this point in time, of our nature, our biological inheritance.

Who have we evolved to become, really? What is our purpose on earth? What have we inherited from our nomadic ancestors, or from our civilized fathers and mothers? Does our biology—our nature and genetic makeup—predestine our gifts, wounds, decisions, and dreams?

Scientists John Stanley D. Bacon, Mihaly Csikszentmihalyi, and Richard Dawkins write with a focus on genes, and what we inherit biologically from our ancestors, and Christine Gorman presents her findings on genetic differences among males and females. Csikszentmihalyi, however, will caution us on how we ought to evaluate our genes' contribution to our identity. All the while we should keep in mind that we have these and all other written words (artifacts of our understanding) because we live civilized lives, allowing us the freedom to think about the questions of life itself.

Heredity and Evolution

John Stanley D. Bacon

John Bacon was born in 1917 and educated at Trinity Hall, Cambridge, where he became interested in the chemical approach to biological problems. His research included work on nutrition, tuberculin, and particularly on the structure and metabolism of carbohydrates, conducted while he was a lecturer in biochemistry at Sheffield University, England.

When Bacon published *The Science of Heredity* in 1951, he wrote that the naked eye had always been the chief method for the study of life, that this study had been basically observational rather than experimental. In fact, it is only recently—in relation to all of the time that the human species has been on earth—that the magnifying glass and subsequent inventions have aided our study.

Much has changed since 1951 in our ability to study human beings, both in the available technology and in regard to the question of what our biological inheritance and our environment contribute to our identity. Ethologists (who explore and explain the nature of animal behavior) have typically asked questions like: What is instinct? What behavior is learned? How does behavior change? How do animals communicate? How do animals behave differently in groups than they do as individuals? Why do animals cooperate? How do they compete? And they use the human eye and language to describe what they find. With the help of technology—from the microscope to computers—we are learning more about our biological inheritance and its relationship to human behavior. In this essay Bacon summarizes the early contributions of biologists and lay people to the study of the human species.

That the offspring of rabbits were rabbits, of monkeys, monkeys, of men, men, and so on, was taken for granted until comparatively recent times. It is true that where their powers of observation failed, our ancestors indulged their imagination, and saw geese as the offspring of barnacles, or permitted the union of the most diverse species in their mythology. 1

Charles Darwin and his forerunners directed attention to the variability of species and postulated an evolutionary scheme in which, to the general horror, the offspring of worms were insects, of reptiles, birds, and of monkeys, men. More exactly, they pictured each species as a transitional stage in the formation of one or more new species; one frame in a cinematograph film of biological history. The offspring of rabbits, they said, are rabbits, but not quite the same rabbits, and in the course of evolution this discrepancy may accumulate, so that the rabbits of today differ considerably from the rabbits of a hundred thousand years ago.

This seemed all the more probable, since in much less than a tenth of that time man had produced breeds of domestic animals which contrasted strikingly with the wild species originally brought into domestication.

Man's experience as a breeder of domestic animals had given him the impression that the link between generation and generation was not so rigid that each offspring was an exact copy of its parents, nor was it so flexible that it could be manipulated at will. Parents and offspring were linked by something having both qualities, so that although animals could be bred for desirable qualities, much time and effort was required for the achievement.

5 The link between generations is what we call "heredity." Since Darwin's day we have begun to study it scientifically, and the name of "genetics" has been given to the branch of science concerned. . . .

The story begins nearly a hundred years ago, but for reasons which will be explained later the bulk of the scientific research was done in the second half of this period. In the first fifty years, however, one great obstacle was surmounted. This was the problem of the relation of the two parents to their offspring. The connection between mother and child is, of course, a very obvious physical one, and the maternity of a child is rarely in doubt. To primitive men, particularly those who did not lead a pastoral life, the relation between the sexual act and childbirth was probably not so obvious, and fatherhood consequently of little significance. Later, the reverse idea was held: that the female provided nothing but nourishment for a seed that came from the father, and motherhood was at a discount. The proof that each sex makes a contribution to the offspring, and that the latter begins its existence as a minute but nevertheless unique speck of living matter, was not obtained until the last decades of the nineteenth century. What was considered probable from general observation became established as one of the fundamental facts of the new science.

Another discovery of the same period, the invention of photography, has helped a large proportion of our countrymen to confirm what had previously been shown only to those of great wealth—that in the members of three generations there can be seen a persistent "family likeness," sometimes strong, sometimes feeble, but never entirely absent. By choosing contemporary photographs of each generation the confusing effect of time can be eliminated, and in each family album we can discern the "Robinson ears," the "Smith nose," just as in the past the examination of paintings revealed the history of the "Hapsburg lip." There can be no doubt that facial characteristics, at least, can be handed down from father to son, from mother to daughter, and (more significantly) from father to daughter and from mother to son. Whether *other* characteristics are inherited is a matter of some dispute; whether "Willie gets his brains from his father" or "Susan gets her temper from her grandmother" is rather more difficult to prove, particularly when the protagonists of opposing views have a personal interest in the answer.

"Little Johnny is *so* like his father, but at times you can see a lot of his mother in him." How often have we heard this? The child cannot resemble one parent without differing in some way from the other; he is usually a mixture of the two. This is understandable if both parents contribute to his origin, but a fact that is not easy to explain is that he and his brothers are not all alike.

It is unquestionable that brothers may differ considerably and yet retain the family likeness. The origin of the variability of our species as a whole evidently lies as much *within the family* as outside it.

Forty years of research into the nature of vitamins, and into many other aspects of human nutrition, have shown us how profoundly inadequate diets, just as surely as severe illness, can alter the human frame. The training of athletes, the development of skill in the techniques of modern industry, reveal the capacity of the body to adapt itself to new demands. Can we explain the differences between members of a family entirely by the action of such influences as these? Does, in fact, each married couple produce boys of one hereditary type and girls of another, which are then changed by the accidents of upbringing and the changes of family fortune into the diverse groups that we see in the family reunion photograph? Most parents would not hesitate to answer an emphatic "No," and they would be right, as later chapters will reveal. Heredity, while preserving the general conformity of the human species, produces a great diversity of detail within these limits.

It is now accepted, for reasons which will be given later, that both parents 10
contribute to the inherited characteristics of their offspring. Taking this for granted and leaving aside the difficulties introduced by sexual differences, the simplest assumption about the nature of heredity would be that the offspring represents an average of the two parents. Thus if the father had black hair and the mother blonde, we might suppose that all their children would have brown hair; or if the father was tall and the mother short (for a woman) that the children would all be of medium height.

The chief objection to such a theory of inheritance is that if it were true one would expect that populations would tend to become less diverse as time passed. The tallest individual would necessarily have to marry someone of shorter stature, and so on, so that after a few centuries we would expect to find everyone looking approximately the same. Since we have no reason to believe that this has happened, it becomes necessary to examine the processes which are working in the other direction—that is to say, which encourage *variation* in the population.

When Darwin was writing his *Origin of Species* (nearly a hundred years ago), he began with the knowledge that the members of natural populations varied considerably, and assumed that the environment among other factors played a big part in producing this effect. Following Lamarck, he thought it most likely that all the individual variations that could be seen in one generation were capable of being transmitted to the next. Among such variations were those due to use or disuse—for example, if an individual developed bigger muscles than his fellows, or (the familiar example) a longer neck by reaching up for food, these advantages would be inherited by his descendants. This was called the "inheritance of acquired characters," and it played an important, though not essential, part in the theory of the origin of new species put forward by Darwin.

That it did so was partly due to uncertainty about the mechanism of heredity which existed at that time. If we assumed the process to be one of averaging, or "blending," as we have just suggested, then these advantageous characteristics would tend to be lost again in the levelling action of inheritance, and to ensure progress in a particular direction a constant repetition of the variation (muscle development or neck stretching) was called for. Thus, in the struggle for survival the same adaptation had to be elicited in generation after generation in order that the whole or a section of the species should change from the old type towards a new one.

By what Darwin called "artificial selection" of particular variable characteristics, cultivated plants and domestic animals had been made to diverge from the original wild type very considerably, and many distinct varieties or breeds had been produced within each species. As examples of these he cited cattle, apples, and in particular pigeons, with which he had conducted experiments on cross-breeding. Very striking results had been achieved by man's efforts within a biologically short period of time, and, as we now know, this process of artificial improvement of plants and animals was to continue unchecked in the next century and to be a powerful stimulus to the scientific study of heredity.

Understanding

1. What is Darwin's evolutionary scheme?
2. How has photography enhanced our understanding of the transmission of hereditary characteristics?
3. According to Bacon, which characteristics did he claim are transmitted by heredity?
4. In Bacon's view, what is the relation of two parents to their offspring? Are the offspring an "average" of the parents? If it were true that offspring represent an average of the two parents, what result would this have on the characteristics of the population?
5. What does Darwin mean by the inheritance of acquired characteristics (paragraph 12)? What examples do we have of this theory?
6. How does the process of artificial selection take place?

Responding

1. In the past, artificial improvement in life forms was limited to plants and animals (producing heartier grass or more juicy tomatoes or leaner cattle). But now attempts are being made to alter human characteristics in the laboratory through manipulating the basic blueprints of life: the genes. What are your thoughts on genetic engineering?
2. What characteristics in yourself can you see as inherited? What characteristics as acquired? Which as a result of inherited and acquired processes?
3. Find out more about social Darwinism, the late-nineteenth-century concept with clear twentieth-century overtones that human social organization was based on the survival of the fittest and the biologically superior? What do you think about this idea?

4. Why are some people upset by the thought that human beings evolved from other life forms?

Connecting

1. In what way is our biology our signature? Develop a brief explication on the use of this metaphor in relation to our biological inheritances.
2. In light of Bacon's essay, consider and draft an answer to at least one of the questions in paragraph 4 of the introduction to "Biology and Identity."
3. Consider the impact of biology on the characters in Gordimer's "Country Lovers" (chapter three). Apply one of Bacon's findings to the situation or the characters in that story.

The Veils of Maya and the World of the Genes

Mihaly Csikszentmihalyi

Born in 1934 in Fiume, Italy, Mihaly Csikszentmihalyi (pronounced "Chick-sent-me-hi") immigrated to the United States in 1956. A former chairman of the Department of Psychology at the University of Chicago and now a professor there, Csikszentmihalyi gained prominence with his bestselling book *Flow: The Psychology of Optimal Experience.* In it he revealed that "What makes people truly satisfied is to be actively involved in a difficult enterprise—a task that stretches our mental and physical abilities." His quarter century of research into "the positive dimensions of experience—creativity, enjoyment, productive involvement," has also yielded some interesting findings on what can compromise that happiness, which he presents in *The Evolving Self: A Psychology for the Third Millennium.*

In "The Veils of Maya and the World of the Genes," Csikszentmihalyi probes the subtle and obvious ways we keep ourselves from reaching a clearer perception of reality. The "veils of Maya" to which he refers is a Hindu concept according to which the world is the product of our own Maya, or illusion, from which we must free ourselves. For Csikszentmihalyi, the veils of illusion overhang the three sources of our human nature: our genes, our culture, and our self. He suggests that the "genetic instructions which were once necessary for our survival . . . are often in conflict with present reality."

The brain is a wonderful mechanism, but it is also deceptive. To guarantee 1
that we don't relax too much, it forces us to strive after forever receding goals. To keep us from settling for daydreams, it begins to project unpleasant information on the screen of consciousness as soon as we stop doing something purposeful. It makes us feel good when we do things that in the past have served survival, but it can't tell us when pleasure trespasses the threshold of danger. Whether we like it or not, it primes us for actions that made sense when people lived in caves, but are now out of place. These are some of the biases built into the machinery of the brain, and in order to gain control of consciousness we must learn how to moderate their influence. But they are not the only obstacles that stand in the way of freeing the self. We normally allow a whole series of illusions to stand between ourselves and reality. Built out of genetic instructions, cultural rules, and the unbridled desires of the self, these distortions are comforting, yet they need to be seen through for the self to be truly liberated.

ILLUSION AND REALITY

A recurring theme in many cultures has been that reality as it appears to us is a deceptive illusion. What we see, think, and believe are not the true outlines of the world. Reality presents itself through a series of veils that distort what lies behind them. Most people look at the illusory veils and are convinced they see the truth, but actually they are only deluding themselves. Only by patiently lifting what the Hindu called the veils of Maya—or illusion—do we get a closer glimpse of what life is really about. This idea is not unique to India, however. Many religions and philosophies the world over hold that common-sense appearances are deceptive and must be seen through to understand the nature of reality. Twenty-four centuries ago, Democritus is supposed to have said: "Nothing is real, or if it is, we don't know it. We have no way of knowing the truth. Truth is at the bottom of an abyss." Christianity did not deny the reality of the material world, but only its importance. All the action that really mattered took place outside this existence. Those who took the events in the physical realm too seriously ran the risk of being deluded by trivial and transient concerns, and thus forfeited the eternal realm of the spirit.

But why should we be concerned, at the threshold of the third millennium, with what ancient religions and philosophies have said about reality? What did they know about truth? It might seem anachronistic that in discussing evolution and the future one should pay any attention to Hindu myths or Christian worldviews. If one takes evolution seriously, however, one appreciates how important the past is in shaping the present and the future. Just as the chemical structure of the human chromosome began to determine, millions of years ago, both the truths and the illusions that we are destined to experience, so, too, do the symbolic representations created by past thinkers help to reveal as well as to conceal reality. The task for us today is to separate the genuine insights of religions and philosophies from the inevitable errors that crept into their explanations. It would be indeed an act of sinful pride to assume that present knowledge is in every way superior to that of the past, and to dismiss what the ancients learned as backward superstition.

"Evolutionary epistemology" is a branch of scholarship that applies the evolutionary perspective to an understanding of how knowledge develops. Knowledge always involves getting information. The most primitive way of acquiring it is through the sense of touch: amoebas and other simple organisms know what happens around them only if they can feel it with their "skins." The knowledge such an organism can have is strictly about what is in its immediate vicinity. After a huge jump in evolution, organisms learned to find out what was going on at a distance from them, without having to actually feel the environment. This jump involved the development of sense organs for processing information that was farther away. For a long time, the most important sources of knowledge were the nose, the eyes, and the ears. The next big advance occurred when organisms developed memory. Now information no longer needed to be present at all, and the animal could recall events and outcomes that happened in the past. Each one of these steps in the evolution of knowledge added important survival advantages to the species that was equipped to use it.

5 Then, with the appearance in evolution of humans, an entirely new way of acquiring information developed. Up to this point, the processing of information was entirely *intrasomatic,* that is, it took place within the body of the organism. But when speech appeared (and even more powerfully with the invention of writing), information processing became *extrasomatic.* After that point knowledge did not have to be stored in the genes, or in the memory traces of the brain; it could be passed on from one person to another through words, or it could be written down and stored on a permanent substance like stone, paper, or silicon chips—in any case, outside the fragile and impermanent nervous system.

The immense increase in our power to control the planet was made possible by the extrasomatic storage of information, a skill that we acquired in only the last few seconds of evolutionary history. At first information was stored in songs, myths, and stories that our ancestors told one another around campfires. Legends encapsulated centuries of useful experience in a few rhymed lines, proverbs, or cautionary tales. The young members of the tribe no longer had to learn only from their own experiences what was dangerous and what was valuable in their environment; instead, they could rely on the collective memory of past generations, and possibly avoid repeating their mistakes. This knowledge helped them to achieve a certain amount of control over the environment, and freed their time to learn the various technologies—such as making weapons, building fires, and working metals—that were also being transmitted extrasomatically.

Of course myths and legends did not just convey useful information; they also passed on an enormous amount of what nowadays would be called "noise"—that is, irrelevant details, or details that make sense only in certain specific historical situations. This is inevitable because anyone who wants to pass on a personally experienced truth usually cannot distinguish the essential element of that truth from its incidental features. For example, suppose a father in our own culture wants to explain to his son the love he felt when he married his wife. Because discussing emotions among males is embarrassing, and because external events are more "real" and easy to describe, the father might recall the wedding primarily in terms of what music was played in the church, the number of guests at the reception, the number of bottles of wine consumed, and so on. The central message concerning his feelings for the bride may hardly be mentioned. So what the son might learn from the father's story is that the significance of weddings depends on music, guests, and drinks, missing the most important part of the message altogether.

When the experiences and thoughts of a culture begin to coalesce into a systematic view of what life and the world are about, religions make their first appearance on the stage of evolution. It is no exaggeration to say that religions have been the most important extrasomatic organs of knowledge created by humans up to now—with the possible exception of science, which is a way of checking objectively the information one obtains, and so allows its users to systematically reject erroneous conclusions. Although religions lack this feature of self-correction, and thus generally fail to adapt to new knowledge and to grow with time, they do have certain other advantages over science that should not be dismissed. Perhaps most important is the fact that religions have existed for centuries, and have had a chance to retain information that is important for human survival for a longer time than science. For this reason alone it would be fatuous to ignore religious insights, especially when, as in the case of the veils of Maya that disguise reality, they recur over and over in very different cultural contexts.

The notion that reality is well hidden from view is not one that only ancient thinkers have entertained. Current scientific thought is beginning to explain, in its own terms, what earlier thinkers may have meant by the metaphor of Maya. The social sciences, for instance, have provided ample evidence to show how different truth appears, depending on where one happens to be born, what sort of early experiences one is exposed to, or what kind of occupation one ends up pursuing.

For example, anthropologists have demonstrated in any number of stud- 10
ies how successfully cultures can inculcate their values and worldviews. Most human groups believe that they are chosen people situated at the center of the universe, and that their ways of life are better than anyone else's. The Amish live in an Amish world, the Zulus in a world of Zulus. Both take it for granted that their understanding of the world is the only one that makes sense. One unfortunate consequence of this attitude is that, believing too strongly in the reality of our culture's world, we miss the larger reality behind it. Many people don't object to toxic waste as long as it is not dumped in their neighborhood. Substances become poisonous only when they threaten one's world. If my world is limited to Chicago, then all the toxins outside the city are not poisonous—as far as I am concerned, they don't exist. The larger the group with which one identifies, the closer to ultimate reality one gets. Only the person who sees the entire planet as her world can recognize a toxic substance as poison no matter where it is dumped.

Similarly, sociologists have pointed out the ways in which reality is socially constructed. As people interact with parents, friends, and co-workers, they learn to see the world from the vantage point of those particular interactions. The world looks very different from a businessmen's club than from a union hall, a military barracks, or a monastery. The chiefs of staff live in a world centered around the Pentagon, where megadeaths, body counts, and fat contracts with defense industries are the main features of the landscape. Theirs is a different world from that of car salesmen, football players, or professors. But it is not just the differences in social position or in ways of making a living that so often result in conflicts of interest, what Marxists call the class struggle. It is that people in different positions in the social system end up living in different physical and symbolic environments—in what are, in effect, alien worlds. Considering how powerful the forces of culture and society are in shaping what we see, what we feel, and what we believe, it is not surprising that the Hindus thought we were all living under spells cast by demonic wizards.

Psychologists find comparable biases at the individual level. Each person, equipped with a more or less unique set of genes and experiences, develops a "cognitive map" of his or her world that makes navigation among its shoals easier. In the same household one child might learn to see the world through rosy glasses, while the other will learn that it is bleak and dangerous. Some children, born with a great sensitivity to sound, will grow up paying attention to the auditory environment and not see many of the colors, lights, and shapes that surround the more visually sensitive child. One person is more interested in quantities, another in feelings; one is open and trusting, the other retiring and suspicious. These individual differences develop with time into habits and then into ways of thinking about and interpreting experience. Such "maps" are useful because they provide consistent directions to those who use them, but they are hardly accurate in the sense of presenting an objective, universally valid picture of reality. In fact, in the same situation two persons using different cognitive maps will see and experience entirely different realities.

The relativity of knowledge is not a concept that only the "soft" social sciences have explored. Even physics, once the paragon of a mechanical and absolute science, has in the last century given up hope of providing unambiguous accounts of what is actually out there—for it turns out that even the most elementary, concrete sense data give unreliable information. Mountains, trees, and houses are not made up of solid matter, but of billions of unpredictably twitching particles. As Democritus already suspected centuries ago, the world we can see is only the part that registers upon the senses. There are all sorts of things happening around us about which we have no idea because they are beyond our perceptual threshold. The eyes, ears, and other senses provide just the minimum of information needed to survive in an average environment. But they leave out so much. It's enough to see a puppy almost going out of its mind with excitement as it explores scents in a meadow to realize how much information we routinely miss.

Why can't we then just make bigger and more sensitive instruments so as to get at those elusive events outside our ken? As physicists have come to realize, every instrument, every measurement gives only a biased view, dependent on the instruments themselves. Reality is created as one tries to apprehend it. Heisenberg's famous uncertainty principle, which describes the logical impossibility of determining both the position and the velocity of a given atomic particle at the same time, was just the first rumble in what has become a veritable earthquake threatening the formerly solid edifice of the physical sciences. Ilya Prigogine, a Nobel laureate in chemistry, expressed the difficulty of getting an accurate picture of absolute reality as follows: "Whatever we call reality, it is revealed to us only through an active construction in which we participate." And the physicist John Wheeler said: "Beyond particles, beyond fields of force, beyond geometry, beyond space and time themselves, is the ultimate constituent [of all there is], the still more ethereal act of observer-participation." In other words, no matter how complex the theory, how precise the measurement, the fact is that it is we who have developed the theories and the measuring instruments—hence, whatever we learn is going to be dependent on our perspective as observers. The limitations of the human nervous system, the particular history of the culture, the idiosyncrasies in the symbol systems used are going to determine the reality one sees. The inelegant acronym used by computer programmers, GIGO (Garbage In, Garbage Out), is applicable to epistemology in general. The output is always a function of the input.

When the Australian aborigines tried to explain the monsoon that each year came to their land from the sea amidst thunder and lightning, they pictured it as a huge snake mating in the clouds and giving birth to rain. Given what they knew, this was the most meaningful account for what they were experiencing. The modern explanation is based on temperature differentials, rate of vapor condensation, wind velocity, and so on. This story sounds much more sensible to us than the one about the giant snake, but would observers looking at it a few hundred years hence not find it equally primitive?

Does this mean, then, that it is useless to worry about what is true, because no matter how much one tries the answer will always be distorted? Many people end up agreeing with this notion. The step from relativism to cynicism is easy to take, yet it is not the best direction in which to go. If we refused to take seriously the reality available here and now because it isn't the absolute truth, we would surely regret that decision in short order. Even though reality can only be seen through distorting glasses, it is better to make do with what one can comprehend, rather than disdain it because it falls short of perfection.

But isn't it discouraging to know that, no matter how much we strive to understand, ultimate reality will always remain hidden? Only if the search for truth is motivated by the desire to reach an absolute, definitive answer. The person looking for certainty is bound to be disappointed. He will be like Faust, who after spending his life studying theology, philosophy, and the sciences despairs at the discovery that he has not learned one single truth he can confidently hold on to. If on the other hand we realize that the partial truths we uncover are all legitimate aspects of the unknowable universe, then we can learn to enjoy the search and derive from it the pleasure one gets from any creative act—whether it is painting a picture or cooking a good meal. In this case, however, it is a question not just of a painting or a meal, but of a way of seeing, of creating an entire world. Shaping one's own reality, living in a world one has created, can be as enjoyable as writing a symphony.

No person who ever lived could apprehend reality as a whole, nor is it imaginable that someone will ever do so. Like evolution itself, the quest for truth never ends. Certainties are always revised, and entirely new vistas open up when we least expect it. Imagine the revolution in understanding when the first farmers discovered that a single seed planted would yield hundreds of new seeds, or when the Copernican view of the planetary system displaced the Ptolemaic view.

But creating a new reality, a personally valid world, is not easy. It is much easier to accept the illusory certainties provided by the genes and by the culture, or to reject all effort and seek refuge in a radical cynicism that denies the value of any effort at understanding. Although the reality we must seek will not contain *the* truth, it must have *a* truth contained in it. A creative product is never random or arbitrary; it must be true to something deeply sensed or felt inside the person. And in order to get to that kernel of inner certainty, one must learn to peel away the various veils of Maya.

There is an old Indian parable that I like to repeat to graduate students 20
who are trying to find topics for their doctoral dissertations. It involves a young disciple who approaches an old and skilled sculptor with a request.

"Master," he says, "I want to become a famous sculptor. What should I do?"

"Well," replies the master, "tell me, what kind of a statue would you like to make?"

The young man thinks for a while, and concludes: "More than anything else, I would like to sculpt a beautiful elephant."

At this the master places in front of the young man a block of stone and a few tools: "Fine. Here is some marble, a mallet, and a chisel. All you have to do now is carve away everything that does not look like a beautiful elephant."

Thus ends the story. Simple? In a way, of course it is, and yet also infuriat- 25
ingly difficult. How do we know what is *not* the elephant? How do we know which is the veil, and which is the reality it conceals? We cannot know in advance. Only after he starts carving does the sculptor begin to sense what must be cast away, and what must be kept; it takes much longer still to know whether he is getting an elephant or just a shapeless lump of stone. Only after many trials does one realize how difficult the simple task actually is. One must painstakingly match one's preconceptions against actual, ongoing experience to begin separating truth from illusion.

This chapter will discuss three major sources of distortion that interfere with a truthful apprehension of what goes on in the world. They include genetic programming, the cultural heritage, and the demands of the self. These distortions are "inside" each one of us—no human being is immune to the illusions they foster. . . .*

THE WORLD OF THE GENES

In the previous chapter we have seen that the brain is built so as to be susceptible to a variety of pleasurable sensations that can be harmful in excessive doses. More generally, it is by now beyond any serious doubt that how we experience the world is limited and structured—but not determined—by the chemical instructions encoded in the genes. These instructions have been passed on more or less unchanged for many millions of years from ancestor to ancestor, and down to our parents. What they tell us to do is to follow the best strategy for survival that our ancestors were able to develop. They tell us to search for food when hungry, defend ourselves if attacked, be interested in members of the opposite sex, and so on.

Genetic instructions are rather generic—they apply to average situations, and prompt us to act in ways that generally tended to be useful in the past.

---

*Csikszentmihilyi's original chapter has been apportioned for this anthology. Of his "three major sources of distortion," you will encounter the first—genetic programming—in this chapter. Cultural heritage is excerpted as "The World of Culture" in chapter six, and the demands of the self are included in "The World of the Self" in chapter seven.

Infants are born with the ability to recognize human faces, because these are the most important features of a baby's early environment. Similarly, babies are programmed to imitate adults, because that is the surest way for them to become independent and survive. These instructions are solidly embedded in the brain, and their effects are automatic. However, when a person is confronted with a new situation, the wisdom of the genes is no longer reliable. An infant will imitate an abusive adult as well as a well-meaning one. Evolution has not been able to build an accurate detector for letting us know which behaviors are worth imitating and which are not. Mammals might be genetically equipped to avoid snakes, but not unscrupulous bond salesmen.

As humans have come to depend more and more on cultural rather than genetic instructions for survival, they have had to unlearn much that was useful in the past. New, artificial rules have had to be adopted instead, such as learning to control anger, to curb sexuality, to tolerate long periods of sitting at desks thinking—often against the promptings of "nature." Yet, despite all this domestication, the voice of the gene is still strong, and the way we experience the world is to a large degree determined by it. Even if a man has learned not to act out aggressive or sexual impulses, much of his inner life, much of his psychic energy, is tied down in emotions and thoughts prompted by instincts. This is the first veil of Maya, and unless one learns to see through it, reality will always be obscured by the needs and desires in the genetic program.

Generally we assume that instincts, drives, and visceral needs constitute 30
the most genuine core of personality, that they are the essence of who we are. But lately evolutionary biologists have begun to argue that the individual person, as far as the genes are concerned, is only a vehicle for their own reproduction and further dissemination. The genes don't really care about us at all, and if it helped their reproduction, they would just as soon have us live in ignorance and misery. Genes are not our little helpers; it is we who are their servants.

The chemical instructions that predispose an unwed teenager to become pregnant were not designed to make her happy or successful in the complex society in which she now lives. They are just a mechanism for making sure that the information in her chromosomes is going to be copied and passed down to another generation. In the past, when the life span was short and infant mortality high, genes that were able to stimulate a young girl to become pregnant as soon as she could bear a child had a better chance of spreading than genes prompting more demure behavior. Whether this was actually good for the individual girl or not is beside the point. The teenager is, of course, blissfully unaware of all this, and obeys the call of nature in the mistaken belief that what feels good at the moment will also be good in the long run.

The genes are programmed to protect us only for as long as we produce viable offspring; afterward we might as well be dead meat. While it is true that our interests as individuals and as carriers of genetic instructions often overlap, this is not always the case. For instance, genes are not interested in how long people live past the time their children are old enough to survive on their own. In fact, it would be to their advantage if the parents died as soon as possible after their children are out of college, so they wouldn't take up room and resources that could be used by still another generation. Not a very friendly bunch, these genes, yet we keep mistaking their interests for ours. As long as we cannot tell the difference between those interests, our minds will not be free to pursue their own ends, but will have to obey garbled commands from the past.

Each person creates the world he or she lives in by investing attention in certain things, and by doing so according to certain patterns. The world constructed on the blueprints provided by the genes is one in which all of a person's attention is invested in furthering the agenda of "reproductive fitness." This is a simple goal: How can I get enough out of the environment to make sure that I reproduce and that my children will also have children? In less complex organisms, like many species of insects, practically the entire life span is dedicated to the project of laying a clutch of eggs; promptly afterward, the parents expire. Like every other organism, the butterfly has evolved to see only those things that will either help or hinder the survival of its offspring. Its world is made up of flowery shapes that provide nectar, and shapes that resemble predators that are best avoided. Poets make much of the majestic eagle soaring freely among the snowy peaks. But the eyes of the eagle are generally focused on the ground, searching for rodents lurking in the shadows. The lives of much of humanity could be summed up in similar terms.

Let us take the example of Jerry, an imaginary young lawyer. On what does he spend his life? Most of it is directed by the requirements of his genes. As he wakes up in the morning, he will spend close to an hour washing, dressing, and sprucing up in an attempt to make his appearance attractive yet at the same time somewhat intimidating—a red power tie might help in that department. Then he spends a few minutes having breakfast, the first of several meals during the day that will boost his spirits and energy by replenishing the sugar level in his bloodstream. The car he drives to work, and the way he drives, are also indirectly influenced by the instructions in his genes. He might drive a Volvo because it is safe, a Ford because it is practical, or he might choose a car that is full of power, or one that projects the image of success. And why does Jerry spend eight, ten, twelve hours a day working? So that he can satisfy his nesting instinct and buy a comfortable house, attract a desirable mate, have children, accumulate some property to pass on, and afford a large insurance policy to protect his offspring.

In all probability Jerry would not say that he spends his psychic energy the way he does because he is trying to humor his genes. He would say that he *chose* to wear the red tie because he likes it better than the others, and drives the Volvo because he feels good driving it. Perhaps he could back up his choices with reasons based on personal experiences, or with objective evidence. In that case, more power to him. But all too often people do not consider options; they do not pause to reflect on alternatives. They simply take the script provided by the genes, and enact it according to the specific directions given by the culture they happen to be born in.

As a teenager I spent a year or so attending a high school in the working-class neighborhood of a southern Italian city. My classmates came from families uprooted by World War II who had moved from traditional farming communities to try their luck in the new urban slums growing up around the factory districts. During the time I spent with them, I felt like an anthropologist visiting a strange tribe; not only their values, but also the ways they looked at the world were so very different from what I had been used to. Although quite a few of the boys (the classes were still segregated by gender) became my friends, I never ceased to wonder at the fact that roughly nine out of ten ideas that went through their heads were about sex. If an unknown teacher or student walked into the classroom for the first time, the boys would comment loudly and at length about his or her primary and secondary sexual characteristics, and speculate about how he or she would be in bed. The high point of the week for these fourteen-year-olds was Wednesday, when the nearby whorehouse gave daytime student discounts. Even though not everyone had access to heterosexual adventures, most of the conversation revolved about real or imaginary exploits. There were also several stable homosexual couples who took their relationships very seriously and with a certain romantic flair.

Not that the school I describe was unique. Teens everywhere must learn to struggle with the hormones flooding their bodies—and their brains—with urgent instructions concerning sexuality and reproduction. It has been estimated that American teenagers think of sex on an average of once every twenty-six seconds—not because they want to, but because the sensations coursing through their flesh make it impossible to do otherwise. Whatever the actual frequency of sex-related thoughts, the point is that psychic energy is not free to go wherever we wish it to go; left to itself, it turns in the direction it was programmed.

Food has a similar grip on the mind. We cannot spend more than a few hours without starting to think of eating. My studies of the psychology of everyday life suggest that average people spend between 10 and 15 percent of their waking life either eating or thinking about food. For people with eating disorders the figure is twice as high—almost one-third of the day is filled with preoccupations about food. In extreme cases, not being able to curb one's hunger can kill. It is uniformly reported by people who have spent time in concentration camps that the prisoners who die first are those who cannot get their minds off food, and are willing to do anything to obtain it. A friend who spent years in the Soviet gulags tells that in one of the camps the kitchen staff amused itself by dumping potato peelings—the only even remotely edible refuse—right next to the latrines, where they would be immediately contaminated with excrement. To eat these raw potato skins was suicide—yet there were always several inmates who could not restrain themselves, and heedless of warnings gorged themselves on the peelings, usually to die soon thereafter of intestinal infections.

Problems of this severity we do not have. Yet in reading popular magazines one gets the impression that even in our society most people are still engaged in a constant battle against obsession with food. It seems that a new diet makes its appearance every week, promising deliverance to the overweight masses. Celebrities discuss their weight-watching strategies with the seriousness once reserved for the salvation of the soul. Sedentary employees in the United States consume as many as 8,000 calories a day—almost three times what the body actually needs—and this inevitably leads to weight gains dangerous to health. Clearly we are far from having gained control of our appetites.

40 Does this mean that it is better to question every move we make, and try to repress sexual desires, or try to stop eating, or refrain from having children, because these are not really *our* goals, but are ones that have been implanted in our minds by selfish genes? Such a course of action would of course be self-defeating. There is no way to escape the facticity of biological existence. It would be presumptuous to try second-guessing the wisdom of millions of years of adaptation, even if it were possible to do so. At the same time, survival in the third millennium will require that we understand better how we are manipulated by chemicals in the body.

As a first step, as we go through daily routines, it is liberating to stop and reflect why we do the things we do. It helps to know, if I get a third rasher of bacon for breakfast, that I am not just exercising free choice or indulging a passing whim, but am probably being manipulated by the instructions of a hungry three-million-year-old gene. It does not matter whether I go ahead and eat that third rasher or not. What counts is that, even if only for a few seconds, I have interrupted the automatic determinism of the genes—that for the moment, I have lifted the first veil of Maya.

Reflecting on the source of impulse, of habits, is the first step in getting control of one's psychic energy. Knowing the origin of motives, and becoming aware of our biases is the prerequisite for freedom. But it is not enough to know how genetic instructions keep us doing what they wish us to do. The second veil is the one with which culture and society—the human systems we are born into—shroud reality, covering up alternatives in order to use our psychic energy for their own ends.

Understanding

1. "Genetic instructions," Csikszentmihalyi explains, "are rather generic—they apply to average situations, and prompt us to act in ways that generally tended to be useful in the past" (paragraph 28). What are genetic instructions? In what ways and through what means do they prompt us to act?
2. In arguing that the brain is a wonderful but deceptive mechanism, Csikszentmihalyi reports that "We normally allow a whole series of illusions to stand between ourselves and reality" (paragraph 1). What does he consider "illusions"?
3. Csikszentmihalyi posits that "with the appearance in evolution of humans, an entirely new way of acquiring information developed" (paragraph 5). When speech appeared, information processing became *extrasomatic*—it could be passed on from one person to another. How has this extrasomatic information-processing mode affected our conception of self?
4. In what ways does Csikszentmihalyi suggest that we are the "servants" of our genes (paragraph 30), manipulated by chemicals in our bodies? What importance does this "servant" role play in our quest for selfhood?

5. From the perspective of science as Csikszentmihalyi outlines it, are stories that a people tell about their origins "veils" that obscure reality? If so, explain. If not, what purpose(s) do they serve?

Responding

1. Where do people today find the "collective memory of past generations"? What value does the generation born after 1960 attach to this kind of memory? How is it demonstrated?
2. Recall an instance when information you received through your senses was challenged or changed through later experience. Describe this situation.
3. Can you identify a belief that you once thought to be true and later learned was not true? What was that belief? How did you come to "unlearn" it? What circumstances would have to exist in order for you to return to that belief?
4. Following the example that Csikszentmihalyi gives of Jerry, the imaginary young lawyer, how much of your daily life is committed to doing things that ensure your reproductive fitness? What activities are they? How do you explain them? Do you think you would do them for any other reason?
5. Over several days, reflect on the things you do on impulse and those that you give conscious thought to doing. Compare the frequency of each type of activity. Which do you do more of? What can you conclude from this distribution of activities?

Connecting

1. How do paragraphs 5 and 6 relate to Jacob Bronowski's assertion in the introduction to "Biology and Identity" regarding nomadic and civilized lives?
2. In paragraph 14, Csikszentmihalyi declares that "Reality is created as one tries to apprehend it." What does he mean? Do you agree? Identify a reading selection from part one, "Self-portraits," where the writer created reality as he or she tried to apprehend it. Analyze how this works.
3. Using a memorable statement from Csikszentmihalyi's discussion of "the truth" in paragraphs 16–19, apply it to a discussion of the writer's thinking (and writing) in Carsen's "The Marginal World" (chapter one), Powell's "Public Announcement" (chapter three), or a selection of your choice in *Signatures.*
4. Jerry, the lawyer in paragraphs 34–35, may have made choices among alternatives regarding what his genes were telling him to do and the actual behavior he employed. Use Csikszentmihalyi's Jerry-the-lawyer distinction to assess what went on between Paulus and Thebedi in Gordimer's "Country Lovers" (chapter three), in Wade-Gayles's essay "Brother Pain: How a Black Woman Came to Terms with Interracial Love" in chapter six, or in any other *Signatures* essay that raises this distinction between truth and reality.

Ancestors and the Digital River

Richard Dawkins

In the preface to *River out of Eden: A Darwinian View of Life,* revolutionary evolutionist Richard Dawkins states that one of the reasons he wrote the book was to acknowledge the incredible contribution of Charles Darwin to our understanding of living things and how they came to be what they are. In fact, all of Dawkins's books have been explorations of Darwin's principles. In the following excerpt from *River out of Eden,* Dawkins presents the metaphor of a river to illustrate how all living things are simply vehicles for information—gene carriers whose primary purpose is propagation of their own DNA (deoxyribonucleic acid)—the fundamental hereditary material of all living organisms; the polymer composing the genes.

Richard Dawkins grew up in East Africa, possibly one of the most diverse bioscapes in the world. He is now a fellow of New College, Oxford University, in England. He lives in Oxford with his wife, Lalla Ward, best known as Romana, Dr. Who's assistant, in the BBC's television series. Dawkins has also written the bestsellers *The Blind Watchmaker* and *The Selfish Gene.*

All peoples have epic legends about their tribal ancestors, and these legends often formalize themselves into religious cults. People revere and even worship their ancestors—as well they might, for it is real ancestors, not supernatural gods, that hold the key to understanding life. Of all organisms born, the majority die before they come of age. Of the minority that survive and breed, an even smaller minority will have a descendant alive a thousand generations hence. This tiny minority of a minority, this progenitorial elite, is all that future generations will be able to call ancestral. Ancestors are rare, descendants are common. 1

All organisms that have ever lived—every animal and plant, all bacteria and all fungi, every creeping thing, and all readers of this book—can look back at their ancestors and make the following proud claim: Not a single one of our ancestors died in infancy. They all reached adulthood, and every single one was capable of finding at least one heterosexual partner and of successfully copulating.[1] Not a single one of our ancestors was felled by an enemy, or by a virus, or by a misjudged footstep on a cliff edge, before bringing at least one child into the world. Thousands of our ancestors' contemporaries failed in all these respects, but not a single solitary one of our ancestors failed in any of them. These statements are blindingly obvious, yet from them much follows: much that is curious and unexpected, much that explains and much that astonishes.

Since all organisms inherit all their genes from their ancestors, rather than from their ancestors' unsuccessful contemporaries, all organisms tend to possess successful genes. They have what it takes to become ancestors—and that means to survive and reproduce. This is why organisms tend to inherit genes with a propensity to build a well-designed machine—a body that actively works as if it is striving to become an ancestor. That is why birds are so good at flying, fish so good at swimming, monkeys so good at climbing, viruses so good at spreading. That is why we love life and love sex and love children. It is because we all, without a single exception, inherit all our genes from an unbroken line of successful ancestors. The world becomes full of organisms that have what it takes to become ancestors. That, in a sentence, is Darwinism. . . .

There is a natural, and deeply pernicious, way to misunderstand the previous paragraph. It is tempting to think that when ancestors did successful things, the genes they passed on to their children were, as a result, upgraded relative to the genes they had received from their parents. Something about their success rubbed off on their genes, and that is why their descendants are so good at flying, swimming, courting. Wrong, utterly wrong! Genes do not improve in the using, they are just passed on, unchanged except for very rare random errors. It is not success that makes good genes. It is good genes that make success, and nothing an individual does during its lifetime has any effect whatever upon its genes. Those individuals born with good genes are the most likely to grow up to become successful ancestors; therefore good genes are more likely than bad to get passed on to the future. Each generation is a filter, a sieve: good genes tend to fall through the sieve into the next generation; bad genes tend to end up in bodies that die young or without reproducing. Bad genes may pass through the sieve for a generation or two, perhaps because they have the luck to share a body with good genes. But you need more than luck to navigate successfully through a thousand sieves in succession, one sieve under the other. After a thousand successive generations, the genes that have made it through are likely to be the good ones.

I said that the genes that survive down the generations will be the ones 5
that have succeeded in making ancestors. This is true, but there is one apparent exception I must deal with before the thought of it causes confusion. Some individuals are irrevocably sterile, yet they are seemingly designed to assist the passage of their genes into future generations. Worker ants, bees, wasps and termites are sterile. They labor not to become ancestors but so that their fertile relatives, usually sisters and brothers, will become ancestors. There are two points to understand here. First, in any kind of animal, sisters and brothers have a high probability of sharing copies of the same genes. Second, it is the environment, not the genes, that determines whether an individual termite, say, becomes a reproducer or a sterile worker. All termites contain genes capable of turning them into sterile workers under some environmental conditions, reproducers under other conditions. The reproducers pass on copies of the very same genes that make the sterile workers help them to do so. The sterile workers toil under the influence of genes, copies of which are sitting in

the bodies of reproducers. The worker copies of those genes are striving to assist their own reproductive copies through the transgenerational sieve. Termite workers can be male or female; but in ants, bees and wasps the workers are all female; otherwise the principle is the same. In a watered-down form, it also applies to several species of birds, mammals and other animals that exhibit a certain amount of caring for young by elder brothers or sisters. To summarize, genes can buy their way through the sieve, not only by assisting their own body to become an ancestor but by assisting the body of a relation to become an ancestor.

The river of my title is a river of DNA, and it flows through time, not space. It is a river of information, not a river of bones and tissues: a river of abstract instructions for building bodies, not a river of solid bodies themselves. The information passes through bodies and affects them, but it is not affected by them on its way through. The river is not only uninfluenced by the experiences and achievements of the successive bodies through which it flows. It is also uninfluenced by a potential source of contamination that, on the face of it, is much more powerful: sex.

In every one of your cells, half your mother's genes rub shoulders with half your father's genes. Your maternal genes and your paternal genes conspire with one another most intimately to make you the subtle and indivisible amalgam you are. But the genes themselves do not blend. Only their effects do. The genes themselves have a flintlike integrity. When the time comes to move on to the next generation, a gene either goes into the body of a given child or it does not. Paternal genes and maternal genes do not blend; they recombine independently. A given gene in you came either from your mother or your father. It also came from one, and only one, of your four grandparents; from one, and only one, of your eight great-grandparents; and so on back.

I have spoken of a river of genes, but we could equally well speak of a band of good companions marching through geological time. All the genes of one breeding population are, in the long run, companions of each other. In the short run, they sit in individual bodies and are temporarily more intimate companions of the other genes sharing that body. Genes survive down the ages only if they are good at building bodies that are good at living and reproducing in the particular way of life chosen by the species. But there is more to it than this. To be good at surviving, a gene must be good at working together with the other genes in the same species—the same river. To survive in the long run, a gene must be a good companion. It must do well in the company of, or against the background of, the other genes in the same river. Genes of another species are in a different river. They do not have to get on well together—not in the same sense, anyway—for they do not have to share the same bodies.

The feature that defines a species is that all members of any one species have the same river of genes flowing through them, and all the genes in a species have to be prepared to be good companions of one another. A new species comes into existence when an existing species divides into two. The river of genes forks in time. From a gene's point of view, *speciation,* the origin of new species, is "the long goodbye." After a brief period of partial separation, the two rivers go their separate ways forever, or until one or the other dries extinct into the sand. Secure within the banks of either river, the water is mixed and remixed by sexual recombination. But water never leaps its banks to contaminate the other river. After a species has divided, the two sets of genes are no longer companions. They no longer meet in the same bodies and they are no longer required to get on well together. There is no longer any intercourse between them—and intercourse here means, literally, sexual intercourse between their temporary vehicles, their bodies. . . .

There are now perhaps thirty million branches to the river of DNA, for 10
that is an estimate of the number of species on earth. It has also been estimated that the surviving species constitute about 1 percent of the species that have ever lived. It would follow that there have been some three billion branches to the river of DNA altogether. Today's thirty million branch rivers are irrevocably separate. Many of them are destined to wither into nothing, for most species go extinct. If you follow the thirty million rivers (for brevity, I'll refer to the branch rivers as rivers) back into the past, you will find that, one by one, they join up with other rivers. The river of human genes joins with the river of chimpanzee genes at about the same time as the river of gorilla genes does, some seven million years ago. A few million years farther back, our shared African ape river is joined by the stream of orangutan genes. Farther back still, we are joined by a river of gibbon genes—a river that splits downstream into a number of separate species of gibbon and siamang. As we push on backward in time, our genetic river unites with rivers destined, if followed forward again, to branch into the Old World monkeys, the New World monkeys, and the lemurs of Madagascar. Even farther back, our river unites with those leading to other major groups of mammals: rodents, cats, bats, elephants. After that, we meet the streams leading to various kinds of reptiles, birds, amphibians, fish, invertebrates. . . .

And now for the point that this has all been leading up to. To the extent that differences between individuals are due to genes (which may be a large extent or a small one), natural selection can favor some quirks of embryological origami or embryological chemistry and disfavor others. To the extent that your throwing arm is influenced by genes, natural selection can favor it or disfavor it. If being able to throw well has an effect, however slight, on an individual's likelihood of surviving long enough to have children, to the extent that throwing ability is influenced by genes, those genes will have a correspondingly greater chance of winning through to the next generation. Any one individual may die for reasons having nothing to do with his ability to throw. But a gene that tends to make individuals better at throwing when it is present than when it is absent will inhabit lots of bodies, both good and bad, over many generations. From the point of view of the particular gene, the other causes of death will average out. From the gene's perspective, there is only the long-term outlook of the river of DNA flowing down through the generations, only temporarily housed in particular bodies, only temporarily sharing a body with companion genes that may be successful or unsuccessful.

In the long term, the river becomes full of genes that are good at surviving for their several reasons: slightly improving the ability to throw a spear, slightly improving the ability to taste poison, or whatever it may be. Genes that, on average, are less good at surviving—because they tend to cause astigmatic vision in their successive bodies, who are therefore less successful spear throwers; or because they make their successive bodies less attractive and therefore less likely to mate—such genes will tend to disappear from the river of genes. In all this, remember the point we made earlier: the genes that survive in the river will be the ones that are good at surviving in the average environment of the species, and perhaps the most important aspect of this average environment is the other genes of the species; the other genes with which a gene is likely to have to share a body; the other genes that swim through geological time in the same river.

Note

1. Strictly speaking, there are exceptions. Some animals, like aphids, reproduce without sex. Techniques such as artificial fertilization make it possible for modern humans to have a child without copulating, and even—since eggs for *in vitro* fertilization could be taken from a female fetus—without reaching adulthood. But for most purposes the force of my point is undiminished.

Understanding

1. In your own words, explain Dawkins's metaphor of the digital river. Imagine that you are explaining it to a group of friends. You may wish to make a drawing (or some kind of visual aid) of the river with various labels. Or, use the T-shirt slogan Dawkins offered when asked to come up with one for the ongoing evolution revolution: LIFE RESULTS FROM THE NON-RANDOM SURVIVAL OF RANDOMLY VARYING REPLICATORS.
2. What is the relationship between genes and the physical bodies that carry them? Does what you accomplish or become in your life have any bearing on the genes you pass to the next generation?
3. Do genes from your father and mother blend to make *you?*
4. Paraphrase what Dawkins means by "a band of good companions marching through geological time" (paragraph 8). Does medical science confound Dawkins's theory by saving people who might have died before being able to reproduce? Does this medical intervention affect the gene pool?
5. How does Dawkins define species? How is *species* equal to *river* in this essay? What is speciation? How many species probably exist on earth today? What percentage of species generally becomes extinct?
6. How is Dawkins's example of a throwing arm useful in explaining natural selection?

Responding

1. At the beginning of "Ancestors and the Digital River," Dawkins claims that "all peoples have epic legends about their tribal ancestors, and these leg-

ends often formalize themselves into religious cults." One such legend, or myth, is the Judeo-Christian one from the Bible, which states that the first humans, Adam and Eve, were created by God in the Garden of Eden. There are as many creation stories as there are peoples. What is yours? Can creation myths coexist with Darwin's scientific theories of evolution? That is, does one set of beliefs necessarily negate the others?

2. Ancestors are an important component of Dawkins's digital river. Their résumés are impressive for what did *not* happen to them. We have much to thank them for. How do you (and your culture) acknowledge your ancestors?
3. What are some traits that you've inherited from your ancestors? How did you come to know and believe that you inherited them?
4. Are any of your gift or wound stories a result of an inherited family characteristic?
5. Write your own signature here. Think of your father's and mother's signatures. Which does yours resemble more? Are your siblings' or relatives' signatures similar to yours? Do you think a signature is an inherited trait?
6. Dawkins has written that we cannot look at the evolution of birds without looking at the evolution of their nests—one of their artifacts. Following that line of thinking, he concludes that both the bird and its nest are the evolutionary extensions of the *egg* to make another egg. Similarly, he suggests that scientists should not look at the evolution of humankind without looking at *our* artifacts—specifically our technologies. If we are co-evolving with our artifacts, it would stand to reason that genes that cannot cope with the new realities will not survive into future millennia. What do you think of this notion?

Connecting

1. Compare Dawkins's ideas with both Bacon's in "Heredity and Evolution" and Csikszentmihalyi's in "The Veils of Maya and the World of the Genes." Where do they differ? Where do they build on each other? Make note of memorable statements, or claims, in each selection.
2. How would Dawkins answer the questions posed in paragraph 4 of the introduction to "Biology and Identity"?

Sizing up the Sexes

Christine Gorman

In a number of visible ways, men and women are different physically. Men tend to be taller than women, weigh more, have more upper-body strength. But are men and women different psychologically? If so, do these differences exist at birth? The following article explores some possible answers to these questions.

Beginning in the 1980s, as you will read in this selection, social, biological, and physical scientists began to challenge the dominant role of environment in shaping human behavior. The reason was increasing attention to the "three-pound monster"—the human brain. Over the past twenty years, the brain has been the subject of some fascinating investigations. Some discoveries about how the brain influences our biological self and our behavior are described in this cover story from *Time* magazine.

The oldest of three daughters of a French mother and an American father, Christine Gorman, an associate editor for *Time,* was born in Bordeaux, France, and taught high school biology in Houston after graduating summa cum laude from Rice University in 1982. Gorman says that storytelling came naturally to her, from listening to her grandmother's tales of life in Europe and the Midwest. She combines her twin passions—biology and writing—to translate the specialized language of science into everyday English.

What are little boys made of?
What are little boys made of?
Frogs and snails
And puppy dogs' tails,
That's what little boys are made of.

What are little girls made of?
What are little girls made of?
Sugar and spice
And all that's nice,
That's what little girls are made of.

—Anonymous

Many scientists rely on elaborately complex and costly equipment to probe the mysteries confronting humankind. Not Melissa Hines. The UCLA behavioral scientist is hoping to solve one of life's oldest riddles with a toybox full of police cars, Lincoln Logs and Barbie dolls. For the past two years, Hines and her colleagues have tried to determine the origins of gender differences 1 by capturing on videotape the squeals of delight, furrows of concentration and myriad decisions that children from 2½ to 8 make while playing. Although both sexes play with all the toys available in Hines' laboratory, her work confirms what most parents (and more than a few aunts, uncles and nursery-school teachers) already know. As a group, the boys favor sports cars, fire trucks and Lincoln Logs, while the girls are drawn more often to dolls and kitchen toys.

But one batch of girls defies expectations and consistently prefers the boy toys. These youngsters have a rare genetic abnormality that caused them to produce elevated levels of testosterone, among other hormones, during their embryonic development. On average, they play with the same toys as the boys in the same ways and just as often. Could it be that the high levels of testosterone present in their bodies before birth have left a permanent imprint on their brains, affecting their later behavior? Or did their parents, knowing of their disorder, somehow subtly influence their choices? If the first explanation is true and biology determines the choice, Hines wonders, "Why would you evolve to want to play with a truck?"

Not so long ago, any career-minded researcher would have hesitated to ask such questions. During the feminist revolution of the 1970s, talk of inborn differences in the behavior of men and women was distinctly unfashionable, even taboo. Men dominated fields like architecture and engineering, it was argued, because of social, not hormonal, pressures. Women did the vast majority of society's child rearing because few other options were available to them. Once sexism was abolished, so the argument ran, the world would become a perfectly equitable, androgynous place, aside from a few anatomical details.

But biology has a funny way of confounding expectations. Rather than disappear, the evidence for innate sexual differences only began to mount. In medicine, researchers documented that heart disease strikes men at a younger age than it does women and that women have a more moderate physiological response to stress. Researchers found subtle neurological differences between the sexes both in the brain's structure and in its functioning. In addition, another generation of parents discovered that, despite their best efforts to give baseballs to their daughters and sewing kits to their sons, girls still flocked to dollhouses while boys clambered into tree forts. Perhaps nature is more important than nurture after all.

Even professional skeptics have been converted. "When I was younger, I 5
believed that 100% of sex differences were due to the environment," says Jerre Levy, professor of psychology at the University of Chicago. Her own toddler toppled that utopian notion. "My daughter was 15 months old, and I had just dressed her in her teeny little nightie. Some guests arrived, and she came into the room, knowing full well that she looked adorable. She came in with this saucy little walk, cocking her head, blinking her eyes, especially at the men. You never saw such flirtation in your life." After 20 years spent studying the brain, Levy is convinced: "I'm sure there are biologically based differences in our behavior."

Now that it is O.K. to admit the possibility, the search for sexual differences has expanded into nearly every branch of the life sciences. Anthropologists have debunked Margaret Mead's work on the extreme variability of gender roles in New Guinea. Psychologists are untangling the complex interplay between hormones and aggression. But the most provocative, if as yet inconclusive, discoveries of all stem from the pioneering exploration of a tiny 3-lb. universe: the human brain. In fact, some researchers predict that the confirmation of innate differences in behavior could lead to an unprecedented understanding of the mind.

Some of the findings seem merely curious. For example, more men than women are lefthanded, reflecting the dominance of the brain's right hemisphere. By contrast, more women listen equally with both ears while men favor the right one.

Other revelations are bound to provoke more controversy. Psychology tests, for instance, consistently support the notion that men and women perceive the world in subtly different ways. Males excel at rotating three-dimensional objects in their head. Females prove better at reading emotions of people in photographs. A growing number of scientists believe the discrepancies reflect functional differences in the brains of men and women. If true, then some misunderstandings between the sexes may have more to do with crossed wiring than cross-purposes.

Most of the gender differences that have been uncovered so far are, statistically speaking, quite small. "Even the largest differences in cognitive function are not as large as the difference in male and female height," Hines notes. "You still see a lot of overlap." Otherwise, women could never read maps and men would always be lefthanded. That kind of flexibility within the sexes reveals just how complex a puzzle gender actually is, requiring pieces from biology, sociology and culture.

10 Ironically, researchers are not entirely sure how or even why humans produce two sexes in the first place. (Why not just one—or even three—as in some species?) What is clear is that the two sexes originate with two distinct chromosomes. Women bear a double dose of the large X chromosome, while men usually possess a single X and a short, stumpy Y chromosome. In 1990 British scientists reported they had identified a single gene on the Y chromosome that determines maleness. Like some kind of biomolecular Paul Revere, this master gene rouses a host of its compatriots to the complex task of turning a fetus into a boy. Without such a signal, all human embryos would develop into girls. "I have all the genes for being male except this one, and my husband has all the genes for being female," marvels evolutionary psychologist Leda Cosmides, of the University of California at Santa Barbara. "The only difference is which genes got turned on."

Yet even this snippet of DNA is not enough to ensure a masculine result. An elevated level of the hormone testosterone is also required during the pregnancy. Where does it come from? The fetus' own undescended testes. In those rare cases in which the tiny body does not respond to the hormone, a genetically male fetus develops sex organs that look like a clitoris and vagina rather than a penis. Such people look and act female. The majority marry and adopt children.

The influence of the sex hormones extends into the nervous system. Both males and females produce androgens, such as testosterone, and estrogens—

although in different amounts. (Men and women who make no testosterone generally lack a libido.) Researchers suspect that an excess of testosterone before birth enables the right hemisphere to dominate the brain, resulting in lefthandedness. Since testosterone levels are higher in boys than in girls, that would explain why more boys are southpaws.

Subtle sex-linked preferences have been detected as early as 52 hours after birth. In studies of 72 newborns, University of Chicago psychologist Martha McClintock and her students found that a toe-fanning reflex was stronger in the left foot for 60% of the males, while all the females favored their right. However, apart from such reflexes in the hands, legs and feet, the team could find no other differences in the babies' responses.

One obvious place to look for gender differences is in the hypothalamus, a lusty little organ perched over the brain stem that, when sufficiently provoked, consumes a person with rage, thirst, hunger or desire. In animals, a region at the front of the organ controls sexual function and is somewhat larger in males than in females. But its size need not remain constant. Studies of tropical fish by Stanford University neurobiologist Russell Fernald reveal that certain cells in this tiny region of the brain swell markedly in an individual male whenever he comes to dominate a school. Unfortunately for the piscine pasha, the cells will also shrink if he loses control of his harem to another male.

Many researchers suspect that, in humans too, sexual preferences are 15
controlled by the hypothalamus. Based on a study of 41 autopsied brains, Simon LeVay of the Salk Institute for Biological Studies announced last summer that he had found a region in the hypothalamus that was on average twice as large in heterosexual men as in either women or homosexual men. LeVay's findings support the idea that varying hormone levels before birth may immutably stamp the developing brain in one erotic direction or another.

These prenatal fluctuations may also steer boys toward more rambunctious behavior than girls. June Reinisch, director of the Kinsey Institute for Research in Sex, Gender and Reproduction at Indiana University, in a pioneering study of eight pairs of brothers and 17 pairs of sisters ages 6 to 18 uncovered a complex interplay between hormones and aggression. As a group, the young males gave more belligerent answers than did the females on a multiple-choice test in which they had to imagine their response to stressful situations. But siblings who had been exposed in utero to synthetic antimiscarriage hormones that mimic testosterone were the most combative of all. The affected boys proved significantly more aggressive than their unaffected brothers, and the drug-exposed girls were much more contentious than their unexposed sisters. Reinisch could not determine, however, whether this childhood aggression would translate into greater ambition or competitiveness in the adult world.

While most of the gender differences uncovered so far seem to fall under the purview of the hypothalamus, researchers have begun noting discrepancies in other parts of the brain as well. For the past nine years, neuroscientists have debated whether the corpus callosum, a thick bundle of nerves that allows the right half of the brain to communicate with the left, is larger in women than in men. If it is, and if size corresponds to function, then the greater crosstalk between the hemispheres might explain enigmatic phenomena like female intuition, which is supposed to accord women greater ability to read emotional clues.

These conjectures about the corpus callosum have been hard to prove because the structure's girth varies dramatically with both age and health. Studies of autopsied material are of little use because brain tissue undergoes such dramatic changes in the hours after death. Neuroanatomist Laura Allen and neuroendocrinologist Roger Gorski of UCLA decided to try to circumvent some of these problems by obtaining brain scans from live, apparently healthy people. In their investigation of 146 subjects, published in April, they confirmed that parts of the corpus callosum were up to 23% wider in women than in men. They also measured thicker connections between the two hemispheres in other parts of women's brains.

Encouraged by the discovery of such structural differences, many researchers have begun looking for dichotomies of function as well. At the Bowman Gray Medical School in Winston-Salem, N.C., Cecile Naylor has determined that men and women enlist widely varying parts of their brain when asked to spell words. By monitoring increases in blood flow, the neuropsychologist found that women use both sides of their head when spelling while men use primarily their left side. Because the area activated on the right side is used in understanding emotions, the women apparently tap a wider range of experience for their task. Intriguingly, the effect occurred only with spelling and not during a memory test.

Researchers speculate that the greater communication between the two 20
sides of the brain could impair a woman's performance of certain highly specialized visual-spatial tasks. For example, the ability to tell directions on a map without physically having to rotate it appears stronger in those individuals whose brains restrict the process to the right hemisphere. Any crosstalk between the two sides apparently distracts the brain from its job. Sure enough, several studies have shown that this mental-rotation skill is indeed more tightly focused in men's brains than in women's.

But how did it get to be that way? So far, none of the gender scientists have figured out whether nature or nurture is more important. "Nothing is ever equal, even in the beginning," observes Janice Juraska, a biopsychologist at the University of Illinois at Urbana-Champaign. She points out, for instance, that mother rats lick their male offspring more frequently than they do their daughters. However, Juraska has demonstrated that it is possible to reverse some inequities by manipulating environmental factors. Female rats have fewer nerve connections than males into the hippocampus, a brain region associated with spatial relations and memory. But when Juraska "enriched" the cages of the females with stimulating toys, the females developed more of these neuronal connections. "Hormones do affect things—it's crazy to deny that," says the researcher. "But there's no telling which way sex differences might go if we completely changed the environment." For humans, educational enrichment could perhaps enhance a woman's ability to work in three dimensions and a man's ability to interpret emotions. Says Juraska: "There's nothing about human brains that is so stuck that a different way of doing things couldn't change it enormously."

Nowhere is this complex interaction between nature and nurture more apparent than in the unique human abilities of speaking, reading and writing. No one is born knowing French, for example; it must be learned, changing the brain forever. Even so, language skills are linked to specific cerebral centers. In a remarkable series of experiments, neurosurgeon George Ojemann of the University of Washington has produced scores of detailed maps of people's individual language centers.

First, Ojemann tested his patients' verbal intelligence using a written exam. Then, during neurosurgery—which was performed under a local anesthetic—he asked them to name aloud a series of objects found in a steady stream of black-and-white photos. Periodically, he touched different parts of the brain with an electrode that temporarily blocked the activity of that region. (This does not hurt because the brain has no sense of pain.) By noting when his patients made mistakes, the surgeon was able to determine which sites were essential to naming.

Several complex sexual differences emerged. Men with lower verbal IQs were more likely to have their language skills located toward the back of the brain. In a number of women, regardless of IQ, the naming ability was restricted to the frontal lobe. This disparity could help explain why strokes that affect the rear of the brain seem to be more devastating to men than to women.

Intriguingly, the sexual differences are far less significant in people with higher verbal IQs. Their language skills developed in a more intermediate part of the brain. And yet, no two patterns were ever identical. "That to me is the most important finding," Ojemann says. "Instead of these sites being laid down more or less the same in everyone, they're laid down in subtly different places." Language is scattered randomly across these cerebral centers, he hypothesizes, because the skills evolved so recently.

What no one knows for sure is just how hardwired the brain is. How far and at what stage can the brain's extraordinary flexibility be pushed? Several studies suggest that the junior high years are key. Girls show the same aptitudes for math as boys until about the seventh grade, when more and more girls develop math phobia. Coincidentally, that is the age at which boys start to shine and catch up to girls in reading.

By one account, the gap between men and women for at least some mental skills has actually started to shrink. By looking at 25 years' worth of data from academic tests, Janet Hyde, professor of psychology and women's studies at the University of Wisconsin at Madison, discovered that overall gender differences for verbal and mathematical skills dramatically decreased after 1974. One possible explanation, Hyde notes, is that "Americans have changed their socialization and educational patterns over the past few decades. They are treating males and females with greater similarity."

Even so, women still have not caught up with men on the mental-rotation test. Fascinated by the persistence of that gap, psychologists Irwin Silverman and Marion Eals of York University in Ontario wondered if there were any spatial tasks at which women outperformed men. Looking at it from the point of view of human evolution, Silverman and Eals reasoned that while men may have developed strong spatial skills in response to evolutionary pressures to be successful hunters, women would have needed other types of visual skills to excel as gatherers and foragers of food.

The psychologists therefore designed a test focused on the ability to discern and later recall the location of objects in a complex, random pattern. In series of tests, student volunteers were given a minute to study a drawing that contained such unrelated objects as an elephant, a guitar and a cat. Then Silverman and Eals presented their subjects with a second drawing containing additional objects and told them to cross out those items that had been added and circle any that had moved. Sure enough, the women consistently surpassed the men in giving correct answers.

What made the psychologists really sit up and take notice, however, was 30
the fact that the women scored much better on the mental-rotation test while they were menstruating. Specifically, they improved their scores by 50% to 100% whenever their estrogen levels were at their lowest. It is not clear why this should be. However, Silverman and Eals are trying to find out if women exhibit a similar hormonal effect for any other visual tasks.

Oddly enough, men may possess a similar hormonal response, according to new research reported in November by Doreen Kimura, a psychologist at the University of Western Ontario. In her study of 138 adults, Kimura found that males perform better on mental-rotation tests in the spring, when their testosterone levels are low, rather than in the fall, when they are higher. Men are also subject to a daily cycle, with testosterone levels lowest around 8 p.m. and peaking around 4 a.m. Thus, says June Reinisch of the Kinsey Institute: "When people say women can't be trusted because they cycle every month, my response is that men cycle every day, so they should only be allowed to negotiate peace treaties in the evening."

Far from strengthening stereotypes about who women and men truly are or how they should behave, research into innate sexual differences only underscores humanity's awesome adaptability. "Gender is really a complex business," says Reinisch. "There's no question that hormones have an effect. But what does that have to do with the fact that I like to wear pink ribbons and you like to wear baseball gloves? Probably something, but we don't know what."

Even the concept of what an innate difference represents is changing. The physical and chemical differences between the brains of the two sexes may be malleable and subject to change by experience: certainly an event or act of learning can directly affect the brain's biochemistry and physiology. And so, in the final analysis, it may be impossible to say where nature ends and nurture begins because the two are so intimately linked.

Understanding

1. This article, written for a popular audience, tries to explain the evidence that supports the idea that many of our behaviors, cognitive skills, and

emotional reactions are really influenced by genetic factors. Which studies cited in this article seem most convincing to you? Why?

2. The results of chemical, biological, and behavioral science research point to the brain as the source of differences—other than the obvious physical ones—between the sexes. These discoveries tend to contradict the explanation that gender differences are the result of environment. Which experiments seem to confirm the influence of environment?
3. According to Gorman, what is the impetus for investigating the origins of differences between the sexes? What do researchers expect to gain from the knowledge they uncover?

Responding

1. What differences in ability do you notice between you and your brother(s) or sister(s)? Between you, your siblings, and your parents? Based on this reading, to what extent might you attribute any differences to genetic factors?
2. As noted in a number of readings in this chapter, the study of family history is one approach to determining the influence of our genes. Research your family history for physical traits (e.g., height, eye color, incidence of breast cancer) and for psychological traits (communication style, temperament) that you can document as being transmitted from one generation of your family to the next. Write a profile of yourself as the recipient of this genetic inheritance.

Connecting

1. How does the evidence in this article correspond to the view of the brain as related in Csikszentmihalyi's "The Veils of Maya and the World of the Genes"? How does it correspond with Goleman's ideas about temperament in "Temperament Is Not Destiny"?
2. Our biologically based sexuality and our more psychologically based sense of gender are important components of who we are (our *self*) and how we express who we are (our *personality*). What do you think of these differences? What more do you need to know in order to come to a conclusion about this question? Can any of your personal experiences be better explained by this distinction between biology (self) and personality (expression of self)?

WRITING OPTION: Biology and Identity

Using your responses from the readings in "Biology and Identity," and the texts themselves as sources, write a short paper that takes a stand or argues a claim. Use one of these assignments as a taking-off point:

1. Take one memorable sentence, or claim, from Csikszentmihalyi's or Gorman's text and supply examples to argue that it is a statement worth arguing (or not).

2. You have written stories about your gifts, wounds, decisions, and dreams and their effects on your identity. Does your biological self control or simply become a factor to work with in these stories?
3. Turn one of your most interesting responses in "Biology and Identity" into a short essay that argues a point. For example, if you turned up some interesting findings in Responding question 1 following Gorman's "Sizing Up the Sexes," state your conclusion and support it in a short essay.

2 Inborn Traits

You may never have thought of your biological parents as a deck of playing cards and of yourself as a hand dealt from the deck, but this is an apt metaphor for the transmission of genetic, or inborn, traits, that cluster of characteristics such as body type, eye color, and the length of our fingers that contributes to the custom-made body we call our self.

The information coded in genes shapes all life on earth, and the science of genetics studies how these genetically borne traits are passed on from one generation to the next. How this transmission occurs is a complex and still not completely understood process: Deciphering the human genetic blueprint involves sequencing 3 trillion letters of genetic code. Although geneticists have made enormous strides in identifying the genes responsible for certain traits, it makes sense to consider what we know as partial and, in some cases, highly debatable. And yet, because so much of who we are reflects our genetic history, the readings in this section give us a tantalizing glimpse into the sources of our human uniqueness. Perhaps, then, it is best to mine these readings for the questions they elicit rather than the answers they give.

Lawrence Wright examines how recent research on twins contributes to our understanding of the extent of genetic influence. Are we victims of our genes? Can we triumph over them to be the person we want to be?

Gillian Turner sums up recent research on the source of intelligence, itself a mysterious quality now thought to be a largely inherited trait. Can we identify which parent contributes the most? Should potential spouses consider intelligence as a factor in choosing their mates?

In the matter of exceptional intelligence, or giftedness, the impact of heredity and environment takes on special significance. What powers the ability to excel is explored in Andrew Solomon's portrait of a young piano virtuoso. Finally, Stanley Crouch foretells the social consequences of a visible inborn trait—our "race." Will we, in a hundred years, regard race as less important than we do today?

We may be the result of a random shuffle of our parents' genetic decks, but as the following selections suggest, and as you will explore in your writing, we may have more choices than previously thought about how to play our hands.

The Biology of Twins

Lawrence Wright

Because identical twins come from one and the same ovum (egg), they have exactly the same genetic makeup and a startling likeness to one another. Reasoned thought would say that if identical twins were raised under the same roof, they would turn out pretty much alike, both physically and mentally, with similar attributes and abilities; if they were separated at birth, on the other hand, and raised by very different families in very different circumstances, they would probably be different, at least in their attitudes, desires, and personal habits. Twins give researchers the opportunity to try to answer the question of whether biology (nature) is a more significant factor in who we turn out to be than our environment (nurture). "The Biology of Twins" explores the most basic assumption in analytical psychology: that the environment we grow up in, particularly our family, makes us into the person we become—not our genetic composition.

Lawrence Wright is a native of Texas, a graduate of Tulane University and the American University in Cairo, Egypt, and the author of four very different books—one on ghetto children from New York City living with farm families during the summer, another on Dallas during the Kennedy assassination, one on six religious leaders, and the last on "recovered memories." He is a staff writer for *The New Yorker* and a contributor to *Rolling Stone.*

A set of identical-twin girls were surrendered to an adoption agency in New York City in the nineteen-sixties. The twins, who are known in psychological literature as Amy and Beth, might have gone through life in obscurity had they not come to the attention of Dr. Peter Neubauer, a prominent psychiatrist at New York University's Psychiatric Institute. Neubauer, who was also an adviser to the adoption agency, believed at the time that twins posed such a burden to parents, and to themselves in the form of certain developmental hazards, that adopted twins were better off being reared apart from each other. 1

It was clear that such a separation would also offer Neubauer exceptional research possibilities. Studies of twins reared apart are the most powerful tool that scholars have for analyzing the relative contributions of heredity and environment to the makeup of individual human natures. Identical twins are rare, however, and twins who have been separated and brought up in different families are particularly unusual. Neubauer knew of only a handful of studies examining twins reared apart, and in many cases the twins being studied had been separated late in their childhood and reunited at some point long before the study began. Amy and Beth presented an opportunity to look at twins from the moment they were separated and to trace them through childhood, observing at each stage of development the parallel or diverging courses of their lives. Such a study might not lay to rest the ancient quarrel over the relative importance of nature and nurture, but one could imagine few other experiments that would be more relevant to understanding the mystery of the human condition.

By the time Amy and Beth were sent to their adoptive homes, an extensive team of psychologists, psychiatrists, pediatricians, and observers was waiting to follow them as they moved from infancy to adolescence. Every step of childhood would be documented through psychological tests, tests of skills and abilities, school records, parental and sibling interviews, films, and the minutes of several hundred weekly conferences. Because the twins had identical genetic constitutions, the team could evaluate the effects of the environment on their personalities, their behavior, their health, their intelligence. Broadly speaking, the differences between the girls as they grew older would be a measure of the validity of the most fundamental assumption of analytical psychology, which is that experience—and, in particular, our family background—shapes us into the people that we become.

The agency that placed the children shortly after their birth informed each set of potential adoptive parents that the girl they were adopting was already involved in a study of child development, and strongly urged the adoptive parents to continue it; however, neither the adoptive parents nor the girls themselves were ever told that the subject of the study was twins. The sisters were fair-skinned blondes with small oval faces, blue-gray eyes, and slightly snub noses. Amy was three ounces heavier and half an inch longer than Beth at birth, an advantage in height and weight that persisted throughout their childhood. The girls were adopted into families that were, in certain respects, quite similar—both were Jewish, and lived in New York State. The mothers stayed at home, and in each family there was a son almost exactly seven years older than the twin. (In Beth's family, there was an older daughter as well.) In other respects, the environments were profoundly different; notably, Amy's family was lower middle class and Beth's was well off. Amy's mother was overweight, low key, and socially awkward. Although she had a compassionate side to her nature, she was an insecure mother, who felt threatened by her daughter's attractiveness. Beth's mother, on the other hand, doted on her daughter and spoke positively of Beth's personality and her place in the family. The team described Beth's mother as pleasant, youthful, slim, chic, poised, self-confident, dynamic, and cheerful. Whereas Amy's mother seemed to regard Amy as a problem, a stubborn outsider, Beth's mother treated her daughter as "the fun child." She went out of her way to minimize the differences between herself and Beth, to the extent of dyeing her own hair to emphasize their similarity. The girls' fathers were alike in many respects—confident, relaxed, at ease with themselves—but were as different as the mothers in their treatment of the girls. Amy's father came to agree with his wife that Amy was a disappointment, whereas Beth's father was more available and supportive.

All in all, the research team characterized Amy's family as a well-knit 5
threesome—mother, father, and son—plus an alienated Amy. It was a family that placed a high value on academic success, simplicity, tradition, and

emotional restraint. Beth's family, on the other hand, was sophisticated and full of energy—"frenetic" at times—and it tended to put more emphasis on material things than on education. Clearly, Beth was more in the center of her home than Amy was in hers.

And how did these identical twins in such contrasting environments turn out? As might be expected, Amy's problems began early and progressed in a disturbing direction. As an infant, she was tense and demanding. She sucked her thumb; she bit her nails; she clung to her blanket; she cried when left alone; she wet her bed; she was prone to nightmares and full of fears. By the time she was ten, she had developed a kind of artificial quality that manifested itself in role-playing, made-up illnesses, and confusion over her sexual identity. Shy, socially indifferent, suffering from a serious learning disorder, pathologically immature, she was a stereotypical picture of a rejected child. If only Amy had had a mother who was more empathic, more tolerant of her limitations, more open and forthcoming (like Beth's mother), Amy's life might have turned out far better. If only her father had been more consistently available and affectionate (like Beth's father), she might have been better able to negotiate the Oedipal dramas of latency and might have achieved a clearer picture of her own sexual role. If only her brother had been less strongly favored (like Beth's brother), Amy would have been spared the mortifying comparisons that were openly drawn in her family. In theory, if Amy had grown up in Beth's family, the sources of her crippling immaturity would have been erased, and she would be another kind of person—happier, one presumes, and more nearly whole.

And yet in almost every respect Beth's personality followed in lockstep with Amy's dismal development. Thumb-sucking, nail-biting, blanket-clenching, and bed-wetting characterized her infancy and early childhood. She became a hypochondriac and, like Amy, was afraid of the dark and of being left alone. She, too, became lost in role-playing, and the artificial nature of her personality was even more pronounced than Amy's. She had similar problems in school and with her peers. On the surface, she had a far closer relationship with her mother than Amy had with hers, but on psychological tests she gave vent to a longing for maternal affection which was eerily the same as her identical sister's. Beth did seem to be more successful with her friends and less confused than Amy, but she was also less aware of her feelings.

The differences between the girls seemed merely stylistic; despite the differences in their environments, their pathology was fundamentally the same. Did their family lives mean so little? Were they destined to become the people they turned out to be because of some genetic predisposition toward sadness and unreality? And what would psychologists have made of either girl if they did not know that she was a twin? Wouldn't they have laid the blame for the symptoms of her neurosis on the parents who raised her? Finally, what did all this say about the fundamental presumptions of psychology?

The separated-twins story is a chestnut of American journalism—one that is guaranteed to gain national exposure, along with stories of pets that have trekked across the country to find their masters. The appeal of the separated-twins story is the implicit suggestion that it could happen to anyone. Babies actually do get lost or separated, and, however rare such an event may be, it feeds the common fantasy that any one of us might have a clone, a doppelgänger—someone who is not only a human mirror but also an ideal companion, someone who understands us perfectly. It is not just the similarity that excites us but the difference: the fantasy of an identical twin is a projection of ourselves living another life, finding other opportunities, choosing other careers, sleeping with other spouses; an identical twin can experience the world and come back to report about choices we might have made.

But the story has a darker and more threatening side, and this may be the real secret of its grip on our imagination. We think we know who we are. We struggle to build our characters through experience; we make ourselves unique by determining what we like, what we don't like, and what we stand for. The premise of free will is that we become the people we *choose* to be. Suppose, then, we meet an Other who is, in every outward respect, ourself. It is one thing to imagine an identical Other who, having lived a separate and distinct life, has been marked by it and become different from us. But what if, in spite of all the differences, we and the Other arrive at the same place? Isn't there a sense of loss? A loss not only of identity but of purpose? We are left wondering not only *who* we are but *why* we are who we are.

The Neubauer twin study is just one among thousands that have raised these questions. Over the last decade, there has been a tidal wave of twin-based scholarship. There are now so many scientists seeking to study twins that every August researchers set up booths under a huge tent at the Twins Day Festival in Twinsburg, Ohio, where some three thousand browsing identicals and fraternals stop to take blood-pressure tests or fill out questionnaires. Recent studies of twinship have challenged our most entrenched views of human development and have capsized cherished beliefs about human nature—in particular, the bedrock notion that character is created by experience. But then twins have been confounding humanity from the earliest times—almost as if they were a divine prank designed to undermine our sense of individuality and specialness in the world. Twins are both an unsettling presence, because they sabotage our sense of personal uniqueness, and a score-settling presence, because their mere existence allows us to pose questions we might not have thought to ask if we lived in a world without them. . . .

If twins are important to science because they allow us to ask how much of our nature arises from our genes and how much from our circumstances, the answers have equally profound implications for social policy. The hallmark of liberalism is that changes in the social environment produce corresponding changes in human development. But if people's destinies are written in their genes, why waste money on social programs? Much of the ferocious argument over individual and group differences in intelligence (which has recently been rekindled by Richard Herrnstein and Charles Murray's "The Bell Curve") draws upon the fact that there is a closer correlation between I.Q.-test scores of identical twins than between those of fraternal twins—the difference being an indication of how much of what we call intelligence is inherited. Even matters that would seem to be entirely a reflection of one's personal experience, such as political orientation or depth of religious commitment, have been shown by various twin studies to be largely under genetic influence.

All this comes after several decades of heightened political struggle between those who believe that people are largely the same, with differences imposed upon them by their environment, and those who conclude that people differ mainly because of their genes, and that their environments are largely of their own making. Obviously, the roots of liberal and conservative views are buried in such contrary presumptions about human nature. The broad movement from environmental determinism to behavioral genetics which has transformed psychology over the last thirty years has also dramatically altered society's view of human development and become a part of the invisible substratum of American politics. This can be demonstrated by comparing the climates of opinion that produced the Great Society, in 1965, and the Contract with America, in 1995.

These days, even the most dogmatic environmentalist is willing to admit that nature influences nurture. The debate has evolved into a statistical war over percentages—*how much* of our personality or behavior or intelligence or susceptibility to disease is attributable to our genes, as compared with such environmental factors as the family we grow up in or the neighborhood we live in or how long we attend school. (What the statistics measure is genetic differences in populations, not in individuals. We cannot infer from the statistics that, say, fifty per cent of any one individual's personality is genetically acquired.) The fulcrum upon which one side rises while the other falls is the concept of heritability. Heritability, decreed the animal geneticist J. L. Lush in 1940, is the fraction of the observed variation in a population that is caused by differences in heredity. For instance, laboratory rats that are bred for their intelligence in escaping mazes will grow smarter over the generations, just as maze-dumb rats will grow dumber when they are bred together. Since there is no difference in their environments, the difference between the two populations must be inherited. It is easy to demonstrate the transmission of traits in plant and animal populations; in fact, the manipulation of observable genetic traits is the basis of selective breeding.

In human beings, however, matters are more complex. Since selective 15
breeding is morally out of the question, scientists must rely on the chance data that society sends their way. One of the principal sources of information about human heritability is twin studies. Theoretically, if a trait is highly heritable then it will approach a hundred per cent concordance in identical twins and fifty per cent in fraternal twins and other siblings. But environmental factors can also affect traits that are genetically transmitted. Height, for instance, is a heritable trait, and in well-nourished Western populations most of the variation in stature is an expression of the genes. But the genes require a supportive environment in order to be expressed in the first place. A population that exists on the brink of starvation can have little variation in height, because growth is arrested; there is no way of telling who has tall genes and who has short ones. If one group within a population enjoys an abundant diet while the rest are starving, the variation in height is largely environmental.

Identical, or monozygotic (MZ), twins are thought to result from the splitting of a single fertilized egg—a zygote—in a form of asexual reproduction. Fraternal, or dizygotic (DZ), twins are thought to be the product of two separate eggs, independently fertilized. Thus, identical twins are clones, having identical genes, whereas fraternal twins share only fifty per cent of their genes on average. The existence of these two types of twins creates a statistical opportunity that has contributed to the expanding field of behavioral genetics, which is built on heritability estimates. Behaviors as diverse as smoking, insomnia, marriage and divorce, choice of careers and hobbies, use of contraceptives, consumption of coffee (but not, oddly enough, of tea), menstrual symptoms, and suicide have all been found to have far higher rates of concordance for identical than for fraternal twins—a finding that suggests these traits to be more influenced by genes than was previously suspected.

A survey of Australian twins in the early nineteen-eighties also found a surprisingly significant genetic component for attitudes toward such wide-ranging political and social issues as apartheid, the death penalty, divorce, working mothers, and some forty other subjects. Only on a motley assortment of topics—coeducation, the use of straitjackets, and pajama parties—was there no meaningful genetic influence on individual attitudes. An especially interesting, and ongoing, Swedish study of elderly twins, begun in 1984 by Professor Robert Plomin, a behavioral geneticist at the Institute of Psychiatry in London and at Pennsylvania State University, looked at life events such as divorce, retirement, illness, the death of a child, the mental illness of a spouse, and financial reverses—many of which might seem, almost by definition, to be accidents of the environment. The researchers concluded that, in many respects, identical twins who had been reared apart were even more alike in terms of their major life events than identical twins who had been reared together.

Underlying these startling findings is an insistent unanswered question: How? Is there a gene for neurosis or Alpine skiing or traditional values? Nothing in molecular biology suggests anything of the sort. It is more likely that configurations of genes shape behavior than that a single gene exercises autonomous control over certain kinds of actions. This is especially true of complex functions such as intelligence.

Because supporting molecular evidence has been slow in coming, in most cases the only proof of genetic influence on personality and behavior still comes from twin and adoption studies, which examine unrelated individuals reared together (thus complementing studies of twins reared apart). Numerous twin studies have shown that alcoholism is an inherited disorder; for example, identical twins are much more alike in their drinking patterns than fraternals, and if these patterns lead to alcoholism it's more likely that both twins will be alcoholics. But even if alcoholism is genetically rooted it is clear that environment plays a significant role in much of drinking behavior. Alcoholism is rarely a problem in religious cultures where drinking is forbidden.

Homosexuality appears to be moderately heritable among males and less 20
so among females. A stretch of X chromosome has been implicated in some

instances of male homosexuality, but it leaves open the question of what, exactly, is inherited. "The fairest thing to say is that nobody knows," Richard C. Pillard, a professor of psychiatry at the Boston University School of Medicine, says. "Is it a propensity to like somebody who is sort of the same as you versus somebody who's different, or to like a man versus a woman, or to be very sensitive, or what? To me that's the payoff question. What is that little brain up there doing that's making you different?"

One reason for the dearth of such knowledge is that research involving the genetic underpinnings of behavior has often been discouraged. When Dutch scientists announced, two years ago, that they had found a connection between a genetic defect and a form of familial aggression, they were denounced for even considering a genetic basis for violent behavior. In this country, the National Institutes of Health, facing charges of racism, pulled the rug out from under a planned 1992 conference on "Genetic Factors in Crime" and scaled back research into the causes of violence. Again and again, when genetic research turns toward human nature, and away from simple biology, politics swamps the discussion and often sinks the research efforts.

The most powerful studies in behavioral genetics are of twins who have been reared apart, and the most influential of these studies have been conducted at the University of Minnesota by Professor Thomas J. Bouchard, Jr. A tall, shambling man of fifty-seven, Bouchard wears suspenders and looks as if he'd be more at home sharing a cup of coffee with the local dairy farmers than sorting through the computerized data bank in the university's Center for Twin and Adoption Research, which he founded. Largely because of Bouchard and his team, the University of Minnesota has been the epicenter of twin studies since 1979. It was then that Bouchard read a newspaper story about Jim Lewis and Jim Springer, identical twins who had been separated at birth and reunited thirty-nine years later.

Each of the Jim twins, as they were called, was six feet tall and weighed a hundred and eighty pounds; they looked as much alike as any other identical pair. At their reunion, they discovered that each had been married twice, first to a woman named Linda and then to a woman named Betty. Jim Lewis had named his firstborn child James Alan, and Jim Springer had named his James Allen. In childhood each twin had owned a dog named Toy. They had enjoyed family vacations on the same beach in Florida and had worked part time in law enforcement. They shared a taste for Miller Lite beer and Salem cigarettes.

At the time, only nineteen cases of reunited identical twins had been reported in the United States. Few had been reared by families who were not biologically related, and that made the Jims all the more exceptional—almost perfect for a behavioral geneticist who had spent his career trying to tease apart the influences of nature and nurture on the human personality. Bouchard excitedly persuaded university officials to provide grant money to initiate a study of the Jim twins. "It was just sheer scientific curiosity," Bouchard says now. "I thought we were going to do a single study of a set of twins reared apart. We might have a little monograph."

The morning the tests were to begin, Bouchard took the Jims to breakfast. 25
He intended to brief them on the particulars of the study, but it was the first time he had ever worked with twins, and he found himself obsessing over little things about them—the way each one had bitten his nails, for example. Each of the Jims had a peculiar whorl in his eyebrow, and Bouchard started absently counting the number of hairs in their brows. "You're staring at us," one told him. Bouchard apologized. He had been staggered by the similarities of their gestures, their voices, and the morphology of their bodies. These two men had lived entirely separate lives, and yet if Bouchard closed his eyes he couldn't tell which Jim was talking.

Since the Jims' first visit, more than a hundred other reared-apart twins have come to the Twin Cities to spend a week in Bouchard's laboratories, in Elliott Hall. In the tests, which usually start on Sunday afternoon and go through the following Saturday, twins undergo a variety of personality assessments and medical examinations, including X-rays, cardiograms, and blood tests. They have their fingerprints taken and their allergies evaluated. They submit to a sexual-history questionnaire that is so intimate that some twins decline to finish it. By the end, Bouchard's team will know as much about each of the twins as it is possible to measure in fifty hours of testing. The researchers will know what both twins eat, the books they read, their sexual orientation and predilections, the television shows they watch, how much their hands quiver when they hold a stick in a hole, their musical tastes and talents, their fears and phobias, their childhood traumas, their pulse rates at rest and under stress, their hobbies, their values, the amount of decay in their teeth, the way they sit in a chair. Because of the Minnesota project, separated twins have become one of the most densely studied populations in the history of psychology.

Besides the Jims, many memorable personalities have passed through Elliott Hall. Among the early pairs were Daphne Goodship and Barbara Herbert, who, like the Jims, had been adopted separately as infants and lived apart for thirty-nine years. Barbara had gone to a modest home in Hammersmith, a borough of London, as the daughter of a city gardener. Daphne had a middle-class childhood north of London, in the town of Luton, where her father was a metallurgist. When they finally met, at King's Cross Station in London, in May of 1979, each was wearing a beige dress and a brown velvet jacket. Right away, they noticed they had identical crooked little fingers—a small defect that had kept both of them from ever learning to type or to play the piano. There were other commonalities that were harder to explain. Both had the eccentric habit of pushing up their noses, which they called "squidging." Both had fallen down the stairs at the age of fifteen and had weak ankles as a result. At sixteen, each had met at a local dance the man she was going to marry. The twins suffered miscarriages with their first children, then proceeded to have two boys followed by a girl. And both laughed more than anyone else they knew, prompting them to be nicknamed the Giggle Twins. Bouchard was interested in the fact that each fell silent whenever the conversation turned to provocative subjects, like politics. In fact, neither had ever voted, except once, when she was employed as a polling clerk.

Among other twins who came to Minnesota to be quizzed and probed and bled and recorded were Jack Yufe and Oskar Stöhr. They were born in Trinidad in 1933 and were split apart a few months later by a bitter divorce, brought on by their father's violent behavior. Jack stayed in Trinidad with their father, a Jewish merchant in Port of Spain. Oskar went to live in the all-female household of their German maternal grandmother. While Oskar was preparing to become a member of the Hitler Youth, Jack was exploring his Jewish identity. At the age of sixteen, he was sent to Israel to work on a kibbutz. In 1954, he decided to emigrate to the United States, and stopped off in Germany to meet his brother for the first time since their separation. The reunion was chilly and brief. Then, twenty-five years later, Jack's wife read about the Jim twins and the Minnesota studies, and Jack decided that it might be a good idea to meet his twin again, this time on neutral ground. He got in touch with Bouchard, and the professor eagerly agreed to fly them both to Minneapolis.

Bouchard was standing with Jack at the Minneapolis airport when Oskar got off the plane. "I remember Jack pulling in his breath, because Oskar walked exactly the same way he did," Bouchard says. "They have a kind of swagger to their bodies." Each sported rectangular wire-rimmed glasses, a short, clipped mustache, and a blue two-pocket shirt with epaulets. They shook hands but did not embrace. Bouchard thought that they would be an ideal pair for detecting environmental influence. The contrasts in their upbringing, their cultures, and their family lives were overwhelming. Moreover, they didn't seem to like each other enough to mythologize their similarities, as critics of twin studies have suggested that twins tend to do.

As it turned out, Jack and Oskar were full of quirky habits in common, 30
such as storing rubber bands on their wrists, reading magazines from back to front, flushing the toilet before using it, and dipping buttered toast in their coffee. They also enjoyed startling people by sneezing in crowded places. They differed in certain obvious respects; Oskar, for instance, was married, while Jack was divorced, but Jack noticed that Oskar expected his wife to take care of all his needs without question—much as he himself had done when he was married. Jack regarded himself as a liberal Californian, and he saw his brother as "very traditionalistic, typically German." Oskar was a skier, Jack was a sailor. Oskar was a devoted union man, Jack a self-employed entrepreneur. Of course, they had lived profoundly different lives, so they differed completely in their memories, their experiences, their religious and political orientations—in other words, their interior worlds, the raw stuff of selfhood. And yet their personality profiles were strikingly similar. Bouchard observed that their tempos, their temperaments, their characteristic mannerisms were far more alike than different—similarities that were all the more surprising because Oskar had been reared entirely by women and Jack had grown up with their father.

The mountain of data compiled by the Minnesota team, along with ongoing twins research in Boulder, Stockholm, and Helsinki, has stunningly tipped the balance in the nature-versus-nurture debate. Bouchard and his team have assessed a variety of personality characteristics, such as sense of well-being, social dominance, alienation, aggression, and achievement, which they described in an important article in the *Journal of Personality and Social Psychology* in 1988. They concluded that identicals reared apart were as much alike as identicals reared together. Moreover, there was not a single one of those personality traits in which fraternal twins reared together were more alike than identicals reared apart. How could this be? Wouldn't twins who had grown up in the same family, gone to the same schools and churches, and been exposed to the same values and traditions have been similarly shaped by those influences? If, as the Minnesota team was claiming, half of the variance in personality in a population was genetic in origin and the other half was environmental, why wouldn't identical twins reared together be far more alike in their personalities than identicals reared apart?

The answer to this paradox had been suggested before, but not with the force of so much data. The Minnesota team asserted that almost none of the environmental variance was due to sharing a common family environment; rather, most of the differences that could be attributed to environmental causes arose from unshared experiences—in other words, the lives the twins led outside the home. Bouchard and his colleagues repeated this assertion in a disturbing 1990 article in *Science.* "The effect of being reared in the same home is negligible for many psychological traits," the Minnesotans wrote. "We infer that the diverse cultural agents of our society, in particular most parents, are less effective in imprinting their distinctive stamp on the children developing within their spheres of influence—or are less inclined to do so—than has been supposed. . . ."

Race and I.Q. are the bugbears of behavioral genetics, because of historically lower I.Q. scores among blacks. At the center of the I.Q. controversy is Sandra Scarr, a former colleague of Lykken and Bouchard at the University of Minnesota, who is now a professor of psychology at the University of Virginia. Scarr was one of the first researchers to conduct twin studies in minority racial populations. Brilliant and dauntingly prolific, much praised and often damned, Scarr has divided the academy because she has insisted on applying the insights of behavioral genetics to developmental psychology.

Early in her career, Scarr began studying why so many black children did poorly on tests and in school achievement. She wondered whether it was a result of sociocultural disadvantage or genetically based racial differences. This was a forbidden question in 1967, when Scarr first started studying the records of black and white twins in the Philadelphia public schools. Two years later, the Berkeley psychologist Arthur Jensen stirred up a nasty debate by airing his theory, based on I.Q.-test scores, that whites are genetically superior to blacks in intelligence. Two years later, Richard J. Herrnstein, a Harvard psychologist, followed with an article in *The Atlantic* on I.Q., in which he disowned his previous environmentalist stance. (That article was widely discussed and became the basis of "The Bell Curve," which was published [in 1994], shortly after his death.) Having observed the public pillorying of Jensen and Herrnstein when their articles appeared, Scarr decided that if her data supported a substantial relationship between African ancestry and low intellectual skills she was prepared to leave the country. "There was no point in documenting yet again that on average blacks score lower than whites," Scarr says.

"So I turned to testing black twins in order to look at the genetic and environmental variation within the black community."

One of the most striking findings of Scarr's early work on twins was that, 35
while studies had shown a closer correlation between the I.Q. scores of white identical twins than between those of white fraternals, the scores of both identical *and* fraternal black twins were similar. A set of black fraternal twins was less likely to range widely in intelligence; there was less likely to be one clever and one slow twin. Scarr speculated that the differences were suppressed by the deprivations of the black children's environment. When she compared the I.Q. scores for white children at the bottom of the socioeconomic ladder, it turned out that environmental differences were just as important for them. Scarr's findings suggested that inner-city black children (and white children in the same severely deprived circumstances) could have the genes for a higher intelligence than their environment permitted them to express. In 1972, soon after Scarr began teaching at the University of Minnesota (a move that seems almost inevitable for anyone interested in twin studies), she and one of her students, Andrew Pakstis, decided to test Jensen's theory that intelligence differences between blacks and whites were genetic in origin. Scarr and Pakstis reasoned that if Jensen was right children of mixed black and white ancestry (as is the case with most African-Americans) would score higher on intelligence tests according to their proportion of white ancestry. But subsequent tests of Philadelphia twins found no relation between intellectual-performance scores and degree of white genetic background.

Then Scarr, along with Richard A. Weinberg, a psychologist who worked with her at Minnesota's Institute of Child Development, went on to study a hundred and thirty black and mixed-race children, ranging in age from four to twelve, who had been adopted by well-off white families. The average I.Q. of these children was 106, which was higher than the average *white* I.Q. and well above the average score of 90 for black children in the region. The earlier the children had been adopted, the better they fared. Scarr and Weinberg estimated that the scores of these early-adopted children could be as much as twenty points higher than those of children of comparable age who had been reared in the black community. It seemed clear to the two researchers that environment influenced I.Q. considerably: specifically, being reared and educated in the culture of the I.Q. tests apparently made a large difference in achievement.

At the same time, however, Scarr and Weinberg were studying a group of white adolescents who had been adopted in early infancy by white families across the middle range of the socioeconomic spectrum. "We were interested in seeing the cumulative effects of the family environment on I.Q. scores," Scarr says. "We were astonished at the results." The hypothesis of the study was that if family environment mattered, then at the end of the child-rearing period adopted children should show the maximum effects of the advantages and disadvantages of the families that had taken them in. But what the Scarr-Weinberg adopted-adolescent study found was that the I.Q. scores of the adopted adolescents bore *no relation at all* to those of the other children reared in the same family or to those of their adoptive parents. "We had expected the children reared in the same family to resemble one another *more* in I.Q. and personality than the young children in our transracial study, but we were dead wrong on both counts," Scarr says. The adopted young black children in the other study were more similar to their white siblings than the adopted adolescents in the new study were to their siblings, despite the fact that the adolescents had spent their entire childhood with their adopted families and were of the same race. "This was really interesting," Scarr says. "First, we were amazed that in an adolescent-adoption study we did not find any resemblances among people unless they were genetic relatives. This did not jibe with previous adoption literature or with our own transracial adoption study. We tried to figure out why adolescents bore so little resemblance to their adoptive families."

Scarr found that children in the same family who were genetically unrelated were alike in their early years but grew to be different over time. They became more like their biological parents, whom they didn't know, than like the adoptive parents who raised them—not only in social attitudes, vocational interests, and certain personality features, such as prejudice and rigidity of belief, but also in I.Q. A follow-up study of the black and mixed-race children who were adopted into white homes found that by adolescence their I.Q. scores had fallen to a point slightly above what would be the average for their racial and ethnic mixture in the area. It was similar to the progression of mental development observed in MZ and DZ twins: the two types start out life being almost equally alike but diverge as they pass through childhood, with the MZ twins becoming even more similar and the DZ twins going their separate ways.

One lesson from the adopted-adolescent study seemed to be that genetic differences caused individuals to respond differently to similar rearing conditions. Another was that adopted children reared in rural or working-class homes did not differ significantly in their intelligence from adopted children reared by parents who were professionals. From these two findings, Scarr concluded that black and white children were essentially alike in their inherent intelligence and in their ability to achieve in schools, provided that they were given realistic opportunities to become part of the culture of the tests and of the schools. As long as children in a population were reasonably nurtured, Scarr observed, the individual differences between them must be genetic. Therefore, efforts to improve intellectual or academic performance should concentrate on rescuing those who were living on the far margins of society—who were genuinely deprived and were unable to gain the skills or knowledge needed to compete in the mainstream culture.

Over the last fifteen years, Scarr has been refining a new theory of devel- 40
opment, based largely on her conviction that environments do influence the intellects of young children. At early stages of life, she observes, enriched environments, such as day-care centers with stimulating programs, can boost a deprived child's achievement. Even young children, however, are genetically programmed to create certain experiences for themselves. For instance, a smiling, gregarious baby is more likely to be cuddled and petted than a fussy and undemonstrative one. If these two dissimilar infants are siblings, their

experiences of living in the same home can be quite different. As children mature, they gain more and more control over their environment, and actively select from the superabundance of opportunities and experiences those which conform to their genetic disposition. The distinction between genes and environment becomes less and less clear. "The dichotomy of nature and nurture has always been a bad one, not only for the oft-cited reasons that both are required for development, but because a false parallel arises between the two," Scarr wrote (in collaboration with her student Kathleen McCartney) in 1983 in the journal *Child Development.* "We propose that development is indeed the result of nature *and* nurture but that genes drive experience. Genes are components in a system that organizes the organism to experience the world."

That is why MZ twins become more similar over time and DZ twins less so. Identical genes compel MZ twins to experience the world in a similar manner, thus reinforcing the similarities of their natures, whereas the genetic variation of DZ twins awakens different interests and talents, which inevitably pull the twins apart into more distinct individuals. Identical twins who have been reared separately may live in different families, and even in different cultures, but they evoke similar responses from their environment and are disposed by their natures to make similar choices and to build similar niches for themselves.

In this school of thought, environment and genes do not represent separate, countervailing forces. To some, it may not even make sense to allocate percentages of heritability to, say, I.Q. or personality traits, because after one reaches a certain age the environment is itself a heritable reflection of one's genetic disposition. We make our environments, rather than the other way around—that is, as long as the environment we find ourselves in is not so impoverished or abusive that normal development cannot occur. "Good enough" parents, who provide an average environment to support development, will have the same effects on their children as "superparents," who press upon their children every cultural advantage.

"The statement that parents have few differential effects on children does *not* mean that not having parents is just as good as having parents," Scarr said, in a 1991 presidential address to the Society for Research in Child Development. "It may not matter much that children have *different* parents, but it does matter that they have parent(s) or some supportive, affectionate person who is willing to be parent-like. To see the effects of having no parents (or parent surrogates), one would have to return to the orphanages of long ago . . . or see children trapped in crack houses of inner cities in the United States, locked in basements and attics by vengeful, crazy relatives. Really deprived, abusive, and neglectful environments do not support normal development for any child." Despite these caveats, Scarr's speech was bitterly attacked by developmental psychologists who oppose her views, believing that they discourage efforts to improve the welfare of children—especially black children—and fail to hold parents accountable for their children's behavior. In fairness, Scarr concedes that parents can have important effects on children's motivation and self-esteem, but she insists that, beyond a minimum level of nurturing, they have little measurable impact on intelligence, interests, and personality.

The assault of behavioral genetics, which has had academe in tumult for the last three decades, has only recently begun to affect politics and social policy, having captured a place in the popular culture. Although twin studies are rarely a conspicuous feature of policy debates, they do exert an underlying force, through the altered understanding of human development which they have engendered. Clearly, we have moved from being a country that believes in the equality of human nature and the effectiveness of government to being one that not only doubts the ability of government to improve people's lives but also denies the possibility of personal transformation. This shift in perspective is reflected in the retreat from the social activism of our recent past. One can look at the cuts in welfare and job-training programs, the attacks on affirmative action, and the erosion of tax support for public education as strong evidence that Americans no longer embrace the ideal that it is possible to change people substantially by improving their circumstances.

Given the consequences, it's not surprising that there has been so much 45
resistance to the portrait of human nature which has been drawn from twin studies. When we read about twins who were separated at birth and are reunited in middle age only to discover that in many respects they have become the same person, it suggests to us that life is somehow a charade: that we only *seem* to react consciously to events; that the life experiences we think have shaped us are little more than ornaments or curiosities we have picked up along the way; and that the injunctions of our parents and the traumas of our youth which we believed to be the lodestones of our character may have had little more effect on us than a book we have read or a show we have seen on television—that, in effect, we could have lived another person's life and still be who we are.

And yet twins may have a different lesson to teach us. "A philosopher who was talking about twins said that maybe it's freedom that makes identical twins different," says Lindon J. Eaves, who is a human geneticist at the Virginia Commonwealth University School of Medicine. "Frankly, I don't believe that for a minute. It could be freedom that makes them alike." Eaves runs one of the largest twin studies in the world, known as the Virginia 30,000, which surveys fifteen thousand twins and their relatives. He is also an Anglican priest, and has consequently reflected on the implications of behavioral genetics for the doctrine of free will. "I think freedom means something about the capacity of the human organism not to be pushed around by external circumstances," he says. "I would argue that evolution has given us our freedom, that natural selection has placed in us the capacity to stand up and transcend the limitations of the environment. So I think the quest for freedom is genetic. I can't prove it, but I think it's a way forward."

It may be threatening to see ourselves as victims of our genes, but that may be preferable to being victims of our environment. To a major extent, after all, our genes are who we are. A trait that is genetically rooted seems somehow more immutable than one that may have been conditioned by the environment. This seems to leave aside the possibility of free choice—or even consciousness of choice at all. And yet people who are aware of their natures are constantly struggling with tendencies they recognize as ingrained or inborn. It makes little difference how such tendencies were acquired—only how they are managed. If it is true that our identical clone can sort through the world of opportunity and adversity and arrive at a similar place, then we may as well see that as a triumph of our genetic determination to become the person we ought to be.

Understanding

1. Wright states in paragraph 2: "Such a study [on twins who have been separated from birth] might not lay to rest the ancient quarrel over the relative importance of nature and nurture, but one could imagine few other experiments that would be more relevant to understanding the mystery of the human condition." What insightful conclusion on the nature-nurture discussion does this article reach? What about the human condition does Wright see as mysterious? What cherished belief has been questioned by the study of twins?
2. Why does Wright raise the "darker side" of the fantasy that there might be someone out there just like us? What does this question have to do with "free will"—usually defined as the human freedom to make choices and decisions without any restraints, compulsions, or previously determined conditions? How does it relate to the doctrine of determinism—that all human actions are determined by a sequence of causes independent of his or her will?
3. How do the answers to the nature-nurture argument play into politics? Why is there so much personal and public resistance to gene studies?
4. What is the effect of the environment on genes? In other words, can a body carry a gene that cannot be expressed?
5. What is the significance of Sandra Scarr's work on black and mixed-race twins? According to her findings, do rich "superparents" who can give their children every cultural advantage have a "better" developmental effect on their children than "good enough" parents?

Responding

1. Are you a twin? If so, explore in your own experience and in observations of you and your twin at least two of the scientific findings discussed in this reading. Do you consider being a twin a gift? Have your actions to be like or unlike your twin been a decision? Do you and your twin share a common wound? A common dream? Are your signatures similar?
2. Do you believe you are the product of your genes or of your environment? Has "The Biology of Twins" changed your beliefs about this question? Explain.

3. Your answer to Responding question 2 may shed light on some of your earlier writing. Has your genetic inheritance been a gift that you are nurturing? Have your genes given you wounds? Do your dreams include wishing for a different genetic makeup? Have you made decisions to struggle with what has been given to you genetically?
4. As we work through *Signatures* to explore our identities and the experiences or givens that mark them, paragraph 45 could be a shock to everything we have thought so far. Summarize these four concluding paragraphs (43–47), and discuss the message in light of a conclusion you made in one of your self-portrait essays. Does Wright's conclusion confirm or complicate your beliefs on the formation of identity by particular experiences?

Connecting

What kinds of traits or characteristics seem to be under genetic control according to this article? Are they the same ones that Bacon describes in "Heredity and Evolution" (chapter five)?

Intelligence and the X Chromosome

Gillian Turner

Gillian Turner is a professor of medical genetics at Hunter Genetics in Newcastle, New South Wales, Australia. *The Lancet,* the British medical journal from which this reading is taken, is an authoritative source of reporting and commentary on recent medical research. This essay comments on the continuing investigations into the source of a primary human trait: intelligence.

Although "Intelligence and the X Chromosome" is an essay—an opinion piece—and not a formal research report, it nevertheless presents some technical language and concepts that may be unfamiliar to the nonprofessional reader. Yet this is as clear and accessible a piece of medical literature as one will read in a medical journal, and we have chosen it precisely for this reason. It is authentic, it actually has some humor, and it is a good example of the type of interactions medical professionals are having about intelligence. It is also an example of the kinds of positions that medical professionals are taking about an issue that has medical as well as social implications.

This much we know: To be a girl, a baby must receive an X chromosome from her mother and an X chromosome from her father. To be a boy, a baby must receive an X from his mother and a Y from his father. What we still don't know, and what Turner comments on in this essay, is what other chemical instructions are contained in the chromosomes, that is, how certain genes are *coded.* Are the instructions or coding for intelligence (and this essay contains an interesting definition of intelligence) found in the genes of the X or the Y chromosomes?

T-shirts that read: "Xq28—Thanks for the genes, Mom!" were produced in the homosexual community in San Francisco when linkage studies first suggested that the gay gene might be at that location. A T-shirt with a wider application might be one that gives thanks to mothers from their children for her X chromosomes for their major contribution to their intelligence. 1

Intelligence has been defined "as the ability to deal adaptively with the changing environment, to benefit from past experience, to proceed in goal-directed fashion, to pursue productive avenues of problem solving, and to perceive common properties in otherwise separate domains of experience."[1] The inheritance of intelligence is reported to be multifactorial, with continuing controversy over the importance of the nature-nurture components. Several studies of monozygotic twins reared apart show a correlation in adult intelligence quotient (IQ) values of about 0.7 "indicating that about 70% of the observed variation in IQ . . . can be attributed to genetic variation."[2] The distribution of IQ scores measuring some aspect of intelligence is bell-shaped, with both sexes having the same mean scores but with wider variability in the male. There are significant differences in scoring between the sexes, with male individuals having better mathematical and musical abilities, and female better verbal abilities.

Lehrke[3,4] was the first to suggest that the genes for coding intellectual function might be on the X chromosome. He based his argument on the known excess of males with mental handicap, the different distributions of IQ in male and female individuals, and from a personal study of ten families in which non-specific mental retardation was segregating in an X-linked pattern. This suggestion was regarded as so unorthodox that Lehrke's first published paper was followed by two invited commentaries,[5,6] both of which were highly critical but offered no evidence to refute his conclusions.[7] In 1992 with Partington,[8] I restated Lehrke's hypothesis, suggesting that there was now molecular evidence to support his proposal. Morton[9] gently replied, stating that on theoretical grounds the evidence presented was not strong enough. The epidemiological and molecular evidence has continued to grow such that there is need for reappraisal.

At the time of the Lehrke controversy our group[10] was studying the epidemiology of mental handicap in New South Wales. We documented the expected excess of males with moderate handicap as 32%. We also found many more families with two affected sons than two affected daughters, which was supportive evidence that genes on the X chromosome were contributing substantially to the male excess. Herbst and Miller[11] recorded the same male and brother pair excess in British Columbia, their data including the mildly handicapped. They suggested that there might be nine to 17 single genes on X that were involved with mental handicap.

Since then at least 154 entities have been described with mental retarda- 5
tion and X-linked inheritance.[12] In some of these, the intellectual handicap is clearly a secondary feature, and one would not suspect that these genes were directly concerned with intelligence. For example, we can reasonably suppose that in X-linked hydrocephalus the mental retardation is secondary to the structural abnormality of the brain and that in the Lesch-Nyhan syndrome it is secondary to the inborn error of purine metabolism. However, there is an increasing number of other conditions in which loss of intelligence (mental retardation or intellectual handicap) is equally clearly the primary or only event.

In primary or non-specific X-linked mental retardation (XLMR) affected males have no phenotypical, neurological, or biochemical features in common apart from mental retardation. The prevalence of XLMR is three times that of the fragile X syndrome (2.5 per 10,000[13]) in the moderately handicapped and may be even more common in the mildly handicapped. There are now 32 extended pedigrees in which linkage studies have localised the genes to areas on the X chromosome. In many the limits of the locations overlap, but eight discrete localisations have emerged, which define the lowest limit of the number of genes involved. They extend over the short and long arm of the X chromosome.[14] The genes themselves are not sequenced and their individual functions are unknown.

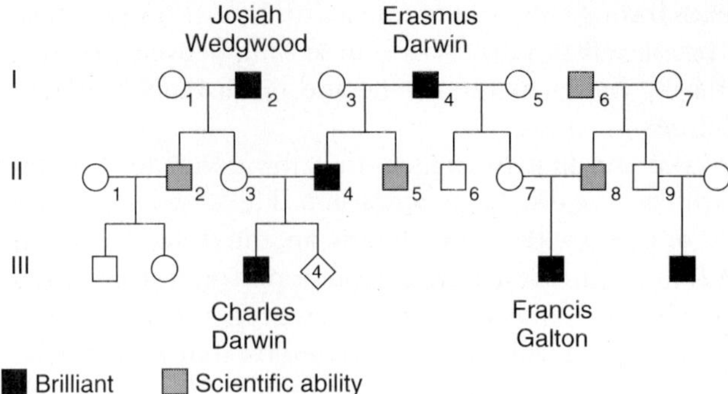

Figure: Abridged pedigree of the Wedgwood, Darwin, Galton family tree[15]
Source: Figure from R. Resta, "Genetic Drift Whispered Hints," *American Journal of Medical Genetics,* vol. 59 (1995): 131–133. Copyright © 1995 by Wiley-Liss, Inc. Reprinted by permission of Wiley-Liss, Inc., a subsidiary of John Wiley & Sons, Inc.

Morton's counterargument was that there were a calculated 325 recessively inherited genes associated with mental retardation. Therefore by calculating total DNA content of all the chromosomes the contribution of the X chromosome should be 17 genes. Theoretically there may be 308 genes on the autosomes that contribute to mental retardation. Indeed there are many recessive or dominantly inherited conditions that are associated with mental retardation but no families listed in the McKusick catalogue in which the single and only feature is mental handicap. The total number of genes on X relating to mental handicap is now at least 154 plus these eight locations for XLMR, which greatly exceeds the theoretical 17 suggested from Morton's calculations.

The conclusion seems inescapable that the genes now localised in families with XLMR indicate mutations in genes coding for aspects of intelligence. These genes are distributed along the whole length of the X chromosome and, presumably, code for various anatomical or functional parts of the neural substratum of intelligence. The female is a mosaic of two X chromosomes, one of which is methylated and inactivated randomly early in embryogenesis. The male with his single X chromosome is, therefore, likely to be more affected by either advantageous genes on the X chromosome or by deleterious mutational events, which may explain the difference in distribution of IQ between the sexes. The variation in patterns of ability between the sexes could result from greater diversity in the female, she being mosaic reflecting the functioning of genes on both her X chromosomes.

A second approach to identifying genes for intelligence would be through linkage studies in families in which high intelligence is segregating. The classic family is that of Charles Darwin (figure). His grandfather was the founder of Wedgwood Pottery and his cousin, Galton, was a prolific writer and the founder of the Eugenic movement. The pedigree shown in the figure was said, at the beginning of the century, to indicate that genius is a Y-linked dominant, but it could equally well be explained by X linkage. Charles Darwin received

Joshua Wedgwood's X chromosome and therefore his intelligence through his mother (II-3), and Erasmus Darwin's brilliance having reappeared in Francis Galton via his mother (II-7), rather than his father. Mary Howard (I-3), was also related to the Galtons.

If the genes coding for intelligence have evolved on the X chromosome this has evolutional advantage. The X or Y system is the mechanism in mammals of sex determination. The X is conserved throughout mammalian evolution.[16] The more intelligent male would be the better provider and may father more children, allowing for rapid propagation of any advantageous change.

In day-to-day practical evolutionary terms for our new millennium the male needs to remember that his primitive urges in mate selection are coded in his genome, and that they target current ideals of sexual attractiveness and youth. His frontal cortex should interpose reminding him that his sons' intelligence, if that is important to him, is solely dependent on his partner, and that is mirrored in both her parents. The female has more freedom of choice; she may be driven to mate by her partner's physique but the brightness of her children lies mainly within her. His daughters are helped by the paternal contribution but it is her potential mother-in-law, not her father-in-law, who needs checking out.

Notes

1. Wilson R. Encyclopedia of neuroscience 1. Boston: Birkhouser, 1987: 539.
2. Bouchard T, Lykkon D, McGue M, Segal N, Tellegen A. Sources of human psychological differences: the Minnesota study of twins reared apart. *Science* 1990; **250:** 223–28.
3. Lehrke R. A theory of X-linkage of major intellectual traits. *Am J Ment Defic* 1972; **76:** 611–19.
4. Lehrke R. X-linked mental retardation and verbal disability. *Birth Defects* 1994; Orig article series, vol X, no 1.
5. Anastasi A. Four hypotheses with a dearth of data: response to Lehrke's "A theory of X-linkage of major intellectual traits". *Am J Ment Defic* 1972; **76:** 620–22.
6. Nance WE, Engel E. One X and four hypotheses: response to Lehrke's "A theory of X-linkage of major intellectual traits." *Am J Ment Defic* 1972; **76:** 623–25.
7. Opitz JM. Editorial comment: on the Gates of Hell and a most unusual gene. *Am J Med Genet* 1986; **23:** 1–10.
8. Turner G, Partington M. Genes for intelligence on the X chromosome. *J Med Genet* 1991; **28:** 429.
9. Morton N. Genes for intelligence on the X Chromosome. *J Med Genet* 1992; **29:** 71.
10. Turner G, Turner B. X-linked mental retardation. *J Med Genet* 1974; **11:** 109–13.
11. Herbst DS, Miller JR. Non-specific X-linked mental retardation II: the frequency in British Columbia. *Am J Med Genet* 1980; **7:** 461–69.
12. Glass I. X-linked mental retardation. *J Med Genet* 1991; **28:** 361–71.
13. Turner G, Webb T, Wake S, Robinson H. The prevalence of the Fragile X syndrome. *Am J Med Genet* (in press).
14. Gedeon A, Donnelly A, Keer B, Turner G, Mulley J. How many genes for non-specific mental retardation are there? *Am J Med Genet* (in press).
15. Resta R. Genetic drift whispered hints. *Am J Med Genet* 1995; **59:** 131–33.
16. Ohno S. Sex chromosomes and sex linkage genes. Berlin: Springer Verlag, 1967.

Understanding

1. What does Turner believe to be the source of intelligence?
2. Find a definition of intelligence from another source (e.g., the dictionary, a book of quotations, a psychology textbook) and compare or contrast it with the definition Turner provides. What commonalities did you find? What differences?
3. The results of studies that Turner reports suggest that "the genes for coding intellectual function might be on the X chromosome" (paragraph 3). How does this event account for variations in patterns of ability between the sexes?
4. What differences in writing style do you detect between Turner's medical journal article and Gorman's "Sizing Up the Sexes," reported in a mass-circulation magazine? Express these differences in terms of the complexity of ideas, vocabulary, frame of reference assumed in the reader, and any other features you think differentiate the two selections.

Responding

1. Turner reports a definition of intelligence as "the ability to deal adaptively with the changing environment, to benefit from past experience, to proceed in goal-directed fashion, to pursue productive avenues of problem solving, and to perceive common properties in otherwise separate domains of experience" (paragraph 2). Choose any two of these attributes of intelligence and describe a behavior that you think demonstrates their presence.
2. Turner cites evidence that shows that "the brightness of a woman's children lies mainly within her." If the intelligence of her children is important to a woman, Turner advises, she should check out her potential mother-in-law, not her father-in-law. If you are a woman seeking this kind of advice, what exactly would you look for in your potential mother-in-law? What does this reveal about you?
3. How important to you is intelligence in a life partner or close friend? What aspects of intelligence as defined in Turner's commentary would you look for? What qualities other than intelligence would form the basis for a friendship or a life partnership?
4. If intelligence is a gift, an endowment from the X chromosome, what is the most appropriate way to use it?

Connecting

In what ways does Turner's hypothesis on the female contribution to intelligence differ from the mother's role as related in Bacon's "Heredity and Evolution"?

Questions of Genius

Andrew Solomon

There are many ways in which a person can be gifted. A genius, however, is someone who demonstrates achievement or aptitude for excellence usually at a very early age. These children, often called prodigies or boy or girl "wonders," can play chess simultaneously with five opponents, solve the most intricate problems in mathematics or physics, invent solutions to troubling technical problems, or create splendid works of art.

For musicians, genius is evident in the abilities described in this essay: an uncommon interest in music and sounds and an extraordinary ability to make music without extensive training. The title of this essay suggests that this gift has a somewhat baffling side, on which the author reflects in this carefully observed portrait of a brilliant Russian pianist.

Andrew Solomon is a contributor to the *New York Times Magazine* and other publications; he writes on cultural issues and is the author of the novel *A Stone Boat.*

At first, when Evgeny Kissin was a small child, his mother did not want him to become a musician. "I had seen how difficult that life was, and I didn't like the education that was given to children training for big careers," she says. "They struggle so hard in those special schools—they lose their childhood. I was afraid for this little son of mine." 1

Anna Pavlovna Kantor, a renowned piano teacher at the prestigious Gnessen Music School for Gifted Children, in Moscow, was astonished when she met the prodigy. "This mother—she had been pressured by a friend to see me—came with her little boy, with curls all over his head like an angel," she recalls. "He opened his bottomless eyes, and I saw a light in him. I took him by the hand and led him inside. I was amazed by this boy—not just by his ears, for many gifted children have such fine hearing, but by the way he used them. When he came to Liszt's Twelfth Rhapsody, he played the octaves, which his tiny hands couldn't reach, with both hands. And he had such imagination, such a sense of fantasy! I asked him to translate a story into music. I said that we were coming into a dark forest, full of wild animals, very scary, and then step by step the sun rises, and the birds start singing. And he began in the lower register of the piano, in a dark and dangerous place, and then, lighter and lighter, the birds awakening, the first rays of the sun, and finally a delightful, almost ecstatic melody.

"I didn't want to teach him. I was afraid, because I knew I would have to teach all the basic things, the notes, how to count the pauses. I thought he would be bored, that he would lose this freshness and interest. Such imagination can be very fragile. But his mother said to me, 'Clever and faithful helper, don't worry. He is interested in whatever is new to him. Try.' And so it began, and ever since then we have been together."

Anna Kantor is still an indispensable adviser to the musical wunderkind of our time, clever and faithful helper to a career that has grown beyond all her early expectations. At the age of twenty-four, Evgeny Kissin has more than two dozen CDs in circulation, many of them best-sellers; his concerts in the world's major halls—whether in New York, Tokyo, Milan, or Buenos Aires—are generally sold out months before they take place. Kissin has kept alive a tradition of larger-than-life virtuoso piano performance that seemed to end with the deaths of Arthur Rubinstein, Vladimir Horowitz, and, last year, Arturo Benedetti Michelangeli. (The last living titan of this older generation is the eighty-one-year-old Sviatoslav Richter.) Kissin's performances are not intellectually conceived interpretations, like those of most modern performers, but magnificent scenes of inspiration that materialize before the audience's very eyes. The forms of genius remain strange to us, and musical genius, which can blossom so suddenly in childhood, is the most mysterious of them all. Kant, in his seminal definition of genius, said, "If an author owes a product to his genius, he himself does not know how he came by the ideas for it; nor is it in his power to devise such products at his pleasure, or by following a plan, or to communicate [his procedure] to others in precepts that would enable them to bring about like products." Watching Kissin perform, one sees a man who seems, literally, possessed by his music.

Though Kissin can speak of music with intellectual clarity, he can no more 5
verbalize how he has arrived at his way of playing the piano than the leopard can explain how he got his spots. "How do you choose your encores?" I asked him when we first met, in London in the early spring, the day after a recital. "They come to me," he said. "How do you judge an audience?" "I feel something in the air." "How do you decide when you are ready for a piece?" "This is always very clear to me." "How do you decide which concerts to attend?" "I attend the ones I'm interested in." It must have been like this to interview the early saints.

Evgeny Kissin is too tall and too thin, with an unusually large head and a mop of crazy-genius Einstein hair. It's the sort of hair in which you could mislay something, and it's his defining physical attribute. He has enormous brown eyes and pale skin, and the overall effect is somehow exaggerated, awkwardly out of proportion, gangly. His bearing is shy and serious, but when inspiration is upon him he seems to fill out his own proportions, taking on a celestial air that can be affecting and, at moments, strangely beautiful. He had been described to me as a "moon child"—peculiar, incomprehensible, closed, impenetrable—and at our first encounter I felt that we were speaking through an unchinked wall. When we started discussing this article, I told him that I would like to plan at least three or four meetings. He replied, sounding genuinely bewildered, "But what on earth will we talk about?"

Evgeny Igorevich Kissin was born in Moscow on October 10, 1971. His mother, Emilia, taught piano to local children; his father, Igor, was a hard-working engineer; his sister, Alla, ten years older than he, was learning piano, and would become an accomplished accompanist. In a cramped apartment, they lived the life of the Soviet Jewish intelligentsia: physically uncomfortable and continually frustrating, with only the pleasures of the mind to make up for ordinary discomforts of the flesh and ideology's intrusions on the spirit. They were a lively but not an obviously remarkable family. The understanding was that the girl would play the piano, like her mother, and the boy would be an engineer, like his father. Little Genya demonstrated remarkable gifts very early, however, and they were not engineering gifts. At eleven months, he sang an entire Bach fugue that his sister had been practicing. He soon began to sing everything he heard: whatever his sister was studying, whatever his mother's pupils were learning, whatever came on the radio. "From that moment on," his mother recalls, "music never left our house. He would start singing immediately after opening his eyes in the morning, and he would sing all day long. It was rather embarrassing to take him out in the streets in Moscow. He would sing all the time, with his very clear baby voice, and people would stop and stare. Sometimes little crowds would gather. At the beginning, it was amusing, but as it went on it became quite eerie. It was relentless, nonstop, and I became frightened by it."

When he was two years and two months old, Genya sat down at the old Bechstein on which his mother taught and picked out with one finger some of the tunes he had been singing. The next day, he did the same again, and on the third day he played with both hands, using all his fingers. As the year progressed, he became more purposeful. He would listen to LPs, and immediately play back a remarkable approximation of the music he'd heard. His mother says, "Chopin's ballades he would play with those little hands, as well as Beethoven sonatas and Liszt rhapsodies. And also songs, children's songs and adult ones, and he would try to play symphonies." That winter, he went to a party for a little girl who was turning two. Frightened by strangers, he stepped back and hid his face in his mother's skirt. But when she whispered, "Genya, there is a piano over there," he marched directly over to the instrument, and entertained the other children all evening.

At three, Kissin began improvising original music. "Unfortunately, no one wrote it down, and those pieces disappeared immediately," he told me. "I especially liked to portray in music the people I knew. I would make the rest of the family guess who it was. As a rule, their answers were right. I don't know how, but I could grasp any form, and I wrote sonatas, rondos, mazurkas—whatever might occur to me." By the age of six, Kissin had been taken on by Anna Pavlovna Kantor.

What most gifted students might take five lessons to learn, the young 10
Kissin learned in one. He read music quickly, and was soon sight-reading everything put in front of him. Virtually anything he played once he had by heart, although he never made, he says, a conscious effort to memorize anything. Anna Pavlovna was very protective of him. "Her greatest triumph is that she preserved his gift," Genya's mother explains. "I am a teacher myself, and understand this. I will be grateful to Anna Pavlovna all my life for what she

did. She understood how to supplement what was there, never replace it. And I, as a mother, tried my best to leave him alone, not to interfere in this development."

As he grew older, Kissin stopped improvising at the keyboard and began to compose. He was often ill—he had pneumonia every winter of his childhood—and when he stayed in bed he would write music all day. All his pieces are inscribed, "Dedicated to my dear teacher, Anna Pavlovna." Kissin never studied composition: "I was afraid that in studying it and doing exercises his inspiration might be destroyed," Anna Pavlovna says. A few years later, he gave up composing. "I had run the gamut of styles, from Baroque to Classical to Romantic," he says, "and then I had nothing more to say. I was increasingly involved in concert performance, and I turned my creative energies there."

From the beginning, the piano was his emancipation. "In my first school years, when I returned from school I would, without taking my coat off, go to the piano and play for a while," he says. "I made my mother understand that this was just what I needed." His earliest public performances, before teachers and classmates, often included his own compositions. He played his first solo recital in May, 1983, at the age of eleven. "I had such a feeling of relief," he recalls. "During intermission, I was impatient to return to the stage. My teacher had said that there is good nervousness and bad nervousness. If you are not prepared, that's bad nervousness. But I think I felt only excitement and pleasure."

After the concert, a friend of Anna Pavlovna's, the wife of the director of the House of Composers, congratulated teacher and pupil. "You play so beautifully," she said. "I will talk to my husband and we will invite you to perform at the House of Composers." This was a great honor, a gateway to fame and comfort in the Soviet period of deprivations. Anna Pavlovna, however, was uneasy. "You know," she replied, "he is still very young. He shouldn't play too much, shouldn't go through the stress of being overexposed." Suddenly, a stranger who was standing nearby interrupted them. "Excuse me," he said, "but I couldn't help overhearing your conversation. I am a doctor, and I have just had the pleasure of attending this concert. I heard you say that it's not good for him to play in public too often, and, of course, in a way that is true. But when, a few minutes ago, I saw in what a state of enthusiasm the boy returned to the stage for his encores I realized that it would be even more dangerous for him to get overburned inside. He needs to perform." He turned to Anna Pavlovna and said, "Madam, you love him, one can easily see it, so you must find the right balance, not to push him, but not to let him consume himself."

Kissin was brought up in the Russian pianistic tradition rooted in the grand style of the nineteenth-century composer and legendary pianist Anton Rubinstein. Josef Hofmann, who studied with Rubinstein, has said of him, "All that he did was done instinctively, which, of course, is far superior to proceeding by rule or instruction because it is vital." The emphasis in Rubinstein's volcanic playing was on freedom of imagination and of feeling, with a reaching for massive effects at the possible expense of precision. (Kissin himself is a virtually note-perfect performer.) Kissin is the latest in a line of Russian "supermen" of the keyboard—a line that includes Sergei Rachmaninoff, Josef Lhévinne, Vladimir Horowitz, Emil Gilels, Sviatoslav Richter, and Lazar Berman, and whose distinguishing characteristic is a belief that the imagination and spirit of the performer should be equal to that of the composer.

Kissin's debut at the House of Composers, on June 23, 1983, was astonishing. The eminent pianist Dmitry Bashkirov was there, and he at once understood that this was an exceptional talent. Bashkirov arranged for Kissin to perform with the Leningrad Philharmonic in November. Two months later, in January, the conductor and pianist Daniel Barenboim visited Moscow, and Bashkirov invited the prodigy to play for him. Barenboim carried to the West the news of an astonishing boy in Moscow, and the legend of Evgeny Kissin began.

On March 27, 1984, Kissin, age twelve, appeared in Moscow with the Moscow Philharmonic under Dmitri Kitaenko and played Chopin's Piano Concertos Nos. 1 and 2. Everyone in the Russian music world was there. Photos from that occasion show a very small boy with a sweet smile and a mass of curls; he is dressed in the outfit of a Young Pioneer, with a red handkerchief tied around his neck and held in place with a badge of Lenin. Musical performance enjoyed a special status among the arts in the Soviet Union, because its abstract nature kept it from being ideologically suspect. The Kremlin, in the post-Stalinist era, was vastly proud of Soviet musicians—who served much the same political function as athletic stars, ballerinas, and cosmonauts—and the Soviet pianistic hothouse of the sixties, seventies, and early eighties was for Olympian victory. Anna Pavlovna kept Kissin away from competitions at which most performers proved themselves with powerhouse ostentatiousness. A recording of the 1984 concert was released in the U.S.S.R. almost immediately, and is still in print in the West. It feels innocent, unstudied, and exquisitely cheerful. Some of the concertos' monumentality is missing, but the playing is astonishingly articulate and beautiful in tone, and it fits Leonard Bernstein's characterization of true artistry—"fresh but inevitable."

As Kissin began to tour and continued to suffer bouts of pneumonia, he had an increasingly irregular schedule at school. Anna Pavlovna negotiated with the authorities for a "free-attendance regimen," in which he received private tutoring ("The usual subjects," he says, "history, literature, mathematics, dialectical materialism, Leninism, military science, and so on") and spent little time in classrooms. He had never been especially connected to his peers and he had few friends his age: some were jealous, others were bewildered by him, and the escape from ordinary schooling came as a relief. Kissin and Anna Pavlovna had become inseparable, and when he was accepted at the Gnessen Institute the authorities gave her special permission to teach him there. He has never had any other teacher.

In May, 1985, Kissin left the U.S.S.R. for the first time, playing at a gala in East Berlin attended by the East German President, Erich Honecker. "There were some circus performers," he recalls, "then I played Schumann and Chopin, and then a magician came out and did tricks." In October, 1986, he went to Japan; in January, 1987, he made his debut in Western Europe, playing with the Berlin Radio Orchestra. On September 30, 1990, he made his Carnegie Hall debut, with a program of Schumann, Prokofiev, Liszt, and Chopin. The response was overwhelming. Hundreds of concertgoers waited outside Carnegie's stage door for autographs, and the reviews were unanimous in their praise.

In 1991, the Kissins invited Anna Pavlovna to live with them. At the end of that year, the Kissins left Moscow for New York to facilitate Genya's growing international career, and Anna Pavlovna came with them. In New York, Genya's command of English progressed rapidly; he is by far the most fluent English-speaker in his family. Settled into an apartment in a modern building on Manhattan's Upper West Side, he found New York's combination of convenience and Moscow-like chaos congenial. He is an avid reader—he likes Russian poetry and musical biographies—but most of his non-performing hours are devoted to music and to the management of his professional life. "Genya's day-to-day existence is completely focussed on who he is as an artist," says Charles Hamlen, who, as Kissin's first American agent, oversaw the pianist's Carnegie Hall debut, and who remains a close friend. "Most of the time he's either practicing, or performing, or recording, or dealing with the minutiae of his career. There's an underlying unity between his artistic and personal lives, and the lack of distinction between them is perhaps the cornerstone of his identity."

20 Despite the urgings of Kissin's various managers, he has consistently resisted hiring a personal assistant. He sorts through the vast number of faxes and phone messages he receives every day, discusses them with his family, and makes decisions about them. He makes most of the choices about the pieces he will perform and where and when he will play them. He is often in touch directly with the conductors with whom he likes to work. Edna Landau, who is his manager at International Management Group, an agency whose roster of clients includes sports as well as music celebrities, says, "The only problem about managing Genya is that he's just too busy to do a fraction of the work for which he's in demand."

Kissin's family remains the center of his social life, and what time he spends away from it is mostly with family and musical friends, many of whom speak Russian. Kissin, who spends more than two-thirds of the year touring, plays approximately fifty engagements. He is usually accompanied by his mother and Anna Pavlovna. Sometimes his father, who is retired, and his sister, who plays only for friends now, come along as well. "Having them with me on my travels is a help," Genya says, "but it's also the pleasure of the company." Anna Pavlovna nods gravely. "For the great part of our lives, we saw nothing, living in the Soviet Union. The days when we were taking Genya Kissin with us are gone. Now are the days when Genya is taking us, and we're very grateful."

Emilia Aronovna and Anna Pavlovna are seldom apart now, shopping together for groceries, in Manhattan, talking about piano literature and how fresh the chickens look and Genya's schedule in a constant pattering dialogue. One critic recalls meeting the pianist just after his Carnegie Hall debut. "This," Kissin said, pointing to his mother, "is my teacher"; then, turning to

Anna Pavlovna, he said, "And this is my mother"; then he blushed and corrected himself. Genya's mother and teacher have always respected each other, and their affection has had twenty years to mature. In her seventies, Kissin's teacher mixes austere seriousness with twinkling enthusiasm. She adores Genya as much as his mother does, but one feels that her love was harder to earn. She has the solid, square dimensions of a Maillol and piercing eyes. As a teacher, she made it a practice never to touch the keyboard, but to teach by speaking, with an expressiveness that goes well beyond the specific meaning of her words.

Anna Pavlovna and Genya's mother are still closely involved in figuring out programs, in discussing how much to play and to record. Upon arriving in any new hall, Genya runs through his program. Anna Pavlovna sits in one place to assess the performance, while Emilia Aronovna walks around the hall to check the acoustics and the distortions. Four lives—father, sister, mother, teacher—have been given over to Kissin's genius and to his enormous earning capacities. (His concert fees are in the highest bracket, averaging twenty-five thousand dollars an appearance.) Kissin seems entirely comfortable with the life of an international virtuoso. "Sometimes I regret that the course of my life was set so early," he told me one day. "But there was never any way to resist it. There is no way to change who I am. Sometimes I wish—I wish that it were different. I wish that I had had more time to bring myself up, in a different atmosphere, without any pressure. But even if my career had begun later, music would always have been the only thing that was important to me. That I would not change."

In his spare evenings, Kissin attends concerts and the opera and the ballet, especially to see or hear performers he knows. He has friends of his own with whom he plays chamber music from time to time, and whom he sometimes entertains by playing ragtime—though he has never performed such material in public. When we went to a party in New York thrown by a mutual friend, he was modest and polite, almost offhand, when other guests came over to praise his abilities. Lately, there have been suggestions in the press that he should get out from under the protective umbrella of his family, that he should somehow become more of an all-American young man. (Similar suggestions were lobbed thirty years ago at Van Cliburn, whose mother was a powerful presence in his career.) Kissin bridles at such talk. "I don't understand why everyone here is so eager to destroy my relationship to my family," he said in an interview shortly after his arrival in this country. Kissin could no more live a "normal" life than could Prince William, and it is part of his dignity not to try. He has dozens of young female admirers but, he says, "I haven't met anyone yet I'd like to spend my life with."

It used to be commonly thought that prodigies were exceptions to the 25
laws of development—repositories of gifts that were categorically different from those of other children. Increasingly, however, child psychologists see prodigies as individuals in whom the pace of development in a single area is vastly accelerated, but whose developmental processes are not otherwise unusual. Some researchers claim that musical predisposition occurs in children

who are hypersensitive to sound, who are driven to order the noise around them, so that it becomes less disturbing. According to the Israeli psychiatrist Pinchas Noy, "The ego . . . is compelled to attain considerable abilities in order to protect itself. . . . [It] develops a superior capacity to organize auditory stimuli, to discern among their various shades, and, in particular, to transform 'painful' stimuli so that [they can provide] gratification and pleasure. . . . Listening to music [becomes] an activity of the ego in the service of mastering auditory stimuli that, in their deeper meaning, are threatening and frightening." This notion that highly discriminative hearing helps deal with overwhelming sound has been argued persuasively. But music is surely more than the reorganization of traumatic noise, just as love is more than the reworking of early losses.

Music, which is a system of abstract sound, is broadly acknowledged as a precursor to speech—a system of *significant* sound. Just as deaf children will begin to communicate with physical gestures, deploying them instead of phonemes to initiate colloquy, musical prodigies begin to use musical sounds as a means of conveying information from an early age. Music for them is not a readaptation of the aural experiments of pre-speech; it is speech itself.

Handel sang before he began to talk; music was, in effect, his first language. Arthur Rubinstein's childhood identification of people was based on the tunes he heard them sing, and he would designate them with these leitmotivs. He expressed his desires through music, singing a mazurka, for example, when he wanted cake. Fortunately, his family was musical enough to be able to decode these communications. Similarly, Kissin interpreted his family, and visiting friends, through musical composition and performance. For prodigies such as Kissin and Rubinstein, fascination with abstract auditory stimuli and the translation of them into concrete meaning represent not a sub-verbal but a super-verbal ability.

The psychologist John Sloboda makes a useful comparison between musical and verbal linguistics: "Musical idioms are not languages, and do not have referential meaning in the way that languages such as English do. They do, however, have complex multi-levelled structural features which resemble syntax or grammar." This suggests that, as we have long known is true of language, a deep structure of music exists in the brain even before the hearing of tunes, and it can be readily vitalized by exposure to musical sounds. Involvement of parents is crucial to the emergence of this faculty in a child: not only must there be a way to speak musically through either the voice or available instruments but also there must be people present to understand that speech. The anthropologist Robert Garfias has asserted that "the roots of each different music structure are inherent and inseparably linked to the structure of spoken language," and that "the two are, in fact, a single system, which is acquired from the earliest stages of infancy through the infant's constant processing of the sounds of human voices around him. . . . I believe that music may be man's primary means of sustaining a process of socialization."

The musicologist John Bailey has posited that early musical performance is contingent on a child's acquiring a "motor grammar"—that the physical dexterity required to produce music early in life far exceeds the level of physical coordination that young children otherwise possess. The prodigy, driven to express himself musically, goes through a process uncannily like the process of acquiring Sign among deaf children.

Conversing with Evgeny Kissin over a period of several months, I realized 30
that he talks the way I play the piano. Musical performance is a mode from which I derive pleasure; but though my level of understanding is adequate my expressive abilities are frustratingly insufficient to what I really have to say. So it is for Kissin and speech. His high intelligence and complex modes of thought are indicated, but not expressed, by his conversation. Kissin has a slight speech impediment, a lingering on explosive consonants that then burst forth like popping balloons. His speech is broken by long pauses; there often seems to be nothing organic leading from one word to the next. Every unexpressive word comes out glacially, always lying in proximity to his meaning and never containing it.

I had been playing with linguistic theories for some time before I put them to him. We were sitting in his simply furnished apartment; he and his family were getting ready to pack up for a move to a larger, older apartment nearby. Our meeting was impromptu; I'd called on the phone, and he'd suggested that I come over. We were both rather tired. He was wearing a pair of old, ill-fitting jeans, a greenish shirt, and bedroom slippers. His mother and Anna Pavlovna were shopping, and his father and sister were out of town. We sat in the small room where the piano—a baby-grand Steinway, on loan from the company—stood, its lid closed, its surface cluttered with greeting cards.

I wanted to know something about the structure of a Rachmaninoff cadenza. "This one?" Genya asked, and played six bars. Suddenly, the little room filled—overflowed—with music. On the tape the effect is alarmingly abrupt. There is perhaps ten minutes of conversation, which, as usual, is a bit stilted, punctuated with long silences broken by the staccato of Genya's speech. And then there is no effort, no forcing, no impediment to communication. Another five minutes of effortful speech, and then Kissin plays two minutes of a Chopin ballade he is preparing for his next season. The sound on my ten-year-old Sony tape recorder was so immense in contrast to the speech that when I first listened to the tape I thought I had bumped the volume control. The notes contained all the feeling absent from the words; the portcullis blocking the inner self from public view seemed to lift. When Genya played, what I heard was a yearning to be understood—the primary source of the beauty of his music. While we had been talking, Genya had several times had to suppress a yawn, explaining that he had not slept well the previous evening; when he was playing, the exhaustion disappeared from his face. It was not the polished way he would perform for a concert audience, and when he performs the piece next year he will doubtless add studied subtleties and intricacies. He was playing only to indicate passages to which I had alluded; but I knew we had by then come to like each other, and I felt, for the first time since we met, that we were in full conversation, that he was conveying something immediate, personal, and emotional. It was like receiving a confidence or a declaration of friendship, as intimate as a physical embrace. I wanted to respond to what I had heard, but I do not speak that language, and when Genya stopped playing I reverted to words, thus bringing him back to words. It was like dragging clouds back across a momentary sun.

I asked whether he thought speech sometimes fell short of conveying his feelings. "Speaking in words is much less for me," he said. "In fact, I don't even know how to convey through speech at all. What I have to say, the music says it. And I don't like to try to speak about the music, either: it speaks for itself. For me, there is no translating this." The fact that music is, in effect, a first language no more guarantees brilliant use of that language than the fact that English is the first language for most American children means that they will all be poets. Apollinaire famously said that artists fall into two categories: that of the perfect virtuoso, who exploits an unmediated "natural" gift (the usual model for the prodigy), and that of the reflective artist, who builds insight around experience. Kissin has managed to enact a musical transformation from the former model to the latter.

His task is to discover the "truth" of the work he is playing through the assertion of his own "truth." For him, the world is, literally, bounded by music. He reminds me of Wallace Stevens's vision of the supreme artist, the beachwalker in the poem "The Idea of Order at Key West," for whom "there never was a world . . . Except the one she sang and, singing, made."

I asked Kissin what he would do if his career were to go awry. "I never 35
thought of it," he replied, "but if my career were suffering, I would be able to find comfort only in music, in the piano. I don't know how I would be able to live if I suddenly became unable to play." For him, music makes sense of the world by ordering—rebalancing—its forces, and it is for this reason that his playing seems to make sense of the world for his audiences. Communicating is supremely important for him. He often has extra seats placed around him on the stage, right next to the piano itself, so that additional people can attend his concerts. "It's strange, but the more people there are in the hall, the better I play," he said. "It's necessary for me to play a piece in public to master it. The whole perception changes. I feel people's attentiveness, and my performance depends on it. . . ."

Next year, he will take six months off from his relentless touring and recording, simply to think and play for himself, as he has not had time to do since his career began. What might come of such a sabbatical? He says cryptically, "Life itself will show me what to do."

Watching Kissin sit down at the piano is like watching a lamp get plugged in: decorative though it may have seemed before, it is only when electricity courses through it that its real use becomes apparent. You do not feel so much that he is pouring energy into the instrument as that he is receiving energy from it. His hands seem actually to *belong* to the piano. In June, I went to the Barbican Hall in London to hear Kissin perform the Rachmaninoff Third Piano Concerto. It was one of the most magnificent concerts I've ever heard. . . .

At the concerto's end, there was a long moment of silence, then a standing ovation. I was sitting with Emilia Aronovna and Anna Pavlovna. Genya's mother counted the number of people standing, while his teacher stayed in her seat. "I think it was good," she said, and I supposed that she was recalling her first encounters with that vast childlike imagination, which under her tutelage had only continued to expand. Kissin was unable to explain the performance. Later, he said, "I just start playing a piece again and it sounds different, not because I *want* it to sound different but simply because I myself have changed. Pushkin said, 'I live in order to think and to suffer.' Life itself brings change. . . ."

I recalled another Kissin concert I'd attended several weeks earlier, in the northern Italian city of Bergamo, where the audience seemed composed largely of local businessmen and their wives. The recital concluded with a Kissin specialty, the monumentally difficult Brahms "Variations on a Theme by Paganini," which he played without boundaries or edges. The applause was tumultuous. Kissin stood up, bowed his stiff bow, and walked off-stage, looking as placid as though he'd just finished lunch. The applause redoubled, and he came back on, gestured up to the balconies, bowed again, and smiled, apparently delighted to discover that all these people had enjoyed what he himself had so evidently enjoyed. For his first encore, he played a Chopin mazurka. It was charming, and the audience clapped merrily. He took a few more bows, then played Weber's "Perpetuum Mobile." Applause; bows. Then Brahms's Hungarian Dances Nos. 6 and 7. After that, some of the concertgoers, perhaps thinking that the encores were over, began to file out of the hall. More bows; then Kissin played a Chopin waltz. Applause, bows, then a fifth encore: Beethoven's "Rage Over a Lost Penny," in an interpretation so playful that the audience burst out laughing.

A game had started: encore, applause, bows, encore. The ovations seemed to challenge Kissin to keep playing. He played the Adagio from the Bach/Busoni Fantasy, Adagio, and Fugue, then Chopin's E-Minor Waltz, after which a woman rushed to the stage, attacked a floral arrangement, grabbed an anthurium, and handed it to him. Next came Rachmaninoff's legendary encore, his own Prelude in C-Sharp Minor, which was followed by the stamping of feet.

They would not let Kissin go. After he had played the Brahms Intermezzo No. 6 from Opus 116, Kissin took six curtain calls. Then a man in one of the upper balconies leaned out, spread his hands like a conductor, and began to clap slowly and rhythmically. Soon the entire audience was clapping in unison. Kissin reemerged and shrugged. Wearing a genial but slightly blank expression, he played the Rondo alla turca from Mozart's A-Major Sonata. More rhythmic clapping. After six more curtain calls, Kissin sat down to play the Intermezzo from Schumann's "Carnaval." After the twelfth encore, someone shouted "Tchaikovsky!" and Kissin, nodding the way rich people acknowledge small charities, sat down and played a Tchaikovsky waltz. Now the audience clapped and stamped in unison, so insistently that the whole building began to tremble. Kissin seemed bewildered. He walked on and off the stage a dozen times before his final encore—the Brahms Rhapsody from Opus 119. It was as colorful and fresh as the first notes he had played that night.

By now, it was well after midnight. "Come," an older woman said, stopping her husband's hands as he clapped. "The boy should go to sleep." Finally, the applause petered out. Kissin did not reappear.

At the stage door, a crowd pressed tight. A guard held people back, letting in thirty or so, then a few more, and then a few more. I got past the guard to find Genya standing backstage, nodding his formal nod to the congratulators and signing "Kissin" in Roman letters on the pieces of paper they held out: photos of him, albums, programs. He smiled politely while one fan and then another posed with him for a snapshot. After he had given perhaps a hundred and fifty signatures, his mother came out of the dressing room. She took his arm very gently and said something in Russian. The disappointed fans who had not got his signature took pictures as he walked between her and Anna Pavlovna to a waiting car. As the engine started, a last round of applause, loud and pulsing, went up from the crowd. When the car was gone, people turned to one another—surprised, apparently, to find themselves on an ordinary spring night in Bergamo. "It's late," the man standing next to me said. "Terribly late," he said, before disappearing down the dark street, as though to explain the sudden silence.

Understanding

1. How would you describe Kissin's life and his personality?
2. What in the description of Kissin's childhood leads you to think that the origin of his gifts is genetic or biological? What might lead you to conclude that the origin is environmental? What role did these two major forces play in the evolution of Kissin's life and talent?
3. Kissin's mother says her son's teacher, Anna Pavlovna, "preserved his gift" (paragraph 10). How did Pavlovna do that?

Responding

1. Solomon speaks of Egveny Kissin as having "remarkable gifts." Do you agree? If so, what are these gifts? What costs are associated with having these gifts?
2. What, in your judgment, are the responsibilities of the teachers of gifted children? Do the child's parents have an obligation to encourage the development of such a gift? If so, to whom? To the child? To society?
3. The psychologist Howard Gardner has proposed the term *multiple intelligences* to describe the many possible ways in which a person may be intelligent or even brilliant. Musical talent is one of these "intelligences." Kissin seems to have found that communicating through music is more productive and satisfying than communicating through words. Music can have such transcendental effects—even on people who are not musically "gifted." Describe a musical experience in your life that conveyed more than words can say.
4. Most of us are consumers rather than producers of music. If you are a musician, what kinds of music do you enjoy? If you are not a musician, what

kinds do you prefer to listen to? What effects does music have on you? Do you think people are genetically "programmed" to like a certain *kind* of music?

5. A popular motivational message says, "The talent you never develop is like having no talent at all." Have you developed a particular talent to an extraordinary level of proficiency? Do you know someone who has? How was this talent first recognized? How was it developed? If you haven't developed a talent, do you recognize one within you that you think can be developed? If so, what is it and how might you go about developing it? What price do you think you might have to pay for developing it?
6. Consider the efforts of professional musicians, athletes, artists, and writers. How much of their "talent" do you think is inborn, and how much is simply the result of discipline and hard work?

Connecting

1. The film *Shine* examines the effects of a demanding environment on a gifted pianist, David Helfgott, who eventually broke under the strain. If you have seen the film, how did Helfgott's environment compare with Solomon's depiction of Kissin's? What other genetic or biological factors, unexamined in the film, might have accounted for Helfgott's breakdown?
2. For an interesting counterpoint to the perils of musical genius, consider Glenn Gould, one of the twentieth century's greatest pianists, who could read music at three and began concertizing at fourteen. If you are interested in film, see *Thirty-Two Short Pieces about Glenn Gould,* which provides a real-life glimpse into his eccentric genius. Gould died in 1982 at age fifty.
3. Listen to one of Kissin's recordings ("more than two dozen CDs in circulation"). Document your reactions to listening to his music.

Race Is Over

Stanley Crouch

In this article the author raises a biological question: What will we Americans look like in a hundred years? His answer has powerful political ramifications. Behind his answer to what we will look like is a strong belief in the importance of humanity (commonality) over race (diversity) in the way he wants his readers to define themselves. He further asks us to think differently than we have in the 1990s.

Social critic Stanley Crouch is the author of *The All-American Skin Game: Or, The Decoy of Race,* in which he urges Americans to focus as much as possible on the human connections that we have and the extraordinary achievements that we have made against what he calls the decoy of race. His arguments are compelling, and "Race Is Over" will give you some new ways to look at the old questions.

BLACK, WHITE, RED, YELLOW—SAME DIFFERENCE

Even though error, chance and ambition are at the nub of the human future, I am fairly sure that race, as we currently obsess over it, will cease to mean as much 100 years from today. The reasons are basic—some technological, others cultural. We all know that electronic media have broken down many barriers, that they were even central to the fall of the Soviet Union because satellite dishes made it impossible for the Government to control images and ideas about life outside the country. People there began to realize how far behind they were from the rest of the modern world. The international flow of images and information will continue to make for a greater and greater swirl of influences. It will increasingly change life on the globe and also change our American sense of race. 1

In our present love of the mutually exclusive, and our pretense that we are something less than a culturally miscegenated people, we forget our tendency to seek out the exotic until it becomes a basic cultural taste, the way pizza or sushi or tacos have become ordinary fare. This approach guarantees that those who live on this soil a century from now will see and accept many, many manifestations of cultural mixings and additions.

In that future, definition by racial, ethnic and sexual groups will most probably have ceased to be the foundation of special-interest power. Ten decades up the road, few people will take seriously, accept or submit to any forms of segregation that are marching under the intellectually ragged flag of "diversity." The idea that your background will determine your occupation, taste, romantic preference or any other thing will dissolve in favor of your perceived identity as defined by your class, livelihood and cultural preferences. Americans of the future will find themselves surrounded in every direction by people who are part Asian, part Latin, part African, part European, part American Indian. What such people will look like is beyond my imagination, but the sweep of body types, combinations of facial features, hair textures, eye colors and what are now unexpected skin tones will be far more common, primarily because the current paranoia over mixed marriages should by then be largely a superstition of the past.

In his essay "The Little Man at Chehaw Station," Ralph Ellison described a young "light-skinned, blue-eyed, Afro-American-featured individual who could have been taken for anything from a sun-tinged white Anglo-Saxon, an Egyptian, or a mixed-breed American Indian. . . ." He used the young man as an example of our central problem—"the challenge of arriving at an adequate definition of American cultural identity. . . ." While the youth's feet and legs were covered by riding boots and breeches, he wore a multicolored dashiki and "a black homburg hat tilted at a jaunty angle." For Ellison, "his clashing of styles nevertheless sounded an integrative, vernacular tone, an American compulsion to improvise upon the given."

The vernacular tone Ellison wrote of is what makes us improvise upon 5
whatever we actually like about one another, no matter how we might pretend we feel about people who are superficially different. Furthermore, the social movements of minorities and women have greatly aided our getting beyond the always culturally inaccurate idea that the United States is "a white man's country."

We sometimes forget how much the Pilgrims learned from the American Indians, or look at those lessons in only the dullest terms of exploitation, not as a fundamental aspect of our American identity. We forget that by the time James Fenimore Cooper was inventing his backwoodsmen, there were white men who had lived so closely to the land and to the American Indian that the white man was, often quite proudly, a cultural mulatto. We forget that we could not have had the cowboy without the Mexican vaquero. We don't know that our most original art-music, jazz, is a combination of African, European and Latin elements. Few people are aware that when the Swiss psychoanalyst Carl Jung came to this country he observed that white people walked, talked and laughed like Negroes. He also reported that the two dominant figures in the dreams of his white American patients were the Negro and the American Indian.

Are we destined to become one bland nation of interchangeables? I do not think so. What will fall away over the coming decades, I believe, is our present tendency to mistake something borrowed for something ethnically "authentic." Regions will remain regions and within them we will find what we always find: variations on the overall style and pulsation. As the density of cross-influences progresses, we will get far beyond the troubles the Census Bureau now has with racial categories, which are growing because we are so hung up on the barbed wire of tribalism and because we fear absorption, or "assimilation." We look at so-called "assimilation" as some form of oppression, some loss of identity, even a way of "selling out." In certain cases and at certain times, that may have been more than somewhat true. If you didn't speak with a particular command of the language—or at a subdued volume—you might have been dismissed as crude. If you hadn't been educated in what were considered the "right places," you were seen as some sort of a peasant.

But anyone who has observed the dressing, speaking and dancing styles of Americans since 1960 can easily recognize the sometimes startling influences that run from the top to the bottom, the bottom to the top. Educated people of whatever ethnic group use slang and terms scooped out from the disciplines of psychology, economics and art criticism. In fact, one of the few interesting things about the rap idiom is that some rappers pull together a much richer vocabulary than has ever existed in black pop music, while peppering it to extremes with repulsive vulgarity.

One hundred years from today, Americans are likely to look back on the ethnic difficulties of our time as quizzically as we look at earlier periods of human history, when misapprehension defined the reality. There will still be squabbling, and those who supposedly speak in the interest of one group or another will hector the gullible into some kind of self-obsession that will influence the local and national dialogues. But those squabbles are basic to upward mobility and competition. It is the very nature of upward mobility and competition to ease away superficial distinctions in the interest of getting the job done. We already see this in the integration of the workplace, in the rise of women and in the increase of corporations that grant spousal-equivalent benefits to homosexuals because they want to keep their best workers, no matter what they do privately as consenting adults. In the march of the world economy, the imbalances that result from hysterical xenophobia will largely melt away because Americans will be far too busy standing up to the challenges of getting as many international customers for their wares as they can. That is, if they're lucky.

Understanding

1. Paraphrase Crouch's thesis.
2. The 1990s have been a time for redefining some popular terms; perhaps you have discussed or debated them yourself. The following are the commonly used definitions in the United States at this time:

   Diversity: In an institution *diversity* is generally defined as the physical presence of members of diverse cultural and social groups.
   Multiculturalism in organizations is generally defined as the integration and full participation of diverse cultural groups in all activities and initiatives of an institution, and especially in decision-making processes.

   How would Crouch respond to these definitions?
3. How does Crouch use African American writer Ralph Ellison's work to support his own argument?

4. In Crouch's opinion, what is the main reason for the politicization of racial and special-interest groups in America? How does this relate to the world economy?
5. People all over the world argue against intermarriage among the races and religions. One reason for the opposition, as Crouch states it, is that we will become "one bland nation of interchangeables" (paragraph 7). Does Crouch agree with that concern?

Responding

1. In paragraph 5, Crouch proclaims that all of us as Americans have gotten "beyond the always culturally inaccurate idea that the United States is 'a white man's country.'" To what extent do you agree? Give examples to support your answer.
2. There is much discussion in universities surrounding the idea that "the personal is the political." Interview several professors or classmates to find out what is meant by this. What does it mean to you? What are the ramifications of such a belief? What would the opposite of this debate be?
3. Crouch says that we as Americans fear "absorption, or 'assimilation.' We look at so-called 'assimilation' as some form of oppression, some loss of identity, even a way of 'selling out.'" What are your views on this assertion? What is it about absorption that some people fear?
4. Check the definition of *xenophobia* in a dictionary. Why, according to Crouch, will xenophobia "melt away" (paragraph 9)? Do you agree?

Connecting

1. When you travel to and from work or school and observe people in your classes, your workplace, on the streets, and on public transportation, do you think that the United States is becoming a *mestizaje* (racial mixture)? Does Crouch's thesis in "Race Is Over" support Anzaldua's in "To Live in the Borderlands Means You (chapter six)? Where might Crouch and Anzaldua differ?
2. Who or what is it that makes defining American cultural identity such an important issue? Does your family claim its cultural roots first, its American affliation second? How does using Ralph Ellison's idea about "the American compulsion to improvise upon the given" (paragraph 4) in his essay "The Little Man at Chehaw Station" relate to other essays or selections in *Signatures?*

WRITING OPTION: Inborn Traits

From your responses to the readings and from the "Inborn Traits" texts themselves, create a short essay around the theme of inborn traits. You may incorporate any of your material from "Self-portraits" and quotations from any of the readings to strengthen your essay where appropriate. Especially helpful is to incorporate strong and memorable statements that hold these authors' claims about the power of inborn traits on our constructions of self. This writing exercise is a chance to focus on those genetic traits that are givens in your lives (and others') which have defining and lasting influences either that you must work with to overcome, or that you have worked to enhance.

Another option is to frame your own question around this topic and develop an essay to answer it. Use your responses to the readings to remind you what was worth extra thought and use this essay as a means to refine your thinking.

3 Nature and Nurture

How do we become who we are? Are we essentially programmed by our genes (nature), or are we determined by our experiences (nurture)? On one level, this question, framed as the "nature-nurture debate," has been resolved: Both influences shape who we become.

As we learn more about how nature and nurture interact, the debate moves to another level. Such aspects of the self as addictive behavior, sexual preference, and some mental disorders, once thought to be the result of environmental insults or faults in our upbringing, are now considered to have a strong genetic component. Thus a new question has emerged: Can nurture, or environment, alter our biology, that is, our chemical composition? Robert Wright shows us how a current controversy over the cause of violence tackles this question. Taking a reproductive strategy to prove his point, Loyal D. Rue argues that education can, and perhaps should, modify the ways in which women select a mate, ultimately affecting the gene pool. Similarly, as Daniel Goleman shows us, temperament, those innate emotional patterns that shade our moods, is a hereditary endowment that we can manipulate.

How much does the average person—the nonscientist—need to know to make sense of these writers' arguments? In what ways do the writers support their points? Are their arguments convincing? How do these issues influence our everyday lives?

Through genetic engineering, scientists have increased their ability to tell the genes what to do. Consider the following readings to be a small sampling of ideas supported by research on a subject that continues to challenge our thinking about the major sources of our identity.

The Biology of Violence

Robert Wright

Violence is as old as time and as new as the latest outbreak of fighting in the world or in your community. This selection explores the idea that some people might inherit a tendency or a predisposition to be violent—a highly controversial and, in many ways, disturbing notion. It also provokes many questions. If violence is part of our genetic makeup, or if it becomes part of our "biology," should we adjust to this condition or strive to overcome it? If we could determine a person's predisposition to violence before birth, should we screen for it during pregnancy? Should people who are shown to be born with this tendency be held accountable for their actions?

Social critic Robert Wright, who has written extensively on American cultural issues, carefully dissects the positions of two medical professionals who have divergent interpretations of the origins of violence and whose conclusions may cause you to rethink your ideas about this ancient yet modern social reality.

Frederick Goodwin has learned a lot during a lifetime of studying human behavior, but no lesson is more memorable than the one driven home to him over the past three years: becoming known as someone who compares inner-city teen-agers to monkeys is not a ticket to smooth sailing in American public life. As of early 1992, Goodwin's career had followed a steady upward course. He had been the first scientist to demonstrate clinically the antidepressant effects of lithium, and had become known as a leading, if not the leading, expert on manic-depressive illness. He had risen to become head of the Alcohol, Drug Abuse and Mental Health Administration, the top position for a psychiatrist in the federal government, and was poised to be the point man in a policy that the Bush Administration was proudly unveiling: the Federal Violence Initiative. The idea was to treat violence as a public-health problem—to identify violently inclined youth and provide therapy early, before they had killed. The initiative had the strong support of the Secretary of Health and Human Services, Louis Sullivan, and Goodwin planned to make it his organization's main focus. 1

Then, in early 1992, while discussing the initiative before the National Mental Health Advisory Council, Goodwin made his fateful remarks. Speaking impromptu—and after a wholly sleepless night, he later said—he got off onto an extended riff about monkeys. In some monkey populations, he said, males kill other males and then, with the competition thus muted, proceed to copulate prolifically with females. These "hyperaggressive" males, he said, seem to be also "hypersexual." By a train of logic that was not entirely clear, he then arrived at the suggestion that "maybe it isn't just a careless use of the word when people call certain areas of certain cities jungles." Goodwin elaborated a bit on his obscure transition from monkeys to underclass males, but no matter; these few fragments are what came to form the standard paraphrase of his remarks. As the Los Angeles *Times* put it, Goodwin "made comparisons between inner-city youths and violent, oversexed monkeys who live in the wild."

As if a few seemingly racist quotes weren't enough of a public-relations bonanza for opponents of the Violence Initiative, Goodwin also injected what some took to be Hitlerian overtones. He talked about "genetic factors" inclining human beings toward violence, and suggested that one way to spot especially troublesome kids might be to look for "biological markers" of violent disposition. Within months, the Violence Initiative was abandoned, amid charges of racism. And Goodwin, facing the same charges, was reassigned to head the National Institute of Mental Health—not a huge demotion, but a conspicuous slap on the wrist. Finally, last year, he left that job for a position in academe after intermittent coolness from the Clinton Administration. Though no Clinton official ever told him he was a political liability, Goodwin found himself no longer invited to meetings he had once attended—meetings on violence, for example.

Goodwin is a victim of a vestigial feature of the American liberal mind: its undiscerning fear of the words "genetic" and "biological," and its wholesale hostility to Darwinian explanations of behavior. It turns out, believe it or not, that comparing violent inner-city males to monkeys isn't necessarily racist, or even necessarily right wing. On the contrary, a truly state-of-the-art comprehension of the comparison yields what is in many ways an archetypally liberal view of the "root causes" of urban violence. This comprehension comes via a young, hybrid academic discipline known as evolutionary psychology. Goodwin himself actually has little familiarity with the field, and doesn't realize how far to the left one can be dragged by a modern Darwinian view of the human mind. But he's closer to realizing it than the people whose outrage has altered his career.

As it happens, the nominally dead Federal Violence Initiative isn't really 5
dead. Indeed, one of the few things Goodwin and his critics agree on is that its "life" and "death" have always been largely a question of labelling. Goodwin, who recently broke a thirty-month silence on the controversy, makes the point while dismissing the sinister aims attributed to the program. "They've made it sound like a cohesive new program that had some uniform direction to it and was directed by one person—namely, me," he told me. "The word 'initiative,' in bureaucratese, is simply a way of pulling stuff together to argue for budgets. In effect, that's what this was—a budget-formulation document, at Sullivan's request." Goodwin's critics look at the other side of the coin: just as the bulk of the Violence Initiative predated the name itself, the bulk of it survived the name's deletion. Thus the war against the violence initiative—lower case—must go on.

The person who was most responsible for turning Goodwin's monkey remarks into a life-changing and policy-influencing event is a psychiatrist named

Peter Breggin, the founder and executive director of the Center for the Study of Psychiatry, in Bethesda, Maryland, just outside Washington. The center doubles as Breggin's home, and the center's research director, Ginger Ross Breggin, doubles as Breggin's wife. (Goodwin says of Peter Breggin, in reference to the center's lack of distinct physical existence, "People who don't know any better think he's a legitimate person.") Both Breggins take some credit for Goodwin's recent departure from government. "We've been all over the man for three years," Ginger Breggin observes.

Goodwin and Peter Breggin interned together at SUNY Upstate Medical Center in the nineteen-sixties. Both took a course taught by Thomas Szasz, the author of "The Myth of Mental Illness," which held that much of psychiatry is merely an oppressive tool by which the powers that be label inconvenient behavior "deviant." Szasz had formed his world view back when the most common form of oppression was locking people up, and Breggin, since founding his center, in 1971, has carried this view into the age of psychopharmacology. He fought lithium, Goodwin's initial claim to fame. He fought the monoamine-oxidase inhibitors, a somewhat crude generation of antidepressants, and now he fights a younger, less crude generation of them. "Talking Back to Prozac," written in collaboration with his wife and published last June, is among the anti-psychopharmacology books he has recently churned out. So is "The War Against Children," published last fall, in which the Breggins attack Goodwin, the Violence Initiative, and also the drug Ritalin. In Breggin's view, giving Ritalin to "hyperactive" children is a way of regimenting spirited kids rather than according them the attention they need—just as giving "anti-aggression" drugs to inner-city kids would be an excuse for continued neglect. And Breggin is convinced that such drugs will be used in precisely this fashion if the Goodwins of the world get their way. This is the hidden agenda of the Violence Initiative, he says. And Goodwin concedes that pharmacological therapy was a likely outcome of the initiative.

Breggin's all-embracing opposition to psychopharmacology has earned him a reputation among psychiatrists as a "flat-earther." Some, indeed, go further in their disparagement, and Breggin is aware of this. "I am not a kook," he will tell a reporter whether or not the reporter has asked. People try to discredit him, Breggin says, because he is a threat to their interests—to the money made by drug companies, which insidiously bias research toward chemical therapy, and to the power of Goodwin and other "biological psychiatrists," who earn their status by "medicalizing" everything they see. "How is it that some spiritually passionate people become labeled schizophrenic and find themselves being treated as mental patients?" he asks in a 1991 book, "Toxic Psychiatry."

Breggin says he is struck by the parallels between the Violence Initiative and Nazi Germany: "the medicalization of social issues, the declaration that the victim of oppression, in this case the Jew, is in fact a genetically and biologically defective person, the mobilization of the state for eugenic purposes and biological purposes, the heavy use of psychiatry in the development of social-control programs." This is the sort of view that encouraged some members of the Congressional Black Caucus to demand that Goodwin be disciplined; it also helped get Breggin on Black Entertainment Television, and led to such headlines in black newspapers as "PLOT TO SEDATE BLACK YOUTH."

Breggin's scenario, the question of its truth aside, did have the rhetorical virtue of simple narrative form. ("He made a nice story of it," Goodwin says, in a tone not wholly devoid of admiration.) There has lately been much interest in, and much federally funded research into, the role that the neurotransmitter serotonin plays in violence. On average, people with low serotonin levels are more inclined toward impulsive violence than people with normal levels. Since Goodwin was a co-author of the first paper noting the correlation between serotonin and violence, he would seem to have a natural interest in this issue. And, since the "serotonin-reuptake inhibitors," such as Eli Lilly's Prozac, raise serotonin levels, there would seem to exist a large financial incentive to identify low serotonin as the source of urban ills. Hence, from Breggin's vantage point it all fell into place—a confluence of corporate and personal interests that helped make serotonin the most talked-about biochemical in federal violence research. But, Breggin says, we musn't lose sight of its larger significance: serotonin is "just a code word for biological approaches."

It was in the late seventies that Goodwin and several colleagues stumbled on the connection between serotonin and violence, while studying servicemen who were being observed for possible psychiatric discharge. Since then, low serotonin has been found in other violent populations, such as children who torture animals, children who are unusually hostile toward their mothers, and people who score high for aggression on standardized tests. Lowering people's serotonin levels in a laboratory setting made them more inclined to give a person electrical shocks (or, at least, what experimenters deceived them into thinking were electrical shocks).

It isn't clear whether serotonin influences aggression per se or simply impulse control, since low serotonin correlates also with impulsive arson and with attempted suicide. But serotonin level does seem to be a rough predictor of misbehavior—a biological marker. In a study of twenty-nine children with "disruptive behavior disorders," serotonin level helped predict future aggression. And in a National Institutes of Health study of fifty-eight violent offenders and impulsive arsonists serotonin level, together with another biochemical index, predicted with eighty-four-per-cent accuracy whether they would commit crimes after leaving prison.

It doesn't take an overactive imagination to envision parole boards screening prisoners for biological markers before deciding their fate—just as Goodwin had suggested that using biological markers might help determine which children need antiviolence therapy. These are the kinds of scenarios that make Breggin worry about a world in which the government labels some people genetically deficient and treats them accordingly. In reply, Goodwin stresses that a "biological" marker needn't be a "genetic" one. Though N.I.H. studies suggest that some people's genes are conducive to low serotonin, environmental influences can also lower serotonin, and federal researchers are studying these. Thus a "biological" marker may be an "environmental" marker, not a "genetic" one. To this Breggin replies, "It's not what they believe, it's not in a million years what they really believe." This attempt to cast biological research as research into environment "shows their desperation, because this was never their argument until they got attacked," he says. "It's a political move."

In truth, federal researchers, including Goodwin, were looking into "environmental influences" on biochemistry well before being attacked by Breggin. Still, they do often employ a narrower notion of the term's meaning than Breggin would like. When Goodwin talks about such influences, he doesn't dwell on the sort of social forces that interest Breggin, such as poverty and bad schools. He says, for example, that he has looked into "data on head injuries, victims of abuse, poor prenatal nutrition, higher levels of lead," and so on.

In other words, he is inclined to view violence as an illness, whether it is the product of aberrant genes or of pathological—deeply unnatural—circumstances, or both. This is not surprising, given his line of work: he is a psychiatrist, a doctor; his job is to cure people, and people without pathologies don't need curing. "Once I learned that seventy-nine per cent of repeated violent offenses were by seven per cent of youth, it began to look to me like a clinical population, a population that had something wrong with it that resulted in this behavior," he says. Other federal researchers on violence tend to take the same approach. After all, most of them work at one of the National Institutes of Health, whether the National Institute of Mental Health, the National Institute on Alcohol Abuse and Alcoholism, or some other affiliate. For the Violence Initiative to be successful in the pragmatic aims that Goodwin acknowledges—as a way "to argue for budgets" for the Department of Health and Human Services—it pretty much had to define violence as a pathology, characteristic of inner-city kids who have something "wrong" with them.

Breggin would rather depict violence as the not very surprising reaction of normal people to oppressive circumstances. A big problem with biological views of behavior generally, he says, is that they so often bolster the medical notions of "deviance" and "pathology"—and thus divert attention from the need to change social conditions.

But "biological" views don't have to be "medical" views. This is where the field of evolutionary psychology enters the picture, and modern Darwinian thought begins to diverge from Goodwin's sketchier and more dated ideas about human evolution. Evolutionary psychologists share Goodwin's conviction that genes, neurotransmitters such as serotonin, and biology more generally are a valid route to explaining human behavior; and they share his belief in the relevance of studying nonhuman primates. Yet they are much more open than he is to the Bregginesque view that inner-city violence is a "natural" reaction to a particular social environment.

To most N.I.H. researchers, evolutionary psychology is terra incognita. Goodwin, for one, professes only vague awareness of the field. But the field offers something that should intrigue him: a theory about what serotonin is, in the deepest sense—why natural selection designed it to do the things it does. This theory would explain, for example, the effect that Prozac has on people. More to the point, this theory would explain the link that Goodwin himself discovered between low serotonin and violence.

The two acknowledged experts on human violence within evolutionary psychology are Martin Daly and Margo Wilson, of McMaster University, in Ontario. Their 1988 book, "Homicide," barely known outside Darwinian-social-science circles, is considered a classic within them. Listening to Margo Wilson talk about urban crime is like entering a time warp and finding yourself chatting with Huey Newton or Jane Fonda in 1969. "First of all, what's a crime?" she asks. It all depends on "who are the rule-makers, who's in power. We call it theft when somebody comes into your house and steals something, but we don't call it theft when we get ripped off by political agendas or big-business practices." And as for gang violence: "It's a coalition of males who are mutually supporting each other to serve their interests against some other coalition. How is that different from some international war?"

To hear this sort of flaming liberal rhetoric from a confirmed Darwinian 20
should surprise not just Peter Breggin but anyone familiar with intellectual history. For much of this century, many people who took a Darwinian view of human behavior embraced the notorious ideology of social Darwinism. They emphatically did not view social deviance as some arbitrary and self-serving designation made by the ruling class; more likely, crime was a sign of "unfitness," of an innate inability to thrive legitimately. The "unfit" were best left to languish in jail, where they could not reproduce. And "unfit" would-be immigrants—those from, say, Eastern Europe, who were congenitally ill equipped to enrich American society—were best kept out of the country.

What permits Margo Wilson to sound a quite different theme is two distinguishing features of evolutionary psychology. First, evolutionary psychologists are not much interested in genetic differences, whether among individuals or among groups. The object of study is, rather, "species-typical mental adaptations"—also known as "human nature." A basic tenet of evolutionary psychologists is that there *is* such a thing as human nature—that people everywhere have fundamentally the same minds.

A second tenet of evolutionary psychologists is respect for the power of environment. The human mind, they say, has been designed to adjust to social circumstances. The vital difference between this and earlier forms of environmental determinism is the word "designed." Evolutionary psychologists believe that the developmental programs that convert social experience into personality were created by natural selection, which is to say that those programs lie in our genes. Thus, to think clearly about the influence of environment we must think about what sorts of influences would have been favored by natural selection.

If, for example, early social rejection makes people enduringly insecure, then we should ask whether this pattern of development might have had a genetic payoff during evolution. Maybe people who faced such rejection saw their chances of survival and reproduction plummet unless they became more socially vigilant—neurotically attentive to nourishing their social ties. Thus genes that responded to rejection by instilling this neurotic vigilance, this insecurity, would have flourished. And eventually those genes could have spread through the species, becoming part of human nature.

These two themes—universal human nature and the power of environment—are related. It is belief in the power of environment—of family milieu, cultural milieu, social happenstance—that allows evolutionary psychologists to see great variation in human behavior, from person to person or from group to group, without reflexively concluding that the explanation lies in genetic variation. The explanation lies in the genes, to be sure. Where else could a program for psychological development ultimately reside? But it doesn't necessarily lie in differences among different people's genes.

This is the perspective that Martin Daly and Margo Wilson bring to the 25
subject of violence. They think about genes in order to understand the role of environment. And one result of this outlook is agreement with Peter Breggin that inner-city violence shouldn't be labelled a "pathology." In a paper published [in 1994] Daly and Wilson wrote, "Violence is abhorrent. . . . Violence is so aversive that merely witnessing an instance can be literally sickening. . . ." There is thus "but a short leap to the metaphorical characterization of violence itself as a sort of 'sickness' or 'dysfunction.'" But, they insisted, this leap is ill advised. Violence is eminently functional—something that people are designed to do.

Especially men. From an evolutionary point of view, the leading cause of violence is maleness. "Men have evolved the morphological, physiological and psychological means to be effective users of violence," Daly and Wilson wrote. The reason, according to modern evolutionary thought, is simple. Because a female can reproduce only once a year, whereas a male can reproduce many times a year, females are the scarcer sexual resource. During evolution, males have competed over this resource, with the winners impregnating more than their share of women and the losers impregnating few or none. As always with natural selection, we're left with the genes of the winners—in this case, genes inclining males toward fierce combat. One reflection of this history is that men are larger and stronger than women. Such "sexual dimorphism" is seen in many species, and biologists consider it a rough index of the intensity of male sexual competition.

To say that during evolution men have fought over women isn't to say that they've always fought directly over women, with the winner of a bout walking over and claiming his nubile trophy. Rather, human beings are somewhat like our nearest relatives, the chimpanzees: males compete for status, and status brings access to females. Hence skills conducive to successful status competition would have a "selective advantage"—would be favored by natural selection. As Daly and Wilson have put it, "if status has persistently contributed to reproductive success, and a capacity for controlled violence has regularly contributed to status, then the selective advantage of violent skills cannot be gainsaid."

It's easy to find anecdotal evidence that status has indeed tended to boost the reproductive success of males. (It was Henry Kissinger who said that power is an aphrodisiac, and Representative Pat Schroeder who observed that a middle-aged congresswoman doesn't exert the same animal magnetism on the opposite sex that a middle-aged congressman does.) But more telling is evidence drawn from hunter-gatherer societies, the closest thing to real-life examples of the pre-agrarian social context for which the human mind was designed. Among the Ache of Paraguay, high-status men have more extramarital affairs and more illegitimate children than low-status men. Among the Aka Pygmies of central Africa, an informal leader known as a *kombeti* gets more wives and offspring than the average Aka. And so on. The Aka, the Ache, and Henry Kissinger all demonstrate that violence against other men is hardly the only means by which male status is sought. Being a good hunter is a primary route to status among the Ache, and being a wily social manipulator helps in all societies (even, it turns out, in chimp societies, where males climb the status ladder by forging "political" coalitions). Still, in all human societies questions of relative male status are sometimes settled through fighting. This form of settlement is, of course, more prevalent in some arenas than others—more in a bikers' bar than in the Russian Tea Room, more in the inner city than on the Upper East Side. But, as Daly and Wilson note, one theme holds true everywhere: men compete for status through the means locally available. If men in the Russian Tea Room don't assault one another, that's because assault isn't the route to status in the Russian Tea Room.

According to Daly and Wilson, a failure to see the importance of such circumstances is what leads well-heeled people to express patronizing shock that "trivial" arguments in barrooms and ghettos escalate to murder. In "Homicide" they wrote, "An implicit contrast is drawn between the foolishness of violent men and the more rational motives that move sensible people like ourselves. The combatants are in effect denigrated as creatures of some lower order of mental functioning, evidently governed by immediate stimuli rather than by foresightful contemplation." In truth, Daly and Wilson say, such combatants are typical of our species, as it has been observed around the world: "In most social milieus, a man's reputation depends in part upon the maintenance of a credible threat of violence." This fact is "obscured in modern mass society because the state has assumed a monopoly on the legitimate use of force. But wherever that monopoly is relaxed—whether in an entire society or in a neglected underclass—then the utility of that credible threat becomes apparent." In such an environment, "a seemingly minor affront is not merely a 'stimulus' to action, isolated in time and space. It must be understood within a larger social context of reputations, face, relative social status, and enduring relationships. Men are known by their fellows as . . . people whose word means action and people who are full of hot air."

That a basic purpose of violence is display—to convince peers that you 30
will defend your status—helps explain an otherwise puzzling fact. As Daly and Wilson note, when men kill men whom they know, there is usually an audience. This doesn't seem to make sense—why murder someone in the presence of witnesses?—except in terms of evolutionary psychology. Violence is in large part a performance.

Thus the dismay often inspired by reports that a black teen-ager killed because he had been "dissed" is naïve. Nothing was more vital to the reproductive success of our male ancestors than respect, so there is nothing that the male mind will more feverishly seek to neutralize than disrespect. All men spend much of their lives doing exactly this; most are just lucky enough to live in a place where guns won't help them do it. These days, well-educated men do their status maintenance the way Goodwin and Breggin do it, by verbally defending their honor and verbally assailing the honor of their enemies. But back when duelling was in vogue even the most polished of men might occasionally try to kill one another.

This view from evolutionary psychology in some ways jibes with a rarely quoted point that Goodwin made during his rambling remarks on monkeys: that inner-city violence may be caused by a "loss of structure in society"; in an environment where violence is deemed legitimate, the male inclination for violence may reassert itself. Of monkeys, Goodwin had said, "that is the natural way of it for males, to knock each other off," and the implicit comparison was supposed to be with all human males, not just black ones; his point was that many black males now live in neighborhoods where social restraints have dissolved. This is the sense in which Goodwin says he meant to compare the inner cities to jungles, and the transcript of his remarks bears him out. His poor choice of imagery still haunts him. "If I had said that in the Wild West, where there was no structure, there was a hell of a lot of violence, no one would have noticed."

There is a crucial difference between this emphasis on social milieu as rendered by Goodwin and as rendered by evolutionary psychologists; namely, they don't abandon it when they start thinking about the interface between biology and environment. Whereas pondering this interface steers Goodwin's thoughts toward "pathology"—the biological effects of malnutrition, or brain damage due to child abuse—evolutionary psychologists try to figure out how normal, everyday experience affects the biochemistry of violence.

Consider serotonin. In particular, consider an extensive study of serotonin in monkeys done by Michael McGuire, an evolutionary psychologist, and his colleagues at U.C.L.A. Vervet monkeys have a clear male social hierarchy: low-status males defer to high-status males over access to limited resources, including females. McGuire found that the highest-ranking monkeys in the male social hierarchy have the highest serotonin levels. What's more, the lower-ranking males tend to be more impulsively violent. Other studies have linked low serotonin to violence in monkeys even more directly.

At first glance, such findings might appear to be what Peter Breggin, and many liberals, would consider their worst nightmare. If this biochemical analogy between monkeys and human beings is indeed valid, the lesson would seem to be this: some individuals are born to be society's leaders, some are born to be its hoodlums; the chairman of I.B.M. was born with high serotonin, the urban gang member was born with low serotonin. And what if it turns out that blacks on average have less serotonin than whites do?

There certainly is evidence that some sort of analogy between the social lives of monkeys and human beings is in order. McGuire has found that officers of college fraternities have higher serotonin levels than the average frat-house resident, and that college athletes perceived as team leaders have higher levels than their average teammate. But grasping the import of the analogy requires delving into the details of McGuire's monkey research.

When McGuire examines a dominant male monkey before he becomes a dominant—before he climbs the social hierarchy by winning some key fights with other males—serotonin level is often unexceptional. It rises during his ascent, apparently in response to sometimes inconspicuous social cues. Indeed, his serotonin may begin to creep upward before he physically challenges any higher-ranking males; the initial rise may be caused by favorable attention from females (who play a larger role in shaping the male social hierarchy than was once appreciated). When, on the other hand, a dominant male suffers a loss of status, his serotonin level drops.

What's going on here? There is no way to look inside a monkey's mind and see how serotonin makes him feel. But there is evidence that in human beings high serotonin levels bring high self-esteem. Raising self-esteem is one effect of Prozac and other serotonin boosters, such as Zoloft. And, indeed, high-ranking monkeys—or, to take a species more closely related to us, high-ranking chimpanzees—tend to behave the way people with high self-esteem behave: with calm self-assurance; assertively, yes, but seldom violently. (This subtle distinction, as Peter Kramer notes in "Listening to Prozac," is also seen in human beings. Prozac may make them more socially assertive, but less irritable, less prone to spontaneous outbursts.) To be sure, an alpha-male chimp may periodically exhibit aggression—or, really, a kind of ritual mock-aggression—to remind everyone that he's the boss, but most alphas tend not to be as fidgety and perturbable as some lower-ranking apes, except when leadership is being contested.

All this suggests a hypothesis. Maybe one function of serotonin—in human and nonhuman primates—is to regulate self-esteem in accordance with social feedback; and maybe one function of self-esteem is, in turn, to help primates negotiate social hierarchies, climbing as high on the ladder as circumstance permits. Self-esteem (read serotonin) keeps rising as long as one encounters social success, and each step in this elevation inclines one to raise one's social sights a little higher. Variable self-esteem, then, is evolution's way of preparing us to reach and maintain whatever level of social status is realistic, given our various attributes (social skills, talent, etc.) and our milieu. High serotonin, in this view, isn't nature's way of destining people from birth for high status; it is nature's way of equipping any of us for high status should we find ourselves possessing it. The flip side of this hypothesis is that low self-esteem (and low serotonin) is evolution's way of equipping us for low status should our situation not be conducive to elevation.

40 This *doesn't* mean what an earlier generation of evolutionists would have thought: that Mother Nature wants people with low status to endure their fate patiently for "the greater good." Just the opposite. A founding insight of evolutionary psychology is that natural selection rarely designs things for the "good of the group." Any psychological inclinations that offer a way to cope with low status provide just that—a way to cope, a way to make the best of a bad situation. The purpose of low self-esteem isn't to bring submission for the sake of social order; more likely, its purpose is to discourage people from conspicuously challenging higher-status people who are, by virtue of their status, in a position to punish such insolence.

And what about the antisocial tendencies, the impulsive behavior linked with low serotonin in both human beings and monkeys? How does evolutionary psychology explain them? This is where the demise of "good of the group" logic opens the way for especially intriguing theories. In particular: primates may be designed to respond to low status by "breaking the rules" when they can get away with it. The established social order isn't working in their favor, so they circumvent its strictures at every opportunity. Similarly, inner-city thugs may be functioning as "designed": their minds absorb environmental input reflecting their low socioeconomic standing and the absence of "legitimate" routes to social elevation, and incline their behavior in the appropriately criminal direction.

The trouble with breaking rules, of course, is the risk of getting caught and punished. But, as Daly and Wilson note by quoting Bob Dylan, "When you ain't got nothin', you got nothin' to lose." In the environment of our evolution, low status often signified that a male had had little or no reproductive success to date; for such a male, taking risks to raise status could make sense in Darwinian terms. In hunter-gatherer societies, Daly and Wilson write, "competition can sometimes be fiercest near the bottom of the scale, where the man on track for total [reproductive] failure has nothing to lose by the most dangerous competitive tactics, and may therefore throw caution to the winds." Even as low self-esteem keeps him from challenging dominant males, he may behave recklessly toward those closer to him on the social ladder. Thus may the biochemistry of low status, along with the attendant states of mind, encourage impulsive risk-taking.

This theory, at any rate, would help make sense of some long-unexplained data. Psychologists found several decades ago that artificially lowering people's self-esteem—by giving them false reports about scores on a personality test—makes them more likely to cheat in a subsequent game of cards. Such risky rule-breaking is just the sort of behavior that makes more sense for a low-status animal than for a high-status animal.

To say that serotonin level is heavily influenced by social experience isn't to say that a person's genetic idiosyncrasies aren't significant. But it is to say that they are at best half the story. There are not yet any definitive studies on the "heritability" of serotonin level—the amount of the variation among people that is explained by genetic difference. But the one study that has been done suggests that less than half the variation in the population studied came from genetic differences, and the rest from differences in environment. And even this estimate of heritability is probably misleadingly high. Presumably, self-esteem correlates with many other personal attributes, such as physique or facial attractiveness. Impressive people, after all, inspire the sort of feedback that raises self-esteem and serotonin. Since these attributes are themselves quite heritable—traceable largely to a person's distinctive genes—some of the "heritability" estimate for serotonin may reflect genes not for high serotonin per se but for good looks, great body, and so on. (The technical term for this oblique genetic effect is "reactive heritability.")

At least some of the variation in serotonin level is grounded more directly in genetic difference. N.I.H. researchers have identified a human gene that helps convert tryptophan, an amino acid found in some grains and fruits, into serotonin, and they have found a version of the gene that yields low serotonin levels. Still, there is no reason to believe that different ethnic groups have different genetic endowments for serotonin. Indeed, even if it turned out that American blacks on average had lower serotonin than whites, there would be no cause to implicate genes. One would expect groups that find themselves shunted toward the bottom of the socioeconomic hierarchy to have low serotonin. That may be nature's way of preparing them to take risks and to evade the rules of the powers that be.

This Darwinian theory integrating serotonin, status, and impulsive violence remains meagrely tested and is no doubt oversimplified. One complicating factor is modern life. People in contemporary America are part of various social hierarchies. An inner-city gang leader may get great, serotonin-boosting respect ("juice," as the suggestive street slang calls it) from fellow gang members while also getting serotonin-sapping signs of disrespect when he walks into a tony jewelry store, or even when he turns on the TV and sees that wealthy, high-status males tend to bear no physical or cultural resemblance to him. The human mind was designed for a less ambiguous setting—a hunter-gatherer society, in which a young man's social reference points stay fairly constant from day to day. We don't yet know how the mind responds to a world of wildly clashing status cues.

Another hidden complexity in this Darwinian theory lies in the fact that serotonin does lots of things besides mediate self-esteem and impulsive aggression. Precisely what it does depends on the part of the brain it is affecting and the levels of other neurotransmitters. Overall serotonin level is hardly the subtlest imaginable chemical index of a human being's mental state. Still, though we don't yet fathom the entire biochemistry of things like self-esteem, impulsiveness, and violence, there is little doubt among evolutionary psychologists that the subject is fathomable—and that it will get fathomed much faster if biomedical researchers, at N.I.H. and elsewhere, start thinking in Darwinian terms.

If evolutionary psychologists are right in even the broad contours of their outlook, then there is good news and bad news for both Frederick Goodwin and Peter Breggin. For Goodwin, the good news is that his infamous remarks were essentially on target: he was right to compare violent inner-city males—or any other violent human males—to nonhuman primates (though he exaggerated the incidence of actual murder among such primates). The bad news is that his Violence Initiative, in failing to pursue that insight, in clinging to the view of violence as pathology, was doomed to miss a large part of the picture; the bulk of inner-city violence will probably never be explained by reference to head injuries, poor nutrition, prenatal exposure to drugs, and bad genes. If violence is a public-health problem, it is so mainly in the sense that getting killed is bad for your health.

Evolutionary psychology depicts all kinds of things often thought to be "pathological" as "natural": unyielding hatred, mild depression, a tendency of men to treat women as their personal property. Some Darwinians even think that rape may in some sense be a "natural" response to certain circumstances. Of course, to call these things "natural" isn't to call them beyond self-control, or beyond the influence of punishment. And it certainly isn't to call them good. If anything, evolutionary psychology might be invoked on behalf of the doctrine of Original Sin: we are in some respects born bad, and redemption entails struggle against our nature.

Many people, including many social scientists and biomedical researchers, 50
seem to have trouble with the idea of a conflict between nature and morality. "I think this is a source of resistance to evolutionary ways of thinking," says John Tooby, a professor at the University of California at Santa Barbara, who along with his wife, Leda Cosmides, laid down some of the founding doctrines of evolutionary psychology. "There's a strong tendency to want to return to the romantic notion that the natural is the good." Indeed, "one modern basis for establishing morals is to try to ground them in the notion of sickness. Anything people don't like, they accuse the person doing it of being sick."

Thomas Szasz couldn't have said it better. Herein lies evolutionary psychology's good news for Peter Breggin: yes, it is indeed misleading to call most violence a pathology, a disorder. The bad news for Breggin is that, even though the causes of violence are broadly environmental, as he insists, they are nonetheless biological, because environmental forces are mediated biologically—in this case by, among other things, serotonin. Thus, a scientist can be a "biological determinist" or a "biological reductionist" without being a genetic determinist. He or she can say—as Daly and Wilson and Tooby and Cosmides do—that human behavior is driven by biological forces impinging on the brain, yet can view those forces largely as a reflection of a person's distinctive environment.

This confronts Breggin with a major rhetorical complication. Much of his success in arousing opposition to the Violence Initiative lay in conveniently conflating the terms "biological" and "genetic." He does this habitually. In suggesting that the initiative grew out of Goodwin's long-standing designs, Breggin says he has Baltimore *Evening Sun* articles from 1984 in which "Goodwin is talking about crime and violence being genetic and biological." In truth, these articles show Goodwin saying nothing about genes—only that violence has some biological correlates and might respond to pharmacological treatment. In Breggin's mind, "genetic" and "biological" are joined at the waist.

That these terms are not, in fact, inseparable—that something utterly biological, like serotonin level, may differ between two people because of environmental, not genetic, differences—poses a second problem for Breggin. The best way to illuminate the environmental forces he stresses may be to study the biological underpinnings of behavior, and that is a prospect he loathes. If serotonin is one chemical that converts poverty and disrespect into impulsiveness or aggression or low self-esteem, then it, along with other chemicals, may be a handy index of all these things—something whose level can be monitored more precisely than the things themselves. (Studies finding that blacks on average don't suffer from low self-esteem are based on asking black people and white people how they feel about themselves—a dubious approach, since expressions of humility seem to be more highly valued in white suburban culture than in black urban culture.)

That Breggin may be wrong in the way he thinks about biology and behavior doesn't mean that the unsettling scenarios he envisions are far-fetched. The government may well try to use biochemical "markers" to select violently inclined kids for therapy, or to screen prisoners for parole. (Then again, if these chemicals aren't simple "genetic markers," but rather are summaries of the way genes and environment have together molded a person's state of mind, how are they different from a standard psychological evaluation, which summarizes the same thing?) There may also be attempts to treat violently inclined teen-agers with serotonin-boosting drugs, as Breggin fears. And, though some teen-agers might thus be helped into the mainstream economy, these drugs could also become a palliative, a way to keep the inner city tranquil without improving it. The brave new world of biochemical diagnosis and therapy is coming; and, for all the insight evolutionary psychology brings, it won't magically answer the difficult questions that will arise.

The point to bear in mind is simply that less eerie, more traditionally 55
liberal prescriptions for urban violence continue to make sense after we've looked at black teen-agers as animals—which, after all, is what human beings are. The view from evolutionary psychology suggests that one way to reduce black violence would be to make the inner cities places where young men have nonviolent routes to social status and the means and motivation to follow them. Better-paying jobs, and better public schools, for example, wouldn't hurt. Oddly enough, thinking about genes from a Darwinian standpoint suggests that inner-city teen-agers are victims of their environment.

Understanding

1. Examine how Wright intercuts the positions of Breggin and Goodwin to highlight their differences. Indicate those points in this essay where he contrasts their points of view on the origins of violence and then summarize their positions.
2. The terms *biological* and *genetic* are distinguished throughout this essay. Those who use them interchangeably are said to "conflate" or merge or fuse them. Explain concisely and in your own words the distinction between *genetic* and *biological.* Use examples to show the difference. Why does "the American liberal mind," as the author states in paragraph 4, "fear" these words?
3. According to the results of the existing biochemical research described in this essay, how does serotonin correlate to violence? Based on this research, what influences its levels in the body? Genes? Biology? The environment? Support your response with examples.

Responding

1. Wright examines three possible explanations for the cause(s) of violence in society. Based on your reading of this selection, is antisocial behavior, such as inner-city violence, a natural reaction to social conditions as evolutionary psychologists might propose? Is it a biological condition? Or is it a genetic program "hardwired" in our brain?

2. According to evolutionary psychologists, the basic purpose of violence—an adaption to the environment at one time in human history—is display, mounted to convince peers that you will defend your status. Do you agree or disagree with this proposal? Explain.
3. Wright suggests that the best ways to counter the biological causes of urban crime are to create better schools and higher-paying jobs so that "young men have nonviolent routes to social status." How effective do you think this suggestion is? What measures would you propose?
4. Should drugs—"psychopharmacological therapies"—be used to curb violent behavior in a young child? Should they be used to control a whole class of disruptive students? How about an entire school of unruly and violent children? Whose responsibility is it to handle such behavior? The children's parents? Society? The government? At what point would you start or stop administering the drug? Explain your position including your view on the place of medical approaches (e.g., drugs) in controlling social behavior.
5. What ideas in this reading are controversial? Explain.

Connecting

1. How does this selection illuminate the violent behaviors described by writers in part one, specifically Carcaterra's "Loving Your Enemy," Fisher's "The Broken Chain," and Spiegelman's "Worse Than My Darkest Dreams"—all from chapter two—or any of your own wound stories? Does any of the violent behavior that appears in your reading or writing suggest a genetic or biological origin? If yes, explain. If not, how would you explain it?
2. How much does violent behavior affect the community in which you live? Compare your answer to Csikszentmihalyi's statement from "The Veils of Maya and the World of the Genes" that "only the person who sees the entire planet as her world can recognize a toxic substance as poison no matter where it is dumped" (paragraph 10).

A Sociobiological Hunch about Educating Women

Loyal D. Rue

Loyal D. Rue has been professor of philosophy and religion at Luther College in Decorah, Iowa, for a quarter century. Aside from the disciplines in which he teaches, he is also an avid reader in sociobiology and environmental philosophy. The book he is currently working on, *Everybody's Story,* is the story of evolution in which he believes everyone has a stake. His earlier books include *Amythia: Crisis in the Natural History of Western Culture* and *By the Grace of Guile: The Role of Deception in Natural History and Human Affairs.* In "A Sociobiological Hunch about Educating Women," Rue discusses the reproductive strategies of males and females, claiming that women have the upper hand regarding the standards of reproductive behavior. In fact, he argues that it is women who control the type and quality of genes that are passed on to future generations.

My wife was one of the many bright and industrious young women of the 1960's who worked their way through college. Somewhere late in her sophomore year, her funds ran low and she inquired at the university about a small loan for books and supplies. She was told that her chances of getting a loan were slim, because university funds were scarce, too, and what resources remained for loans were being given almost exclusively to male students. The only women getting loans at the moment were seniors who were about to graduate. 1

She wasn't surprised—disappointed, but not surprised. The priorities were well known: male students first, regardless of academic status, and then if there was enough money left it would go to advanced female students. The university's loan policy was not unusual; it was just one more expression of an ancient value in the Western tradition: Education for males is practical but for females it is luxurious. It is the males, after all, who are destined to hold jobs that require learning; the females—well, a measure of common sense is sufficient for bringing up children.

While these attitudes have been soundly rejected in many quarters in more recent years, there is still enough evidence of their persistence to justify one more argument in favor of education for women. I want to argue that the education of women in a civilized society is a practical thing. In fact, I shall assert that a civilized society should take greater pains to educate its young women than to educate its young men.

The argument I am about to advance comes out of an interest I have had for some time now in the nascent field of sociobiology. The fundamental theoretical claim of sociobiology is that organisms may be expected to behave in ways that will maximize their reproductive success (fitness). Millions of years of evolution have produced a stunning variety of mechanisms employed by life forms to assure that their own genes are replicated in future generations.

For animals, the method for gene replication is sexual reproduction. Each 5
surviving offspring carries genes from each parent into the future. Not all genes survive. Many are selected out of the game because they are carried in bodies that for one reason or another cannot or do not reproduce. Things go wrong on the way toward reproduction. Some bodies die as a result of illness, malnutrition, or predation. Where there is competition for mating partners, some will not win out. The genes in those bodies are not replicated.

On the other hand, genes that are replicated by successful reproducers will find expression in the physical and behavioral traits of future generations. Such traits are, almost by definition, successful or adaptive traits. It is tempting to think of adaptive traits as being called forth by the challenges of the environment. But it is more accurate to say that adaptive traits and the genes that control them are simply those that are left over after the editorial pen of nature has done its work.

Given sufficient time and variation in the environment, we would expect nature to produce many variations in both the physical and behavioral traits that survive. A short walk in the woods or a trip to the zoo provides plenty of evidence for this conclusion. There are fish, fowl, insects, reptiles, and mammals, and there are small, medium, and large varieties in each category. But some of the most interesting variations have to do with the behavioral traits that have survived, and some of the most interesting variations in behavioral traits have to do with reproductive strategy.

All animals are strategists in the reproductive game. Some have invested in the strategy of quantity, producing large numbers of offspring in the hope that enough of them will survive more or less on their own until they reach reproductive age. Others go for quality, producing only a small number of offspring and then investing their energies in nurturing their young toward maturity. Both strategies work reasonably well, given specific environmental challenges.

Even within a single species there are variations in reproductive strategy. The most fundamental is between the male and female. The male produces a large number of small reproductive cells; the female produces a small number of large reproductive cells. This difference between the sexes has been attended by characteristically different reproductive strategies on the parts of males and females, a difference that is more exaggerated in the higher vertebrates. Males tend toward the quantitative strategy while females tend toward the qualitative.

For most males, the act of sexual reproduction requires a limited invest- 10
ment of time. A quick encounter will do. As a consequence, the male's reproductive success will be enhanced by his directing his energies toward encountering as many females as possible. For females, the strategy is different. Since during gestation she is unavailable for further reproductive activity, her reproductive success is enhanced by more careful attention to the welfare of a few young.

Females, in other words, have fewer tries than males in the reproductive game and must discriminate more in mating. If you have an unlimited supply of arrows you might let them fly in great numbers and with abandon, for the chances are that some will hit the target. But if you have only a few arrows, you will take careful aim with each. Evolution has created a biological double standard rewarding promiscuity among males and discrimination among females. The males who are most successful in getting their genes replicated are the ones who have fired the most arrows; the most successful females are the ones who have fired theirs most carefully.

The result of all this is that in the business of reproduction the males compete and the females select. Therefore we cannot escape the conclusion that the "standards" of natural selection are set by the females. In most species the males have been naturally selected for the traits—size, speed, strength, color—that have been most beneficial in competing with other males for access to females. The females have been selected for having the most discriminating eye for mating with the most competitive males.

In civilized societies, of course, the rules have changed. While polygyny still exists in some cultures, it is evident that monogamous mating patterns are the general rule. Also, in civilized societies there are few reproductive premiums on traits that would be advantageous in the wild. But no matter how severely civilization has imposed limitations on the reproductive strategies of contemporary human beings, the vestiges of the past are still at work.

There may be new rules to limit the philanderings of males, but the genetic programming for it is still there—the male is still programmed to compete with other males for the favors of females. And the female is still programmed to respond to the male who, by her standards, offers her genes the best chance for reproductive success. Civilization hasn't changed the fact that males compete and females select. The standards of reproductive behavior are still governed by the females.

This is the feature that has implications for education in a civilized society. 15
The whole idea is that any modification in the selective standards of females will result in a modification in the behavior of males. Male behavior is keyed on the female's criteria for responding to it; her standards of choice become his standards of achievement.

I have heard it argued that while sociobiological principles may be useful in describing life in the wild, they have little relevance to life in a civilized environment. To the contrary, it is precisely because we are civilized that the principles are useful. The values of a civilized society ensure that every male and female will have the opportunity to succeed in the reproductive game. This means that almost any standard of mate selection can pay off. Females may respond to males because they are good at street-fighting or because they drive fast cars or because they treat females abusively. On the other hand, they may respond to males who are sensitive and attentive and able to make music and refined conversation.

Reproductive success in a civilized society is consistent with any of these values; in the long haul, however, the interests of a civilized society will be best served by cultivating other values such as reasoned cooperation, tolerance, and respect for the integrity of others.

The way to enforce such values is to inculcate them in females so that they will be applied in their selection of a mate. If there are no females showing signs of being impressed by fast cars and abusive behavior, then there will be fewer fast cars and less abusive behavior. If all females show disgust at the behavior of "macho" males, then macho behavior will disappear. By educating women, society creates a powerful incentive for the education of men.

I am aware of the accusations of sexism that have been directed at sociobiology by feminists. But there is a new feminism on the horizon, one that takes account of the important and undeniable differences between the sexes and works within their boundaries to bring an end to discrimination. It is clear that the principles of sociobiology may be used to justify the double standard of sexual behavior that is nearly universal in human culture. I am opposed to this double standard for all sorts of reasons, as most sociobiologists are. It isn't even biologically significant under civilized conditions, but the genetic predispositions for behavioral asymmetry still exist. All I am arguing, really, is that the practice of educating women gives us the means for turning the ancient programming of sexual behavior against itself.

Understanding

1. Whether or not you agree with its premise, "A Sociobiological Hunch about Educating Women" is nevertheless a "perfect" deductive essay: Its introduction uses an appeal, or "hook," to establish a common ground with the reader—statements or anecdotes about what the reader might already know and relate to, or be able to find believable. It then moves, at the end of the introduction, to a well-stated thesis—a full sentence which is an opinion, not a fact. This thesis, or "contract" with the reader, is a claim that Rue must prove to the best of his ability by the end of the essay. Sentence by sentence, paragraph by paragraph, Rue must build his support for that thesis. Otherwise the contract is useless—null and void; the reader feels cheated. Identify Rue's thesis. Does he argue it well? (Answer this question objectively, regardless of whether you agree with his ideas.)
2. What behavior traits among living species does Rue find the most interesting?
3. Rue makes explicit the point that he is talking about behavior in a "civilized" society. What has civilization not been able to change?
4. Rue's argument seems to encourage a *decision* on the part of males and females to change their genetically predispositioned reproductive behaviors in order to serve the interests of a civilized society. What are the interests of a civilized society? What can we infer are Rue's values and interests?
5. In Rue's argument, how does educating women create a powerful incentive for educating men?

Responding

1. Do you agree with the statement in paragraph 14 that "the standards of reproductive behavior are . . . governed by the females"? Record experiences that would support your position.

2. Has "A Sociobiological Hunch about Educating Women" changed your opinion of things to consider when looking for a mate? That is, did Rue prove his thesis?

Connecting

1. Explain, according to Rue, the quantitative and qualitative reproductive strategies and purposes of male and female higher vertebrates. What are the purposes and results of these two separate strategies? Compare and contrast them with Csikszentmihalyi's notions on "reproductive fitness" in "The Veils of Maya and the World of the Genes."
2. What qualities do you look for in a mate? Do you consider the genes you want to provide your descendants and future generations, or are you thinking of the here and now? From your observations, do you think people in general calculate the genetic material in potential mates? If not, what is the main attraction? Compare your answer to the recommendation Turner makes in "Intelligence and the X Chromosome."
3. Does Wright's "The Biology of Twins" support or contradict what Rue advises young females?

Temperament Is Not Destiny

Daniel Goleman

For Daniel Goleman, intelligence and a high IQ (intelligence quotient)—the two are not the same—are not the keys to success and happiness. The fifty-year-old concept of IQ, he concludes, is far too narrow to explain the broad range of mental abilities. As he reports in *Emotional Intelligence,* from which this selection is drawn, when the Harvard classes of the 1940s were surveyed, it was determined that the most successful members of the class were not those with the highest IQs; rather, success favored those who could exercise self-restraint, be persistent, and empathize and relate with others. They had what Goleman calls "emotional intelligence." According to Goleman, all emotional activities—feelings—have an evolutionary origin and an adaptive context. They are, he says, learned reactions or adjustments that have been built into our brains to enhance our survival in the world. Though recent research on the human brain shows that infants have strong tendencies toward one sort of temperament, proper parenting and teaching can help any child learn the empathy and self-control necessary for a happy life.

In "Temperament Is Not Destiny," Goleman, who has a Ph.D. in psychology from Harvard and reports on science for the *New York Times,* explores how emotions originate in the brain and how they might be managed to achieve a truly integrated and satisfying life.

Temperament can be defined in terms of the moods that typify our emotional life. To some degree we each have such a favored emotional range; temperament is a given at birth, part of the genetic lottery that has compelling force in the unfolding of life. Every parent has seen this: from birth a child will be calm and placid or testy and difficult. The question is whether such a biologically determined emotional set can be changed by experience. Does our biology fix our emotional destiny, or can even an innately shy child grow into a more confident adult? 1

The clearest answer to this question comes from the work of Jerome Kagan, the eminent developmental psychologist at Harvard University.[1] Kagan posits that there are at least four temperamental types—timid, bold, upbeat, and melancholy—and that each is due to a different pattern of brain activity. There are likely innumerable differences in temperamental endowment, each based in innate differences in emotional circuitry; for any given emotion people can differ in how easily it triggers, how long it lasts, how intense it becomes. Kagan's work concentrates on one of these patterns: the dimension of temperament that runs from boldness to timidity.

For decades mothers have been bringing their infants and toddlers to Kagan's Laboratory for Child Development on the fourteenth floor of Harvard's William James Hall to take part in his studies of child development. It was there that Kagan and his coresearchers noticed early signs of shyness in a group of twenty-one-month-old toddlers brought for experimental observations. In free play with other toddlers, some were bubbly and spontaneous, playing with other babies without the least hesitation. Others, though, were uncertain and hesitant, hanging back, clinging to their mothers, quietly watching the others at play. Almost four years later, when these same children were in kindergarten, Kagan's group observed them again. Over the intervening years none of the outgoing children had become timid, while two thirds of the timid ones were still reticent.

Kagan finds that children who are overly sensitive and fearful grow into shy and timorous adults; from birth about 15 to 20 percent of children are "behaviorally inhibited," as he calls them. As infants, these children are timid about anything unfamiliar. This makes them finicky about eating new foods, reluctant to approach new animals or places, and shy around strangers. It also renders them sensitive in other ways—for example, prone to guilt and self-reproach. These are the children who become paralyzingly anxious in social situations: in class and on the playground, when meeting new people, whenever the social spotlight shines on them. As adults, they are prone to be wallflowers, and morbidly afraid of having to give a speech or perform in public.

Tom, one of the boys in Kagan's study, is typical of the shy type. At every 5
measurement through childhood—two, five, and seven years of age—Tom was among the most timid children. When interviewed at thirteen, Tom was tense and stiff, biting his lip and wringing his hands, his face impassive, breaking into a tight smile only when talking about his girlfriend; his answers were short, his manner subdued.[2] Throughout the middle years of childhood, until about age eleven, Tom remembers being painfully shy, breaking into a sweat whenever he had to approach playmates. He was also troubled by intense fears: of his house burning down, of diving into a swimming pool, of being alone in the dark. In frequent nightmares, he was attacked by monsters. Though he has felt less shy in the last two years or so, he still feels some anxiety around other children, and his worries now center on doing well at school, even though he is in the top 5 percent of his class. The son of a scientist, Tom finds a career in that field appealing, since its relative solitude fits his introverted inclinations.

By contrast, Ralph was one of the boldest and most outgoing children at every age. Always relaxed and talkative, at thirteen he sat back at ease in his chair, had no nervous mannerisms, and spoke in a confident, friendly tone, as though the interviewer were a peer—though the difference in their ages was twenty-five years. During childhood he had only two short-lived fears—one of dogs, after a big dog jumped on him at age three, and another of flying, when he heard about plane crashes at age seven. Sociable and popular, Ralph has never thought of himself as shy.

The timid children seem to come into life with a neural circuitry that makes them more reactive to even mild stress—from birth, their hearts beat faster than other infants' in response to strange or novel situations. At twenty-one months, when the reticent toddlers were holding back from playing, heart rate monitors showed that their hearts were racing with anxiety. That easily aroused anxiety seems to underlie their lifelong timidity: they treat any new person or situation as though it were a potential threat. Perhaps as a result, middle-aged women who remember having been especially shy in childhood, when compared with their more outgoing peers, tend to go through life with more fears, worries, and guilt, and to suffer more from stress-related problems such as migraine headaches, irritable bowel, and other stomach problems.[3]

THE NEUROCHEMISTRY OF TIMIDITY

The difference between cautious Tom and bold Ralph, Kagan believes, lies in the excitability of a neural circuit centered on the amygdala. Kagan proposes that people like Tom, who are prone to fearfulness, are born with a neurochemistry that makes this circuit easily aroused, and so they avoid the unfamiliar, shy away from uncertainty, and suffer anxiety. Those who, like Ralph, have a nervous system calibrated with a much higher threshold for amygdala arousal, are less easily frightened, more naturally outgoing, and eager to explore new places and meet new people.

An early clue to which pattern a child has inherited is how difficult and irritable she is as an infant, and how distressed she becomes when confronted with something or someone unfamiliar. While about one in five infants falls into the timid category, about two in five have the bold temperament—at least at birth.

10 Part of Kagan's evidence comes from observations of cats that are unusually timid. About one in seven housecats has a pattern of fearfulness akin to the timid children's: they draw away from novelty (instead of exhibiting a cat's legendary curiosity), they are reluctant to explore new territory, and they attack only the smallest rodents, being too timid to take on larger ones that their more courageous feline peers would pursue with gusto. Direct brain probes have found that portions of the amygdala are unusually excitable in these timid cats, especially when, for instance, they hear a threatening howl from another cat.

The cats' timidity blossoms at about one month of age, which is the point when their amygdala matures enough to take control of the brain circuitry to approach or avoid. One month in kitten brain maturation is akin to eight months in a human infant; it is at eight or nine months, Kagan notes, that "stranger" fear appears in babies—if the baby's mother leaves a room and there is a stranger present, the result is tears. Timid children, Kagan postulates, may have inherited chronically high levels of norepinephrine or other brain chemicals that activate the amygdala and so create a low threshold of excitability, making the amygdala more easily triggered.

One sign of this heightened sensitivity is that, for example, when young men and women who were quite shy in childhood are measured in a laboratory while exposed to stresses such as harsh smells, their heart rate stays elevated much longer than for their more outgoing peers—a sign that surging norepinephrine is keeping their amygdala excited and, through connected neural circuits, their sympathetic nervous system aroused.[4] Kagan finds that timid children have higher levels of reactivity across the range of sympathetic nervous system indices, from higher resting blood pressure and greater dilation of the pupils, to higher levels of norepinephrine markers in their urine.

Silence is another barometer of timidity. Whenever Kagan's team observed shy and bold children in a natural setting—in their kindergarten classes, with other children they did not know, or talking with an interviewer—the timid children talked less. One timid kindergartener would say nothing when other children spoke to her, and spent most of her day just watching the others play. Kagan speculates that a timid silence in the face of novelty or a perceived threat is a sign of the activity of a neural circuit running between the forebrain, the amygdala, and nearby limbic structures that control the ability to vocalize (these same circuits make us "choke up" under stress).

These sensitive children are at high risk for developing an anxiety disorder such as panic attacks, starting as early as sixth or seventh grade. In one study of 754 boys and girls in those grades, 44 were found to have already suffered at least one episode of panic, or to have had several preliminary symptoms. These anxiety episodes were usually triggered by the ordinary alarms of early adolescence, such as a first date or a big exam—alarms that most children handle without developing more serious problems. But teenagers who were timid by temperament and who had been unusually frightened by new situations got panic symptoms such as heart palpitations, shortness of breath, or a choking feeling, along with the feeling that something horrible was going to happen to them, like going crazy or dying. The researchers believe that while the episodes were not significant enough to rate the psychiatric diagnosis "panic disorder," they signal that these teenagers would be at greater risk for developing the disorder as the years went on; many adults who suffer panic attacks say the attacks began during their teen years.[5]

The onset of the anxiety attacks was closely tied to puberty. Girls with few 15
signs of puberty reported no such attacks, but of those who had gone through puberty about 8 percent said they had experienced panic. Once they have had such an attack, they are prone to developing the dread of a recurrence that leads people with panic disorder to shrink from life.

NOTHING BOTHERS ME: THE CHEERFUL TEMPERAMENT

In the 1920s, as a young woman, my aunt June left her home in Kansas City and ventured on her own to Shanghai—a dangerous journey for a solitary woman in those years. There June met and married a British detective in the colonial police force of that international center of commerce and intrigue. When the Japanese captured Shanghai at the outset of World War II, my aunt and her husband were interned in the prison camp depicted in the book and movie *Empire of the Sun.* After surviving five horrific years in the prison camp, she and her husband had, literally, lost everything. Penniless, they were repatriated to British Columbia.

I remember as a child first meeting June, an ebullient elderly woman whose life had followed a remarkable course. In her later years she suffered a stroke that left her partly paralyzed; after a slow and arduous recovery she was able to walk again, but with a limp. In those years I remember going for an outing with June, then in her seventies. Somehow she wandered off, and after several minutes I heard a feeble yell—June crying for help. She had fallen and could not get up on her own. I rushed to help her up, and as I did so, instead of complaining or lamenting she laughed at her predicament. Her only comment was a lighthearted "Well, at least I can walk again."

By nature, some people's emotions seem, like my aunt's, to gravitate toward the positive pole; these people are naturally upbeat and easygoing, while others are dour and melancholy. This dimension of temperament—ebullience at one end, melancholy at the other—seems linked to the relative activity of the right and left prefrontal areas, the upper poles of the emotional brain. That insight has emerged largely from the work of Richard Davidson, a University of Wisconsin psychologist. He discovered that people who have greater activity in the left frontal lobe, compared to the right, are by temperament cheerful; they typically take delight in people and in what life presents them with, bouncing back from setbacks as my aunt June did. But those with relatively greater activity on the right side are given to negativity and sour moods, and are easily fazed by life's difficulties; in a sense, they seem to suffer because they cannot turn off their worries and depressions.

In one of Davidson's experiments volunteers with the most pronounced activity in the left frontal areas were compared with the fifteen who showed most activity on the right. Those with marked right frontal activity showed a distinctive pattern of negativity on a personality test: they fit the caricature portrayed by Woody Allen's comedy roles, the alarmist who sees catastrophe in the smallest thing—prone to funks and moodiness, and suspicious of a world they saw as fraught with overwhelming difficulties and lurking dangers. By contrast to their melancholy counterparts, those with stronger left frontal activity saw the world very differently. Sociable and cheerful, they typically felt a sense of enjoyment, were frequently in good moods, had a strong sense of self-confidence, and felt rewardingly engaged in life. Their scores on psychological tests suggested a lower lifetime risk for depression and other emotional disorders.[6]

People who have a history of clinical depression, Davidson found, had 20
lower levels of brain activity in the left frontal lobe, and more on the right, than did people who had never been depressed. He found the same pattern in patients newly diagnosed with depression. Davidson speculates that people who overcome depression have learned to increase the level of activity in their left prefrontal lobe—a speculation awaiting experimental testing.

Though his research is on the 30 percent or so of people at the extremes, just about anyone can be classified by their brain wave patterns as tending toward one or the other type, says Davidson. The contrast in temperament between the morose and the cheerful shows up in many ways, large and small.

For example, in one experiment volunteers watched short film clips. Some were amusing—a gorilla taking a bath, a puppy at play. Others, like an instructional film for nurses featuring grisly details of surgery, were quite distressing. The right-hemisphere, somber folks found the happy movies only mildly amusing, but they felt extreme fear and disgust in reaction to the surgical blood and gore. The cheerful group had minimal reactions to the surgery; their strongest reactions were of delight when they saw the upbeat films.

Thus we seem by temperament primed to respond to life in either a negative or a positive emotional register. The tendency toward a melancholy or upbeat temperament—like that toward timidity or boldness—emerges within the first year of life, a fact that strongly suggests it too is genetically determined. Like most of the brain, the frontal lobes are still maturing in the first few months of life, and so their activity cannot be reliably measured until the age of ten months or so. But in infants that young, Davidson found that the activity level of the frontal lobes predicted whether they would cry when their mothers left the room. The correlation was virtually 100 percent: of dozens of infants tested this way, every infant who cried had more brain activity on the right side, while those who did not had more activity on the left.

Still, even if this basic dimension of temperament is laid down from birth, or very nearly from birth, those of us who have the morose pattern are not necessarily doomed to go through life brooding and crotchety. The emotional lessons of childhood can have a profound impact on temperament, either amplifying or muting an innate predisposition. The great plasticity of the brain in childhood means that experiences during those years can have a lasting impact on the sculpting of neural pathways for the rest of life. Perhaps the best illustration of the kinds of experiences that can alter temperament for the better is in an observation that emerged from Kagan's research with timid children.

TAMING THE OVEREXCITABLE AMYGDALA

The encouraging news from Kagan's studies is that not all fearful infants grow up hanging back from life—temperament is not destiny. The overexcitable amygdala can be tamed, with the right experiences. What makes the difference are the emotional lessons and responses children learn as they grow. For the timid child, what matters at the outset is how they are treated by their parents, and so how they learn to handle their natural timidness. Those parents who engineer gradual emboldening experiences for their children offer them what may be a lifelong corrective to their fearfulness.

About one in three infants who come into the world with all the signs of 25
an overexcitable amygdala have lost their timidness by the time they reach kindergarten.[7] From observations of these once-fearful children at home, it is clear that parents, and especially mothers, play a major role in whether an innately timid child grows bolder with time or continues to shy away from novelty and become upset by challenge. Kagan's research team found that some of the mothers held to the philosophy that they should protect their

timid toddlers from whatever was upsetting; others felt that it was more important to help their timid child learn how to cope with these upsetting moments, and so adapt to life's small struggles. The protective belief seems to have abetted the fearfulness, probably by depriving the youngsters of opportunities for learning how to overcome their fears. The "learn to adapt" philosophy of childrearing seems to have helped fearful children become braver.

Observations in the homes when the babies were about six months old found that the protective mothers, trying to soothe their infants, picked them up and held them when they fretted or cried, and did so longer than those mothers who tried to help their infants learn to master these moments of upset. The ratio of times the infants were held when calm and when upset showed that the protective mothers held their infants much longer during the upsets than the calm periods.

Another difference emerged when the infants were around one year old: the protective mothers were more lenient and indirect in setting limits for their toddlers when they were doing something that might be harmful, such as mouthing an object they might swallow. The other mothers, by contrast, were emphatic, setting firm limits, giving direct commands, blocking the child's actions, insisting on obedience.

Why should firmness lead to a reduction in fearfulness? Kagan speculates that there is something learned when a baby has his steady crawl toward what seems to him an intriguing object (but to his mother a dangerous one) interrupted by her warning, "Get away from that!" The infant is suddenly forced to deal with a mild uncertainty. The repetition of this challenge hundreds and hundreds of times during the first year of life gives the infant continual rehearsals, in small doses, of meeting the unexpected in life. For fearful children that is precisely the encounter that has to be mastered, and manageable doses are just right for learning the lesson. When the encounter takes place with parents who, though loving, do not rush to pick up and soothe the toddler over every little upset, he gradually learns to manage such moments on his own. By age two, when these formerly fearful toddlers are brought back to Kagan's laboratory, they are far less likely to break out into tears when a stranger frowns at them, or an experimenter puts a blood-pressure cuff around their arm.

Kagan's conclusion: "It appears that mothers who protect their high[ly] reactive infants from frustration and anxiety in the hope of effecting a benevolent outcome seem to exacerbate the infant's uncertainty and produce the opposite effect."[8] In other words, the protective strategy backfires by depriving timid toddlers of the very opportunity to learn to calm themselves in the face of the unfamiliar, and so gain some small mastery of their fears. At the neurological level, presumably, this means their prefrontal circuits missed the chance to learn alternate responses to knee-jerk fear; instead, their tendency for unbridled fearfulness may have been strengthened simply through repetition.

In contrast, as Kagan told me, "Those children who had become less timid 30
by kindergarten seem to have had parents who put gentle pressure on them to be more outgoing. Although this temperamental trait seems slightly harder

than others to change—probably because of its physiological basis—no human quality is beyond change."

Throughout childhood some timid children grow bolder as experience continues to mold the key neural circuitry. One of the signs that a timid child will be more likely to overcome this natural inhibition is having a higher level of social competence: being cooperative and getting along with other children; being empathic, prone to giving and sharing, and considerate; and being able to develop close friendships. These traits marked a group of children first identified as having a timid temperament at age four, who shook it off by the time they were ten years old.[9]

By contrast, those timid four-year-olds whose temperament changed little over the same six years tended to be less able emotionally: crying and falling apart under stress more easily; being emotionally inappropriate; being fearful, sulky, or whiny; overreacting to minor frustration with anger; having trouble delaying gratification; being overly sensitive to criticism, or mistrustful. These emotional lapses are, of course, likely to mean their relationships with other children will be troubled, should they be able to overcome their initial reluctance to engage.

By contrast, it is easy to see why the more emotionally competent—though shy by temperament—children spontaneously outgrew their timidity. Being more socially skilled, they were far more likely to have a succession of positive experiences with other children. Even if they were tentative about, say, speaking to a new playmate, once the ice was broken they were able to shine socially. The regular repetition of such social success over many years would naturally tend to make the timid more sure of themselves.

These advances toward boldness are encouraging; they suggest that even innate emotional patterns can change to some degree. A child who comes into the world easily frightened can learn to be calmer, or even outgoing, in the face of the unfamiliar. Fearfulness—or any other temperament—may be part of the biological givens of our emotional lives, but we are not necessarily limited to a specific emotional menu by our inherited traits. There is a range of possibility even within genetic constraints. As behavioral geneticists observe, genes alone do not determine behavior; our environment, especially what we experience and learn as we grow, shapes how a temperamental predisposition expresses itself as life unfolds. Our emotional capacities are not a given; with the right learning, they can be improved. The reasons for this lie in how the human brain matures.

Notes

1. See, for example, Jerome Kagan et al., "Initial Reactions to Unfamiliarity," *Current Directions in Psychological Science* (Dec. 1992). The fullest description of the biology of temperament is in Kagan, *Galen's Prophecy.*
2. Tom and Ralph, archetypically timid and bold types, are described in Kagan, *Galen's Prophecy,* pp. 155–57.
3. Lifelong problems of the shy child: Iris Bell, "Increased Prevalence of Stress-related Symptoms in Middle-aged Women Who Report Childhood Shyness," *Annals of Behavior Medicine* 16 (1994).

4. The heightened heart rate: Iris R. Bell et al., "Failure of Heart Rate Habituation During Cognitive and Olfactory Laboratory Stressors in Young Adults With Childhood Shyness," *Annals of Behavior Medicine* 16 (1994).
5. Panic in teenagers: Chris Hayward et al., "Pubertal Stage and Panic Attack History in Sixth- and Seventh-grade Girls," *American Journal of Psychiatry* vol. 149(9) (Sept. 1992), pp. 1239–43; Jerold Rosenbaum et al., "Behavioral Inhibition in Childhood: A Risk Factor for Anxiety Disorders," *Harvard Review of Psychiatry* (May 1993).
6. The research on personality and hemispheric differences was done by Dr. Richard Davidson at the University of Wisconsin, and by Dr. Andrew Tomarken, a psychologist at Vanderbilt University: see Andrew Tomarken and Richard Davidson, "Frontal Brain Activation in Repressors and Nonrepressors," *Journal of Abnormal Psychology* 103 (1994).
7. The observations of how mothers can help timid infants become bolder were done with Doreen Arcus. Details are in Kagan, *Galen's Prophecy.*
8. Kagan, *Galen's Prophecy,* pp. 194–95.
9. Growing less shy: Jens Asendorpf, "The Malleability of Behavioral Inhibition: A Study of Individual Developmental Functions," *Developmental Psychology* 30, 6 (1994).

Understanding

1. What evidence does Goleman offer for the assertion that temperament is not destiny?
2. Although Harvard psychologist Jerome Kagan reports that his research uncovered four temperaments—bold, timid, upbeat, and melancholy—the idea of four temperaments is an ancient one. The Greek physician Hippocrates identified the four as choleric (irritable), melancholic (depressed), sanguine (optimistic), and phlegmatic (listless) and related them to the influence of bodily "humors," or fluids. What does Goleman indicate is the source of temperament?

Responding

1. How would you characterize your temperament? How much a part of your self is it? What childhood experiences do you think reinforced or altered it? Have you struggled with it? Are there other members in your family with the same temperament or a similar disposition? How did their childhood experiences compare or contrast with yours?
2. Goleman concludes in *Emotional Intelligence* that "There is an old-fashioned word for the body of skills that emotional intelligence represents, character." From your life experience and your reading so far, summarize how "character" is interpreted in American society today. For what endeavors in life does it have the most relevance? Who values it? How, in your estimation, can it be built?
3. If a high IQ is not a requirement for happiness, what is it good for?

Connecting

1. Compare Goleman's point of view on the source of temperament and the role of the brain to Csikszentmihalyi's in "The Veils of Maya and the World of the Genes."

2. How do childhood experiences influence a person's emotional reactions in later life? To support your view, provide one or two examples from your own life, from the gifts, wounds, decisions, and dreams stories in part one, or from other sources with which you are familiar.

Writing Option: Nature and Nurture

So which is more powerful—nature or nurture—in defining who we are? Write a short essay in which your answer to this long and hotly debated question is recorded, or where *you* raise a question regarding nature and nurture. You may frame your essay in any way to address this issue, but you will probably use at least one of the readings as source material. Document the source whether you challenge it or use it to support your views.

To get started, read over your responses to these readings to find one that you wrote quite a bit about at the time. Is the issue still interesting? For example, how did you feel about Crouch's view that xenophobia will melt away? What about using drugs to alter genetically carried traits? Can educating a male or a female to selectively choose a mate according to biological traits alter our collective gene pool or somehow make it "better"? (Better for what?) How much of us can be altered by recognizing and tapping into our emotional intelligence?

The best papers, and the most fulfilling to you, will be those in which you pose a question that you have a genuine interest in answering—and then answer it (the answer is your thesis), and argue using anything appropriate you have written or read earlier in *Signatures* to support your answer.

6

Community and Culture

In chapter 5, "Biology and Identity," the writers tackle a big subject: the world of genes—the units of heredity that determine our human nature. But in tracing the course of our biological evolution, these writers leave a fundamental question unanswered: How does a three-dimensional person emerge from a one-dimensional string of chemicals? With this humbling inquiry into our origins in the background, the writers in chapter 6, "Community and Culture," turn our attention to the more familiar social overlay of our biological selves: the influences of our community and culture.

Communities are the social networks that connect us to one another. If our genes unfold in the solitary prenatal environment of our mothers, it is in the community that we play out the rest of our lives. Families, neighborhoods, schools, churches, nations—these are the communities or institutions that try to satisfy our needs for safety and security, love and belonging, dignity and self-expression. We form attachments in communities, invest our feelings in them, develop our ideas through them, and, as the writers do in this section, create our standpoints—our own particular "take" on them.

Of singular importance in meeting these needs is the family, one of the largest of these institutions. The 1990 U.S. census reports that of the almost 95 million households in this country, 70 percent are families. Based on the inescapable bond of kinship, families are how societies have come to organize this physical fact of life. Consider the readings in the "Family Ties" section of this chapter as an exhibit of portraits of family life in the twentieth century. As the readings illustrate, families, whether rambunctious or serene, make indelible impressions on our young selves. Researchers try to measure their effectiveness as Maggie Scarf does in "The Beavers Scale of Family Health and Competence." Memoirists Phyllis Rose, Susan Cheever, Floyd Skloot, and Julia Alvarez describe their potent influences in fine detail.

Learning is typically thought of as an individual pursuit, but the readings in the "Learning Communities" section focus on its social context. Leslie Marmon Silko's "Through the Stories We Hear Who We Are" tells how the oral histories of the Pueblo people reaffirm her tribal identity; Mike Rose describes how his education was influenced by the sharing of one teacher. In Frank Conroy's "Think About It," we see that the sharing of ideas goes on in many places outside of school and well beyond what we think of as our "school years." Michel de Montaigne shares his passion for the exchange of ideas in "On the Art of Conversation"; and in "The Ascent to Wisdom," in his classic allegory of the cave, Plato counsels that education involves the responsibility of sharing what has been learned.

If families try to meet our needs for security and intimacy, and education is a means of socializing our knowledge, the readings in "Communities of Faith" show how religion tends to our spiritual striving. We are the only creatures who think in abstract terms and struggle to reach intangible goals. Perhaps for these reasons, we feel drawn to worship powers we believe to be greater than ourselves. Gordon Allport, in "A Solitary Quest," explains how we move to find our way in the world through religion; In "Choosing My Religion," Stephen J. Dubner shows how a community of believers is necessary to fulfill the need for spiritual rootedness; Shirley Park Lowry interprets religion as a provider of comfort in dealing with the unknown. Each of these writers teaches us how to see through and into what is hidden in the universe.

Whether we relate to others in households we call home (the family community), in cities we call our hometown (the local community), in countries we call our native land (the national community), or through "home pages" and chatrooms on the Internet (the cyber community), we seem to have an irrepressible need to connect with people. Evolutionary explanations aside, we do not "know" why this is true, only that it is so. As the social philosopher Martin Buber writes, "The essence of man . . . can be directly known only in a living relation." John Blaha, the American astronaut who spent four months in the Russian space station *Mir,* puts it more directly: "Isolation is tough."

Combating isolation and creating a sense of togetherness are functions of *culture,* which is usually defined as an organized way of life shared by a group of people and transmitted from generation to generation. Culture respects history, tradition, and the values they embody by trying to preserve them. Through culture, we encounter the time-honored ways of doing things: cooking, farming, making deals, composing music. Through culture, we learn how to play by the rules and, whether we like it or not, we learn our place. Culture, psychologist B. F. Skinner concluded, is "one gigantic exercise in self-control."

The section "In Public and Private" comprises readings that show how we deal with this need for control. As Richard Rodriguez explores in "The New, New World," we feel compelled to express our public and private selves in different ways. Luc Sante reveals in "Living in Tongues" that each of the languages he speaks exposes different facets of himself and that his "multiply rooted self" makes it impossible for him "to fence off a plot of the world and decide that everyone dwelling outside is 'other.'" In "Cyberhood vs. Neighborhood: Community," Howard Rheingold bridges his public and private selves through virtual relationships, whereas in "Storytellers and Scribes," Elias Canetti, as an unobtrusive public observer, tries to demystify the private transactions he observes in a Moroccan marketplace.

Although cultural norms and values are handed down by the generations that preceded us, communities allow us some degree of freedom to live according to our preferences. As adults we can choose where we want to live and with whom we want to associate; we can create new communities. To a large extent, the mosaic of communities defines a culture and imparts its character. To give the notions of community and culture an evolutionary spin, communities are the "nests" we build in our culture to ensure our survival in it.

With nesting comes territoriality and erection of boundaries. From earliest times, people the world over have thought of the earth as having a center. Each group has envisioned its own land as near to this place or its people as having come from it. The notion of "us versus them" may have originated from this ethnocentric world view. In the "Boundaries" section, Ina Russell, who edited her uncle "Jeb's" diaries from which "Love and Affection, Damn It!" is excerpted, collects his thoughts on living within the limits created by his sexual preference. Gloria Wade-Gayles, in "Brother Pain: How a Black Woman Came to Terms with Interracial Love," rues the boundary crossings of interracial couples; and in "To Live in the Borderlands Means You," Gloria Anzaldúa offers her view of what it means to be living *sin fronteras,* or "without borders," carrying five races of Mexican American heritage yet not being grounded in any one. In "Ageism in the Sisterhood," Barbara MacDonald confronts the attitudes she perceives in younger feminists. Boundaries may protect our nests, but they also limit our experience. In "The World of Culture," Mihaly Csikszentmihalyi cautions us to realize how "partial a view of reality even the most sophisticated culture affords."

There may be more-enduring influences on our identity, but none is more rich in imagery and fantasy than popular culture, the environments of everyday life that round out our cultural literacy. The themes of the four readings in "Popular Culture": how a sports legend defines an era in Michael Ventura's "Mickey Mantle's Summer"; how the aggressive synergy between teenage consumers and marketing mavens in Malcolm Gladwell's "The Coolhunt" brings us new products; how a talk-radio host functions as personal therapist to millions of listeners in Rebecca Johnson's "The Just-Do-It Shrink"; and how television and films shade the mood of a nation of viewers in Michiko Kakutani's "Bound by Suspicion" provide a glimpse into this influence. Each of these readings conveys the interplay between the pop culture artifacts and icons and who we think we are and who we want to be.

As you read the selections in this chapter, you will see that the interaction among individuals and community and culture is far from simple. In almost every reading, the writers calculate the costs as well as the benefits of being connected and disengaging. But these readings offer more than a literary arc between the writers and you—the reader—and you are much more than a member of their "audience": Allow these readings to stimulate you to think about your experiences in your communities and your cultures, to come to a richer awareness of your place and your significance in them; then write about them, perhaps for the first time, in ways that reflect this awareness.

1 Family Ties

Few institutions are more routinely scrutinized than the family. Researchers, writers, politicians—everyone discusses its values, its impact on individuals, its evolving shape and function, its ability to survive within the changing demands—both personal and public—of its individual members. Whether families are biologically produced—a random shuffle of our parents' genetic decks of cards—or contemplated choices made by individuals to compose a family by adoption or by claiming a family tie, these lifelong connections are the most powerful first lens through which we interpret the larger world.

According to sociologists, families provide crucial socialization experiences that inform the way we learn to live with others. Even though the ways in which these socialization experiences take place around the world, and even though all families are not successful in raising healthy individuals, families still exist to do the following four things: they provide close emotional ties for their individual members; they care for and socialize the young; they control sexual expression; and they provide for the continuation of the species.

Although parents may not necessarily be consciously aware of these driving forces as they carry out their familial interactions, a particular family life develops, as Maggie Scarf's selection will show, to establish *coherence* and *control* among its members through rules that attempt to provide security, stability, and predictability for its members' behavior. A further task is for its members to establish both a *capacity for intimacy* and a *personal autonomy,* which allows them to grow into separate individuals without losing their sense of belonging within the larger family group—even if they choose life paths radically different from what the shared family values have been accustomed to. Such accomplishments—and pitfalls—are explored in the family reminiscences of writers Phyllis Rose, Susan Cheever, Floyd Skloot, and Julia Alvarez. Exploring the varied family lives of others may enhance your understanding of your own.

The Beavers Scale of Family Health and Competence

Maggie Scarf

Although stories about families are interesting in their details and make for engrossing memoirs, some researchers have attempted to use objective methods to classify the ways in which families interact. Such is the case with "The Beavers Scale of Family Health and Competence," which guided Maggie Scarf's understanding of family functioning. Developed by psychiatrist W. Robert Beavers, the Beavers Scale shows how all family systems operate at differing but very clearly recognizable levels of health.

Maggie Scarf experienced the power of family members to influence one another's mental and physical health while researching and writing *Intimate Worlds: Life Inside the Family,* from which this selection is excerpted. Families, she found, present a dizzying array of dramas and dances which testify to their power.

Scarf, a senior fellow at the Bush Center in Child Development and Social Policy at Yale University, has written widely on relationships. Although she had dealt with difficult, emotionally charged subjects in her previous books on women and depression, *Unfinished Business: Pressure Points in the Lives of Women,* and on marital relationships in *Intimate Partners: Partners in Love and Marriage,* she admits that "nothing had quite prepared me for what happened when I began exploring the subject of the family. Here was every charged topic and every emotional dilemma that I could possibly have thought of and some I couldn't possibly have imagined."

As you read through the Beavers Scale, you may be unable to resist the temptation to cast your own family in one of the levels. Although this is not our intention in presenting the scale, you may find it useful in beginning to think analytically about family functioning. Because family worlds until quite recently have been intensely private ones, it may be illuminating to recognize yours among the constellation of families that operate in similar ways.

It is by now well recognized that the famous opening line of Leo Tolstoy's *Anna Karenina*—"All happy families resemble one another; every unhappy family is unhappy in its own way"—is a beautiful statement but a fallacious one. It is *unhappy* families who are more likely to resemble one another, for they tend to rigidify into certain recognizable, limited stances. The hallmark of the happy family is its variability, its ability to be flexible and to cherish its members' individuality, whereas unhappy families tend to become trapped in 1 fixed patterns of responding and in nonnegotiable positions—to get stuck, in other words.

It is of course obvious that radically different emotional climates, rules, roles, and patterns of being exist within different families; but in what *specific* ways do these families actually differ? In recent years, researchers have been attempting to codify and to examine rigorously what transpires within a relatively competent, harmonious, well-functioning family group, as contrasted with one whose members are distressed and disturbed.

Among the many family assessment instruments now available is the well-known Beavers Systems Model. This is a clinical scale that researchers use to classify families according to level of health and competence. All families are viewed as existing on a continuum that ranges from the most perturbed family system at one end to the least troubled system at the other.

The Beavers Systems Model (formerly the Beavers-Timberlawn Family Assessment Scale) is named after its principal originator, the psychiatrist W. Robert Beavers, who was for many years director of the Southwest Family Institute in Dallas. In over thirty years of work with this assessment/diagnostic instrument, Beavers and his colleagues have been subjecting their hypotheses about how families function to ongoing scientific testing; they use both individual family members' self-reports, and observational ratings of the family as a whole. Thus, their evolving theories have been buttressed by valid empirical findings—a rarity in the teeming family theory and therapy marketplace, where an astonishing variety of competing points of view, sects, gurus, charismatic leaders, and schools of serious thought abound.

In its simplest terms, the central, compelling theme that has emerged 5
from the Beavers research is that *different family systems operate at differing, but very clearly recognizable, levels of health and competence;* and any given family's current level of functioning can usually be described with a surprising degree of precision. Beavers has, moreover, taken a maverick approach within the field of family assessment, inasmuch as he and his co-workers have made healthy, competent families as important a focus of their attention as families that are distressed and perturbed.

The Beavers Systems Model is thus not primarily pathology-oriented (as many such family diagnostic instruments are). Rather than limit themselves to the study of what can go wrong—of processes that are destructive to the members of the system and to the system itself—these scientists have also looked carefully at healthy, competent families over an extended (five-year) period. A considerable part of this effort has, in other words, been geared toward understanding, in the most exact terms possible, what can go *right* within the family setting, and what specific sorts of family interactions tend to make it do so.

THE BEAVERS SYSTEMS MODEL: FIVE FAMILY DEVELOPMENTAL LEVELS

Briefly, the five major family developmental levels on the Beavers health and functioning graph are as follows. Families at Level 1, "optimal" families, are the most competent on the scale. Next to this topmost group are the Level 2 "adequate" families. Level 3 is called "midrange." This is the most densely populated cluster; in most studies, about 60 percent of families seem to fit into this "midrange" category. After the midrange is Level 4, the "borderline" family; and finally, at Level 5, the least well functioning end of the spectrum are families that are "severely disturbed."

Family systems operating at these five different planes of emotional development are, as will become quite evident, not only struggling with profoundly different kinds of dilemmas, but struggling to deal with these dilemmas in profoundly different kinds of ways.

Levels 1–5: An Overview

A brief overview of the different kinds of family worlds described in the 10
Beavers Systems Model follows. . . . I will begin with the chaotic systems at the bottom rung of the competence ladder, for the movement upward on the scale, from worse to better, clearly illuminates the basic nature of the developmental tasks that must be mastered along the way to a family's healing and improvement.

Level 5: The Family in Pain (Severely Disturbed) The *family in pain* is an emotional system in a state of confusion and turmoil. This kind of family world is comparable to a nation in a state of civil disorder; nobody seems to have authority; no one is able to enforce rules or effect needed changes; real leadership is totally lacking.

In this disjointed family realm, there are no durable, straightforward predictabilities, no clear-cut ways of behaving that one can be certain will lead to good outcomes. The operational rules of the system, to the extent that such rules exist, are in perpetual flux, always mystifying, always changing. And if one member of the group (say, the mother) attempts to articulate an idea, someone else inside the emotional system (father, grandparent, teenage child) will negate or dispute it in an almost automatic, reflexive fashion. To add to the general air of confusion, the mother may then acquiesce to the opposing idea, without acknowledging that it is at total variance with her own suggestion. Or, if never contradicted, she may simply backtrack and contradict herself.

This is an amorphous world, a world without any reliable or even discernible hierarchy or governance. *No* member of the system is capable of achieving clarity, of taking a personal stand and maintaining it long enough to ensure that new and better things can happen. A sense of murky uncertainty pervades the entire system, creating feelings of terrible apprehension and danger—a sense of danger that is by no means limited to the present or to fears of what may happen in the future. For severely disturbed families are ghost-ridden, haunted by the unmourned, unmetabolized, unresolved sorrows and miseries of the past. Indeed, if the severely disturbed family had a motto emblazoned upon the gate to its domain, it would be "Loss (and therefore change of any sort) is intolerable."

In these severely compromised systems, even the expectable losses and partings associated with the passage of time (children growing up and leaving the nest; the decline of aging parents) are frequently denied and disavowed, for there is an underlying sense that change and loss will prove intolerably painful, far too painful to be managed. For this reason, what emerges is a sticky, pervasive sense of stasis and stagnation; it is as if biological time itself isn't even ticking along (or as if its ticking can be disregarded and ignored).

While life itself, with its expectable transitions as well as its unforeseen disruptions and setbacks, will bring a train of demands for adaptive change, these chaotic and yet fundamentally rigid systems can come up with nothing other than the most stilted and stereotypic modes of responding. The family in pain tends to do what it has always done before, without ever seeming to notice that what it does has not been working.

What one tends to see, at this developmental level, are the same dreary, no-win sequences recurring over and over again. It is as if the members of the system are in an unspoken collusion to keep their collective attention away from the real sources of their suffering—for the underlying issues are too freighted with pain to bear consciously knowing about, much less reflecting upon, experiencing, feeling.

Depending upon the nature of the family's relational style ("family style" is itself an important topic, which I shall discuss), the dilemmas and conflicts within the system may be covert and smoldering or they may be overt and explosive; but they are, in any case, perennially unresolvable. For the members of the Level 5 family can neither focus on their issues and concerns with any reasonable degree of clarity nor can they even think about them in a coherent fashion.

To an outsider, it sometimes seems as if the people in this kind of family cosmos are oddly dedicated to promoting a state of mutual obfuscation. Their discussions are riddled with sudden, evasive shifts of topic—the question asked is not the question that is answered—and there is a frequent failure to recall certain facts that are of monumental emotional importance to the hearer ("I thought I'd told you about the abortion; maybe I didn't"). Certain remarks, moreover, are simply met with silence, as if the statement itself had been dropped into a well—which has the effect of disqualifying both the speaker and whatever words he or she has spoken.

The net result of these, and a host of other confusing and disorienting conversational techniques, is that in severely disturbed systems, meaning is routinely fragmented and *life itself makes no sense.* What families at this level of development lack, in the most fundamental way, is *coherence.* A sense of coherence and clarity is, in fact, what everyone in this terrifyingly chaotic kind of system is struggling desperately to achieve.

Level 4: The Polarized Family (Borderline) In the *polarized family,* matters have improved somewhat, but only to a limited degree. For as part of a desperate effort to master the disorder seen in the severely disturbed systems below them, borderline families have gone to the opposite extreme. Instead of having no rules, they have nothing but *inflexible, black-and-white rules*—rules designed not only to control the actions, but the thoughts and feelings of everyone within the intimate system.

Borderline families live in the polarized world of either/or: You're either in control or you're out of control; you're either all bad or you're all good; you're either all right or you're in the wrong entirely. You are the parent of a perfect family or the parent of a family full of monstrous ingrates. In this kind of emotional universe, there is not much gray area, nor is there space for negotiation of individual differences. For at this developmental level, the terrifying disorganization of the severely disturbed Level 5 system has been replaced by a dictatorship. Utter disorder has been supplanted by strict overcontrol, and anarchy overcome by the advent of a tyrant.

And disagreeable as life in this kind of emotional system might appear to be, it does represent a developmental advance over the terrifying chaos that exists below it on the scale. For the authoritarian family world that has been created *is* preferable to the confusion and formlessness that lurk at Level 5.

An analogy might be made to the welcoming of a strong dictatorship in a country whose cultural institutions are breaking down, whose criminal justice system has ceased to function, and whose economy is out of control. In the face of total disorganization, the loss of personal freedom seems a small sacrifice; *any* government, however repressive, is felt to be preferable to no government at all.

Seen from this point of view, the emergence of the tyrant feels—and *is* in truth—adaptive for everyone concerned. Life is not so incoherent and unstructured that what happens is likely to be unpredictable and unintelligible. The family despot has imposed his own ironclad expectations, rules, and regulations upon the group, and thus replaced potential disarray and confusion with a state of martial law.

The problem is that while his behavior may, in the short run, have brought order out of disarray, in the long run it becomes untenable to everyone. For the tyrant, in his struggle to maintain control, has imposed *rigid ways not only of behaving but of thinking and feeling* upon the members of the intimate group. His stern jurisdiction extends into the internal life of every person in the household; it is he who hands down the decrees about which ideas, wishes, emotions, and behaviors fall within the range of the acceptable. The overlord then defends these edicts with a force buttressed by his own underlying panic—for in this world of polar opposites, he experiences himself as being either in total control or as having no control whatsoever. And if he is out of control, chaos threatens.

In these polarized families, the organizational rules have come into existence not only in order to stave off family-wide chaos but to impose a sense of order in the internal world of everyone within the household. The intractable problem that pervades these intimate systems is, however, that maintaining total dominion over other people's thoughts and feelings—their wishes, longings, strivings (such as a growing adolescent's striving for autonomy)—may be effective in the short run but is doomed in the long one. For, like murder, human complexity will out—and inevitably, as in other totalitarian systems, a rebellious fifth column develops.

For even if the individuals in the family have no conscious wish to defy or resist the prevailing order, they cannot remain in their highly oversimplified roles and positions forever. Being human, they will find themselves experiencing a great variety of diverse thoughts, ideas, and emotions, even if such thoughts and feelings are forbidden in their family world. They may feel angry, sad, inadequate, or just plain ambivalent—even though mutually inconsistent or just plain unwelcome thoughts and feelings are unforgivable violations of the system's operational code.

In borderline, Level 4 families, an air of constraint settles on everyone; the rules of the emotional system cannot be challenged. This is not due solely to fear of the dictator's power; it is also due to a prevalent dread that once control is lost, the system itself will go completely haywire; the family itself may splinter and fall apart.

It is for these reasons that the members of the intimate group live under mutual surveillance, struggling to think and feel the permissible thoughts and emotions. But they live, always, with the lurking fear of the family bogeyman—the ever-present threat that someone's essential individuality, differentness, actual thoughts, wishes, and ideas will suddenly burst out and come into view. And when this happens (as it will, because human nature cannot be suppressed indefinitely), it will be seen, within this emotional framework, as vile badness or utter insanity—but in any case, as treachery of the most inexcusable sort. For it flies in the face of one of the polarized system's most basic precepts, which is that nobody in this family world is supposed to state an individual, differentiated position—"I disagree with what you said"; "I'd prefer staying home this afternoon"; "I feel upset by what you did"; and the like—or, worse yet, to maintain that position in the face of the tyrant's disapproval.

The tyrant runs the system, not by means of conflict resolution and compromise, but by means of intimidation and control. Control is, in fact, the paramount issue that families at this level of emotional development are grappling with, and the intermittent power struggles they experience can be truly ferocious.

Thus, while Level 4, borderline families have actually solved the problem of coherence that pervades the formless Level 5 system below them, they have done so at great psychic cost—by establishing a despotic, totalitarian mode of existence. It is nevertheless true that the Level 4 family system *has* developed structure—rules which make life predictable—and the people in this system are truly better off.

Level 3: The Rule-Bound Family (Midrange) The *rule-bound, Level 3 family* represents yet another advance upward on the family developmental continuum. In this midrange emotional system, the issues of both coherence *and* control have been dealt with and resolved. Midrange families are not formless and confused; neither do they need to exist under a state of martial law. They certainly do *not* (as do Level 4, borderline families) require a tyrant whose decrees are handed down in terms of strict absolutes.

This is because the midrange, Level 3 family has figured out how to maintain order and control in a less primitive, cartoonlike fashion. In these families, control is no longer external—something imposed upon its members by an oppressive dictator—but rather comes from within each individual member of the group. Midrange families use the tremendous power and influence inherent in close relationships in order to keep the people within the emotional system in line. And indeed, if the members of this system were to devise a motto for their own family coat of arms, it would be *If you loved me, you would always do all the particular things that you well know will meet with my approval.*

In the midrange family, feeling worthy, loved and lovable, good about oneself is contingent on obeying the dictates of the emotional system.

If, for example, a wife takes it as a given and obvious rule of living that "A good man spends all his free time with his family," then being a "good man" clearly involves behaving in this particular fashion.

Suppose, however, that the husband is invited to go off on a weekend expedition with his old college buddies—and suppose, furthermore, that he wants very much to go. Given that his relationships with his wife and children are important to him, and that he does want to be a good spouse and parent (as defined by the emotional system's rules), he is immediately confronted with one of two possible—and equally disagreeable—choices.

He can either abide by the family by-law (and feel disappointed and resentful) or he can defy the rule and go off for the weekend feeling like a rotten louse—that is, guilty. Whichever of these courses he chooses, the regulation itself remains inflexibly in place, because at this developmental level, the rules of the system are far more important than anyone within it.

The Invisible Referee In the rule-bound family's world, the coercion to behave in certain acceptable ways does not come from external sources (which is why the tyrant can be dispensed with); the coercion comes from within each member of the group and from the manifold rules for being a good person that have been taken in by every one of them. Thus, rules such as "A good woman always keeps a spotless house" and "A loving wife always wants to have sex whenever her partner does" may be among the code of regulations for living that the people in the emotional system have internalized. And if rules like these are indeed on the family books, then the female partner (like the husband in the earlier example) can follow either the path of compliance or that of defiance and guilt.

If she takes the former path and abides by the rules of the emotional system, she may find herself—for reasons that are often quite unclear to her—tense, irate, and perhaps suffering from a good deal of unexplained depression (because the rules of the system impel her to harshly suppress her own authentic thoughts and feelings). If she takes the latter path—lets the house get untidy from time to time, or tells him that she's not in the mood for sex—she may be perceived as a bad, slovenly creature or as a "frigid," unfeminine, and unloving sexual partner *not only by her spouse but by herself.*

The rule-bound emotional system is one in which the regulations for honorable living are ubiquitous and dominate almost every aspect of existence. The omnipresent difficulty is, however, that when obedience to the rules takes precedence over any effort to figure out what one actually wants, it is almost impossible to make contact with one's own psychological insides—that is, with one's real thoughts, true wishes, and actual preferences.

If, for instance, the wife in the above example happens to be someone who doesn't want to put her energies into keeping her house impeccably clean, she may feel compelled to do so, because a spotless home is written into the marital and family by-laws. Or it may be that the wife actually prefers to have sex less often than her spouse does, or in a less routinized manner—and in their intimate world the policy is that it happens every other night. She may conform and feel resentful, or not conform and feel guilty; but what she *won't* have, in the midrange system, is the option to think about whether or not the rule itself makes much sense to her.

Doing something because one "ought" to do so is very different from doing it because it is an expression of one's own genuine preference. But in the rule-bound family what one does is, by and large, what one is supposed to do and what is expected of one—or one feels culpable, blameworthy.

In such an atmosphere, the members of the Level 3 family often behave as if they are being surveilled by a spectral watcher or what psychiatrist Robert Beavers has termed "the invisible referee"—a faceless judge or perhaps an entire imagined audience of "good people" who are scrutinizing every aspect of one's thoughts, feelings, and behavior. Under the sway of this invisible referee's authority and domination, the people in the system become genuinely confused about whether they are thinking certain thoughts or acting in certain ways because they want to or because it is wanted of them.

For example, the father who might like to go off on a camping weekend with his friends may not even be capable of knowing consciously that he does want to go. The system's rules take precedence over the capacity to experience certain wishes, thoughts, needs, feelings; and even though the pressure to be one's own real self continues to exert itself, the family's regulations for being a worthy person exert counterpressures of even greater strength and force. The rules and regulations feel vitally necessary, because *midrange systems are pervaded by the belief that human beings are basically uncaring and untrustworthy.*

There is no faith that a family member will behave in loving ways sponta- 45
neously. Thus, an adult daughter may faithfully obey the rule "You should call your parents once a week," but it feels vastly different to call home because it's expected rather than to call home because one is really eager to talk to the folks. The very need for such a rule betrays a lack of confidence that she would ever want to call home if left to her own devices.

In families at the midrange level, the rules are felt to be critically necessary because they keep the people in the system behaving in the ways that good, close, and loving family members *ought to.* The dilemma is, however, that even though the rules *do* serve to regulate everyone's behavior very effectively, they throw up an invisible yet very real barrier against spontaneous, authentic, close relating.

For one cannot say to the partner or to the family, "This is who I am," if doing so flies in the face of the system's operational regulations. And if one ever did so, the feedback would very likely be a reprimand: "A good, loving person would think (or feel or be) otherwise." It is as if, in the backdrop of the family theater, there is a kind of Greek chorus commenting on everyone's behavior. Their constant refrains are "They say—" and "Everyone knows—."

But who, actually, are "they" or "everyone"? Driven by the rules as they all are, the members of the midrange family would find this a difficult question to answer.

The Problem of Intimacy The rules have, of course, been brought into play to provide security, stability, and predictability to the behavior of everyone in the system; the difficulty is that these selfsame rules interfere seriously with the development of genuine closeness. For true intimacy has to begin with people trying to come to grips with who they really are and what they actually do think and feel (as distinct from knowing what they "should" think and feel) and being willing to come to one another with this honest, if not always perfectly congenial and welcome, information.

Real relationship involves having a place to go with one's not-so-pretty thoughts. Real relationship involves being able to bring one's ambivalent feelings out into the open, and to do so with a sense of safety, which in turn must derive from the knowledge that one will be heeded and attended. But in the rule-bound emotional system, it is far more important to be who one "should be" than to be who one actually is at the moment.

Admittedly there is, in *all* family systems, a certain amount of tension between meeting the needs of the self and meeting the needs of the group as an emotional entity. But what tends to happen at the midrange level is that the richness of the individual's subjective experience becomes truncated as he or she struggles valiantly to be the person that "they" or "everyone" will find acceptable.

The problem intrinsic to the midrange system is that if a person cannot get in touch with his own real feelings—cannot become connected to his or her own inner world in a manner that is vivid, genuine, and alive—it is truly impossible ever to get to know another person intimately either. Being heard as who one is, and hearing the other as who he or she is, is the loving service that true intimates offer to one another routinely.

In truth, when it comes to getting intimate, no stand-in for the real self will do. For intimacy involves the capacity to expose one's genuine (if not always palatable) thoughts, feelings, and needs to the close person or people in one's life. It involves making oneself vulnerable by daring to say forthrightly, "This is who I am, warts and all." This could only be hazarded if one were fairly confident that the feedback would be supportive—that to be honestly oneself would be within the pale of what is humanly permissible.

In the midrange family, however, the internalized rules themselves preclude this from happening. *The rules rule, because the system is operating on the basic assumption that the guidelines to behavior must be in place because no one would ever do the right and loving thing of his or her own accord.* What has been sacrificed, in the service of the manifold "shoulds" and "oughts," is intimacy itself, and intimacy is indeed the major issue with which the people in this rule-bound world are struggling.

Level 2: The Adequate Family; and Level 1: The Optimal Family *Adequate* and *optimal* families may be referred to in the same categorical breath, so to speak, because these relational systems are in many ways far more similar than they are different. Families at this healthier end of the clinical ladder share fundamental characteristics—most especially, their ability to be comfortable with both their loving feelings and with their feelings of annoyance and frustration. The members of the intimate group can, in other words, take personal responsibility for their mixed, ambivalent thoughts and emotions.

Adequate and optimal families are also much alike in their ability to display flexible responses to life events, and to focus on their issues and on the tasks at hand with a good degree of goal-direction and clarity. While these competent systems are, of course, not totally devoid of conflict—there is no group of individuals, indeed no individual human being, without mixed thoughts and feelings about a great variety of matters—there is, in such families, generally very little conflict that is found to be unresolvable.

For while the members of any family group do have to struggle with their share of strong differences, matters of disagreement, and occasional outright battles, these more capable, successful families are pervaded by a deep sense of trust in the dependability and reliability of their underlying connection. Because their fundamental relationships with one another *feel* so secure, there is always the sense that "We can work it out"; the vitally important relational web that links them will not be dangerously threatened.

POWER, CONTROL, INTIMACY: CORE FAMILY ISSUES

Power is always a major focus of concern, overtly or covertly, in every human grouping. As one ascends the Beavers Scale from the least competent and functional families to the most competent and functional families, clear differences in the ways in which power, control, and intimacy issues are managed become strikingly apparent.

In families at the bottom of the clinical ladder (Level 5, severely disturbed), no member of the family is clearly in charge. These basically structureless, ungoverned families are without any real, discernible hierarchy; the only rule is that there is no reliably consistent rule; "Anything goes" is the household's basic credo. In this kind of emotional system, efforts to establish control are generally covert and indirect, and since *no one* in this family world has real power that can be used effectively, the system itself feels dangerously random and chaotic.

In families at the next level up (Level 4, borderline), the situation has of course improved, but only to a certain degree. While some sense of order has been established, these polarized systems are characterized by persistent (but never completely successful) efforts to establish patterns of dominance and submission. The all-pervasive difficulty here is that while dictatorial rule is certainly better than no coherent structure at all, this form of family government eventually does become completely untenable. Fierce power struggles—which always involve some family member's desperate effort to establish his or her own separateness and individual humanity—inevitably erupt.

Such control battles may surface in the overt form of emotional explosions, or in the more covert form of emotional symptoms (for example, anorexia nervosa). In the polarized family, however, the power struggle can never really be resolved and settled. For in this kind of extravagantly oversimplified either/or system, all is understood in terms of diametric opposites (you are either omnipotent *or* you are totally helpless). Thus, the more subtle, intricate, complex gray areas of negotiation and compromise have no place or existence whatsoever. At this level of family functioning, the ongoing struggle for control has—and can have—no imaginable conclusion, so the unresolvable conflict rages on endlessly.

At the next higher rung of the Beavers ladder (Level 3, midrange), the people in the system have certainly recognized the tremendous power and influence inherent in close relationships; they also know very well how to use that power to keep the emotional system running smoothly. Families at this developmental plane have mastered the problem of control by establishing a more complex and differentiated set of organizational rules. The disconcerting difficulty pervading the system is, however, that the stable structure thus created is being maintained by means of manipulation, intimidation, and guilt. Even though the emotional system does operate effectively, everyone within it is feeling emotionally constricted, guilt-laden, and discomfited. The myriad rules about what a "good person" should think and feel make the members of these families feel controlled from within.

Furthermore, because certain thoughts and feelings are not acceptable within the system, the internal world of every member of the family starts feeling "bad" and dangerous. Indeed, it is often the case that people in a rule-bound world will confuse having had a "bad," unacceptable thought with actually having done something terrible.

Very commonly, in order to defend themselves from the sense of shame, guilt, and inner badness, the members of the midrange group will deny, repress, or project onto others thoughts and feelings that have been deemed impermissible and unthinkable. It is almost as if the family members have labored together to build a tall prison, whose walls are made entirely of rules, and then they've all leaped inside it and locked the door behind them.

FLEXIBILITY AND STRUCTURE: KEY ASPECTS OF FAMILY HEALTH

As one moves upward on the health and competence continuum, it will 65
be useful to bear in mind the fact that families at Level 2 (adequate) are located between the midrange and optimal families on the Beavers Scale. Adequate, Level 2 is, in fact, an in-between kind of category, for while families assessed as "adequate" have a great deal in common with the optimal families

above them on the Beavers ladder, they also bear some resemblance to the less capable, rule-bound families one rung below them.

The adequate family is like the rule-bound family in its occasional tendency to use emotionally coercive tactics—to try to resolve conflicts by means of intimidation and guilt. There will also be times when the members of an adequate family are not supposed to think certain thoughts, or to have certain feelings, which are considered out of bounds within the emotional framework. *Such methods of control are by no means the norm* in adequate families (as they are in midrange families) but to the extent that they are present in the system they do impose limits on the closeness, trust, and good feeling that the members of the intimate group can confidently share.

Adequate families are more like optimal, Level 1 families in their performance rating; both groups do extremely well when it comes to meeting the developmental needs of their individual members. The parents in the adequate family have formed an effective coalition, and they work well as a team (though their marital relationships may not be quite as emotionally rewarding as are those of the optimal couples above them on the scale). At these higher levels of family development, the nature of the rules and the structure of the hierarchy are in dramatically sharper focus; the way in which the organization operates (who is in charge, and under which circumstances) are now well defined and clear to all concerned.

Most important of all, however, the rules of the family system are not viewed as edicts that have been engraved in stone; they are seen as human rules, made by fallible human beings—rules that can, under the appropriate circumstances, come into question and undergo change. And it is in this particularly crucial respect that adequate families and optimal families are most similar.

Healthy, competent emotional systems are flexible—although families assessed as adequate are somewhat less so. While both these emotional systems operate very effectively, in terms of doing the right thing, the adequate system's wheels don't always move around easily; some pain and individual loneliness are present. In adequate families, one simply doesn't see the same relatively constant sense of closeness and delight—that real pleasure in one another's company—so evident in the optimal families above them at the top of the scale.

FAMILY HAPPINESS AND POWER SHARING

The most competent family systems are egalitarian ones, in which *equal* 70
overt power is shared by the parents in a manner that is mutually attentive to and respectful of each other's sometimes different viewpoints. In purely political terms, one would call the optimal family a democratically organized group, with strong, clear, joint leadership at the head of its government, and a citizenry (the younger generation) with a voice that will be heard and responded to reliably.

In these workable intimate systems, negative affects such as anger, frustration, sadness, discouragement—even despair—are viewed as part of the human package, rather than as unwelcome, dangerous, or potentially destructive forces. In this kind of emotional atmosphere, a full range of feeling can be expressed because *all feelings (not just those that are in line with the family's agenda and self-image) are taken to be the "facts" of someone's existence at that particular moment*—at that particular moment, it must be emphasized, and not until the end of time.

In these families, angry feelings and sad feelings are thus not merely "allowed" or "permitted"; they are expected to exist, welcomed, and even embraced as aspects of a loved family member's own unique humanity. It is, in truth, this readiness to acknowledge and experience the hard and distressing parts of life that makes it possible for the people in the system to own and take responsibility for their genuine feelings and to feel quite naturally entitled to do so.

In this familial environment, individual differences are not viewed as threatening; simply being oneself is never seen as badness or a betrayal of the group. Differences are not merely tolerated by the group; they are seen as enriching to everyone. Here, as well, space is allotted—a plot of personal autonomy in which each member of the family can grow as a separate being without sacrificing his or her sense of belonging within the larger relational system. And it is this very comfortable sense that one can get close without being swallowed up in other peoples' needs, or in their communal mythmaking, that makes intimacy feel safe—or, indeed, possible at all.

Understanding

1. In each of the five levels of the Beavers Scale, there are at least one or two drivers of behaviors of the family members. At each level indicate the behavior or motivation that propels those behaviors.
2. Identify a fictional or "media" family that resembles one of the levels of family functioning described in the scale. Describe those aspects that conform to its dimensions.
3. Scarf states that *power* is a major focus of concern in every human grouping, including the family. What is the function of power in family operations? How is it demonstrated?
4. What purposes do instruments like the Beavers Scale serve? To which levels of family described by the scale do you think they can be most useful? Why?

Responding

1. If you were to undertake an analysis similar to Scarf's of your family as compared with other families you know, with what conceptual distinctions would you begin? Why?
2. The family is a social invention that is associated with particular problems or tasks: that of creating new persons to replace aging ones, for example, and of instructing or socializing the younger generation in what it must know and do in order to continue the social structure. But other institutions

or actions can produce the same result; for example, a single act of sexual intercourse can result in new life, and a daycare center can socialize young children relatively effectively. What, then, do you see as the unique purpose of the family unit?

3. What differences in family life—even among families described as optimally functioning—can be expected in American society in the twenty-first century? Indicate the sources of the expected differences as they appear in today's families.
4. During the course of her interviews with families, Scarf usually posed this question to everyone in the group who was old enough and willing to try to answer it: "If you were going to tell or write the story of your life—which would, of course, begin when you were a small infant in your own family—what would the first sentence of your autobiography sound like?" Respond to this question.

Connecting

1. In England, America, and northern France, even as early as the seventeenth century, the overwhelming majority of married couples lived with their dependent children in separate domestic units. This beginning of what we today call the "nuclear family" has become the norm in these and many other countries and is the basis of Scarf's analysis. How important is this kind of domestic unit to the "health and competence" of people? Are there other family structures depicted in this text that challenge the utility or the wisdom of the nuclear family? Consider, for example, Bettelheim's "Creating a New Way of Life" (chapter four).
2. Recall the narratives of the men in Tollefson's "Choosing Not to Fight" (chapter three), who deviated from the norms of accepted behavior at the time and resisted the draft. Review their descriptions of their family structures with respect to the Beavers Scale. What tentative conclusions about their families' influence on their behavior can you draw from your analysis?

Hating Goldie

Phyllis Rose

Author Phyllis Rose received her bachelor's degree from Radcliffe, her master's from Yale, and her doctorate from Harvard. Having taught briefly at the latter two schools, she went to Wesleyan University in 1969 and remained there as a professor of English. Rose has written extensively on the Victorian era. One of her most interesting books is *Parallel Lives: Five Victorian Marriages,* wherein she explores her notion that marriage is *the primary political experience* of an adult life. In the preface, she writes:

> I believe, first of all, that living is an act of creativity, and that, at certain moments of our lives, our creative imaginations are more conspicuously demanded than at others. At certain moments, the need to decide upon the story of our own lives becomes particularly pressing—when we choose a mate, for example, or embark upon a career. . . . There is a kind of arranging and telling and choosing of detail—of narration, in short—which we must do so that one day will prepare for the next day, one week prepare for the next week. In some way we all decide when we have grown up and what event will symbolize for us that state of maturity—leaving home, getting married, becoming a parent, losing our parents, making a million, writing a book.

Though not a marriage story, in "Hating Goldie" Rose has chosen an object—and her story around it—to symbolize such a state of maturity. Perhaps "Hating Goldie" will remind you of a symbol that has accompanied your life thus far.

The childhood my parents gave me could hardly have been more privileged. Yet for many years, in the fashion of spoiled middle-class girls of my generation, that was exactly what I held against them. 1

Take Goldie. For my sixth birthday, I had asked for a trip to Texas, where I intended to be a cowboy. My parents told me Texas wasn't like what I imagined and gave me a canary instead, which without much thought I named Goldie. I hated Goldie from the first time I had to clean his cage, sandpapering his wooden bars to remove the bird shit and replacing the soiled paper at the bottom of his cage. Nothing about him gave me esthetic pleasure. At night I had to cover his cage with a plastic wrapper whose very smell and feel offended me. Goldie's song I found insipid. Like my mother, I was interested in lyrics, and "instrumentals" bored me. Goldie was kept in the same room as the radio, which stimulated him to song. Often we had to cover his cage before his bedtime, so we could listen to our favorite shows without his caterwauling in competition. I hated Goldie all the more because he was what I had received for my sixth birthday instead of the trip to Texas. I waited for him to die, but he lived on and on. He was still alive when I got out of elementary school and started high school. He was still alive when I went to college and my parents sold the family house. Goldie had to be given away. Eventually it occurred to me to remark to my mother on the longevity of this extraordinary bird, and eventually she thought I was old enough to know the truth.

"There wasn't just one Goldie, dear, there were several. They died every few years. Canaries don't live that long, you know. But Daddy and I thought you'd be upset, so we replaced each one with another as quickly as we could, and you never noticed the difference."

Never noticed the difference! No wonder! I hated the damned thing! Never gave it a glance, if I could avoid it. For years I held Goldie against my parents, especially my mother. Look at the gilded cage I lived in! I said to whoever would listen. Look how my parents kept me from reality! It was my equivalent of the story of how Dickens was put to work in a blacking factory at the age of 12, deprived of his education, hopeless, abandoned by his parents who had turned the world upside down and relied on him to support them. As I'd learned from reading Edmund Wilson, all of Dickens's novels had proceeded from this experience. Why didn't I have something awful like that in my past? Instead I had Goldie. No wonder I hadn't become a great novelist. My parents hadn't allowed me to suffer.

I was a difficult, ungrateful child, and this lasted well into my 40's. It wasn't 5
until I told this story to Dr. S., a wise man in New Haven, that I got a handle on it. I told it to him as an example of how I'd been coddled as a child, trying to gain his sympathy. ("Poor little fly on the wall," I can hear my mother say. "Nebbish!") Wasn't it at least partly my parents' fault if I hadn't yet written what I wanted to write? Hadn't my parents deprived me of the pain I needed to be nourished as an artist? My doctor said, with the insight and subtlety achieved only after the most sophisticated theoretical and orthodox Freudian training, "She sounds like a very good mother."

Understanding

1. Good memoir and narrative tell a story, relate a salient anecdote, and make a point, either stated or clear enough to be inferred. In "Hating Goldie," the reader needs to infer the point. What analysis does Rose settle on to convey what she learned from her doctor's comment? What symbolizes a new "state of maturity" for Rose?
2. In "Hating Goldie," Rose said, "Look at the gilded cage I lived in!" (paragraph 4). Did she use the notion of *cage* accidentally? Was the reason Rose never noticed that her parents replaced each canary as it died really because she hated it? What else did she *not* notice during that time?

Responding

1. Like Phyllis Rose, many if not all of us blame our parents for something real or imagined. In her case, Rose says, "No wonder I hadn't become a

great novelist. My parents hadn't allowed me to suffer" (paragraph 4). As readers we might laugh, say "Get off it" or "Oh, you *poor* baby." It's easy for outsiders to see how convenient it is to blame our parents for situations over which we actually do have choices. Have you been carrying such a grudge? Claim it and write about it. When you discover the point of the story, analyze whether it is symbolic of a "state of maturity" such as the one Rose offers in the quote in the introduction to this reading.

2. Did Rose actually suffer from finding out that her parents had replaced the dead Goldies over the years? Though her mother explained the deception as trying to protect her daughter, what may have been her mother's real reason for exchanging the canaries? Do you think parents should try to ease the pain they think a child might suffer even though one might say that they are telling "little white lies"? Explain.
3. In an interview Phyllis Rose stated: "I love the essay form, because I very often don't know when I start on a subject where I'm going to end up. I find out what I think, and sometimes too, in the process I find consolation." Try this kind of exploratory writing about a pet or object that accompanied your younger life. Reflect later on the consoling features of the process.

Connecting

1. One school of literary biography seeks to establish how "life" has had an influence on a writer's work. Rose, in contrast, believes that what people *read* influences their lives—their views of their own experience; that is, that "certain imaginative patterns—call them mythologies or ideologies—determine the shape of a writer's life as well as his or her work." She has commented on her own "addictive" writing process this way: "In many cases I would start with a very personal experience and connect it with things I'd read or that friends had told me and work that way from the individual and personal to the general and shared." Trace this writing process—and the resulting rhetorical form (narrative shape)—in "Hating Goldie." What other selections seem to make a connection between what you read or hear from others and its effect on your identity?
2. In chapter one, "Gifts," we asked if there was ever a gift you wanted and didn't receive. (A canary instead of a trip to Texas produced a lifelong tapestry of events for Rose.) If you wrote a gift-story response, take another look at it and revise it (or its ending).

Eating, Breathing, Drinking

Susan Cheever

Susan Cheever is the daughter of Pulitzer Prize–winning author John Cheever (1912–82). A substantial writer in her own right, Cheever began her career as a journalist and then turned to fiction, biography, and memoir. Her topics are people, places, and events close to home—she explores an intensely personal world. About her own writing, Cheever has said: "I write to bear witness, whether about my three failed marriages or my crazy family. If I have any usefulness on this planet, it is to tell the story of my life and 'to tell the truth truly,' as Emerson said."

"Eating, Breathing, Drinking" bears witness to one family's way of being within its ritual alcohol consumption. Cheever's narrative-commentary style moves the piece along rapidly with its abrupt changes in mood and vision.

My grandmother Cheever taught me how to embroider, how to say the Lord's Prayer and how to make a dry martini. She showed me how to tilt the gin bottle into the tumbler, strain the icy liquid into the martini glass and add the vermouth. "Just pass the bottle over the gin," she explained in her genteel Yankee voice as she twisted the lemon peel with her tiny hands and its oil spread across the surface of the drink. I was 8. 1

New York in the 40's was a postwar paradise. Soldiers brought back bamboo hats from the Philippines and lacquered boxes from Japan. The streets were safe; the shopkeepers knew everyone on the block. The women wore dresses and the men all wore hats. Every evening at 6 o'clock, right on schedule—because everything in those days was right on schedule—the adults would prepare for what they called their preprandial libation. They opened the clinking, golden bottles and filled the opalescent ice bucket, brought out the silver martini shaker and the strainer and the glasses, and the entire mood would change. I loved those mood changes even then. I loved the paraphernalia of drinking, the ice trays that I was allowed to refill and the gin-soaked olives that were my first childhood treat. I loved the way the adults got loose and happy and forgot that I was a child, and the way the men would sit down so close to me that I smelled tweed and cigarette smoke and whisky.

I knew that I would grow up and marry a man who also smelled of tweed and cigarette smoke and whisky. I would iron his shirts; I would learn to cook pork chops in cream sauce and serve cheese and crackers at parties and take care of the children. In the evenings, I would greet my husband with the ice bucket and martini shaker. In the summer we would stay cool with gin and tonics. In the winter we would drink Manhattans. In good times we would break out Champagne, in bad times we would dull the pain with stingers. I was already acquainted with the miraculous medicinal powers of alcohol.

My mother dispensed two fingers of whisky for stomach pains and beer for digestive problems. Gin was our family's all-purpose disinfectant and anesthetic.

I learned about divorce around the same time I learned that the Russians had enough atomic power to blow us all up. These two ways in which my life could be brutally shattered by outside forces seemed equally terrifying. My father liked to tell divorce stories; he loved the story of how Janie Simon had left her husband while he was at work—taking the children, the furniture and even the pets, so that her husband came back home that night to an empty house. Divorce was rare, though. If you ask me, people back then were too dressed up to submit to the indignities of divorce court. They still had their hats on every time they went out. When they got clinically depressed, when their adulteries caught up with them, when all the martinis in the world weren't enough to blot out the pain of their humanness, they killed themselves quietly. No one talked about it. They hanged themselves with their hats on.

There were a lot of things I didn't learn in college. I didn't learn the date 5
of the Magna Carta or the succession of the Roman emperors, but I learned something much more important: I learned how to manipulate men. I combed the assigned literature for clues. I studied the behavior of successful girls with anthropological zeal, and in the beginning of my sophomore year, I stumbled onto a boy as confused as I was. In the anger of our breakup after a few miserable months together, he told me the truth. "You tell me everything," he said with real disgust. "I know everything you're feeling." There might as well have been an audible click. Overnight I became desirable. I knew how to make men want me! The exhilaration of that knowledge lasted through three unsuccessful marriages.

It was simple. You were often too busy to see them. You told them nothing. When you were with them you focused your mind on something pleasurable you were going to do as soon as they left—you were going to read a trashy book, you were going to pick up adoring messages from other more desirable men, you were going to have a drink. I learned without knowing what I was learning that love is a fantasy, and that fantasy thrives in a vacuum. I became good at creating that vacuum. I learned that love smolders along until it encounters an obstacle, and then it flames up and catches fire, creating the most delicious kind of heat. I became very good at creating those obstacles.

In the spring I took my First Love home for a visit. My father hated him, and he forbade any physical contact between us. "No necking in the parlor!" he shouted, and he meant it. I soon learned, again without knowing I had learned it, that I could keep my father's disapproval at bay by restricting my sexual activity to the sons of his friends, and later to the friends of his friends. By September my First Love had been kicked out of school, and this made him even more attractive to me—and less attractive to my father. He took an apartment off campus in a seedy Italian neighborhood at the bottom of College Hill. After the classes I deigned to attend, I would coast down the hill in my precious red Volkswagen convertible, down-shifting to save the worn-out brakes. I parked in the street and ran up the uneven staircase to the room he had rented. Our happiest times were already over.

After a Christmas Eve party that year another man drove me home and kissed me. If I was looking for a place to park my car after Christmas, he said, I might think of his house. He had a deep voice and a reassuring, plummy accent; they had kicked him out of prep school, but not before he learned how to elongate his A's and rattle his R's. He was the son of a friend of my father's, and I'll call him Harry. I was dazzled by his sexy condescension, his tweeds and pink Brooks Brothers shirts and the way he moaned, "Oh, Susie," using my childhood name.

There were always guests at Christmas dinner. That year—it must have been 1964—the guests were Ralph and Fanny Ellison. The Ellisons walked right into the battle over whether I could spend the weekend with Harry. My father, thrilled to be playing the part of protective Victorian parent, cleared his throat and said I shouldn't go. "A young woman does not spend a weekend alone with a man unchaperoned," he harrumphed. Ralph, God bless him, took my side.

He had always been a friend of mine. He acted as if anything I did was all 10
right, as if I might have a mind all my own. Ralph was the only one of my parents' friends who didn't drink a lot. He was always the same sensible and gentle man. Even William Maxwell, who has lived into a distinguished old age, cheerfully remembers drinking so much at my parents' house that he couldn't remember whether they were still friends the next morning. That Christmas Day Ralph reached over the table, over the turkey and the cranberry sauce and the creamed onions, and gently pulled my hair up off my face. "I think Susie should go," he said. "Let her go, John."

And so I went. It was an odd rainy weekend. Harry had torn out one wall of his house and planned to build an addition. The rain came in through the holes. In the mornings we hacked away with rusty shovels at what was supposed to be a new foundation; in the afternoons we drank. We drew plans for bay windows and grand flights of stairs and told stories about the parties we would have when they were finished.

At the parties in my father's house, guests were always falling down the stairs. People who came for lunch frequently had to be put to bed during the afternoon—sometimes they stayed for days. The cars were often at the body shop. In the evenings there were terrible fights. Almost any disagreement escalated into an apocalyptic rage. Drinking seemed as much a part of life as eating or breathing. We laughed while alcohol twined itself around our family like a choking, deadly, invisible vine. No one talked about it. No one saw what was happening. And all that time we had no idea why my mother was crying upstairs in her room, or why my father was always on the way to the hospital, or why I had to marry the wrong man—and then marry the wrong man again, and again.

Understanding

1. Who (which readers) was Cheever writing for in this essay? Explain.
2. Explore the title of the selection in relation to the point Cheever makes.

3. Examine the narrative shaping of this essay by making a time line of the events. Is it developed sequentially, or are flashbacks involved? What else happens within the chronological development? Examine when Cheever "tells" the story as opposed to when she "shows" what was happening. You might refer back to the "To the Student: Essential Reading before You Get Started" section on "How to Craft a Good Story" for a refresher on telling and showing.
4. Knowing her through this story, what do you think Cheever might truly wish had been different about her family life? Does she wish anything had been different? Does Cheever consider alcohol to have been a major problem in her family?
5. Before writer Mary Karr went on a book tour to promote her memoir *The Liars' Club,* she thought her family—her "less-than-perfect Texas clan"—was "full of freaks." The response she got from the book tour was overwhelmingly positive. She says that "After eight weeks of travel, I ginned up this working definition for a dysfunctional family: any family with more than one person in it."

   At her readings on her promotional book tour, over and over again her listeners would thank her for sharing her "dysfunctional" family, because it made them feel less isolated. Would you agree with Karr's comment on family stories that "The good ones I've read confirm my experience of a flawed family. They reassure the same way belonging to a community reassures." How do *you* feel about reading others' private lives, such as Cheever's?

Responding

1. African American writer Ralph Ellison (1914–94), author of the highly acclaimed *Invisible Man,* was at Christmas dinner in the Cheever household in 1964—several years before the civil rights movement and before many blacks and whites socialized in their homes. Do you think Ellison and Susan Cheever were close up until he died? Do you recall a grownup family friend, like Ralph Ellison in Cheever's family—with another racial identity from yours or not—who took your side in a battle? Write about that situation. Is that person still on your side?
2. Did or does alcohol affect your family ties? If so, explore its effect.

Connecting

1. Cheever wrote a biographical memoir, *Home Before Dark,* about her father, John Cheever, after his death from cancer. John Blades, in the *Chicago Tribune,* suggests that Cheever omits very few details of her father's life, "telling of a turbulent marriage, his long and frustrating struggle to make a living as a writer, his alcoholism, his paternal inadequacies, his aristocratic pretensions and his confused sexual life." What issues with her father does Cheever allude to in "Eating, Breathing, Drinking"? Does she come to any conclusions in this process of her "bearing witness"? Compare or contrast the themes of this essay with Rose's "Hating Goldie."

2. All families have traditions and rituals. What is the difference between the two? The clinking of glasses at 6 P.M. was framed as her family's ritual by Susan Cheever. What ritual (as opposed to tradition) presents itself as memorable in your family? Describe it and its effect on your family. Have you or your siblings retained it in adult life? Relate it, if you wish, to the Beavers Scale of descriptors in Scarf's "The Beavers Scale of Family Health and Competence."

The Royal Family

Floyd Skloot

In this short story, Floyd Skloot presents the theme of youthful idealization: the process of exaggerating the virtues (and minimizing the faults) of someone special. Idealization is an inevitable part of falling in love, but it is also a common element in many parent-child relationships. Those who study families suggest that idealization is a reflection of doubt about one's own self-reliance, which seems reasonable in a young child.

Through young Danny Webb, Skloot reveals some of that irresistible power of family members to influence one another—as part of a system—which Scarf describes in the first selection of this chapter. The title "The Royal Family" is a wry commentary on the workaday life of an "average" American family in the 1950s.

Born in Brooklyn, New York, in 1947, Floyd Skloot now lives in rural Oregon. His stories, poems, and essays have been published in a number of journals. His novels *Pilgrim's Harbor, Summer Blue,* and *The Open Door* were published by Story Line Press in the fall of 1992, and *Music Appreciation,* a collection of his poems, appeared in 1994; *The Night-Side,* a collection of essays about the illness experience, appeared in 1996.

1 Saturday morning always smelled like meat. When Milton Webb woke his son Danny in the dark, an odor of raw pork was already on his hands.

One hand was spread across Danny's brow, the thumb and pinky squeezing his temples in a steady massage. His eyes fluttered open. It never occurred to him that his father was a small man. Everything about Milton Webb seemed large. He spoke in salvos and his whisper was like the eye of a hurricane. Danny could hear him breathing anywhere in the apartment. Milt had corded, hairy arms and fingers that were so thick he had trouble buttoning shirts. His nose, smashed twice by falling chicken coops, sheered his shadowed face toward the jutting jaw and seemed stretched to a point by its own weight. His huge belly didn't jiggle when he walked. He would make Danny punch him there as hard as he could and would never flinch.

Even when his father stood near the old fighter Simon Sabbeth, Danny didn't think of him as small. It just seemed that Si, who had boxed under the name of Kid Sunday and was his father's best friend, was a giant. Maybe Si would show up at the market today.

Milt was dressed for work, wearing black corduroys and a maroon flannel shirt that didn't show blood. His socks sagged into boots he wouldn't tie until leaving the apartment. Their lace tips clicked on the linoleum when he walked.

5 "C'mon, pal, it's past time to get up. Now what's the slogan?"

"Kill or be killed," Danny mumbled.

"Right you are. And don't forget, Mr. Alfred J. Honts, who used to be my friend Alf, will gladly take every one of my customers if I'm not careful."

"Except the chink restaurants."

"Except the chinks, right. That's another thing to remember. Your uncle Joseph wanted no part of the chink trade, which is why he's selling hats today. Makes me laugh."

Danny turned his head away and gazed at the map hung on his wall. A 10
huge red oval seemed to glow down at him. Ask him to find any volcano in the Ring of Fire and Danny would jab a finger right to it on the map. From Chile up to Alaska and down from Siberia to New Zealand, he could place more than six hundred of the world's most furious mountains. Someday, he promised himself, he would walk within the Valley of Ten Thousand Smokes. He would visit Burney and Barren Island, Tarawera and Ulawun, Purace, Mount Saint Helens. He loved just saying their names.

"Uncle Joe's a hatdasher, right?"

"Haberdasher." Milt rolled Danny's head back away from the wall. "Now let's get moving, we open at five."

Danny's clothes were in a tall chest that was backed into his closet. He found a pair of dungarees with their cuffs still rolled properly—his father got furious when cuffs were too high or uneven, when they sagged against his sneakers, when they had fade marks. Danny's mother always unrolled the cuffs when she did the wash. He wished she'd leave them alone, since it was always so hard to get the cuffs right again, but he didn't have the nerve to ask her. When he asked questions about her housekeeping, she would scream, wide-eyed, "Just like your father!"

He slipped on a sweatshirt the same shade of blue as his dungarees. He thought his father might appreciate the match. If so, then this could be his market uniform from now on. Then his father would take him along more Saturdays, like he used to. Danny hoped he might have finally figured out the right thing to do.

Before leaving the room, Danny checked to be sure he hadn't disturbed 15
his brother. Ricky slept on his back with his bad eye half open, so it was difficult to be sure.

Saturdays, Ricky had to meet all morning with his tutor. He hadn't been allowed to go to the market since failing algebra and history.

Ricky's bad eye had been bad since before Danny was born, so he knew it couldn't be his fault. Something about a broken lens, glass in Ricky's eye, one entire summer of surgeries. Danny dreamed about it sometimes. In the dreams, he always saw their father's fist, with its black hairs standing sharp and tall as spikes, that made his brother's glasses explode in his face.

Ricky was asleep. Danny could tell by checking whether the bad eye moved.

He could remember to call him Rick when his brother was awake, but Danny still thought of him as Ricky. It had only been a few weeks since Ricky demanded the name change. Every time Danny forgot, his brother would punch him on the arm. There was a big bruise now on his biceps, but Danny hadn't told his mother the truth about how he'd gotten it. Ricky said that if he did, it would cost him his leg.

Danny had trouble keeping up with Ricky's names. Not too long ago, he had a long struggle replacing Richie with Ricky. Now he had to remember Rick.

He checked himself out in the mirror behind their door. Everything looked neat enough, but you could never be sure. He wiped the residue of sleepstring from the corner of his eye.

Whenever Danny dressed to visit his grandparents, or for Sunday dinner at Lundy's, his father made him go back to his room to change shirts. Shirt selection was his real problem, all right. No matter which one he chose, Danny's first selection was always wrong.

He kept hoping Saturday mornings would be different. As he checked his sweatshirt one more time for cleanliness and color, he thought he might be getting the knack of dressing right.

Milton Webb flung open the furrowed gray doors of his poultry market. They rumbled in their tracks like subway train cars, and disappeared.

"Wake up and fly right!"

Webb's Live Poultry flapped wildly in the coops that lined one wall. As they screamed back at him, their cries ricocheted through the air.

"Help! Help!"

Danny stared at the faces of three scales, which threw dawn light onto him. The market's floors were covered with fresh sawdust spread last night by his father's helper, a grizzled old man named Gabe.

Soon, Danny knew, the floors would be patched with clots of feathers and blood. He would feel their lumps under his soles all day. There would also be more meat smell. It would remind him of breakfast and make him want to skip lunch. But he couldn't refuse to eat Saturday lunch with his father. That got him madder than anything.

Besides, his father said he would get used to the smell. He said Danny would get used to the racket from the coops, too. But it hadn't happened yet.

He stood on the tracks listening to the birds go crazy. His father hurried to the plucking room for aprons. Danny watched him move, the massive shoulders rolling through the air as though he were swimming.

Suddenly, out of the darkness behind him, two hands folded themselves around Danny's face. He was yanked backward, feet off the ground like a fryer being snatched from its coop, and his head struck something solid. He sank into a heavy stench of offal.

"Ayyyyy, little Milt! Guess who?"

Danny squirmed in the iron grip of his father's helper. Gabriel Kozey once told Danny his hands were so strong because he'd been pulling feathers out of freshly killed birds for forty years.

"You think they wanna come outta there, the plumages?" Gabe had laughed. "It's like jerking out a lady's eyelashes, you know what I mean?"

Danny hated to have Gabe's hands on him. The hands were mottled with blank patches, scaly sections paler than the rest and hairless. Probably from all the blood and feather juice, which Danny could imagine staining like acid.

He thought Gabe must never wash his hands right, the way Milt had taught Danny. He'd bet Gabe didn't flush toilets with his feet, either. He smelled even worse than liver.

No wonder Gabe never got invited home for dinner. Danny liked to imagine his father sending Gabe away from the table to wash better, then his mother checking to make sure Gabe had cleaned the sink after himself. She would probably throw the napkin he used into the incinerator when Gabe left.

Before letting him go, Gabe rolled Danny's head a few times across his belt buckle. Then he nudged him toward the coops and headed back to the plucking room to find Milt.

Danny approached the coops. The chickens crowded into the far corner. 40

"It's just me. I won't hurt you."

They kept backing up, bunching together and beginning to cry out. Danny stuck a finger in to attract them.

"Here, girls."

"Help!" they squawked.

"GET INNA THE OFFICE!" Milt yelled from behind him. Danny hadn't 45
heard him coming. "How many times I gotta tell you keep your hands to yourself? Here, home, everywhere. The hell am I gonna do with you, anyway?"

He threw an apron over Danny's head. Despite the fresh soap, he could still smell old blood on it.

"Now don't touch anything." He drew a knife from someplace beneath his apron. "You want to lose a finger, here, I'll chop it off for you."

Danny put his hands in his pants pockets. "I'm sorry."

The office was small and warm. The squat cash register filled most of the table. Above it was a shelf that held the old radio. Danny didn't like hearing it talk about the new H-bomb, so he climbed onto the table and turned the dial until he found a song he knew. "Hey there, you with the stars in your eyes." His mother could play that one on the piano. He climbed back down. There was a chair on wheels with a flattened cushion sheathed in old aprons. Danny sat in the chair, wheeled it over to the damp window, and wiped a circle clear to watch his father getting the market ready.

First, Milt reached back to slide his hand under the apron and draw out a 50
small plaid flask. He took a deep drink, replaced the flask, and rubbed his arms hard to warm up. Next, he tested the scales. He swept the entryway and put out a fresh roll of brown paper to wrap the dead chickens in. Finally, he lit a cigar, first biting off its tip and screwing on the brown plastic holder that was the same color as the floor of the market.

The last time Danny was here, it was midmorning when things started going wrong. He remembered his father glaring at him from in front of the coops. The knife he used to cut the chickens' necks gleamed in his hand.

By noon, Milt had called Faye to come down on the bus and get Danny out of there. When his mother arrived, Danny had burst into tears and his father had thrown a rag at him covered in blood and feather juice.

Now, Danny wanted to stay out of trouble. He just wished he knew what he'd done wrong last time.

That sort of thing kept happening. Last Sunday, Danny had done things to get his father so angry that Milt had kicked his ass like a football. Danny landed on his knees against the bed. His mother had quickly come over to smooth out the bedspread and lead Danny out of the room.

Milt yanked open the door to a coop. He snatched a capon's feet and swept him facedown through the gate.

Wrists snapping, arms flapping faster than wings, he wrapped the legs above the spurs with wire and dangled the capon from the scale's hook.

"Four pounds six," he called over his shoulder.

The old woman, who looked like Grandmother Webb, shrugged her shoulders. She looked over toward the office, where Danny peered back at her.

"Why not?" she said.

Milt produced a knife from under his apron and cut the capon's neck. He took it back to Gabe and then came back to talk to the woman.

Danny came out of the office to watch Gabe thrust the bird, squawking blood, legs kicking air, slit neck down into a can to die. Gabe turned to the plucking machine. He removed a pullet he'd been cleaning for someone who said she'd pick it up at ten.

He addressed Danny without looking at him, as though they'd been chatting all morning. "So, you gonna be a lawyer when you grow up?"

"I don't know." Danny couldn't stop watching the capon's legs. "Maybe."

"A doctor?"

The bird let out a weird rattle and was still. "I don't think so."

"Right, too much school." Gabe put the capon into the plucker and turned the machine on. Danny stood on his toes to watch the feathers fly. "You like school?"

"Can I take her out to my dad?"

"This is an it, not a her." He lifted the carcass and brushed it vigorously. "But sure, do it."

He ripped paper from the fat roll and wrapped the capon quickly. Danny carried the spotted package, taped shut, back to the office. Milt came in to ring the sale.

"Nice job," he said, patting Danny on the head.

When Milt left to hand the package over to the old woman, Danny ran a hand through his hair to check for feather juice.

He didn't see anything special about the man. It was just before noon when he sauntered in, hands in his jacket pockets, and smiled an anteater's jagged smile.

Milt jerked a thumb over his shoulder like an umpire signaling an out. The man, dressed in a gray overcoat and a hat with one long gray feather, nodded and walked back toward the plucking room.

Gabe burst out of the room at once, as though ejected. He wiped his hands on a towel strung through his apron string, then hurried to the front. He whispered something to Milt, who shook his head.

75 Danny watched his father come toward the office. Milt's face was suddenly drawn tight, as it had looked on Sunday just before he'd kicked Danny's ass. Danny took a few steps back from the office door until he reached the wall, wondering what he'd done wrong. He hadn't been letting his nose touch the glass, hadn't spoken, he hadn't handled anything. (Except the radio! Milt would hear the music!)

Milt stuck his head into the office, but didn't enter. "Stay put," he hissed. "I'm going out back for a while."

Danny was so relieved he wasn't the cause of his father's anger that he couldn't ask any questions. Milt went to where the stranger was waiting, brushed by him without a word, and disappeared.

Danny didn't know Gabe was allowed to wait on customers. He worried that people wouldn't want to buy anything from a man who looked so gory. If somebody came, Danny thought he'd better go out and keep an eye on things.

No one did, though. Gabe stood outside in the morning sun, eyes shut and head tilted skyward. Soon Remo Santselmo, the man who owned the meat market next door, came to stand with Gabe, who accepted the proffered flask and drank deeply as Milt had earlier.

80 It was still cool, despite the growing brightness. Gabe offered Mr. Santselmo a Lucky Strike.

Danny hung back in the shadows of the coops, watching the men pass time. Mr. Santselmo, who always traded sausage for chicken with Milt on Friday nights, seemed angry.

"*Criminale,*" he muttered. "Let's talk about something else, huh? We don't gotta talk about those bastards."

"Sure, sure. What about the Series? You ever see anything like that catch?"

"Willie Mays, you know he's gonna do good. That Dusty Rhodes, he's the guy wins you a Series."

85 "The pitching. Indians give us twenty-one runs in four games. You and me coulda won it, we don't need no Willie Mays."

"The hell with it. I like Brooklyn next year anyhow." Mr. Santselmo threw his cigarette down and stomped on it. "How much longer's Milt gonna put up with this? Makes me embarrassed I'm Italian, even. Goddam."

"Milt's tough."

"That don't make no difference. We're all tough. I'm tough. I been tough since Brooklyn was still a city. Hell, now you can't make no money at all. You gotta keep giving to these people more all the time."

A woman entering Mr. Santselmo's market brought the conversation to a stop. Gabe watched him leave, then turned around and saw Danny standing there. He looked over the boy's shoulder and frowned. Danny understood. He went back into the office and stood as far from the door as he could.

90 Later that evening, Danny watched from the floor of their room as his parents dressed for a costume party. It was his mother's annual Raskin Cousins' Club meeting, a tradition every Halloween weekend. He stayed out of their way, but listened to everything they said. The air was filled with the scent of Old Spice and rye whiskey.

"What's Red going as this year?" Milt asked. It was his father's mild voice, the one Danny hadn't heard since first thing in the morning.

"Oh, you know Red. My brother wouldn't tell me the truth if I begged him."

"Probably doesn't even know, himself. I bet you his commie wife plans their whole life."

"Sasha's no communist. What's wrong with you? She's simply a nice rich girl from Scarsdale, which you know perfectly well."

"Got a name like a Cossack is all I know. Whispers all the time, like she's got something to hide."

Last year, Danny remembered, they'd dressed as gangsters. Milt had worn an overcoat and hat like the man who'd come to the market. He carried a bottle of liquor under his arm. Danny had thought they'd decided not to wear costumes. But Faye explained that his father was pretending to be Al Capone and she, with a fox stole around her neck and rolling pin in her hand, was his moll.

This year, Danny thought the costumes were much better. His father had a mustache painted on and wore a gold satiny cape that matched his crown. He looked like some movie star king. Faye had made a queen costume for herself out of sky-blue material seasoned with sequins.

"We're the Royal Family," she said.

"Right," Milt grumbled. "King Tut and his wife Nut."

All day, she'd been practicing her queen dance. She showed Danny the routine, putting her hands together above her head, shutting her eyes, and bobbing like a turtle going in and out of its shell. Her eyes were encased in black triangles that matched her thickened lips.

"You're doing your head wrong," Milt said.

"What do you know about it?"

"I know that your head should go side to side."

"Mr. King of Egypt, the dance expert."

"I've seen it done right, if that's what you mean. Seen it lots of times."

Faye turned away from Milt and spoke to Danny. "Your father, whose idea of world travel is a weekend at Lake George, is going to tell *me* about foreign culture. This is a man who thinks Picasso is some kind of flower."

"Drop it," Milt said. "What do I care if your damn cousins think you're a turtle."

Danny kept playing with his baseball cards on the floor. He had them spread into a field between this parents' beds. Using a pencil for a bat and penny for a ball, he conducted a full nine-inning game, announcing each at-bat to himself in Red Barber's Mississippi accent.

He liked to be near his parents as they prepared to go out, even if they argued. He had to fight back tears when Mrs. Auer, the gray-haired baby-sitter, would arrive from the sixth floor and make him go out into the living room.

"Who's better, Dad? Johnny Antonelli or Johnny Podres?"

"Podres. No doubt about it. I mean, Antonelli's Italian."

"Mr. Santselmo thinks Antonelli won the pennant for the Giants last year. I heard him tell Gabe."

"Well, Mr. Santselmo doesn't know anything about anything. Not baseball, not business, not anything. He's as bad as Alf Honts, but at least he sells sausage instead of poultry."

"Who was that man who came in today when you had to leave? I didn't like him."

Milt looked over at Faye, who was watching them in the mirror. He spoke to her, not Danny, when he said, "Guy who used to be my friend."

"Now what is he?"

"He told me today he's the future. Now go answer the door, pal. Mrs. Auer's here."

Understanding

1. How does Danny reveal the character of his father? What actions are most revealing?
2. As a character in this story, does Danny have any limitations that influence his interpretation of the persons or events in it? If so, what are they and how do they influence it?
3. The sociologist Christopher Lasch, in his book *Haven in a Heartless World,* has suggested that families can and should be a refuge from the harshness of the outside world. Is this the case with Danny's family? What drives the relationships in his family?
4. When Danny asks his father, "Who was that man who came in today . . . ?" Milton Webb responds, "He told me today he's the future." What does he mean?
5. In what ways does the title of this story describe the Webbs?

Responding

1. Milton and Faye Webb are obviously a large part of Danny's socialization, but other characters also play a role: his brother, Ricky; Mr. Alfred J. Honts; Gabriel Kozey; and even the members of the Brooklyn Dodgers. Describe at least two individuals, other than members of your immediate family, who played a similar role in your life. Whom have *you* influenced in this way?
2. Some critics of contemporary society suggest that family ties, especially in advanced industrial societies like the United States, may be loosening. They point to the greater varieties of family structure, the general acceptance of divorce and remarriage, and the increase in sexual freedom as evidence of this relaxation in the bonds of kinship. Indicate your disagreement or agreement with this conclusion using examples and evidence to support your position.
3. Choose a television show, a movie, a play, or a song that you think best describes the state of family organization in America today. Explain why you think your choice exemplifies it.

Connecting

1. Compare Danny's description of his father to other father-son relationships described in this anthology, for example, Hamill's in "Steel Memories from Father's Toolbox" (chapter one), Carcaterra's in "Loving Your Enemy" (chapter two), or Spiegelman's in "Worse Than My Darkest Dreams" (chapter two).
2. Do you see any places in this selection where the Webb family is, as Scarf states in "The Beavers Scale of Family Health and Competence" (earlier in this chapter), "trapped in fixed patterns of responding and in non-negotiable positions"? Describe them. On which level of the Beavers Scale would you place the Webb family?

The Kiss

Julia Alvarez

As other immigrant writers have said, you have to leave home to uncover what is so special about it. Only from a distance can you know its lasting effect on you. Julia Alvarez, a professor of English at Middlebury College in Vermont, explores what she lost and what she found through the stories of four sisters in her first novel, *How the Garcia Girls Lost Their Accent,* from which "The Kiss" is excerpted. Caught between the new world and the old, Sofía reveals her relationship to her father.

When she was ten, Alvarez and her parents were forced to leave the Dominican Republic shortly before its dictator, General Rafael Leónidas Trujillo, was assassinated. Since writing about the Garcia girls, Alvarez has written a second book, *In the Time of the Butterflies,* the story of four beautiful, convent-educated Dominican sisters, three of whom were believed to have been assassinated by Trujillo. On November 25, 1960, their bodies were found near their wrecked Jeep at the bottom of a 150-foot cliff on the north coast of the island. Because these sisters were so well loved, and also known as fervent opponents of Trujillo's regime, Alvarez wanted their story told. Like the Garcia girls stories, *In the Time of the Butterflies* depicts a family struggling with its beliefs and bridging its needs to survive in its beloved homeland. Her most recent book is *¡Yo!*

As explored further in "In Public and Private" later in this chapter, there are joys and tensions inherent in belonging to two cultures. A third experience—one's family—is yet another cultural layer in working out an identity. The following selection is a father-daughter story with a surprise at the end.

Even after they'd been married and had their own families and often couldn't make it for other occasions, the four daughters always came home for their father's birthday. They would gather together, without husbands, would-be husbands, or bring-home work. For this too was part of the tradition: the daughters came home alone. The apartment was too small for everyone, the father argued. Surely their husbands could spare them for one overnight? 1

The husbands would just as soon have not gone to their in-laws, but they felt annoyed at the father's strutting. "When's he going to realize you've grown up? You sleep with us!"

"He's almost seventy, for God's sake!" the daughters said, defending the father. They were passionate women, but their devotions were like roots; they were sunk into the past towards the old man.

So for one night every November the daughters turned back into their father's girls. In the cramped living room, surrounded by the dark oversized furniture from the old house they grew up in, they were children again in a smaller, simpler version of the world. There was the prodigal scene at the door. The father opened his arms wide and welcomed them in his broken English: "This is your home, and never you should forget it." Inside, the mother fussed at them—their sloppy clothes; their long, loose hair; their looking tired, too skinny, too made up, and so on.

5 After a few glasses of wine, the father started in on what should be done if he did not live to see his next birthday. "Come on, Papi," his daughters coaxed him, as if it were a modesty of his, to perish, and they had to talk him into staying alive. After his cake and candles, the father distributed bulky envelopes that felt as if they were padded, and they were, no less than several hundreds in bills, tens and twenties and fives, all arranged to face the same way, the top one signed with the father's name, branding them his. Why not checks? the daughters would wonder later, gossiping together in the bedroom, counting their money to make sure the father wasn't playing favorites. Was there some illegality that the father stashed such sums away? Was he—none of the daughters really believed this, but to contemplate it was a wonderful little explosion in their heads—was he maybe dealing drugs or doing abortions in his office?

At the table there was always the pretense of trying to give the envelopes back. "No, no, Papi, it's *your* birthday, after all."

The father told them there was plenty more where that had come from. The revolution in the old country had failed. Most of his comrades had been killed or bought off. He had escaped to this country. And now it was every man for himself, so what he made was for his girls. The father never gave his daughters money when their husbands were around. "They might receive the wrong idea," the father once said, and although none of the daughters knew specifically what the father meant, they all understood what he was saying to them: Don't bring the men home for my birthday.

But this year, for his seventieth birthday, the youngest daughter, Sofía, wanted the celebration at her house. Her son had been born that summer, and she did not want to be traveling in November with a four-month-old and her little girl. And yet, she, of all the daughters, did not want to be the absent one because for the first time since she'd run off with her husband six years ago, she and her father were on speaking terms. In fact, the old man had been out to see her—or really to see his grandson—twice. It was a big deal that Sofía had had a son. He was the first male born into the family in two generations. In fact, the baby was to be named for the grandfather—Carlos—and his middle name was to be Sofía's maiden name, and so, what the old man had never hoped for with his "harem of four girls," as he liked to joke, his own name was to be kept going in this new country!

During his two visits, the grandfather had stood guard by the crib all day, speaking to little Carlos. "Charles the Fifth; Charles Dickens; Prince Charles." He enumerated the names of famous Charleses in order to stir up genetic ambition in the boy. "Charlemagne," he cooed at him also, for the baby was large and big-boned with blond fuzz on his pale pink skin, and blue eyes just like his German father's. All the grandfather's Caribbean fondness for a male heir and for fair Nordic looks had surfaced. There was now good blood in the family against a future bad choice by one of its women.

"You can be president, you were born here," the grandfather crooned. 10
"You can go to the moon, maybe even to Mars by the time you are of my age."

His macho babytalk brought back Sofía's old antagonism towards her father. How obnoxious for him to go on and on like that while beside him stood his little granddaughter, wide-eyed and sad at all the things her baby brother, no bigger than one of her dolls, was going to be able to do just because he was a boy. "Make him stop, please," Sofía asked her husband. Otto was considered the jolly, good-natured one among the brothers-in-law. "The camp counselor," his sisters-in-law teased. Otto approached the grandfather. Both men looked fondly down at the new Viking.

"You can be as great a man as your father," the grandfather said. This was the first compliment the father-in-law had ever paid any son-in-law in the family. There was no way Otto was going to mess with the old man now. "He is a good boy, is he not, Papi?" Otto's German accent thickened with affection. He clapped his hand on his father-in-law's shoulders. They were friends now.

But though the father had made up with his son-in-law, there was still a strain with his own daughter. When he had come to visit, she embraced him at the door, but he stiffened and politely shrugged her off. "Let me put down these heavy bags, Sofía." He had never called her by her family pet name, Fifi, even when she lived at home. He had always had problems with his maverick youngest, and her running off hadn't helped. "I don't want loose women in my family," he had cautioned all his daughters. Warnings were delivered communally, for even though there was usually the offending daughter of the moment, every woman's character could use extra scolding.

His daughters had had to put up with this kind of attitude in an unsympathetic era. They grew up in the late sixties. Those were the days when wearing jeans and hoop earrings, smoking a little dope, and sleeping with their classmates were considered political acts against the military-industrial complex. But standing up to their father was a different matter altogether. Even as grown women, they lowered their voices in their father's earshot when alluding to their bodies' pleasure. Professional women, too, all three of them, with degrees on the wall!

Sofía was the one without the degrees. She had always gone her own way, 15
though she downplayed her choices, calling them accidents. Among the four sisters, she was considered the plain one, with her tall, big-boned body and large-featured face. And yet, she was the one with "non-stop boyfriends," her sisters joked, not without wonder and a little envy. They admired her and were always asking her advice about men. The third daughter had shared a room with Sofía growing up. She liked to watch her sister move about their room, getting ready for bed, brushing and arranging her hair in a clip before easing herself under the sheets as if someone were waiting for her there. In the dark, Fifi gave off a fresh, wholesome smell of clean flesh. It gave solace to the third daughter, who was always so tentative and terrified and had such troubles with men. Her sister's breathing in the dark room was like having a powerful, tamed animal at the foot of her bed ready to protect her.

The youngest daughter had been the first to leave home. She had dropped out of college, in love. She had taken a job as a secretary and was living at home because her father had threatened to disown her if she moved out on her own. On her vacation she went to Colombia because her current boyfriend was going, and since she couldn't spend an overnight with him in New York, she had to travel thousands of miles to sleep with him. In Bogotá, they discovered that once they could enjoy the forbidden fruit, they lost their appetite. They broke up. She met a tourist on the street, some guy from Germany, just like that. The woman had not been without a boyfriend for more than a few days of her adult life. They fell in love.

On her way home, she tossed her diaphragm in the first bin at Kennedy Airport. She was taking no chances. But the father could tell. For months, he kept an eye out. First chance he got, he went through her drawers "looking for my nail clippers," and there he found her packet of love letters. The German man's small, correct handwriting mentioned unmentionable things—bed conversations were recreated on the thin blue sheets of aerogramme letters.

"What is the meaning of this?" The father shook the letters in her face. They had been sitting around the table, the four sisters, gabbing, and the father had come in, beating the packet against his leg like a whip, the satin hair ribbon unraveling where he had untied it, and then wrapped it round and round in a mad effort to contain his youngest daughter's misbehavior.

"Give me those!" she cried, lunging at him.

The father raised his hand with the letters above both their heads like the 20
Statue of Liberty with her freedom torch, but he had forgotten this was the daughter who was as tall as he was. She clawed his arm down and clutched the letters to herself as if they were her baby he'd plucked from her breast. It seemed a biological rather than a romantic fury.

After his initial shock, the father regained his own fury. "Has he deflowered you? That's what I want to know. Have you gone behind the palm trees? Are you dragging my good name through the dirt, that is what I would like to know!" The father was screaming crazily in the youngest daughter's face, question after question, not giving the daughter a chance to answer. His face grew red with fury, but hers was more terrible in its impassivity, a pale ivory moon, pulling and pulling at the tide of his anger, until it seemed he might drown in his own outpouring of fury.

Her worried sisters stood up, one at each arm, coaxing him like nurses, another touching the small of his back as if he were a feverish boy. "Come on, Papi, simmer down now. Take it easy. Let's talk. We're a family, after all."

"Are you a whore?" the father interrogated his daughter. There was spit on the daughter's cheeks from the closeness of his mouth to her face.

"It's none of your fucking business!" she said in a low, ugly-sounding voice like the snarl of an animal who could hurt him. "You have no right, no right at all, to go through my stuff or read my mail!" Tears spurted out of her eyes, her nostrils flared.

The father's mouth opened in a little zero of shock. Quietly, Sofía drew 25
herself up and left the room. Usually, in her growing-up tantrums, this daughter would storm out of the house and come back hours later, placated, the

sweetness in her nature reasserted, bearing silly gifts for everyone in the family, refrigerator magnets, little stuffed hairballs with roll-around eyeballs.

But this time they could hear her upstairs, opening and closing her drawers, moving back and forth from the bed to the closet. Downstairs, the father prowled up and down the length of the rooms, his three daughters caging him while the other great power in the house, tidily—as if she had all the time in the world—buttoned and folded all her clothes, packed all her bags, and left the house forever. She got herself to Germany somehow and got the man to marry her. To throw in the face of the father who was so ambitious for presidents and geniuses in the family, the German nobody turned out to be a world-class chemist. But the daughter's was not a petty nature. What did she care what Otto did for a living when she had shown up at his door and offered herself to him.

"I can love you as much as anybody else," she said. "If you can do the same for me, let's get married."

"Come on in and let's talk," Otto had said, or so the story went.

"Yes or no," Sofía answered. Just like that on a snowy night someone at his door and a cold draft coming in. "I couldn't let her freeze," Otto boasted later.

"Like hell you couldn't!" Sofía planted a large hand on his shoulder, and anyone could see how it must be between them in the darkness of their lovemaking. On their honeymoon, they traveled to Greece, and Sofía sent her mother and father and sisters postcards like any newlywed. "We're having a great time. Wish you were here."

But the father kept to his revenge. For months no one could mention the daughter's name in his presence, though he kept calling them all "Sofía" and quickly correcting himself. When the daughter's baby girl was born, his wife put her foot down. Let him carry his grudge to the grave, *she* was going out to Michigan (where Otto had relocated) to see her first grandchild!

Last minute, the father relented and went along, but he might as well have stayed away. He was grim and silent the whole visit, no matter how hard Sofía and her sisters tried to engage him in conversation. Banishment was better than this cold shoulder. But Sofía tried again. On the old man's next birthday, she appeared at the apartment with her little girl. "Surprise!" There was a reconciliation of sorts. The father first tried to shake hands with her. Thwarted, he then embraced her stiffly before taking the baby in his arms under the watchful eye of his wife. Every year after that, the daughter came for her father's birthday, and in the way of women, soothed and stitched and patched over the hurt feelings. But there it was under the social fabric, the raw wound. The father refused to set foot in his daughter's house. They rarely spoke; the father said public things to her in the same tone of voice he used with his sons-in-law.

But now his seventieth birthday was coming up, and he had agreed to have the celebration at Sofía's house. The christening for little Carlos was scheduled for the morning, so the big event would be Papi Carlos's party that night. It was a coup for the youngest daughter to have gathered the scattered family in the Midwest for a weekend. But the real coup was how Sofía had managed to have the husbands included this year. The husbands are coming, the husbands are coming, the sisters joked. Sofía passed the compliment off on little Carlos. The boy had opened the door for the other men in the family.

But the coup the youngest daughter most wanted was to reconcile with her father in a big way. She would throw the old man a party he wouldn't forget. For weeks she planned what they would eat, where they would all sleep, the entertainment. She kept calling up her sisters with every little thing to see what they thought. Mostly, they agreed with her: a band, paper hats, balloons, buttons that broadcast THE WORLD'S GREATEST DAD. Everything overdone and silly and devoted the way they knew the father would like it. Sofía briefly considered a belly dancer or a girl who'd pop out of a cake. But the third daughter, who had become a feminist in the wake of her divorce, said she considered such locker-room entertainments offensive. A band with music was what she'd pitch in on; her married sisters could split it three ways if they wanted to be sexists. With great patience, Sofía created a weekend that would offend no one. They were going to have a good time in her house for the old man's seventieth, if it killed her!

The night of the party, the family ate an early dinner before the band and the guests arrived. Each daughter toasted both Carloses. The sons-in-law called big Carlos, "Papi." Little Carlos, looking very much like a little girl in his long, white christening gown, bawled the whole time, and his poor mother had not a moment's peace between serving the dinner she'd prepared for the family and giving him his. The phone kept ringing, relatives from the old country calling with congratulations for the old man. The toasts the daughters had prepared kept getting interrupted. Even so, their father's eyes glazed with tears more than once as the four girls went through their paces.

He looked old tonight, every single one of his seventy years was showing. Perhaps it was that too much wine had darkened his complexion, and his white hair and brows and mustache stood out unnaturally white. He perked up a little for his gifts, though, gadgets and books and desk trophies from his daughters, and cards with long notes penned inside "to the best, dearest Papi in the world," each one of which the old man wanted to read out loud. "No you don't, Papi, they're private!" his daughters chimed in, crowding around him, wanting to spare each other the embarrassment of having their gushing made public. His wife gave him a gold watch. The third daughter teased that that's how companies retired their employees, but when her mother made angry eyes at her, she stopped. Then there were the men gifts—belts and credit card wallets from the sons-in-law.

"Things I really need." The father was gracious. He stacked up the gift cards and put them away in his pocket to pore over later. The sons-in-law all knew that the father was watching them, jealously, for signs of indifference or self-interest. As for his girls, even after their toasts were given, the gifts opened, and the father had borne them out of the way with the help of his little granddaughter, even then, the daughters felt that there was something else he had been waiting for which they had not yet given him.

But there was still plenty of party left to make sure he got whatever it was he needed for the long, lonely year ahead. The band arrived, three middle-aged men, each with a silver wave slicked back with too much hair cream.

DANNY AND HIS BOYS set up a placard with their name against the fireplace. There was one on an accordion, another on a fiddle, and a third was miscellaneous on maracas and triangle and drums when needed. They played movie themes, polkas, anything familiar you could hum along to; the corny songs were all dedicated to "Poppy" or "his lovely lady." The father liked the band. "Nice choice," he congratulated Otto. The youngest daughter's temper flared easily with all she'd had to drink and eat. She narrowed her eyes at her smiling husband and put a hand on her hip. As if Otto had lifted a finger during her long months of planning!

The guests began to arrive, many with tales of how they'd gotten lost on the way; the suburbs were dark and intricate like mazes with their courts and cul-de-sacs. Otto's unmarried colleagues looked around the room, trying to single out the recently divorced sister they'd heard so much about. But there was no one as beautiful and funny and talented as Sofía had boasted the third oldest would be. Most of these friends were half in love with Sofía anyway, and it was she they sought out in the crowded room.

40 There was a big chocolate cake in the shape of a heart set out on the long buffet with seventy-one candles—one for good luck. The granddaughter and her aunts had counted them and planted them diagonally across the heart, joke candles that wouldn't blow out. Later, they burned a flaming arrow that would not quit. The bar was next to the heart and by midnight when the band broke out again with "Happy Birthday, Poppy," everyone had had too much to eat and drink.

They'd been playing party games on and off all night. The band obliged with musical chairs, but after two of the dining room chairs were broken, they left off playing. The third daughter, especially, had gotten out of hand, making musical chairs of every man's lap. The father sat without speaking. He gazed upon the scene disapprovingly.

In fact, the older the evening got, the more withdrawn the father had become. Surrounded by his daughters and their husbands and fancy, intelligent, high-talking friends, he seemed to be realizing that he was just an old man sitting in their houses, eating up their roast lamb, impinging upon their lives. The daughters could almost hear his thoughts inside their own heads. He, who had paid to straighten their teeth and smooth the accent out of their English in expensive schools, he was nothing to them now. Everyone in this room would survive him, even the silly men in the band who seemed like boys—imagine making a living out of playing birthday songs! How could they ever earn enough money to give their daughters pretty clothes and send them to Europe during the summers so they wouldn't get bored? Where were the world's men anymore? Every last one of his sons-in-law was a kid; he could see that clearly. Even Otto, the famous scientist, was a schoolboy with a pencil, doing his long division. The new son-in-law he even felt sorry for—he could see this husband would give out on his strong-willed second daughter. Already she had him giving her backrubs and going for cigarettes in the middle of the night. But he needn't worry about his girls. Or his wife, for that matter. There she sat, pretty and slim as a girl, smiling coyly at everyone when a song was dedicated to her. Eight, maybe nine, months he gave her of widowhood, and then she'd find someone to grow old with on his life insurance.

The third daughter thought of a party game to draw her father out. She took one of the baby's soft receiving blankets, blindfolded her father, and led him to a chair at the center of the room. The women clapped. The men sat down. The father pretended he didn't understand what all his daughters were up to. "How does one play this game, Mami?"

"You're on your own, Dad," the mother said, laughing. She was the only one in the family who called him by his American name.

"Are you ready, Papi?" the oldest asked.

"I am perfect ready," he replied in his heavy accent.

"Okay, now, guess who this is," the oldest said. She always took charge. This is how they worked things among the daughters.

The father nodded, his eyebrows shot up. He held on to his chair, excited, a little scared, like a boy about to be asked a hard question he knows the answer to.

The oldest daughter motioned to the third daughter, who tiptoed into the circle the women had made around the old man. She gave him a daughterly peck on the cheek.

"Who was that, Papi?" the oldest asked.

He was giggling with pleasure and could not get the words out at first. He had had too much to drink. "That was Mami," he said in a coy little voice.

"No! Wrong!" all the women cried out.

"Carla?" he guessed the oldest. He was going down the line. "Wrong!" More shouts.

"Sandi? Yoyo?"

"You guessed it," his third oldest said.

The women clapped; some bent over in hilarious laughter. Everyone had had too much to drink. And the old man was having his good time too.

"Okay, here's another coming at you." The eldest took up the game again. She put her index finger to her lips, gave everyone a meaningful glance, quietly circled the old man, and kissed him from behind on top of his head. Then she tiptoed back to where she had been standing when she had first spoken. "Who was that, Papi?" she asked, extra innocent.

"Mami?" His voice rode up, exposed and vulnerable. Then it sank back into its certainties. "That was Mami."

"Count me out," his wife said from the couch where she'd finally given in to exhaustion.

The father never guessed any of the other women in the room. That would have been disrespectful. Besides, their strange-sounding American names were hard to remember and difficult to pronounce. Still he got the benefit of their kisses under cover of his daughters. Down the line, the father went each time: "Carla?" "Sandi?" "Yoyo?" Sometimes, he altered the order, put the third daughter first or the oldest one second.

Sofía had been in the bedroom, tending to her son, who was wild with all the noise in the house tonight. She came back into the living room, buttoning her dress front, and happened upon the game. "Ooh." She rolled her eyes. "It's getting raunchy in here, ha!" She worked her hips in a mock rotation, and the men all laughed. She thrust her girlfriends into the circle and whispered to her little girl to plant the next kiss on her grandfather's nose. The women all pecked and puckered at the old man's face. The second daughter sat briefly on his lap and clucked him under the chin. Every time the father took a wrong guess, the youngest daughter laughed loudly. But soon, she noticed that he never guessed her name. After all her hard work, she was not to be included in his daughter count. Damn him! She'd take her turn and make him know it was her!

Quickly, she swooped into the circle and gave the old man a wet, open-mouthed kiss in his ear. She ran her tongue in the whorls of his ear and nibbled the tip. Then she moved back.

"Oh la la," the oldest said, laughing. "Who was that, Papi?"

The old man did not answer. The smile that had played on his lips throughout the game was gone. He sat up, alert. There was a long pause; everyone leaned forward, waiting for the father to begin with his usual, "Mami?"

But the father did not guess his wife's name. He tore at his blindfold as if 65
it were a contagious body whose disease he might catch. The receiving blanket fell in a soft heap beside his chair. His face had darkened with shame at having his pleasure aroused in public by one of his daughters. He looked from one to the other. His gaze faltered. On the face of his youngest was the brilliant, impassive look he remembered from when she had snatched her love letters out of his hands.

"That's enough of that," he commanded in a low, furious voice. And sure enough, his party was over.

Understanding

1. Thinking in sociological terms of the functions of families, which role did the grandfather play in relation to his grandson, his granddaughter, and his daughters? What sorts of things did he say or do to "socialize" Sofía's sexual behavior?
2. In the fight Sofía's father was concerned about her virginity whereas Sofía was concerned about her privacy—he had read her love letters. Virginity versus privacy—these values were the issue. Are these two values at an equal level in this selection?
3. What changed the old man's mind about Sofía?
4. What role does Sofía's mother play in the story?

Responding

1. How did Sofía's last action strike you? Was it authentic? Why did she choose to do that in particular?
2. Have you ever been accused of something because someone in authority found letters that revealed your secret life? Write about what you were

accused of in relation to your thoughts about your right to the privacy. Thinking of "The Kiss," what does your personal value system say about virginity and privacy? Where are they in the hierarchy of your values?

Connecting

1. Which of the Beavers Scale descriptions fit the Garcia family? Support your opinion with examples from the text.
2. What similarities or differences do you see in this family and Cheever's?

WRITING OPTION: Family Ties

In response to the Responding questions in the "Family Ties" section of this chapter, choose a piece that you became particularly involved in writing. Analyze the questions and answers that arose in the course of your writing. Revise the piece as an essay or as a narrative, using any of the "Family Ties" readings as models. Be sure that you are included as a character *and* as the writer who provides an analysis and ultimate point. Your essay should treat the reader to a unique view of a family's impact on one of its members. Think about this question as you begin to write: How did your family—as a community—provide clues to your identity?

What is learning? How and where does it take place? On the surface these questions seem simplistic, and easy answers are ready on the tongue. But thoughtfully considered, our definitions of *learning* change over time as we recognize that we *have* learned—sometimes in schools, others in unlikely settings or on serendipitous occasions.

Deciding *where* learning takes place is negotiable according to our definition of it. And *how* it takes place is ever a mystery, though educators from Plato to modern educational theorists have continued to dissect how the magic of learning takes place. Most would agree, however, that learning *has* taken place when, on the one hand, we have mastered a skill or, on the other, we have had a brilliant burst of insight—a breakthrough where new knowledge powerfully illuminates or augments the old. It is no wonder people say that learning is one of the peak experiences in life.

We may never know exactly how learning takes place, but growth and development require that we continually learn and that we hone our knowledge to fit our needs or desires for survival. In identifying moments of insight or synthesis, we have for a time come upon the excitement of being somehow changed or altered by our new knowledge. And while true that powerful learning may occur when we are struggling alone in the wee hours of the morning, or solitary and vulnerable on a dark street in a foreign country, our thoughts, insights, and epiphanies are generally provoked by an issue, a question, or a situation raised *because we are part of a community.*

"Learning Communities" investigates this idea; the readings in this section present various explorations into the value and responsibilities of education, illustrating how indelible moments of truth have taken place in the presence of others, in communities. The narratives of Leslie Marmon Silko and Mike Rose explore the learning communities that formed their early ways of knowing; Frank Conroy demonstrates how learning is making connections among ordinary events. Michel de Montaigne presents his criteria for his rules of a stimulating conversation and for the types of people with whom he enjoys sparring—those who make his mind soar; and finally Plato advises us of our responsibility once we have learned—once we have seen the truth, the beautiful, the just, and the good.

Strong on insight, each of these readings opens a door to a community of learners. You may find yourself identifying with and learning from all of them. As the writers show, learning communities are very powerful. They will remind you of the ones to which you already belong.

Through the Stories We Hear Who We Are

Leslie Marmon Silko

Born in 1948, Leslie Marmon Silko grew up in Laguna Pueblo in New Mexico. In this essay her style and tone convey the authority of "insider writing" as she explores the storytelling history of her people.

Language creates our world view, and each language gives those who speak it the means of defining who they are in relation to the world they inhabit. In an earlier portion of "Through the Stories We Hear Who We Are," Silko explains that the English definition of *landscape*—"a portion of territory the eye can comprehend in a single view"—does not adequately describe the notion of landscape in Pueblo memory: the relationship between the people and their surroundings. The English definition, she writes, "assumes the viewer is somehow *outside* or *separate from* the territory he or she surveys." But for the Pueblo, "The land, the sky, and all that is within them—the landscape—includes human beings." Writing on the Pueblo definition of *landscape,* Silko's essay explores the history and functions of storytelling in Pueblo life.

All summer the people watch the west horizon, scanning the sky from south to north for rain clouds. Corn must have moisture at the time the tassels form. Otherwise pollination will be incomplete, and the ears will be stunted and shriveled. An inadequate harvest may bring disaster. Stories told at Hopi, Zuñi, and at Acoma and Laguna describe drought and starvation as recently as 1900. Precipitation in west-central New Mexico averages fourteen inches annually. The western pueblos are located at altitudes over 5,600 feet above sea level, where winter temperatures at night fall below freezing. Yet evidence of their presence in the high desert plateau country goes back ten thousand years. The ancient Pueblo people not only survived in this environment, but many years they thrived. In A.D. 1100 the people at Chaco Canyon had built cities with apartment buildings of stone five stories high. Their sophistication as sky-watchers was surpassed only by Mayan and Inca astronomers. Yet this vast complex of knowledge and belief, amassed for thousands of years, was never recorded in writing. 1

Instead, the ancient Pueblo people depended upon collective memory through successive generations to maintain and transmit an entire culture, a world view complete with proven strategies for survival. The oral narrative, or "story," became the medium in which the complex of Pueblo knowledge and belief was maintained. Whatever the event or the subject, the ancient people perceived the world and themselves within that world as part of an ancient continuous story composed of innumerable bundles of other stories.

The ancient Pueblo vision of the world was inclusive. The impulse was to leave nothing out. Pueblo oral tradition necessarily embraced all levels of human experience. Otherwise, the collective knowledge and beliefs comprising ancient Pueblo culture would have been incomplete. Thus stories about the Creation and Emergence of human beings and animals into this World continue to be retold each year for four days and four nights during the winter solstice. The "humma-hah" stories related events from the time long ago when human beings were still able to communicate with animals and other living things. But, beyond these two preceding categories, the Pueblo oral tradition knew no boundaries. Accounts of the appearance of the first Europeans in Pueblo country or of the tragic encounters between Pueblo people and Apache raiders were no more and no less important than stories about the biggest mule deer ever taken or adulterous couples surprised in cornfields and chicken coops. Whatever happened, the ancient people instinctively sorted events and details into a loose narrative structure. Everything became a story.

Traditionally everyone, from the youngest child to the oldest person, was expected to listen and to be able to recall or tell a portion, if only a small detail, from a narrative account or story. Thus the remembering and retelling were a communal process. Even if a key figure, an elder who knew much more than others, were to die unexpectedly, the system would remain intact. Through the efforts of a great many people, the community was able to piece together valuable accounts and crucial information that might otherwise have died with an individual.

Communal storytelling was a self-correcting process in which listeners 5
were encouraged to speak up if they noted an important fact or detail omitted. The people were happy to listen to two or three different versions of the same event or the same humma-hah story. Even conflicting versions of an incident were welcomed for the entertainment they provided. Defenders of each version might joke and tease one another, but seldom were there any direct confrontations. Implicit in the Pueblo oral tradition was the awareness that loyalties, grudges, and kinship must always influence the narrator's choices as she emphasizes to listeners this is the way *she* has always heard the story told. The ancient Pueblo people sought a communal truth, not an absolute. For them this truth lived somewhere within the web of differing versions, disputes over minor points, outright contradictions tangling with old feuds and village rivalries.

A dinner-table conversation, recalling a deer hunt forty years ago when the largest mule deer ever was taken, inevitably stimulates similar memories in listeners. But hunting stories were not merely after-dinner entertainment. These accounts contained information of critical importance about behavior and migration patterns of mule deer. Hunting stories carefully described key landmarks and locations of fresh water. Thus a deer-hunt story might also serve as a "map." Lost travelers, and lost piñon-nut gatherers, have been saved by sighting a rock formation they recognize only because they once heard a hunting story describing this rock formation.

The importance of cliff formations and water holes does not end with hunting stories. As offspring of the Mother Earth, the ancient Pueblo people could not conceive of themselves within a specific landscape. Location, or "place," nearly always plays a central role in the Pueblo oral narratives. Indeed, stories are most frequently recalled as people are passing by a specific geographical feature or the exact place where a story takes place. The precise date of the incident often is less important than the place or location of the happening. "Long, long ago," "a long time ago," "not too long ago," and "recently" are usually how stories are classified in terms of time. But the places where the stories occur are precisely located, and prominent geographical details recalled, even if the landscape is well-known to listeners. Often because the turning point in the narrative involved a peculiarity or special quality of a rock or tree or plant found only at that place. Thus, in the case of many of the Pueblo narratives, it is impossible to determine which came first: the incident or the geographical feature which begs to be brought alive in a story that features some unusual aspect of this location.

There is a giant sandstone boulder about a mile north of Old Laguna, on the road to Paguate. It is ten feet tall and twenty feet in circumference. When I was a child, and we would pass this boulder driving to Paguate village, someone usually made reference to the story about Kochininako, Yellow Woman, and the Estrucuyo, a monstrous giant who nearly ate her. The Twin Hero Brothers saved Kochininako, who had been out hunting rabbits to take home to feed her mother and sisters. The Hero Brothers had heard her cries just in time. The Estrucuyo had cornered her in a cave too small to fit its monstrous head. Kochininako had already thrown to the Estrucuyo all her rabbits, as well as her moccasins and most of her clothing. Still the creature had not been satisfied. After killing the Estrucuyo with their bows and arrows, the Twin Hero Brothers slit open the Estrucuyo and cut out its heart. They threw the heart as far as they could. The monster's heart landed there, beside the old trail to Paguate village, where the sandstone boulder rests now.

It may be argued that the existence of the boulder precipitated the creation of a story to explain it. But sandstone boulders and sandstone formations of strange shapes abound in the Laguna Pueblo area. Yet most of them do not have stories. Often the crucial element in a narrative is the terrain—some specific detail of the setting.

A high dark mesa rises dramatically from a grassy plain fifteen miles south- 10
east of Laguna, in an area known as Swanee. On the grassy plain one hundred and forty years ago, my great-grandmother's uncle and his brother-in-law were grazing their herd of sheep. Because visibility on the plain extends for over twenty miles, it wasn't until the two sheepherders came near the high dark mesa that the Apaches were able to stalk them. Using the mesa to obscure their approach, the raiders swept around from both ends of the mesa. My great-grandmother's relatives were killed, and the herd lost. The high dark mesa played a critical role: the mesa had compromised the safety which the openness of the plains had seemed to assure. Pueblo and Apache alike relied upon the terrain, the very earth herself, to give them protection and aid. Human activities or needs were maneuvered to fit the existing surroundings and conditions. I imagine the last afternoon of my distant ancestors as warm

and sunny for late September. They might have been traveling slowly, bringing the sheep closer to Laguna in preparation for the approach of colder weather. The grass was tall and only beginning to change from green to a yellow which matched the late-afternoon sun shining off it. There might have been comfort in the warmth and the sight of the sheep fattening on good pasture which lulled my ancestors into their fatal inattention. They might have had a rifle whereas the Apaches had only bows and arrows. But there would have been four or five Apache raiders, and the surprise attack would have canceled any advantage the rifles gave them.

Survival in any landscape comes down to making the best use of all available resources. On that particular September afternoon, the raiders made better use of the Swanee terrain than my poor ancestors did. Thus the high dark mesa and the story of the two lost Laguna herders became inextricably linked. The memory of them and their story resides in part with the high black mesa. For as long as the mesa stands, people within the family and clan will be reminded of the story of that afternoon long ago. Thus the continuity and accuracy of the oral narratives are reinforced by the landscape—and the Pueblo interpretation of that landscape is *maintained.*

Understanding

1. What counts as knowledge for a Pueblo? How is knowledge taught?
2. Is the conveyance of knowledge in Pueblo oral culture strictly storytelling, or is conversation in general also used? What's the difference between the two when "what is true" is being created by a group of people? What seems most important in a Pueblo story? Time? People? Place? Event? Does Pueblo culture intend to explain and describe events, or is its purpose to control them?
3. Do the Pueblo discover themselves or create themselves through storytelling? Why might this distinction matter?
4. What is the point of Silko's story about her great-grandmother's relatives? How is the landscape crucial to this story?
5. Is Pueblo storytelling practiced nowadays?

Responding

1. Philosopher Richard Rorty has written widely on the "postmodern experience" and how humans everywhere create our own world views—our situations. Contrary to early Western philosophical views, where reason and evidence contained the basis for learning and knowledge, Rorty asserts that *language* provides the conceptual starting point for all organized thought about the world; that is, we recognize as real only that for which we have language. Similarly, we create our lives and views of them because we have the language to do so. Is Silko's essay an instance of Rorty's claim? Explain.
2. Compare or contrast *your* primary learning community with Silko's. How did students learn about the world around them? What counted as "knowl-

edge" in that learning environment? How did you know? What was valuable about your "learning training"? What changes would you make to that community or pedagogy?

Connecting

In "Temperament Is Not Destiny" (chapter five), Goleman defines different kinds of intelligences. Which kind might the best Pueblo storytellers have?

I Just Wanna Be Average

Mike Rose

Plato said that each person who has seen a truth has the responsibility of providing those less fortunate with access to the same truth. Though we might debate the meaning of *truth* here, what Mike Rose demonstrates in *Lives on the Boundary* is a commitment to education for all America's students.

The only son of Italian immigrants, Rose grew up in south Los Angeles; "I Just Wanna Be Average" recounts his teenage schooling when he was placed by mistake on the vocational track, where he met kids who were figuring out ways to live up to the "Voc. Ed." image. Rose's story does not wallow in the stigmas—remedial, illiterate, intellectually deficient—placed on kids in the educational underclass; instead he tells his stories to show how the cycle of despair can be broken. He takes his truth to educators, parents, and policymakers in order to break the cycle of the self-fulfilling prophecy that so often handicaps young lives. Much of what he suggests resides in the exploitation of language, literature, expression, and untapped potential.

It's popular these days to claim you grew up on the streets. Men tell violent tales and romanticize the lessons violence brings. But, though it was occasionally violent, it wasn't the violence in south L.A. that marked me, for sometimes you can shake that ugliness off. What finally affected me was subtler, but more pervasive: I cannot recall a young person who was crazy in love or lost in work or one old person who was passionate about a cause or an idea. I'm not talking about an absence of energy—the street toughs and, for that fact, old Cheech had energy. And I'm not talking about an absence of decency, for my father was a thoughtful man. The people I grew up with were retired from jobs that rub away the heart or were working hard at jobs to keep their lives from caving in or were anchorless and in between jobs and spouses or were diving headlong into a barren tomorrow: junkies, alcoholics, and mean kids walking along Vermont looking to throw a punch. I developed a picture of human existence that rendered it short and brutish or sad and aimless or long and quiet with rewards like afternoon naps, the evening newspaper, walks around the block, occasional letters from children in other states. When, years later, I was introduced to humanistic psychologists like Abraham Maslow and Carl Rogers, with their visions of self-actualization, or even Freud with his sober dictum about love and work, it all sounded like a glorious fairy tale, a magical account of a world full of possibility, full of hope and empowerment. Sindbad and Cinderella couldn't have been more fanciful. 1

Budding manhood. Only adults talk about adolescence budding. Kids have no choice but to talk in extremes; they're being wrenched and buffeted, rabbit-punched from inside by systemic thugs. Nothing sweet and pastoral here. Kids become ridiculous and touching at one and the same time: passionate about the trivial, fixed before the mirror, yet traversing one of the most important rites of passage in their lives—liminal people, silly and profoundly human. Given my own expertise, I fantasized about concocting the fail-safe aphrodisiac that would bring Marianne Bilpusch, the cloakroom monitor, rushing into my arms or about commanding a squadron of bosomy, linguistically mysterious astronauts like Zsa Zsa Gabor. My parents used to say that their son would have the best education they could afford. Maybe I would be a doctor. There was a public school in our neighborhood and several Catholic schools to the west. They had heard that quality schooling meant private, Catholic schooling, so they somehow got the money together to send me to Our Lady of Mercy, fifteen or so miles southwest of Ninety-first and Vermont. So much for my fantasies. Most Catholic secondary schools then were separated by gender.

It took two buses to get to Our Lady of Mercy. The first started deep in South Los Angeles and caught me at midpoint. The second drifted through neighborhoods with trees, parks, big lawns, and lots of flowers. The rides were long but were livened up by a group of South L.A. veterans whose parents also thought that Hope had set up shop in the west end of the county. There was Christy Biggars, who, at sixteen, was dealing and was, according to rumor, a pimp as well. There were Bill Cobb and Johnny Gonzales, grease-pencil artists extraordinaire, who left Nembutal-enhanced swirls of "Cobb" and "Johnny" on the corrugated walls of the bus. And then there was Tyrrell Wilson. Tyrrell was the coolest kid I knew. He ran the dozens like a metric halfback, laid down a rap that outrhymed and outpointed Cobb, whose rap was good but not great—the curse of a moderately soulful kid trapped in white skin. But it was Cobb who would sneak a radio onto the bus, and thus underwrote his patter with Little Richard, Fats Domino, Chuck Berry, the Coasters, and Ernie K. Doe's mother-in-law, an awful woman who was "sent from down below." And so it was that Christy and Cobb and Johnny G. and Tyrrell and I and assorted others picked up along the way passed our days in the back of the bus, a funny mix brought together by geography and parental desire.

Entrance to school brings with it forms and releases and assessments. Mercy relied on a series of tests, mostly the Stanford-Binet, for placement, and somehow the results of my tests got confused with those of another student named Rose. The other Rose apparently didn't do very well, for I was placed in the vocational track, a euphemism for the bottom level. Neither I nor my parents realized what this meant. We had no sense that Business Math, Typing, and English–Level D were dead ends. The current spate of reports on the schools criticizes parents for not involving themselves in the education of their children. But how would someone like Tommy Rose, with his two years of Italian schooling, know what to ask? And what sort of pressure could an exhausted waitress apply? The error went undetected, and I remained in the vocational track for two years. What a place.

My homeroom was supervised by Brother Dill, a troubled and unstable 5
man who also taught freshman English. When his class drifted away from him,

which was often, his voice would rise in paranoid accusations, and occasionally he would lose control and shake or smack us. I hadn't been there two months when one of his brisk, face-turning slaps had my glasses sliding down the aisle. Physical education was also pretty harsh. Our teacher was a stubby ex-lineman who had played old-time pro ball in the Midwest. He routinely had us grabbing our ankles to receive his stinging paddle across our butts. He did that, he said, to make men of us. "Rose," he bellowed on our first encounter; me standing geeky in line in my baggy shorts. " 'Rose'? What the hell kind of name is that?"

"Italian, sir," I squeaked.

"Italian! Ho. Rose, do you know the sound a bag of shit makes when it hits the wall?"

"No, sir."

"Wop!"

Sophomore English was taught by Mr. Mitropetros. He was a large, bejew- 10
eled man who managed the parking lot at the Shrine Auditorium. He would crow and preen and list for us the stars he'd brushed against. We'd ask questions and glance knowingly and snicker, and all that fueled the poor guy to brag some more. Parking cars was his night job. He had little training in English, so his lesson plan for his day work had us reading the district's required text, *Julius Caesar,* aloud for the semester. We'd finish the play way before the twenty weeks was up, so he'd have us switch parts again and again and start again: Dave Snyder, the fastest guy at Mercy, muscling through Caesar to the breathless squeals of Calpurnia, as interpreted by Steve Fusco, a surfer who owned the school's most envied paneled wagon. Week ten and Dave and Steve would take on new roles, as would we all, and render a water-logged Cassius and a Brutus that are beyond my powers of description.

Spanish I—taken in the second year—fell into the hands of a new recruit. Mr. Montez was a tiny man, slight, five foot six at the most, soft-spoken and delicate. Spanish was a particularly rowdy class, and Mr. Montez was as prepared for it as a doily maker at a hammer throw. He would tap his pencil to a room in which Steve Fusco was propelling spitballs from his heavy lips, in which Mike Dweetz was taunting Billy Hawk, a half-Indian, half-Spanish, reed-thin, quietly explosive boy. The vocational track at Our Lady of Mercy mixed kids traveling in from South L.A. with South Bay surfers and a few Slavs and Chicanos from the harbors of San Pedro. This was a dangerous miscellany: surfers and hodads and South-Central blacks all ablaze to the metronomic tapping of Hector Montez's pencil.

One day Billy lost it. Out of the corner of my eye I saw him strike out with his right arm and catch Dweetz across the neck. Quick as a spasm, Dweetz was out of his seat, scattering desks, cracking Billy on the side of the head, right behind the eye. Snyder and Fusco and others broke it up, but the room felt hot and close and naked. Mr. Montez's tenuous authority was finally ripped to shreds, and I think everyone felt a little strange about that. The charade was over, and when it came down to it, I don't think any of the kids really wanted it to end this way. They had pushed and pushed and bullied their way into a freedom that both scared and embarrassed them.

Students will float to the mark you set. I and the others in the vocational classes were bobbing in pretty shallow water. Vocational education has aimed at increasing the economic opportunities of students who do not do well in our schools. Some serious programs succeed in doing that, and through exceptional teachers—like Mr. Gross in *Horace's Compromise*—students learn to develop hypotheses and troubleshoot, reason through a problem, and communicate effectively—the true job skills. The vocational track, however, is most often a place for those who are just not making it, a dumping ground for the disaffected. There were a few teachers who worked hard at education; young Brother Slattery, for example, combined a stern voice with weekly quizzes to try to pass along to us a skeletal outline of world history. But mostly the teachers had no idea of how to engage the imaginations of us kids who were scuttling along at the bottom of the pond.

And the teachers would have needed some inventiveness, for none of us was groomed for the classroom. It wasn't just that I didn't know things—didn't know how to simplify algebraic fractions, couldn't identify different kinds of clauses, bungled Spanish translations—but that I had developed various faulty and inadequate ways of doing algebra and making sense of Spanish. Worse yet, the years of defensive tuning out in elementary school had given me a way to escape quickly while seeming at least half alert. During my time in Voc. Ed., I developed further into a mediocre student and a somnambulant problem solver, and that affected the subjects I did have the wherewithal to handle: I detested Shakespeare; I got bored with history. My attention flitted here and there. I fooled around in class and read my books indifferently—the intellectual equivalent of playing with your food. I did what I had to do to get by, and I did it with half a mind.

But I did learn things about people and eventually came into my own 15
socially. I liked the guys in Voc. Ed. Growing up where I did, I understood and admired physical prowess, and there was an abundance of muscle here. There was Dave Snyder, a sprinter and halfback of true quality. Dave's ability and his quick wit gave him a natural appeal, and he was welcome in any clique, though he always kept a little independent. He enjoyed acting the fool and could care less about studies, but he possessed a certain maturity and never caused the faculty much trouble. It was a testament to his independence that he included me among his friends—I eventually went out for track, but I was no jock. Owing to the Latin alphabet and a dearth of *R*s and *S*s, Snyder sat behind Rose, and we started exchanging one-liners and became friends.

There was Ted Richard, a much-touted Little League pitcher. He was chunky and had a baby face and came to Our Lady of Mercy as a seasoned street fighter. Ted was quick to laugh and he had a loud, jolly laugh, but when he got angry he'd smile a little smile, the kind that simply raises the corner of the mouth a quarter of an inch. For those who knew, it was an eerie signal. Those who didn't found themselves in big trouble, for Ted was very quick. He loved to carry on what we would come to call philosophical discussions: What is courage? Does God exist? He also loved words, enjoyed picking up big ones like *salubrious* and *equivocal* and using them in our conversations—laughing at himself as the word hit a chuckhole rolling off his tongue. Ted didn't do all that well in school—baseball and parties and testing the courage he'd speculated about took up his time. His textbooks were *Argosy* and *Field and Stream,* whatever newspapers he'd find on the bus stop—from *the Daily Worker* to pornography—conversations with uncles or hobos or businessmen he'd meet in a coffee shop, *The Old Man and the Sea.* With hindsight, I can see that Ted was developing into one of those rough-hewn intellectuals whose sources are a mix of the learned and the apocryphal, whose discussions are both assured and sad.

And then there was Ken Harvey. Ken was good-looking in a puffy way and had a full and oily ducktail and was a car enthusiast . . . a hodad. One day in religion class, he said the sentence that turned out to be one of the most memorable of the hundreds of thousands I heard in those Voc. Ed. years. We were talking about the parable of the talents, about achievement, working hard, doing the best you can do, blah-blah-blah, when the teacher called on the restive Ken Harvey for an opinion. Ken thought about it, but just for a second, and said (with studied, minimal affect), "I just wanna be average." That woke me up. Average?! Who wants to be average? Then the athletes chimed in with the clichés that make you want to laryngectomize them, and the exchange became a platitudinous melee. At the time, I thought Ken's assertion was stupid, and I wrote him off. But his sentence has stayed with me all these years, and I think I am finally coming to understand it.

Ken Harvey was gasping for air. School can be a tremendously disorienting place. No matter how bad the school, you're going to encounter notions that don't fit with the assumptions and beliefs that you grew up with—maybe you'll hear these dissonant notions from teachers, maybe from the other students, and maybe you'll read them. You'll also be thrown in with all kinds of kids from all kinds of backgrounds, and that can be unsettling—this is especially true in places of rich ethnic and linguistic mix, like the L.A. basin. You'll see a handful of students far excel you in courses that sound exotic and that are only in the curriculum of the elite: French, physics, trigonometry. And all this is happening while you're trying to shape an identity; your body is changing, and your emotions are running wild. If you're a working-class kid in the vocational track, the options you'll have to deal with this will be constrained in certain ways: You're defined by your school as "slow"; you're placed in a curriculum that isn't designed to liberate you but to occupy you, or, if you're lucky, train you, though the training is for work the society does not esteem; other students are picking up the cues from your school and your curriculum and interacting with you in particular ways. If you're a kid like Ted Richard, you turn your back on all this and let your mind roam where it may. But youngsters like Ted are rare. What Ken and so many others do is protect themselves from such suffocating madness by taking on with a vengeance the identity implied in the vocational track. Reject the confusion and frustration by openly defining yourself as the Common Joe. Champion the average. Rely on your own good sense. Fuck this bullshit. Bullshit, of course, is everything you—and the others—fear is beyond you: books, essays, tests, academic scrambling, complexity, scientific reasoning, philosophical inquiry.

The tragedy is that you have to twist the knife in your own gray matter to make this defense work. You'll have to shut down, have to reject intellectual stimuli or diffuse them with sarcasm, have to cultivate stupidity, have to convert boredom from a malady into a way of confronting the world. Keep your vocabulary simple, act stoned when you're not or act more stoned than you are, flaunt ignorance, materialize your dreams. It is a powerful and effective defense—it neutralizes the insult and the frustration of being a vocational kid and, when perfected, it drives teachers up the wall, a delightful secondary effect. But like all strong magic, it exacts a price.

20 My own deliverance from the Voc. Ed. world began with sophomore biology. Every student, college prep to vocational, had to take biology, and unlike the other courses, the same person taught all sections. When teaching the vocational group, Brother Clint probably slowed down a bit or omitted a little of the fundamental biochemistry, but he used the same book and more or less the same syllabus across the board. If one class got tough, he could get tougher. He was young and powerful and very handsome, and looks and physical strength were high currency. No one gave him any trouble.

I was pretty bad at the dissecting table, but the lectures and the textbook were interesting: plastic overlays that, with each turned page, peeled away skin, then veins and muscle, then organs, down to the very bones that Brother Clint, pointer in hand, would tap out on our hanging skeleton. Dave Snyder was in big trouble, for the study of life—versus the living of it—was sticking in his craw. We worked out a code for our multiple-choice exams. He'd poke me in the back: once for the answer under *A,* twice for *B,* and so on; and when he'd hit the right one, I'd look up to the ceiling as though I were lost in thought. Poke: cytoplasm. Poke, poke: methane. Poke, poke, poke: William Harvey. Poke, poke, poke, poke: islets of Langerhans. This didn't work out perfectly, but Dave passed the course, and I mastered the dreamy look of a guy on a record jacket. And something else happened. Brother Clint puzzled over this Voc. Ed. kid who was racking up 98s and 99s on his tests. He checked the school's records and discovered the error. He recommended that I begin my junior year in the College Prep program. According to all I've read since, such a shift, as one report put it, is virtually impossible. Kids at that level rarely cross tracks. The telling thing is how chancy both my placement into and exit from Voc. Ed. was; neither I nor my parents had anything to do with it. I lived in one world during spring semester, and when I came back to school in the fall, I was living in another.

Switching to College Prep was a mixed blessing. I was an erratic student. I was undisciplined. And I hadn't caught onto the rules of the game: Why work hard in a class that didn't grab my fancy? I was also hopelessly behind in math. Chemistry was hard; toying with my chemistry set years before hadn't prepared me for the chemist's equations. Fortunately, the priest who taught both chemistry and second-year algebra was also the school's athletic director. Membership on the track team covered me; I knew I wouldn't get lower than a C. U.S. history was taught pretty well, and I did okay. But civics was taken over by a football coach who had trouble reading the textbook aloud—and reading aloud was the centerpiece of his pedagogy. College Prep at Mercy was certainly an improvement over the vocational program—at least it carried some status—but the social science curriculum was weak, and the mathematics and physical sciences were simply beyond me. I had a miserable quantitative background and ended up copying some assignments and finessing the rest as best I could. Let me try to explain how it feels to see again and again material you should once have learned but didn't.

You are given a problem. It requires you to simplify algebraic fractions or to multiply expressions containing square roots. You know this is pretty basic material because you've seen it for years. Once a teacher took some time with you, and you learned how to carry out these operations. Simple versions, anyway. But that was a year or two or more in the past, and these are more complex versions, and now you're not sure. And this, you keep telling yourself, is ninth- or even eighth-grade stuff.

Next it's a word problem. This is also old hat. The basic elements are as familiar as story characters: trains speeding so many miles per hour or shadows of buildings angling so many degrees. Maybe you know enough, have sat through enough explanations, to be able to begin setting up the problem: "If one train is going this fast . . ." or "This shadow is really one line of a triangle. . . ." Then: "Let's see . . ." "How did Jones do this?" "Hmmmm." "No." "No, that won't work." Your attention wavers. You wonder about other things: a football game, a dance, that cute new checker at the market. You try to focus on the problem again. You scribble on paper for a while, but the tension wins out and your attention flits elsewhere. You crumple the paper and begin daydreaming to ease the frustration.

25 The particulars will vary, but in essence this is what a number of students go through, especially those in so-called remedial classes. They open their textbooks and see once again the familiar and impenetrable formulas and diagrams and terms that have stumped them for years. There is no excitement here. *No* excitement. Regardless of what the teacher says, this is not a new challenge. There is, rather, embarrassment and frustration and, not surprisingly, some anger in being reminded once again of long-standing inadequacies. No wonder so many students finally attribute their difficulties to something inborn, organic: "That part of my brain just doesn't work." Given the troubling histories many of these students have, it's miraculous that any of them can lift the shroud of hopelessness sufficiently to make deliverance from these classes possible.

Through this entire period, my father's health was deteriorating with cruel momentum. His arteriosclerosis progressed to the point where a simple nick on his shin wouldn't heal. Eventually it ulcerated and widened. Lou Minton would come by daily to change the dressing. We tried renting an oscillating bed—which we placed in the front room—to force blood through the constricted arteries in my father's legs. The bed hummed through the night, moving in place to ward off the inevitable. The ulcer continued to spread, and the doctors finally had to amputate. My grandfather had lost his leg in a stockyard accident. Now my father too was crippled. His convalescence was slow but steady, and the doctors placed him in the Santa Monica Rehabilitation Center, a sun-bleached building that opened out onto the warm spray of the Pacific. The place gave him some strength and some color and some training in walking with an artificial leg. He did pretty well for a year or so until he slipped and broke his hip. He was confined to a wheelchair after that, and the confinement contributed to the diminishing of his body and spirit.

I am holding a picture of him. He is sitting in his wheelchair and smiling at the camera. The smile appears forced, unsteady, seems to quaver, though it is frozen in silver nitrate. He is in his mid-sixties and looks eighty. Late in my junior year, he had a stroke and never came out of the resulting coma. After that, I would see him only in dreams, and to this day that is how I join him. Sometimes the dreams are sad and grisly and primal: my father lying in a bed soaked with his suppuration, holding me, rocking me. But sometimes the dreams bring him back to me healthy: him talking to me on an empty street, or buying some pictures to decorate our old house, or transformed somehow into someone strong and adept with tools and the physical.

Jack MacFarland couldn't have come into my life at a better time. My father was dead, and I had logged up too many years of scholastic indifference. Mr. MacFarland had a master's degree from Columbia and decided, at twenty-six, to find a little school and teach his heart out. He never took any credentialing courses, couldn't bear to, he said, so he had to find employment in a private system. He ended up at Our Lady of Mercy teaching five sections of senior English. He was a beatnik who was born too late. His teeth were stained, he tucked his sorry tie in between the third and fourth buttons of his shirt, and his pants were chronically wrinkled. At first, we couldn't believe this guy, thought he slept in his car. But within no time, he had us so startled with work that we didn't much worry about where he slept or if he slept at all. We wrote three or four essays a month. We read a book every two to three weeks, starting with the *Iliad* and ending up with Hemingway. He gave us a quiz on the reading every other day. He brought a prep school curriculum to Mercy High.

MacFarland's lectures were crafted, and as he delivered them he would pace the room jiggling a piece of chalk in his cupped hand, using it to scribble on the board the names of all the writers and philosophers and plays and novels he was weaving into his discussion. He asked questions often, raised everything from Zeno's paradox to the repeated last line of Frost's "Stopping by Woods on a Snowy Evening." He slowly and carefully built up our knowledge of Western intellectual history—with facts, with connections, with speculations. We learned about Greek philosophy, about Dante, the Elizabethan world view, the Age of Reason, existentialism. He analyzed poems with us, had us reading sections from John Ciardi's *How Does a Poem Mean?*, making a potentially difficult book accessible with his own explanations. We gave oral reports on poems Ciardi didn't cover. We imitated the styles of Conrad, Hemingway, and *Time* magazine. We wrote and talked, wrote and talked. The man immersed us in language.

Even MacFarland's barbs were literary. If Jim Fitzsimmons, hung over and 30
irritable, tried to smart-ass him, he'd rejoin with a flourish that would spark the indomitable Skip Madison—who'd lost his front teeth in a hapless tackle—

to flick his tongue through the gap and opine, "good chop," drawing out the single "o" in stinging indictment. Jack MacFarland, this tobacco-stained intellectual, brandished linguistic weapons of a kind I hadn't encountered before. Here was this *egghead,* for God's sake, keeping some pretty difficult people in line. And from what I heard, Mike Dweetz and Steve Fusco and all the notorious Voc. Ed. crowd settled down as well when MacFarland took the podium. Though a lot of guys groused in the schoolyard, it just seemed that giving trouble to this particular teacher was a silly thing to do. Tomfoolery, not to mention assault, had no place in the world he was trying to create for us, and instinctively everyone knew that. If nothing else, we all recognized MacFarland's considerable intelligence and respected the hours he put into his work. It came to this: The troublemaker would look foolish rather than daring. Even Jim Fitzsimmons was reading *On the Road* and turning his incipient alcoholism to literary ends.

There were some lives that were already beyond Jack MacFarland's ministrations, but mine was not. I started reading again as I hadn't since elementary school. I would go into our gloomy little bedroom or sit at the dinner table while, on the television, Danny McShane was paralyzing Mr. Moto with the atomic drop, and work slowly back through *Heart of Darkness,* trying to catch the words in Conrad's sentences. I certainly was not MacFarland's best student; most of the other guys in College Prep, even my fellow slackers, had better backgrounds than I did. But I worked very hard, for MacFarland had hooked me. He tapped my old interest in reading and creating stories. He gave me a way to feel special by using my mind. And he provided a role model that wasn't shaped on physical prowess alone, and something inside me that I wasn't quite aware of responded to that. Jack MacFarland established a literacy club, to borrow a phrase of Frank Smith's, and invited me—invited all of us—to join.

There's been a good deal of research and speculation suggesting that the acknowledgment of school performance with extrinsic rewards—smiling faces, stars, numbers, grades—diminishes the intrinsic satisfaction children experience by engaging in reading or writing or problem solving. While it's certainly true that we've created an educational system that encourages our best and brightest to become cynical grade collectors and, in general, have developed an obsession with evaluation and assessment, I must tell you that venal though it may have been, I loved getting good grades from MacFarland. I now know how subjective grades can be, but then they came tucked in the back of essays like bits of scientific data, some sort of spectroscopic readout that said, objectively and publicly, that I had made something of value. I suppose I'd been mediocre for too long and enjoyed a public redefinition. And I suppose the workings of my mind, such as they were, had been private for too long. My linguistic play moved into the world; like the intergalactic stories I told years before on Frank's berry-splattered truck bed, these papers with their circled, red B-pluses and A-minuses linked my mind to something outside it. I carried them around like a club emblem.

One day in the December of my senior year, Mr. MacFarland asked me where I was going to go to college. I hadn't thought much about it. Many of the students I teach today spent their last year in high school with a physics text in one hand and the Stanford catalog in the other, but I wasn't even aware of what "entrance requirements" were. My folks would say that they wanted me to go to college and be a doctor, but I don't know how seriously I ever took that; it seemed a sweet thing to say, a bit of supportive family chatter, like telling a gangly daughter she's graceful. The reality of higher education wasn't in my scheme of things: No one in the family had gone to college; only two of my uncles had completed high school. I figured I'd get a night job and go to the local junior college because I knew that Snyder and Company were going there to play ball. But I hadn't even prepared for that. When I finally said, "I don't know," MacFarland looked down at me—I was seated in his office—and said, "Listen, you can write."

My grades stank. I had A's in biology and a handful of B's in a few English and social science classes. All the rest were C's—or worse. MacFarland said I would do well in his class and laid down the law about doing well in the others. Still, the record for my first three years wouldn't have been acceptable to any four-year school. To nobody's surprise, I was turned down flat by USC and UCLA. But Jack MacFarland was on the case. He had received his bachelor's degree from Loyola University, so he made calls to old professors and talked to somebody in admissions and wrote me a strong letter. Loyola finally accepted me as a probationary student. I would be on trial for the first year, and if I did okay, I would be granted regular status. MacFarland also intervened to get me a loan, for I could never have afforded a private college without it. Four more years of religion classes and four more years of boys at one school, girls at another. But at least I was going to college. Amazing.

In my last semester of high school, I elected a special English course 35
fashioned by Mr. MacFarland, and it was through this elective that there arose at Mercy a fledgling literati. Art Mitz, the editor of the school newspaper and a very smart guy, was the kingpin. He was joined by me and by Mark Dever, a quiet boy who wrote beautifully and who would die before he was forty. MacFarland occasionally invited us to his apartment, and those visits became the high point of our apprenticeship: We'd clamp on our training wheels and drive to his salon.

He lived in a cramped and cluttered place near the airport, tucked away in the kind of building that architectural critic Reyner Banham calls a *dingbat.* Books were all over: stacked, piled, tossed, and crated, underlined and dog eared, well worn and new. Cigarette ashes crusted with coffee in saucers or spilled over the sides of motel ashtrays. The little bedroom had, along two of its walls, bricks and boards loaded with notes, magazines, and oversized books. The kitchen joined the living room, and there was a stack of German newspapers under the sink. I had never seen anything like it: a great flophouse of language furnished by City Lights and Café le Metro. I read every title. I flipped through paperbacks and scanned jackets and memorized names: Gogol, *Finnegan's Wake,* Djuna Barnes, Jackson Pollock, *A Coney Island of the Mind,* F. O. Matthiessen's *American Renaissance,* all sorts of Freud, *Troubled Sleep,* Man Ray, *The Education of Henry Adams,* Richard Wright, *Film as Art,* William Butler Yeats, Marguerite Duras, *Redburn, A Season in Hell, Kapital.* On the cover of Alain-Fournier's *The Wanderer* was an Edward Gorey drawing of a young man on a road winding into dark trees. By the hotplate sat a strange Kafka novel called *Amerika,* in which an adolescent hero crosses the Atlantic to find the Nature Theater of Oklahoma. Art and Mark would be talking about a movie or the school newspaper, and I would be consuming my English teacher's library. It was heady stuff. I felt like a Pop Warner athlete on steroids.

Art, Mark, and I would buy stogies and triangulate from MacFarland's apartment to the Cinema, which now shows X-rated films but was then L.A.'s premiere art theater, and then to the musty Cherokee Bookstore in Hollywood to hobnob with beatnik homosexuals—smoking, drinking bourbon and coffee, and trying out awkward phrases we'd gleaned from our mentor's bookshelves. I was happy and precocious and a little scared as well, for Hollywood Boulevard was thick with a kind of decadence that was foreign to the South Side. After the Cherokee, we would head back to the security of MacFarland's apartment, slaphappy with hipness.

Let me be the first to admit that there was a good deal of adolescent passion in this embrace of the avant-garde: self-absorption, sexually charged pedantry, an elevation of the odd and abandoned. Still it was a time during which I absorbed an awful lot of information: long lists of titles, images from expressionist paintings, new wave shibboleths, snippets of philosophy, and names that read like Steve Fusco's misspellings—Goethe, Nietzsche, Kierkegaard. Now this is hardly the stuff of deep understanding. But it was an introduction, a phrase book, a Baedeker to a vocabulary of ideas, and it felt good at the time to know all these words. With hindsight I realize how layered and important that knowledge was.

It enabled me to do things in the world. I could browse bohemian bookstores in far-off, mysterious Hollywood; I could go to the Cinema and see events through the lenses of European directors; and, most of all, I could share an evening, talk that talk, with Jack MacFarland, the man I most admired at the time. Knowledge was becoming a bonding agent. Within a year or two, the persona of the disaffected hipster would prove too cynical, too alienated to last. But for a time it was new and exciting: It provided a critical perspective on society, and it allowed me to act as though I were living beyond the limiting boundaries of South Vermont.

Understanding

1. The last sentence in *Lives on the Boundary,* from which this reading is excerpted, is: "But it is not terror that fosters learning, it is hope, everyday heroics, the power of the common play of the human mind." How does "I Just Wanna Be Average" support this claim?
2. Identify the teachers who contributed to Rose's estimation of himself. Consider their attributes. What did each bring out in Rose?

Responding

1. Harvard University professor of psychology Howard Gardner has documented seven forms of intelligence: linguistic, logical-mathematical, spa-

tial, musical, bodily-kinesthetic, interpersonal (knowing how to deal with others), and intrapersonal (knowledge of oneself). (He explains them fully in his 1985 book *Frames of Mind: the Theory of Multiple Intelligences.*) Gardner claims that when we say someone is "smart," we are really talking about either linguistic or logical-mathematical ability, that these two intelligences are what our society values. What sorts of intelligences are evident in "I Just Wanna Be Average"? Which were most recognized in your schooling experience? Which were least acknowledged?

2. Underline all the well-known and classical books and authors mentioned in this essay. Apparently, Rose feels that they combine to equal a certain cultural literacy and are important in living a full life. How many of the titles have you spent time with? What's the value of knowing the references that an author cites in a literary work?
3. Recall a student from your K–12 days who had gifts that, for whatever reason, teachers, other students, or even his or her parents couldn't see. Perhaps *you* were a student of that kind. Write that student's (or your) story and suggest how his or her gift could have been noticed and valued. What did others miss out on by not seeing this person's gift? Draw on Gardner's notion of multiple intelligences (Responding question 1 above).
4. What commitment should America have to educating all its students? What forms should it take? What outcomes should emerge?

Connecting

If Silko's idea that "through the stories we hear who we are" is true, what stories did Mike Rose and his friends in south L.A. hear and what did they hear that they were through them? Contrast Silko's stories with Rose's. How did they affect the lives of each group? How powerful are stories in forming a person's identity? Are they everlasting? Do Silko and Rose believe that people can change their stories (their beliefs) about themselves?

Think About It

Frank Conroy

The power of educational institutions is undeniable. But outside those walls, a person is bombarded by the values and activities of many other institutions, social communities, and individuals as well. By sifting through all this influence and combined experience, we incorporate some of it (consciously or not) and we make our own way—develop our own standpoints and live them out as our statement of who we are.

In "Think About It," jazz pianist and writer Frank Conroy shares his own views on education. Though he has been quoted as saying that the lessons from experience are elusive, he makes a powerful argument that experience is well worth pondering, and he mines ordinary topics for his reflections. Conroy is the director of the famous Iowa Writers' Workshop and a contributor to many magazines such as *The New Yorker.* Conroy's memoir of his childhood is *Stop Time* (1967), and the "small liberal arts college outside Philadelphia" that he mentions in "Think About It" is Haverford.

In this essay, Conroy refers to a legal case, *Dennis et al. v. United States,* which was decided by the U.S. Supreme Court on June 4, 1951. In it eleven leaders of the Communist Party were convicted of willfully and knowingly conspiring to organize and teach people to advocate the overthrow and destruction of the government of the United States by force of violence. Justice William O. Douglas (1898–1980) was one of two Supreme Court justices to write a dissenting opinion. His dissent focused on his belief that these people and their teachings did not present a "clear and present danger" to the United States.

When I was sixteen I worked selling hot dogs at a stand in the Fourteenth Street subway station in New York City, one level above the trains and one below the street, where the crowds continually flowed back and forth. I worked with three Puerto Rican men who could not speak English. I had no Spanish, and although we understood each other well with regard to the tasks at hand, sensing and adjusting to each other's body movements in the extremely confined space in which we operated, I felt isolated with no one to talk to. On my break I came out from behind the counter and passed the time with two old black men who ran a shoeshine stand in a dark corner of the corridor. It was a poor location, half hidden by columns, and they didn't have much business. I would sit with my back against the wall while they stood or moved around their ancient elevated stand, talking to each other or to me, but always staring into the distance as they did so. 1

As the weeks went by I realized that they never looked at anything in their immediate vicinity—not at me or their stand or anybody who might come within ten or fifteen feet. They did not look at approaching customers once they were inside the perimeter. Save for the instant it took to discern the color of the shoes, they did not even look at what they were doing while they worked, but rubbed in polish, brushed, and buffed by feel while looking over their shoulders, into the distance, as if awaiting the arrival of an important person. Of course there wasn't all that much distance in the underground station, but their behavior was so focused and consistent they seemed somehow to transcend the physical. A powerful mood was created, and I came almost to believe that these men could see through walls, through girders, and around corners to whatever hyperspace it was where whoever it was they were waiting and watching for would finally emerge. Their scattered talk was hip, elliptical, and hinted at mysteries beyond my white boy's ken, but it was the staring off, the long, steady staring off, that had me hypnotized. I left for a better job, with handshakes from both of them, without understanding what I had seen.

Perhaps ten years later, after playing jazz with black musicians in various Harlem clubs, hanging out uptown with a few young artists and intellectuals, I began to learn from them something of the extraordinarily varied and complex riffs and rituals embraced by different people to help themselves get through life in the ghetto. Fantasy of all kinds—from playful to dangerous—was in the very air of Harlem. It was the spice of uptown life.

Only then did I understand the two shoeshine men. They were trapped in a demeaning situation in a dark corner in an underground corridor in a filthy subway system. Their continuous staring off was a kind of statement, a kind of dance. Our bodies are here, went the statement, but our souls are receiving nourishment from distant sources only we can see. They were powerful magic dancers, sorcerers almost, and thirty-five years later I can still feel the pressure of their spell.

The light bulb may appear over your head, is what I'm saying, but it may 5
be a while before it actually goes on. Early in my attempts to learn jazz piano, I used to listen to recordings of a fine player named Red Garland, whose music I admired. I couldn't quite figure out what he was doing with his left hand, however; the chords eluded me. I went uptown to an obscure club where he was playing with his trio, caught him on his break, and simply asked him. "Sixths," he said cheerfully. And then he went away.

I didn't know what to make of it. The basic jazz chord is the seventh, which comes in various configurations, but it is what it is. I was a self-taught pianist, pretty shaky on theory and harmony, and when he said sixths I kept trying to fix the information into what I already knew, and it didn't fit. But it stuck in my mind—a tantalizing mystery.

A couple of years later, when I began playing with a bass player, I discovered more or less by accident that if the bass played the root and I played a sixth based on the fifth note of the scale, a very interesting chord involving both instruments emerged. Ordinarily, I suppose I would have skipped over the matter and not paid much attention, but I remembered Garland's remark and so I stopped and spent a week or two working out the voicings, and greatly strengthened my foundations as a player. I had remembered what I hadn't understood, you might say, until my life caught up with the information and the light bulb went on.

I remember another, more complicated example from my sophomore year at the small liberal-arts college outside Philadelphia. I seemed never to be able to get up in time for breakfast in the dining hall. I would get coffee and a doughnut in the Coop instead—a basement area with about a dozen small tables where students could get something to eat at odd hours. Several mornings in a row I noticed a strange man sitting by himself with a cup of coffee. He was in his sixties, perhaps, and sat straight in his chair with very little extraneous movement. I guessed he was some sort of distinguished visitor to the college who had decided to put in some time at a student hangout. But no one ever sat with him. One morning I approached his table and asked if I could join him.

"Certainly," he said. "Please do." He had perhaps the clearest eyes I had ever seen, like blue ice, and to be held in their steady gaze was not, at first, an entirely comfortable experience. His eyes gave nothing away about himself while at the same time creating in me the eerie impression that he was looking directly into my soul. He asked a few quick questions, as if to put me at my ease, and we fell into conversation. He was William O. Douglas from the Supreme Court, and when he saw how startled I was he said, "Call me Bill. Now tell me what you're studying and why you get up so late in the morning." Thus began a series of talks that stretched over many weeks. The fact that I was an ignorant sophomore with literary pretensions who knew nothing about the law didn't seem to bother him. We talked about everything from Shakespeare to the possibility of life on other planets. One day I mentioned that I was going to have dinner with Judge Learned Hand. I explained that Hand was my girlfriend's grandfather. Douglas nodded, but I could tell he was surprised at the coincidence of my knowing the chief judge of the most important court in the country save the Supreme Court itself. After fifty years on the bench Judge Hand had become a famous man, both in and out of legal circles—a living legend, to his own dismay. "Tell him hello and give him my best regards," Douglas said.

10 Learned Hand, in his eighties, was a short, barrel-chested man with a large, square head, huge, thick, bristling eyebrows, and soft brown eyes. He radiated energy and would sometimes bark out remarks or questions in the living room as if he were in court. His humor was sharp, but often leavened with a touch of self-mockery. When something caught his funny bone he would burst out with explosive laughter—the laughter of a man who enjoyed laughing. He had a large repertoire of dramatic expressions involving the use of his eyebrows—very useful, he told me conspiratorially, when looking down on things from behind the bench. (The court stenographer could not record the movement of his eyebrows.) When I told him I'd been talking to William O. Douglas, they first shot up in exaggerated surprise, and then lowered and moved forward in a glower.

"*Justice* William O. Douglas, young man," he admonished. "Justice Douglas, if you please." About the Supreme Court in general, Hand insisted on a tone of profound respect. Little did I know that in private correspondence he had referred to the Court as "The Blessed Saints, Cherubim and Seraphim," "The Jolly Boys," "The Nine Tin Jesuses," "The Nine Blameless Ethiopians," and my particular favorite, "The Nine Blessed Chalices of the Sacred Effluvium."

Hand was badly stooped and had a lot of pain in his lower back. Martinis helped, but his strict Yankee wife approved of only one before dinner. It was my job to make the second and somehow slip it to him. If the pain was particularly acute he would get out of his chair and lie flat on the rug, still talking, and finish his point without missing a beat. He flattered me by asking for my impression of Justice Douglas, instructed me to convey his warmest regards, and then began talking about the Dennis case, which he described as a particularly tricky and difficult case involving the prosecution of eleven leaders of the Communist party. He had just started in on the First Amendment and free speech when we were called in to dinner.

William O. Douglas loved the outdoors with a passion, and we fell into the habit of having coffee in the Coop and then strolling under the trees down toward the duck pond. About the Dennis case, he said something to this effect: "Eleven Communists arrested by the government. Up to no good, said the government; dangerous people, violent overthrow, etc. First Amendment, said the defense, freedom of speech, etc." Douglas stopped walking. "Clear and present danger."

"What?" I asked. He often talked in a telegraphic manner, and one was expected to keep up with him. It was sometimes like listening to a man thinking out loud.

"Clear and present danger," he said. "That was the issue. Did they consti- 15
tute a clear and present danger? I don't think so. I think everybody took the language pretty far in Dennis." He began walking, striding along quickly. Again, one was expected to keep up with him. "The FBI was all over them. Phones tapped, constant surveillance. How could it be clear and present danger with the FBI watching every move they made? That's a ginkgo." he said suddenly, pointing at a tree. "A beauty. You don't see those every day. Ask Hand about clear and present danger."

I was in fact reluctant to do so. Douglas's argument seemed to me to be crushing—the last word, really—and I didn't want to embarrass Judge Hand. But back in the living room, on the second martini, the old man asked about Douglas. I sort of scratched my nose and recapitulated the conversation by the ginkgo tree.

"What?" Hand shouted. "Speak up, sir, for heaven's sake."

"He said the FBI was watching them all the time so there couldn't be a clear and present danger," I blurted out, blushing as I said it.

A terrible silence filled the room. Hand's eyebrows writhed on his face like two huge caterpillars. He leaned forward in the wing chair, his face settling, finally, into a grim expression. "I am astonished," he said softly, his eyes holding mine, "at Justice Douglas's newfound faith in the Federal Bureau of Investigation." His big, granite head moved even closer to mine, until I could smell the martini. "I had understood him to consider it a politically corrupt, incompetent organization, directed by a power-crazed lunatic." I realized I had been holding my breath throughout all of this, and as I relaxed, I saw the faintest trace of a smile cross Hand's face. Things are sometimes more complicated than they first appear, his smile seemed to say. The old man leaned back. "The proximity of the danger is something to think about. Ask him about that. See what he says."

I chewed the matter over as I returned to campus. Hand had pointed out 20
some of Douglas's language about the FBI from other sources that seemed to bear out his point. I thought about the words "clear and present danger," and the fact that if you looked at them closely they might not be as simple as they had first appeared. What degree of danger? Did the word "present" allude to the proximity of the danger, or just the fact that the danger was there at all—that it wasn't an anticipated danger? Were there other hidden factors these great men were weighing of which I was unaware?

But Douglas was gone, back to Washington. (The writer in me is tempted to create a scene here—to invent one for dramatic purposes—but of course I can't do that.) My brief time as a messenger boy was over, and I felt a certain frustration, as if, with a few more exchanges, the matter of *Dennis* v. *United States* might have been resolved to my satisfaction. They'd left me high and dry. But, of course, it is precisely because the matter did not resolve that has caused me to think about it, off and on, all these years. "The Constitution," Hand used to say to me flatly, "is a piece of paper. The Bill of Rights is a piece of paper." It was many years before I understood what he meant. Documents alone do not keep democracy alive, nor maintain the state of law. There is no particular safety in them. Living men and women, generation after generation, must continually remake democracy and the law, and that involves an ongoing state of tension between the past and the present which will never completely resolve.

Education doesn't end until life ends, because you never know when you're going to understand something you hadn't understood before. For me, the magic dance of the shoeshine men was the kind of experience in which understanding came with a kind of click, a resolving kind of click. The same with the experience at the piano. What happened with Justice Douglas and Judge Hand was different, and makes the point that understanding does not always mean resolution. Indeed, in our intellectual lives, our creative lives, it is perhaps those problems that will never resolve that rightly claim the lion's share of our energies. The physical body exists in a constant state of tension as it maintains homeostasis, and so too does the active mind embrace the tension of never being certain, never being absolutely sure, never being done, as it engages the world. That is our special fate, our inexpressibly valuable condition.

Understanding

1. How did Conroy eventually interpret the shoeshine men's staring off into the distance? If he told them his interpretation, what are the chances they

would agree? That is, does the fact that Conroy gave their actions this meaning make him right? Is any interpretation of experience the truth? Why would this question matter? How does Conroy tie this experience into the whole essay?

2. According to Conroy, what is "our special fate, our inexpressibly valuable condition"? How do his examples illustrate his claim?
3. How would Conroy define education? How much of it goes on at school? If there was one sentence in Conroy's essay that you would want carved in granite, which would it be? Why?
4. The case of *Dennis v. United States* was decided during the McCarthy era, a period during the Cold War between the United States and the Soviet Union, which had just exploded an atomic weapon. In this context of fear, the House Committee on Un-American Activities was formed to investigate the activities of Communist Party "sympathizers." FBI surveillance was put into high gear, and artists and screenwriters were particular targets. Some have said "tough times make bad law," and perhaps this notion is what Justice William O. Douglas and Learned Hand, a highly esteemed judge (though not on the Supreme Court), were discussing through the young Conroy. Both men felt that free speech was of utmost importance, and their questions centered on whether Dennis's and the others' reading of Marxist doctrine made them a clear and present danger to the country.

   Learned Hand (1872–1961) has said that in order not to lead ourselves into savagery, "we must not yield a foot upon demanding a fair field and an honest race to all ideas"; and Conroy notes Hand as having said that our Constitution and our Bill of Rights are but pieces of paper to be interpreted wisely—not by those who do not want to give a controversial idea full voice. Conroy writes that it was many years before he understood what Hand meant. What does Conroy finally learn? How does his insight illuminate his notion of education?

Responding

1. It has been said that in five years you will be the same person that you are today except for two things: the people you meet and the books you read. Conroy's essay seems to support this armchair philosophy. Write your own "Think About It" regarding people you have known or books you have read in the past five years that made the kind of difference to you that Conroy's meant to him.
2. Active readers are always interrupted (in a positive way) when they're reading by what comes up for them or what gets sparked as they connect, validate, or consider a writer's position against their own experience or belief. Describe such a "light bulb" experience which appeared as you read "Think About It." Relate it to points Conroy makes in his final paragraph. Include the people like Douglas and Hand who helped you "turn on the light."
3. How many times do you find your learning, your creativity, your responses to everyday challenges unsatisfactory? Could it be that you are stifled by the

way you look at them? Consider Conroy's statement: "I kept trying to fix the information into what I already knew, and it didn't fit." How is this real phenomenon both a boon and an impediment to the act of creating our lives? What can you do to change it?

4. Have you ever been in a situation that you would call "clear and present danger"? Describe it and why the quoted words are important to the event. Relate your answer, if possible, to the concept, or word, *punundrum,* which Justice Douglas used in his Bill of Rights activism.

Connecting

I Just Wanna Be Average is a sentence that took a long time for Mike Rose to understand. Recall what was so powerful about the statement when he finally understood it. How does this delayed understanding relate to Conroy's "Think About It"?

On the Art of Conversation

Michel de Montaigne

Conversation is a uniquely human way to start and sustain a relationship, as Michel de Montaigne examines in this essay. Montaigne (1533–92) was, in fact, the originator of the personal essay. He first used the word *essay* (from the French *essayer,* to try or try on) in 1580 as a title to what we know today as a short, reflective, prose piece. Prior to that time, public writing was less personal and introspective. In Montaigne's view we must use as much judgment as possible in all things, but when those things surpass our understanding, we must try them out; we must *essay* them. This is what Montaigne did in "On the Art of Conversation," his personal attempt to try out what he thought constituted the elements of this intimate interaction between human minds. At the time he wrote this essay, the ability to engage in "good conversation" or argument was the sign of a well-educated person.

Trained in the law and for four years the mayor of Bordeaux, France, Montaigne produced essays that are now considered his intellectual autobiography. His motto *"Que sais-je?"* (What do I know?) reflected his doubting spirit or what some have called his "conservative skepticism."

One point is worth clarifying: Montaigne's exclusive reference to men as practitioners of the art of conversation was a product of his time: Learning communities at universities in sixteenth-century Europe did not typically include women. The publication of the third edition of his *Essais* in 1595 was, however, supervised by a woman, Marie de Gournay, who was his intellectual disciple. The following is a translation from the original French.

To my taste the most fruitful and most natural exercise of our minds is conversation. I find the practice of it the most delightful activity in our lives. That is why, if I were now obliged to make the choice, I think I would rather lose my sight than my powers of speech or hearing. In their academies the Athenians, and even more the Romans, maintained this exercise in great honour. In our own times the Italians retain some vestiges of it—greatly to their benefit, as can be seen from a comparison of their intelligence and ours. Studying books has a languid feeble motion, whereas conversation provides teaching and exercise all at once. If I am sparring with a strong and solid opponent he will attack me on the flanks, stick his lance in me right and left; his ideas send mine soaring. Rivalry, competitiveness and glory will drive me and raise me above my own level. In conversation the most painful quality is perfect harmony. 1

Just as our mind is strengthened by contact with vigorous and well-ordered minds, so too it is impossible to overstate how much it loses and deteriorates by the continuous commerce and contact we have with mean and ailing ones. No infection is as contagious as that is. I know by experience what that costs by the ell. I love arguing and discussing, but with only a few men and for my own sake: for to serve as a spectacle to the great and indulge in a parade of your wits and your verbiage is, I consider, an unbecoming trade for an honourable gentleman.

* * *

I do truly seek to frequent those who manhandle me rather than those who are afraid of me. It is a bland and harmful pleasure to have to deal with people who admire us and defer to us. Antisthenes commanded his sons never to give thanks or show gratitude to anyone who praised them.[1] I feel far prouder of the victory I win over myself when I make myself give way beneath my adversary's powers of reason in the heat of battle than I ever feel gratified by the victory I win over him through his weakness. In short I admit and acknowledge any attacks, no matter how feeble, if they are made directly, but I am all too impatient of attacks which are not made in due form. I care little about what we are discussing; all opinions are the same to me and it is all but indifferent to me which proposition emerges victorious. I can go on peacefully arguing all day if the debate is conducted with due order. It is not so much forceful and subtle argument that I want as order—the kind of order which can be found every day in disputes among shepherds and shop-assistants yet never among us. If they go astray it is in lack of courtesy. So do we. But their stormy intolerance does not make them stray far from their theme: their arguments keep on course. They interrupt each other. They jostle, but at least get the gist. To answer the point is, in my judgement, to answer very well. But when the discussion becomes turbulent and lacks order, I quit the subject-matter and cling irritably and injudiciously to the form, dashing into a style of debate which is stubborn, ill-willed and imperious, one which I have to blush for later.

It is impossible to argue in good faith with a fool. Not only my judgement is corrupted at the hands of so violent a master, so is my sense of right and wrong. Our quarrels ought to be outlawed and punished as are other verbal crimes. Since they are always ruled and governed by anger, what vices do they not awaken and pile up on each other? First we feel enmity for the arguments and then for the men. In debating we are taught merely how to refute arguments; the result of each side's refuting the other is that the fruit of our debates is the destruction and annihilation of the truth.[2] That is why Plato in his *Republic* prohibits that exercise to ill-endowed minds not suited to it.[3]

You are in quest of what *is.*[4] Why on earth do you set out to walk that road 5
with a man who has neither pace nor style? We do no wrong to the subject-matter if we depart from it in order to examine the way to treat it—I do not mean a scholastic, donnish way, I mean a natural way, based on a healthy intellect. But what happens in the end? One goes east and the other west; they lose the fundamental point in the confusion of a mass of incidentals. After a tempestuous hour they no longer know what they are looking for. One man is beside the bull's eye, the other too high, the other too low. One fastens on a word or a comparison; another no longer sees his opponent's arguments,

being too caught up in his own train of thought: he is thinking of pursuing his own argument not yours. Another, realizing he is too weak in the loins, is afraid of everything, denies everything and, from the outset, muddles and confuses the argument, or else, at the climax of the debate he falls into a rebellious total silence, affecting, out of morose ignorance, a haughty disdain or an absurdly modest desire to avoid contention. Yet[5] another does not care how much he drops his own guard provided that he can hit you. Another counts every word and believes they are as weighty as reasons. This man merely exploits the superior power of his voice and lungs. And then there is the man who sums up against himself; and the other who deafens you with useless introductions and digressions. Another is armed with pure insults and picks a groundless 'German quarrel' so as to free himself from the company and conversation of a mind which presses hard on his own.

Lastly, there is the man who cannot see reason but holds you under siege within a hedge of dialectical conclusions and logical formulae. Who can avoid beginning to distrust our professional skills and doubt whether we can extract from them any solid profit of practical use in life when he reflects on the use we put them to? *'Nihil sanantibus litteris.'* [such erudition as has no power to heal.][6] Has anyone ever acquired intelligence through logic? Where are her beautiful promises? *'Nec ad melius vivendum nec ad commodius disserendum.'* [She teaches neither how to live a better life nor how to argue properly.] Is there more of a hotchpotch in the cackle of fishwives than in the public disputations of men who profess logic? I would prefer a son of mine to learn to talk in the tavern rather than in our university yap-shops.

Take an arts don; converse with him. Why is he incapable of making us feel the excellence of his 'arts' and of throwing the women, and us ignoramuses, into ecstasies of admiration at the solidity of his arguments and the beauty of his ordered rhetoric! Why cannot he overmaster us and sway us at his will? Why does a man with his superior mastery of matter and style intermingle his sharp thrusts with insults, indiscriminate arguments and rage? Let him remove his academic hood, his gown and his Latin; let him stop battering our ears with raw chunks of pure Aristotle; why, you would take him for one of us—or worse. The involved linguistic convolutions with which they confound us remind me of conjuring tricks: their sleight-of-hand has compelling force over our senses but it in no wise shakes our convictions. Apart from such jugglery they achieve nothing but what is base and ordinary. They may be more learned but they are no less absurd.

I like and honour erudition as much as those who have it. When used properly it is the most noble and powerful acquisition of Man. But in the kind of men (and their number is infinite) who make it the base and foundation of their worth and achievement, who quit their understanding for their memory, *'sub aliena umbra latentes'* [hiding behind other men's shadows],[7] and can do nothing except by book, I loathe (dare I say it?) a little more than I loathe stupidity.

In my part of the country and during my own lifetime school-learning has brought amendment of purse but rarely amendment of soul. If the souls it meets are already obtuse, as a raw and undigested mass it clogs and suffocates them; if they are unfettered, it tends to purge them, strip them of impurities and volatilize them into vacuity. Erudition is a thing the quality of which is neither good nor bad, almost: it is a most useful adjunct to a well-endowed soul: to any other it is baleful and harmful; or rather, it is a thing which, in use, has great value,[8] but it will not allow itself to be acquired at a base price: in one hand it is a royal sceptre, in another, a fool's bauble.

But to get on: what greater victory do you want than to teach your enemy that he cannot stand up to you? Get the better of him by your argument and the winner is the truth; do so by your order and style, then you are the winner!

Notes

1. Plutarch (tr. Amyot), *De la mauvaise honte,* 81 B.
2. Renaissance rhetoric and dialectic in school and university did indeed often encourage *pro et contra* debates rather than a search for truth.
3. Plato, *Republic,* 539 A–C.
4. '88: of *the truth:* why . . .
5. '88: muddles *and ruffles the debate.* Yet another . . .
6. Seneca, *Epist. moral.,* LIX, 15; then, Cicero, *De finibus,* I, xix, 63, criticizing Epicurean logic.
7. Seneca, *Epist. moral.,* XXXIII, 7.
8. '88: great *nobility and* value . . .

Understanding

1. According to Montaigne, what are some of the characteristics of a "good conversation"?
2. Montaigne paints an unflattering picture of university professors, or "dons." What fault does he find in them? What other opinions does he relate about university life?
3. In Montaigne's view, what is the purpose of conversation?
4. Do you find the tone of this essay "personal"? Indicate those elements that support your view.

Responding

1. Describe your conversational skills. How have you developed them? In what situations is it easy for you to converse? In what situations is it difficult? How important are your conversational skills to your sense of self?
2. In Montaigne's day the ability to converse was the hallmark of an educated person. In today's society, as you know it, what place does "conversation" have in distinguishing such a person? Where do the most interesting conversations take place today?
3. How has the presence of women changed the quality of "conversation" among educated people?
4. If you could have dinner with three people (from the past or the present), who would they be? Why would you choose them? What do you think you

would converse about? What do your choices of dinner guests suggest about you and the values you hold?

Connecting

1. How does Montaigne's description of a good conversation compare with Rheingold's notion in "Cyberhood vs. Neighborhood: Community" in the "In Public and Private" section later in this chapter?
2. What characteristics of Montaigne's description correspond to Conroy's description of the mediated conversation between Justice William O. Douglas and Learned Hand in "Think About It"?

The Ascent to Wisdom

Plato

According to Plato (circa 427–347 B.C.), education is the central public concern of any well-ordered government. In today's society education is also a primary means of socializing people to the expectations of society.

Although schools are the most obvious institutions for providing an "education," according to Plato, they provide only the basics—the tools of learning. It is futile and dangerous, he believed, to expect schools to bring immature pupils to an awareness of higher truths. Formal schooling should lead to the mastery of a method for a lifelong pursuit of wisdom.

"Nowhere is Plato's vision of education more powerfully expressed than in the parable of the cave from *The Republic,* which French philosopher Jean-Jacques Rousseau said was "the finest treatise on Education ever written." In this parable one of the prisoners in an underground cave, who has never seen anything more substantial than shadows, is unchained and brought out into the blazing sunlight. At first he wants to withdraw from the painful brightness, but eventually he comes to realize that seeing things as they are is the only way to live life. He resists returning to the cave and its world of illusion but finally realizes that he has an inescapable duty to go back and help others see through their illusions.

At about age forty, after having traveled widely through Greece, Egypt, and Italy, Plato returned to Athens, where he founded a school of advanced studies in mathematics and philosophy, teaching there until his death.

And now, I said, let me show in a parable what education means in human life. Behold! human beings living in an underground den, which has a mouth open towards the light and reaching all along the den; here they have been from their childhood, and have their legs and necks chained so that they cannot move, and can only see before them, being prevented by the chains from turning round their heads. Above and behind them a fire is blazing at a distance, and between the fire and the prisoners there is a raised way; and you will see, if you look, a low wall built along the way, like the screen which marionette players have in front of them, over which they show the puppets. 1

I see.

And do you see, I said, men passing along the wall carrying all sorts of vessels, and statues and figures of animals made of wood and stone and various materials, which appear over the wall? Some of them are talking, others silent.

You have shown me a strange image, and they are strange prisoners.

Like ourselves, I replied; and they see only their own shadows, or the shadows of one another, which the fire throws on the opposite wall of the cave?

True, he said; how could they see anything but the shadows if they were never allowed to move their heads?

And of the objects which are being carried in like manner they would only see the shadows?

Yes, he said.

And if they were able to converse with one another, would they not suppose that they were naming what was actually before them?

Very true.

And suppose further that the prison had an echo which came from the other side, would they not be sure to fancy when one of the passers-by spoke that the voice which they heard came from the passing shadow?

No question, he replied.

To them, I said, the truth would be literally nothing but the shadows of the images.

That is certain.

And now look again, and see what will naturally follow if the prisoners are released and disabused of their error. At first, when any of them is liberated and compelled suddenly to stand up and turn his neck round and walk and look towards the light, he will suffer sharp pains; the glare will distress him, and he will be unable to see the realities of which in his former state he had seen the shadows; and then conceive someone saying to him, that what he saw before was an illusion, but that now, when he is approaching nearer to being and his eye is turned towards more real existence, he has a clearer vision—what will be his reply? And you may further imagine that his instructor is pointing to the objects as they pass and requiring him to name them—will he not be perplexed? Will he not fancy that the shadows which he formerly saw are truer than the objects which are now shown to him?

Far truer.

And if he is compelled to look straight at the light, will he not have a pain in his eyes which will make him turn away to take refuge in the objects of vision which he can see, and which he will conceive to be in reality clearer than the things which are now being shown to him?

True, he said.

And suppose once more, that he is reluctantly dragged up a steep and rugged ascent, and held fast until he is forced into the presence of the sun himself, is he not likely to be pained and irritated? When he approaches the light his eyes will be dazzled, and he will not be able to see anything at all of what are now called realities.

Not all in a moment, he said.

He will require to grow accustomed to the sight of the upper world. And first he will see the shadows best, next the reflections of men and other objects in the water, and then the objects themselves; then he will gaze upon the light of the moon and the stars and the spangled heaven; and he will see the sky and the stars by night better than the sun or the light of the sun by day?

Certainly.

Last of all he will be able to see the sun, and not mere reflections of him in the water, but he will see him in his own proper place, and not in another; and he will contemplate him as he is.

Certainly.

He will then proceed to argue that this is he who gives the season and the years, and is the guardian of all that is in the visible world, and in a certain way the cause of all things which he and his fellows have been accustomed to behold?

Clearly, he said, he would first see the sun and then reason about him.

And when he remembered his old habitation, and the wisdom of the den and his fellow prisoners, do you not suppose that he would felicitate himself on the change, and pity them?

Certainly, he would.

And if they were in the habit of conferring honors among themselves on those who were quickest to observe the passing shadows and to remark which of them went before, and which followed after, and which were together; and who were therefore best able to draw conclusions as to the future, do you think that he would care for such honors and glories, or envy the possessors of them? Would he not say with Homer,

"Better to be the poor servant of a poor master,"

and to endure anything, rather than think as they do and live after their manner?

Yes, he said, I think that he would rather suffer anything than entertain these false notions and live in this miserable manner.

Imagine once more, I said, such a one coming suddenly out of the sun to be replaced in his old situation; would he not be certain to have his eyes full of darkness?

To be sure, he said.

And if there were a contest, and he had to compete in measuring the shadows with the prisoners who had never moved out of the den, while his sight was still weak, and before his eyes had become steady (and the time which would be needed to acquire this new habit of sight might be very considerable), would he not be ridiculous? Men would say of him that up he went and down he came without his eyes; and that it was better not even to think of ascending; and if any one tried to loose another and lead him up to the light, let them only catch the offender, and they would put him to death.

No question, he said.

This entire allegory, I said, you may now append, dear Glaucon, to the previous argument; the prison house is the world of sight, the light of the fire is the sun, and you will not misapprehend me if you interpret the journey upwards to be the ascent of the soul into the intellectual world according to my poor belief, which, at your desire, I have expressed—whether rightly or wrongly God knows. But, whether true or false, my opinion is that in the world of knowledge the idea of good appears last of all, and is seen only with an effort; and, when seen, is also inferred to be the universal author of all things beautiful and right, parent of light and of the lord of light in this visible world, and the immediate source of reason and truth in the intellectual; and that this is the power upon which he who would act rationally either in public or private life must have his eye fixed.

I agree, he said, as far as I am able to understand you.

Moreover, I said, you must not wonder that those who attain to this beatific vision are unwilling to descend to human affairs; for their souls are ever hastening into the upper world where they desire to dwell; which desire of theirs is very natural, if our allegory may be trusted.

Yes, very natural.

And is there anything surprising in one who passes from divine contemplations to the evil state of man, misbehaving himself in a ridiculous manner; if, while his eyes are blinking and before he has become accustomed to the surrounding darkness, he is compelled to fight in courts of law, or in other places, about the images or the shadows of images of justice, and is endeavoring to meet the conceptions of those who have never yet seen absolute justice?

Anything but surprising, he replied.

Any one who has common sense will remember that the bewilderments of the eyes are of two kinds, and arise from two causes, either from coming out of the light or from going into the light, which is true of the mind's eye, quite as much as of the bodily eye; and he who remembers this when he sees any one whose vision is perplexed and weak, will not be too ready to laugh; he will first ask whether that soul of man has come out of the brighter life, and is unable to see because unaccustomed to the dark, or having turned from darkness to the day is dazzled by excess of light. And he will count the one happy in his condition and state of being, and he will pity the other; or, if he have a mind to laugh at the soul which comes from below into the light, there will be more reason in this than in the laugh which greets him who returns from above out of the light into the den.

That, he said, is a very just distinction.

But then, if I am right, certain professors of education must be wrong when they say that they can put a knowledge into the soul which was not there before, like sight into blind eyes.

They undoubtedly say this, he replied.

Whereas, our argument shows that the power and capacity of learning exists in the soul already; and that just as the eye was unable to turn from darkness to light without the whole body, so too the instrument of knowledge can only by the movement of the whole soul be turned from the world of becoming into that of being, and learn by degrees to endure the sight of being, and of the brightest and best of being, or in other words, of the good.

Very true.

And must there not be some art which will effect conversion in the easiest and quickest manner; not implanting the faculty of sight, for that exists already, but has been turned in the wrong direction, and is looking away from the truth?

Yes, he said, such an art may be presumed.

And whereas the other so-called virtues of the soul seem to be akin to bodily qualities, for even when they are not originally innate they can be implanted later by habit and exercise, the virtue of wisdom more than anything else contains a divine element which always remains, and by this conversion is rendered useful and profitable; or, on the other hand, hurtful and useless. Did you never observe the narrow intelligence flashing from the keen eye of a clever rogue—how eager he is, how clearly his paltry soul sees the way to his end; he is the reverse of blind, but his keen eyesight is forced into the service of evil, and he is mischievous in proportion to his cleverness?

Very true, he said. 50

But what if there had been a circumcision of such natures in the days of their youth; and they had been severed from those sensual pleasures, such as eating and drinking, which, like leaden weights, were attached to them at their birth, and which drag them down and turn the vision of their souls upon the things that are below—if, I say, they had been released from these impediments and turned in the opposite direction, the very same faculty in them would have seen the truth as keenly as they see what their eyes are turned to now.

Very likely.

Yes, I said; and there is another thing which is likely, or rather a necessary inference from what has preceded, that neither the uneducated and uninformed of the truth, nor yet those who never make an end of their education, will be able ministers of State; not the former, because they have no single aim of duty which is the rule of all their actions, private as well as public; nor the latter, because they will not act at all except upon compulsion, fancying that they are already dwelling apart in the islands of the blest.

Very true, he replied.

Then, I said, the business of us who are the founders of the State will be 55
to compel the best minds to attain that knowledge which we have already shown to be the greatest of all—they must continue to ascend until they arrive at the good; but when they have ascended and seen enough we must not allow them to do as they do now.

What do you mean?

I mean that they remain in the upper world: but this must not be allowed; they must be made to descend again among the prisoners in the den, and partake of their labors and honors, whether they are worth having or not.

But is not this unjust? he said; ought we to give them a worse life, when they might have a better?

You have again forgotten, my friend, I said, the intention of the legislator, who did not aim at making any one class in the State happy above the rest; the happiness was to be in the whole State, and he held the citizens together by persuasion and necessity, making them benefactors of the State, and therefore benefactors of one another; to this end he created them, not to please themselves, but to be his instruments in binding up the State.

True, he said, I had forgotten. 60

Observe, Glaucon, that there will be no injustice in compelling our philosophers to have a care and providence of others; we shall explain to them that in other States, men of their class are not obliged to share in the toils of politics: and this is reasonable, for they grow up at their own sweet will, and the government would rather not have them. Being self-taught, they cannot be expected to show any gratitude for a culture which they have never received. But we have brought you into the world to be rulers of the hive, kings of yourselves and of the other citizens, and have educated you far better and more perfectly than they have been educated, and you are better able to share in the double duty. Wherefore each of you, when his turn comes, must go down to the general underground abode, and get the habit of seeing in the dark. When you have acquired the habit, you will see ten thousand times better than the inhabitants of the den, and you will know what the several images are, and what they represent, because you have seen the beautiful and just and good in their truth.

Understanding

1. Plato introduces the idea of knowledge-sharing as a criterion of responsible citizenship. What justifications does he provide for this assertion?
2. According to Plato, where is this perfect world? If it doesn't exist, where does the idea of a perfect world come from?
3. Plato believed that in some supernatural realm there exists a truly just and good society—an ideal world—in which social life on earth as we know it is a pale and distorted reflection. He believed that, through reasoning, philosophers could incorporate knowledge of this perfect reality and that they should organize a universal compulsory school system where boys and girls could be "taught" as much about this reality as their capacities would permit. Why is this important?

Responding

1. In what ways do you see lifelong learning occurring in the adults you know? Are they conscious of this process? What value does it have for them? How do you imagine you will proceed in your quest for lifelong learning?
2. If you were working for political development in some traditional, nontechnological society, what specific techniques of adult education or training would you use and for what purposes?
3. Typically, *education* encourages people to acquire knowledge through discussion and independent thinking. *Training*, on the other hand, requires that people develop skills without extensive research and, sometimes, without much independent thinking. What is the relationship between these two enterprises? How do they characterize formal schooling today? Explain.

Connecting

1. Rodriguez indicates in "The New, New World" ("In Public and Private" later in this chapter) that he greatly values the education he received: "We were in the 13th century, but the 13th-century skills prepared us in some remarkable way to belong." What does he mean? What would Plato say about his statement?
2. The concept of illusion to which Plato refers in the parable of the cave has also been taken up by Csikszentmihalyi in "The Veils of Maya and the World of the Genes" in chapter five. What is an illusion? In what ways does it cloud people's perception of reality?
3. How does Plato's parable of "what education means in a human life" compare with the schooling experiences Mike Rose describes in "I Just Wanna Be Average"?

WRITING OPTION: Learning Communities

From your store of responses to the Responding questions in this "Learning Communities" section, choose the one in which you felt most intellectually or emotionally involved in writing. Revise or expand that response as an essay or a narrative using any of the "Learning Communities" readings as guides to the style and the concepts presented.

Whatever form you choose, it should reflect your unique perspective on how your membership in a learning community influenced your view of education, schooling, or some other learning venue *and* led to some change in you through that experience. Some possibilities include: how specific learning experiences socialized you; how they influenced you positively or negatively to continue your schooling; how one or two pivotal teachers influenced your attitude toward learning or school; how you responded to Plato's theory of education in "The Ascent to Wisdom" or Rose's views in "I Just Wanna Be Average." Focus your thoughts on developing one strong position or theme.

3 Communities of Faith

Over time and throughout the world, faith in a power beyond our human capabilities has inspired the formation of religions—organized communities of faith that offer consolation and certainty in an uncertain world. Adhering to a religion, whether through birth or by choice, also offers us membership in a community of believers. Our faith becomes part of who we are, and our religion a way of identifying ourselves to the outside world. Until declared illegal in the United States, for example, it was a common practice for employers to ask job applicants to state their religion.

This section offers three perspectives on experiences of faith. As a psychologist, Gordon Allport traces the evolution of religious belief and the very personal contribution it makes to "completing our personality." Shirley Park Lowry examines how and why religious "myths," as she calls them, reconcile us to life's limitations. Tucked between these two academic views of religion and faith is Stephen J. Dubner's personal narrative of how he made the momentous decision to change his religion.

According to some social observers, mainline religions in the United States are waning, but spirituality, an individual's personal connection with the divine or the all-powerful, is on the rise. Whatever form religious expression takes—solitary meditation, ecstatic frenzy, or traditional community worship—religions and the faith that nourishes them add an otherworldly dimension to who we are. These readings and your written responses to them may add to your appreciation of how we grapple with what many believe goes on beyond our own earthly steps.

A Solitary Quest

Gordon Allport

Religion is a defining institution in many cultures. It has provoked wars and impelled peace, inspired great works of art and literature and presided over their destruction, united individual aspirations toward common goals and divided families against each other. Written in 1950, the essays collected under the title *The Individual and His Religion* were psychologist Gordon Allport's attempt to reconcile psychology with religion. It was his value judgment that individuals have the right to work out their own philosophies and find their own personal niches in creation. Religion is one path in this quest.

A native of Indiana and a graduate of Harvard, Allport (1897–1967) wrote extensively on the human personality and was an advocate of "trait psychology," the theory that a person's fundamental uniqueness flows from certain consistent thoughts and actions. He also believed that the "early self" is formed by the age of three and that this self consists of a bodily sense, a sense of personal identity which is related to the development of language, and a feeling of self-esteem, essential bases for the formation of the "mature self." In Allport's view, religion has a unique contribution to make to the integrity of the mature self.

I stated that belief normally seems to develop in three stages. There is first 1
a period of raw credulity, most clearly seen in the child who believes indiscriminately in the evidence of his senses, of his imagination, and in what he hears. His first religious beliefs are derived chiefly from what he hears, that is, from "verbal realism." To him words are as good as facts. That some of this primitive credulity lasts throughout life is evident, but chiefly, I think, in minds marked by arrested development, or in areas where we are starkly ignorant or in the face of strong prestige suggestion. Some religious belief among adults is of this unquestioning variety—childish, authoritarian, and irrational.

Normally, however, a second stage of development disrupts the first. Doubts of the many sorts we have considered flood into one's life. They are an integral part of all intelligent thinking. Until one has faced the improbabilities involved in any commitment one is not free to form an independent conviction based on productive thinking and observing.

Mature belief, the third stage, grows painfully out of the alternating doubts and affirmations that characterize productive thinking. We evolve our important beliefs *pari passu* with our values and our sentiments. When I say I believe in education, in civil rights, in the United Nations, I mean that these intangible objects are regarded by me not only as *existing* but also as *desirable* and wholly consonant with my personal sentiment-structure. They are necessary to me if I am to fulfill the course of development that has now become my essential style of life. All positive sentiments entail belief of this sort. For without belief one could not act in keeping with one's sentiments, and if one could not act out one's sentiments one soon would lose them. It is important to remark that beliefs may be held with all grades of certainty. Even a relatively unsure belief can marshal a great deal of energy. One does not know for certain that the United Nations can save civilization from collapse, but one can be loyal and helpful if one at least believes there is a good chance.

Is "faith" the same as "belief"? Often the words are used interchangeably, although more often there is a difference in connotation. We tend to speak of faith when we are designating the less sure beliefs. We believe our eyes, and we believe the proposition that twice two are four, but we have faith in America, or in the ultimate triumph of good over evil. There is, of course, a borderline of discourse where we can use either term. "I believe in the United Nations" means much the same as "I have faith in the United Nations."

"Faith" also seems to carry a warmer glow of affection than does bare 5
"belief." It suggests that though the risk may be greater, still the commitment is stronger and the outcome of the wager more precious. Most people, when asked, say they believe in God. But in many of these cases the reply seems perfunctory, and one suspects that the religious sentiment behind the statement is rudimentary. But when an individual says, "I have faith in God," it seems almost certain that the religious sentiment holds a prominent place in his personality-structure.

This excursion into semantics has no particular importance for our purpose excepting to indicate that faith is probably more complex psychologically than is simple belief. Although the term may be used in connection with any sentiment, it is most characteristically used in connection with the religious sentiment. And this fact seems to signify that we are dimly aware of the special intricacies involved in the affirmations arising from this sentiment. . . .

We come at last to the question how the religious individual justifies his faith. Even while his religious intentions are active he is incapable of cross-questioning himself. Is there a God or an orderly purpose to which he can reasonably address these intentions? It is important for him to know. How he goes about the process of validation is psychologically an interesting if complex story.

The basic phase in the process I have already described. A certain measure of confidence in the intended object is necessarily resident in every intention. Man knows his striving is real enough, and he suspects, from repeated experiences of reaching goals, that an appropriate object resides at the terminus of any persistent striving.

Is he thirsty? There is water to assuage his thirst. Is he tired? There is rest to be had. Cold? There is such a thing as warmth. Extending this reasoning to the religious striving, C. S. Lewis adds: "If I find in myself a desire which no experience in this world can satisfy, the most probable explanation is that I was made for another world. If none of my earthly pleasures satisfy it, that does not prove that the universe is a fraud. Probably earthly pleasures were never *meant* to satisfy it, but only to arouse it, to suggest the real thing."[1]

Thus people find that belief is both a reflex of their striving, and on the 10
whole a reasonable consequence to draw from the very fact of striving. A Mohammedan legend puts the matter picturesquely. A dervish was tempted by the devil to stop calling on Allah because Allah did not answer, "Here am I." The prophet Khadir appeared to the dervish in a vision with a message from Allah: "Was it not I who summoned thee to my service? Did I not make thee busy with My name? Thy calling 'Allah' was My 'Here am I.'"

According to this homily the fact of seeking is all that is required to validate the seeking.

In that thou seekest thou hast the treasure found,
Close with thy question is the answer bound.

One step beyond this modest validation takes us to the so-called ontological argument for the existence of God which derives the necessity of God's existence from the idea of God that man has. Although philosophers have been harsh in their rejection of the a priori statement of this proposition, an empirical or psychological version of the argument appeals to many people. Since my longing for perfect wisdom could not be the product of so finite a being as I (I would not be able to endow myself with glimpses of anything more perfect than myself), then it is inevitable for me to assume that God implanted in me the desire to know Him. The mere fact that I do undoubtedly have the idea of a perfect sovereign Being is a sign that the Creator has put this idea into my mind "as the mark of the workman imprinted on his work." Descartes is an ardent defender of this view. According to his reasoning, a nonentity cannot produce an entity; that which is imperfect cannot produce an idea of that which is perfect. Peter Abelard in the twelfth century expressed the same thought:

Wish and fulfillment can severed be ne'er,
Nor the thing prayed for come short of the prayer.

Values that cannot be achieved in this world *require* a Kingdom of Heaven.

The question may now be asked whether anyone is ever convinced by a simon-pure rational argument for the existence of God. It is certainly true that men do try to reason the matter through to a logically tight solution, just as they endeavor to find sound explanations for every riddle that confronts them. People want a rationally achieved answer. Some find it in the so-called cosmological argument which demands a sufficient first cause to explain the existence of matter, mind, and values. Yet is it not also true that unless one is awe-struck at the overpowering structure of the physical and moral universe, one could not feel the cogency of the cosmological argument? Without emotion and value he would not build a system of faith around it. Similarly, unless an individual is moved by evidences of intelligence and design in the universe, he would not take the teleological argument as support for his faith, because it would answer no lively questions for him.

What reasoning does is to lend support to a relationship that is already inherent in every sentiment—the relationship between an intention and the idea which is its object. Having first believed in the object because of the intended relationship that is set up, we normally continue to do so only if there is independent reinforcement. Sense perception and reasoning provide such support. Whenever belief receives a great deal of such reinforcement so that it conforms with sense perception, with reason, and with the beliefs of others, we are likely to call it *knowledge.* At the other extreme, when belief is deprived of all these supports, we call it *delusion.* In between these limits, where belief rests on probabilities, as the majority of beliefs do, we speak of *faith.* In all states of faith doubt is still theoretically possible though not actually dominating the mental situation at the moment.

Degrees of religious faith, as with all faith, range from high to low. Perhaps the highest is the unshakable certainty of the mystic that his immediate experience (for him the equivalent of sensory knowledge) confirms the existence of God. Perhaps the lowest degree is found in the aesthetic make-believe of Santayana who maintains that the great drama of religion would be marvelous if it were justified, so marvelous that we are entitled to act as if it were justified.

As I have previously pointed out, a relatively low degree of faith may be able to direct an enormous output of energy. One can be half-sure without being half-hearted. You and I may not have complete faith in the United Nations, but since it is our one and only hope we can and do back it with all our might. If our faith were zero we would not back it at all, but one chance in a thousand is enough for us. One recalls Descartes' reflections on this point. He remarks that a traveler who finds himself astray in some forest ought not to wander about, turning now to one side and now to another. He should walk as straight as he can in one direction, and not change it for trivial reasons. By so doing he is bound to arrive at some place probably far better than the middle of the forest.[2] Though it is not within our power to discern certain knowledge we do well to act decisively on the basis of whatever probability attends the object of our faith.

Where does revealed religion enter into the individual's struggle for validation? It unquestionably assists him if he is persuaded that God of His free generosity has chosen to give dependable, if partial, knowledge of Himself through the devices of the intelligible universe that affect our senses, including, for example, those divinely ordained symbols employed in the sacraments which are sensible signs of what is hidden in Him. It helps to assume that God chooses to declare Himself to us in our own language.[3] Faith, based on this premise, is enjoined by the historic church, and is for millions the decisive consideration. But it is well to note that the church allows also supporting means of faith, including the rational arguments of theology, and the avenue of mystical contemplation or immediate experience. It shows psychological wisdom in multiplying the avenues through which various individuals may achieve the heightened degree of confidence in the validity of their own beliefs.

There are two final modes of validation, different in type: the mystical and the pragmatic.

Although I have no conclusive evidence on the point, I suspect that the most commonly accepted type of verification is some form of immediate experience, convincing to oneself though not as a rule to others. It is religion's peculiar secret that it brings to the individual a solemn assurance unlike anything else in life, a tranquility, an ever-present help in trouble, that makes next steps easier no matter what mesh of circumstances may entangle the life. A person who finds that the practice of faith has brought a genuine solution of conflict is convinced, for to discover order and felicity where there were chaos and distress is to find something extraordinarily real. This experience of a "solution found" is often attended by some degree of mystical perception. One feels that one has reached out a hand and received an answering clasp. One has sent up a cry and heard a response. Whoever verifies his faith in this manner has evidence no less convincing to him than the sensory perception which validates his beliefs in the world about him. Immediacy of this sort persuades him that revelation comes from God to man. In passing, it may be remarked that what has been called "functional revelation" seems to be more common than is "cognitive revelation." That is to say, apparently more people report an access of strength and power than claim clarifying knowledge.

Swinging abruptly to a less introverted mode of validation we wonder how 20
many people in the present century owe their religious faith to William James's insistence that "a true thought is a thought that is an invaluable instrument of action." No need to embroil oneself in "snarling logicality" when the "will-to-believe" is available through a simple act of choice. For everyone there are higher and lower limits of attainment, and whatever leads the individual to the higher level is worth believing in. Good, believed in, finds itself embodied simply because faith changes aspiration into realization, transforms the possible into the actual. If I refuse to believe in democracy, regarding it as the dream of a fool, I shall not act democratically, and democracy will not come into being. Take the more productive option, says James. Religious faith is such an option. The core of its validation lies in the values generated and unity of life attained.

This outlook has marked appeal to action-minded individuals who have seen so many instances in life where faith in a fact (the optimistic bias) helps create the fact. Practically speaking, faith has undeniably good effects. Blending the pragmatic mode of thought with the rational one asks, "Must not that which has good effects likewise exist?" There are no effects without sufficient cause. Theism, as James himself points out, is a not infrequent accompaniment of pragmatism. Every other way of explaining value seems to break down halfway to its conclusion. The theist, for example, is persuaded that while nothing that contradicts science is likely to be true, still nothing that stops with science can be the whole truth. A more complete world view is to be achieved through affirming that the natural order is under divine rule.[4] Having committed oneself to this position the theistic-pragmatist finds his vision clarifying and his faith strengthened as he acts upon it. When, in the third chapter, I called attention to the heuristic character of mature religion I had in mind this fruitfulness of faith both for value and for understanding.

Any given individual is likely to accept several forms of validation, finding them in combination sufficient to sustain the degree of faith that he has achieved. Modes of validation do not clash; they are mutually supportive. Both reason and pragmatic sanction, for example, may blend in the individual's mind with memories of his own mystical experiences. The latter, in turn, may persuade him that divine grace is in fact available from above to help one's unbelief, and to enable one to complete the edifice of faith that no aspirant can build entirely alone.

With these many aids to verification the individual may achieve considerable certitude in the validity of his religion. Lacking, as he necessarily must, tests of absolute certainty, his own mode of validation is not necessarily convincing to others. But it may be deeply convincing to him.

THE SOLITARY WAY

My theme has been the diversity of form that subjective religion assumes. Many different desires may initiate the religious quest, desires as contrasting as fear and curiosity, gratitude and conformity. Men show a varying capacity to outgrow their childhood religion, and to evolve a well-differentiated mature religious sentiment. There are many degrees in the comprehensiveness of this sentiment and in its power to integrate the life. There are different styles of doubting, different apperceptions of symbols, contrasting types of content that vary both with the culture and with the temperament and capacity of the believer. There are innumerable types of specific religious intentions. How the individual justifies his faith is a variable matter, and the certitude he achieves is his alone.

From its early beginnings to the end of the road the religious quest of the 25
individual is solitary. Though he is socially interdependent with others in a thousand ways, yet no one else is able to provide him with the faith he evolves, nor prescribe for him his pact with the cosmos.

Often the religious sentiment is merely rudimentary in the personality, but often too it is a pervasive structure marked by the deepest sincerity. It is the portion of personality that arises at the core of the life and is directed toward the infinite. It is the region of mental life that has the longest-range intentions, and for this reason is capable of conferring marked integration upon personality, engendering meaning and peace in the face of the tragedy and confusion of life.

A man's religion is the audacious bid he makes to bind himself to creation and to the Creator. It is his ultimate attempt to enlarge and to complete his own personality by finding the supreme context in which he rightly belongs.

Notes

1. C. S. Lewis. *Christian Behaviour,* New York: Macmillan Co., 1943, pp. 57 f. Quoted by permission.
2. Réné Descartes. *Discourse on Method,* Part III.
3. Cf. J. Maritain. Science, Philosophy, and Faith in *Science, Philosophy and Religion: A Symposium,* New York: Conference on Science, Philosophy and Religion, 1941, Chapter 10.
4. W. James. Reflex action and theism in *The Will to Believe and Other Essays,* New York: Longmans Green, 1897.

Understanding

1. Allport distinguishes between *faith* and *belief.* What are the distinctions? Which of the two is more complex? Why?
2. Allport refers to two arguments for the existence of God: the ontological and the cosmological. What are these arguments and how do they relate to a person's religious "strivings"?
3. "Practically speaking," Allport asserts, "faith has undeniably good effects." What does he indicate are these "good effects"?
4. Why is the religious quest of the individual solitary?
5. Allport suggests that some form of immediate experience often moves individuals to believe in God. According to Allport, on what basis or bases does most people's faith in God reside? What purposes does faith serve?

Responding

1. Allport states that people "show a varying capacity to outgrow their childhood religion, and to evolve a . . . mature religious sentiment." How does this statement relate to your experience of faith?
2. For some people religion is an answer; for others, it is a question. How would you characterize its role in your life?
3. Although the religious quest is solitary, people often need a societal context—a place and like-minded people—in which to pursue it. Is it possible to be religious without some form of community support? Explain.

Connecting

In "The Ascent to Wisdom" in the "Learning Communities" section of this chapter, Plato relates that education entails a social responsibility, that the "best minds" have an obligation to "descend again among the prisoners in the den, and partake of their labors and honors" (paragraph 57). On the other hand, Allport explains that the religious quest is solitary, that no one else is able to provide us with the faith we evolve. What about these two quests requires that people take two such different paths to reach them?

Choosing My Religion

Stephen J. Dubner

For many people religion embodies the plain truth; for others it is a shackle on personal freedom. Perhaps because of its intensely personal significance in people's lives, religion has been a topic to avoid in social encounters. Recently, however, religion has entered into the public domain as a part of our national dialogue and has received even more attention in light of current debate on such issues as using federal tax dollars to support parochial schools, displaying religious symbols in public places, and sanctioning prayer in schools.

Stephen J. Dubner reflects this new openness in "Choosing My Religion," which appeared as a cover story in the *New York Times Magazine.* Dubner, an editor at the *New York Times,* explains that "There has never been a more liberal time and place than pre-millennial America to explore a given religion, both intellectually and spiritually." In "Choosing My Religion," he traces the path of faith that his parents scrupulously followed and reconstructs his own and others' conversion experiences.

What is particularly revealing is how the men and women he profiles view not just the importance of religion in their lives but the idea that they feel free to choose what they wish to believe. Equally fascinating is the fact that although all of them rejected their childhood religions, they embraced new communities of faith, revealing what Dubner calls the "fiercely personal nature of any religious search."

Not long ago, I was having Shabbos dinner with three friends. I am still new to all this. As the candles were lighted and a song was sung, I stumbled along. We washed our hands, then said the blessing as we dried them. I did know that you weren't supposed to speak until the bread had been blessed, so I went back to the table. 1

As I sat there, another silent ritual came to mind. I was raised in upstate New York and was the last of eight children. When it was your birthday, you had to eat your entire piece of cake without saying a word. If you broke your silence, a penalty awaited: molasses would be poured over your bare feet, then chicken feed sprinkled on, and you'd have to walk through the chicken coop and let the hens peck away.

Although the penalty was carried out a few times (never on me), what I remember best is the struggle to keep the silence, no matter how much everyone baited you. The whole thing was nonsense, and I had never thought about where it came from—until that Shabbos dinner a few weeks ago, when I suddenly wondered if one silence weren't somehow related to the other.

I did not grow up Jewish, but my parents did. Florence Greenglass and Solomon Dubner, both born in Brooklyn, were the children of Russian and

Polish immigrants. On Christmas Eve of 1942, when Florence was a 21-year-old ballet dancer, she was baptized as a Roman Catholic. Two years later, she met Sol, a 28-year-old soldier home on furlough. The son of Orthodox Jews, he, too, was about to become a Catholic.

Unlike St. Augustine or Thomas Merton, my parents did not embrace 5
Catholicism to atone for a wanton past. Unlike Saul of Tarsus, who became St. Paul, they saw no visions, heard no voices. Theirs were sober conversions of faith, brought about by no force or crises, or at least none visible from the surface.

The fallout was dramatic: no one in their families went to their wedding, and Sol's father never spoke to him again. They built new lives from top to bottom. They even changed their names. My mother chose Veronica as her baptismal name and has used it ever since; Sol, not surprisingly, became Paul.

They began having children, moved to a rural sprawl outside Albany and continued having children. After Joseph, the first son, and Mary, the first daughter, the rest of us had to settle for Joseph or Mary as our middle names. My namesake was St. Stephen, the first Christian martyr, who, I remember learning early on, was stoned to death by Jews.

We took our Catholicism very seriously. We never missed Mass; our father was a lector, and both our parents taught catechism. At 3 in the afternoon on Good Friday, we gathered in the living room for 10 minutes of silence in front of a painting of the Crucifixion. On top of a battered bookcase, our mother kept a simple shrine: a large wooden crucifix, a statue of a beatific Virgin Mary and several devotional candles, all nestled on a thick piece of red felt. Once a year, when our grandmother was due to visit, the shrine was packed away in a cardboard box. This wasn't a sin, our mother assured us, and was absolutely necessary, to keep our grandmother "from getting hysterical."

It did seem strange that our Jewish aunts and uncles and cousins almost never visited—not that I had the slightest idea of what a Jew or Judaism was. Our neighbors were farmers and auto mechanics named O'Donnell and Vandemeer. Only when our father died, when he was 57 and I was 10, did a handful of Jewish relatives make the trip upstate. Because our grandmother was dead by then, the shrine stayed put.

The matter of our having been Jewish was half footnote, half secret. A jar 10
of gefilte fish sometimes found its way into the refrigerator, and our parents occasionally resorted to Yiddish for private conversation. But their ardent Catholicism allowed for scant inquiry into a different religious past. My brother Dave remembers asking our mother, when he was 7, why they had become Catholic. "Because we were young and we were searching for the truth, and we found it," she told him.

If I had known then what I know now, I might have recognized the remnants of my parents' past—for a religious conversion, I have come to learn, is imperfect. At best, the convert is a palimpsest. The old writing will always bleed through. The gefilte fish, the birthday cake routine, the way our father would burst into "My Yiddishe Mama"—it all reminds me of the Marranos, the Jews who were forced during the Spanish Inquisition to convert to Catholicism and wound up practicing their Judaism in secret. Hundreds of years later, some fully assimilated Marrano families still clung to old Jewish rituals with no idea where they had come from.

But for my parents—and now, for me, as I am becoming a Jew—there is a pointed difference. We have *chosen* our religion, rejecting what we inherited for what we felt we needed. This is a particularly American opportunity and one that is being exploited in ever-increasing numbers. To be convinced, you only need to stick your head into an overflowing Catholic conversion workshop, a mosque filled with American-born blacks, a 5,000-member "megachurch" that caters to forward-looking Protestants or a tiny Pentecostal church packed with Hispanic immigrants who came here as Catholics. "Religious switching is more common now than it has ever been in American history," says Dean Hoge, a sociology professor at Catholic University in Washington, D.C., who has conducted many religious surveys.

Statistics on religious affiliation are notoriously slippery: the Government isn't allowed to gather such data, and the membership claims of religious organizations aren't entirely reliable. But, according to "One Nation Under God" (1993), by Barry A. Kosmin and Seymour P. Lachman, perhaps the most ambitious study to date of Americans and their religions, about 30 percent of Americans now switch denominations in their lifetimes. Kosmin and Lachman, who used a survey of 113,000 people, conclude that the most common reason for a switch is, predictably, intermarriage, followed by a shift in religious conviction and a geographical change.

To be sure, the majority of shifts are not particularly dramatic, tending to be from one Protestant denomination to another. (In a study of 500 people from 33 to 42 years old who had been confirmed as Presbyterians, Hoge found that 33 percent had already made a move, usually to another mainline Protestant denomination.) Still, Kosmin says, "There are more spiritual searches now than ever before, mainly because people are freer than ever before to search."

There is also the common phenomenon of intensely renewing your reli- 15
gion of birth as an adult—an especially strong movement among American Jews and middle-class blacks. Such journeys often fall under what is known as Hansen's Law, or the third-generation syndrome, noted by the sociologist Marcus Lee Hansen in the 1930's. According to Hansen's Law, a person looks beyond his parents' religion, which was watered down by assimilation, to the religion of his grandparents, splicing traditional rituals and beliefs into his modern life.

Americans born after World War II, simultaneously facing their parents' deaths and watching their children grow up with a flimsy religious identity, are particularly susceptible to Hansen's Law. The recent surge in American spirituality has sent even the most secular adults into what has become a religion bazaar, where the boundaries are far more fluid and the rules less rigid than when they were children. As late as 1960, even a Protestant-Catholic marriage might have kept at least one set of in-laws out of the church; since then, the charge toward ecumenism has been relentless.

Jack Miles, a former Jesuit and the author of the recent "God: A Biography," told me why he thought this is so: because America has long been that rare country where a religious identity, as opposed to a political identity, is optional. As citizens of a country that has absorbed, with a fair amount of grace, so many different religious traditions, we are bound to be more tolerant and experimental. Miles himself is proof: after leaving the seminary in 1970, he considered converting to Judaism, then flirted with Buddhism and is now a practicing Episcopalian.

By now, choosing a religion is no longer a novel idea. And sometimes all the switching can seem comically casual. At the first meeting of a Judaism class I've been taking, we all announced why we had come. "I grew up Catholic in New Zealand—Catholic school, the whole bit," said one earnest young man, who was there with his Jewish girlfriend. "I had more than my share of whacks on the behind. And, well, as I learned more about Judaism, I thought it was a cracking good religion, so I'm here to see more about it."

The movement toward choosing religion, rampant as it is, shouldn't be surprising. Ours is an era marked by the desire to define—or redefine—ourselves. We have been steadily remaking ourselves along ethnic, political, sexual, linguistic and cultural lines, carefully sewing new stripes into our personal flags and waving them with vigor. Now, more than ever, we are working on the religious stripe.

That, of course, is a tricky proposition, since religion comprises practically 20
every strand of identity we possess, and since so many religious rituals are also our most important family rituals. Disengaging yourself from your family's religion often means disengaging yourself, to some extent, from your family.

Lately, I have fallen in with and sought out a variety of converts—or seekers or returnees or born-agains, as they variously call themselves. Judith Anderson, 34, is a practicing Buddhist who was raised, she said, in a "devoutly atheistic" Jewish family in Teaneck, N.J. Like many Jews who practice Buddhism, she hasn't renounced her Jewishness; still, her parents are distressed with the spiritual layer she has added to her life, and she is torn between satisfying herself and appeasing them.

"My heart really hurts right now," she told me. "If they knew half of what goes on in the Buddhist center I belong to, or half of what I say in the morning when I do chants, it would absolutely freak them out. So I will probably always edit what I say and what I expose them to." She keeps a small Buddhist shrine in her Manhattan apartment; when her parents visit, she takes most of it down.

Three of my four sisters are still practicing Catholics; none of my brothers are. Most of them are curious about my God-wrestling, as we sometimes call it, but they don't seem to want or need it for themselves. My mother, meanwhile, remains the most devoted Catholic I have ever known. Two summers ago, I was sitting with her on a screened-in porch in the Adirondacks. Everyone else was off swimming or fishing. To that point, I hadn't asked her how she felt about my push toward Judaism, since I was pretty sure I knew. Now, though, I decided to go ahead with the question.

She tilted her face toward me and almost smiled. "How can I tell you what to believe?" she said. "You have to be true to your own conscience, and you have to do what you think is right." Her answer surprised me and pleased me.

"But," she went on, "I see this as the loss of a great opportunity for 25
you." She respected Judaism, she explained, but only as the foundation for Catholicism.

Her tone of voice encouraged no argument. A door slammed, and my niece ran in, dripping wet, wanting to tell Grandma about her swim. I was relieved to be interrupted. For the first time, I had felt the sting of rebuke that, a half-century ago, my parents must have felt tenfold.

* * *

It may be that the transcendent mystery of a religious conversion, like the transcendence of sex, is incommunicable. A conversion is a tangle of loneliness, ambition, fear and, of course, hope. It is never tidy. The memoirs written by converts are generally one of two kinds: the breathless account of an irreversible epiphany (I tend to be skeptical of these) and the story wherein a convert pokes around his soul and his mind, yet arrives at no more concrete an explanation than a pressing desire to change the course of his life.

The current boom in choosing religion exists precisely because such inquiry is allowed today—as opposed to when my parents converted. There has never been a more liberal time and place than pre-millennial America to explore a given religion, both intellectually and spiritually. Fifty years ago, challenging a religious text or arguing with doctrine bordered on the heretical; now it is fashionable. Most denominations have become adept at packaging themselves, at disseminating their doctrines and rewards. "It's supply-side religion," Barry Kosmin says. "It's a free-market situation, and anything you can do to survive in that market, you'll do."

What the trends don't reveal, of course, is the fiercely personal nature of any religious search. Daniel Dunn, 26, a database programmer in Boca Raton, Fla., who grew up in the United Church of Christ, became a Catholic after a serious water-skiing accident left him wondering why he hadn't died. "I would go every Sunday and sit in the back pew, just watching and listening to the weekly Scriptures," Dunn says. "I was able to relate to each one in some way, which I hadn't been able to do as a young person."

Everyone who chooses a religion is running toward—and away from—his 30
own mountain of questions. As adults, at least people know how to ask those questions and, just as important, how to argue—with their religions, their consciences, their families. They experience the intoxicating jolt of learning a religion with the intellect of an adult rather than the rote acceptance of a child.

I recently met a 22-year-old woman named Fatima Shama, whose mother is a devout Catholic from Brazil and whose father, a Palestinian Muslim, isn't very religious, Shama said. Shama grew up Catholic in the Bronx; she saw Islam, as practiced by her aunts, as exceedingly anti-female. At college, though, she discovered literary interpretations of the Koran, many written by women.

"I realized that everything I'd been taught as a child was wrong," she told me. "I began to separate out the Islamic religion from the Arabic culture, to learn what was really what." She now practices Islam, albeit a more liberal form than her aunts do, and insists that she will marry an Arab-American Muslim. "All my brothers and sisters, they think I'm whacked," Shama said. "They always say to me, 'Where did you come from?' "

I have been asked the same question, now that I am becoming a Jew—or, as some would argue, as I am learning to be the Jew that I have always been. I was, after all, born of a Jewish mother; curious as my religious provenance may be, my bloodline would provide entry into either the state of Israel or a concentration camp.

Four years ago, I first sat down with my mother and a tape recorder. I had to know at least a little bit about my Jewish family, and how Florence Greenglass became Veronica Dubner. And I had to understand what made me so badly want to be Jewish when both my mother and father wanted so badly not to be.

* * *

What could be called the first existential thought of Florence Greenglass's 35
life occurred in 1931, when she was 10. In bed with a cold, she heard her friends playing stickball outside and realized that, with or without her, life would go rambling on. From that day, she pondered the ephemerality of her existence, and her fate.

Her father, Harry, was an agnostic, a quietly affable man who ran a candy store on Lincoln Place in Brooklyn. Florence had an older sister and a mother, Esther, who disapproved of most things that Florence was interested in. Harry and Esther, born poor in Russia, were now inching toward the middle class. They were the only Jews in their neighborhood, which was mostly Catholic. Florence's grandmother was Orthodox and devout, but the rest of the family observed only Passover and a few other holidays.

Florence considered her Jewishness largely inconsequential. "Except I do remember one time, this girl standing up in class, in sixth grade," she told me. "This very, very blond girl, her name was Ann Ross. And she said, 'My father thinks that Hitler has the right idea about the Jews.' That was kind of a blow, to hear somebody come out and say that."

When Florence was 13, she began studying ballet in Manhattan. Her teacher, Asta Souvorina, was about 60, a former Russian ballerina and actress who had fled Moscow in 1917. Madame Souvorina, as her students always called her, had converted to Catholicism from Russian Orthodoxy. She was domineering, charming, melodramatic; an intellectual, a storyteller—a mentor in every sense. Florence became her star dancer, performing in her small company and later in nightclub acts.

Florence and some of the other girls virtually lived at the studio, where Mme. Souvorina held forth on many subjects. When she mentioned the Epistles of St. Paul, Florence was curious: she had no idea that a living, breathing person, a Jew no less, had left behind such a dramatic record of his newfound faith, and such a compelling explanation of everlasting life. She read Paul's letters and felt they had the ring of truth.

"Well, if you really believe, you ought to do something about it," Mme. 40
Souvorina told her. "You ought to get baptized, because that's what Jesus said you should do."

But Florence had much to reconcile—the Virgin Birth, for instance, seemed highly implausible. Her search was long and gradual. She devoured literature and asked endless questions of priests and her Catholic friends. One day, she went to Mass at the Church of the Blessed Sacrament, on West 71st Street in Manhattan, just down Broadway from Mme. Souvorina's studio. She was 21.

Even now, after more than 50 years, my mother's eyes brighten at the memory, and her voice shoots up an octave: "The priest was saying, 'God said, "This is my beloved son in whom I am well pleased. Hear Him." ' Those words were the key to my conversion, actually—'*hear* Him,' listen to Jesus and do what He said. And all of a sudden, everything made sense."

About two years ago, I asked my mother how she ultimately came to accept the Virgin Birth and the Resurrection on a literal level. "First of all, it's told in Scripture," she said. But how had she come to believe Scripture? "Because you feel that Scripture was divinely inspired, for one thing—it's not a fairy tale that's made up." But how was she convinced that the Gospels canonized in the New Testament were divinely inspired, as opposed to all the conflicting gospels that didn't make it in?

A long, jagged pause. "It's the gift of faith," she said, "and faith is a gift."

It's the gift of faith, and faith is a gift. Where could I go with that? I recalled how our parents used to parry any questions about Catholicism: faith, they told us, is a treasure that can neither be questioned nor fully explained.

Florence was baptized at Blessed Sacrament, and her new faith immediately became the most valuable thing in her life. Esther, her mother, was heartsick and furious—what kind of daughter would betray the family, betray the Jews? Esther tried to plead, bully, threaten her daughter out of it. Veronica, as she now called herself, put up a font of holy water in her bedroom; when she came home, it was missing. "My mother told me I was to blame for her arthritis," she remembers. "And when my father died, she said he died because of me."

She had anticipated her mother's anger. "But you see, this was calculated—you know what you're going to have to give up," she says. "And to me, it was worth it. It's like the story in the Scripture, where you sell everything you have to buy this pearl of great value. That's what you do when you find that pearl—you pay the price. And I could not have lived with myself if I hadn't done it."

A confession: Much of the time my mother is telling me about her conversion, I am thinking about my father. When she mentions a book that influenced her, I ask if he read it, too. I prod her to remember more of his life, to think of more people I can interview about what he was like as a Jew and why he converted.

Instead, she sends me a letter from a nun named Sister June. "Dear Mrs. Dubner," it says. "I was with Paul when he died—it was very peaceful. I was praying with him—he opened his eyes halfway and seemed to look at me. I kept saying the name of Jesus in his ear. I rejoice that he sees the Lord face to face."

I have the urge to round up 10 Jews and drive upstate to the Catholic 50 cemetery where he is buried, to recite the Mourner's Kaddish.

The evidence of my father's Catholicism is overwhelming. Yet in re-creating his life, I found myself thinking of him as a Jew. I would cling to the un-Catholic stories I heard, no matter how wispy, like the time he came back to New York and immediately picked up a copy of The Jewish Daily Forward. He was proud he could still read Yiddish.

I never got to ask him what led to his conversion, but it probably wouldn't have mattered. He seems to have told no one. Even my mother's recollections are painfully featureless. His only significant written traces are 18 wartime letters he sent to my mother, all from after his baptism. I studied them endlessly—even the envelopes held potential clues—and scurried off to read the books he mentioned in them. I tracked down relatives who knew of my existence only as a shadowy member of "the Catholic part of the family" (or, occasionally, worse). Some of the reunions were cathartic: "What's this I hear about you becoming Jewish again?" one aunt asked me. "Oh, that's good, that's good."

* * *

In late 1944, Sol Dubner was home in New York on furlough. As a teenager, he had been sharp and full of ambition, but the war had worn him down, made him lonely, set him searching. He had spent two years with a medical unit at Army hospitals, most recently on Christmas Island. He had written home that he was the only Jew there. What he didn't write home was that after encountering a group of Christian missionaries, he had undergone a non-denominational baptism. And he was pretty sure he wanted to become a Catholic.

Back in Manhattan, he saw a posting for a dance sponsored by the Church of the Blessed Sacrament, and he went around to talk to the priest. "Tell me, Father," he said, "did you ever hear of another creature like me, a Jew who wants to become a Catholic?"

Actually, there were a few such creatures, the priest told him, whom Sol 55 could find at a meeting of young Catholics the following night.

Although my mother insists that in the beginning it was only a friendship, other evidence suggests that she and Sol fell in love at the meeting that night. He asked question after question, especially about the Virgin Mary and why she was so key to Catholicism. Veronica, because she had asked the same questions herself two years earlier, could answer them. They spent much of Sol's furlough together, going to Mass regularly.

Sol returned to duty in January, at an Army hospital in Hawaii. "There's a good chance of my being baptized at this post as the chaplain here is pretty interested in my case," he wrote to Veronica.

The chaplain was a German-born Catholic priest named Ulrich J. Proeller. He is now 92 and lives in San Antonio. I called him to see what he could tell me of my father's conversion.

He said he couldn't recall a thing. A wartime conversion, he explained, was often no more than "a momentary transaction." Then he suddenly said: "I remember he was a very alert young fellow, very interested. It was a joy to instruct him."

"There were not many Jewish converts," he went on. "He took confidence 60
in me somehow. And I was grateful—I wanted to create better feelings between the Christians and the Jews, since I had the experience of the Jews in Germany."

Father Proeller paused for a minute. "Wartime is good for converts," he finally said. "The Jews felt kind of lonely, you know, because they were so few, so they picked out what they thought was the best, as far as services were concerned, and they stuck with that."

He made it sound so casual! Like a recipe from an Army cookbook: Take one New York City Jew; place him in the middle of nowhere (preferably during a war that's killing Jews by the millions); add a flock of missionaries; top with a gung-ho priest (German if possible). Yield: one Catholic.

Sol, ecstatic after his baptism, wrote to Veronica steadily. March 29, 1945: "I know it would knock you for a loop to know that I am toying with the notion of becoming a priest after the war." Aug. 16, 1945: "At long last we have peace again! . . . If God wills it, I may be back home in four or five months!" Sept. 14, 1945: "It's going to be hard to make my family understand why I am a Catholic. . . . Perhaps I will find some room and board in New York till I decide what my future plans will be."

Sol's father, Shepsel, was one of the most rigorously observant Orthodox men in the neighborhood. He and his wife, Gussie, had come from a small Polish town called Pultusk, north of Warsaw. They settled in the Brownsville section of Brooklyn, where they ran a tiny kosher restaurant.

Sol, the fifth of six children, had wanted to be a writer, to play the saxo- 65
phone, to study in France after high school. "Whatever he thought about doing, Shepsel would slap down," my Aunt Dottie told me. Sol never got along with his father, and often stayed with an older brother. "Shepsel was very, very strict, to a fault really," Dottie says. "It was because of the religion."

Gussie, meanwhile, was as gentle and encouraging as Shepsel was harsh, and Sol was extremely close to her. One day, he was walking home from high school, whistling. A neighbor shouted out the window: "Hey, Sol, what are you whistling for? Don't you know your mother's dead?" Gussie, 51, had had high blood pressure and died suddenly. On the day of her funeral, the street was packed with mourners.

Last year, before Rosh ha-Shanah, I went to a Judaica shop on West 30th Street to buy a tallis—a prayer shawl—and a yarmulke. A man with short red hair and eyeglasses, about 35, grabbed my arm as I walked in. "Come on, we need you," he said. It was time for afternoon prayers, and they were one man shy of the necessary 10.

"I can't—I have to get back to my office," I lied.

"Come *on*," he said. "A couple of minutes."

I sputtered again: *can't . . . can't . . . can't*. Finally: "I don't know *how*." 70

From behind the counter, a woman's voice: "Leave him alone already. You'll get someone else."

A minute later, a 10th man came in and I slunk off to buy my things. At home that night, I stood in front of a mirror, put on the yarmulke and started to wrap myself in the prayer shawl. I was feeling the deep tug of ritual. I got the shawl around my shoulders, though not without a struggle, but then the yarmulke fell off my head. I put it back on, then got my forearms tangled in the shawl, like a mummy. The yarmulke fell off again. As I grabbed for it, I heard the shawl rip.

For about two seconds, I laughed. Then I got sad, and angry—that I don't even know how to put on a prayer shawl. That, at 32, I have to sound out my Hebrew like a first grader. That, even if I had wanted to, I couldn't have been the 10th man.

My father was never overwhelmingly religious; none of Shepsel's children turned out to be. But he certainly knew his way around Judaism and what it would mean to abandon it. I tried to imagine his mind-set on Christmas Island. I knew that the war had depressed him, and that it was hardly an easy time to be even an American Jew. Ever since his mother died, his home situation had been rocky, and he wasn't exactly flush with career opportunities after the war.

Reading the New Testament with my father in mind, I came across any 75
number of passages that might have seized him. In Matthew 19:29, for instance: "And everyone who has left houses, brothers, sisters, father, mother, children or land for the sake of my name will be repaid a hundred times over, and also inherit eternal life." But I couldn't imagine the son of an Old World Jew, even one who was willing to shed his Judaism, being satisfied by the Gospels alone, no matter how deft their politics and psychology.

One day, my mother mentioned a book that my father said had greatly influenced him: "Rebuilding a Lost Faith," by John L. Stoddard. Dots began to connect. In one wartime letter, Sol mentioned giving the same book to a friend, and his first job after the war was at P. J. Kenedy & Sons, the Catholic publisher that had put out the Stoddard book—surely not a coincidence.

I was nervous about reading the book. I wanted it to reveal the mystery of his conversion, and I dreaded that it wouldn't. It turned out to be a fairly dry piece of hard-sell apologetics; the last chapter is called "Some Catholic Privileges and Compensations." The moment I read Stoddard's passage about the special appeal of the Virgin Mary, I felt that I owned my father's secret:

"All hearts are not alike. Some unimpassioned souls prefer to pray to God alone. . . . Others are moved to hold communion with their Saviour only. . . . And there are others still, lone, orphaned hearts, who crave a mother's love and care, and find the greatest surcease of their pain by coming to the Mother of their crucified Redeemer. . . . There are in every life some moments when a mother's tenderness outweighs the world, and prayer to Mary often meets this want, especially when one's earthly mother is forever gone."

I wish I had my father's copy. Would those sentences be underlined? Tear-stained? From the day he became a Catholic, my father was deeply devoted to Mary. He started a local chapter of the Blue Army, a group dedicated to Mary and the rosary, and constantly wore a scapular around his neck that contained her likeness. He took public-speaking courses, my mother told me, "because he wanted to go to church societies and speak about the Blessed Mother Mary."

After the war, Sol did move back in with his family, keeping his conversion 80
secret. His father had grown even more religious in his old age. One day, while

Sol was out of the house, Shepsel went to fold a pair of pants that Sol had draped over a chair. A rosary dropped out of the pocket. "If a knife had been plunged into him, I don't think he would have bled," my Aunt Irene told me. "I thought he was going to take his own life."

Instead, Shepsel went into a quiet rage. He declared his son dead and sat shiva, the seven-day mourning period. He announced that Sol was not to enter the house, nor was his name to be spoken. Sol was crushed. He tried to visit his father with Veronica, whom he was now planning to marry.

My mother, whose memory is amazingly Catholic-centric, cannot recall this meeting (which exasperates me to no end); I can only imagine the young couple, remotely hopeful and deathly nervous, standing before the seething old man.

They were married on March 2, 1946, at St. Brigid's Catholic Church in Brooklyn. Only a small group of friends, nearly all Catholics, attended. Shepsel kept his word about Sol, never even inquiring about his grandchildren.

Within a few years, Shepsel was dying of cancer in Kings County Hospital. Very near the end, he cried out: "Solly! Solly! Solly!" Maybe he regretted cutting off his son. Or maybe he was still angry. At the funeral, Sol wasn't allowed inside the chapel, or to stand near the grave. When I learned about this in interviews with relatives, I couldn't believe that my mother had never told me. As it turns out, she didn't know—my father never told *her.* Nor had anyone ever told Sol that his father had been calling his name in the hospital.

I wonder how his life might have been different had he known. Perhaps 85
he—and my mother—wouldn't have been so determined to live as though their families and their Jewishness had never existed. As it was, they would build a future from the ground up, a foundation of secrets and hurt feelings plastered over by a seemingly endless supply of faith.

Like the graduates of some notorious boot camp, my brothers and sisters and I look back with a sort of perverse glee at the rigors of our Catholicism. My oldest sister, Mary, was so convinced of the church's omnipotence that when she walked into a Protestant church with some high-school friends, she was sure its walls would crash down on her head. We were expected to say our prayers with feeling, to go to Mass with joy and to confession with contrition. The boys were to become altar boys, and the girls were to emulate the Virgin Mary, in every way. Dating, if absolutely necessary, was to involve only other Catholics.

Our rebellions were many, but seldom vehement. When she went to college, Mary changed her name to Mona, for whom no saint is named. "*Mary* was just so religious," she says now. "I never told Mom and Dad why I changed, though, because I didn't want to hurt them. I resented them for requiring us to be *so* Catholic, but even then, I think, I knew that we had very decent parents."

They were, indeed, unerringly decent—and inexorably Catholic. Soon after they were married, they visited a Pennsylvania farm retreat run by the Catholic Worker organization. Between the sessions on social activism and prayer, they learned about baking bread and growing vegetables, and saw the appeal of living off the land. It made sense: they could embrace the proud poverty of Catholicism and still produce a large and healthy family. In 1959, they bought an old farmhouse on 36 acres upstate near a town called Duanesburg.

Our father had been scraping by on two and three blue-collar jobs. Now, he became a journalist, which he had wanted to be all along. He worked as a copy editor at The Schenectady Gazette and then as the religion page editor at The Troy Record, for about $150 a week. Our mother ran the home operation: we milked our cow, slaughtered our chickens, baked our bread, tapped our maple trees and canned, pickled or froze anything that was remotely edible. We were eight Catholic Workers, obedient if reluctant. (We scraped the wheat germ off our oatmeal when Mom wasn't looking and fed our vitamins to the dogs.)

At school, we were the kids who could never pull off a trade from our bag 90
lunches. But we were also a sort of minor dynasty, one Dubner rolling through after the next. We played music and sports, occasionally made class president or valedictorian. We were a dependable brand name—a serendipitously un-Jewish-sounding brand name. All told, we passed beautifully as a Catholic family. Our father started the parish library, and our mother was the prime link on the local prayer chain, phoning other parishioners when someone took ill. When abortion was legalized, she helped start the local Right-to-Life chapter; as a 10-year-old, I was enlisted to help make up "Abortion Is Murder" posters with Magic Markers and yellow cardboard.

Along the way, our parents had discovered the charismatic renewal movement. I remember those prayer meetings more vividly than anything else from that time. About a dozen adults would gather in a ring of folding metal chairs; I was the only child there. They'd close their eyes and start to pray, quietly, addressing Jesus and God in what seemed to me startlingly intimate voices. They would open their pale blue booklets to sing, the melodies and words far more ethereal than our regular hymns. More silence, then they would start to mumble, their faces twisted in what looked like pain, and their voices would leap up and over one another's, jagged bursts of unknown syllables.

I peeked through half-shut eyelids. Why were they making up this absurd language? Was I supposed to know it, too? It was several months before I heard someone refer to this drama as speaking in tongues; still, I didn't understand. The prayer meetings scared me, and I dreaded going, but in our family it was impractical to refuse a religious duty.

Our father was now in his mid-50's. He had had a number of health problems, but since finding the charismatic movement, he was on an upswing. It lasted about two years. At a large meeting of charismatics in Albany in late 1973, he gave a short inspirational talk, then sat down and slumped forward in his seat. My mother thought he had fallen asleep. He spent a month in the hospital, and died just before Christmas.

At his funeral Mass, I served as an altar boy while the rest of my family sat in the front pew. Afterward, in the sacristy, I remember coolly stripping off my cassock and hanging it neatly, the job done. I didn't cry, then or later: my mother, the priest, my parents' friends all told me how happy my father was in heaven, and how proud I should be that God wanted him.

95 I knew they really believed this, but I could neither believe nor disbelieve. To me, God was some sort of complicated magic trick, a foreign tongue I couldn't speak. Every Sunday, I let the communion wafer dissolve on my tongue undisturbed, as the nuns had taught; I waited for the transubstantiation, to feel God filling up my body, a feeling I dearly wanted. Week after week, it didn't happen.

After my father died, my mother began going to church even more often, every morning during the summer, and I usually went with her. I now believe that she may have mistaken my obedience for devotion, and that I encouraged her to do so. I had neither the courage nor the language to challenge her faith, much less reject it. I thought about God less and less, primarily as a punisher whose wrath I could escape by cleverness. Going off to college, I had a sharply defined religious identity that I was eager to shed.

For Rosh ha-Shanah last year, I decided to go with a friend, Ivan Kronenfeld, to an old Orthodox synagogue on the Lower East Side. Even though the service would last into the night and would be totally in Hebrew, I felt armed to the teeth. I had bought a prayer book with English transliterations; I had been taking my classes; I was wearing my brand-new tallis. No doubt about it, I thought: Today, I am a Jew.

I sat in the second row with Ivan, who is in his late 40's. In front of us were a tall, straight-backed man and his 15-year-old son. The boy wore eyeglasses and a suit like his father's, and the two of them moved like a dancer and his shadow: standing-bowing-sitting-standing-singing, all with effortless passion. The boy was called up to sing from the Torah, and his voice was sweet and clear.

For the first hour or so, I hung in. But I kept losing my way in the prayer book. The tallis felt scratchy on my neck. The Hebrew was flying by too fast to sing along. Watching the boy and his father, I hated them. I had come here to pray, to account for my jealousy and selfishness of the past year; now I was jealous of the boy and selfish enough to pretend that I wasn't. At the first break, I told Ivan I'd had enough, folded up my tallis and went home.

100 I had fallen in with Ivan a few years earlier, when I was studying and teaching writing in graduate school. A wise but decidedly unorthodox Jew, he was a brilliant, controlling mentor—an actor, a deal-maker, a raconteur, a scholar of boxing and psychology, of Marx and Maimonides. Once he heard my family's story, he became my Virgil, shuttling me from a claustrophobic little Hasidic shul in Brooklyn to the sagging Judaica shops and bookstores on the Lower East Side. He lectured me on Akiba, Spinoza, Disraeli, Salk, Arthur Miller, Hank Greenberg, and most of it stuck. I felt as though I were growing into my skin, as though I were coming home to a place that I hadn't known to exist. My mother, meanwhile, was sending me stacks of Catholic literature; for Easter, she gave me the New Testament on cassette.

Ivan introduced me to several rabbis, most of whom unhesitatingly pronounced me a Jew. I was proud, and confused. At shul, Ivan showed me how to touch the fringes of my tallis to the Torah, then to my lips, but I felt painfully awkward—half intruder, half impostor. As enthusiastic as I was about this new identity, I was growing leery of having it decreed by someone else. And Ivan, for all his sincerity, was, like Mme. Souvorina, not inclined to subtle encouragements.

I stopped trying to go to synagogue. Besides, I was busy exploring the secular precincts of an unspent Jewish youth: klezmer music, Ratner's deli, Jewish girlfriends, Sholem Aleichem and The Forward, now published in English. One friend bought a mezuza for my door; he didn't spend much, he joked, because he figured I'd be moving to Israel soon. I became what I wanted to become, a cultural and intellectual Jew—which left me wanting, as it had my parents.

But it left us wanting different things. My mother, recognizing life's temporality, was determined to insure a life everlasting. For reasons I can't explain, I was less consumed with beating back the darkness of death than with finding a schematic for the here and now.

About 18 months ago, I called my mother to tell her that I had taken on a book project, helping to put together the teachings of Menachem Mendel Schneerson, the late Lubavitcher Rebbe. Her first reaction was that it might be dangerous, because the Hasids were such obvious targets for anti-Semites. Then she said that it might be good for me, since understanding Judaism would deepen my understanding of Catholicism.

Working on the book meant thinking and reading about God a great deal, from the simplest Hasidic parables to the Talmud, the writings of Martin Buber and the medieval French scholar Rashi. It didn't take long to realize what a painfully narrow view of God I had grown up with. Now, my mind purged of fairy-tale images, unencumbered by fear, able to see that religion itself is man-made, I began to wrestle with a new idea of God. And I came to understand that the very act of wrestling is paramount. Quite organically, I had begun to think Jewishly about God.

For several months, I was content simply to relish this understanding. But I was bombarded by small, sacred moments. Now that my head was engaged, my soul demanded the same attention. I started going to synagogue again (and learning my way around the service), reading the Torah, having Shabbos dinner and studying the Talmud with friends. I started spending more time with Ivan.

As a Jew, I am still astoundingly ignorant, and sometimes compensate with enthusiasm, like trying to tackle the Orthodox Rosh ha-Shanah service last fall. I recognized my parents in this enthusiasm; it is common to the convert—a giddy rush to gather up the promises of a new and better life and hold them so tightly to your breast that they might pass through to your heart.

Sometimes they do. Eight days after the Rosh ha-Shanah service, I went back to Ivan's shul for Yom Kippur: I had decided that I didn't need to be perfect to be a good Jew. The straight-backed man and his son were in the front pew again, singing beautifully. The rabbi, a soft-voiced, sad-eyed old man, turned out to be the boy's grandfather. He stepped forward to give a sermon. During these days of reflection, he said, he had been asking himself what makes us keep on being Jews when it's such a struggle. "And I found the answer in six words," he said. "Six words in the Talmud, written by Rashi: *'He will not let us go.'*"

It isn't a matter of our choosing whether to quit God, the old rabbi explained; it is God who chooses not to quit us.

Of course! I immediately understood that, as much as I had chosen my 110
religion, I chose the one that had chosen me. I had come to Judaism for many, many reasons, but the journey soon developed its own relentless, inexplicable momentum—the same sort of momentum, obviously, that had moved my parents in the opposite direction.

But was it even the opposite direction? True, the relative merits of Catholicism and Judaism could be argued endlessly, as my mother and I have tried; but hadn't my parents and I ultimately trodden the same path? Like Abraham, we left our native land and our father's house for a land we did not know. As much as ours were spiritual acts, they were cultural, familial and psychological acts as well. Choosing a religion means far more than choosing a new perspective on God—it informs how we talk, eat and vote, how we think about justice and history, money and sex. We choose a new religion to choose a new self, to set ourselves apart from where we have come. My parents, as it turns out, were practicing identity politics long before it had a name.

The day after Yom Kippur, I left on a trip to Poland. When I got to Pultusk, where my father's parents came from, I wanted to see where their parents were buried. As in most of Europe, the Nazis had made the Jews of Pultusk tear down their families' gravestones for building material. My hotel, a sprawling hilltop castle, was a former bishop's residence; during the war, it had been commandeered by the Nazis. The Jewish gravestones, I was told, had been used to pave the courtyard where I was just strolling.

My first taste of Jewish rage was deep; it was a shock to realize what I had become a part of. That night, lying in bed, I recognized how thoroughly my siblings and I had been spared that rage. I also recognized, for the first time, that had my parents not become such fervent Catholics, I probably wouldn't have been born—how many Jewish families of the 1950's and 60's, after all, had eight children?

My mother is a gentle woman, but her Catholicism runs so deep that I was sure she couldn't accept her youngest son as a Jew. Long after my intentions were known, she gave me for my birthday a coffee-table book called "The Living Gospels of Jesus Christ."

The first sign of détente was a newspaper clipping she sent last year, just 115
after the Easter and Passover holidays. It was about a group of Jews in Sarajevo who had celebrated Passover with a famous 14th-century Haggadah that had miraculously survived the Bosnian war.

When the Rabbi Schneerson book came out, she sent me a note: "Great work! And I can see why you're attracted to Judaism. For me, Catholicism is the blossoming or fruition or completion of Judaism. Lots of love, Mom."

When we had first sat down to talk about her conversion, she was cooperative but unenthusiastic. Now she was calling to reminisce about her family seders. She would even call to talk about the family story that pained her the most: David Greenglass and Ethel Greenglass, who married Julius Rosenberg, were my mother's first cousins; she had known them fairly well as a girl. No one in my family was aware of this until a few years ago, and when I first asked my mother about it, she reached out and turned off the tape recorder.

Ours is still a fragile understanding, built as it is over such powerful waters. I believe it *is* an understanding, though, not a capitulation. I think she realizes that I did indeed inherit her faith, and the faith of my father, but that it has taken a different shape.

Just before Christmas, I drove upstate to my father's cemetery. I was ready to carry out my act of spiritual subterfuge: I had a yarmulke and the Mourner's Kaddish in my pocket. It took me a while to find his marker. I scraped off the snow, saw the cross and then his name. I never reached for the yarmulke. Would I want some son of mine saying the rosary when I'm lying in a Jewish cemetery? Painful as it has been to accept my father's choice, it *was* his choice, just as I've been free to make mine. I ended up having a conversation with him; it cleared up a lot of things. I did leave a little stone at the corner of his plot.

When I got home, there was a Christmas card from my mother, offering 120
me a novena. And, in a separate envelope, a Hanukkah card. "I don't remember my letters enough to translate this," she wrote beneath the Hebrew lettering, "but I'm sure it's a good wish."

On the phone a few days later, she told me about spending Christmas Eve alone. With eight children, Christmas had always been a rambunctious affair, and in the past she had missed it. This year, she just quietly reflected on her faith: Dec. 24 was the anniversary of her baptism, 53 years ago. She thought about all her blessings, she said, and about my father, "happy as he can be, because he's got it all, face to face with God."

In the past, I would have shut out a comment like that—it's too far removed from what I believe. Now I just listened to the serenity in her voice. There was a long silence on the line. It was the sound of forgiveness, I'm sure, and it was traveling in two directions.

Understanding

1. Dubner reports that, unlike what is occurring in other countries, in America today a religious identity is optional. What does he mean?
2. What reasons does Dubner offer for his conversion to Judaism? How are they different from the reasons for his parents' conversion to Catholicism? How do his family's reactions to his conversion differ from those of his grandparents to his parents' conversion? What commonalities can you discern from these differences?
3. Dubner indicates that choosing one's religion is "rampant." What does he mean by this assertion and how does he support it?
4. Examine how Dubner tells the story of his conversion to Judaism. How does he relate his past experiences as a Catholic to his decision to convert? What about the tone of the piece? What effect does he seek to produce in the reader? Sympathy? Anger? What about his *style* creates this tone or effect? Outline those elements of the selection that support your response.

Responding

1. Several of the conversion experiences that Dubner recounts involve a mentor, someone who guides the seeker to the threshold of choice (e.g., Madame Souvorina for Veronica Dubner and his friend Ivan Kronenfeld). How important is a mentor to a life choice such as choosing a religion? Why? For what other choices is a mentor important? What qualities would you look for in a mentor?
2. As Dubner indicates, "choosing a religion means far more than choosing a new perspective on God—it informs how we talk, eat and vote, how we think about justice and history, money and sex. We choose a new religion to choose a new self" (paragraph 111). The idea of the "self" is a relatively new one in human history. What do you think inspires dissatisfaction with the "old self"? How, in your judgment, does religion enable the development of this new self? Give examples from your own life experience to support your response.
3. A recent *US News & World Report* poll reveals that 65 percent of voters said religion is losing its influence on American life, but 62 percent said its influence is growing in their *own* lives. What factors might explain the apparent discrepancy in these findings?
4. Dubner reports on individuals who continue to see meaning in religion, yet many people have abandoned it altogether. Do you know such a person? If so, what accounts for the rejection?
5. If you practice a religion, would you ever consider changing it? Under what circumstances? Explain.

Connecting

Is Dubner's conversion a particular example of outgrowing one's childhood religion and evolving a "mature religious sentiment," as Allport discusses in "A Solitary Quest"? If so, what elements of Dubner's experience correspond to Allport's claim? If not, examine the differences.

Climbing Jacob's Ladder

Shirley Park Lowry

"Death and taxes" used to be the humorous answer to an old question: "What two things can you always be certain of?" In "Climbing Jacob's Ladder," Shirley Park Lowry deals with the first of these certainties and relates how religions meet a people's need to conquer death by assuring their personal survival in another world. The title is a biblical allusion to Jacob, an Old Testament patriarch who dreamed he saw a ladder reaching straight to heaven, where God stood and uttered a blessing. "Awesome," Jacob proclaimed the experience which spurred his spiritual growth throughout the rest of his life.

Shirley Park Lowry is professor of English at Los Angeles Valley College, where she teaches mythology. In *Familiar Mysteries,* from which this selection is excerpted, she describes myth as a story about a culture's gods or heroes that gives purpose, direction, and meaning to those peoples' lives. Myths can give personal guidance through stages of development, garner support for a nation's superpower status, or provide answers to the most important of life's mysteries: Who am I? Why was I born? What happens when I die? Myths, Lowry claims, "help people accept life's great mysteries with serenity rather than with horror."

We are climbing Jacob's ladder,
Soldiers of the Cross. . . .
Every rung goes higher, higher,
Soldiers of the Cross. . . .
Sinner, do you love your Jesus?
Soldiers of the Cross. . . .
If you love Him, why not serve Him?
Soldiers of the Cross. . . .

—A hymn

Christianity has never seen humankind only as piteous and insufficient. Everything that God made is good, and even fallen humankind is part of God's creation. Furthermore, Christianity has always held that each person is going to live with himself—his unique, conscious self—forever, and that his own choices will shape his happiness for all time. This phase of Christianity sees the individual as supremely important and effective. The vision drew on two powerful pre-Christian forces in Western thought: Greek humanism and the Judaism of the last centuries before Christ. The Greeks saw people not as servants or glorifiers of the gods but as beings intrinsically valuable. In behaving with dignity, courage, or generosity, the Greeks held, a person honored not the gods but himself and his humanity. The notion that people *could* 1 achieve a godlike excellence of mind and body invited them to reach for excellence.

Meanwhile, Judaism had affirmed not only a personal survival after death but affirmed also the individual's profound effect on the quality of that survival. One could secure one's own eternal felicity by following religious laws and easing others' earthly woes.

The Greek and the later Judaic traditions converged in a Christian view of the individual as valuable and efficacious. Over the centuries, the doctrine of salvation through one's own efforts has had a far stronger attraction than Paul's and, later, Calvin's denial of the doctrine. The doctrine is so deeply embedded in our culture that in a variety of ways it affects the religious and nonreligious alike. Most important, it has engendered the myth of the Superself.

According to this myth, everyone, even the poor, the untalented, the seemingly helpless, can control his final fate. The value of that belief is so great as to be incalculable. Not only does it reconcile us to unavoidable troubles; it predisposes us to good cheer, self-reliance, and persistence in the face of adversity. Countless people, sure that virtue will be rewarded and vice punished in an afterlife, have passed through the world confident that their griefs are not heartbreaking by-products of impersonal processes but have been ordained by a loving God for their improvement; that God will wash all griefs away in the afterlife; and that a person's efforts to bend the world a bit toward his vision of heaven will open heaven to him. These beliefs have made people's lives rich and meaningful to them and often beneficent to their neighbors.

Furthermore, the Superself myth, in assigning the individual great poten- 5
tial worth, fosters twin institutions—representative government and public education—that do extend personal power. Representative government demands educated citizens. Although public education cannot develop the best in every person, it does give large numbers of people the means to participate in their society, and it does awaken in some the desire to develop themselves. Representative government and the free ventilation of ideas provide an orderly way to improve ideas and to promote the social stability needed for elaborate projects. To be sure, our raising of the individual to such heights results in much loud honking by the fatuous, the self-indulgent, the pretentious—but also for many people, lives of otherwise impossible fullness; and for a few, lives that bestow on the rest of us the gifts of untrammeled genius.

All great myths—those that help people make good lives—exact a price. Our habit of investing people with power that they often do not really command confuses us. The United States contains not one Superman disguised as Clark Kent but many Clark Kents disguised as Superman. Americans say, "You can do anything you really want to" and "If you really try, you'll succeed." Faithfully we buy books explaining how to be happy, popular, rich, beautiful, slim without exercising more or eating less; how to speak fluent German in two weeks; how to raise our children and our I.Q.s. Our sense of what is possible has an extraordinary amplitude. We tend to believe not only that effort is good for its own sake but that effort or even confidence alone ensures success. We are all going to be the best, all dance on the pinhead.

When we fail to achieve what we have expected, we may preserve our sense of efficacy by explaining that we did not try hard enough, and then go off to find something we are better at. No harm done. But too often, when a person does not meet unrealistic expectations, he and others conclude that he is lazy, burdening him with a sense of guilt in a culture that takes moral failure very seriously. When we know full well that he is trying, yet failing, we are so discomfited that we often pretend he is succeeding. The American educational system often awards the mediocre and the outstanding alike, fostering mediocrity. ("Because psychology is such a tough graduate program to get into, I don't jeopardize the chances of my psych majors by giving any of them less than an A.") In such a muddled atmosphere, when we do clearly fail, we tend to collapse in helpless despair.

Another cost of the Superself myth is that it encourages rashness. In rueful moods, we characterize Western civilization of the Protestant era as Faustian, after the legendary scholar so restless for universal knowledge and technical mastery that he paid for a twenty-year spree with eternal damnation. During that spree, for the adolescent joy of doing what he *could* do, Faust changed the Rhine's course, summoned Helen's spirit from the dead, played crude magical jokes on the Pope, and looped the loop among the planets. Sometimes in a similar exercise of power and greed, we broadcast deadly chemicals intended to take the ping out of our gasoline, the bugs off our broccoli. We more readily turn our minds to producing atomic energy than to disposing of its deadly wastes. Making something happen now is more to our taste than pondering its effect twenty or two hundred years from now. Critics warn that our heedlessness may doom all life.

Obviously, we must learn to behave more responsibly than has been our custom, but we might also give our characteristic zest its due. Most members of "contemplative" Eastern societies are really too poor, sick and uneducated to know and enjoy the benefits of contemplation. These millions have no choice but to shuffle resignedly from day to day, their greatest hope not a better life but a final release from life. To foster the contemplative response may be best where climate, soil, and debilitating diseases relentlessly cancel human effort; in our luckier circumstances, however, the experimental habit of mind still seems, for all its risks, preferable.

Perhaps not Faust, after all, but Hamlet is the figure who says most to us 10
about ourselves. Both the Faust and the Hamlet in us stem from the Superself myth, but the latter may be the more dangerous precisely because it has undermined our zest. Although we have always held the individual responsible for his own fate, he became more emphatically so with the loosening of Church authority in the Renaissance. Whereas the clergy, sacraments, and saints of the medieval Church had been one's conduits to God, with the Reformation each Protestant became in effect his own conduit, listening for God within himself. Protestants held that God had created each person sufficient, through reading and reflecting on the Bible, to understand and heed God's will.

In secular thought, too, people grew more independent, more intensely aware of the private world within their own skulls—and more preoccupied with the implications of that privacy. The brooding Hamlet, so tortured by the burden of solitary introspection, catches the imagination again and again, not only in English-speaking countries but throughout the Western world. Clever, charming, analytical though he be, Hamlet is insufficient because he cannot move outside himself. He lacks both robust convictions and the ability to love wholeheartedly anyone but himself. There he stands, unsupported, unsupporting.

Many Western minds, whether Catholic or Protestant, religious or secular, large or small, have, like Hamlet's, trembled at their own solitude, at the burden of living alone in that vast inner space. Some have thought of God as peering from afar, while they heave themselves seallike over the sharp rocks, never knowing whether their absurd, gelatinous selves will finally *do* or will be thrust into hell's fire. Gerard Manley Hopkins's cry is the cry of many: "O the mind, mind has mountains; cliffs of fall / Frightful, sheer, no-man-fathomed" ("No Worst, There Is None"). But many, like Camus, suspect worse, that even the god is a mirage, and the solitary journey not a test but the sum and meaning of it all.

Despite the Neoclassical interruption of the late seventeenth and the eighteenth centuries—with its reassertion of the communal, the shared, the generic—our awareness of each person's singularity has on the whole deepened since the Renaissance. In fact, the sense of solitude had reaffirmed itself even more strongly by the end of the eighteenth century with the commonplace speculation that perhaps *only* one's self existed, that other people and all the moiling world were mere dreams invented by one's mind. The individual had become in speculation not just his own Pope, his own world, but his own crack-brained god, living quite alone with his disordered dreams, not the controller yet the sole source of all.

Today, many of a less philosophical bent can see well enough that the world exists. They just cannot get very excited about it. Generations before them went climbing Jacob's ladder, higher, higher, ever higher, but not they. Climbing is tough work, and they suspect they know what they would find up there. Squinting in the thin air, one would see no God, no heaven—only the swaying ladder and one's own spent self clinging to it in otherwise vacant space. The literature of the last two centuries is full of cosmic abandonments, betrayals, expressions of shock and dismay. Characters helplessly witness the collapse of their meaningful world. They cry out that, contrary to John Donne's assertion, *every* man is an island. A striking number of characters either think of themselves as wandering alone in the snow or actually perish that way.[1]

Although our singularity has never seemed more true than it does today, the late twentieth century has domesticated it. No big deal. Some shrug, work enough to keep the paychecks coming, slip through their lives by watching TV, eating out, taking up and putting down a series of attitudes, projects, lovers, none very disturbing for long. Yet a pervasive unease suggests that, without knowing how, people want to do something significant. Even the extreme narcissism so evident in the past decade tends to express itself in efforts to connect, if temporarily, with other people.[2] These efforts range from casual copulations to encounter sessions in which the nude participants loll in hot tubs, touching toes, or shut themselves up together for a weekend to lay before one another, in stupefying detail, the contents of their minds.

To be sure, each person is irrevocably singular. He cannot even share his child's earache, only remember his own. Each person does wander through his shadowy, puzzling life alone, often hungering for the impossible contact, the revelation. All are unhoused, vulnerable. Many twentieth-century people are existentialists—whether or not they have heard the word—spinning a kind of meaning as they go along, out of their personal experience. Each one makes his way through the void of time by the light of his singular consciousness, and waves to the other people in the dim light of their collective glimmers.

But that light is real and precious. We may agree with the Hindu philosopher that one person's effort is unlikely to improve the world for long. We may suspect that the "soul" dies with the body. We may believe that the earth, the universe itself, is dying. But the ancient Egyptian god Re thought it worthwhile to battle Apep every single night in order to make one day more, and the Egyptians rejoiced for that one day. To believe in the eternal life of individual souls or in the permanence of one's acts is not the only path to a meaningful life on this earth. Perhaps few people today see themselves as ever standing before the Great Judge and perhaps most muddle through the anomie of our age, but they sometimes come upon a truth that their forebears knew: Individuals become significant and effective as they spend themselves for something larger than themselves. The human community is still there.

Notes

1. Many recent short stories use snow as a symbol of sterile singularity, a loss of value, especially of meaningful connections: James Joyce's "The Dead," Ernest Hemingway's "The Snows of Kilimanjaro," Willa Cather's "Paul's Case," F. Scott Fitzgerald's "The Ice Palace," Ted Hughes's "Snow." Novels include D. H. Lawrence's *Women in Love* and Margaret Drabble's *The Ice Age.* In their very different ways, Hans Christian Anderson's tale "The Snow Queen" and Randall Jarrell's poem "90 North" use the same symbol. Examples of anomie in Western literature, philosophy, and social commentary of the last two centuries are too numerous to need citation.
2. Although the phenomenon of widespread narcissism, as Christopher Lasch cogently demonstrates in *The Culture of Narcissism,* has developed over the past two centuries, it has recently taken startingly extreme forms.

Understanding

1. In what ways does Lowry suggest that "Christianity sees the individual as supremely important and effective" rather than as a helpless sinner?
2. Lowry concludes that two institutions—representative government and education—sprang from the acceptance of the "Superself" myth. What is the Superself myth and what is its connection with representative government and education?

3. Lowry argues that one consequence of a culture's acceptance of the Superself myth is apparent in the shunning of failure and the need to reward all despite their apparent lack of accomplishment. What is her perspective on this refusal to accept mediocrity?

Responding

1. How would you describe "a meaningful life"? Does it depend on the existence of your personal survival in another world? Explain.
2. Lowry suggests that the Superself myth assigns the individual great potential worth. Does this myth enhance personal relationships, or does it carry the seeds of their dissolution? Does it reinforce competition among people or engender cooperation? How can two or more "Superselves" get along?
3. Death, uncertainty, and inequality are facts of the human condition. Faith and the religions it has spawned have been seen as a response to these realities. Using Lowry's definition of myth as a story about a culture's heroes or gods, how do religious myths help us deal with these limitations?
4. "Service learning," a recent trend in American education that involves students in some form of social action or community work, is, in the view of its advocates, one path to a responsible and meaningful life. Have you ever been involved in such an activity? If so, did you perform it voluntarily or was it required of you? What meaning did it have for you? Would you do it again, voluntarily? If you have never been involved in service learning, under what circumstances would you engage in it? Why might this kind of activity be considered a kind of "stairway to heaven"—a modern-day Jacob's ladder?
5. The myth of the Superself can inspire great personal achievement and material success. Consider the outcome if an entire community or culture believes itself to be a collection of Superselves. Discuss the consequences of such a determination on the supposed Superselves and on the "less endowed."

Connecting

1. Interpret one of the stories in chapter two, "Wounds," in light of the myth of the Superself. How would this myth give consolation to the people who experience grief or sorrow?
2. How does Lowry's claim that "without knowing how, people want to do something significant" relate to Allport's assessment in "A Solitary Quest" of the place of religion in the life economy of the individual?

WRITING OPTION: Communities of Faith

From the Responding questions in "Communities of Faith," choose a response that has special relevance to your experiences—either satisfying or disturbing—with faith or with communities of faith.

If your response was short, consider expanding it to an essay that includes the insights you gained from the readings in this section. Or you might choose a modified narrative form modeled on Dubner's "Choosing My Religion." If you choose this model, be sure to import the learnings or insights you gained from the other readings that support or strengthen your point. As with the other writing options, consider your reader as you relate your experiences to their impact on who you are now.

One final note: Because religion is a sensitive topic for many, take care in developing the *tone* of your writing so that it "tunes in" rather than "turns off" your reader.

4 In Public and Private

One of the surest ways to continue growing throughout our lives is to make contact with others. Opening our "private" selves to public view through writing, chatting on the Internet, traveling, or just getting dressed and walking down the street primes us for new awarenesses. More than that, the social experience of making contact requires that we suspend our self-sufficient individualism to enter into, or try to enter into, relationships with others who can play a vital role in the discovery of ourselves as significant.

Making contact with others can also be a risky, bruising process. What we reveal can be misunderstood, rejected, ridiculed, or, even worse, ignored, but we do it nonetheless. Swiss psychiatrist Paul Tournier says, "It is impossible to overemphasize the immense need humans have to be really listened to, to be taken seriously, to be understood." If what he says is true, we will take a chance, as the writers in this section do, on revealing ourselves by the language we use, the friends we keep, and the communities we inhabit.

In "The New, New World," Richard Rodriguez tells us that we share the experience of our individuality but at the same time hunger for "deep communal and intimate assurance." As these readings show, we seek ways to satisfy this hunger: through clinging to some part of the comfortable culture of our childhood, as Luc Sante does through language in "Living in Tongues"; through the exchange of concerns and resources on the Web, which Howard Rheingold documents in "Cyberhood vs. Neighborhood: Community"; or through courageous travel in unfamiliar places, such as Elias Canetti negotiates in "Storytellers and Scribes." Their writing exposes the very different and creative ways in which they try to make all of who they are, public and private, work in their own best interests.

There is a sense in which we can know only that much of ourselves that we have the courage to reveal. These writers show us how they have taken the risk to traverse the border between their public and private selves. It is for you, the reader, to decide if they have made contact.

The New, New World

Richard Rodriguez interviewed by Viriginia I. Postrel & Nick Gillespie

Probably the least controversial way to identify Richard Rodriguez is as *essayist.* His views on bilingual education, multiculturalism, and on becoming an American have rankled critics who consider his ideas assimilationist, a betrayal of his ethnic heritage. His admirers describe him as looking toward complexity and away from sentimentality and carefully avoiding ideology.

Anyone who has viewed Rodriguez's occasional video essays on the PBS *NewsHour* will recognize his style as respectful of the delicate and dynamic balance between individuals and the communities to which they say they belong. His delivery, a mix of rhetorical intensity and personal calm, seems to invite listening. And yet, as distinctive as Rodriguez's views are, he does not present them to promote himself or his own identities. Judge for yourself in the following interview, which is a shorthand representation of some of his more popularized views.

A Mexican American writer who is currently identified as "an editor of the Pacific News Service," Rodriguez gained celebrity for his 1982 book *Hunger of Memory: The Education of Richard Rodriguez.* His most recent book, published in 1993, is *Days of Obligation: An Argument with My Mexican Father.*

Essayist Richard Rodriguez, best known for his 1982 book *Hunger of Memory: The Education of Richard Rodriguez,* is usually classified as an iconoclastic Mexican-American writer with little patience for political correctness. The description is accurate but incomplete. He is, more broadly, a student of America—a subtle and perceptive observer of the tension between individual and community, self and culture, optimism and pessimism, in contemporary life. He is also deeply ambivalent, especially in his more-recent work, including *Days of Obligation: An Argument with My Mexican Father.* In that book, Rodriguez struggles with the loss of optimism, both his and California's, since his youth in the 1950s—the discovery of what Thomas Sowell might call "the constrained vision," the knowledge that "much in life is failure or compromise," just as his Mexican father said. For Rodriguez, though, this sense of life's limits is wedded to an appreciation for its possibilities. Editor Virginia Postrel and Assistant Editor Nick Gillespie talked with Rodriguez in Los Angeles in late April.

Reason: You became famous in the early 1980s for opposing bilingual education and affirmative action—specifically for turning down jobs as an English professor that you thought you were offered on the basis of your ethnicity. Have you changed your mind about that?

Richard Rodriguez: No, I guess I haven't. Although I miss teaching, I go back to the university campuses today with some reluctance.

Reason: Why is that?

Rodriguez: For example, I was at CSUN [Cal State, Northridge] a few months ago, and I had to pass through some kind of approval of the Chicano studies program for my visit to be sanctioned. And it just becomes too tiresome. There is some etiquette—that I have to meet with the Chicano students to defuse whatever their anger is.

Reason: And what are those meetings like?

Rodriguez: Well, they're usually tedious. At Northridge there was a long 5
speech where I was harangued by a woman from the history department, but clearly Chicano studies also, about my misunderstanding of Mexicans, about how Mexico has come to terms with its Indian identity. There have been a few times—for example, at U.C.-San Diego last year—where I did lose control of the audience. There were a number of students who were so disruptive that it was difficult to go on.

Reason: What do you make of that sort of attitude among college students?

Rodriguez: As it applies to me, I find it curious. I think of myself as left of center. I'm horrified that the left in America is as intolerant as it is these days. The level of incivility among people who are otherwise engaged in discussion of ideas also is surprising to me.

Reason: Where do you think it comes from?

Rodriguez: If you ask me about these individual students, I think they are required to think of themselves as representing a cause. Their admission is in the name of a larger population for whom they feel responsible, and they do claim to have a kind of communal voice to speak in the name of the people. If you have a different opinion, then you are not of the people.

Multiculturalism, as it is expressed in the platitudes of the American campus, is not multiculturalism. It is an idea about culture that has a specific genesis, a specific history, and a specific politics. What people mean by multiculturalism is different hues of themselves. They don't mean Islamic fundamentalists or skinheads. They mean other brown and black students who share opinions like theirs. It isn't diversity. It's a pretense to diversity. And this is an exposure of it—they can't even tolerate my paltry opinion.

Reason: *Days of Obligation* got a friendlier response than *Hunger of Memory,* 10
partly because it was more Mexican.

Rodriguez: I think of it as more Catholic rather than more Mexican. An older man is writing this book. I thought of my earlier book as a more deeply Protestant book: my objection to the popular ideology of that time; my insistence that *I am this man,* contrary to what you want to make me; my declaration of myself, of my profession—political and personal; my defiance of my mother's wishes in publishing this memoir. It seemed to me very Protestant and very self-assertive—in the best sense.

This later book is much more Catholic and much more troubled. I'm much more interested in the intervention of the tragic in my life now. The AIDS epidemic has been a large part of that, but that isn't the only aspect. I quite clearly live in a California that has lost its charm, in a place that no longer quite believes in a future.

Reason: You suggest in your book that Mexico itself and Mexicans in America have become the comic side, the optimistic side, and that it is actually blond California that is getting pessimistic.

Rodriguez: That's part of the great irony. We've always assumed that America somehow belonged on this land. Well, maybe you can put America in a suitcase and take it to Hong Kong. Maybe you can take it to Shanghai. And maybe what our Scandinavian ancestors of the 19th century would recognize as America, or as an American city, they would see more clearly in Tijuana now than they would in San Diego.

15 **Reason:** What do you mean by the America that you could take to Hong Kong?

Rodriguez: The notion of self-reliance. The notion of re-creation. More and more I'm sensing that that kind of optimism belongs now to immigrants in this country—certainly to Mexicans that I meet—and less and less so to the native-born.

Americans seem to be tired. They talk about a lot of problems. I'm not depressed about the problems on the horizon, because I think that's where you get solutions. We'll start growing our spinach in space only when we run out of space. What I worry about is that when you talk about zero population growth and that sort of thing you are really talking about a sort of stopped time, where the whole process of evolution gets called into question.

Reason: Why do you think people today talk so much about culture?

Rodriguez: Because there is an enormous sense of discontinuity in our lives. A friend of mine who was writing a book on Orange County once took me to this enormous shopping center—South Coast Plaza—where there were Iranians and Mexicans and everybody, and I said to him, "Do you feel flattered that the whole world has come to where you used to bicycle across open fields?" And he said, "Of course I feel flattered. It's an extraordinary idea that the entire world would come to your playground. But at some other level I feel enormously besieged, and in some sense displaced, that here they're coming and they have no memory that I was here." We may become some new tribe of American Indians, who remember a California once upon a time and now are in the presence of rude people whose memory doesn't extend that far.

20 So we start asking questions about what our culture was and what their culture seems to be. Most people tend to use *culture* in a static sense—he represents this culture and I represent this culture. I think culture is much more fluid and experiential. I belong to many cultures. I've had many cultural experiences. And the notion that I've lost my culture is ludicrous, because you can't lose a culture. You can change a culture in your lifetime, as in fact most of us do. I'm not my father. I didn't grow up in the state of Colima in Western Mexico. I grew up in California in the 1950s. The notion that I've lost his culture is, of course, at some level true, but not interesting. The interesting thing is that my culture is *I Love Lucy*.

Reason: Are there political implications to this view of culture versus the static view?

Rodriguez: The interesting thing about America, the risky thing about America, is that when it opened itself up to immigrants, it opened itself to the possibility that it was going to become fluid and a stranger to itself. The great 19th-century argument against immigrants was not racial or ethnic but primarily religious. The argument against the Irish migration was a very interesting one, and one I've always taken seriously: whether or not an Irish Catholic can become a good American. Because in some way, as a Catholic in this country, I'm at odds with America. There is a prevailing ideology, a culture, which we change and adapt and resist and in various ways ignore and become part of. But in some sense it's not an easy relationship for the outsider, nor is it an easy relationship for those who are within the culture to know what to do with these outsiders.

The argument ends in the 19th century with this remarkable reversal from the anti-immigrant biases of the 1850s. Americans start talking about themselves as belonging to the tradition of the immigrant—we are all immigrants. And we see ourselves in the disheveled figure of the woman loaded down with the suitcase and garlic and crucifix. Who knew what she was saying? But we recognize in that movement away from her past that there was some great American drama that we saw ourselves as part of.

Reason: How do you account for the fact that in the beginning of the 20th century, as we were accepting the myth of the immigrant as the true American, the first broad-based restrictions on mass immigration started to be discussed in an active way?

Rodriguez: How do I account for the fact that, at a time when black and white relationships are so difficult in America, blond kids are listening to rap? Within what is desired is also what is feared. The stranger is the figure of the American but also the threat to American stability. Surely there is some part of us that wants to settle down, that doesn't want to keep moving.

25 **Reason:** You've written, "Protestantism taught Americans to believe that America does not exist—not as a culture, not as a shared experience, not as a communal reality. Because of Protestantism, the American *ideology* of individualism is always at war with the experience of our lives, our *culture.* As long as we reject the notion of culture we are able to invent the future." Isn't the paradox of American culture that it emerges out of the living of individualism?

Rodriguez: What I was arguing in that paragraph is that it is possible to share the experience of individuality but that it is always paradoxically so. And that there is an anti-intellectual bias in America based upon a constant rejection of the elder, of authority, of the past. There is in the American experience continually this notion that we have sort of stumbled upon experience, that we have discovered sex, that we have discovered evil. I quote a woman at Columbia University who said, in the 1970s, "After Vietnam I will never believe that America is the good and pure country that I once thought it to be." I thought to myself, "Where has she been all this time? Did she miss the part about the slaves? Did she miss that page about the Indians? Where does that notion of innocence come up?" We are innocent of history, of memory.

What I'm arguing is that there is a tradition that immigrants should be taught as much as native-born Californians. A tradition of America which connects us to one another, despite the fact that the strongest thing that we could say about one another is that we are disconnected. But the woman I know in Berkeley who drives her red Volkswagen around to this day with a bumper sticker that says "Question Authority"—there is not a more conventional American ideal than "Question Authority."

Reason: In the context of immigrants, you've said that America is irresistible, that parents think that their children can pick and choose but that you can't resist it. Does that mean that the concern about assimilation is needless?

Rodriguez: Some part of it will be natural and inevitable. But no one is more American than the person who insists that he's not. I said to these kids in Corpus Christi the other day, "I don't mind that you go around pretending that you live in Mexico, and wear sombreros and so forth. I just want you to know that that's an American thing to do—that insistence that *I* can decide whether I'm going to be Mexican or not."

I was doing a documentary for the BBC a few years ago on American 30
teenagers, and there was this girl in North Carolina who was telling us about how she wanted to become more Scottish. She was going to bicycle that summer in Scotland and get in touch with her Scottish ancestors. And my film crew, these Brits, said, "This idea of becoming more Scottish. That's a very American idea, isn't it?" Nobody in Scotland talks that way. And that's exactly the point, that the American arrogance has always been that the individual is in control of the culture. In some way, the people who are most individualistic, and most insistent on their refusal to assimilate, are the people who are most deeply assimilated.

The joke on Mexican Americans is that Mexicans now are Americanizing themselves at probably a faster rate than we are, and we may turn into British Columbians. You go up to British Columbia, and there are these more-British-than-the-British Canadians, with their picture of the queen in their dining room and tea cozies and so forth. My fear is that Mexican Americans may turn into people who are in some kind of bubble in history, while these new Mexicans are going back and forth.

Reason: You talk a lot about two things that are related. One is intimacy, and the other is the tension between the public and the private. How do you reconcile the public and the private, the communal and the individual life?

Rodriguez: I don't have any large scheme for that settlement. I do think that we go in cycles as a society. Remember Reinhold Niebuhr wrote a book called *Moral Man and Immoral Society* about 40 years ago, 50 years ago? If one were to write a book like that today you would have to almost reverse the title, *Immoral Man and Moral Society*. Dealing with a problem like the homeless, we have almost no sense that as individuals we can make any difference. We seem not to believe that we can change the condition of the American household, which is in disrepair—mothers unhappy, mothers being beaten by papa, the children being abused by somebody. We refer our problems to agencies or to the public realm because we sense more and more that some intimate circle has been fragmented.

Maybe Hillary Clinton's generation is the great generation of this belief that if you can reorganize the public realm all will be well, that the public can redeem the private. I'm beginning to sense among the young today that there is some reversal now in the other direction, that the kids I talk to—I'm talking about the children we would normally describe as troubled children—are more and more looking for more intimate ways of organizing themselves and restoring themselves.

Reason: Like? 35

Rodriguez: Like Nation of Islam, Victory Outreach. The most successful rescue structures in this society are not governmental but are cases of one person taking another person. There is a man named Joe Marshall in San Francisco who has something called the Omega Boys Club. He used to be a junior-high-school teacher, and he realized that these kids basically did not have a home. He was expecting them to study a geography lesson, and they hadn't had breakfast. They were without such preliminaries in their intimate life that they had no way of living in the public life. So he committed himself as an individual to becoming their father essentially and to relating to them one on one—"I will be here for you." And he's had enormous success. He's sent over 100 kids to college—kids who would not normally fall under any umbrella of the ideal student. I'm more and more taken with that possibility, that what we are looking for now is some way to redeem the house.

I write in the "Late Victorians" chapter [in *Days of Obligation*] about the homosexuals who did not have a family, whose deepest secret was not held against the city but was held against their own parents. And they came to San Francisco in the 1970s and moved into the Victorian houses. They loved those symbols of 19th-century domestic stability, with four generations raised—one story upon the other—behind this great wooden door. This woman came up to me the other day and said, "The only happily married people I know are gay couples." I said to her, "Maybe that's part of the irony of our time, that people who didn't have that intimacy have been spending more time on it." I sense that there are very large groups of people who are without intimate life and who are looking for it now. And increasingly these people are not looking to government.

That's partly the reason for the rise of certain sorts of religious fundamentalism, which has within it a deep communal assurance and intimate assurance. There is down the block in my yuppie neighborhood this Filipino evangelical church. If you do not come tonight they will come looking for you. I don't want to say that ominously, because that's not the way they would describe it. But they miss you. And they eat together. They are there in the morning—I go jogging at 6:30 some mornings and they're coming out of church, and I think to myself, "This is insane. What have they been doing? When did they sleep?" Clearly something is going on in there that's not liturgical, or is so powerfully liturgical that it engages the re-creation of community in a city that is otherwise oblivious and hostile to them.

Reason: What do you think about the attraction of Latin Americans, both here and in Latin America, to evangelical Protestantism?

Rodriguez: Catholicism is a religion that stresses to you constantly that 40
you can't make it on your own, that you need the intercession of the Virgin Mary, and the saints, St. Jude, and your grandmother—candles and rosaries and indulgences and the pope. There are all these intermediaries, because you facing God would be hopeless.

Suddenly, into the village comes this assurance that you don't need *padrecito.* You can read the bible yourself—you don't need someone to tell you what it says. You don't need the Virgin Mary, you don't need the saints, you don't need anybody. God is speaking to *you.* And just because your father beat your mother, just because your grandfather was poor, doesn't mean it has to happen to you. You can change your whole life around. This is all based on the Easter promise and not, as the Catholic church has always based it, on some Good Friday suffering.

Reason: Protestants always have empty crosses.

Rodriguez: It is an enormously powerful motif, the notion that Christ just got off the cross and walked away somewhere—went off to L.A.—and you could do it too. I think Protestantism is most successful in those cases where people are beginning to taste and sense discontinuity. And they begin to make sense out of it as providential. Protestantism also establishes, in a time of social change, the memory of the village. Within the storefront church, you can hold hands and remember what it was like in another time.

It will be one of the great changes of Latin America, the Protestantization of Latin America, and I think in some way that it will change the United States. The relationship of the evangelicals in places like Texas where there are rednecks and Mexicans together is really very interesting. The new Mexican who is now appearing in places like police departments—this is a new face of Latin America, and it is not necessarily one that we want.

Reason: How so?

Rodriguez: I think there has always been a charm to Latin America as 45
being sort of morally lazy. We've always used it as a place where we could go to after dark and do whatever we wanted that we couldn't do here. We never really expected that Latin America was going to become a moral Clorox for our society, and maybe there's a ferocity there that we don't expect.

Reason: Aside from the desire to have this Latin America of easy virtue, are there bad consequences to that?

Rodriguez: How shall I put this? Mexican cops have never been cops I like to deal with. And there can be this ferocity—you see it in New York now with a lot of Puerto Rican and Hispanic households, the ferocity against the gay movement, the Rainbow Curriculum, for example. I see myself—as a homosexual man—much freer in America than in Latin America.

Reason: So that the danger is that in adopting a sort of American Protestantism, a religious version of individualism, they will not, do not, adopt the tolerant individualism, the political individualism?

Rodriguez: We're talking about a low-church Protestantism. It is part of the paradox of the Protestant tradition that there has been this intolerance within a religion otherwise powerfully concerned with the individual. It is a paradox within Catholicism that a religion so communal would otherwise be so individualistic—in the sense that people are so private.

50 **Reason:** The association of immigration with welfare in the political discourse, particularly in California, has become very tight, and yet of course everywhere you go in L.A. all you see are immigrants working. What do you make of that?

Rodriguez: It may have something to do with some Anglo-Saxon prejudice about the South—that these people really are not workaholics. In fact, every Mexican I've ever known has been haunted by a kind of work lust that is just extraordinary to me—it terrifies me.

It may also be that, well fine, this generation is going to scrape the dishes and wipe your grandmother's ass when she's an invalid, but that's not what their kids are going to do. When they start becoming American, we're going to have to pay for the kids, who are not going to do that work and who are going to be bitter. There is some logic in that. Ironically so. Isn't it interesting that we find that their Americanization is meaning that they would work less?

There is also this fear of the workaholic, which expresses itself especially against Asian immigrants. That they're working too hard. I've quoted that man who said to me, "Asians are unfair to my children because they work too hard." For a lot of people, the complaint about Asians is that not only do they work very hard but their work is multiplied—that it is entire families working, while I'm working here as a solitary being.

There is not a great deal of praise given to these immigrants, who have sometimes two and three jobs. A lot of these people are maintaining the quality of life in California. They're the ones who are planting the trees, mowing the lawns, cooking the Italian food in the yuppie restaurants. They are the ones who are maintaining what's left of the California dream, and of course they are the ones who are accused of destroying it.

55 **Reason:** Where do you think this backlash against immigrants is going?

Rodriguez: In the short term, I think it could be very ferocious. What worries me most is the black and immigrant split—the threat that blacks feel as they are replaced, literally, in places like Miami and Los Angeles. I think that could be very dangerous. I do know a number of black kids whom I've tried to get work for—as dishwashers, bus boys—and I'm told by employers that they don't hire black. They'll say, we hire Chinese, or we hire Mexican, or we hire Central Americans.

Reason: Much of the debate about immigration gets into issues involving public schools. There is this very powerful myth of the public schools as the conveyors of American culture and American ideas—the great assimilating mechanism. You went to parochial schools. You were taught by nuns who were not even American born, Irish nuns. You grew up with an incredible sense of difference from the surrounding culture. And yet you say those schools Americanized you. What does that tell us about the public schools?

Rodriguez: The irony is a true one. We used a lot of skills that came out of a medieval faith. The stress that the nuns placed on memorizing. The notion that education was not so much little Junior coming up with a new idea, but little Junior having to memorize what was already known. Education was not about learning something new. It was about learning something old. The nuns said about my sister, criticizing her to my parents, that she has a mind of her own.

At the same time, that taught us some basic things. We knew certain dates of American history. I knew certain poems by Longfellow. I knew how to multiply. I had a sense of the communal within that tradition. I could not only name popes, but I could also name presidents. I memorized the 48 state capitals. We were in the 13th century, but the 13th-century skills prepared us in some remarkable way to belong.

Reason: Do you think more education like yours, in terms of curriculum and structure, would be a better form of education?

Rodriguez: Absolutely, because I think that education in that sense 60
should be anti-American. There is enough in America out on the street to convince little Johnny that he's the center of everyone's universe—that his little "I" on his skateboard matters more than anybody else's right to walk on the sidewalk. What the classroom should insist on is that he belongs to a culture, a community, a tradition, a memory, and that in fact he's related to all kinds of people that he'll never know. That's the point of education.

It is, curiously, because of the Americanness of the public schools that they are less able to do what private schools can do, and that is teach us our communal relationships. American institutions end up becoming very American, and you have schools now that are supposed to teach little Hispanic kids to be privately Hispanic. That's not the point and never was. The point of education is to teach Hispanic kids that they're black.

Reason: What do you mean by that?

Rodriguez: Education is not about self-esteem. Education is demeaning. It should be about teaching you what you don't know, what you yet need to know, how much there is yet to do. Part of the process of education is teaching you that you are related to people who are not you, not your parents—that you are related to black runaway slaves and that you are related to suffragettes in the 19th century and that you are related to Puritans. That you are related to some continuous flow of ideas, some linkage, of which you are the beneficiary, the most recent link. The argument for bilingual education, or for teaching black children their own lingo, assumes that education is about self-esteem. My argument is that education is about teaching children to use language of other people.

Reason: The public language.

Rodriguez: If you all decided tomorrow that you wanted to speak Spanish, 65
I would be the first one insisting that that's the issue. One of the reasons I haven't gotten involved in the English Only movement is because I thought they were misplacing the emphasis. I support the use of English in the classroom because that's what this society tends to use. English is the de facto official language of the classroom, of the country. If you all changed tomorrow and decided you all wanted to speak Esperanto, then I would become the great defender of Esperanto. I'm not an Anglophile.

Reason: Your writing has become increasingly private. The reason *Hunger of Memory* was so controversial was that, even though it was a personal memoir, it took stands on public issues—bilingual education, affirmative action.

Rodriguez: I do think there are public issues in *Days of Obligation.* Religion is a public issue. The majority of reviewers ignored the fact that this book was primarily about being Catholic in America, not about being Hispanic in America. I'm not Catholic to them. I'm Hispanic. And I'm not gay to them. I'm brown to them. And I'm not Indian to them, because they know who the Indians are—the Indians live in Oklahoma.

The issue of the Indian, which very few people have remarked on, is a public issue. My rewriting of the Indian adventure [into a story in which the conquistadors' culture was in effect conquered, absorbed, and transformed by Indians through conversion and miscegenation] was not only to move the Indian away from the role of victim but to see myself in relationship to Pocahontas, to see myself as interested in the blond on his horse coming over the horizon. It occurred to me there was something aggressive about the Indian interest in the Other, and that you were at risk in the fact that I was watching you, that I wanted you, that I was interested in your religion, that I was prepared to swallow it and to swallow you in the process.

Maybe what is happening in the Americas right now is that the Indian is very much alive. I represent someone who has swallowed English and now claims it as *my language,* your books as *my books,* your religion as my religion—maybe this is the most subversive element of the colonial adventure. That I may be truest to my Indian identity by wanting to become American is really quite extraordinary.

Understanding

1. Rodriguez conceives of education as a means of preparing people "to belong." How does he describe this process?
2. Explain Rodriguez's response—"Within what is desired is also what is feared—" (paragraph 24) to the interviewer's question, "How do you account for the fact that in the beginning of the 20th century . . . the first broad-based restrictions on mass immigration started to be discussed . . . ?" What possible fears could mass immigration have engendered then? What fears does it raise today?
3. Rodriguez uses the term *ironic* and *irony* throughout this interview. What is irony? How is his final statement "I may be truest to my Indian identity by wanting to become American" ironic?
4. Rodriguez refers to his personal experience to illustrate and support his ideas. How effective is this approach to dealing with the "larger issues"?

Responding

1. Rodriguez's appearances on *NewsHour* do not occur on a predictable schedule, but if you have a chance to see one of his video essays, or if any of them

are on file in a library or media center, view one or two of them. Identify the themes around which they are created. What questions would you ask Rodriguez after viewing his work?

2. Do you think that knowing a person's race, gender, and religion is necessary to understand that person's views? What is so illuminating about these personal attributes? Which of these (or other) attributes would be necessary for others to understand *you?* Explain.
3. If you were to create a video essay examining your borders and your sense of belonging, what images would you include and with whom would you ally yourself? How would you begin it? How would you end it? In what language(s) would you present it?
4. Rodriguez esteems his ethnicity yet recognizes "I belong to many cultures." He has either avoided or overcome a hypersensitivity to discussions of this aspect of his identity by placing it in a larger perspective: "I think we go in cycles as a society." How do you think he has reached this kind of understanding? In what other ways might people from a minority culture appreciate their ethnic heritage without succumbing to a "victim" mentality?

Connecting

1. Connect Rodriguez's characterization of the way students discuss ideas today to Montaigne's ideal of conversation in "On the Art of Conversation" in "Learning Communities."
2. Read ahead in "Boundaries" to Anzaldúa's poem "To Live in the Borderlands Means You." How does this poem support or contradict Rodriguez's points?
3. Which of Csikszentmihalyi's ideas strike you as similar to Rodriguez's?
4. Do Rodriguez's hopes relate to the dreams expressed in Bettelheim's "Creating a New Way of Life" in chapter four?

Living in Tongues

Luc Sante

The "tongues" that Luc Sante (pronounced "luke sahnt") "lives in" are Walloon, French, and English, and he says they "revolve around and inform one another." Born in 1954 to a middle-class Belgian family of Walloon ancestry, Sante and his family moved back and forth between Belgium and the United States four times before they actually settled in New York City. (The *Walloon* are a French-speaking people of Celtic descent who inhabit southern and southeast Belgium and adjacent regions of France. The term also refers to the dialect of French spoken by these people.)

Having developed a penchant for obscure history while working in the paperback section of a New York bookstore, Sante became obsessed with long forgotten history, particularly of the Lower East Side, where he lived for fourteen years after graduating from Columbia University. The outcome was two books: *Low Life,* where he gives detailed and lurid accounts of life in the "underside of New York" from around 1840 to 1919, and *Evidence,* a collection of gruesome photographs and stories about New Yorkers who died mysteriously (mostly of murder) around the time of World War I. Aside from this particular fascination with forgotten lives, Sante has been a freelance journalist and critic. He currently teaches writing at Columbia University (School of the Arts) in New York City.

"Living in Tongues" is adapted from *The Factory of Facts,* Sante's memoir reflecting on his "Belgian birth, Walloon ethnicity, the experience of immigration, his upbringing in two cultures, and the acquisition of language." The essay offers another view on the debate surrounding multiculturalism and on capturing the other world that one leaves behind upon emigrating from it.

The first thing you have to understand about my childhood is that it mostly took place in another language. I was raised speaking French, and did not begin learning English until I was nearly 7 years old. Even after that, French continued to be the language I spoke at home with my parents. (I still speak only French with them to this day.) This fact inevitably affects my recall and evocation of my childhood, since I am writing and primarily thinking in English. There are states of mind, even people and events, that seem inaccessible in English, since they are defined by the character of the language through which I perceived them. My second language has turned out to be my principal tool, my means for making a living, and it lies close to the core of my self-definition. My first language, however, is coiled underneath, governing a more primal realm. 1

French is a pipeline to my infant self, to its unguarded emotions and even to its preserved sensory impressions. I can, for example, use language as a measure of pain. If I stub my toe, I may profanely exclaim, in English, "Jesus!" But in agony, like when I am passing a kidney stone, I become uncharacteristically reverent, which is only possible for me in French. *"Petit Jésus!"* I will cry, in the tones of nursery religion. When I babble in the delirium of fever or talk aloud in my sleep, I have been told by others, I do so in French. But French is also capable of summoning up a world of lost pleasures. The same idea, expressed in different languages, can have vastly different psychological meanings. If, for example, someone says in English, "Let's go visit Mr. and Mrs. X," the concept is neutral, my reaction determined by what I think of Mr. and Mrs. X. On the other hand, if the suggestion is broached in French, *"Allons dire bonjour,"* the phrasing affects me more powerfully than the specifics. "*Dire bonjour*" calls up a train of associations: for some reason I see my great-uncle Jules Stelmes, dead at least 30 years, with his fedora and his enormous white mustache and his soft dark eyes. I smell coffee and the raisin bread called *cramique,* hear the muffled bong of a parlor clock and the repetitive commonplaces of chitchat in the drawling accent of the Ardennes, people rolling their R's and leaning hard on their initial H's. I feel a rush-caned chair under me, see white curtains and starched tablecloths, can almost tap my feet on the cold ceramic tiles, perhaps the trompe-l'oeil pattern that covered the entire floor surface of my great-uncle Albert Remacle's farmhouse in Viville. I am sated, sleepy, bored out of my mind.

A large number of French words and turns of phrase come similarly equipped with dense associative catalogues, which may contain a ghostly impression of the first time I understood their use in speech. On the other hand, nearly all English words and phrases have a definite point of origin, which I can usually recall despite the overlaying patina acquired through years of use. Take that word "patina," for example. I don't remember how old I was when I first encountered it, but I know that I immediately linked it to the French *patiner,* meaning "to skate," so that its use calls up an image of a crosshatched pond surface.

Other English words have even more specific histories. There is "coffee," which I spotted on a can of Chock Full o'Nuts in our kitchen in Westfield, N.J., in 1960, when I was 6. I learned to spell it right away because I was impressed by its insistent doubling of F's and E's. The creative spellings reveled in by commerce in the early 1960's tended to be unhelpful. I didn't know what to make of "kleen" or "Sta-Prest," and it took me some time to appreciate the penguin's invitation on the glass door of the pharmacy: "Come in, it's KOOL inside." Then there was the local dry-cleaning establishment whose signs promised "one-hour Martinizing." I struggled for years to try and plumb that one, coming up with increasingly baroque scenarios.

When I started first grade, my first year of American schooling—I had 5
begun school in Belgium at 3½, in a prekindergarten program that taught basic reading, writing and arithmetic—I knew various words in English, but not how to construct a sentence. My first day remains vivid in its discomfort; I

didn't know how to ask to go to the toilet. In addition, my mother had dressed me in a yellow pullover over a white shirt-collar dickey. It was a warm day, and the nun in charge suggested I take off my sweater. Since I didn't understand, she came over and yanked it off me, revealing my sleeveless undershirt.

As the weeks and months went on, I gradually learned how to speak and comprehend the new language, but between home and school, and school and home, I would pass through a sort of fugue state lasting an hour or two during which I could not use either language. For a while, my mother tackled this problem by tutoring me in French grammar and vocabulary as soon as I got home. It never crossed my parents' minds that we should begin employing English as the household tongue. For one thing, my parents' command of it was then rudimentary—I was rapidly outpacing them—and for another, they were never certain that our American sojourn was to be permanent. We were economic refugees, to use the current expression, victims of the collapse of the centuries-old textile industry centered in my native city of Verviers, but my parents' loyalty to their own country was unquestioned.

For several years our family kept up a sort of double role. We were immigrants whose income bobbed just above the poverty line, thanks to my father's capacity for working swing shifts and double shifts in factories (and thanks to the existence of factory jobs); but we were also tourists. As soon as we could afford a used car we began methodically visiting every state park, historical site and roadside attraction within a reasonable radius, taking hundreds of snapshots—some to send to my grandparents, but many more that were intended for our delectation later on, when we were safely back in Belgium, recalling our fascinating hiatus in the land of large claims and vast distances. This was not to be, owing to family deaths and diverse obligations and uneasily shifting finances, but my parents kept up their faith in an eventual return, and a concomitant relative detachment from the American way of life.

* * *

Our household was a European outpost. My parents made earnest attempts to replicate Belgian food, a pursuit that involved long car trips to the then-rural middle of Staten Island to purchase leeks from Italian farmers, and expeditions to German butcher shops in Union and Irvington, N.J., to find a version of *sirop*—a dense concentrate of pears and apples that is the color and texture of heavy-gauge motor oil and is spread on bread—and various unsatisfactory substitutions. Neither cottage cheese nor ricotta could really pass for the farmer cheese called *makée* (*sirop* and *makée* together make *caca de poule*), but we had little choice in the matter, just as club soda had to stand in for *eau gazeuse,* since we lived in suburbs far from the seltzer belt, and parsley could only ever be a distant cousin to chervil. Desires for gooseberries and red currants, for familiar varieties of apricots and strawberries and potatoes and lettuce, for "real" bread and "real" cheese and "real" beer, simply had to be suppressed.

It wasn't easy constructing a version of Belgium in an apartment in a wooden house, with wood floors and Salvation Army furniture and sash windows and no cellar—not that the situation didn't present certain advantages, like central heating, hot running water and numerous appliances, none of which my parents could afford in Belgium, where we had actually been more prosperous. "Belgium" became a mental construct, its principal constituent material being language. We spoke French, thought in French, prayed in French, dreamed in French. Relatives kept us supplied with a steady stream of books and periodicals, my father with his Marabout paperbacks, my mother with the magazine *Femme d'Aujourd'hui* (Woman of Today), and me with history books for kids and comic magazines, in particular Spirou, which I received every week. Comics occupy a place in Belgian popular culture roughly comparable to that held in America by rock-and-roll, and like every other Belgian child, I first aspired to become a cartoonist. The comics I produced were always in French and clearly set in Belgium. (I couldn't abide American superhero adventures, although I did love Mad and the Sunday funnies, which were more commensurate with a Belgian turn of mind.) Somehow, though, I decided I wanted to become a writer when I was 10, and having made that decision never thought of writing in any language but English. Even so I continued to conduct my internal monologues in French until late adolescence. For me the French language long corresponded to the soul, while English was the world.

My parents learned the language of their adopted country not without 10
some difficulty. My father could draw on what remained of his high-school English, complete with pronunciation rules that wavered between Rhenish German and the BBC, but otherwise my parents had arrived equipped only with the 1945 edition of a conversation manual entitled "L'Anglais sans peine" (English Without Toil). This volume, published by the Assimil firm of Paris and Brussels, is sufficiently embedded in Francophone consciousness that you can still raise a snicker by quoting its opening phrase, "My tailor is rich." (English speakers, of course, will have no idea what you are talking about.) The book could not have been much help, especially since its vocabulary and references were attuned not to 1960's America but to Britain in the 1930's: "The Smiths had wired ahead the time of their arrival, and were expected for lunch at Fairview." This was also true of their other textbook, a reader called "Short Narratives" published in Ghent: "The proprietor of an eating-house ordered some bills to be printed for his window, with the words, 'Try our mutton pies!'" There were also some evening classes at the Y.M.C.A. in Summit, N.J., where we eventually settled, but I don't recall their lasting very long.

My parents' circle of acquaintances was almost entirely Belgian. My father had grown up in a tenement apartment in Verviers downstairs from the Dosquet family, whose children became his closest friends. The second daughter, Lucy, married an American G.I. after the war and they went to live in his native northern New Jersey. In 1953, her younger brother, Léopold (known as Pol), who was the same age as my father, followed suit with his wife, Jeanne. They were enthusiastic about the States and wrote rapturous letters. In 1957, when the prospects of my father's employer, an iron foundry that manufactured wool-carding machinery, were beginning to look grim, Jeanne Dosquet returned on a visit, and we all spent a week at the seaside resort of De Panne, at a socialist hostelry called the Hôtel Germinal, where plans were made for our own emigration.

After our arrival, we briefly shared an apartment with the Dosquets, a tight and uncomfortable situation. They introduced my parents to such Belgians as they had met by chance, in particular the three Van Hemmelrijk sisters and their mother, bourgeois French-speaking Antwerpers who had somehow ended up in America in straitened circumstances. There were others, too: a couple from Dolhain, near Verviers, who worked as caretakers of an estate in Tuxedo Park, N.Y., and another French-speaking Fleming, whom I only ever knew as Marie-Louise *"du facteur,"* because she had once been married to a mailman. She contributed another item to my burgeoning English vocabulary. One evening, while we were all watching television, Cesar Romero appeared on the screen: "Such a handsome man!" Marie-Louise exclaimed in English. To this day any appearance of the word "handsome" calls up the faint but unmistakable impression of Cesar Romero, in my mind's eye.

Even non-Belgian acquaintances tended to be foreigners whose grasp of the local tongue was as limited as ours. In Summit, our downstairs neighbors for a while were Hungarians named Szivros, who had fled their country after the doomed Budapest uprising of '56. Since we did not yet own a television, Mrs. Szivros would stand at the foot of the stairs of an evening and call up, "Missis, missis! 'Million Dollar Movie!'" Given the landscape, then, it is not surprising that my parents were somewhat at sea, knocked about among languages.

Sometimes, especially under pressure, my parents would reach for one tongue or the other and find themselves instead speaking Walloon, the native patois of southern Belgium. Walloon, now moribund, is usually identified as a dialect of French, whereas it is actually as old as the patois of Île-de-France, which became the official language—the 11th edition of the Encyclopedia Britannica in fact describes it as the northernmost Romance language. Like English, Walloon incorporates a substantial body of words that derives from Old Low German, so that it could, if unconsciously, seem like the middle ground between English and French. An often-told story in my family related how Lucy Dosquet, when her G.I. suitor arrived looking like a slob, angrily ordered him in Walloon, "*Louke-tu el mireu!*" He understood perfectly, and studied his reflection.

* * *

Walloon was the household tongue of all the relatives of my grandparents' 15
generation. Their parents in turn might have spoken nothing else; that no one bothered to establish rules for the writing of Walloon until the very beginning of this century, just in time for its decline in currency, partly accounts for the fact that nearly everyone in the family tree before my grandparents' time was illiterate. Walloon enjoyed a brief literary flowering that started in the 1890's but was largely killed off by World War I. My paternal grandfather acted in the Walloon theater in Verviers during its heyday, and my father followed in his footsteps after World War II, but by then it had largely become an exercise in nostalgia. Today, only old people still speak Walloon, and poor ones at that, since its use is considered rude by merchants, businessmen and

the middle class in general, and young people simply don't care. Young Walloons nowadays have been formed by television, movies and pop music, much of it emanating from France, and they have seemingly acquired the Parisian accent *en bloc.*

I was raised in a Belgian bubble, though, which means, among other things, that my speech is marked by the old Verviers Walloon accent, which causes observant Belgians some confusion. They can't reconcile that accent with the American flavor that has inevitably crept in, nor with my age and apparent class status. My French speech is also peppered with archaisms; I find myself unconsciously saying, for example, *"auto"* instead of *"voiture"* to mean "car," or "*illustré*" instead of *"revue"* to mean "magazine," expressions redolent of the 30's and 40's, if not earlier.

The sound of Walloon, on those rare occasions when I hear it, affects me emotionally with even more force than French does. Hearing, as I did a few months ago, an old man simply greeting his friend by saying, *"Bôdjou, Djôsef,"* can move me nearly to tears. But, of course, I hear much more than just "Hiya, Joe"—I hear a ghostly echo of my maternal grandfather greeting his older brother, Joseph Nandrin, for one thing, and I also hear the table talk of countless generations of workers and farmers and their wives, not that I particularly wish to subscribe to notions of collective ethnic memory. Walloon is a good-humored, long-suffering language of the poor, naturally epigrammatic, ideal for both choleric fervor and calm reflection, wry and often psychologically acute—reminiscent in some ways of Scottish and in some ways of Yiddish. Walloon is often my language of choice when, for instance, I am sizing up people at a party, but I have no one to speak it with at home. (My wife hails from Akron, Ohio.) I sometimes boast that, among the seven million people in New York City, I am the only Walloon speaker, which may or may not be true.

My three languages revolve around and inform one another. I live in an English-speaking world, of course, and for months on end I may speak nothing else. I do talk with my parents once a week by phone, but over the years we have developed a family dialect that is so motley it amounts to a Creole. I cannot snap back and forth between languages with ease, but need to be surrounded by French for several days before I can properly recover its rhythm, and so recover my idiomatic vocabulary—a way of thinking rather than just a set of words—and not merely translate English idioms. This means that I am never completely present at any given moment, since different aspects of my self are contained in different rooms of language, and a complicated apparatus of air locks prevents the doors from being flung open all at once. Still, there are subterranean correspondences between the linguistic domains that keep them from stagnating. The classical order of French, the Latin-Germanic dialectic of English and the onomatopoeic-peasant lucidity of Walloon work on one another critically, help enhance precision and reduce cant.

I like to think that this system helps fortify me in areas beyond the merely linguistic. I am not rootless but multiply rooted. This makes it impossible for me to fence off a plot of the world and decide that everyone dwelling outside those boundaries is "other." I am grateful to the accidents of my displaced upbringing, which taught me several kinds of irony. Ethnically, I am about as homogenous as it is possible to be: aside from one great-grandmother who came from Luxembourg, my gene pool derives entirely from an area smaller than the five boroughs of New York City. I was born in the same town as every one of my Sante forebears at least as far back as the mid-16th century, which is as far back as the records go. Having been transplanted from my native soil, though, and having had to construct an identity in response to a double set of demands, one from my background and one from my environment, I have become permanently "other." The choice I am faced with is simple: either I am at home everywhere or I am nowhere at all; either I realize my ties to human beings of every race and nationality or I will die, asphyxiated by the vacuum. Mere tolerance is idle and useless—if I can't recognize myself in others, no matter how remote in origin or behavior they might appear, I might as well declare war upon myself.

Understanding

1. Like Rue's "A Sociobiological Hunch About Educating Women" in chapter 5, "Biology," Luc Sante has written a "perfect" deductive essay. Identify Sante's thesis. What kinds of support/evidence does he use to illuminate it? Is Sante's essay convincing?
2. How did Sante *feel* about his younger life? Does he consider his three languages a burden or a gift?
3. Sante claims that he has become "permanently 'other'" (paragraph 19). What does he mean? Was his a "liminal" existence? Explain this possibility in relation to others on the planet and to his community or communities. What values are in evidence here?
4. What is the difference between *language learning* and *language acquisition?* Which did Sante do—learn or acquire? How? Did going to school in English cause Sante to lose his native tongue and culture? How does your answer support or refute arguments in favor of bilingual education in American schools?

Responding

1. If your first language is other than English, describe your "balancing act." Do you consider your languages gifts or burdens?
2. If you have lived in another country for an extended time, or even if you have just traveled through, you have been unnerved or tickled by language experiences. Write a story about one of them. Or, if you have studied another language in school, describe words and experiences (smells, feelings, food tastes) that you associate with that learning experience—that classroom, that teacher, those classmates.

3. What is your definition of language? Define it anyway you want, or use the formal definition formula:
   Language is a _______ which _____________________________________.
   (New word) (Class) (Differentia: How does this thing differ from all other members of this class?)
   Example: *A ring* is a *piece of jewelry* which *is worn on a finger or toe.*
4. Research by linguists and anthropologists shows that a community's language is a way of viewing the world. Language is in fact both a limiting factor and an illuminating one. Some cultures have no terms of endearment; others have words for different kinds of snow or different colors. Does not recognizing a phenomenon and therefore not naming it cause one not to notice it? Explore this notion further for your responses to questions 1, 2, or 3.

Connecting

Rodriguez in "The New, New World" distinguishes between *public* and *private* language—the school language and the intimate "home" language. Does Sante make the same distinction? Explain. Do you?

Cyberhood vs. Neighborhood: Community

Howard Rheingold

Howard Rheingold is a science fiction novelist and a nonfiction writer. His enthusiastic work showcases his love of language and vast knowledge of science and technology. His books on computers offer both history and speculation on future development and their possible ramifications on human communities. His books, mostly written for the general public, have been commended for their clarity and wit.

A "group" or "community" may be described as a number of people who experience shared or patterned interaction and who feel bound together by a like consciousness. Sociologists call collections of people who lack these traits "categories," if they have a particular characteristic in common, or "aggregates," if they are located in a specific area. In "Cyberhood vs. Neighborhood: Community," which is excerpted from his book *The Virtual Community,* Rheingold explores the characteristics of the newly emerging cyberspace community.

1 In the summer of 1986, my then-2-year-old daughter picked up a tick. There was this blood-bloated *thing* sucking on our baby's scalp, and we weren't quite sure how to go about getting it off. My wife, Judy, called the pediatrician. It was 11 o'clock in the evening. I logged onto the WELL, the big Bay Area infonet, and contacted the Parenting conference (a conference is an on-line conversation about a specific subject). I got my answer on-line within minutes from a fellow with the improbable but genuine name of Flash Gordon, M.D. I had removed the tick by the time Judy got the callback from the pediatrician's office.

What amazed me wasn't just the speed with which we obtained precisely the information we needed to know, right when we needed to know it. It was also the immense inner sense of security that comes with discovering that real people—most of them parents, some of them nurses, doctors, and midwives—are available, around the clock, if you need them. There is a magic protective circle around the atmosphere of the Parenting conference. We're talking about our sons and daughters in this forum, not about our computers or our opinions about philosophy, and many of us feel that this tacit understanding sanctifies the virtual space.

The atmosphere of this particular conference—the attitudes people exhibit to each other in the tone of what they say in public—is part of what continues to attract me. People who never have much to contribute in political debate, technical argument, or intellectual gamesmanship turn out to have a lot to say about raising children. People you knew as fierce, even nasty, intellectual opponents in other contexts give you emotional support on a deeper level, parent to parent, within the boundaries of this small but warmly human corner of cyberspace.

In most cases, people who talk about a shared interest don't disclose enough about themselves as whole individuals on-line to inspire real trust in others. But in the case of the subcommunity called the Parenting conference, a few dozen of us, scattered across the country, few of whom rarely if ever saw the others face to face, have a few years of minor crises to knit us together and prepare us for serious business when it comes our way. Another several dozen read the conference regularly but contribute only when they have something important to add. Hundreds more read the conference every week without comment, except when something extraordinary happens.

Jay Allison and his family live in Massachusetts. He and his wife are public- 5
radio producers. I've never met them face to face, although I feel I know something powerful and intimate about the Allisons and have strong emotional ties to them. What follows are some of Jay's postings on the WELL:

"Woods Hole. Midnight. I am sitting in the dark of my daughter's room. Her monitor lights blink at me. The lights used to blink too brightly so I covered them with bits of bandage adhesive and now they flash faintly underneath, a persistent red and green, Lillie's heart and lungs.

"Above the monitor is her portable suction unit. In the glow of the flashlight I'm writing by, it looks like the plastic guts of a science-class human model, the tubes coiled around the power supply, the reservoir, the pump.

"Tina is upstairs trying to get some sleep. A baby monitor links our bedroom to Lillie's. It links our sleep to Lillie's too, and because our souls are linked to hers, we do not sleep well.

"I am naked. My stomach is full of beer. The flashlight rests on it, and the beam rises and falls with my breath. My daughter breathes through a white plastic tube inserted into a hole in her throat. She's 14 months old."

Sitting in front of our computers with our hearts racing and tears in our 10
eyes, in Tokyo and Sacramento and Austin, we read about Lillie's croup, her tracheostomy, the days and nights at Massachusetts General Hospital, and now the vigil over Lillie's breathing and the watchful attention to the mechanical apparatus that kept her alive. It went on for days. Weeks. Lillie recovered, and relieved our anxieties about her vocal capabilities after all that time with a hole in her throat by saying the most extraordinary things, duly reported online by Jay.

Later, writing in *Whole Earth Review,* Jay described the experience:

"Before this time, my computer screen had never been a place to go for solace. Far from it. But there it was. Those nights sitting up late with my daughter, I'd go to my computer, dial up the WELL, and ramble. I wrote about what was happening that night or that year. I didn't know anyone I was "talking" to. I had never laid eyes on them. At 3:00 a.m. my "real" friends were asleep, so I turned to this foreign, invisible community for support. The WELL was always awake.

"Any difficulty is harder to bear in isolation. There is nothing to measure against, to lean against. Typing out my journal entries into the computer and over the phone lines, I found fellowship and comfort in this unlikely medium."

Many people are alarmed by the very idea of a virtual community, fearing that it is another step in the wrong direction, substituting more technological ersatz for yet another natural resource or human freedom. These critics often voice their sadness at what people have been reduced to doing in a civilization that worships technology, decrying the circumstances that lead some people into such pathetically disconnected lives that they prefer to find their companions on the other side of a computer screen. There is a seed of truth in this fear, for communities at some point require more than words on a screen if they are to be other than ersatz.

Yet some people—many people—who don't do well in spontaneous spoken interaction turn out to have valuable contributions to make in a conversation in which they have time to think about what to say. These people, who might constitute a significant proportion of the population, can find written communication more authentic than the face-to-face kind. Who is to say that this preference for informal written text is somehow less authentically human than opting for audible speech? Those who critique computer-mediated communication because some people use it obsessively hit an important target, but miss a great deal more when they don't take into consideration people who use the medium for genuine human interaction. Those who find virtual communities cold places point at the limits of the technology, its most dangerous pitfalls, and we need to pay attention to those boundaries. But these critiques don't tell us how the Allisons, my own family, and many others could have found the community of support and information we found in the WELL when we needed it. And those of us who do find communion in cyberspace might do well to pay attention to the way the medium we love can be abused.

Although dramatic incidents are what bring people together and stick in their memories, most of what goes on in the Parenting conference and most virtual communities is informal conversation and downright chitchat. The model of the WELL and other social clusters in cyberspace as "places" emerges naturally whenever people who use this medium discuss its nature. In 1987, Stewart Brand quoted me in his book *The Media Lab* about what tempted me to log onto the WELL as often as I did: "There's always another mind there. It's like having the corner bar, complete with old buddies and delightful newcomers and new tools waiting to take home and fresh graffiti and letters, except instead of putting on my coat, shutting down the computer, and walking down to the corner, I just invoke my telecom program and there they are. It's a place."

I've changed my mind about a lot of aspects of the WELL over the years, but the sense of place is still as strong as ever. As Ray Oldenburg proposes in his 1989 book *The Great Good Place,* there are three essential places in people's lives: the place we live, the place we work, and the place we gather for conviviality. Although the casual conversation that takes place in cafés, beauty shops, pubs, and town squares is universally considered to be trivial, idle talk, Oldenburg makes the case that such places are where communities can come into being and continue to hold together. These are the unacknowledged agoras of modern life. When the automobilecentric, suburban, fast-food, shopping-mall way of life eliminated many of these "third places" from traditional towns and cities around the world, the social fabric of existing communities started shredding.

Oldenburg puts a name and a conceptual framework on a phenomenon that every virtual community member knows instinctively, the power of informal public life:

"Third places exist on neutral ground and serve to level their guests to a condition of social equality. Within these places, conversation is the primary activity and the major vehicle for the display and appreciation of human personality and individuality. Third places are taken for granted and most have a low profile. Since the formal institutions of society make stronger claims on the individual, third places are normally open in the off hours, as well as at other times. The character of a third place is determined most of all by its regular clientele and is marked by a playful mood, which contrasts with people's more serious involvement in other spheres. Though a radically different kind of setting for a home, the third place is remarkably similar to a good home in the psychological comfort and support that it extends.

"Such are the characteristics of third places that appear to be universal and essential 20
to a vital informal public life. . . .

"The problem of place in America manifests itself in a sorely deficient informal public life. The structure of shared experience beyond that offered by family, job, and passive consumerism is small and dwindling. The essential group experience is being replaced by the exaggerated self-consciousness of individuals. American lifestyles, for all the material acquisition and the seeking after comforts and pleasures, are plagued by boredom, loneliness, alienation, and a high price tag. . . .

"Unlike many frontiers, that of the informal public life does not remain benign as it awaits development. It does not become easier to tame as technology evolves, as governmental bureaus and agencies multiply, or as population grows. It does not yield to the mere passage of time and a policy of letting the chips fall where they may as development proceeds in other areas of urban life. To the contrary, neglect of the informal public life can make a jungle of what had been a garden while, at the same time, diminishing the ability of people to cultivate it."

It might not be the same kind of place that Oldenburg had in mind, but many of his descriptions of third places could also describe the WELL. Perhaps cyberspace is one of the informal public places where people can rebuild the aspects of community that were lost when the malt shop became a mall. Or perhaps cyberspace is precisely the *wrong* place to look for the rebirth of community, offering not a tool for conviviality but a life-denying simulacrum of real passion and true commitment to one another. In either case, we need to find out soon.

Because we cannot see one another in cyberspace, gender, age, national origin, and physical appearance are not apparent unless a person wants to make such characteristics public. People whose physical handicaps make it difficult to form new friendships find that virtual communities treat them as they always wanted to be treated—as thinkers and transmitters of ideas and feeling beings, not carnal vessels with a certain appearance and way of walking and talking (or not walking and not talking).

One of the few things that enthusiastic members of virtual communities 25
in places like Japan, England, France, and the United States all agree on is that expanding their circle of friends is one of the most important advantages of computer conferencing. It is a way to *meet* people, whether or not you feel the need to affiliate with them on a community level. It's a way of both making contact with and maintaining a distance from others. The way you meet people in cyberspace puts a different spin on affiliation: In traditional kinds of communities, we are accustomed to meeting people, then getting to know them; in virtual communities, you can get to know people and *then* choose to meet them. Affiliation also can be far more ephemeral in cyberspace because you can get to know people you might never meet on the physical plane.

How does anybody find friends? In the traditional community, we search through our pool of neighbors and professional colleagues, of acquaintances and acquaintances of acquaintances, in order to find people who share our values and interests. We then exchange information about one another, disclose and discuss our mutual interests, and sometimes we become friends. In a virtual community we can go directly to the place where our favorite subjects are being discussed, then get acquainted with people who share our passions or who use words in a way we find attractive. In this sense, the topic is the address: You can't simply pick up a phone and ask to be connected with someone who wants to talk about Islamic art or California wine, or someone with a 3-year-old daughter or a 40-year-old Hudson; you can, however, join a computer conference on any of those topics, then open a public or private correspondence with the previously unknown people you find there. Your chances of making friends are increased by several orders of magnitude over the old methods of finding a peer group.

You can be fooled about people in cyberspace, behind the cloak of words. But that can be said about telephones or face-to-face communication as well; computer-mediated communications provide new ways to fool people, and the most obvious identity swindles will die out only when enough people learn to use the medium critically. In some ways, the medium will, by its nature, be forever biased toward certain kinds of obfuscation. It will also be a place where people often end up revealing themselves far more intimately than they would be inclined to do without the intermediation of screens and pseudonyms.

Point of view, along with identity, is one of the great variables in cyberspace. Different people in cyberspace look at their virtual communities through differently shaped keyholes. In traditional communities, people have a strongly shared mental model of the sense of place—the room or village or city where their interactions occur. In virtual communities, the sense of place requires an individual act of imagination. The different mental models people have of the electronic agora complicate the question of why people seem to want to build societies mediated by computer screens. A question like that leads inexorably to the old fundamental questions of what forces hold any society together. The roots of these questions extend farther than the social upheavals triggered by modern communications technologies.

When we say "society," we usually mean citizens of cities in entities known as nations. We take those categories for granted. But the mass-psychological transition we made to thinking of ourselves as part of modern society and nation-states is historically recent. Could people make the transition from the close collective social groups, the villages and small towns of premodern and precapitalist Europe, to a new form of social solidarity known as society that transcended and encompassed all previous kinds of human association? Ferdinand Tönnies, one of the founders of sociology, called the premodern kind of social group *gemeinschaft,* which is closer to the English word *community,* and the new kind of social group he called *gesellschaft,* which can be translated roughly as *society.* All the questions about community in cyberspace point to a similar kind of transition, for which we have no technical names, that might be taking place now.

Sociology student Marc Smith, who has been using the WELL and the Net 30
as the laboratory for his fieldwork, pointed me to Benedict Anderson's *Imagined Communities,* a study of nation-building that focuses on the ideological labor involved. Anderson points out that nations and, by extension, communities are imagined in the sense that a given nation exists by virtue of a common acceptance in the minds of the population that it exists. Nations must exist in the minds of their citizens in order to exist at all. "Virtual communities require an act of imagination," Smith points out, extending Anderson's line of thinking to cyberspace, "and what must be imagined is the idea of the community itself."

Understanding

1. How is it that real trust can be inspired online, in some cases more so than in face-to-face communication?
2. Define *community.* What kinds of people use the Parenting (and other) conferences? How does it fit your definition of community? And how powerful is this one?
3. What are the criticisms of computer-mediated communications?
4. Rheingold quotes writer Ray Oldenburg claiming that WELL (Whole Earth 'Lectronic Link) is a "place," an *agora,* a "third place." What are the characteristics of a third place according to Oldenburg? What is Oldenburg's concern about informal public life? Do you share his forecast?
5. What is the difference between traditional communities and virtual communities? Do people generate actual communities by imagining them and creating them, or do communities simply happen and then become recognized and named? Which do you think happened in the WELL communities?

Responding

1. Do you participate in a conference in cyberspace? If so, write about its contribution to you and yours to it. If you don't have a virtual community, find out how to get there, log on to one, participate in it, and report your findings. Try writing it as a historical narrative or a log book of the experience.

2. Do you agree with Oldenburg when he claims in paragraph 17 that the conversations we hold in "third places"—those where we gather for conviviality—are "universally considered to be trivial, idle talk"? Do you agree with his claim that Americans "are plagued by boredom, loneliness, alienation, and a high price tag"?
3. Using Oldenburg's criteria, describe a noncyberspace "third place" of your own. What is your attraction to it? What kind of sustenance does it provide?
4. John Perry Barlow, a cattle rancher in Wyoming for seventeen years while he wrote songs for the Grateful Dead, began speaking and writing about cyberspace in 1988 and is currently on the board of directors of WELL. Though he says we ought to go into cyberspace with hope, almost like unconditional love, he is also critical of the "community" that currently inhabits it—there is no diversity. He claims that it is populated "as near as I can tell, by white males under fifty with plenty of computer terminal time, great typing skills, high math SATs, strongly held opinions on just about everything, and an excruciating face-to-face shyness, especially with the opposite sex." Do you agree with him? If you are a user of cyberspace, what are your demographics in relation to his claims? What are your suggestions or dreams for creating virtual communities? What can the human spirit and our basic desire to connect create out there? Using WELL as a model, write a proposal for your virtual community.

Connecting

Rick Smolan and Jennifer Erwitt's book (and Web site) *24 Hours in Cyberspace: Painting on the Walls of the Digital Cave,* had one purpose: "to create a one-day 'digital snapshot' of the people whose lives are being dramatically transformed by the wave of online technology sweeping over them." They wanted to chronicle this new community, where humanity gathers to meet, romance, discuss, buy, and sell. From the 200,000 photographs that were taken and sent to "Mission Control" in San Francisco, 150 were published on the *24 Hours in Cyberspace* Web site. There were 4 million "hits" that day—a huge "community" response. Find this book or log on to the project's home page (http://www.cyber24.com). Describe what kind of community values you find there. What is this virtual community's power? Does this kind of effort make a difference in people's lives? Discuss this community *(24 Hours in Cyberspace)* or the Parenting conference Rheingold describes in relation to other communities in chapter six. For example, how are the values or activities of the Parenting conference similar to (or different in significant ways from) others in this chapter?

Storytellers and Scribes

Elias Canetti

Elias Canetti, winner of the 1981 Nobel Prize for Literature, is one of the major intellectual figures of the twentieth century. *Voices of Marrakesh: A Record of a Visit,* from which this selection is taken, is Canetti's travel book, but it describes no ordinary visit and no ordinary traveler. Along with the voices of the city, with the words of its Arab, European, and Jewish residents, Canetti records his own mental voyage. The stories in this book subtly present some of Canetti's great themes: mortality, the crowd, the sounds and smells of life in all their tragedy and complexity.

Voices of Marrakesh is a collection of stories—rather like beautifully polished journal entries—of his trip to Marrakesh, one of the great cities of Morocco. Early in the book, Canetti writes:

> During the weeks I spent in Morocco I made no attempt to acquire either Arabic or any of the Berber languages. I wanted to lose none of the force of those foreign-sounding cries. I wanted sounds to affect me as much as lay in their power, unmitigated by deficient and artificial knowledge on my part. I had not read a thing about the country. Its customs were as unknown to me as its people.

Once we know how Canetti traveled, we can understand the idiosyncratic nature of his observations. In "Storytellers and Scribes," he creates Djema el Fna, the square, and its special inhabitants as well as an intense internal dialogue full of questions that come from the people he sees.

The largest crowds are drawn by the storytellers. It is around them that people throng most densely and stay longest. Their performances are lengthy; an inner ring of listeners squat on the ground and it is some time before they get up again. Others, standing, form an outer ring; they, too, hardly move, spellbound by the storyteller's words and gestures. Sometimes two of them recite in turn. Their words come from farther off and hang longer in the air than those of ordinary people. I understand nothing and yet whenever I came within hearing I was rooted to the spot by the same fascination. They were words that held no meaning for me, hammered out with fire and impact: to the man who spoke them they were precious and he was proud of them. He arranged them in a rhythm that always struck me as highly personal. If he paused, what followed came out all the more forceful and exalted. I sensed the solemnity of certain words and the devious intent of others. Flattering compliments affected me as if they had been directed at myself; in perilous situations I was afraid. Everything was under control; the most powerful words flew precisely as far as the storyteller wished them to. The air above the listen- 1 ers' heads was full of movement, and one who understood as little as I felt great things going on there.

In honour of their words the storytellers wore striking clothes. They were always dressed differently from their listeners. They favoured the more splendid materials; one or other of them always appeared in blue or brown velvet. They gave the impression of exalted yet somehow fairy-tale personages. They spared few glances for the people by whom they were surrounded. Their gaze was on their heroes, their characters. If their eye did fall on someone who just happened to be there it surely gave him an obscure feeling of being someone else. Foreigners were simply not there as far as they were concerned, did not belong in the world of their words. At first I refused to believe I was of so little interest to them; this was too unfamiliar to be true. So I stood there more than usually long, though I already felt the tug of other sounds in that place so replete with sounds—but they were still taking no notice of me when I was beginning to feel almost at home in the group of listeners. The storyteller had seen me, of course, but to him I was and remained an intruder in his magic circle: I did not understand him.

There were times when I would have given a great deal to be able to, and I hope the day will come when I can appreciate these itinerant storytellers as they deserve to be appreciated. But I was also glad I could not understand them. For me they remained an enclave of ancient, untouched existence. Their language was as important to them as mine to me. Words were their nourishment, and they let no one seduce them into exchanging it for a better form of nourishment. I was proud of the power of storytelling that I witnessed them wielding over their linguistic fellows. I saw them as elder and better brothers to myself. In happy moments I told myself: I too can gather people round me to whom I tell stories; and they too listen to me. But instead of roaming from place to place never knowing whom I will find, whose ears will receive my story, instead of living in utter dependence on my story itself I have dedicated myself to paper. I live now behind the protection of desk and door, a craven dreamer, and they in the bustle of the marketplace, among a hundred strange faces that are different every day, unburdened by cold, superfluous knowledge, without books, ambition, or empty respectability. Having seldom felt at ease among the people of our zones whose life is literature—despising them because I despise something about myself, and I think that something is paper—I suddenly found myself here among authors I could look up to since there was not a line of theirs to be *read.*

But a little farther on in the same square I had to admit how seriously I had blasphemed against paper. Only a few steps from the storytellers the scribes had their pitch. It was very quiet here, the quietest part of the Djema el Fna. The scribes did nothing to recommend their skill. Delicate little men, they sat there in silence, their writing things in front of them, and never once gave you the impression they were waiting for clients. When they looked up they considered you with no particular curiosity, and their eyes soon travelled on to something else. Their benches were set up some distance apart, far enough for it to be impossible to hear from one to another. The more modest or possibly more conservative among them squatted on the ground. Here they cogitated or wrote in a confidential world apart, surrounded by the tumultuous din of the square and yet cut off from it. It was as if they were used to being consulted about secret complaints and, since this took place in public, had got into a certain habit of effacement. They themselves were barely present; all that counted here was the silent dignity of paper.

People came up to them singly or in pairs. Once I saw two veiled young 5
women sitting on the bench before a scribe, moving their lips almost imperceptibly as he nodded and almost as imperceptibly wrote. Another time I noticed a whole family, extremely proud and respectable. It consisted of four people, who had arranged themselves on two benches at right angles with the scribe between them. The father was an elderly, powerful-looking, magnificently handsome Berber, experience and wisdom plainly legible in his face. I tried to imagine a situation in which he would be inadequate and could think of none. Here he was, in his one and only inadequacy, his wife beside him; her bearing was as impressive as his, for the veil over her face left only the enormous dark eyes exposed, and beside her on the bench sat two similarly-veiled daughters. All four sat erect and extremely solemn.

The scribe, who was very much smaller, accepted their respect. His features evinced a keen attentiveness, which was as palpable as the prosperity and beauty of the family. I watched them from only a short distance away without hearing a sound or observing a single movement. The scribe had not yet begun his actual business. He had probably asked for and received an account of the matter and was now considering how this could best be encompassed in terms of the written word. The group gave such an impression of unity that its members might have known one another for ever and occupied the same positions since the beginning of time.

So intimately did they belong together that I did not even ask myself what they had all come for, and it was not until much later, when I had long left the square, that I began to think about it. What on earth could it have been that had required the whole family's attendance before the scribe?

Understanding

1. Why do you think Canetti refused to believe that he himself was of little interest to the storyteller in the square, and that this situation—being uninteresting—was "too unfamiliar to be true" (paragraph 2).
2. What is the difference between the storytellers Canetti observes and himself as a storyteller?
3. What are scribes? What do they do? Who are their clients? Are there scribes in the United States?
4. Italian filmmaker Federico Fellini said, "A different language is a different version of life." What versions of life was Canetti missing? What version was the family in the square missing? What do you make of Canetti's desire *not* to learn anything about Moroccan culture or language?

Responding

1. Canetti is not Moroccan and he does not know Arabic or any of the Berber languages spoken in Morocco. He is a foreigner who admitted that he knew nothing (and wanted to know nothing) about Moroccan culture. In truth, he is writing about Morocco from the point of view of an outsider. Have you ever written about another culture as an outsider? What is the advantage of writing as an outsider? What is the disadvantage?
2. Did you come from a culture (or family) of storytellers? If so, describe your earliest memories of those events. Where did the stories take place? Who told? Who listened? What were the usual topics? Which were your favorite, and which would you tell your own children? Do you consider yourself a storyteller now?
3. Canetti was a Sephardic Jew who grew up in many different European cities, speaking German, English, French, and Bulgarian. He wrote in German, and *Voices of Marrakesh* was translated into English by J. A. Underwood. In your opinion, was Underwood a kind of scribe for Canetti? What kinds of power do a translator and a scribe have?
4. If the storytellers who fascinated Canetti were from an oral culture, we can infer that what counts as knowledge is that which is handed down from ancestors. Canetti, on the other hand, is from a writing-based culture, where knowledge is based on evidence, consistency, and precise reasoning. He exhibits those cultural characteristics in his own writing. In this case, Canetti and the storytellers are "others" to each other because of differences in their backgrounds; however, we have only Canetti's view (interpretation) of this scene in the square. Write this passage from the point of view of the "other"—the storyteller.

Connecting

Compare Canetti's "borders" with those in Sante's "Living in Tongues." How does language play in each essay?

Writing Option: In Public and Private

Your life experiences have put you in contact with many communities to which you belong either by choice, as in Rheingold's "Cyberhood vs. Neighborhood: Community," or by birth, as in Sante's "Living in Tongues." The readings in this section only suggest the varieties of these communities.

Examine your responses to the "In Public and Private" Responding questions and cull those that provide your most insightful thinking about your experiences of belonging, or of trying to belong, to a community.

If you select a community to which you have chosen to belong, you might explain the need that motivated your choice, your expectations, and the costs and rewards of membership. If you belong by birth, analyze and explain how you are coming to terms with this membership, as Sante does in examining his "multiply rooted self."

Try to crystallize your main point(s) in one or two sentences before you begin. You should certainly be able to do it by the end. Use your own experiences to support your point, as well as ideas and the justification for them from your readings. Your writing may take the form of a personal narrative, like Sante's, an exchange interview with a classroom colleague modeled after Rodriguez's "The New, New World" (but with fewer questions), or a more conventional essay.

5 Boundaries

> *"I am conscious of myself and become myself only while revealing myself for another, through another, and with the help of another.* To be *means* to communicate . . . *To be means to be for another, and through the other for oneself. A person has no internal sovereign territory, he is wholly and always on the boundary: looking inside himself, he looks* into the eyes of another *or* with the eyes of another . . . *I cannot imagine without another; I must find myself in another by finding another in myself."*
>
> —Mikhail Banktin

Here/there, love/hate, mine/yours. The couplings of these words betoken boundaries, dividing lines between ourselves and what we define as "other." We usually think of boundaries as physical separations designed to protect our property, ensure our privacy, or control our behavior. Fences, doors, national borders, and velvet ropes serve this function. But boundaries are also psychological—invisible "do not enter" signs that we put up between ourselves and others to protect the original personal property, our "self." We are not singular, though; we are a composite structure that has been formed since the day we were born and continues to be formed by countless and never-ending exchanges with others. So if we deliberately bring the outside world *inside* of us in order to be who we are, on what basis do we create boundaries?

We begin by examining some of the boundaries that spring from our contact with and rejection of the "other." The personal characteristics reflected in the following readings—gender, color, age, and ethnicity—show how persistent the tendency is to "draw the line" between ourselves and others; and yet by writing about boundaries these writers take a step over them. Jeb Alexander reveals his secrets in a diary which he hopes the reader will approach with understanding, a true "crossover" dream. Gloria Wade-Gayles shares her indignation toward those who have crossed a racial boundary she hoped to preserve and, in so doing, distances herself from her own self-imposed boundaries. Barbara MacDonald, in a clenched and angry speech, shows that the boundary crossings between age groups with similar sympathies and interests may not be all that they seem. Gloria Anzaldúa exhorts us with heat: "Live *sin fronteras* / be a crossroads."

Whether boundaries are physical or psychological, they give us a safe but blinkered view of our world. Mihaly Csikszentmihalyi proposes that boundaries may be the price we must pay for living in a reasonably civilized society. If so, these writers show how those of us who create or live within boundaries also have the capacity to transcend them. In so doing, we change our personal context and reconfigure how and what we think about our individuality.

Love and Affection, Damn It!

Ina Russell, editor

> It occurred to me today with something of a shock how horrible it would be for this diary of mine to be pawed over and read unsympathetically after I am dead, by those who are incapable of understanding . . . And then the thought of one thing even more dreadful and terrible than that—for my diary never to be read by the one person who would or could understand. For I do want to be read—there is no use concealing the fact—by somebody like me, who would understand.

And so in a paragraph, the man known by the pseudonym of Jeb Alexander expresses his desire to be read and understood—probably the desire of every writer. But Jeb never achieved his desire to be an author by conventional standards; instead, what we know of his life is found in his journals, portions of which are excerpted here.

In them, Jeb traces his extraordinary on-again, off-again love affair with C. C. Dasham ("Dash"), whom he met on the train on his way to college and with whom he maintained a lifelong friendship. From 1918 to the late 1950s, Jeb chronicled in unsparing detail his daily life first as a college student, then as an editor for the U.S. Department of State, and as a gay man.

Ina Russell inherited the fifty-volume diary from her uncle "Jeb" when he died in 1965. She culled what she considered the most significant insights from this monumental chronicle of life in old Washington, D.C. It is a record that conveys the texture of daily life from a singular perspective, leaving readers with an account of an ordinary gay life that has few, if any, parallels.

1919

Thursday, 2 January 1919

I left with only Mama to part from. I was almost sick with nervous antici- 1
pation. She told me, "Try to make friends at school. Begin over. Don't get the reputation of being quiet." Well meant, but when the stars sing to the moon, then shall I be talkative and likable.

My two suitcases, heavy and clumsy, were a hindrance. On Fourteenth Street hill, from the streetcar window, I saw Henry's friends Leroy and Ford. They turned into a tobacco store. Then to the station, and into the train and a pair of seats, red-plush covered. The train pulled out of the station and I told Washington good-bye. We flew on through Virginia. I looked through the misty windowpanes at the sodden country in winter. Night closed in. Beyond the pale glow from the train lights, a void of rain and darkness. At Strasburg Junction, C. C. Dasham got on.

He looked about the car, then sat with me. He has the palest green eyes I ever saw. He admired my tie and in his Mississippi drawl asked about my copy of *Dubliners*. He said, "It looks like a fine book." In a while he asked me what my goals were; my goals for life. After some hesitation I told him, "Authorship." He remarked, "I have no such specific dream for myself. I'm still in the 'having-fun' stage of my youth." The rain changed to snow and the flying flakes brushed against the window with a faint scratching sound. We reached Harrisburg and walked out into the storm. Dasham carried one of my valises for me, as he had only a satchel.

We climbed into the cavern of a hack and were driven to the Hotel Kavanaugh. The snow sailed horizontally into our faces. Dasham helped me bring my suitcases into the lobby. His cheeks were mottled red from the cold. We came upon two other fellows from school, and arranged to share two rooms, four beds, leaving instructions to call us at six in the morning. Dasham was in the other room. . . .

Sunday, 23 March 1919 (Lexington, Virginia)

As I returned from the cemetery with daffodils I had picked there, I passed 5
Dasham and Agneau. "Hey, Alexander," said Dasham, "those are lovely." I gave some daffodils to him. On my desk as I write, the rest are radiant with beauty. O, I know I am shy and weak, but I believe that with Dasham I would be godlike, and he would be godlike with me. I declare, he is the most beautiful thing I ever saw—so wholesome and healthy, so full of youth. I imagine us on the high seas; I imagine us shipwrecked and cast adrift to lost islands. Every day I live a joyous life with him, if only in my imagination.

Sunday, 1 June 1919

D.C. sizzles under a blazing hot spell. I walked down to the National Art Gallery, and it was like walking over an oven. Still, I was glad I went. I like Corot better than any other artist. I should love to paint beautiful landscapes. It ought to be a happy life.

At dinner tonight a general argument, in which I took my part, about the South, Mama saying she was sick of talk about the Southern Gentleman and so on—but tonight, especially, I hate to write about Mama; she is contemptible and small. I pity her. Today is the anniversary of the death of my real mother. Who knows how much richer my life might have been had Mother lived. I was so young when she died. Henry was a sturdy lad of eight, but I was a frightened four-year old. The lilacs and the pinks were in full bloom. The nurse came on to the porch and stood looking about in her cat-and-mouse way. When she saw Henry and me, she approached us where we sat in the green swing under the cedar tree, and told us that Mother had "gone away to heaven." It hurt so much, to think my mother would leave me. And then, there came a day when Henry asked the little nurse, "Why are you going to live with us?" She told him, "He needs someone to take care of his boys." After that she and Dad were married, and she was Mama. What a starved, repressed childhood I had. . . .

Friday, 26 September 1919 (Lexington, Virginia)

Lansing Tower told me that he is writing a novel; has been for almost a year. We had a long talk on the topic. Later at night I saw him at the post office and suggested going up to the cemetery. On the way up we discussed long hair and independence of ordinary conventions. Lansing spoke affectionately of "cranks," and I told him, "I should like to be considered a 'crank,' by being independent." He said, "You are pretty sure to be thought a 'crank' by at least a few."

The cemetery was quiet at that hour, though the stones gleamed uncannily. Except for one start of nervousness on coming round a tomb I felt at ease. But I didn't mind confessing to Lansing that I shouldn't like to go there alone, not that I am afraid of ghosts, but just from nervousness at being in such a place at that time.

Friday, 17 October 1919 (Lexington, Virginia)

Wore my new suit and when I came down to breakfast everyone gave a 10
W&L yell-yell for "Puny Alexander's suit." They didn't know today was my twentieth birthday. Later we had a rally at Wilson Field, with yells and singing. Agneau and Dasham sat in the bleachers. Dasham waved to me, his eyes pale green and beautiful, his face full of life. He, a young god on his throne—and I in dumb adoration and abasement, dreaming dreams of ourselves . . . and as much as I long for him, I am fearful of the slightest response, fearful that it will pull him from his pedestal, afraid that a touch of earth will destroy the celestial vision. Dear boy, would that I knew what he thinks of me, how much of that beautiful smile of his is contempt, or whether it is serene wonderment and nothing more.

Saturday, 8 November 1919 (Lexington, Virginia)

Football! We beat Georgia Tech, unbeaten by a Southern team for six years! The score was W&L—3, Georgia Tech—0. It took W&L to blow up the "Golden Tornado," to take the sting out of the Yellow Jackets! The Lyric had a wire to Atlanta, so it was almost like seeing the game, with each play described and a diagram on a blackboard showing the location of the ball. By the time I got up there, a surging mob of students was struggling to get in. Dasham and Agneau beckoned over the crowd, and behind them I squeezed through the door. We were in a fever pitch of excitement. The W&L orchestra played jazz, stopping short when every few minutes a telegram came. Jimmie Mattox was taken out injured in the first quarter, Silverstein with a wrenched shoulder at the half, and Paget with a broken arm. In spite of it all we triumphed. *O, what joy* when Mattox kicked a field goal!

Afterward, as we spilled outdoors among the excited crowd, Dasham and Agneau told me that they were going into town. They didn't invite me. Oh, well! I walked back alone, joyously reliving every play our team had made. Beautiful night, the air bracing, stars glittering frostily in the sky. Up to my room and found Lansing Tower had made a fire, was sitting in my chair, reading my *New Republic,* with his feet propped on my table and *attired in my bathrobe,* all of which I could forgive except the last. He said there was too much noise outside his own room. The arrogant idiot still refuses to join in the excitement about football.

> **New Republic.** *Jeb was an ardent reader of magazines that offered a strong blend of social criticism and literature, including the* Freeman *(1920–1924),* The Nation, *and the* New Republic.

1920

Thursday, 18 March 1920 (Lexington, Virginia)

Instead of studying, tonight like a fool I went to the show, just as I have gone every night this week. The show was Mildred Harris in another splendidly true to life picture of Lois Weber's, *Home.* Like *Borrowed Clothes,* the photoplay follows the Griffith school of realism that I used to glory in at the Strand and Garden. Bennet sat beside me. Several rows ahead I saw Dasham and Agneau. Bennet and I walked home together, he with his arm in mine. Above us in the night sky there came a thunder storm. I was glad, because thunder is a sure sign of spring. Bennet talked of himself and of how much he likes me, and said I won't talk, but he never took any interest when I did try to say something. Repeatedly he has invited me to his room; again tonight I refused.

> ***Lois Weber*** *(1883–1939) started out as an actress; by 1920 she had become, at Universal Studios, Hollywood's first important woman producer.* Borrowed Clothes *was produced by Weber in 1918 and, like* Home, *starred Mildred Harris.*

Monday, 20 April 1920 (Lexington, Virginia)

As I went down the steps I saw Dasham in front of the "bulletin board." It made me feel refreshed just to see his beautiful face. He was tanned, as he had been playing tennis. He turned about, and with a sweet, friendly smile, greeted me. It was the first warmth he has shown me in such a long time that I thrilled all over. We might have spoken more but just then Lansing passed by and asked if I were going to the library. I walked off with him before I could think of a reason not to, and immediately was filled with the bitterest grief. I glanced back and Dasham was still standing there—my beloved lad! I hardly listened to Lansing's chatter but was plunged into melancholy imagining what I might have done or said.

Walked later along the river bank. The bloodroots were getting into their prime. The hepaticas were just past it. I picked a bunch of each. I longed for my real mother, to be kneeling at her lap saying my prayers, a trusting child. Thought of a wife, which I have not done in a long time. She was different from the woman I usually imagine. Instead of a passionate brunette creature of powerful intellect and artistic tendencies, she was a homebody, a tender, motherly woman who would coddle me and take care of me. Longed for comfort and love.

Monday, 19 July 1920

At the Municipal Beach the sun shone across the water into my eyes. I waded into the cool ticklish water and plunged forward, delighting to strongly bear my body through the water. Then my enthusiasm vanished. Nobody paid attention to me; all were shouting and frolicking. I sat on the sea-wall, picking up pebbles and sifting and catching them. Later I checked my bathing suit and wandered about. At that time of evening the streets are crowded, then all of a sudden people disappear and there are only aimless strollers. In all the great city I have not one friend. Those who might be my friends, who are capable of giving me companionship, are hidden away from me, buried in the crowds.

Municipal Beach. *People used to swim in the Potomac River, in this case at the beach which is now the reconstructed Tidal Basin.*

Friday, 23 July 1920

Henry has been indulging in his old pastime of scolding me for writing in my diary. I cannot imagine why he objects so idiotically to it. Tonight he tried to persuade me to go with him to the Krazy Kat, a "Bohemian" joint in an old stable up near Thomas Circle. He told me about the conversation in there, of artists, musicians, atheists, professors. I wanted to see something of the place, but was afraid I'd make a fool of myself by my backwardness. In a crowd Henry's ready tongue would give him mastery of me.

I left for town instead. Drops of rain began falling from a gloomy sky.

Listened to the Salvation Army band, to "Brother Hammond," "the Ensign," "the Cadet," and "Mother," who was known in the Bowery Corps as "Sunshine." They had an organ and a trombone to aid in the work of washing sins away. The Ensign, a stout red-haired girl, sang unaffectedly, as though she were really speaking to us.

A robe of white, a cross of gold,
A harp, a home, a mansion fair,
A victor's palm, and joy untold,
Are mine when I get there . . .

I don't know why I should take such pleasure in these exhibitions. The 20
crude music attracts me, I guess, making more significant the surroundings I am looking on, as music does for me. I wandered on. I thought of writing and determined to get a theme this very night. If I can't make myself write now, how can I *ever* expect to do so? Roamed past dismal houses, steep steps and no yards, across from the Pension Building. A girl on a dim step with dreamy eyes

stared into the darkness. From another house, the wistful tones of a piano in a gloomy parlor.

Saturday, 21 August 1920

The Salvation Army service was the farewell service of the Ensign and the Cadet. They will leave for Pennsylvania on Tuesday. I am sorry to see them go. It was their beautiful singing, and a personal interest in the Cadet, that has been the chief attraction for me. They sang tonight and each one gave a moving talk. Yes, the Cadet's talk moved me, because I felt sadness at the earnestness with which he spoke.

Later on I went into Lafayette Square and near the Von Steuben statue watched two fellows furtively engaged in mutual masturbation under cover of the dimness. They were frequently interrupted by the passersby. When I left, I walked close by to see their faces. Both were handsome, clean-looking chaps, refined and cultured.

Wandered down to the Union Station. The dreamy girl I used to watch in Child's is now in the Union Station soda fountain. Hair bobbed. Gazes melancholily over the great waiting rooms. Russian-looking. With a resolution to get a story written, I thought of an idea about the girl, and worked over it as I wandered about on *the* three streets whereon life concentrates, Pennsylvania Avenue, Ninth Street and F Street.

Lafayette Square *was* the *place in Washington to cruise for homosexual encounters. The park is directly across from the White House.*

Wednesday, 25 August 1920

I have at last found a friend, a lovable, handsome fellow, a realization of the friend I have dreamed of during all those lonely nights while I walked alone through the streets. Above all, our friendship is mutual. It has burst into full blossom like a glowing, beautiful flower. It happened like this: I went to Lafayette Square and found a seat in the deep shade of the big beech. It is the best bench in the park. A youth sat down beside me, a youth in a green suit with a blue dotted tie. He has beautiful eyes and sensuous lips. He wants to become a diplomat, but is devoted to music. Earlier tonight he had been singing at the Episcopalian Church, and is taking vocal lessons. His name is Randall Hare.

We strolled down to the Ellipse, where we sat affectionately together on a dim bench. Later we came to rest in the moon-misted lawns near the Monument. With an excess of nervous caution I gazed about, watching for some prowling figure. "We are safe," Randall whispered. And he was right. Nothing disturbed us and we lay in each other's arms, my love and I, while the moon beamed from a spacious sky and the cool night breezes rustled our hair. The black trees stood like sentinels against the silvery grass. Afterward, we lay close together and gazed at the stars above, becoming fast friends, exchanging confidences. Ah, happiness! As Wilde said, "Youth! Youth! There is absolutely nothing in the world but youth!"

Oscar Wilde *(1854–1900). Wilde's relationship with "Bosie" (Lord Alfred Douglas, the son of the marquess of Queensberry) resulted in his being found "guilty of homosexual practices," for which he spent two years in prison. Wilde's writing, such as the plays* The Importance of Being Earnest *and* Lady Windermere's Fan, *assure him a permanent place in English letters, but Jeb was more interested in Wilde as a victim of Victorian hypocrisy.*

Sunday, 5 September 1920

Randall and his mother live with Randall's uncle in one of the oldest houses in Georgetown, a rambling stone mansion on Prospect Avenue. Several apartments occupy the house. We entered from a court. The walls are mostly of large bricks and the living room has an enormous fireplace and ceilings with heavy rafters. Randall told me that the rafters are said to have been taken from Thomas Jefferson's house in Georgetown. I was delighted. "This is most unusual, charming, quaint, artistic, ancient—" Randall smiled, "—and other adjectives. Now look at my room." He has fixed up his room in jade green, like a sunlit green bower. The whole apartment is filled with interesting objects—bric a brac, unusual furniture, paintings, and old musical instruments.

The uncle came in while we were there. He is a painter named Mr. Dieterlie. He wore yellow walking shoes, an old checkered suit and a green tie with a green-striped shirt. They showed me the painting that "Uncle Dieterlie" is working on right now. It shows a round moon rising, and fairies dancing in its light. On the right is a Lombardy poplar silvered by moonlight, and on the left is a shrub. Mr. Dieterlie showed me other paintings, various Japanese prints, and ornaments. Randall burned incense in a bronze brazier. We were late in leaving Randall's house and the streetcar trip to Brookland was a long one, but I sat back comfortably, savoring the pleasure of companionship with Randall. Out in Brookland we entered the Catholic monastery and went into a great cross-shaped hall. The service was profoundly beautiful. The monks chanted in Latin high up in the gallery. At little altars in the wings were clusters of colored candles, blazing like jewels, a wonderful sight.

During the ride back Randall had his hand lying on mine, and a girl across the aisle made an audible remark about it to her companions. But Randall in his melodious voice said, "We should worry," and kept his hand on mine. He said, "Be glad she noticed, so she won't be shocked the next time she sees it." He said there was no reason boys should not be demonstrative toward one another, as girls and Frenchmen were.

Monastery. *The Franciscan monastery, catacombs, and gardens are located at Fourteenth and Quincy Streets, N.E., in the Brookland section of Washington.*

Sunday, 12 September 1920

On this day I realized complete disillusionment. My "friendship" with Randall Hare was a fabrication! Friendship indeed! We went to Washington Cathedral. As we left the beautiful open air service and strolled together across the lawns, we had an unpleasant exchange with some rudeness on his part. I became somewhat stammering. Randall said scornfully, "What *have* you been believing? Did you think that when I wasn't with you I was *singing?*" I replied, "I did think that, and I feel deceived." He leaned back looking disgusted. "If I wanted a clinging vine I'd find—a woman." End of my friendship with him! I shall never find real friendship, never!

1921

Wednesday, 12 January 1921 (Lexington, Virginia)

In English class I told Lansing I had changed my mind concerning what 30
he spoke about last night. He said, "This afternoon." Before supper I went to his room. There I found Howard, the light-colored negro youth who works in the kitchen. Howard had the pint of corn whiskey but said he hadn't been able to find "the $4.25 man" and had to go to another place. He wanted another dollar, and a quarter for himself. Lansing loaned me the additional money.

It is the first time I have ever drunk whiskey, except when I was a child and took it for medicine. I opened up my Keats and sipped the fiery liquid while I read the "Ode to a Nightingale"—that sensuous poetry that many a time has made me long for wine. But the poetry was more beautiful than the taste—at least of this wine of the Land of the Fire!

Friday, 11 February 1921 (Lexington, Virginia)

Scurrying clouds; flakes of snow. In the library I was reading "Modern Love" in George Meredith's poems when Dasham in his quick way strode in and seated himself to study. I gazed at that dear head bent over a publication. My fingers longed to stroke that lovely brown hair.

I want love and affection. Damn it! All that Stevenson said about journals is true. This diary of mine is a tissue of posturing. My real thoughts on such matters as sex are not admitted even to myself. I *will* be frank. I am madly in love with C. C. Dasham. "Sexual inversion," Havelock Ellis calls it. I always had some "hero" whom I adored and observed at every opportunity. It is not only Dasham with whom I've had visionary adventures, shipwrecks, desert isles, and the like. For years I have loved and worshipped other boys and youths. Before college there was Henry's schoolmate Bunny Alcott (think of it!). Then Hennessey, a god-like fellow, never seen or heard of since; and Morphew, a boy now gone to Tulane. The only one I even *spoke* to was Dasham. I have had a big-brotherly interest in some, an artistic sympathy for others. With Randall Hare the attraction was purely physical.

I left the library, not knowing where to go or what to do. Walked to the river bank, coat collar upturned, in the teeth of the chilling cold wind.

Havelock Ellis *(1859–1939) was an English psychologist and specialist in human sexuality. Jeb somehow acquired Ellis's book in Lexington in 1921. No* *doubt as a result of having read Ellis's work, Jeb in his youth sometimes labels a male homosexual an "invert," and a female homosexual a "female invert."*

Understanding

1. Jeb is the author of his own personality rather than the product of another writer's imagination or reconstruction, and the reader can determine much about Jeb's personality from his diary entries. What is Jeb's assessment of himself?
2. Jeb expresses a number of "enthusiasms" in the short period reflected in these excerpts. Which of them appear to be enduring and which short-lived?
3. How important is friendship to Jeb? How would he define friendship? What in his entries supports your view?
4. Feelings of marginality make sense only within the possibility of community. What is it about Jeb's life that makes him feel marginal? In what sense does community provide the context for Jeb's feelings of marginality?

Responding

1. Jeb discovered his "sexual inversion" in the writings of the English psychologist Havelock Ellis, a revelation that seemed to validate it. Have you ever discovered a "truth" about yourself or someone you care about through the writings of others? If so, describe this discovery and the source or sources that enabled you to uncover it.
2. Jeb was a college freshman when he wrote these entries. In what ways does his collegiate life seem the same as or different from college life today?
3. Have you ever recorded your experiences in a way similar to Jeb's? If so, what does your writing reveal about what you regarded as important or meaningful at the time? If not, what prevented you from committing your experiences to paper? Under what circumstances might you do so? Explain.

Connecting

Friendship between two people depends on intimacy or at least a sharing of concerns at some level that is meaningful to both. Compare Jeb Alexander's notion of friendship to Wiesel's in "What Is a Friend?" (chapter one).

Brother Pain: How a Black Woman Came to Terms with Interracial Love

Gloria Wade-Gayles

Without a society that views some of us as people of color, the issue of interracial love which Gloria Wade-Gayles examines in this reading would be less charged. Or would it? What is unarguable is the pain and anger that fill this coming-to-terms piece on a "hot-button" topic. A burning issue during the late 1960s and 1970s, when black awareness and the black power movement gave a new resonance to a situation that had largely been considered a province of white racists, interracial love is now more prevalent in American society than it was twenty-five years ago. Interracial marriages, in fact, doubled from 1960—when they constituted fewer than half a million—to 1970 and tripled from 1970 to 1980. By 1990 the U.S. census counted 1.5 million interracial couples.

Although somewhat softened by time and a different perspective, the pain and indignation that Wade-Gayles and her friends express about interracial love in this essay seem fresh and unremitting. Gloria Wade-Gayles is professor of English and women's studies at Spelman College in Atlanta. This piece is excerpted from her *Rooted Against the Wind,* which was published in 1996.

"How could he?" one student asked.

"It hurts," said another. "When I see a black man with a white woman, I think that I have not measured up. That something is lacking in me."

I understand the pain and anger of these young black women because their pain and anger were once mine. The passing of decades has not removed the abandonment I once felt when my newest heartthrob on screen, record, or the playing field married a white woman. The news would flash, and my friends and I would go into mourning, grieving our own deaths. That was how we felt: nonexistent in the eyes of those men who gave us visibility and voice in a world that denied us both. 1

I remember in my high school and college years being proud of the black man in *Mod Squad.* He was so very hip, so very visible, so very much an equal in the trio that fought crime. "Day-o. Day-o. Daylight come and me wan' go home." I would calypso dance in front of the mirror to Harry Belafonte's scratchy voice singing melodiously. And like other black women, I was proud of Sidney Poitier, that ebony brother of tight smoothness, who was the first of the big stars. There was something in the way he walked, leaning down in his hips, in the way he talked with his eyes, in the way his deep blackness spoke of a power that was mine to claim.

All of those men married white women.

The pain we experience as teenagers follows many of us into adulthood, and if we are professional women, it follows with a vengeance. As a colleague explains the situation, "Black men don't want us as mates because we are independent; white men, because we are black." The only difference between us and black teenagers is the language we use, our attempt at some kind of analysis, and our refusal to mourn. Teenagers see an individual heart throb; we see an entire championship basketball team. Teenagers know about athletes and entertainers; we know about politicians and scholars.

I look at my past participation in venting sessions with gratitude for the 5
liberation I now experience, a liberation that was slow and gradual, yet seems to have happened overnight, as if while I slept someone or something cut the straps of the straitjacket that was stealing my breath and I awoke, miraculously, with arms freed for embracing. It must have been a good spirit who knew that the weight of anger had become too much for me: anger over the deterioration of black schools, over the battering and homicide of black women, over the violence against our children, our elderly, and our young men. It was a long list; it was a weight I had to lighten or lose my mind.

The question was, What could I remove from the list? What was really important? What could make a difference in the world?

The answer came to me with the clarity of a mockingbird singing from the rooftop in the North Carolina dawn, identifying herself and the place she had claimed as her own. I could see myself flying to a spiritually high place, identifying myself as the woman who loves herself and claiming as my own a different place for struggle. Perched there, singing, I knew I would never again give my mind and my emotions over to something I could not change, and something that was not the cause of suffering in the world. I decided to focus my anger, to be more useful in the struggle for change, for the new justice we so desperately need. Anger over black men with white women, I sang, took me out of focus.

From this perspective, I made a new list of concerns I feel I have a moral obligation to address. Black men with white wives didn't make the cut. I wouldn't be telling the truth if I said I believe that most black men married to white wives don't have problems with themselves, with the race, and with black women. I will not lie. I believe many of them wear the aroma of disdain we can smell miles away. I believe that for most of them the choice is not a matter of the heart, but not knowing who in the group followed his heart, I have decided not to judge. Like a recovering alcoholic who can be hooked all over again with one sip, I have written my own recovery program. It has one step: Remember how much lighter you feel without the weight of anger, the weight of judging.

That must have been the spirit I was projecting when a male friend revealed the pain that, even in my recovery, I didn't realize ran so deep for some black men married to white women. "This," he said, referring to the O. J. Simpson case, "implicates us in the eyes of many people. They think all of us are obsessed with white women." He paused. "Obsessed to the point of violence."

I had met my friend two years earlier in a long-distance phone conversa- 10
tion. He had called to tell me that my rememberings in my book *Pushed Back to Strength* were his rememberings as well. He was reminiscing about growing up black and male in segregated South Carolina when he said suddenly, "My wife is white." Had the phone fallen, he would have known not to continue. Had my energy changed, he would have regretted the call. I made no response. Only in retrospect did I realize I had passed a crucial test.

That conversation was followed by another and yet another until, finally, we met in person at a Unitarian-Universalist anti-racist conference in Spokane, Washington. My friend was a mover and shaker in the group and through him I met another black man married to a white woman. The three of us stole time to discuss "the problem." The question was not "How could you?" but rather "How does it feel to be a black man in racist America married to a white woman?"

"People never come right out and ask," my friend said.

"How can we?" I interrupted. "It's such a personal matter. We don't dare ask without . . ."

"Without judging," he replied. "They don't ask, but I see the question in their eyes. Why? Why did you marry a white woman?"

Most black women, he explained, reject him instantly when he says, "My 15
wife is white." It's in their eyes. "Disdain. Disgust. Immediately, they pull out their mental list of misconceptions about black men with white wives."

"I need her in order to feel good about myself and to feel more powerful."

"She's from a lower socioeconomic group or, if she's economically privileged, she's angry with her family."

"He has always been interested in white women. Dated them rather than us."

"He doesn't like who he is as an African-American—therefore he doesn't like black women."

But none of this was true of my friend. The one thing my friend did not 20
ever want to do was marry white. Some experts say we can choose whom we love, which means that the heart beats only when the mind commands. But are we ever in charge of where and with whom we find ourselves? Can we dictate to the heart? This business of romantic love might be just what Toni Morrison says it is: one of the three dangerous concepts in human thinking.

"If I could not have loved her," my friend confessed, "I would not have loved her." I know some revolutionary-talking "brothers" and "sisters" who say black men should make a political decision not to marry white, not to *love* white. But what black woman or black man wants to be married to someone who loves another but cannot marry him or her for political reasons? Romantic love might be a dangerous concept, but it has its hold on me. I'm an incurable romantic who believes that people should marry because they love each other. Period. Mix in a political agenda and you have real problems. I remember a black man who confessed his love for a white woman to a "sister" he later married. They are now divorced.

Twenty years after they wed, my friend and his wife are still together. They are both activists working for racial justice. To see my friend and his son together is to see two men comfortable enough with their manhood and their racial identity to hold hands and embrace in public. "Our children's psychological health is the strongest proof of what we feel for each other," my friend said.

It is true, he admitted, that interracial parentage can create problems for children. Are they black? Are they white? What exactly are they? But he hasn't seen any data that document the absence of confusion for children of same-race marriages. Neither have I.

At first, my friend feared that falling in love would mean giving up home. He was in Germany when he met his future wife in a train station. "We spent hours just talking," he said. "We found a comfort zone. You know how it is when someone knows your secrets and you didn't know they knew." It was that way with them. Not her race but a "comfort zone" brought them together.

25 How could he return to the States with a white wife? The derision, disdain, and rejection—he didn't want his family to be subjected to it. So they remained in Germany for ten years until both he and his wife found the courage to return. Re-entry was difficult. At first, friends and associates were in denial, saying to themselves that his wife was German, not white. Then many—though certainly not all—went the expected route, he explained, reviewing the list of misconceptions with which our conversation began. "Not all, thank God," he said.

One day he was with his wife and ran into a former sweetheart, a black woman. There was a moment of dread. The breath left his body. "She paused," he recalled, "and then with her eyes she told me 'It's OK.'" He was fighting the tears. "I can't tell you how good it felt to breathe again."

"Is it that important for black women to embrace you?" I asked.

His eyes were moist. "More than you can imagine," he replied. "The pain for me is that I am expected to cut myself off from the wisdom of all those black women I grew up with. It's a deep pain, cutting off a lifeline." I knew that some black men married to white women experienced discomfort, but this kind of pain was beyond my imagining.

Their courage lightens the pain. Together, he and his wife are fighting to dispel the misconceptions. It's not easy for either of them and, in many ways, it's more difficult for her. As a man, he has a voice that she is denied. But still they awake every morning relieved that they moved here. It is the heart that makes them so.

30 The other man had remained silent during most of this conversation. "Talk about irony," he said, finally, explaining that once he judged black men married to white women, judged them harshly. *That* was definitely not something *he* would ever do. Have sex with white women? Yes. Marry one of them? No. Absolutely, no. He was one of those "brothers" in the '60s who devoted a lot of their revolutionary time to sleeping with white women. "I set out to get them as my revenge against the Man," he admitted. "As many conquests as possible."

Marrying white, however, was never an option for him because of the difficulties he believed it would pose for children. It was not an option because he was wed emotionally, psychologically, spiritually, and politically to black women—to all black people.

His wife was not someone he used to seek revenge against "the Man." In fact, he met her by chance after that period in his life had ended. She was "a little lady on somebody else's arm," and though he was drawn to her, he pulled back because, he said, "that was never something I would consider." As if by fate, they found themselves together again and again until "it happened," he recalled. "And I knew she was my soul mate." He smiled. "I wanted it to go away, but it wouldn't."

He had no other option but to marry. "One of the rarest gifts is to find someone whom you love and who loves you," he said. Full of fire, talented, and charming, he was on his way to leadership in the black empowerment struggle. "I gave it up," he added, neither his tone nor his eyes suggesting regret. "I took myself out of the leadership track." Married happily for over 20 years, he does not regret the sacrifice. He gave up leadership in the movement, but not his commitment to racial justice. That is his passion, his life's work, his other heart.

When I asked him whether he understands the pain that black women feel, he replied, "In a way you can't imagine." The thought that they hurt because of him makes him want to weep. And sometimes he does. "I can't get away from black women's pain," he said, his voice breaking. "I can't, and as crazy as it sounds for a black man married to a white woman, I am motivated in my work in part by my sensitivity to black women's pain. Because I know we brothers haven't made it easy for black women. We've got our pain, but it doesn't begin to compare with yours."

My eyelids are cups, but I dare not tilt them, lest rivers of pain rush from me. The pain is not his marriage, but rather the negative reading of relationships between black men and white women. How different that reading is from this man's description of his marriage-friendship.

As the conversation ended, he said, "Can we talk again? We only scratched the surface of my feelings. I need to talk. I *have* to talk." Then he added, "Those were good questions."

"Not too offensive?"

"Are you kidding? It's as if you read my mind." He paused. "But, Sister Glo, I'm more worried about you than I am about me."

I was confused.

"I'm used to being beat up on when the subject is black men and white wives. I'm used to the fights. But you?"

It was only then that I began to wonder how my friends would interpret my new attitude. So much for your spiritual spinning, they would say, but let us get to the critical question: Would you want your daughter or your son to marry a white person? To be honest, I hope that they will not, but if they are following their heart, I pray that they will.

What, if anything, do these stories prove? Certainly the fact that there are two black men married to white women—two out of thousands—who remain committed to our people and want to do what they can to erase the pain of black women doesn't eradicate "the problem." But it might make us pause before we judge individuals. It might make us rethink giving an interracial couple that look of disdain my friends say hurts so much.

"But how can these men be so sure that their analysis is right?" some black women will ask. "How do *they* know that whiteness did not make 'it' happen? After all, there is this thing, this monster, called conditioning, called psychological scarring. The truth is, they *can't* be sure."

Perhaps my friends can't prove that race did not make "it" happen, but can we prove that race *did* make it happen? How will we measure that? And with what instrument? If we could enter the heart and know, would our pain be altered? Would our knowing create jobs, build better schools, stop the trafficking in drugs, or dethrone patriarchy? Would it save the children and care for the elderly? Would it jettison our people from the dark side of the moon, where injustice never sleeps? In the long run, does it matter whom my friends marry and whom they say they love? For me, it no longer does. I have already taken my anger elsewhere.

Understanding

1. What in this essay suggests that Wade-Gayles has come to terms with interracial love? What suggests that, despite her claims, she has not?
2. One of Wade-Gayles's friends indicates that he "believes people should marry because they love each other." This is one facet of romantic love. Can you think of others? How significant is romantic love as a factor in most marriages?
3. So far as we can tell, no black man has rejected Wade-Gayles personally for a white woman. What is it then that drove her anger against interracial love? What does her anger reveal about the self-perceptions of the black women with whom she identifies?
4. The French have an aphorism: "Whatever can be understood can be forgiven." Is this the case with Wade-Gayles? What has she understood? What has she forgiven?

Responding

1. Do you know anyone who has "loved interracially"? If so, how does your response to this situation compare with Wade-Gayles's?
2. How would you respond to a close friend or family member who was contemplating or was involved in an interracial marriage?
3. Marrying "across racial lines" is really an act of betrayal against the family, which is a repository of traditional values, rather than a break from the larger social order. Do you agree or disagree with this assessment? Explain.

4. Respond to one or both of these statements:
   a. By connecting her "pain" with the choices that other people make, Wade-Gayles overinvests herself in the lives of others and shows her intolerance of their freedom to act.
   b. Victory over institutional racism or "jettisoning our people from the dark side of the moon, where injustice never sleeps" is impossible when black men choose to "marry white."
5. Are racial "boundaries" really necessary? What purposes do they serve?

Connecting

How would Crouch in "Race Is Over" (chapter five) respond to Wade-Gayles?

Ageism in the Sisterhood

Barbara MacDonald

Growing old is inevitable in the life of all living things. Depending on differing values and beliefs among various cultures, our communities delineate the ways members are to be treated at different ages and stages of life. While in America we may cherish the cultural value of inclusiveness, in reality, age groups are sharply segmented. For the most part, children are left in preschools and with nannies and babysitters while their parents attend social and community events; adults work with adults; retired people live in retirement communities or nursing homes. Boundaries are inevitable as a result of this compartmentalized lifestyle determined by age.

Writer Barbara MacDonald considers generational relations among women in terms of alienation, abandonment, and ageism. Her voice powerfully expresses an opinion most of us have not heard before because of the boundaries created in a culture that is very mobile and exclusive in the way it views people at different ages.

From the beginning of this wave of the women's movement, from the beginning of Women's Studies, the message has gone out to those of us over 60 that your "Sisterhood" does not include us, that those of you who are younger see us as men see us—that is, as women who used to be women but aren't any more. You do not see us in our present lives, you do not identify with our issues, you exploit us, you patronize us, you stereotype us. Mainly you ignore us. 1

Has it never occurred to younger women activists as you organized around "women's" issues, that old women are raped, that old women are battered, that old women are poor, that old women perform unpaid work in the home and out of the home, that old women are exploited by male medical practitioners, that old women are in jail, are political prisoners, that old women have to deal with racism, classism, homophobia, anti-semitism? I open your feminist publications and not once have I read of any group of younger women enraged or marching or organizing legal support because of anything that happened to an old woman. I have to read the *L.A. Times* or *Ageing International* to find out what's happening to the women of my generation, and the news is not good. I have to read these papers to find out that worldwide old women are the largest adult poverty group, or that 44 percent of old Black women are poor, or about the battering of old women, about the conditions in public housing for the elderly in which almost all of the residents are women, or that old women in nursing homes are serving as guinea pigs for experimental drugs—a practice forbidden years ago for prison inmates.

But activists are not alone in their ageism. Has it never occurred to those of you in Women's Studies as you ignore the meaning and the politics of the lives of women beyond our reproductive years, that this is male thinking? Has it never occurred to you as you build feminist theory that ageism is a central feminist issue?

* * *

Meanwhile, as the numbers of old women rapidly increase, the young women you taught five years ago are now in the helping professions as geriatricians and social workers because the jobs are there. They still call themselves feminists but, lacking any kind of feminist analysis of women's aging from your classrooms, they are defining old women as needy, simple-minded, and helpless—definitions that correlate conveniently with the services and salaries they have in mind . . .

But it is worse than that. For you yourselves—activists and acade- 5
micians—do not hesitate to exploit us. We take in the fact that you come to us for "oral histories"—for your own agendas, to learn *your* feminist or lesbian or working-class or ethnic histories—with not the slightest interest in our present struggles as old women. You come to fill in some much-needed data for a thesis, or to justify a grant for some "service" for old women that imitates the mainstream and which you plan to direct, or you come to get material for a biography of our friends and lovers. But you come not as equals, not with any knowledge of who we are, what our issues may be. You come to old women who have been serving young women for a lifetime and ask to be served one more time, and then you cover up your embarrassment as you depart by saying that you felt as though we were your grandmother or your mother or your aunt. And no one in the sisterhood criticizes you for such acts.

But let me say it to you clearly: We are not your mothers, your grandmothers, or your aunts. And we will never build a true women's movement until we can organize together as equals, woman to woman, without the burden of these family roles.

Mother. Grandmother. Aunt. It should come as no surprise to us that ageism has its roots in patriarchal family.

* * *

But if we are to understand ageism, we have no choice but to bring family again under the lens of a feminist politic. In the past, we examined the father as oppressor, we examined his oppression of the mother and the daughters, in great detail we examined the mother as oppressor of the daughters, but what has never come under the feminist lens is the daughters' oppression of the mother—that woman who by definition is older than we are.

The source of your ageism, the reason why you see older women as there to serve you, comes from family. It was in patriarchal family that you learned that mother is there to serve you, her child, that serving you is her purpose in life. This is not woman's definition of motherhood. This is man's definition of motherhood, a male myth enforced in family and which you still believe—to your peril and mine. It infantilizes you and it erases me.

Understanding

1. What does MacDonald mean by "male thinking"? How is ageism a central feminist issue?
2. Who is "you" in this essay? What point do we come away with, and what is MacDonald arguing for?
3. What does MacDonald mean when she asserts that ageism is rooted in the patriarchal family?
4. How are the issues of older women similar to or different from those of college-age women?
5. How does MacDonald's use of *old woman* strengthen the impact of the piece?

Responding

1. Thinking carefully about MacDonald's argument, do you agree that younger women, specifically feminists, are oppressors of older women? If so, how and why has this come to be the case? Was it ever different? How does her feeling diminished diminish you?
2. Are younger men guilty of the same oppression of old men?
3. For those of you who are from other countries, apply MacDonald's points to women in your native culture. Could she make the same case for elderly women in your country? Why or why not?
4. MacDonald doesn't actually prescribe remedies for the problems she depicts. How would *you* remedy the oppressive situation MacDonald describes?
5. Think of an older woman with whom you could share this essay; ask her to read it. Record her views about the essay as accurately as possible, and ask her for suggestions on how to cross these boundaries.

Connecting

1. Apply MacDonald's opinion to Mansfield's "Miss Brill" (chapter two). Are there instances of alienation, abandonment, and loneliness caused by younger women in this short story?
2. Refer to Elkind's summary of Erikson's eight stages of human development (chapter seven). Situate yourself and Barbara MacDonald in your appropriate stages. How are each of your developmental tasks different at this point? Since she has been through the stages after yours, what might you want to ask her?
3. What boundaries or borders are created in this essay? How might Rodriguez ("The New, New World") incorporate MacDonald's argument in his essay? What would he say about her issues?
4. If you did an observation of older people for the Responding questions following Mansfield's "Miss Brill" (chapter two), review your "field" notes in light of MacDonald's piece.

To Live in the Borderlands Means You

Gloria Anzaldúa

Writer, teacher, lecturer, seventh-generation American, Chicana, lesbian, Third World woman—Gloria Anzaldúa is all of these, and she has worked hard to fashion a life that is truly her own. Born in 1942 in South Texas, a *mestiza* (a combination of Mexican, Native American, and Anglo), she grew up among *campesinos* (farm workers) and knew the life of a farmer. She also did well in school, but her mother was adamantly against education for women and called her reading and writing "laziness." As a result, much of her early life was spent rebelling against her mother and her Chicana culture. Reading, Anzaldúa says, "was the only avenue that gave me an entry into a different way of being."

Anzaldúa's major publication, *Borderlands/La Frontera: The New Mestiza,* from which this poem was taken, is a kind of literary autobiography written in a combination of English, Castilian Spanish, northern Mexican dialect, Tex-Mex, and Nahuatl, a Native American dialect. It also combines a number of different genres—poetry, prose, academic theoretical writing—to produce a kind of blueprint for *la nueva cultura* (the new culture), which she defines as a consciousness and a physical reality—a *mestizaje* (a racial mixture) that Anzaldúa believes is currently in the making.

The "border" that Anzaldúa references is the U.S.-Mexico border, which stretches from Brownsville, Texas, to San Diego, California, with all of its political, cultural, and linguistic history.

[To live in the Borderlands means you]
are neither *hispana india negra española*
ni gabacha, eres mestiza, mulata, half-breed
caught in the crossfire between camps
while carrying all five races on your back
not knowing which side to turn to, run from;

To live in the Borderlands means knowing
  that the *india* in you,
  betrayed for 500 years,
  is no longer speaking to you,
  that *mexicanas* call you *rajetas,*
  that denying the Anglo inside you
  is as bad as having denied
  the Indian or Black;

---

gabacha a Chicano term for a white woman.
rajetas literally, "split," that is, having betrayed your word.

Cuando vives en la frontera
people walk through you, the wind steals your voice,
you're a *burra, buey,* scapegoat,
forerunner of a new race,
half and half—both woman and man, neither—
a new gender;

To live in the Borderlands means to
put *chile* in the borscht,
eat whole wheat *tortillas,*
speak Tex-Mex with a Brooklyn accent;
be stopped by *la migra* at the border checkpoints;

Living in the Borderlands means you fight hard to
resist the gold elixir beckoning from the bottle,
the pull of the gun barrel,
the rope crushing the hollow of your throat;

In the Borderlands
you are the battleground
where enemies are kin to each other;
you are at home, a stranger,
the border disputes have been settled
the volley of shots have shattered the truce
you are wounded, lost in action
dead, fighting back;

To live in the Borderlands means
the mill with the razor white teeth wants to shred off
your olive-red skin, crush out the kernel, your heart
pound you pinch you roll you out
smelling like white bread but dead;

To survive the Borderlands
you must live *sin fronteras*
be a crossroads.

Understanding

1. The brilliance of a poem or a piece of prose is its ability to generate personal meaning in the individuals who read it. Though Anzaldúa is writing for a specific audience (the different interest groups who make up the feminist movement of women of color), can readers who are neither women nor persons of color personalize this poem's message to *their* an-

---

burra donkey.
buey oxen.
sin fronteras without borders.

cestors who came to be in whatever borderlands they found themselves? Explain.

2. How does the tone of the poem complement the message?
3. Anzaldúa's final stanza is powerful advice. How would you paraphrase that advice? Do you agree with it?
4. In an essay entitled "En Rapport, in Opposition," Anzaldúa writes: "So if we won't forget past grievances, let us forgive. Carrying the ghosts of past grievances *no vale la pena.* It is not worth the grief." Where does her poem suggest this admonition and how does its expression serve her purpose?
5. Are there any Spanish words in the poem that you need to know in order to fully understand it? If so, use the language resources among your colleagues. Someone you know speaks Spanish. Gather your own list of "glosses" for the Spanish words.

Responding

1. Do you have an ancestor who is such a mixture—"Carrying all five races on your back"? If so, tell his or her story.
2. Write your own words for stanza 4 (or any of the stanzas that touch you). Start with "To live in the Borderlands means to . . ."
3. Where are *your* borderlands if not the U.S.-Mexico border? Do you conceive of them as gifts or wounds or both? How else do you conceive of them?
4. Though the border that she references is the U.S.-Mexico border, elsewhere in *Borderlands/La Frontera* Anzaldúa describes her "Borderlands" (with a capital *B*) as symbolic of the psychological, cultural, sexual, and spiritual differences represented among people. Those differences for Anzaldúa are framed in her Borderlands metaphor. How useful is this metaphor to you?
5. Have you ever had a relationship with another person that could be illuminated by using Anzaldúa's concept of Borderland with a capital *B?* What were the Borderlands—the contact points—that each of you had to negotiate? What was the experience like?

Connecting

1. Though the two pieces are wildly different, what in Anzaldúa's poem could relate to Dawkins's "Ancestors and the Digital River" (chapter five)?
2. How does Anzaldúa's advice that *no vale la pena* to carry the ghosts of past grievances relate to the issue that Wade-Gayles discusses in "Brother Pain: How a Black Woman Came to Terms with Interracial Love"?

The World of Culture

Mihaly Csikszentmihalyi

If genetic instructions give us the capacity to speak and act, as Csikszentmihalyi advised us in "The Veils of Maya and the World of the Genes" (chapter five), then cultural instructions influence how we use this capacity by what we say and do. These instructions are delivered through the values, rules, habits, and attitudes we inherit as members of a culture and which we often accept unthinkingly. Sometimes we accept them quite self-consciously, as the readings in the "Popular Culture" section will illustrate.

According to Csikszentmihalyi, belonging to a culture gives us a sense of power and invulnerability, which can lead to great accomplishment or to ethnocentrism, a rootedness in the assumptions, values, and beliefs of the culture with which we most identify (to the exclusion of others). Becoming aware of how this second veil shrouds reality, and how it affects our descriptions of what is "real" in the world around us, is yet another step toward the freedom that the writer says can increase our happiness.

Examine this reading to see how the potent mixture of community and cultural influences that you read about in the preceding selections are reflected in Csikszentmihalyi's analysis.

Peasants living in the tiny hamlets of the Hungarian plains occasionally told visitors: "Did you know that our village is the center of the world? No? You can check it out for yourself easily enough. All you have to do is go to the square in the middle of the village. In the middle of the square is the church. If you climb its tower, you can see the fields and forests spreading out in a circle all around, with our church in the center." The fact that the neighboring villages also thought they were at the hub of the world didn't matter—after all, what did foreigners living on the periphery of the universe know? Their delusions were not to be taken seriously. These traditional peasants based their views on perfectly sensible bits of information: When they were looking down from the church spire the village did in fact look as if it stood at the center of the world, and the traditions they learned in infancy from their elders held a stronger truth value than anything they learned later. From their isolated vantage point, the reality they knew made perfectly good sense. 1

Unfortunately, every isolated culture must come to the same locally plausible yet ultimately erroneous conclusion. When living in Calabria, in the far south of Italy, I spent many frustrating hours debating other teenagers who claimed they were much more civilized than the people who lived far north in Naples, or in Rome: "After all," they said, "everyone knows that the farther south you go, the higher the level of civilization." It did no good to point out

power to run, the power to throw. The power to be Mickey Mantle. It was *his* summer, it was *all* his—and the next summer, and the next. Pain didn't seem to bother him. Nothing seemed to bother him. He played with joy, and it was a joy to see. That much was real: the joy of his playing. Watch the footage. You can't mistake it. He seemed the very embodiment of America—of what America wanted to be, of what they told us America was: an innocent giant with power that was good for everyone.

He's dying as I write this. The harsh thing is that he's dying ashamed of himself, ashamed of his drinking, ashamed of his evasions—the way America has become ashamed of itself. It seems he can't help but reflect us. Can't help but reflect how we see ourselves. That was his glory then and that is his destruction now. (The cancer is merely the finale; the destruction goes so much deeper.) And his wan ravaged face, so frightened and unsure—you want to cup that face in your hands, you want to say, "Don't be ashamed, don't die in shame, you did something beautifully once, and you took the projection of our innocence upon yourself the way Marilyn took the projection of our lust, and it was too much for you, and your demons ate you alive, you hurt yourself and your loved ones like we all do but you never went out of your way to do harm and you kept the joy of your hardball game, you never sullied *that,* not ever, and in a time of evasions, in a summer of lies, *that* wasn't a lie. You lived it out, and you didn't betray us. Nobody, nobody at all, begrudges you that summer. Go well."

Understanding

1. Ventura claims that what Americans interpreted as security in the 1950s now seems like "ignorance—an ignorance that they called, and believed to be, 'security'" (paragraph 1). What aspects of American life, viewed from the perspective of forty years, does Ventura translate as ignorance? How does he explain it?
2. In this essay Ventura uses a classic rhetorical device more commonly found in formal speeches—*anaphora*—the repetition of a word or a phrase at the beginning of successive lines. The phrase *Mickey Mantle's summer,* repeated at the beginning of seven of the thirteen paragraphs, references not just the ballplayer but the quality of American life in the 1950s. What effect does using this device have on the reader? What other aspects of Ventura's writing style contribute to this effect?
3. In the last paragraph, Ventura claims Mantle was "dying ashamed of himself, ashamed of his drinking, ashamed of his evasions—the way America has become ashamed of itself." What means does Ventura use to connect these two events? How does the rest of the essay support the connection? Explain.

Responding

1. Some of your relatives—parents, aunts, and uncles—probably grew up during Mickey Mantle's summer, and it is likely that the values Ventura

expresses in his essay were part of their upbringing as well. What do you think of American life during Mickey Mantle's summer as Ventura describes it? In what ways do you detect some of the cultural influences he describes as part of your own or your family's value system?

2. Identify a cultural icon from your childhood or adolescence who fired your imagination the way Mickey Mantle sparked Ventura's. What about this individual was so compelling? What aspects of the culture of the time reinforced the power of this person to be so fascinating? In what ways has this person influenced who you are today?
3. At a press conference following his surgery for liver replacement, Mantle warned young people: "Don't be like me. God gave me a body and the ability to play baseball. I had everything and I just . . ." At this point he threw his hands up and bowed his head. How relevant do you think the personal lives of public figures are to the assessment of their professional contributions? How much of an impact would Mantle's statement have on young people of today?
4. Fans of pop culture heros like Mickey Mantle often have a hard time accepting the human frailties of their idols. As we mentioned earlier in Skloot's "The Royal Family," this may be the result of idealization, or it may be the outcome of the media's projection of the image rather than the reality of a pop culture star's life. What do you think is responsible for this phenomenon?
5. Using a style similar to Ventura's, write a valedictory to a cultural idol with whom you identified in your younger years, incorporating the cultural markers of the time as a context for your message.

Connecting

Relate Ventura's evaluation of security versus ignorance or "the refusal to see or admit the obvious" (paragraph 2) to Csikszentmihalyi's view of culture in "The World of Culture."

The CoolHunt

Malcolm Gladwell

Every year, the world's most famous designers present their newest ideas in clothing on the runways of Paris, Milan, and New York for upscale critics and buyers. But in the turbulent fashion markets of ready-to-wear footwear and related apparel, this top-down approach doesn't always work. Increasingly, designers' inspirations come from the street and not the other way around. As writer Malcolm Gladwell claims, the fashion scene is witnessing "the ascendancy in the marketplace, of high school."

The ready-to-wear fashion scene is a brutal one. Misidentifying the next trend can be costly, but anticipating it can be immensely profitable. A relatively new tool in the search for cool are "coolhunters," whose job it is to seek out "innovators," discover what they like, and pass it on to designers. From the Converse One Star to Hush Puppies, from Tommy Hilfiger to the North Face, and from Nike's Air Jordans to Reebok's DXT, the designs were consecrated on the streets. Their designers are constantly on the hunt for a new look. Malcolm Gladwell takes us on just such a search with two very established coolhunters, DeeDee and Baysie, and he introduces us to *diffusion research*—the study of how ideas and innovations spread.

Malcolm Gladwell is a staff writer for *The New Yorker* and a contributor to the *New Republic* and *Slate,* an online magazine.

Baysie Wightman met DeeDee Gordon, appropriately enough, on a coolhunt. It was 1992. Baysie was a big shot for Converse, and DeeDee, who was barely twenty-one, was running a very cool boutique called Placid Planet, on Newbury Street in Boston. Baysie came in with a camera crew—one she often used when she was coolhunting—and said, "I've been watching your store, I've seen you, I've heard you know what's up," because it was Baysie's job at Converse to find people who knew what was up and she thought DeeDee was one of those people. DeeDee says that she responded with reserve—that "I was like, 'Whatever' "—but Baysie said that if DeeDee ever wanted to come and work at Converse she should just call, and nine months later DeeDee called. This was about the time the cool kids had decided they didn't want the hundred-and-twenty-five-dollar basketball sneaker with seventeen different kinds of high-technology materials and colors and air-cushioned heels anymore. They wanted simplicity and authenticity, and Baysie picked up on that. She brought back the Converse One Star, which was a vulcanized, suède, low-top classic old-school sneaker from the nineteen-seventies, and, sure enough, the One Star quickly became the signature shoe of the retro era. Remember what Kurt Cobain was wearing in the famous picture of him lying dead on the 1 ground after committing suicide? Black Converse One Stars. DeeDee's big score was calling the sandal craze. She had been out in Los Angeles and had kept seeing the white teen-age girls dressing up like *cholos,* Mexican gangsters, in tight white tank tops known as "wife beaters," with a bra strap hanging out, and long shorts and tube socks and shower sandals. DeeDee recalls, "I'm like, 'I'm telling you, Baysie, this is going to hit. There are just too many people wearing it. We have to make a shower sandal.'" So Baysie, DeeDee, and a designer came up with the idea of making a retro sneaker-sandal, cutting the back off the One Star and putting a thick outsole on it. It was *huge,* and, amazingly, it's still huge.

Today, Baysie works for Reebok as general-merchandise manager—part of the team trying to return Reebok to the position it enjoyed in the mid-nineteen-eighties as the country's hottest sneaker company. DeeDee works for an advertising agency in Del Mar called Lambesis, where she puts out a quarterly tip sheet called the *L Report* on what the cool kids in major American cities are thinking and doing and buying. Baysie and DeeDee are best friends. They talk on the phone all the time. They get together whenever Baysie is in L.A. (DeeDee: "It's, like, how many times can you drive past O. J. Simpson's house?"), and between them they can talk for hours about the art of the coolhunt. They're the Lewis and Clark of cool.

What they have is what everybody seems to want these days, which is a window on the world of the street. Once, when fashion trends were set by the big couture houses—when cool was trickle-down—that wasn't important. But sometime in the past few decades things got turned over, and fashion became trickle-up. It's now about chase and flight—designers and retailers and the mass consumer giving chase to the elusive prey of street cool—and the rise of coolhunting as a profession shows how serious the chase has become. The sneakers of Nike and Reebok used to come out yearly. Now a new style comes out every season. Apparel designers used to have an eighteen-month lead time between concept and sale. Now they're reducing that to a year, or even six months, in order to react faster to new ideas from the street. The paradox, of course, is that the better coolhunters become at bringing the mainstream close to the cutting edge, the more elusive the cutting edge becomes. This is the first rule of the cool: The quicker the chase, the quicker the flight. The act of discovering what's cool is what causes cool to move on, which explains the triumphant circularity of coolhunting: because we have coolhunters like DeeDee and Baysie, cool changes more quickly, and because cool changes more quickly, we need coolhunters like DeeDee and Baysie.

DeeDee is tall and glamorous, with short hair she has dyed so often that she claims to have forgotten her real color. She drives a yellow 1977 Trans Am with a burgundy stripe down the center and a 1973 Mercedes 450 SL, and lives in a spare, Japanese-style cabin in Laurel Canyon. She uses words like "rad" and "totally," and offers non-stop, deadpan pronouncements on pop culture, as in "It's all about Pee-wee Herman." She sounds at first like a teen, like the same teens who, at Lambesis, it is her job to follow. But teen speech—particularly girl-teen speech, with its fixation on reported speech ("so she goes," "and I'm like," "and he goes") and its stock vocabulary of accompanying grimaces and gestures—is about using language less to communicate than to fit in. DeeDee uses teen speech to set herself apart, and the result is, for lack of a better word, *really* cool. She doesn't do the teen thing of climbing half an octave at the end of every sentence. Instead, she drags out her vowels for emphasis, so that if she mildly disagreed with something I'd said she would say "Maalcolm" and if she strongly disagreed with what I'd said she would say "Maaalcolm."

5 Baysie is older, just past forty (although you would never guess that), and went to Exeter and Middlebury and had two grandfathers who went to Harvard (although you wouldn't guess that, either). She has curly brown hair and big green eyes and long legs and so much energy that it is hard to imagine her asleep, or resting, or even standing still for longer than thirty seconds. The hunt for cool is an obsession with her, and DeeDee is the same way. DeeDee used to sit on the corner of West Broadway and Prince in SoHo—back when SoHo was cool—and take pictures of everyone who walked by for an entire hour. Baysie can tell you precisely where she goes on her Reebok coolhunts to find the really cool alternative white kids ("I'd maybe go to Portland and hang out where the skateboarders hang out near that bridge") or which snowboarding mountain has cooler kids—Stratton, in Vermont, or Summit County, in Colorado. (Summit, definitely.) DeeDee can tell you on the basis of the *L Report's* research exactly how far Dallas is behind New York in coolness (from six to eight months). Baysie is convinced that Los Angeles is not happening right now: "In the early nineteen-nineties a lot more was coming from L.A. They had a big trend with the whole Melrose Avenue look—the stupid goatees, the shorter hair. It was cleaned-up aftergrunge. There were a lot of places you could go to buy vinyl records. It was a strong place to go for looks. Then it went back to being horrible." DeeDee is convinced that Japan *is* happening: "I linked onto this future-technology thing two years ago. Now look at it, it's huge. It's the whole resurgence of Nike—Nike being larger than life. I went to Japan and saw the kids just bailing the most technologically advanced Nikes with their little dresses and little outfits and I'm like, 'Whoa, this is trippy!' It's performance mixed with fashion. It's really superheavy." Baysie has a theory that Liverpool is cool right now because it's the birthplace of the whole "lad" look, which involves soccer blokes in the pubs going superdressy and wearing Dolce & Gabbana and Polo Sport and Reebok Classics on their feet. But when I asked DeeDee about that, she just rolled her eyes: "Sometimes Baysie goes off on these tangents. *Man,* I love that woman!"

I used to think that if I talked to Baysie and DeeDee long enough I could write a coolhunting manual, an encyclopedia of cool. But then I realized that the manual would have so many footnotes and caveats that it would be unreadable. Coolhunting is not about the articulation of a coherent philosophy of cool. It's just a collection of spontaneous observations and predictions that differ from one moment to the next and from one coolhunter to the next. Ask a coolhunter where the baggy-jeans look came from, for example, and you might get any number of answers: urban black kids mimicking the jailhouse look, skateboarders looking for room to move, snowboarders trying not to look like skiers, or, alternatively, all three at once, in some grand concordance.

Or take the question of exactly how Tommy Hilfiger—a forty-five-year-old white guy from Greenwich, Connecticut, doing all-American preppy clothes—came to be the designer of choice for urban black America. Some say it was all about the early and visible endorsement given Hilfiger by the hip-hop auteur Grand Puba, who wore a dark-green-and-blue Tommy jacket over a white Tommy T-shirt as he leaned on his black Lamborghini on the cover of the hugely influential "Grand Puba 2000" CD, and whose love for Hilfiger soon spread to other rappers. (Who could forget the rhymes of Mobb Deep? "Tommy was my nigga/And couldn't figure/How me and Hilfiger/used to move through with vigor.") Then I had lunch with one of Hilfiger's designers, a twenty-six-year-old named Ulrich (Ubi) Simpson, who has a Puerto Rican mother and a Dutch-Venezuelan father, plays lacrosse, snowboards, surfs the long board, goes to hip-hop concerts, listens to Jungle, Edith Piaf, opera, rap, and Metallica, and has working with him on his design team a twenty-seven-year-old black guy from Montclair with dreadlocks, a twenty-two-year-old Asian-American who lives on the Lower East Side, a twenty-five-year-old South Asian guy from Fiji, and a twenty-one-year-old white graffiti artist from Queens. That's when it occurred to me that maybe the reason Tommy Hilfiger can make white culture cool to black culture is that he has people working for him who are cool in both cultures simultaneously. Then again, maybe it *was* all Grand Puba. Who knows?

One day last month, Baysie took me on a coolhunt to the Bronx and Harlem, lugging a big black canvas bag with twenty-four different shoes that Reebok is about to bring out, and as we drove down Fordham Road, she had her head out the window like a little kid, checking out what everyone on the street was wearing. We went to Dr. Jay's, which is the cool place to buy sneakers in the Bronx, and Baysie crouched down on the floor and started pulling the shoes out of her bag one by one, soliciting opinions from customers who gathered around and asking one question after another, in rapid sequence. One guy she listened closely to was maybe eighteen or nineteen, with a diamond stud in his ear and a thin beard. He was wearing a Polo baseball cap, a brown leather jacket, and the big, oversized leather boots that are everywhere uptown right now. Baysie would hand him a shoe and he would hold it, look at the top, and move it up and down and flip it over. The first one he didn't like: "*Oh*-kay." The second one he hated: he made a growling sound in his throat even before Baysie could give it to him, as if to say, "Put it back in the bag—now!" But when she handed him a new DMX RXT—a low-cut run/walk shoe in white and blue and mesh with a translucent "ice" sole, which retails for a hundred and ten dollars—he looked at it long and hard and shook his head in pure admiration and just said two words, dragging each of them out: "No *doubt*."

Baysie was interested in what he was saying, because the DMX RXT she had was a girls' shoe that actually hadn't been doing all that well. Later, she explained to me that the fact that the boys loved the shoe was critical news, because it suggested that Reebok had a potential hit if it just switched the shoe to the men's section. How she managed to distill this piece of information from the crowd of teen-agers around her, how she made any sense of the two dozen shoes in her bag, most of which (to my eyes, anyway) looked pretty much the same, and how she knew which of the teens to really focus on was a mystery. Baysie is a Wasp from New England, and she crouched on the floor in Dr. Jay's for almost an hour, talking and joking with the homeboys without a trace of condescension or self-consciousness.

Near the end of her visit, a young boy walked up and sat down on the 10
bench next to her. He was wearing a black woollen cap with white stripes pulled low, a blue North Face pleated down jacket, a pair of baggy Guess jeans, and, on his feet, Nike Air Jordans. He couldn't have been more than thirteen. But when he started talking you could see Baysie's eyes light up, because somehow she knew the kid was the real thing.

"How many pairs of shoes do you buy a month?" Baysie asked.

"Two," the kid answered. "And if at the end I find one more I like I get to buy that, too."

Baysie was onto him. "Does your mother spoil you?"

The kid blushed, but a friend next to him was laughing. "Whatever he wants, he gets."

Baysie laughed, too. She had the DMX RXT in his size. He tried them on. 15
He rocked back and forth, testing them. He looked back at Baysie. He was dead serious now: "Make sure these come out."

Baysie handed him the new "Rush" Emmitt Smith shoe due out in the fall. One of the boys had already pronounced it "phat," and another had looked through the marbleized-foam cradle in the heel and cried out in delight, "This is bug!" But this kid was the acid test, because this kid knew cool. He paused. He looked at it hard. "Reebok," he said, soberly and carefully, "is trying to get *butter.*"

In the car on the way back to Manhattan, Baysie repeated it twice. "Not better. *Butter!* That kid could totally tell you what he thinks." Baysie had spent an hour coolhunting in a shoe store and found out that Reebok's efforts were winning the highest of hip-hop praise. "He was so *fucking* smart."

If you want to understand how trends work, and why coolhunters like Baysie and DeeDee have become so important, a good place to start is with what's known as diffusion research, which is the study of how ideas and innovations spread. Diffusion researchers do things like spending five years studying the adoption of irrigation techniques in a Colombian mountain village, or developing complex matrices to map the spread of new math in the Pittsburgh school system. What they do may seem like a far cry from, say, how the Tommy Hilfiger thing spread from Harlem to every suburban mall in the country, but it really isn't: both are about how new ideas spread from one person to the next.

One of the most famous diffusion studies is Bruce Ryan and Neal Gross's analysis of the spread of hybrid seed corn in Greene County, Iowa, in the nineteen-thirties. The new seed corn was introduced there in about 1928, and it was superior in every respect to the seed that had been used by farmers for decades. But it wasn't adopted all at once. Of two hundred and fifty-nine farmers studied by Ryan and Gross, only a handful had started planting the new seed by 1933. In 1934, sixteen took the plunge. In 1935, twenty-one more followed; the next year, there were thirty-six, and the year after that a whopping sixty-one. The succeeding figures were then forty-six, thirty-six, fourteen, and three, until, by 1941, all but two of the two hundred and fifty-nine farmers studied were using the new seed. In the language of diffusion research, the handful of farmers who started trying hybrid seed corn at the very beginning of the thirties were the "innovators," the adventurous ones. The slightly larger group that followed them was the "early adopters." They were the opinion leaders in the community, the respected, thoughtful people who watched and analyzed what those wild innovators were doing and then did it themselves. Then came the big bulge of farmers in 1936, 1937, and 1938—the "early majority" and the "late majority," which is to say the deliberate and the skeptical masses, who would never try anything until the most respected farmers had tried it. Only after they had been converted did the "laggards," the most traditional of all, follow suit. The critical thing about this sequence is that it is almost entirely interpersonal. According to Ryan and Gross, only the innovators relied to any great extent on radio advertising and farm journals and seed salesmen in making their decision to switch to the hybrid. Everyone else made his decision overwhelmingly because of the example and the opinions of his neighbors and peers.

Isn't this just how fashion works? A few years ago, the classic brushed- 20
suède Hush Puppies with the lightweight crêpe sole—the moc-toe oxford known as the Duke and the slip-on with the golden buckle known as the Columbia—were selling barely sixty-five thousand pairs a year. The company was trying to walk away from the whole suède casual look entirely. It wanted to do "aspirational" shoes: "active casuals" in smooth leather, like the Mall Walker, with a Comfort Curve technology outsole and a heel stabilizer—the kind of shoes you see in Kinney's for $39.95. But then something strange started happening. Two Hush Puppies executives—Owen Baxter and Jeff Lewis—were doing a fashion shoot for their Mall Walkers and ran into a creative consultant from Manhattan named Jeffrey Miller, who informed them that the Dukes and the Columbias weren't dead, they were dead chic. "We were being told," Baxter recalls, "that there were areas in the Village, in SoHo, where the shoes were selling—in resale shops—and that people were wearing the old Hush Puppies. They were going to the ma-and-pa stores, the little stores that still carried them, and there was this authenticity of being able to say, 'I am wearing an original pair of Hush Puppies.'"

Baxter and Lewis—tall, solid, fair-haired Midwestern guys with thick, shiny wedding bands—are shoe men, first and foremost. Baxter was working the cash register at his father's shoe store in Mount Prospect, Illinois, at the age of thirteen. Lewis was doing inventory in his father's shoe store in Pontiac, Michigan, at the age of seven. Baxter was in the National Guard during the 1968 Democratic Convention, in Chicago, and was stationed across the street from the Conrad Hilton downtown, right in the middle of things. Today, the two men work out of Rockford, Michigan (population thirty-eight hundred), where Hush Puppies has been making the Dukes and the Columbias in an old factory down by the Rogue River for almost forty years. They took me to the plant when I was in Rockford. In a crowded, noisy, low-slung building, factory workers stand in long rows, gluing, stapling, and sewing together shoes in dozens of bright colors, and the two executives stopped at each production station and described it in detail. Lewis and Baxter know shoes. But they would be the first to admit that they don't know cool. "Miller was saying that there is something going on with the shoes—that Isaac Mizrahi was wearing the shoes for his personal use," Lewis told me. We were seated around the conference table in the Hush Puppies headquarters in Rockford, with the snow and the trees outside and a big water tower behind us. "I think it's fair to say that at the time we had no idea who Isaac Mizrahi was."

By late 1994, things had begun to happen in a rush. First, the designer John Bartlett called. He wanted to use Hush Puppies as accessories in his spring collection. Then Anna Sui called. Miller, the man from Manhattan, flew out to Michigan to give advice on a new line ("Of course, packing my own food and thinking about 'Fargo' in the corner of my mind"). A few months later, in Los Angeles, the designer Joel Fitzpatrick put a twenty-five-foot inflatable basset hound on the roof of his store on La Brea Avenue and gutted his adjoining art gallery to turn it into a Hush Puppies department, and even before he opened—while he was still painting and putting up shelves—Pee-wee Herman walked in and asked for a couple of pairs. Pee-wee Herman! "It was total word of mouth. I didn't even have a sign back then," Fitzpatrick recalls. In 1995, the company sold four hundred and thirty thousand pairs of the classic Hush Puppies. In 1996, it sold a million six hundred thousand, and that was only scratching the surface, because in Europe and the rest of the world, where Hush Puppies have a huge following—where they might outsell the American market four to one—the revival was just beginning.

The cool kids who started wearing old Dukes and Columbias from thrift shops were the innovators. Pee-wee Herman, wandering in off the street, was an early adopter. The million six hundred thousand people who bought Hush Puppies last year are the early majority, jumping in because the really cool people have already blazed the trail. Hush Puppies are moving through the country just the way hybrid seed corn moved through Greene County—all of which illustrates what coolhunters can and cannot do. If Jeffrey Miller had been wrong—if cool people hadn't been digging through the thrift shops for Hush Puppies—and he had arbitrarily decided that Baxter and Lewis should try to convince non-cool people that the shoes were cool, it wouldn't have worked. You can't convince the late majority that Hush Puppies are cool, because the late majority makes its coolness decisions on the basis of what the early majority is doing, and you can't convince the early majority, because the early majority is looking at the early adopters, and you can't convince the early adopters, because they take their cues from the innovators. The innovators do get their cool ideas from people other than their peers, but the fact is that they are the last people who can be convinced by a marketing campaign that a pair of suède shoes is cool. These are, after all, the people who spent hours sifting through thrift-store bins. And why did they do that? Because their definition of cool is doing something that nobody else is doing. A company can intervene in the cool cycle. It can put its shoes on really cool celebrities and on fashion runways and on MTV. It can accelerate the transition from the innovator to the early adopter and on to the early majority. But it can't just manufacture cool out of thin air, and that's the second rule of cool.

At the peak of the Hush Puppies craziness last year, Hush Puppies won the prize for best accessory at the Council of Fashion Designers' awards dinner, at Lincoln Center. The award was accepted by the Hush Puppies president, Louis Dubrow, who came out wearing a pair of custom-made black patent-leather Hush Puppies and stood there blinking and looking at the assembled crowd as if it were the last scene of "Close Encounters of the Third Kind." It was a strange moment. There was the president of the Hush Puppies company, of Rockford, Michigan, population thirty-eight hundred, sharing a stage with Calvin Klein and Donna Karan and Isaac Mizrahi—and all because some kids in the East Village began combing through thrift shops for old Dukes. Fashion was at the mercy of those kids, whoever they were, and it was a wonderful thing if the kids picked you, but a scary thing, too, because it meant that cool was something you could not control. You needed someone to find cool and tell you what it was.

When Baysie Wightman went to Dr. Jay's, she was looking for customer 25
response to the new shoes Reebok had planned for the fourth quarter of 1997 and the first quarter of 1998. This kind of customer testing is critical at Reebok, because the last decade has not been kind to the company. In 1987, it had a third of the American athletic-shoe market, well ahead of Nike. Last year, it had sixteen per cent. "The kid in the store would say, 'I'd like this shoe if your logo wasn't on it,' " E. Scott Morris, who's a senior designer for Reebok, told me. "That's kind of a punch in the mouth. But we've all seen it. You go into a shoe store. The kid picks up the shoe and says, 'Ah, man, this is nice.' He turns the shoe around and around. He looks at it underneath. He looks at the side and he goes, 'Ah, this is Reebok,' and says, 'I ain't buying this,' and puts the shoe down and walks out. And you go, 'You was just digging it a minute ago. What happened?' " Somewhere along the way, the company lost its cool, and Reebok now faces the task not only of rebuilding its image but of making the shoes so cool that the kids in the store *can't* put them down.

Every few months, then, the company's coolhunters go out into the field with prototypes of the upcoming shoes to find out what kids really like, and come back to recommend the necessary changes. The prototype of one recent Emmitt Smith shoe, for example, had a piece of molded rubber on the end of the tongue as a design element; it was supposed to give the shoe a certain "richness," but the kids said they thought it looked overbuilt. Then Reebok gave the shoes to the Boston College football team for wear-testing, and when they got the shoes back they found out that all the football players had cut out the rubber component with scissors. As messages go, this was hard to miss. The tongue piece wasn't cool, and on the final version of the shoe it was gone. The rule of thumb at Reebok is that if the kids in Chicago, New York, and Detroit all like a shoe, it's a guaranteed hit. More than likely, though, the coolhunt is going to turn up subtle differences from city to city, so that once the coolhunters come back the designers have to find out some way to synthesize what was heard, and pick out just those things that all the kids seemed to agree on. In New York, for example, kids in Harlem are more sophisticated and fashion-forward than kids in the Bronx, who like things a little more colorful and glitzy. Brooklyn, meanwhile, is conservative and preppy, more like Washington, D.C. For reasons no one really knows, Reeboks are coolest in Philadelphia. In Philly, in fact, the Reebok Classics are so huge they are known simply as National Anthems, as in "I'll have a pair of blue Anthems in nine and a half." Philadelphia is Reebok's innovator town. From there trends move along the East Coast, trickling all the way to Charlotte, North Carolina.

Reebok has its headquarters in Stoughton, Massachusetts, outside Boston—in a modern corporate park right off Route 24. There are basketball and tennis courts next to the building, and a health club on the ground floor that you can look directly into from the parking lot. The front lobby is adorned with shrines for all of Reebok's most prominent athletes—shrines complete with dramatic action photographs, their sports jerseys, and a pair of their signature shoes—and the halls are filled with so many young, determinedly athletic people that when I visited Reebok headquarters I suddenly wished I'd packed my gym clothes in case someone challenged me to wind sprints. At Stoughton, I met with a handful of the company's top designers and marketing executives in a long conference room on the third floor. In the course of two hours, they put one pair of shoes after another on the table in front of me, talking excitedly about each sneaker's prospects, because the feeling at Reebok is that things are finally turning around. The basketball shoe that Reebok brought out last winter for Allen Iverson, the star rookie guard for the Philadelphia 76ers, for example, is one of the hottest shoes in the country. Dr. Jay's sold out of Iversons in two days, compared with the week it took the store to sell out of Nike's new Air Jordans. Iverson himself is brash and charismatic and faster from foul line to foul line than anyone else in the league. He's the equivalent of those kids in the East Village who began wearing Hush Puppies way back when. He's an innovator, and the hope at Reebok is that if he gets big enough the whole company can ride back to coolness on his coattails, the way Nike rode to coolness on the coattails of Michael Jordan. That's why Baysie was so excited when the kid said Reebok was trying to get *butter* when he looked at the Rush and the DMX RXT: it was a sign, albeit a small one, that the indefinable, abstract thing called cool was coming back.

When Baysie comes back from a coolhunt, she sits down with marketing experts and sales representatives and designers, and reconnects them to the street, making sure they have the right shoes going to the right places at the right price. When she got back from the Bronx, for example, the first thing she did was tell all these people they had to get a new men's DMX RXT out, *fast,* because the kids on the street loved the women's version. "It's hotter than we realized," she told them. The coolhunter's job in this instance is very specific. What DeeDee does, on the other hand, is a little more ambitious. With the *L Report,* she tries to construct a kind of grand matrix of cool, comprising not just shoes but everything kids like, and not just kids of certain East Coast urban markets but kids all over. DeeDee and her staff put it out four times a year, in six different versions—for New York, Los Angeles, San Francisco,

Austin-Dallas, Seattle, and Chicago—and then sell it to manufacturers, retailers, and ad agencies (among others) for twenty thousand dollars a year. They go to each city and find the coolest bars and clubs, and ask the coolest kids to fill out questionnaires. The information is then divided into six categories—You Saw It Here First, Entertainment and Leisure, Clothing and Accessories, Personal and Individual, Aspirations, and Food and Beverages—which are, in turn, broken up into dozens of subcategories, so that Personal and Individual, for example, includes Cool Date, Cool Evening, Free Time, Favorite Possession, and on and on. The information in those subcategories is subdivided again by sex and by age bracket (14–18, 19–24, 25–30), and then, as a control, the *L Report* gives you the corresponding set of preferences for "mainstream" kids.

Few coolhunters bother to analyze trends with this degree of specificity. DeeDee's biggest competitor, for example, is something called the *Hot Sheet*, out of Manhattan. It uses a panel of three thousand kids a year from across the country and divides up their answers by sex and age, but it doesn't distinguish between regions, or between trendsetting and mainstream respondents. So what you're really getting is what *all* kids think is cool—not what cool kids think is cool, which is a considerably different piece of information. Janine Misdom and Joanne DeLuca, who run the Sputnik coolhunting group out of the garment district in Manhattan, meanwhile, favor an entirely impressionistic approach, sending out coolhunters with video cameras to talk to kids on the ground that it's too difficult to get cool kids to fill out questionnaires. Once, when I was visiting the Sputnik girls—as Misdom and DeLuca are known on the street, because they look alike and their first names are so similar and both have the same *awesome* New York accents—they showed me a video of the girl they believe was the patient zero of the whole eighties revival going on right now. It was back in September of 1993. Joanne and Janine were on Seventh Avenue, outside the Fashion Institute of Technology, doing random street interviews for a major jeans company, and, quite by accident, they ran into this nineteen-year-old raver. She had close-cropped hair, which was green at the top, and at the temples was shaved even closer and dyed pink. She had rings and studs all over her face, and a thick collection of silver tribal jewelry around her neck, and vintage jeans. She looked into the camera and said, "The sixties came in and then the seventies came in and I think it's ready to come back to the eighties. It's totally eighties: the eye makeup, the clothes. It's totally going back to that." Immediately, Joanne and Janine started asking around. "We talked to a few kids on the Lower East Side who said they were feeling the need to start breaking out their old Michael Jackson jackets," Joanne said. "They were joking about it. They weren't doing it yet. But they were going to, you know? They were saying, 'We're getting the urge to break out our Members Only jackets.'" That was right when Joanne and Janine were just starting up; calling the eighties revival was their first big break, and now they put out a full-blown videotaped report twice a year which is a collection of clips of interviews with *extremely* progressive people.

What DeeDee argues, though, is that cool is too subtle and too variegated 30
to be captured with these kind of broad strokes. Cool is a set of dialects, not a

language. The *L Report* can tell you, for example, that nineteen-to-twenty-four-year-old male trendsetters in Seattle would most like to meet, among others, King Solomon and Dr. Seuss, and that nineteen-to-twenty-four-year-old female trendsetters in San Francisco have turned their backs on Calvin Klein, Nintendo Gameboy, and sex. What's cool right now? Among male New York trendsetters: North Face jackets, rubber and latex, khakis, and the rock band Kiss. Among female trendsetters: ska music, old-lady clothing, and cyber tech. In Chicago, snowboarding is huge among trendsetters of both sexes and all ages. Women over nineteen are into short hair, while those in their teens have embraced mod culture, rock climbing, tag watches, and bootleg pants. In Austin-Dallas, meanwhile, twenty-five-to-thirty-year-old women trendsetters are into hats, heroin, computers, cigars, Adidas, and velvet, while men in their twenties are into video games and hemp. In all, the typical *L Report* runs over one hundred pages. But with that flood of data comes an obsolescence disclaimer: "The fluctuating nature of the trendsetting market makes keeping up with trends a difficult task." By the spring, in other words, everything may have changed.

The key to coolhunting, then, is to look for cool people first and cool things later, and not the other way around. Since cool things are always changing, you can't look for them, because the very fact they are cool means you have no idea what to look for. What you would be doing is thinking back on what was cool before and extrapolating, which is about as useful as presuming that because the Dow rose ten points yesterday it will rise another ten points today. Cool people, on the other hand, are a constant.

When I was in California, I met Salvador Barbier, who had been described to me by a coolhunter as "the Michael Jordan of skateboarding." He was tall and lean and languid, with a cowboy's insouciance, and we drove through the streets of Long Beach at fifteen miles an hour in a white late-model Ford Mustang, a car he had bought as a kind of ironic status gesture ("It would look good if I had a Polo jacket or maybe Nautica," he said) to go with his '62 Econoline van and his '64 T-bird. Sal told me that he and his friends, who are all in their mid-twenties, recently took to dressing up as if they were in eighth grade again and gathering together—having a "rally"—on old BMX bicycles in front of their local 7-Eleven. "I'd wear muscle shirts, like Def Leppard or Foghat or some old heavy-metal band, and tight, tight tapered Levi's, and Vans on my feet—big, like, checkered Vans or striped Vans or camouflage Vans—and then wristbands and gloves with the fingers cut off. It was total eighties fashion. You had to look like that to participate in the rally. We had those denim jackets with patches on the back and combs that hung out the back pocket. We went without I.D.s, because we'd have to have someone else buy us beers." At this point, Sal laughed. He was driving really slowly and staring straight ahead and talking in a low drawl—the coolhunter's dream. "We'd ride to this bar and I'd have to carry my bike inside, because we have really expensive bikes, and when we got inside people would freak out. They'd say, 'Omigod,' and I was asking them if they wanted to go for a ride on the handlebars. They were like, 'What is wrong with you. My boyfriend used to dress like that in the eighth grade!' And I was like, 'He was probably a lot cooler then, too.' "

This is just the kind of person DeeDee wants. "I'm looking for somebody who is an individual, who has definitely set himself apart from everybody else, who doesn't look like his peers. I've run into trendsetters who look completely Joe Regular Guy. I can see Joe Regular Guy at a club listening to some totally hardcore band playing, and I say to myself 'Omigod, what's that guy doing here?' and that totally intrigues me, and I have to walk up to him and say, 'Hey, you're really into this band. What's up?' You know what I mean? I look at everything. If I see Joe Regular Guy sitting in a coffee shop and everyone around him has blue hair, I'm going to gravitate toward him, because, hey, what's Joe Regular Guy doing in a coffee shop with people with blue hair?"

We were sitting outside the Fred Segal store in West Hollywood. I was wearing a very conservative white Brooks Brothers button-down and a pair of Levi's, and DeeDee looked first at my shirt and then my pants and dissolved into laughter: "I mean, I might even go up to *you* in a cool place."

Picking the right person is harder than it sounds, though. Piney Kahn, 35
who works for DeeDee, says, "There are a lot of people in the gray area. You've got these kids who dress ultra funky and have their own style. Then you realize they're just running after their friends." The trick is not just to be able to tell who is different but to be able to tell when that difference represents something truly cool. It's a gut thing. You have to somehow just *know.* DeeDee hired Piney because Piney clearly *knows:* she is twenty-four and used to work with the Beastie Boys and has the formidable self-possession of someone who is not only cool herself but whose parents were cool. "I mean," she says, "they named me after a *tree.*"

Piney and DeeDee said that they once tried to hire someone as a coolhunter who was not, himself, cool, and it was a disaster.

"You can give them the boundaries," Piney explained. "You can say that if people shop at Banana Republic and listen to Alanis Morissette they're probably not trendsetters. But then they might go out and assume that everyone who does that is not a trendsetter, and not look at the other things."

"I mean, I myself might go into Banana Republic and buy a T-shirt," DeeDee chimed in.

Their non-cool coolhunter just didn't have that certain instinct, that sense that told him when it was O.K. to deviate from the manual. Because he wasn't cool, he didn't know cool, and that's the essence of the third rule of cool: you have to be one to know one. That's why Baysie is still on top of this business at forty-one. "It's easier for me to tell you what kid is cool than to tell you what things are cool," she says. But that's all she needs to know. In this sense, the third rule of cool fits perfectly into the second: the second rule says that cool cannot be manufactured, only observed, and the third says that it can only be observed by those who are themselves cool. And, of course, the first rule says that it cannot accurately be observed at all, because the act of discovering cool causes cool to take flight, so if you add all three together they describe a closed loop, the hermeneutic circle of coolhunting, a phenomenon whereby not only can the uncool not see cool but cool cannot even be adequately described to them. Baysie says that she can see a coat on one of her friends and think it's not cool but then see the same coat on DeeDee and think that it is cool. It is not possible to be cool, in other words, unless you are—in some larger sense—already cool, and so the phenomenon that the uncool cannot see and cannot have described to them is also something that they cannot ever attain, because if they did it would no longer be cool. Coolhunting represents the ascendancy, in the marketplace, of high school.

Once, I was visiting DeeDee at her house in Laurel Canyon when one of 40
her *L Report* assistants, Jonas Vail, walked in. He'd just come back from Niketown on Wilshire Boulevard, where he'd bought seven hundred dollars' worth of the latest sneakers to go with the three hundred dollars' worth of skateboard shoes he'd bought earlier in the afternoon. Jonas is tall and expressionless, with a peacoat, dark jeans, and short-cropped black hair. "Jonas is good," DeeDee says. "He works with me on everything. That guy knows more pop culture. You know: What was the name of the store Mrs. Garrett owned on 'The Facts of Life'? He knows all the names of the *extras* from eighties sitcoms. I can't believe someone like him exists. He's fucking unbelievable. Jonas can spot a cool person a *mile* away."

Jonas takes the boxes of shoes and starts unpacking them on the couch next to DeeDee. He picks up a pair of the new Nike ACG hiking boots, and says, "All the Japanese in Niketown were really into these." He hands the shoes to DeeDee.

"Of *course* they were!" she says. "The Japanese are all into the tech-looking shit. Look how exaggerated it is, how bulbous." DeeDee has very ambivalent feelings about Nike, because she thinks its marketing has got out of hand. When she was in the New York Niketown with a girlfriend recently, she says, she started getting light-headed and freaked out. "It's cult, cult, cult. It was like, 'Hello, are we all drinking the Kool-Aid here?'" But this shoe she loves. It's Dr. Jay's in the Bronx all over again. DeeDee turns the shoe around and around in the air, tapping the big clear-blue plastic bubble on the side—the visible Air-Sole unit—with one finger. "It's so fucking rad. It looks like a platypus!" In front of me, there is a pair of Nike's new shoes for the basketball player Jason Kidd.

I pick it up. "This looks . . . cool," I venture uncertainly.

DeeDee is on the couch, where she's surrounded by shoeboxes and sneakers and white tissue paper, and she looks up reprovingly because, of course, I don't get it. I *can't* get it. "Beyooond cool, Maalcolm. Beyooond cool."

Understanding

1. What are the three rules of "cool"?
2. How has the coolhunter influenced consumerism and production? Is it the coolhunter who has the impact, or is it people spreading new ideas from one person to the next?
3. What types of people has diffusion research categorized to identify the stages of an established product? Trace them in relation to the hybrid seed corn study and the Hush Puppy craze. When Baysie is at Dr. Jay's, interviewing kids about cool shoes, one of them uses *butter* to describe what she's

attempting. Are the kids to whom she is showing the shoes "innovators" or "early adopters"? Apply the designations from diffusion research to those kids. How would you categorize them as a diffusion researcher?

4. Where did the name *coolhunter* come from? How do you get to be one? Do you reinvent yourself as one and just do it?
5. "Cool is a set of dialects, not a language." What does Gladwell mean by this?

Responding

1. Do you wear or have you worn (or do you know kids who have worn) the shower sandal or the Converse One Star? If so, describe the group that wore them and analyze why. If not, describe a type of clothing that has identified you as cool or as part of a particular crowd. Identify how that item or style became the item of choice among that group and how it felt to wear it. What did wearing it say about you and about the group with which you associated?
2. Can you identify a time when you were an innovator, an early adopter, an early or late majority, or a laggard for something? Explain. Can you predict what will be cool next?
3. How would you characterize cool in your city? Make an *L Report* entry for your city following the categories in the article for DeeDee's *L Report.* As you do it, analyze who gives your choices credibility—who are you picturing in your mind as cool as you describe what they do and like? Are you among them?
4. Since the 1980s, popular culture has been preoccupied with name-brand clothing. Describe your experiences with name-brand clothing. Do you wear it? Why? Who didn't wear it and why not? Do you think the name-brand fad in clothing is over? Why or why not?

Connecting

What do you make of the 1997 return to cool of the *Star Wars* film series? Do you think it had anything to do with input from innovators or coolhunters?

The Just-Do-It Shrink

Rebecca Johnson

If popular culture at the threshold of the new millennium is represented in rap, ska, and jungle music; retro, old-lady, and designer clothing; prime-time television programs, sports of choice, and chic coffee drinks for the under-thirty crowd, then talk radio must be included in over-thirty popular culture. With so many of this age group commuting in cars, millions tune in to their favorite talk-show "communities" (a twenty-year-old phenomenon) to listen and, sometimes, talk about their own personal relationships. Like on the Internet, the participants on talk radio—both callers and listeners—are invisible voices; but unlike the Internet, where the topics range widely, the talk radio community shares the issues that all of us think about—how to get along with others, and how to fashion a life we consider meaningful—one which meets our personal standards for success. 1-800-DR-LAURA, featuring "the just-do-it shrink" Dr. Laura Schlessinger, is one of those talk shows.

With a Ph.D. in physiology from Columbia University for her research on the impact of insulin on fat tissues (not psychotherapy), Dr. Laura Schlessinger is second only to conservative host Rush Limbaugh in popularity on the talk radio air waves. "Dr. Laura," however, does not discuss politics; instead, she does a kind of talk therapy by telling people to "get over themselves." Writer Rebecca Johnson, contributing editor at *Vogue,* writes that Dr. Schlessinger's show "may well represent the end of therapy as we know it." Popular culture originates in innovative responsiveness to people's needs. "The Just-Do-It Shrink," originally published in the *New York Times Magazine,* is a provocative commentary on the state of communication and leadership in American culture today.

"Jan! Welcome to the program." 1

"Hi. I'm kind of nervous calling you, because I know you tell people how it is."

"I don't blame you. I'd really think about calling me."

But call they do. Every weekday thousands of people dial 1-800-DR-LAURA to pour out the most intimate details of their messed-up lives to Laura Schlessinger, a once-divorced, conservative Jewish mother with a Ph.D. in physiology and a license in marriage and family counseling, who introduces herself as "my kid's mom" and may well represent the end of therapy as we know it.

Consider Jan, a 28-year-old mother of two who began her call to Dr. Laura 5
all bubbly and jokey, seeking advice about her 50-year-old husband, a man she began seeing while he was married to someone else.

"My problem is—and it's a serious problem—that he has children from his first marriage."

"Who are probably older than you. He has ties older than you."

"Correct," Jan answered, sustaining the first blow, "but I don't want to seem like the blond bimbo, because I'm not. I'm an educated redhead."

"Oh, O.K., a redheaded bimbo with a degree."

"No, not yet, but I'm working on it. However, his children treat me like . . ." 10

"You have to understand one very important point—their father acted like a bum, but they don't want to be orphans, so they're probably putting the onus on you, because they don't know how to look into their father's face and say, 'You're a disgusting bum.'"

"O.K.," Jan said, the bubble in her voice gone flat.

"He screwed up the family, and then everybody's demanding that everybody act like it's O.K. and normal and be accepting. You're asking for a lot. So, minimally, we can hope for polite. But you're asking to be accepted as though you were kosher, and—trust me—there's been no blessing on this dinner."

"So what do I do? Do I leave him?"

"With two little kids, and break up yet another family? That *sounds like a* 15
wise idea."

"No, I mean, I love the man to death, but I don't want to—"

"I'm glad! But you didn't love him enough to leave him alone with his family. You wanted him for yourself, so you have their rage. Well, no kidding. What do you expect? Waltz in, take a guy, make babies with him out of wedlock, then marry him and then everybody is supposed to go, 'Well, since you got married, I guess it's O.K.'?"

"But they already told me that their parents' marriage was over."

"It wasn't over till it's over! Any opportunity for it not to be over was destroyed when you came into the picture, the cute little bimbo redhead."

"Don't call me a bimbo." Now her voice was tiny, dissolving into a whimper, and 20
Dr. Laura's was getting bigger, gathering, with each word, the rage and indignation of not just the scorned wife but of all of society against the transgressors of the social order. Vixen! Harlot! Slut!

"But that's what it's like to everybody else!" Dr. Laura said, finishing her off. "He didn't get a grown woman who was his peer. He got a little girl who adores him. . . ."

You could hear the beginning of an agonized wail, but just as it grew, the music cut it off. "This is Dr. Laura, and you're listening to WABC."

* * *

Laura Schlessinger is not interested in your pain, your suffering, your heartbreak. She does not care about your low self-esteem and your lousy childhood. She is shrink as aerobics teacher: Stop feeling sorry for yourself. Stop blaming other people. Stop thinking about yourself so much. Forget victimhood, empathy or therapy as anodyne. In other words, Suck it up, bucko.

If the numbers mean anything (and they do), we are listening. Just two years after her Los Angeles–based call-in show went national, it can be heard in 80 percent of the country. Every day, some 12 million people tune in. (In New York she can be heard live on WABC-AM from 3 to 4 P.M.) Her two self-help books, "Ten Stupid Things Women Do to Mess Up Their Lives" and "How Could You Do That?! The Abdication of Character, Courage and Conscience," have been best-sellers for more than two years. On the airwaves, she is second in popularity only to Rush Limbaugh. Both share a conservative agenda based on what have come to be known as family values, but that's where the similarities end. Schlessinger doesn't discuss issues or politics and demurs when asked about her own. "It's not relevant," she says, though it's pretty clear where she stands. In her office I spied copies of The Weekly Standard, and she often directs listeners to the book "Who Stole Feminism? How Women Betrayed Women," Christina Hoff Sommers's withering denunciation of the women's movement. "Feminism," Schlessinger says, "is anti-men, anti-family and anti-children."

In person, the woman who has tapped into America's confused superego 25
so successfully is an intense, 49-year-old size 2 with permed hair, a jeweled Star of David around her neck, red-lacquered nails and the unmistakable air of someone who is sure she's always right. When asked if she has ever given anyone the wrong advice, she does not hesitate: No, never. Which may be what makes her such an irresistible figure for these ambivalent times when, given a choice, many of us would prefer to have no choice. Tell me what to do, her callers ask, and I'll do it. I'd do the right thing if I knew what the right thing was. And if the authority figure is a little mean and a little harsh, if she calls your behavior "stupid" instead of "self-defeating," isn't that what we all think anyway? When I bought a copy of "Ten Stupid Things Women Do to Mess Up Their Lives," the sad-eyed clerk rang up the sale and said, "I ought to read that book, too." No wonder the therapeutic community can't stand Dr. Laura. "Her information is not the kind that a psychologist gives," says Dr. Lilli Friedland, a past president of the media-psychology division of the American Psychological Association. "We're supposed to guide people, not lead them."

It has been 20 years since Toni Grant, a Los Angeles psychologist who also wrote the best-selling advice book "Being a Woman: Fulfilling Your Femininity and Finding Love," put radio therapy on the map. Her show was such a success that talk-radio programmers began adding therapists to lineups that had once included only sports, politics and the occasional gardening show. One of television's top-rated shows, "Frasier," is based on the burgeoning profession of radio shrink, though they got the sex wrong: the hosts of the two biggest national therapy shows are women, society's traditional empaths. But even as the industry has grown, bringing therapy—or an approximation of it—to ever larger numbers of people, traditionalists have watched these developments with dismay.

"When I first started, the A.P.A. tried to take my license away," says Dr. Joy Browne, a radio psychologist who is syndicated on 250 stations. "People kept saying, 'Joy shouldn't be doing this.' Then they'd slip me their card and say, 'If you ever need a replacement, call me.'" Like Dr. Laura, who says her show deals with "moral health, not mental health," Browne says that what she does on the air is not therapy. "It's Problem Solving 101," she says, "and it may be Voyeurism 102," but she thinks these call-in shows correspond to a deep need to be recognized. "People would rather be praised than punished," she says, "but they'd rather be punished than ignored. How else to explain why they call?" Still, except to say that Dr. Laura "doesn't have a license to worry about" (a radio therapist doesn't need one), Browne hesitates to make a direct hit. "I feel we should all be more gentle and careful with one another," she says. "There are no simple answers for complicated questions. Until we've walked in someone else's shoes, we don't know what their lives are like."

Noble sentiments, but not necessarily the stuff of high ratings. "The best way to ensure the failure of a radio therapy show is to concentrate on psychology," says David Bartlett, president of the Radio–Television News Directors Association and a former radio programmer who has conducted workshops for the A.P.A. "Good talk radio is done for the listener, not the caller. That may not always be compatible with the role of therapist. Let me give you an extreme example: someone who is on the ledge of a window contemplating suicide calls up a show. The therapist wants to talk the person down, but the program director wants her to hang up. You've got to be ruthless to survive."

The fact is, therapy in general has had to change to survive. Outside the neurotic sliver of Manhattan, very few people have the time, the money or the inclination for traditional analysis. "Therapy is not a dinosaur, but it is a luxury," Browne says. "Now that managed care limits the visits an insurer will pay for, we've all had to figure out how to get results more quickly. Even Woody Allen has joked, 'I'm going to give it one more year and then try Lourdes.' "

* * *

On most days, Laura Schlessinger rises before dawn, lifts weights, practices 30
martial arts (she has a black belt in Hapkido) and gets to her office—which is decorated with a framed photo of Linda Hamilton in "Terminator 2"—by 10 A.M. to prepare for her three-hour show. Of the 60,000 calls a day made to the show at her home station of KFI-AM, in Los Angeles, Schlessinger's producer, Carolyn Holt, screens about 100 every hour. Holt looks for people who have a dilemma, a conflict, something that will make good radio but not anything too dark like suicide or sex abuse. True psychosis does not entertain, and nobody wants to hear about the abyss on the way to the grocery store.

When Holt, who honed her skills as a customer-service representative for a credit card company where she was allowed only three minutes a call, finds a problem she likes, she distills it into a sentence and sends it to Dr. Laura via computer:

> "Colin having a problem being nice 2 Dad in Law he can't stand.
> —Colin in OH, M 31"
>
> "Nt sure abt giving up position to find out if Beau loves her."
> —Karen in Pitts, PA, F 24"
>
> "Nt sure abt talking 2 son w/family or alone re hm Being Gay.
> —Louis, M 47"

Schlessinger chooses the call that appeals to her and begins to work. On 35
the day I observed her in the studio, I was impressed with her wit, her mostly good sense and her timing. It was easy to see why she is popular, and I was beginning to wonder why therapists dislike her so much. Then Aubrey called. Aubrey sounded intelligent and educated, but too needy, too eager to please. You just knew he was the kid who got picked on in high school. Aubrey was living with a woman whom he had taken in four years earlier when her mother kicked her out of the house. The woman had a child that Aubrey had raised as his own. There was, however, nothing romantic in the relationship. Well, not true—they had necked and petted "on rare occasions," but there was no

sex. The problem was that the woman had turned into a "thoroughly unpleasant person," and he was afraid she was going to take the child away. What, Aubrey wanted to know, should he do?

"Whose interests are first here? Hers? The kid's? Or yours?"

"The kid's."

"Then you try to get along with her so that at least he has the balance of one, I assume, reasonably decent, sane human being helping him grow up. But at some point, she's likely to want to get herself a guy."

"Well, I've asked her to marry me, and she has been putting me off."

"You're not it."

"Apparently not."

"You're the one who can be used. You're not the kind of guy she's going to go for."

Ow. Was I the only one who found that exchange painful? Afterward I asked Schlessinger if she had been too hard on the man.

"No," she answered. "The people who call me are not fragile and frail. They don't stay on the line for 30 minutes on hold if they are. I could tell from the tone of his voice, the word choice, the way he spoke, that he could take it. It's like with a car mechanic. When you drive up, he can tell a lot about a car by the way it sounds. I don't have a lot of time with people, so I need to distill it down and make it bold with lights flashing."

Radio professionals say that is precisely her talent. "When Laura became so successful, I started to get a lot more tapes from therapists who wanted their own show," says David Hall, program director at KFI. "But they didn't get it. They'd send tapes of themselves being meaner or harder on people, but that's not what makes her successful. What she has is an ability to focus on the heart of someone's story and say whatever is the right thing. I think Oprah does that, too."

Still, I couldn't get Aubrey out of my mind. He had seemed like a bright man in serious pain, somebody who was struggling with a severely dysfunctional relationship and needed help. Who could be a better candidate for traditional therapy? Schlessinger disagreed. "There would be no value for that person to go into therapy," she said. "The typical therapist would say: 'Let go of this woman. You're not in a real relationship. It's sad for the kid, but life is sad.' Whether something is right or wrong is not an issue in therapy. Modern therapy promotes self-centeredness. Everything is rational or relative. I'm not. My morality is based on the Old Testament and the Talmud. Whenever I can, I try and push people toward religion."

"Revelations," as Schlessinger likes to say, "don't change lives." True enough. Even Freud once observed that giving a patient insight into the causal connection between his current problems and his childhood experiences has "as much influence on the symptoms of nervous illness as a distribution of menu cards in a time of famine has upon hunger." Still, it's hard not to wonder what happened to Laura Schlessinger to make her the way she is. It comes, therefore, as no surprise to anyone versed in the most basic of therapeutic principles—we either become what we hate or become the opposite—to learn that her own childhood was less than ideal. She would, by the way, hate to be analyzed like this and is certainly no fan of Freud or anyone else for that matter. When asked to name her influences, she says: "Nobody. I do what I do in spite of influences."

Laura Schlessinger grew up on Avenue U in Brooklyn, one of two daughters born to Monroe Schlessinger, a civil engineer, and Yolanda Ceccovini, a young Italian beauty he met and married during World War II. The marriage was not a happy one, partly because Schlessinger's Jewish family did not accept his Catholic wife. As a child, Laura Schlessinger reacted to the chilly emotional landscape of her home by retreating into the seemingly rational world of science. When the family prospered and moved to Long Island, she set up a laboratory in the basement, got a B.S. in biology from the State University of New York at Stony Brook and eventually got her Ph.D. from Columbia for her research on the impact of insulin on fat cells. She moved to California for the weather and began teaching courses in biology, physiology and human sexuality at the University of Southern California. Enrollment in those classes began to double and triple as students discovered Schlessinger's frank and mordant humor. One day she called a radio talk show to answer the question "Which would you rather be—divorced or a widow?" Schlessinger, who was divorced at the time, answered "Widow." The host was so taken with her banter that he kept her on the air for 20 minutes and hired her as a guest expert on human sexuality. One year later she was able to parlay this exposure into her own show on a radio station in Orange County.

These days Schlessinger refuses to talk about her mother, who is still alive but with whom she has not spoken in 10 years. In 1994, however, she told People magazine that the rift occurred when Schlessinger suggested that her mother, who was working as her secretary, learn how to type. She walked out and has not been heard from since. When Schlessinger speaks of her father, who died of stomach cancer in 1990, she recalls a "dad who never said he was proud of me or loved me." She cried when she said it, and I couldn't help but notice that she had also cried when discussing the lack of love in her family during an interview on the television program "20/20." Either she is capable of producing tears on cue or her upbringing was so troubled that she is still traumatized by it.

So the underloved and underpraised daughter of a religiously mixed marriage grows up to become a national phenomenon, a radio personality who, among other things, discourages people from marrying outside their religion. It should please the ironists to learn that her husband, Dr. Lew Bishop, a former professor of neurophysiology at the University of Southern California, was brought up as an Episcopalian. Schlessinger said he had converted to Judaism, but when I asked him about it, Bishop, a laid-back yin to her high-strung yang, said he was still in the process. "I've been busy," he said (he works full time managing her career), "and there are some things about it I'm still struggling with." Like what? "Oh, the problem of evil."

The fact that Schlessinger felt underpraised as a child almost makes her own self-aggrandizing easier to take. The biographical note for her first book ran a page and a half and ended with the wince-producing sentence "She is certainly a woman from whom to learn courage." Her acknowledgments for the second book, a windy, somewhat unreadable rehash of her daily show, begins: "I'll admit it. I slaved on this book by myself for most of a year. And that's after 18 years of studying, teaching, counseling and on-air work. . . . I thank myself for all that effort." Asked if she sees herself as part of a larger movement toward conservative values in this country, she says: "I'm not part of a movement. I am a movement."

* * *

There is a saying in talk radio that the average listener is 35 to death, but Schlessinger says that when she tried to figure out the demographics of her show, she found a flat line. She appealed equally to men and women, young and old. To see who these fans were, I attended a book signing and a live broadcast of her show in Lake Arrowhead, Calif. Driving west out of the endless sprawl and murky gloom of Los Angeles toward the faux Tyrolean village of Lake Arrowhead, site of second homes of Roseanne, Patrick Swayze and Schlessinger herself, you understand why Southern California has spawned so many national personalities in talk radio. Everyone here is on the move, sealed into the car, radio on.

The fans on this day were mostly white, mostly female and mostly in the throes of man trouble. "She changed my life," said Leanne Combs, a 35-year-old telephone repairer who cradled a dog-eared copy of "Ten Stupid Things" while standing in line. "I married a man for all the wrong reasons. I was looking for a father, for someone to save me." Displaying that disconcerting, peculiarly American willingness to reveal inner life to a complete stranger that makes shows like Schlessinger's possible, Combs added that she was so miserable she considered suicide. Then she found Dr. Laura.

She now listens daily, though she has never tried to call the show. "I know what she'd say," Combs said. "I'm married and I have two kids. I need to make this marriage work, so that's what I'm trying to do." But as she spoke, her eyes went watery. "My husband is not a bad man, he's just selfish," she said. "But now I'm taking a hardball attitude. Just this week, I came home from work—he's between jobs—and he asked me, 'What's for dinner?' I told him he has got to start taking some responsibility around the house." And had she ever considered therapy? "It occurred to me," she answered, "but I don't know what they'd tell me that Dr. Laura hasn't."

Curious to see what men thought of Schlessinger, I went looking for a 55
male fan and found Wayne Burns, a 46-year-old street-sweeper operator from Rancho Cucamonga who looked like a character out of a Jimmy Buffett song. He wore a mustache, a floral-print shirt, aviator sunglasses and a straw fedora and was deeply, but humorously, alive to the class divisions in American society. "This place is snobsville, Richie Rich land," he said. "Those houses on the lake go for $5 million apiece. This is as close as they let a person like me get."

Burns turned out to be the most devout and thoughtful fan I met. He'd been listening to Schlessinger for years while he drove his street sweeper. "In the beginning I'd lie to the guys at work and say I'd been listening to Rush and hadn't bothered to change the station," he said. "But now a lot of them listen, too." This was the first time Burns had ever seen Schlessinger in person, and he said he was shocked that she was selling paraphernalia like $16 T-shirts emblazoned with her motto "Take on the day" or stuffed teddy bears wearing "I am my kid's mom" T-shirts. I couldn't tell if he was being ironic.

"I got divorced a few years ago," Burns said, "and I went to a psychologist for a year, but all he did was sit there and go 'Mmm-hmm, mmm-hmm' while I whined and whined. It was more helpful for me to listen to her. My biggest problem has always been my career. I always thought it was someone else's fault that I hadn't advanced more. I blamed a lot of other people, especially my father, because he quit school in the eighth grade and didn't encourage me to go to college. He said people in college were snobby. But then I started listening to Dr. Laura and I heard caller after caller try to blame someone else for what had gone wrong in their life and I really recognized myself in them. I realized: 'It's you. It's yourself.' It's not someone else's fault. It sounds simple, I know, but I didn't get it for a long time."

Wayne Burns was still a street sweeper at 46, he was still frustrated that his own child wasn't more interested in school and he was still divorced, but somehow Laura Schlessinger had made him feel better about it. She had given him a way to reframe his past, to forgive his father and make him less bitter about the promise that had once been his life. "What does she say?" he asked. "'Dreams are just unrealized goals.' I write a lot of her sayings down." No therapist could ask for more.

Understanding

1. Who is the target market of talk radio? Why?
2. Why do traditional therapists dislike Schlessinger's work?
3. How does Schlessinger characterize modern therapy in regard to morality?
4. What do her fans say is most powerful in Dr. Laura's advice?

Responding

1. What does Jan, in the opening interview, want from Dr. Schlessinger? What did she get? That is, how did Schlessinger leave her? Of what value to Jan was the interchange? What might Jan have done after the phone call? How about Aubrey's call? Analyze it in the same way.
2. The article says that talk-show listeners are age "35 to death." Maybe you are one of them. If you are, describe your experience as a listener or caller with one of these shows, or try 1-800-DR-LAURA if you haven't yet heard her. Take into account this article's point that talk radio is done for the listener, not the caller. If you are not a "35 to death" talk-show listener, do a little field work. Tune in to one of Dr. Laura's shows. Take notes on what you hear. Analyze and describe your listening experience in writing.
3. Compare and contrast the methods of calling a complete stranger (effectively with 100,000 people listening) to tell your troubles to as opposed to the traditional shoulder of a friend or family member. What does this show

about our family ties when we opt to confide in a talk-radio stranger? What does this do to the border between our public and private lives?

4. With the exception of fashion and its performance aspects, popular culture seems to include mostly voyeuristic activities on the part of its consumers. Does the fact that it offers a predominantly voyeur's menu mean that popular culture does not create communities? Respond to this proposition using the articles you've read and your own experience.
5. Some people say that watching and listening to people "air their dirty laundry" on the television and radio waves is another form of mass voyeurism, that there is an infinite consumer market for other people's misery and misfortune. They can't get enough of it. Do you agree or disagree? Support your position with your own interests and behavior regarding these kinds of shows.

Connecting

1. Relate what Schlessinger does to "socialize" her listeners to Goleman's notions in "Temperament Is Not Destiny" (chapter five).
2. Connecting the notions in "The Just-Do-It Shrink" with Chekhov's short story "Grief" in chapter two, "Wounds," gives us a way to look at where we turn to share our grief. What do Chekov and Schlessinger reveal as they respond to humans sharing their pain?

Bound by Suspicion

Michiko Kakutani

Cultural anthropologists—those who study cultures for a living—typically examine five institutions or markers to distinguish one culture from another: laws, customs, language, values, and ideology. Sometimes, if only for a few years, events in some of these markers align to produce a wave of thinking and feeling that ripples through a culture, infiltrates its artifacts, and invades its conversation. Such is the issue that Michiko Kakutani explores in "Bound by Suspicion," a look at how storytelling carried through the media affects our national consciousness.

Suspicion can provide a healthy balance to gullibility, but true paranoia is a sign of disordered thinking. Although there is no clear distinction between behaviors that can be called "normal" and those that are classified as disordered, psychologists and psychiatrists often diagnose a person who exhibits extreme sensitivity, suspiciousness, envy, and mistrust of others for no apparent reason as suffering from paranoid personality disorder (PPD). A person with this disorder also has a restricted range of emotions and, understandably, avoids closeness or intimacy with others.

The paranoia that Kakutani unveils in this essay has some noticeable similarities to PPD but, as the title suggests, it seems to attract rather than alienate people, heighten rather than lower the pitch of their emotions, and provoke wildly interesting, if improbable, stories.

Kakutani, who writes a weekly "Culture Zone" essay for the Sunday *New York Times,* looks at the manifestations of paranoia as a current blip on the pop culture radar screen affecting enough people in American society to merit a closer look.

What do "the X-Files," "Independence Day" and Joan Didion's latest novel have in common? What outlook do Louis Farrakhan and Pat Robertson share? What mind-set lumps together the C.I.A., space aliens, Communists, the Mafia and the United Nations as evil threats to our well being? 1

The answer, of course, is paranoia.

Back in the 70's, Henry Kissinger observed that "even a paranoid can have enemies," and in recent years his observation seems to have become a kind of watchword in American politics, embraced by everyone from right-wing radicals who believe that the Federal Government planned the Oklahoma City bombing to black militants who believe that the AIDS virus was deliberately created in a laboratory to infect blacks.

Although millennial anxieties seem to have fanned the flames of conspiracy thinking, paranoia itself is nothing new in American politics. (Remember the Communist plot to fluoridate American water?) What is new is the domino effect that this paranoid style is beginning to have in the realm of culture. In the last year or so, conspiracy thinking has been used as a narrative model by everyone from novelists to the makers of blockbuster movies. Paranoia is the motor that drives the cult TV show "The X-Files" as well as such new shows as "Millennium," "Dark Skies," "The Pretender" and "Profiler." It's also the premise behind Mel Gibson's next movie, "Conspiracy Theory," which is about a paranoid cabdriver whose outlandish fears start coming true. The new card game Netrunner is set in a "dark techno-future" in which "ruthless corporations scheme to accomplish secret agendas." And even the popular cult game that suggests that the actor Kevin Bacon is linked to every other actor in the world by no more than six degrees of separation conjures a universe of hidden connections.

Why, it's almost enough to make Oliver Stone sound like a sensible human 5
being.

No doubt the new paranoid style in American arts reflects the national mood: Watergate taught us to be suspicious, and later investigations (from Iran-contra to Whitewater) further fueled those suspicions. As for the demise of the Communist threat, it left us not with a new sense of security but with a flurry of free-floating suspicions.

At the same time, however, the art of paranoia is also a reflection of that oldest of human instincts—the narrative impulse. In Didion's new novel, "The Last Thing He Wanted," which pivots around an elaborate assassination plot, she describes storytellers as "weavers of conspiracy" who appreciate how every act has "logical if obscure consequences." And in the work of Thomas Pynchon, vast conspiratorial networks metastasize, symbols of either the overwhelming nature of reality in our information-mad world or simply the yearning for meaning, experienced by poor delusional human beings.

Add to this the fact that paranoia is a remarkably efficient narrative device. It enables its practitioners to build suspense, to indulge in portentous foreshadowing and to tie together incongruous loose ends into something that can be called a story. It can be used to create thrill-a-minute action films in which every offhand remark has a frightening payoff and huge, sprawling epics in which plausible resolutions exist only as projections in the paranoid audience's mind. After all, as every "X-Files" fan knows, the corollary to "Trust No One" is "The Truth Is Out There"—somewhere.

And yet the very notion that an explanation exists, that life is not random, is an old-fashioned, conservative view. Indeed, the last response to fin-de-siècle tensions—that is, the modernism forged in the upheavals of turn-of-the-century Europe and galvanized by World War I—produced not paranoia but an age (and art) of anxiety. A reaction against Enlightenment rationalism, modernism posited a world in which truth is, at best, subjective and logical explanations are suspect. Its esthetic lessons were the very opposite of those advanced by today's purveyors of paranoia. Instead of connecting events into conspiratorial plots, modernism gave us an esthetic of irony, ambiguity and fragmentation. (Think Kafka, think T. S. Eliot.) Instead of a world of secret cabals, it gave us a shadowy realm of radical discontinuity. Instead of omnipotent fixers like Cancer Man—the "X-Files" figure, supposedly involved in everything from J.F.K.'s assassination to the rigging of Buffalo Bills games—it gave us alienated loners acting on whim and impulse.

We are once again on the brink of a new century, faced with mind- 10
boggling changes like the breakdown of cold-war politics, the proliferation of new technologies and growing tensions among the races and sexes. One reaction—apparent in rap music and avant-garde fiction—has been to push discontinuity further, to celebrate incoherence. Another reaction, the paranoid reaction, has been to embrace an esthetic that does not mirror indeterminacy but defies it.

Shows like "The X-Files," "Dark Skies" (which suggests that many recent historical events, including the assassination of J.F.K., are connected to a secret alien invasion) and "Millennium" (which suggests that "all of this violence you read about in the paper these days may not be random") supposedly play to our worst neurotic fears. In reality, they actually help contain those worries by offering pat, systematic answers and a rationalistic (if ultimately irrational) view of the world.

Indeed, the art of paranoia turns out to be a profoundly traditional form, as reassuring, in its twisted way, as the old-fashioned detective story, which offers a similar Manichaean realm of clearly defined villains and innocents, victims and victimizers and readily decodable patterns.

A Government cover-up of pyramids discovered on Mars? An alien conspiracy to accelerate the greenhouse effect and wreak havoc on Earth? The mark of the beast in the Universal Product Code? However upsetting such beliefs may be, they also imply an orderly cosmos in which causality still obtains, human (or alien) will is paramount and inefficiency and accidents are unknown. Nothing is unexplained in the paranoid's universe; nothing is incoherent.

No wonder a poster in Mulder's "X-Files" office reads, "I Want to Believe."

Understanding

1. Test your media literacy. How many of the proper nouns in this piece can you identify?
2. Kakutani views paranoia as a reaction to modernism "in which truth is, at best, subjective and logical explanations are suspect" (paragraph 9). How does she support her view?
3. Besides the TV shows *The X Files* and *The Pretender* and the films *Independence Day* and *Conspiracy Theory,* other films such as *The Treasure of the Sierra Madre, The Caine Mutiny, Taxi Driver,* and Oliver Stone's *JFK* have depicted paranoid individuals or conjured up conspiracy theories. It could be, as Kakutani concludes, that "paranoia is a remarkably efficient narrative device" (paragraph 8)—it makes an interesting story. What makes paranoia such an interesting storytelling device?

4. People who are alert to social issues frequently ask specific questions to help them in their search for explanations. After gathering evidence from various points of view, they weigh what they have found and make a decision. Trace, through this essay, the questions that Kakutani asks about paranoia, how she sifts through what she found, and the conclusions she reaches.

Responding

1. How influenced are you by the paranoia that Kakutani describes? What do you think accounts for its continuing presence in American culture? Is it the result of a tainted water supply, the consequence of recreational drug use, the side effects of physician-prescribed medication, a reaction to powerlessness in the face of big government, or a nasty but harmless way to defy authority? Is any one of these interpretations more credible than another? Do they all apply? Are there other source(s) of this thinking? Explain.
2. Sometimes beliefs like the ones that Kakutani describes in paragraph 3—that the federal government planned the Oklahoma City bombing, that the AIDS virus was created in a laboratory to infect blacks—have some historical basis or a kernel of truth that grows into a conspiracy claim. Can you cite other conspiracy beliefs that have some basis in fact? What fact "kernels" got them started? What keeps them alive?
3. Kakutani conjectures that "millennial anxieties seem to have fanned the flames of conspiracy thinking." Americans enjoy an extremely high standard of living; our life expectancy is the longest ever in recorded history; no enemies threaten our shores; opportunities to work, go to school, and express our ideas freely abound. What possible "millennial anxieties" can Americans be prey to? What millennial anxieties do you experience?
4. All disorders suggest certain kinds of treatment to manage or cure them. Is the paranoia that Kakutani describes a "cultural personality disorder" that requires therapy? If so, what would you recommend? Or is paranoia, as she implies in the title of her essay, a bonding device that all cultures need from time to time to affirm their identity? Does it have this effect on you? Explain your position.

Connecting

1. So far as we know, paranoia is not an inborn trait but develops over the course of our growing up. Using Elkind's summary of "Erik Erikson's Eight Ages of Man" (chapter seven), consider in what stage(s) of development a person might be most vulnerable to developing this mind-set. What circumstances in a person's upbringing might cause it to develop?
2. What ideas from the readings in chapter five, "Biology and Identity," provide evidence either for or against the notion that the world is *not* random and that there is an orderly cosmos. Cite specific readings and references that reflect this view.

3. What specifics from Ventura's "Mickey Mantle's Summer" might contribute to Kakutani's exposition of paranoia in America today?

WRITING OPTION: Popular Culture

As you have seen from the readings in this section, *popular culture* refers to the cultural practices, artifacts, and icons of everyday life that appeal to large numbers of people.

From your responses to the questions following the readings, choose one that you think reflects your most careful observations, descriptions, or analysis. Revise that response as a narrative or as an essay using the *style* of any of the "Popular Culture" readings as models. Notice that the style is rich in descriptive detail, specific examples, and proper nouns.

If you choose a mostly narrative form, identify your point and then organize your experiences to demonstrate it clearly; for example, you might indicate what aspect of popular culture appeals to you, tell of an event that demonstrates its effect on you, the extent of your participation in or acceptance of it, and, especially, how it has affected who you express yourself to be (which may be different from who you are).

If you choose an analytical essay, confine your analysis to one trend and show what you think it means as viewed through your critical eyes.

Whatever your approach, assume that your reader is *not* familiar with the fad, fashion, or fascination that you are exploring.

PART TWO WRITING OPTION: Origins and Influences

Review the writing options you have written in this chapter and choose *three* that you would like to revise and develop for the "Origins and Influences" Writing Option. There are two ways to approach this:

1. You could choose one response from chapter five, "Biology and Identity," and two from chapter six, "Communities and Culture," and revise each of the three to demonstrate—under one cover—three different aspects of your identity, your self.
2. You could choose three from "Biology and Identity" *or* three from "Communities" *or* three from "Culture" to do a more intensive and focused study of how that particular influence has molded your identity.

This exploration will show an increased command of both inductive narrative writing (if you choose to continue to use the narrative form) and deductive writing (if your paper develops from a thesis to examples to support that claim). For example, if you write something similar to Mike Rose's "I Just Wanna Be Average," you will be using narrative development. However, note that the writer interjects himself into the story with analyses of what's going on *during* the story itself. He is commenting on his own story.

On the other hand, if you write a more issue-oriented paper like Loyal D. Rue's, you will state your claim up front and support that claim with examples from your own stories or from the other writers you have read. In this case, the analysis may come from what others say, and you will document your sources.

Both form and content are important and, where possible, each needs to show a relationship to or use the ideas from the selections you have been reading. In addition, this paper may incorporate material from your part one writing option as examples to support the points you make.

Part Three

Living Out Loud

The longest journey is the journey inwards Of him who has chosen his destiny . . . who has started upon his quest for the source of his being.

—Dag Hammarskjöld
Markings

Signatures ends with a flourish of individuality. It is, however, an individuality enriched by experience, reflection, and empathy. In part three, "Living Out Loud," the writers speak in voices of commitment and of responsibility for their choices. Here in chapter seven, "Taking Stands," are moments of assertion—moments of living out loud—when discovering what they believe and then acting on it becomes paramount in their lives.

We all have histories that culminate in these moments. As the readings in part two, "Origins and Influences," show, each person's identity emerges from the swirl of genetic potential, biological impact, and the traditions of community and culture. In our earliest years, the voices of others—parents, teachers, friends—make deep impressions on our thinking. It is likely, too, that we were touched by music. We listened to and identified with the songs of love and loneliness, of being footloose and of being tough. As much as for the sheer pleasure as for the affirmation of the messages, we sang along out loud, our voices blending with the vocals. These are some of the formative experiences that compose what psychotherapist Susan Vaughan calls our "story synthesizer," whose function is "to provide the plot lines and characters for the unique personal stories we bring to life whenever we interact with others." Some of these stories are included in part one, "Self-portraits"—the rich, authentic voices that told of gifts, wounds, decisions, and dreams. And throughout this anthology, you have told some of your own stories.

In much the same way that age deepens the voices of our childish selves and gives them resonance, time and circumstance alter how we see ourselves. We consider what others say but begin to develop our own opinions and speak for ourselves on matters that are important to us. We still sing songs, but we may try writing our own lyrics. We create our own style of dressing and speaking. We cultivate distinct preferences for what we like to eat and how we like to be entertained. These expressions of our identity, which Mihaly Csikszentmihalyi in "The World of the Self" calls "the illusion of selfhood," can empower us to do bold things, but, as he warns, they can also misguide us and be a source of trouble. Yet, as David Elkind tells us in "Erik Erikson's Eight

Ages of Man," we go through predictable stages of development. If we negotiate these stages successfully, we can emerge from them with "a basic confidence in [our] inner continuity amid change," a clearer notion of who we are and what we stand for.

At times when our identity is anchored in established social structures—family, church, school, work—we see ourselves primarily as parent, partner, student, or stockbroker. At these times we may give voice to how we should interpret these roles. In doing so we may even take stands against our own history, as William Raspberry does in "A Father, His Daughters, and a Lesson."

At other times, which may be painful or disorienting, our anchors are removed or we choose to throw them off. For the writers in "Taking Stands," these are opportunities to redirect or even reinvent themselves. Viktor E. Frankl wrote *Man's Search for Meaning,* from which "The Push and Pull of Values" is excerpted, after his experiences in a concentration camp; Martin Dugard writes "Running on Empty" after his involvement in extreme sports; Rafael Campo's stand in " 'Give Back to Your Community,' She Said" follows on an exhortation from his medical school dean; and Václav Havel in "Dear Olga" finds meaning in the "difficult circumstances" of his imprisonment.

Some experiences transcend the ordinary. James McBride in "A Jew Discovered" emerges with a new sense of self after a trip to his mother's hometown; John C. Glidewell links freedom to the availability of resources—at a fair price. In "Spring Storm" Yōko Mori uses the plot-turning device of a career move as an occasion for personal redirection; and Kweisi Mfume in "Nowhere to Run, Nowhere to Hide" finds that he will never be the same after a street-corner moment of truth. Others, like physician Victoria L. Macki's powerful stand on death and dying in "We Have No Real Choice about Death" result from quotidian experience.

Taking a few steps back from these personal affirmations, Daniel C. Dennett in "The Reality of Selves" investigates the source of our multiple selves, whereas in "Identity Crisis" Sherry Turkle expands on the times when we try to "get ourselves together," to find the "glue" that is the "essential us." Finally, Sarah Cirese in her manifesto, "Ultimately," makes her case for the importance of living one's life to the fullest.

The readings in "Living Out Loud" give voice to the human capacity to make sense of things and to construct a meaningful and well-measured life, a life whose commitments we are willing to make public. We present them as examples of the kinds of uncommon awarenesses we get when we venture beneath the surfaces of our selves, claim our consciousnesses, and take a stand. We hope that through them and through the questions that follow, you too will accept the challenge of living out loud.

7

Taking Stands

As explored in the readings in part two, "Origins and Influences," each person's identity emerges from genetic and biological history and from the stories, rituals, and legends of community and culture. The readings in part three, "Living Out Loud," move us to consider how we negotiate these epic influences on our lives and how we recognize and reposition the multiple aspects of our selves.

We do not delve here into the philosophy, the psychology, or the science of the "self," although some of the readings approach the subject from these points of view. Rather we offer them to you as an incentive to experience, through the final writing option, what psychologist Erik Erikson called "a basic confidence in one's inner continuity amid change"—*identity.*

Three facets of the self come forward in these readings: the *physical* self; the social or *expressive* self; and the *transcendent* self, the self that goes beyond ordinary perception and feeling. Realistically, of course, we cannot separate the self into distinct "parts." The physical self cannot function without a social context, and the transcendent self cannot function without both. Yet there are moments when one of these selves moves to center stage while the others play supporting roles. Equally important are those moments when we try to "get ourselves together," to find the "glue" that is the "essential us," as Sherry Turkle remarks in "Identity Crisis." These moments represent our moving toward an integrated self.

The most intimate guide to our physical self is the brain. Is this structure, the "three-pound monster" explored in chapter five, "Biology and Identity," the same as the "mind"? Is it a host for the mind? Is it the source of our "self," as Daniel C. Dennett argues in "The Reality of Selves"? We know that the brain is the "executive service center" of all our actions, but it may mislead us. In "The World of the Self," Mihaly Csikszentmihalyi explains how this executive function—the ego—or the "illusion of selfhood" can be a "source of trouble" in our search for a good life.

The social or expressive self takes center stage in this search. In order for this self to play the roles for which it was born, other people—real or imagined—are necessary to complete the story line.

Some roles are temporary; others, such as the role of parent, last a lifetime. In "A Father, His Daughters, and a Lesson," William Raspberry faults himself for not performing the role of father to his daughters in ways that would have benefitted them most. But how was he to know? For some roles we get no scripts and little rehearsal.

From time to time amid all the roles we play—parent, friend, free spirit—we think about what they add up to. The process of sorting through and integrating our social roles and "masks"—what Carl Jung called *individuation*—is what Rafael Campo tries to do in " 'Give Back to Your Community,' She Said" and what Sherry Turkle unravels in "Identity Crisis."

We suspect that if Raspberry, Campo, and Turkle were to write their essays five years from now, they might have an entirely different slant. That's because, as David Elkind conveys in "Erik Erikson's Eight Ages of Man," we have the capacity to "become," to develop ourselves in a continuous lifelong process. This awareness of ourselves as continuously becoming opens up the world of possibilities. It fills many with the confidence that sends Sarah Cirese singing a hymn to her possibilities in "Ultimately." The perception of possibilities also leads people to great achievements and life-threatening challenges, like the Raid Gauloises that Martin Dugard chronicles in "Running on Empty." For those who push themselves to the limits of their endurance out of choice and not necessity, the *freedom* to act may mean as much as the action itself.

Viktor E. Frankl's excerpt from *Man's Search for Meaning* tells us that this freedom can empower us to make moral and personally meaningful decisions and make us vulnerable to what he calls the "pull of values." John C. Glidewell in "On Freedom and Resources" explains how being free is related to the resources at our disposal. The characters in Mori Yōko's "Spring Storm" spend an uncomfortable afternoon sifting through possibilities before deciding on how to express their freedom.

Freedom, in the physical sense, is something that Václav Havel lacked when he wrote "Dear Olga." And yet the "difficult circumstances" of his imprisonment did little to prevent him from finding meaning in his existence—a mission to which he has committed his creative and his public life.

There are moments when one feels utterly free of the "veils of Maya" that Csikszentmihalyi keeps reminding us cloud our perception. James McBride in the excerpt from *The Color of Water* and Kweisi Mfume in "Nowhere to Run, Nowhere to Hide" describe moments when, liberated from their own identification with human limitations and labels, they transcended their ordinary "self" to arrive at an altered state of awareness.

Nowhere does freedom matter more than in questions of life and death. Many believe, as does Sarah Cirese, that their "quests are ultimately fulfilled in the living" of their lives. Others regard the living of their earthly lives as a prelude to eternal life. This may be the meaning behind Victoria Macki's standpoint on physician-assisted suicide in "We Have No Real Choice about Death." The questions she invites the reader to answer may help you frame yours.

Moving toward an integrated self means recognizing your links with the past, your engagement in the present, and your intentions for the future that only you can discover by looking within yourself. The Responding questions at the end of each reading are meant to open all ports to the memory, perception, and feeling of your self so that you can accept the challenge of discovery that awaits you in your writing.

The World of the Self

Mihaly Csikszentmihalyi

Through the title of his book *The Evolving Self,* Csikszentmihalyi communicates his view that we are dynamic, continually changing individuals. He argues that we can, and must, change for the better. To begin to do that, he advises the reader to be aware of those distortions—the veils of Maya—that keep us from moving in this direction.

Csikszentmihalyi has already presented two veils of Maya: our *genes* which, through evolution, carry extremely detailed scripts for certain behaviors which may or may not be useful today, and our *culture,* the web of values, norms, and viewpoints that influence our behavior from the outside, sometimes without our knowing it. In "The World of the Self," he presents what he calls the illusion of selfhood or the ego as the third and last veil.

Happy people, the author asserts, can overcome the constraints imposed by biology and culture to carve out a small freedom of choice. This description of a "self" liberated to make choices from alternatives makes Csikszentmihalyi's an optimistic blueprint for personal development.

Instinctual desires and cultural values work their way into consciousness from the outside, so to speak. The first start as chemical impulses that we interpret as true needs, the second begin as social conventions that we internalize as inevitable. The third distortion of reality begins in the mind and works itself out: it is the side effect of being conscious—the illusion of selfhood. 1

As we have seen earlier, self-reflective consciousness is a recent development in human evolution, but exactly how recent, no one knows. Certainly the genetic instructions are much older; probably cultural instructions also developed earlier than the advent of self-reflection. It has even been proposed that it was only about three thousand years ago that people began to realize that they were thinking. Before that point, ideas and emotions passed through the mind on their own, without any conscious control. A Greek warrior or a Sumerian priest followed instinct and convention; when a new idea occurred to him, he believed it was sent by a god or spirit.

It is unlikely that we will ever be able to determine with any precision when people started to realize that they could control their mental processes. Unlike arrowheads and pots, traces of self-reflection cannot be dug out of the remains of early settlements. The event was so inconspicuous that it left no evidence: not with a bang but a whisper did the era of consciousness begin. Whenever the ability developed, it was one of the most momentous events that happened on our planet. Not even the asteroids alleged to have put an end to the age of the dinosaurs some 65 million years ago brought so great a change into the world.

Why was this event so important? Partly, of course, it was because conscious manipulation of mental content made new inventions and new technology much easier to envision, and to adopt once invented. But even more significantly, once the mind realized its autonomy, individuals were able to conceive of themselves as independent agents with their own self-interest. For the first time, it was possible for people to emancipate themselves from the rule of genes and of culture. A person could now have unique dreams, and take an individual stance based on personal goals.

While the self brought the gift of personal freedom, it also spun another 5
veil, as thick as the two earlier ones: the illusions of the ego. Selfishness is an eternal part of living, and ruthless bullies must have been abundant long before men and women started to control their own minds through the ability to reflect. But once the self developed, it brought its own distortions to bear. Let us consider Zorg, the imaginary leader of a group of hominids far enough in the past to be prior to the advent of self-reflective consciousness. Zorg knows he is the leader because if he decides to walk in a certain direction the tribe will follow. Likewise, if he snarls, the others cringe. When prompted by hunger or sexual desires, Zorg takes advantage of his dominant position to take more than his share. Occasionally he may throw a tantrum and hurt some of his fellows. He is clearly selfish, but his selfishness lacks an essential component that only a person with a reflective ego can have: Zorg is not ambitious, and he does not try to accumulate power in an abstract sense. His bids for dominance are the result of genetic instructions and the feedback he receives from others; they are temporary, context-driven attempts. He does not even try to accumulate more property than his peers; after all, hunter-gatherers own no real estate, and movable goods are a great burden to carry around.

It could be said that Zorg's perspective is severely limited by what biology and culture allow him to experience. But he remains free from all those biases that are the by-product of a mind conscious of itself. The Pharaohs, the rulers of Mesopotamia, of the Indus River valley, of ancient China, were different from Zorg not only in that they had immensely greater resources to draw upon, but also because each had a sense of his own unique individuality. And once an ego is present, its foremost goal becomes that of protecting itself at all costs. Thus tens of thousands of Egyptian slaves had to give up their lives to build the pyramids so that the Pharaoh's ego could live on; the thousands of statues buried in the tombs of the Chinese emperors were laboriously shaped for the same purpose.

On a smaller scale, insatiable egos were devouring the psychic energy of people in almost every ancient human group we know about. When the chieftain of one of those nomadic troops of horsemen who were constantly swooping down from the steppes of Central Asia to ravage the more settled regions of Europe and Asia happened to die, he was buried with his horses, weapons, and jewelry—and also his women and servants, so they could serve the dear departed in the afterlife.

The *Iliad,* that most revered epic of the European past, gives an excellent description of how the ego of a Greek warrior worked. The poem begins with a meeting of the leaders of the Greek army that is besieging the enemy city of Troy. The siege has lasted for many years and so far has been a fiasco; the Greeks are tired, homesick, and ravaged by disease. The council is trying to resolve a squabble between two great chiefs that is threatening to disrupt the Greek alliance and end the war in an ignominious retreat. Agamemnon, leader of the largest of the army's factions, claims that the meager spoils the Greeks have won so far have been distributed unfairly: Achilles got more than he deserved. Achilles, the young prince whose reckless valor has made him the most admired among the Greeks, objects heatedly that he is entitled to all the prizes he has won. Agamemnon insists that, unless he is granted Briseis, a Trojan princess who had been awarded to Achilles, he will pull out with his troops. The other leaders fear that if Agamemnon and his many soldiers leave, the war will be lost, so they reluctantly force Achilles to give up the girl. The rest of the *Iliad* tells of the consequences of this action: sulking Achilles refuses to fight any longer; without him the war turns even worse for the Greeks; the gods descend from Olympus to take sides with the various factions and against each other . . . and so on and on, until the proud towers of Troy finally fall, engulfed in flames.

The point is that the conflict that sets the stage for the *Iliad* is a contest between two men caught in the need to satisfy their egos. Neither Achilles nor Agamemnon particularly values the wretched Trojan princess: she simply happens to be a symbol, a prize that publicly identifies the best man. But the two great warriors are ready to ruin themselves, their families and friends, in order to protect the idea of self nurtured in their minds. As soon as a hero becomes self-conscious, he identifies his whole being with his reputation. And once he does that, in order to continue existing, he must keep up his reputation at whatever cost.

The example from the *Iliad* also illustrates that, with the advent of reflec- 10
tive consciousness, the ego begins to use possessions to symbolize the self. As William James clearly saw: "A man's Self is the sum-total of all that he can call his, not only his body, and his psychic powers, but his clothes and his house, his wife and children, his ancestors and friends, his reputation and works, his land and horse and yacht and bank account."

The problem is that the more the ego becomes identified with symbols outside the self the more vulnerable it becomes. James goes on to write that the sudden loss of one's possessions results in a "shrinkage of our personality, a partial conversion of ourselves to nothingness." To prevent its annihilation, the ego forces us to be constantly on the watch for anything that might threaten the symbols on which it relies. Our view of the world becomes polarized into "good" and "bad"; to the first belong those things that support the image of the self, to the second those that threaten it. This is how the third veil of Maya works: it distorts reality so as to make it congruent with the needs of the ego.

The ideas that become central representations of the self are those in which a person invests the most psychic energy. For the Greek warriors it was honor, for the early Christians it was religious faith. There were times when Christians forced to choose between death and rejection of their faith chose death, because annihilation of a self built upon a religious foundation would have been worse. In the thirteenth century the Cathars of southern France let themselves be killed by the thousands rather than give up their worldview, a view that other Christians believed to be heresy. Of the major religions today only Islam seems to command this degree of total allegiance. At least in technological societies, people rarely build their egos around religious faith any longer.

Currently the symbols of the self tend to be more of the material kind. Scratch the paint on someone's new car, and he's liable to kill you. If psychic energy is invested in a home, furniture, a retirement plan, or stocks, then these will be the objects that must be protected in order to ensure the safety of the self. The advantages of identifying the self with possessions are obvious. The man who drives a Rolls-Royce is immediately recognized by everyone as someone successful and important. Objects give concrete evidence of their owner's power, and the ego can increase its boundaries almost indefinitely by claiming control over greater quantities of material possessions. But the more the self becomes identified with external objects, the more vulnerable it becomes. After all, nobody can really control fame and fortune—not an absolute ruler like Alexander the Great, not a multibillionaire like Robert Maxwell—and for those who depend too much on them to define who they are, any threat to acquisitions will threaten the core of being. It is for this reason that religious and philosophical systems have always been so ambivalent about material strivings, and prescribed instead the development of a self that has a value independent of external accomplishments.

Objects are not the only external symbols by which the ego represents the self. Kinship and other human relationships are also very important. We invest a great deal of attention in those who are close to us, and thus they become indispensable to our sense of who we are. Especially in societies where fewer material possessions are available, ties with others are the central, defining components of the self. Even the war described in the *Iliad* started because Paris, one of the sons of the Trojan king, eloped with the wife of Agamemnon's brother. The symbolism of her leaving was intolerable to the egos of the principals involved.

Human relationships seem a much sounder basis for building an image 15
of the self than material possessions. Unfortunately the temptation to use other people to aggrandize one's ego is also quite strong, and many people find it difficult to resist. Parents who are overprotective of their children, lovers who are exceedingly jealous, paternalistic employers, revolutionaries ready to sacrifice lives for the good of humankind often do not care much for the well-being of the people with whom they interact. The effort to "help" or "protect" is often a way of demonstrating the ability to control, and therefore the power of the self.

Because the ego is such a source of trouble, there have been many efforts made to abolish it. Some of the Eastern religions have come up with the most radical prescriptions to this effect. Their arguments are quite logical: If a person refuses to invest psychic energy in goals, gives up desires, and does not identify with any idea, belief, object, or human relationship, then in a certain sense he or she becomes invulnerable. By our nature we want certain things to happen; when our desires are frustrated, we suffer. By giving up expectation and desire—in effect, by giving up the self—one can no longer be frustrated. Whatever happens will be acceptable. A vulgarized version of this solution seems to have imbued the attitude of many young people these last few decades. The expression "It's no problem," and the statement "I'm O.K., you're O.K." are distant cousins of that detached stance.

Could the radical project of ridding oneself of the self succeed? It is unlikely that a society would survive if a majority of its people were to become entirely selfless. And even if one were successful in giving up desires, one must at the same time by necessity also give up hope, ambition, and striving for a better, or even for a different, future. The person without an ego—if he or she actually exists—is a great rarity, an exemplary specimen that is a useful model to show us that this also is a possibility. But it is not likely to be the way of the third millennium.

If there are to be a thousand years longer in which we will evolve, however, it will be necessary to find better ways to build selves. The type of ego that might pull us through is one secure enough to forgo desires beyond what are necessary. It will be one that relies on possessions that are not scarce. Instead of competing for the same symbolic resources, as Achilles and Agamemnon did, it will be satisfied with what is unique about itself and its experiences. And despite greater individuality, it will be a self identified with the greatest common good—not only with kin and country, but with humanity as a whole, and beyond humanity, with the principle of life itself, with the process of evolution. It is difficult to see at this point how humanity can survive otherwise.

The first stages toward constructing such a self involve clearing the mind of the illusions that drain psychic energy and leave us impotent to control our lives. These illusions are the inevitable consequence of being born of flesh, in a human culture, with a brain complex enough to have become conscious of its own workings. They are inevitable, but they are not inescapable. To become free of the facticity of existence, at first we need only to step back and reflect on what makes us function. As we begin to see behind our acts the control being exerted by genes, by the culture, and by the ego, and as we realize the extent to which we are following their instructions, we might become discouraged and hopeless. But the harsh winds of reality are bracing as well. The realization that many of our actions are not of our choosing is the first step toward the development of a more authentic, more genuinely individual agenda.

20 People who lead a satisfying life, who are in tune with their past and with their future—in short, people whom we would call "happy"—are generally individuals who have lived their lives according to rules they themselves created. They eat according to their own schedules, sleep when they are sleepy, work because they enjoy doing it, choose their friends and relationships for good reasons. They understand their motives and their limitations. They have carved out a small freedom of choice. Typically they are not people who want

much for themselves. They may be ambitious dreamers, great builders and doers, but their goals are not selfish in any of the three senses of serving the goals of the genes, the culture, or the ego. They do what they do because they enjoy meeting the challenges of life, because they enjoy life itself. They feel that they are part of the universal order, and identify themselves with harmonious growth. It is this kind of self that will make survival into the third millennium possible.

Understanding

1. What is "self-reflective consciousness"? If, as Csikszentmihalyi imagines, Zorg is the leader of an imaginary group of hominids predating self-reflective consciousness (paragraph 5), how could Zorg "know" he is the leader?
2. Based on Csikszentmihalyi's observations, define *ego*. What are the advantages and disadvantages of the ego representing itself by objects and by kinship?
3. Csikszentmihalyi indicates that in technological societies the ego has supplanted religious faith. Why is this so? Under what circumstances might this trend be reversed? Under what circumstances might it be reinforced?
4. Csikszentmihalyi has a millennarian view of evolution, that is, that it will produce a better self, one that is happier, less destructive, and more humane. How does he see this movement happening?

Responding

1. Recall a time in your life when you were aware that you were aware of yourself, other people, and your environment. What was that time? Capture that awareness in a narrative. How much of what you recall has been flavored by the telling and retelling of stories in your family? How much is a product of your own experience?
2. Usually, a proposal to improve a condition in society is based on some clue within society already. In medieval times in Christian societies, men and women formed religious communities apart from the world, dedicated to selflessness; and in the Far East, many eastern religions sought the abandonment of "self" as a means of purification. Where in today's society might an interested observer find a clue to the kind of society that Csikszentmihalyi envisions? How realistic is his proposal that we must "find better ways to build selves" (paragraph 18)? Explain.
3. If you were asked to devise a plan to find better ways to build selves, whom would you call upon to assist you in working it out? What particular attributes or gifts would these people bring to the discussion? To what readings or resources would you refer? What would the challenges in formulating such a plan be?
4. Many social and cultural constructions contribute to our sense of personal importance. Once we acquire our language, we use it without much

thought as to how it contributes to our sense of self. Yet if it is challenged, or if we were denied its use, we would think ourselves deprived of an important marker of our identity. Other than language, what social or cultural aspects of your life contribute to your sense of self?

5. Identify those social interactions that produce a feeling of violation of your "self" (for example, when a driver cuts you off on an expressway) and those that you think enhance your self (e.g., when a work of which you are proud is recognized as such by others). Which of these kinds of reactions expand your freedom to be you? Which limit them?
6. What is it that you must absolutely hold on to in order to keep your self?

Connecting

Relate Csikszentmihalyi's explanation of William James's statement in paragraph 10 that "A man's Self is the sum-total of all that he can call his . . ." to the experiences of the people profiled in Bragg's "Big Holes Where the Dignity Used to Be" (chapter four).

Erik Erikson's Eight Ages of Man

David Elkind

A basic confidence in one's inner continuity amid change. This is how psychoanalyst and author Erik Erikson (1903–94) has described *identity.*

A friend and disciple of Sigmund Freud, Erikson is best known for the theory that each stage of life is associated with a particular struggle that contributes to defining one's personality. This view extended Freud's notions that identity was shaped primarily in infancy and childhood. One identity-shaping event not pointed out in this reading is worth noting: Erik Erikson never met his birth father or his mother's first husband and was known throughout his youth as Erik Homburger—the name of his pediatrician, who later became his mother's second husband.

Known primarily for the stage theory presented in this reading, Erikson's ideas shaped the field of child development and life-span studies and added credibility to a form of historical reporting called *psychobiography,* the approach to history that considers personal lives as well as historical forces. Optimistic until the last years of his life, Erikson wrote *The Life Cycle Completed* in 1982 and, in 1986, *Vital Involvements in Old Age,* with Joan Serson, his wife of more than fifty years, and Helen Kwnick. The eight stages of development first appeared in Erikson's landmark work, *Childhood and Society.*

Child psychologist David Elkind is currently professor of child study at Tufts University in Medford, Massachusetts. Prior to Tufts he was professor of psychology, psychiatry, and education at the University of Rochester. He is best known for three recent books, *The Hurried Child, All Grown Up and No Place to Go,* and *Miseducation.*

At a recent faculty reception I happened to join a small group in which a young mother was talking about her "identity crisis." She and her husband, she said, had decided not to have any more children and she was depressed at the thought of being past the child-bearing stage. It was as if, she continued, she had been robbed of some part of herself and now needed to find a new function to replace the old one. 1

When I remarked that her story sounded like a case history from a book by Erik Erikson, she replied, "Who's Erikson?" It is a reflection on the intellectual modesty and literary decorum of Erik H. Erikson, psychoanalyst and professor of developmental psychology at Harvard, that so few of the many people who today talk about the "identity crisis" know anything of the man who pointed out its pervasiveness as a problem in contemporary society two decades ago.

Erikson has, however, contributed more to social science than his delineation of identity problems in modern man. His descriptions of the stages of the life cycle, for example, have advanced psychoanalytic theory to the point where it can now describe the development of the healthy personality on its own terms and not merely as the opposite of a sick one. Likewise, Erikson's emphasis upon the problems unique to adolescents and adults living in today's society has helped to rectify the one-sided emphasis on childhood as the beginning and end of personality development.

Finally, in his biographical studies, such as "Young Man Luther" and "Gandhi's Truth" (which has just won a National Book Award in philosophy and religion), Erikson emphasizes the inherent strengths of the human personality by showing how individuals can use their neurotic symptoms and conflicts for creative and constructive social purposes while healing themselves in the process.

5 It is important to emphasize that Erikson's contributions are genuine advances in psychoanalysis in the sense that Erikson accepts and builds upon many of the basic tenets of Freudian theory. In this regard, Erikson differs from Freud's early co-workers such as Jung and Adler who, when they broke with Freud, rejected his theories and substituted their own.

Likewise, Erikson also differs from the so-called neo-Freudians such as Horney, Kardiner and Sullivan who (mistakenly, as it turned out) assumed that Freudian theory had nothing to say about man's relation to reality and to his culture. While it is true that Freud emphasized, even mythologized, sexuality, he did so to counteract the rigid sexual taboos of his time, which, at that point in history, were frequently the cause of neuroses. In his later writings, however, Freud began to concern himself with the executive agency of the personality, namely the ego, which is also the repository of the individual's attitudes and concepts about himself and his world.

It is with the psychosocial development of the ego that Erikson's observations and theoretical constructions are primarily concerned. Erikson has thus been able to introduce innovations into psychoanalytic theory without either rejecting or ignoring Freud's monumental contribution.

The man who has accomplished this notable feat is a handsome Dane, whose white hair, mustache, resonant accent and gentle manner are reminiscent of actors like Jean Hersholt and Paul Muni. Although he is warm and outgoing with friends, Erikson is a rather shy man who is uncomfortable in the spotlight of public recognition. This trait, together with his ethical reservations about making public even disguised case material, may help to account for Erikson's reluctance to publish his observations and conceptions (his first book appeared in 1950, when he was 48).

In recent years this reluctance to publish has diminished and he has been appearing in print at an increasing pace. Since 1960 he has published three books, "Insight and Responsibility," "Identity: Youth and Crisis" and "Gandhi's Truth," as well as editing a fourth, "Youth: Change and Challenge." Despite the accolades and recognition these books have won for him, both in America and abroad, Erikson is still surprised at the popular interest they have generated and is a little troubled about the possibility of being misunderstood and misinterpreted. While he would prefer that his books spoke for themselves and that he was left out of the picture, he has had to accede to popular demand for more information about himself and his work.

The course of Erikson's professional career has been as diverse as it has been unconventional. He was born in Frankfurt, Germany, in 1902 of Danish parents. Not long after his birth his father died, and his mother later married the pediatrician who had cured her son of a childhood illness. Erikson's stepfather urged him to become a physician, but the boy declined and became an artist instead—an artist who did portraits of children. Erikson says of his post-adolescent years, "I was an artist then, which in Europe is a euphemism for a young man with some talent and nowhere to go." During this period he settled in Vienna and worked as a tutor in a family friendly with Freud's. He met Freud on informal occasions when the families went on outings together.

These encounters may have been the impetus to accept a teaching appointment at an American school in Vienna founded by Dorothy Burlingham and directed by Peter Blos (both now well known on the American psychiatric scene). During these years (the late nineteen-twenties) he also undertook and completed psychoanalytic training with Anna Freud and August Aichhorn. Even at the outset of his career, Erikson gave evidence of the breadth of his interests and activities by being trained and certified as a Montessori teacher. Not surprisingly, in view of that training, Erikson's first articles dealt with psychoanalysis and education.

It was while in Vienna that Erikson met and married Joan Mowat Serson, an American artist of Canadian descent. They came to America in 1933, when Erikson was invited to practice and teach in Boston. Erikson was, in fact, one of the first if not the first child-analyst in the Boston area. During the next two decades he held clinical and academic appointments at Harvard, Yale and Berkeley. In 1951 he joined a group of psychiatrists and psychologists who moved to Stockbridge, Mass., to start a new program at the Austen Riggs Center, a private residential treatment center for disturbed young people. Erikson remained at Riggs until 1961, when he was appointed professor of human development and lecturer on psychiatry at Harvard. Throughout his career he has always held two or three appointments simultaneously and has traveled extensively.

Perhaps because he had been an artist first, Erikson has never been a conventional psychoanalyst. When he was treating children, for example, he always insisted on visiting his young patients' homes and on having dinner with the families. Likewise, in the nineteen-thirties, when anthropological investigation was described to him by his friends Scudder McKeel, Alfred Kroeber and Margaret Mead, he decided to do field work on an Indian reservation. "When I realized that Sioux is the name which we [in Europe] pronounced "See ux" and which for us was *the* American Indian, I could not resist." Erikson thus antedated the anthropologists who swept over the Indian reservations in the post-Depression years. (So numerous were the field workers at that time that the stock joke was that an Indian family could be defined as a mother, a father, children and an anthropologist.)

Erikson did field work not only with the Oglala Sioux of Pine Ridge, S.D. (the tribe that slew Custer and was in turn slaughtered at the Battle of Wounded Knee), but also with the salmon-fishing Yurok of Northern California. His reports on these experiences revealed his special gift for sensing and entering into the world views and modes of thinking of cultures other than his own.

It was while he was working with the Indians that Erikson began to note syndromes which he could not explain within the confines of traditional psychoanalytic theory. Central to many an adult Indian's emotional problems seemed to be his sense of uprootedness and lack of continuity between his present life-style and that portrayed in tribal history. Not only did the Indian sense a break with the past, but he could not identify with a future requiring assimilation of the white culture's values. The problems faced by such men, Erikson recognized, had to do with the ego and with culture and only incidentally with sexual drives.

The impressions Erikson gained on the reservations were reinforced during World War II when he worked at a veterans' rehabilitation center at Mount Zion Hospital in San Francisco. Many of the soldiers he and his colleagues saw seemed not to fit the traditional "shell shock" or "malingerer" cases of World War I. Rather, it seemed to Erikson that many of these men had lost the sense of who and what they were. They were having trouble reconciling their activities, attitudes and feelings as soldiers with the activities, attitudes and feelings they had known before the war. Accordingly, while these men may well have had difficulties with repressed or conflicted drives, their main problem seemed to be, as Erikson came to speak of it at the time, "identity confusion."

It was almost a decade before Erikson set forth the implications of his clinical observations in "Childhood and Society." In that book, the summation and integration of 15 years of research, he made three major contributions to the study of the human ego. He posited (1) that, side by side with the stages of psychosexual development described by Freud (the oral, anal, phallic, genital, Oedipal and pubertal), were psychosocial stages of ego development, in which the individual had to establish new basic orientations to himself and his social world; (2) that personality development continued throughout the whole life cycle; and (3) that each stage had a positive *as well as* a negative component.

Much about these contributions—and about Erikson's way of thinking—can be understood by looking at his scheme of life stages. Erikson identifies eight stages in the human life cycle, in each of which a new dimension of "social interaction" becomes possible—that is, a new dimension in a person's interaction with himself, and with his social environment.

TRUST VS. MISTRUST

The first stage corresponds to the oral stage in classical psychoanalytic theory and usually extends through the first year of life. In Erikson's view, the new dimension of social interaction that emerges during this period involves

Freud's "Ages of Man"

Erik Erikson's definition of the "eight ages of man" is a work of synthesis and insight by a psychoanalytically trained and worldly mind. Sigmund Freud's description of human phases stems from his epic psychological discoveries and centers almost exclusively on the early years of life. A brief summary of the phases posited by Freud:

Oral stage—roughly the first year of life, the period during which the mouth region provides the greatest sensual satisfaction. Some derivative behavioral traits which may be seen at this time are *incorporativeness* (first six months of life) and *aggressiveness* (second six months of life).

Anal stage—roughly the second and third years of life. During this period the site of greatest sensual pleasure shifts to the anal and urethral areas. Derivative behavioral traits are *retentiveness* and *expulsiveness.*

Phallic stage—roughly the third and fourth years of life. The site of greatest sensual pleasure during this stage is the genital region. Behavior traits derived from this period include *intrusiveness* (male) and *receptiveness* (female).

Oedipal stage—roughly the fourth and fifth years of life. At this stage the young person takes the parent of the opposite sex as the object or provider of sensual satisfaction and regards the same-sexed parent as a rival. (The "family romance.") Behavior traits originating in this period are *seductiveness* and *competitiveness.*

Latency stage—roughly the years from age 6 to 11. The child resolves the Oedipus conflict by identifying with the parent of the opposite sex and by so doing satisfies sensual needs vicariously. Behavior traits developed during this period include *conscience* (or the internalization of parental moral and ethical demands).

Puberty stage—roughly 11 to 14. During this period there is an integration and subordination of oral, anal and phallic sensuality to an overriding and unitary genital *sexuality*. The genital sexuality of puberty has another young person of the opposite sex as its object, and discharge (at least for boys) as its aim. Derivative behavior traits (associated with the control and regulation of genital sexuality) are *intellectualization* and *estheticism.*

basic *trust* at the one extreme, and *mistrust* at the other. The degree to which the child comes to trust the world, other people and himself depends to a considerable extent upon the quality of the care that he receives. The infant whose needs are met when they arise, whose discomforts are quickly removed, who is cuddled, fondled, played with and talked to, develops a sense of the world as a safe place to be and of people as helpful and dependable. When, however, the care is inconsistent, inadequate and rejecting, it fosters a basic mistrust, an attitude of fear and suspicion on the part of the infant toward the world in general and people in particular that will carry through to later stages of development.

It should be said at this point that the problem of basic trust-versus- 20
mistrust (as is true for all the later dimensions) is not resolved once and for all during the first year of life; it arises again at each successive stage of development. There is both hope and danger in this. The child who enters school with a sense of mistrust may come to trust a particular teacher who has taken the trouble to make herself trustworthy; with this second chance, he overcomes his early mistrust. On the other hand, the child who comes through infancy with a vital sense of trust can still have his sense of mistrust activated at a later stage if, say, his parents are divorced and separated under acrimonious circumstances.

This point was brought home to me in a very direct way by a 4-year-old patient I saw in a court clinic. He was being seen at the court clinic because his adoptive parents, who had had him for six months, now wanted to give him back to the agency. They claimed that he was cold and unloving, took things and could not be trusted. He was indeed a cold and apathetic boy, but with good reason. About a year after his illegitimate birth, he was taken away from his mother, who had a drinking problem, and was shunted back and forth among several foster homes. Initially he had tried to relate to the persons in the foster homes, but the relationships never had a chance to develop because he was moved at just the wrong times. In the end he gave up trying to reach out to others, because the inevitable separations hurt too much.

Like the burned child who dreads the flame, this emotionally burned child shunned the pain of emotional involvement. He had trusted his mother, but now he trusted no one. Only years of devoted care and patience could now undo the damage that had been done to this child's sense of trust.

AUTONOMY VS. DOUBT

Stage Two spans the second and third years of life, the period which Freudian theory calls the anal stage. Erikson sees here the emergence of *autonomy*. This autonomy dimension builds upon the child's new motor and mental abilities. At this stage the child can not only walk but also climb, open and close, drop, push and pull, hold and let go. The child takes pride in these new accomplishments and wants to do everything himself, whether it be pulling the wrapper off a piece of candy, selecting the vitamin out of the bottle or flushing the toilet. If parents recognize the young child's need to do what he is capable of doing at his own pace and in his own time, then he develops a sense that he is able to control his muscles, his impulses, himself and, not insignificantly, his environment—the sense of autonomy.

When, however, his caretakers are impatient and do for him what he is capable of doing himself, they reinforce a sense of shame and doubt. To be sure, every parent has rushed a child at times and children are hardy enough to endure such lapses. It is only when caretaking is consistently overprotective and criticism of "accidents" (whether these be wetting, soiling, spilling or breaking things) is harsh and unthinking that the child develops an excessive sense of shame with respect to other people and an excessive sense of doubt about his own abilities to control his world and himself.

If the child leaves this stage with less autonomy than shame or doubt, he will be handicapped in his attempts to achieve autonomy in adolescence and adulthood. Contrariwise, the child who moves through this stage with his sense of autonomy buoyantly outbalancing his feelings of shame and doubt is well prepared to be autonomous at later phases in the life cycle. Again, however, the balance of autonomy to shame and doubt set up during this period can be changed in either positive or negative directions by later events.

It might be well to note, in addition, that too much autonomy can be as harmful as too little. I have in mind a patient of 7 who had a heart condition. He had learned very quickly how terrified his parents were of any signs in him of cardiac difficulty. With the psychological acuity given to children, he soon ruled the household. The family could not go shopping, or for a drive, or on a holiday if he did not approve. On those rare occasions when the parents had had enough and defied him, he would get angry and his purple hue and gagging would frighten them into submission.

Actually, this boy was frightened of this power (as all children would be) and was really eager to give it up. When the parents and the boy came to realize this, and to recognize that a little shame and doubt were a healthy counterpoise to an inflated sense of autonomy, the three of them could once again assume their normal roles.

INITIATIVE VS. GUILT

In this stage (the genital stage of classical psychoanalysis) the child, age 4 to 5, is pretty much master of his body and can ride a tricycle, run, cut and hit. He can thus initiate motor activities of various sorts on his own and no longer merely responds to or imitates the actions of other children. The same holds true for his language and fantasy activities. Accordingly, Erikson argues that the social dimension that appears at this stage has *initiative* at one of its poles and *guilt* at the other.

Whether the child will leave this stage with his sense of initiative far outbalancing his sense of guilt depends to a considerable extent upon how parents respond to his self-initiated activities. Children who are given much freedom and opportunity to initiate motor play such as running, bike riding, sliding, skating, tussling and wrestling have their sense of initiative reinforced.

Initiative is also reinforced when parents answer their children's questions (intellectual initiative) and do not deride or inhibit fantasy or play activity. On the other hand, if the child is made to feel that his motor activity is bad, that his questions are a nuisance and that his play is silly and stupid, then he may develop a sense of guilt over self-initiated activities in general that will persist through later life stages.

INDUSTRY VS. INFERIORITY

Stage Four is the age period from 6 to 11, the elementary school years 30
(described by classical psychoanalysis as the *latency phase*). It is a time during which the child's love for the parent of the opposite sex and rivalry with the same sexed parent (elements in the so-called family romance) are quiescent. It is also a period during which the child becomes capable of deductive reasoning, and of playing and learning by rules. It is not until this period, for example, that children can really play marbles, checkers and other "take turn" games that require obedience to rules. Erikson argues that the psychosocial dimension that emerges during this period has a sense of *industry* at one extreme and a sense of *inferiority* at the other.

The term *industry* nicely captures a dominant theme of this period during which the concern with how things are made, how they work and what they do predominates. It is the Robinson Crusoe age in the sense that the enthusiasm and minute detail with which Crusoe describes his activities appeals to the child's own budding sense of industry. When children are encouraged in their efforts to make, do, or build practical things (whether it be to construct creepy crawlers, tree houses, or airplane models—or to cook, bake or sew), are allowed to finish their products, and are praised and rewarded for the results, then the sense of industry is enhanced. But parents who see their children's efforts at making and doing as "mischief," and as simply "making a mess," help to encourage in children a sense of inferiority.

During these elementary-school years, however, the child's world includes more than the home. Now social institutions other than the family come to play a central role in the developmental crisis of the individual. (Here Erikson introduced still another advance in psychoanalytic theory, which heretofore concerned itself only with the effects of the parents' behavior upon the child's development.)

A child's school experiences affect his industry-inferiority balance. The child, for example, with an I.Q. of 80 to 90 has a particularly traumatic school experience, even when his sense of industry is rewarded and encouraged at home. He is "too bright" to be in special classes, but "too slow" to compete with children of average ability. Consequently he experiences constant failures in his academic efforts that reinforces a sense of inferiority.

On the other hand, the child who had his sense of industry derogated at home can have it revitalized at school through the offices of a sensitive and committed teacher. Whether the child develops a sense of industry or inferiority, therefore, no longer depends solely on the caretaking efforts of the parents but on the actions and offices of other adults as well.

IDENTITY VS. ROLE CONFUSION

When the child moves into adolescence (Stage Five—roughly the ages 35
12–18), he encounters, according to traditional psychoanalytic theory, a reawakening of the family-romance problem of early childhood. His means of resolving the problem is to seek and find a romantic partner of his own generation. While Erikson does not deny this aspect of adolescence, he points out that there are other problems as well. The adolescent matures mentally as well as physiologically and, in addition to the new feelings, sensations and desires he experiences as a result of changes in his body, he develops a multitude of new ways of looking at and thinking about the world. Among other things, those in adolescence can now think about other people's thinking and wonder about what other people think of them. They can also conceive of ideal families, religions and societies which they then compare with the imperfect families, religions and societies of their own experience. Finally, adolescents become capable of constructing theories and philosophies designed to bring all the varied and conflicting aspects of society into a working, harmonious and peaceful whole. The adolescent, in a word, is an impatient idealist who believes that it is as easy to realize an ideal as it is to imagine it.

Erikson believes that the new interpersonal dimension which emerges during this period has to do with a sense of *ego identity* at the positive end and a sense of *role confusion* at the negative end. That is to say, given the adolescent's newfound integrative abilities, his task is to bring together all of the things he has learned about himself as a son, student, athlete, friend, Scout, newspaper boy, and so on, and integrate these different images of himself into a whole that makes sense and that shows continuity with the past while preparing for the future. To the extent that the young person succeeds in this endeavor, he arrives at a sense of psychosocial identity, a sense of who he is, where he has been and where he is going.

In contrast to the earlier stages, where parents play a more or less direct role in the determination of the result of the developmental crises, the influence of parents during this stage is much more indirect. If the young person reaches adolescence with, thanks to his parents, a vital sense of trust, autonomy, initiative and industry, then his chances of arriving at a meaningful sense of ego identity are much enhanced. The reverse, of course, holds true for the young person who enters adolescence with considerable mistrust, shame, doubt, guilt and inferiority. Preparation for a successful adolescence, and the attainment of an integrated psychosocial identity must, therefore, begin in the cradle.

Over and above what the individual brings with him from his childhood, the attainment of a sense of personal identity depends upon the social milieu in which he or she grows up. For example, in a society where women are to some extent second-class citizens, it may be harder for females to arrive at a sense of psychosocial identity. Likewise at times, such as the present, when rapid social and technological change breaks down many traditional values, it may be more difficult for young people to find continuity between what they learned and experienced as children and what they learn and experience as adolescents. At such times young people often seek causes that give their lives meaning and direction. The activism of the current generation of young people may well stem, in part at least, from this search.

When the young person cannot attain a sense of personal identity, either because of an unfortunate childhood or difficult social circumstances, he shows a certain amount of *role confusion*—a sense of not knowing what he is, where he belongs or whom he belongs to. Such confusion is a frequent symptom in delinquent young people. Promiscuous adolescent girls, for example, often seem to have a fragmented sense of ego identity. Some young people seek a "negative identity," an identity opposite to the one prescribed for them by their family and friends. Having an identity as a "delinquent," or as a "hippie," or even as an "acid head," may sometimes be preferable to having no identity at all.

In some cases young people do not seek a negative identity so much as 40
they have it thrust upon them. I remember another court case in which the defendant was an attractive 16-year-old girl who had been found "tricking it" in a trailer located just outside the grounds of an Air Force base. From about the age of 12, her mother had encouraged her to dress seductively and to go out with boys. When she returned from dates, her sexually frustrated mother demanded a kiss-by-kiss, caress-by-caress description of the evening's activities. After the mother had vicariously satisfied her sexual needs, she proceeded to call her daughter a "whore" and a "dirty tramp." As the girl told me, "Hell, I have the name, so I might as well play the role."

Failure to establish a clear sense of personal identity at adolescence does not guarantee perpetual failure. And the person who attains a working sense of ego identity in adolescence will of necessity encounter challenges and threats to that identity as he moves through life. Erikson, perhaps more than any other personality theorist, has emphasized that life is constant change and that confronting problems at one stage in life is not a guarantee against the reappearance of these problems at later stages, or against the finding of new solutions to them.

INTIMACY VS. ISOLATION

Stage Six in the life cycle is young adulthood; roughly the period of courtship and early family life that extends from late adolescence till early middle age. For this stage, and the stages described hereafter, classical psychoanalysis has nothing new or major to say. For Erikson, however, the previous attainment of a sense of personal identity and the engagement in productive work that marks this period gives rise to a new interpersonal dimension of *intimacy* at the one extreme and *isolation* at the other.

When Erikson speaks of intimacy he means much more than love-making alone; he means the ability to share with and care about another person without fear of losing oneself in the process. In the case of intimacy, as in the case of identity, success or failure no longer depends directly upon the parents but only indirectly as they have contributed to the individual's success or failure at the earlier stages. Here, too, as in the case of identity, social conditions may help or hinder the establishment of a sense of intimacy. Likewise, intimacy need not involve sexuality; it includes the relationship between friends. Soldiers who have served together under the most dangerous circumstances often develop a sense of commitment to one another that exemplifies intimacy in its broadest sense. If a sense of intimacy is not established with friends or a marriage partner, the result, in Erikson's view, is a sense of isolation—of being alone without anyone to share with or care for.

GENERATIVITY VS. SELF-ABSORPTION

This stage—middle age—brings with it what Erikson speaks of as either *generativity* or *self-absorption,* and stagnation. What Erikson means by *generativity* is that the person begins to be concerned with others beyond his immediate family, with future generations and the nature of the society and world in which those generations will live. Generativity does not reside only in parents; it can be found in any individual who actively concerns himself with the welfare of young people and with making the world a better place for them to live and to work.

Those who fail to establish a sense of generativity fall into a state of self- 45
absorption in which their personal needs and comforts are of predominant concern. A fictional case of self-absorption is Dickens's Scrooge in "A Christmas Carol." In his one-sided concern with money and in his disregard for the interests and welfare of his young employe, Bob Cratchit, Scrooge exemplifies the self-absorbed, embittered (the two often go together) old man. Dickens also illustrated, however, what Erikson points out: namely, that unhappy solutions to life's crises are not irreversible. Scrooge, at the end of the tale, manifested both a sense of generativity and of intimacy which he had not experienced before.

INTEGRITY VS. DESPAIR

Stage Eight in the Eriksonian scheme corresponds roughly to the period when the individual's major efforts are nearing completion and when there is time for reflection—and for the enjoyment of grandchildren, if any. The psychosocial dimension that comes into prominence now has *integrity* on one hand and *despair* on the other.

The sense of integrity arises from the individual's ability to look back on his life with satisfaction. At the other extreme is the individual who looks back upon his life as a series of missed opportunities and missed directions; now in the twilight years he realizes that it is too late to start again. For such a person the inevitable result is a sense of despair at what might have been.

These, then, are the major stages in the life cycle as described by Erikson. Their presentation, for one thing, frees the clinician to treat adult emotional problems as failures (in part at least) to solve genuinely adult personality crises and not, as heretofore, as mere residuals of infantile frustrations and conflicts. This view of personality growth, moreover, takes some of the onus off parents and takes account of the role which society and the person himself play in the formation of an individual personality. Finally, Erikson has offered hope for us all by demonstrating that each phase of growth has its strengths as well as its weaknesses and that failures at one stage of development can be rectified by successes at later stages.

The reason that these ideas, which sound so agreeable to "common sense," are in fact so revolutionary has a lot to do with the state of psychoanalysis in America. As formulated by Freud, psychoanalysis encompassed a theory of personality development, a method of studying the human mind and, finally, procedures for treating troubled and unhappy people. Freud viewed this system as a scientific one, open to revision as new facts and observations accumulated.

The system was, however, so vehemently attacked that Freud's followers were constantly in the position of having to defend Freud's views. Perhaps because of this situation, Freud's system became, in the hands of some of his followers and defenders, a dogma upon which all theoretical innovation, clinical observation and therapeutic practice had to be grounded. That this attitude persists is evidenced in the recent remark by a psychoanalyst that he believed psychotic patients could not be treated by psychoanalysis because "Freud said so." Such attitudes, in which Freud's authority rather than observation and data is the basis of deciding what is true and what is false, has contributed to the disrepute in which psychoanalysis is widely held today.

Erik Erikson has broken out of this scholasticism and has had the courage to say that Freud's discoveries and practices were the start and not the end of the study and treatment of the human personality. In addition to advocating the modifications of psychoanalytic theory outlined above, Erikson has also suggested modifications in therapeutic practice, particularly in the treatment of young patients. "Young people in severe trouble are not fit for the couch," he writes. "They want to face you, and they want you to face them, not as a facsimile of a parent, or wearing the mask of a professional helper, but as a kind of over-all individual a young person can live with or despair of."

Erikson has had the boldness to remark on some of the negative effects that distorted notions of psychoanalysis have had on society at large. Psychoanalysis, he says, has contributed to a widespread fatalism—"even as we were trying to devise, with scientific determinism, a therapy for the few, we were led to promote an ethical disease among the many."

Understanding

1. According to Erikson, which cultural forces play major roles in helping children negotiate each stage of their development? What are the consequences of completing each stage successfully?
2. In advancing a "stage" theory, Erikson implies that we naturally experience the resolution of each conflict or crisis and that facing any one crisis usually occurs at a certain age. Are there other implications of this kind of stage theory? If so, what are they?
3. Erikson deals primarily with the *effects* of passing through each stage and with the process itself. What ideas from your reading might suggest the *cause(s)* of these stages?
4. Compare Erikson's developmental stages with the behavior traits identified in Freud's "Ages of Man." How do they complement each other? Or do they? Which seems most useful to you?
5. Erikson's theory tries to explain the intellectual, social, and emotional stages of human development. In which stage(s) do you think moral development or the capacity to judge between right and wrong is developed? Through what agencies?

Responding

1. Which of Erikson's stages have you negotiated? Did you confront the crisis or challenge associated with each stage at the time that he suggests? Choose at least one of the passages and describe your crisis, how you perceived it, how you resolved it, and what, if anything, you learned from it.
2. Which of Erikson's developmental stages do you think is particularly difficult to resolve in contemporary society? Why?
3. How important are families in the development of a wholesome personality?

Connecting

1. Keen in "The Peach-Seed Monkey" (chapter one) refers to Erikson's eight stages to illustrate the trust-versus-mistrust continuum. What allowed Keen to accept the monkey without bitterness years after it was promised?
2. Reflect back on "The Beavers Scale of Family Health and Competence" in Scarf's article in the "Family Ties" section of chapter six in relation to issues of intimacy, power, and self-control. Using both Beavers's and Erikson's work, what hypotheses could you make surrounding these issues for both individuals and families?

A Father, His Daughters, and a Lesson

William Raspberry

Everyone is someone's son or daughter. Sounds simplistic, doesn't it? But when you look at others in your classes or at work, you don't often—if ever—think of them in the role of father or mother or son or daughter. Yet family relationships are all-powerful for parents as well as children. Each of your parents has soul-searched for the right way to parent you. Parents do well, and they also make mistakes. They are guilt-ridden over things they did or didn't do, or they are smug when their children seem perfect. Whatever the case, William Raspberry's soul-searching has revealed a powerful synthesis of advice worth noting. In "A Father, His Daughters, and a Lesson," he shares a lesson he wishes he had learned earlier.

William Raspberry is a highly respected journalist who has been called "The Lone Ranger of Columnists" for taking an independent view on national and international issues. He writes three columns a week, and two are syndicated. In addition to his columns, he has taught journalism at Howard University, served numerous times as a television commentator and panelist, and been a member of the Pulitzer Prize board. The following glimpse into his private life is illuminating.

I've just left a meeting with Nan Keohane, the new president of Duke 1
University, where I'm now teaching. The first person I meet upon my return to *The Washington Post* is Keohane's sister: former editor of *The Des Moines Register* and new *Post* ombudsman, Geneva Overholser.

And I'm thinking: What was their father's secret, and why couldn't I have raised my daughters like that?

I have a son, too, but men generally think we know how to raise sons to be confident and competent adults. But our daughters . . .

My daughters aren't exactly chopped liver, mind you. One has just completed a master's degree, and the other is a dissertation short of a doctorate. Both are smart, pretty, confident. Nor do I wish to give the impression that there was no *maternal* contribution to their (or the Overholsers') success.

I'm saying only that fathers are more important to our daughters' sense 5
of self than most of us know in time to do much good.

Stepfathers, too, my colleague Judy Mann reminds me. Mann, who makes as much sense on the subject of raising daughters as anybody I've come across, recalls one of those illuminating flashes from her own household.

Her daughter Katherine had just signed up for ninth-grade math, and Mann's husband, Richard Starnes, wanted to know which math she had chosen.

"I'm taking geometry."

"Oh, great! You're going to have so much fun with geometry!"

And she did. Mann, who admits being particularly terrified by geometry 10
during her own math-hating high school years, says she even heard Katherine chatting on the phone with friends about how much fun she was having in geometry. She has no doubt that that one small father-daughter exchange, which may have registered as only a blip in Starnes' own recollection, made the critical difference.

Mann, who has written a terrific book on the subject ("The Difference: Growing up Female in America"), knows well that Starnes' encouraging response might as easily have come from a mother as from a father. But she believes that a father's words and attitudes play a special role in helping daughters find their place in the world.

"We live in a culture that glorifies men and talks about how important men are," she says. "And men are perfectly willing to believe it all. And yet men are far more important in raising and influencing their daughters than they realize. Just by their own attitudes, they can enable their daughters to soar or cripple them into psychological dependency."

I know, in these days of androgyny cum equality, to expect the quick response: Mothers, too. And sons.

It's true. But it is also true that fathers and stepfathers—perhaps because of the importance men are accorded in the society—have special power to lift their daughters' sense of self. And, more often than not, we waste the power—not through neglect but through failure to understand the importance of the subtle signals we send. Says Mann:

"A girl who accomplishes something outstanding might be complimented 15
on her effort, a boy on his ability. There's a powerful difference between, 'You really worked hard, and I'm so proud of you,' and 'Boy, you're good!' "

Or, she says, boys will be praised for their accomplishments while girls will be praised for their appearance.

Did Bill Clinton fall into that trap the other day at Yellowstone National Park? There he was, posing for a photograph with Hillary, Chelsea and Chelsea's girlfriend. "Look at my girls," the beaming president sang out. "Aren't they cute?"

I'm willing to concede that that may have been a joke. After all, just a day or so earlier, Clinton had approved mountain-climbing lessons for Chelsea, who then went rappelling down a 130-foot cliff. Such things build confidence, the president said.

Joke or not, girls do learn early that being attractive can get them more positive attention than being brave or smart. And when they learn this lesson from their own fathers, it's bound to affect the way they view themselves.

My children—all three of them—are good-looking and smart. I'm incred- 20
ibly proud of them. They will do just fine. Still, it occurs to me that they might have done even better if their father had been a little smarter.

I know, belatedly, that fathers matter an awful lot. I wish I'd known it sooner.

Understanding

1. Who is Raspberry writing for? What does he want his audience to take from the piece?
2. What conflict is Raspberry working through here?
3. Analyze Raspberry's style in terms of narrative, observation, and judgement. How do his questions work to strengthen the piece?

Responding

1. Do you think men are generally confident, as Raspberry says, about how to raise their sons to be "confident and competent adults"? Is it the same with mothers and daughters?
2. At what might Raspberry think his children would have done better if he had been a "smarter" father? How do you think his children responded to this article?
3. In an interview, Raspberry revealed that he preferred writing to verbal presentations on television. "I like being able to think things through in a column rather than delivering hard opinions as though from on high. I think readers deserve to know how I reach a conclusion." Is it rhetorically clear in "A Father, His Daughters, and a Lesson" how he reached his conclusion? Are you more comfortable sharing your opinions in writing or in speaking? What are the advantages in each medium for you?
4. Compose a letter to your parent (or guardian) of the opposite sex, acknowledging his or her contribution to you. (Do this even if you can't find anything positive to say right now. Just begin to write an acknowledgment.) Use Raspberry's criteria. Finish with what you learned about yourself in the writing.
5. Are there any things you think your father should have done differently in rearing you? Use them for an advice letter to yourself on how to bring up your own children (or any child you might love enough to be responsible for at a given time, even as a babysitter.) If you have children of your own, do you agree with Raspberry's lesson? How has being a parent caused you to explore another more (or less) integrated self?

Connecting

1. How does Raspberry's article relate to Conroy's point in "Think About It" (chapter six)?
2. Which of Erikson's eight developmental stages would Raspberry be working through at the time he wrote this article? Why would his questions be important to that stage? According to Erikson, which developmental tasks was he involved in during the time his daughters were growing up? How might they have influenced his parenting?

The Push and Pull of Values

Viktor E. Frankl

German philosopher Friedrich Nietzsche (1844–1900) said: "He who has a *why* to live can bear with almost any *how.*" Author and psychiatrist Viktor E. Frankl (1905–1997) has demonstrated Nietzsche's statement in his life's work as the founder of *logotherapy,* his own version of existential therapy. (In Greek, *logos* is "meaning.") Frankl traced the problems in his patients' lives to their inability to find meaning and a sense of responsibility in their existence. The purpose of logotherapy is to weave these broken lives into firm patterns of meaning and responsibility.

Frankl's ideas about therapy come from his own life experience. A survivor of horrific conditions in concentration camps and the deaths there of his father, mother, brother, and wife, he was still able to find life worth living. Frankl says that in suffering, the last of our distinctively human capacities remains: our freedom and ability to choose one's attitude in a given set of circumstances. Though it may not seem possible to find any meaning in suffering, Frankl has dedicated his life to working with patients to do just that.

Man's search for meaning is a primary force in his life and not a "second- 1
ary rationalization" of instinctual drives. This meaning is unique and specific in that it must and can be fulfilled by him alone; only then does it achieve a significance which will satisfy his own *will* to meaning. There are some authors who contend that meanings and values are "nothing but defense mechanisms, reaction formations and sublimations." But as for myself, I would not be willing to live merely for the sake of my "defense mechanisms," nor would I be ready to die merely for the sake of my "reaction formations." Man, however, is able to live and even to die for the sake of his ideals and values!

A poll of public opinion was conducted a few years ago in France. The results showed that 89 per cent of the people polled admitted that man needs "something" for the sake of which to live. Moreover, 61 per cent conceded that there was something, or someone, in their own lives for whose sake they were even ready to die. I repeated this poll at my clinic in Vienna among both the patients and the personnel, and the outcome was practically the same as among the thousands of people screened in France; the difference was only 2 per cent. In other words, the will to meaning is in most people *fact,* not *faith.*

Of course, there may be some cases in which an individual's concern with values is really a camouflage of hidden inner conflicts; but, if so, they represent the exceptions from the rule rather than the rule itself. In these instances a psychodynamic interpretation is justified in an attempt to disclose the underlying unconscious dynamics. In such cases we have actually to deal with pseudo-values (a good example of this is that of the bigot), and as such they have to be unmasked. Unmasking, or debunking, however, should stop as soon as one is confronted with what is authentic and genuine in man, e.g., man's desire for a life that is as meaningful as possible. If it does not stop then, the man who does the debunking merely betrays his own will to depreciate the spiritual aspirations of another.

We have to beware of the tendency to deal with values in terms of mere self-expression of man himself. For *logos,* or "meaning," is not only an emerging from existence itself but rather something confronting existence. If the meaning which is waiting to be fulfilled by man were really nothing but a mere expression of self, or no more than a projection of his wishful thinking, it would immediately lose its demanding and challenging character; it could no longer call man forth or summon him. This holds true not only for the so-called sublimation of instinctual drives but for what C. G. Jung[1] called the "archetypes" of the "collective unconscious" as well, inasmuch as the latter would also be self-expressions, namely, of mankind as a whole. This holds true as well for the contention of some existentialist thinkers who see in man's ideals nothing but his own inventions. According to Jean-Paul Sartre, man invents himself, he designs his own "essence"; that is to say, what he essentially is, including what he should be, or ought to become. However, I think the meaning of our existence is not invented by ourselves, but rather detected.

Psychodynamic research in the field of values is legitimate; the question is 5
whether it is always appropriate. Above all, we must keep in mind that any exclusively psychodynamic investigation can, in principle, only reveal what is a driving force in man. Values, however, do not drive a man; they do not *push* him, but rather *pull* him. This is a difference, by the way, of which I am constantly reminded whenever I go through the doors of an American hotel. One of them has to be pulled while the other has to be pushed. Now, if I say man is *pulled* by values, what is implicitly referred to is the fact that there is always freedom involved: the freedom of man to make his choice between accepting or rejecting an offer, i.e., to fulfill a meaning potentiality, or else to forfeit it.

However, it should be made quite clear that there cannot exist in man any such thing as a *moral drive,* or even a *religious drive,* in the same manner as we speak of man's being determined by basic instincts. Man is never driven to moral behavior; in each instance, he decides to behave morally. Man does not do so in order to satisfy a moral drive and to have a good conscience. Man does not behave morally for the sake of having a good conscience but for the sake of a cause to which he commits himself, or for a person whom he loves, or for the sake of his God. If he actually did it for the sake of having a good conscience, he would become a case of Pharisaism and cease to be a truly moral person. I think that even the saints did not care for anything other than simply to serve God, and I doubt that they ever had it in mind to become saints. If that were the case they would have become only perfectionists rather than saints. Certainly, "a good conscience is the best pillow," as a German saying goes; but true morality is more than just a sleeping pill, or a tranquilizing drug.

Note

1. Carl Jung (1875–1961) expanded Sigmund Freud's idea of the unconscious to include the *collective unconscious* which, according to Jung, contains basic patterns and symbols—*archetypes*—which are common to all humanity, e.g., heroes, goddesses, and behaviors such as creative or inspirational thinking, nurturing, sexuality, as well as impulses to destroy, absorb, and reproduce.

Understanding

1. What is the difference between the ideas of existentialist Jean-Paul Sartre and Viktor Frankl?
2. According to Frankl, are morality and religion inherently human? What causes human beings to behave morally? What role does choice play in moral behavior? What is conscience? Why does Frankl argue that it is inadequate for a person to behave morally only for the sake of having a good conscience?
3. What is *Pharisaism?* Explain Frankl's use of the term (paragraph 6).
4. What function do values serve in contributing to the meaning of life? What is the difference between pushing and pulling with regard to values?
5. What is "meaning" with regard to a person's life?

Responding

1. Using Frankl, your best dictionary, and informal interviews with people you respect, construct a definition of *values.* List ten values that your daily actions support. Using one of your essays from a writing option assignment, or another piece of your writing generated by *Signatures,* identify an operative value or set of values at work in that narrative. Examine that narrative again from Frankl's notions of push or pull. What does your analysis reveal?
2. Conduct a poll of your own with the following questions. You will need to interview about five or ten people. Write a summary of your interviewees' answers.
   - Do people need something to live for?
   - If yes, what is it? Explain.
   - If no, why not?
3. Is being truly moral one of your values? Explain.
4. Do you know anyone who is truly moral in the sense described by Frankl? Describe that person. If you have your own definition of morality—different from Frankl's—describe it using a person who fits *your* definition.

Connecting

1. Are there some values or people you would be prepared to die for because without them life would have no meaning? Are there ideals, like those of Havel (see "Dear Olga" later in this chapter), that you would be willing to go to prison for? What or who are they? What values would your sacrifices reveal? What other writers have you encountered in this anthology

who have been willing to suffer extreme consequences as a result of their choices?

2. Frankl has said elsewhere in his writing that humans are not necessarily better off in a tensionless state. Instead he feels that we actually need the tension of "striving and struggling for a worthwhile goal, a freely chosen task." Examine this proposition in terms of your own daily life. What happens to you when you are in a state of tension? What causes it? How is tension a positive factor in our lives, according to Frankl?

   Look at Csikszentmihalyi's description of "happy" people in "The World of Self" (paragraph 20). Compare or contrast Frankl's proposition with Csikszentmihalyi's description of people who lead a satisfying life—a life with meaning. What is most strikingly similar about the two?

3. Gordon Allport, former professor of psychology at Harvard University, is the person responsible for introducing Frankl's work in the United States. Looking back to Allport's essay "A Solitary Quest" (chapter six), how do these two writers' ideas differ? How do they complement each other?

Running on Empty

Martin Dugard

A search for who we are can take us down many roads. To push one's body to its limits is one such avenue for this quest. The Raid Gauloises, "the toughest race on earth," has provided this challenge for men and women since 1989 at its first site, New Zealand. Though no one (as of this writing) has ever died in the competition, participants are constantly on the edge of their worst fears. Nevertheless, adventure races have become so popular that regional imitations of the Raid Gauloises have sprung up throughout the world. They include the Raid Corsica, the Raid Madagascar, and, in Spain, the Raiverd (Green Raid). In North America the Eco-Challenge is emerging to great popularity as are Speight's Coast to Coast and the Southern Traverse in New Zealand.

Having been an avid two-year Raid spectator, Martin Dugard, frequent contributor to *Sports Illustrated, Outside,* and *Running World,* decided to compete in the 1995 Raid in the Argentine region of Patagonia. He did so in order to break out of his "comfort zone." This is the story of his quest. Dugard is a full-time writer and lives in southern California. He went back to the Raid in 1997—and finished.

The Raid Gauloises is a French stage-race held in a different part of the world each year. Five-person teams, each having at least one woman, race night and day from start to finish by means appropriate to the host country's terrain. Over mountains and down rivers, on horseback and on foot, by kayak and canoe. The ordeal can last more than a week, and teams rarely sleep more than an hour a day. Some competitors emerge as nothing more than human rubble, while others limp away revitalized. All, however, talk soulfully of going beyond their known abilities, of the Raid being a metaphor for life, and, in that vein, of discovering that the journey is more enriching than its completion. 1

The Raid has earned its infamous reputation by constantly reinventing the definition of "extreme." In the words of founder Gerard Fusil, "It is designed to push individuals to their mental, physical, and emotional limits." Since its inception in 1989, the Raid has seen competitors race everywhere from Costa Rica to Oman, competing in events ranging from skydiving to camel riding. In 1994's race in Borneo, for instance, the disciplines of jungle orienteering, white-water rafting and canoeing, mountain biking, and spelunking took advantage of Borneo's rivers, narrow jungle trails, and the legendary Mulu caves. For hazards, there were cobras, alligators, and monitor lizards, as well as millions of bats who made the caves their home—in fact, many competitors remember Borneo more for the sharp ammonia smell of guano than the musty-green aroma that defines the jungles.

However, though the conditions were as hazardous and challenging as ever, a combined team of Mulu cave guides and New Zealander ultramarathoners managed to sweep through the course in an unheard-of four days. There were rumors they had been fed insider information, a fact that enraged other squads.

Fusil said nothing at the time, but later vowed publicly that the 1995 event in the mountainous Argentine region of Patagonia would be the toughest Raid ever. It would last at least eight days. No locals would be allowed to compete. The events—kayaking, mountaineering, canoeing, snowshoeing, horseback riding, and orienteering—were endurance-oriented, with nothing frivolous in the mix. Adding to the difficulty, teams would be required to carry more gear than at other Raids, making for packs that weighed anywhere from forty to sixty pounds. “I want to slow them down,” Fusil said, explaining the need for heavier packs. “I want them to remember that the Raid should feel like an expedition.”

Though I had spent many years as both a runner and triathlete, when I 5
first heard of the Raid, I was only too happy to watch from the sidelines, sure that it was a race for the obsessive-compulsive or merely insane. Toward the end of Borneo, the second Raid I witnessed, I changed. Watching what the competitors were enduring, and having talked to enough of them to know that they were actually calmly adventurous instead of insane or otherwise dysfunctional, I began to actually consider competing. My life, I realized, had been lived within a comfort zone. I embraced personal mediocrity instead of striving to do my absolute best. I felt the need to break out of that rut, to take a flying leap outside the comfort zone.

There’s a chance I might have gone home and tucked those thoughts deep into my subconscious if not for the intriguing words of a competitor. “The worst time was at night,” Karen Fry of Team Australia said, describing what it was like to walk through the same jungles once roamed by headhunters. “We’d be walking with our headlamps on, and though we never saw or heard really big animals, when we’d shine our lights into the jungle we could always see eyes shining back at us.”

Chilling. Exciting. Motivating. I returned home with definite plans to be on the starting line in Patagonia. Having run for so many years, I figured that I had the proper endurance base. That I had no knowledge whatsoever of how to rappel, climb, canoe, snowshoe, kayak, or ride horseback didn’t matter. Those, I rationalized, were things I could learn.

And I did. Bit by bit I stepped outside the comfort zone. I learned each required skill. I increased my running mileage and increased my upper-body strength. I spent hours on the phone trying to raise the thousands of dollars it takes to compete ($50,000 is the average cost for a team of five and two support people, including gear, transportation, and entry fee). The Raid became not just a physical challenge, but the sort of long-range goal that makes life interesting, the kind that gets you out of bed in the morning with the promise of some greater reward.

I recruited an incredibly solid team to help me see that goal through. There was Susan Hemond-Dent, a tough woman who had done the Raids in Oman and Madagascar, and had crewed for the all-female America^3 syndicate during the 1992 America's Cup. Jay Smith, the ornery lead climber, had climbed Everest. And Mike Sammis and Robert Finlay were ex-commandos with an extreme take on life.

Our training was severe, filled with twenty-four-hour hikes and long kayaks in the roiling Pacific that would prepare us for the Raid. Over the course of the 400-mile-long race, two days would be spent kayaking along enormous Lago Nahuel Huapi, three days mountaineering, a day white-water canoeing, two days horseback riding, then a quick section of orienteering and rappelling before the finish. We were known as Team Dockers. When we left for Patagonia in late November, I was certain we possessed the talent to become the first American team ever to win the Raid Gauloises.

The Raid began on a Sunday. One-hundred and forty-seven bright-red kayaks departed en masse from a gravel beach north of Villa la Angostura—forty-nine teams from thirteen countries were entered (including twenty from France and seven from the United States). A frenzied scene, with boats and paddles and rudders colliding, it was a literal clash of cultures, with a multilingual screech of profanities to match.

Out of the tangle, French teams InterSport, Coflexip, and Hewlett-Packard emerged as leaders, beginning a battle that would continue until the Raid's final hours. Team Dockers was twenty-first. And while kayaking was our weakest event, we knew we couldn't afford to lag too far behind. For reasons of safety (and to divide the field), Fusil had mandated a "door" atop a peak known as Cerro López, which we would climb immediately after kayaking. Teams that did not make it to the summit of López by 9 p.m. on the Raid's second day would be forced to stop for the night. The "door," in other words, would close. Those teams that summitted before then would find the door open, and could continue through the night. In effect, they would gain at least a six-hour lead. When things got tough during the long hours of kayaking through three-foot swells and thirty-knot winds, when our forearms and shoulders burned from effort and the urge to take a break grew strong, images of that door slamming and Raid victory slipping away propelled us forward.

We finished kayaking at 4 p.m. of day two and began the mad dash upward to the door. We climbed at breakneck pace to the summit, a beastly 8,000 feet away—legs on fire, lungs heaving, and me not allowing myself to look down while scaling sections that dropped thousands of feet into the lake. This was the toughest thing I had ever done in my life. Forget the marathons and triathlons. Part of me thrilled at the wonder of overcoming both a fear of heights and pre-race jitters about being a Raid competitor. Another reminded me that it was an awful, punishing climb, and I wouldn't do it again on a bet.

Only six teams made it through the door that night, and Team Dockers wasn't one of them. Bitterly disappointed, the five of us camped below the summit, an enclave of rocks and scrub protecting us from the raging wind (pilots of the Argentine Air Force once complained that the winds over the Patagonian Andes actually forced their jet fighters *backward*) but not from the below-freezing temperature. Fully dressed, we shivered in our lightweight sleeping bags and waited for dawn. Sue, who was in the throes of altitude sickness and severe dehydration, threw up all night, and when we began moving again at 4 a.m., her movements were feeble. Half-delirious, using a free hand to slip stomach-friendly Gummi Bears in her mouth to get a jolt of energy, she was petrifying to watch as we snaked up the knife-edge ridge to the summit. One side fell thousands of feet into Nahuel Huapi. The other fell a mere 100 feet onto a snowfield.

15 The Raid, I was finding, is like that: a continual process of overcoming. Each moment of each day is lived with incredible intensity. There are extremes of pain and exhaustion. Something as simple as putting one foot in front of the other for hours on end becomes a major accomplishment. A competitor told me that in Borneo the emphasis on moving forward—of being positive—made it impossible to think of something as heretical as quitting. "You can't," he said. "You just think about putting one foot in front of the other until you finish." This was the mind-set of Team Dockers on day three. Quitting wasn't an option; only forward progress. We didn't make the door, but we muddled on, just twelve hours off the lead, in seventeenth place. The Raid is such a long race that anything can happen. "They've gotta sleep sometime," Mike reminded us, referring to the lead teams.

With that in mind, we moved as swiftly as Sue's deteriorating condition would allow. As we worked to make up ground, the "wonders" of nature became adversaries instead of merely beautiful backdrops. The once-in-a-lifetime splendor of standing atop Cerro López as the sun rises is not awe-inspiring if you must descend that peak (sliding at breakneck speeds down a snowfield) and climb two others before noon, all the while haunted by the specter of the 11,600-foot Monte Tronador, which must be summitted the next day. Likewise, there was nothing stunning about the cliff-lined shore of Nahuel Huapi stretching over the horizon once I realized that we had to kayak the entire length of that coast. And while I finally appreciated Patagonia's beauty after my Raid ended, during the race I saw nothing but suffering in those summits plumed with snow and gray shale. The tumbling mountain streams, so clear and swift from record snowfall, held not a trace of allure beyond their ability to refuel water bottles. And more often, they were an obstacle.

The inevitable finally happened. After three days and nights of her body rejecting all food and water, Sue was forced to abandon the race. We all knew it was coming. In fact, it had been a source of unspoken tension because it would mean the official end of our team at the 1995 Raid Gauloises. The second that the helicopter settled to the ground and Sue climbed aboard, Team Dockers was out. Though the four of us would be allowed to go on without her, our finish would be unofficial.

I had a hard time believing Sue was gone. From the moment I decided to field a team of my own, it was Sue who drove me crazy with niggling phone calls about the special equipment we would need and with input on the skills required of prospective team members. Left to her own devices, Sue wouldn't have abandoned, no matter what. It was Raid doctors who made the decision for her. After observing her condition at a checkpoint, they forbade her from continuing and called in the chopper.

Mike, Jay, Robert, and I went on, but the disappointment had fractured us. We spent the morning of day four trekking up a near-vertical snowfield, then had a bitter argument at the summit. We screamed crazy words, fueled by frustration and fatigue. When we finally shut up, calmed down, and shouldered our packs again, each was still too angry to speak. We walked ten meters apart, each in his own universe. It was a good example of why, more than the physical or mental aspect, the team dynamic of the Raid is what makes it a true test of character. Getting along with four other people for more than a week is a chore under normal circumstances, but almost impossible when you're cold, tired, hungry, wet, and miserable.

Our split would have healed with time, but things took another turn for 20
the worse. As we picked our way through a field of shale on a steep descent, my right foot slipped into a hole. Two manhole-size chunks of shale fell on top of it, trapping and wrenching my knee. I felt a pop in my knee, then a bone-on-bone grinding behind the patella. The wind was blowing so my teammates couldn't hear me yell for help. It took forever, but I hobbled three miles to the checkpoint, where I knew there was a doctor.

The diagnosis was immediate: My Raid was over.

Gerard Fusil himself carried me to the helicopter—the same one that had lifted Sue out just hours before. As the copter rose straight up off the ground, and I watched Jay and Mike and Robert move forward without me, I knew why those Germans in Madagascar were so saddened. It wasn't that their race had come to an end. In fact, it had nothing to do with racing, or even competition. They were sad because the Raid is a miserable, painful process that demands nothing but personal excellence at all times. The conditions are so severe that you have no choice but to comply. Touching excellence is uplifting and addictive in a way that no drug can ever be. It is the reward that lies beyond the comfort zone, and to be ripped from that by fate is grievous.

As I rested my strained ligaments over the next week, I slowly started to see the wondrous beauty of Patagonia. I watched from the sidelines as Coflexip canoed the swollen Rio Manso and rode horseback across the Pampas, then came from behind to defeat InterSport on the last day. In a move that will go down in Raid lore for its drama, Coflexip cinched their packs down tightly and ran four consecutive hours to catch, and pass, InterSport. The thought of running for four hours on fresh legs is staggering. On legs eight days into the Raid and burdened by a pack is almost superhuman.

Coflexip's time was eight days, two hours. The remains of Team Dockers finished three days later. Almost two-thirds of the forty-nine starting teams did not finish at all, many citing both injury and overwhelming fatigue. My injury seemed almost slight next to the French woman whose foot was broken by tumbling rock. Mike Sawyer of the United States' Team Odyssey had his entire right hand crushed by shale. But despite the Raids' hazards, not a single competitor has ever died. Such good luck will be necessary this year, when the Raid will take place in Lesotho, South Africa, where alligators, snakes, and even bigger predators will shine their eyes on competitors in the night.

As I prepared to fly home, Fusil asked me, "Will you be coming back 25
next year?"

I thought for a moment of being miserable, tired, cold, and wet. I thought of the heights, of that epic team argument, of my despair-filled helicopter ride, of bones crushed and knees torn in the blink of an eye. But mostly, I thought of how devastated I was after my Raid came to an end. Did I really want to come back again and suffer? Were my midrace moments of life outside the comfort zone really worth another year of training?

"Of course," I answered, meeting his gaze. The answer had come in a flash. "Of course."

Understanding

1. What exactly is the Raid Gauloises? Describe it fully as if to someone whom you are asking for money to support your team's participation in the Raid.
2. Dugard claims that the Raid Gauloises is "much more than a simple race." Explain his assertion.
3. What made Dugard compete? Why would he do it again?

Responding

1. Raid Gauloises founder Gerard Fusil says the Raid is "designed to push individuals to their mental, physical, and emotional limits." What is the value in this endeavor, especially if you are ordered out of the Raid by doctors and your team is disqualified as a result?
2. Would you do the Raid course if it were not a race? What are the advantages and disadvantages of each set of conditions?
3. Have you ever participated in (or found yourself in) an event or situation requiring extreme physical endurance? Describe it and what you learned about yourself and others.
4. It seems that Raid (or even Olympic) competitors have plenty of time and money to train and then compete. Do you know anyone who is a competitor in this sense? Describe them, or research what kinds of people actually compete in the Raid or other adventure races. What do these competitors have in common?
5. The 1997 Raid Gauloises was held in Lesotho, South Africa, in January 1997. Use this e-mail address to find the location of the next Raid (nifusil@aol.com), or call (310) 271-8335; ask for a brochure and application. Imagine yourself competing. Whom would you enroll on your team? List each person (including yourself) and describe what each would contribute. Also analyze each participant's liabilities.

Connecting

1. Compare Dugard's exertion and perseverence with a challenge of one of the other writers in this anthology. What does a commitment as complete

as this one to the Raid Gauloises cause for each person who undertakes such demanding tasks?

2. Analyze Dugard's quest with regard to Frankl's notion that the search for meaning is a primary force in one's life. (See "The Push and Pull of Values" earlier in this chapter.) What does Frankl claim? What does Dugard claim?
3. Apply Glidewell's notion of freedom and resources (see "On Freedom and Resources" later in this chapter) to Dugard's quest. Analyze it in terms of Glidewell's definitions.

"Give Back to Your Community," She Said

Rafael Campo

The struggle to find meaning for ourselves through our communities is ongoing and dynamic. At once we are members of many communities. Which are more important? Which exact our most thoughtful inquiries? Which cause us to take a stand? Which define us in our membership? Rafael Campo promises answers in choosing the subtitle of his article " 'Give Back to Your Community,' She Said"—*But which one? A doctor's struggle with identity politics.*

Campo's article examines how he found meaning and responsibility—himself—in his life. His discussion centers around how he identified the community to which he would dedicate his life and through which he would integrate the many aspects of himself. Something or someone sets us on the path on which we journey, and Campo acknowledges that love led him to his current commitment to his occupation and the attitude he has toward it. He is a doctor (and a poet) who teaches and practices at Beth Israel Hospital in Boston. This selection provides a wonderful example of someone who has integrated his gifts, dreams, wounds, and decisions with his community and biological inheritance.

A Harvard Medical School dean was musing over my future career options as a doctor the first time I heard the phrase "giving back to the community." Puzzled by what she might mean, I wondered what it was that I could have unwittingly stolen. (Having grown up in white America, I suppose I must have been taught that the dark one in the room must always be guilty of *something;* in my case especially, this was usually in fact true.) It seemed virtually impossible to me that I owed anybody anything, given the history of numbing loss that was all that I had inherited from my Cuban family. Indeed, it seemed to me that someday reparations would have to be made to *me,* for the lost sugar plantation and the 1,000 slaughtered head of cattle, for the nameless stream that ran with our blood and the salt and sand quarries in which our murdered bodies were dumped. 1

So what could I now give back, one who had so very little, one who was still so busy trying to make his selections? Yes, the Americans had turned their backs on us at a crucial moment, but in the end they had given us a new home in a glaring white supermarket of opportunities, bargains and possibilities. The point of my American journey seemed to be what else I could acquire for *myself*—the state-of-the-art home entertainment center or the swank beachfront vacation home in Florida; each of these was more clearly imaginable to me than my grandfather's out-of-tune guitar or his modest house by the sea.

As I listened impatiently to the dean hold forth on the needs of poor Latinos who lived in neighborhoods through which I would avoid driving if at all possible, people who might try to pay me for my services with chickens or tortillas, people whose teen-age sons might mug me on my way home from a night shift in the emergency room, I grew more and more concerned about paying back the $60,000 in student loans I had amassed during my academic career. I was contemplating a lucrative career in diagnostic radiology—whatever youthful idealism I had brought with me to medicine had long since evaporated. I had started to like the fluid look of my reflection in the shiny Volvos and BMW's parked around the hospital in the spaces reserved for the radiologists; I liked having my boundaries blurred. What could be wrong with the soft, pink, perfectly made body of success? I wanted to wear America like an expensive suit, the best that money could buy. I deserved it.

Of course, I conceded on some level that there were others like me who had been dispossessed as well, perhaps just as unfairly, those same Spanish-speaking people who were fast becoming my patients as I embarked on my first ward rotations. I saw, too, how what they had lost oftentimes was recorded physically upon their bodies: the missing limb, amputated after an inadvertent step on a land mine; the empty eye socket where the globe had been ruptured after a gun butt's brutal blow to the face; the lost uterus, removed during a Government-promoted sterilization program.

5 Sometimes their illnesses were less obviously caused by the conditions in which they were now forced to live, or by the jobs hunger urged them to take: the green-eyed woman from Mexico who burned her arm in the maw of a laundry press, the gray-haired Salvadoran man with scarred lungs and a nerve disorder, who had probably inhaled pesticides sprayed while he was picking fruit; the cinnamon-black man from Cuba whose infant daughter was bitten by a hungry rat in the housing projects where they lived. I felt sorry for them, to be sure, but if there was one thing I had by then learned during medical school, it was how to protect myself.

Moreover, my own once-downtrodden family of immigrants had not only survived but prospered. Despite their own personal litany of hardships—the omnipresent language barrier, the matter-of-fact but subtle discrimination and the especially savored moments of blatant persecution—their durability, much more than their industrious achievements, had been always a source of great pride to them. So I expected no less of these people for whom I was beginning to care, whose bodies were my laboratories and my classrooms. If they were vaguely "my people," it was more in the sense of "property" or "baggage" as opposed to "spirit." The myth of the uniqueness of fingerprints was making a dangerous kind of sense to me: human beings are so unalterably different, even when they share a mother tongue or a susceptibility to bullets, I believed it was impossible for an embrace or a prayer or a handshake or a poem to bring them together.

Then there was the larger problem of what was meant by "community" in the first place. Was this well-intentioned dean referring, when she pronounced this polysyllabic word, only to the Cuban expatriate community, whose rabid patriotism and reactionary anti-Communist/anti-Castro right-wing politics repulsed me, but to whom I nonetheless belonged in the most obvious ways?

Or did she mean the more broadly defined Latino community, which in Boston at the time comprised not only Cubans but also much larger contingents of Dominicans and Salvadorans, as well as a significant number of Puerto Ricans (some born on the mainland, some back on the island itself) and a growing number of Mexican-Americans?

Or, perhaps worst of all, did she simply relegate me to the most broadly defined category available, that clamoring, undifferentiated heap of the darker-skinned oppressed, those pitiably disadvantaged and generically "poor" people in America? Or were there other groups of people—ones I was afraid to acknowledge in her genteel presence, or even others at the moment unknown to both of us—with whom I shared yet another different homeland?

I had felt many times, or had been made to feel, that I had been admitted 10
to Harvard Medical School for a very specific reason. I was not really expected to think independently or to have original ideas but to satisfy a quota. It was a thankless role: the one who desperately needs that life-changing hand up. This identity was especially painful to bear, because it was created by the kindly liberal people whom I knew were allies—people who wanted to do something to help, as long as they did not have to reach out into those needy communities themselves with their own clean, well-manicured hands.

These liberals were preferable, at least, to the outright bigots who angrily bemoaned my presence among them. To them, I was the reason their sons did not get into Harvard. Perhaps they imagined I was another 10th baby born out of wedlock who would someday have 10 illegitimate children myself and thus take over the world by outbreeding white people. Or I was a beneficiary of Head Start, food stamps and other expensive Government-sponsored entitlement programs that siphoned off their tax dollars from more worthy uses like Star Wars or the B-1 bomber. I was responsible for the resurgence of tuberculosis in the United States, the illegal immigrant who smuggled the organism into the country hidden in my lungs like contraband. I was not human to them, so I myself could not suffer; I was simply a vector.

I was all the potentially lethal vermin and the terrible scourges they carried, the fierce African killer bee, the blood-sucking mosquito, the typhus-infected rat. I was the pathetic monkey trying to imitate them, to steal their precious American know-how and cutting-edge technology and take it back to my own country. I was dragging their gloriously free society down the tubes.

Then there were the few other Latinos in medicine whom I encountered, mostly older, disgruntled men who worked in chronically underfinanced primary-care programs. I recall vividly the harrowing interview with the director of minority recruitment at one West Coast medical school, who demanded to know why I had not checked any of the boxes next to the various categories that allowed the school to identify minority-group candidates. He implied that either I was ashamed of my heritage or I was a sellout too eager for the promised assimilation that would never come. Affirmative action was not special consideration, he argued, but redress of past inequities. He then accused me of possibly the worst of all crimes, namely the abandonment of my own community. That word again: "community."

There were other reasons for my ambivalence about "giving back." That Latino culture is stereotypically seen as welcoming, colorful and musical made its rejection of me when I came out as a gay man all the more painful. The quietly closed doors of the Anglo world literally paled in comparison with the melodramatic tears this revelation caused in my own family, the near-violent disowning of my lover by his father and the sanctimonious sermons I endured from Catholic priests. The Latino "community," the one place where I expected to be unconditionally loved, turned out to have a virulent hostility to homosexuality. I came to think of myself as doubly illegal, at once the unwanted immigrant and the sinful castaway who would shame the culture that had given me life.

Ultimately, it was this unspeakable love that led me to the place where I 15
am now, to a career not in diagnostic radiology but in general internal medicine, which allows me to provide primary care mostly to Latino patients in Boston. It was the love of another man, Latino himself, who taught me to appreciate my culture and led me to my place at the banquet table. It was his nurturing that sustained me through the cold winters of my New England college and later through the chilling anatomy labs of medical school. It did not matter to him whether on occasion I listened to old Broadway show tunes or to Led Zeppelin instead of salsa; we could still communicate in Spanish, we could still cook paella, *plátanos* and rice and beans, still discuss politics late into the night while chain-smoking cigarettes. We created our own country of origin, crossed oceans to our own undiscovered continent. We would invent our own utopian political system, we who belonged neither to Spain nor to the United States but to each other.

Under the tutelage of his love, I began over the years to understand democracy and human rights in a revolutionary way. I saw particularly that in illness, as in desire, all people are indeed created equal. Suffering did not respect national boundaries nor speak in only one approved language. The color of blood in every flag was monotonously the same unfathomable red. Need paid no attention to what part of whose body was placed where. Death visited every neighborhood, riding in on the subway or in a stretch limousine at any hour of the day or night. Though wealth might have the power to promote health, and maybe even to prolong life, in the end all my patients needed me to hold their hands, to smile and touch their faces. Everyone needed a witness; all of them wanted someone to whom they could tell their final stories. Afterward, the agonal last breaths always followed the same basic pattern, and the flat green line on the monitor always failed to be rekindled with the electrical wave form of a beating heart.

Oppression, too, transcended class. The infected rat bite, the debilitating toxic exposure and the relentless spread of AIDS were no longer simply the documentation of losses that I had learned to compile passively from the history of my own family, losses about which nothing could be done; rather, each became a form of active violence perpetrated by the powerful against the weak, calling for an immediate, drastic and equally purposeful response.

I began to understand how one atrocity led to another: from the genocide of this land's indigenous peoples (a fact I had once haughtily questioned), in which European diseases wiped out native people, to the American embargo of Cuba, where because of the lack of vaccines and antibiotics children continue to die each day.

I learned from reading the newspapers many things that were never mentioned in my medical textbooks. The contentious debates over Government spending to combat AIDS raged in ever-more-hostile terms during my four years of medical school. It was for all intents and purposes a war, one that had led desperate and misguided Act Up members to disrupt Mass at St. Patrick's Cathedral by blocking the aisles, throwing condoms and spitting out the host.

20 It was a war in which the rhetoric of hate and bigotry was venomously expressed by Jesse Helms, the senior Republican Senator from North Carolina, who spoke the following words on the Senate floor: "What originally began as a measured response to a public health emergency has become a weapon, frankly, for the deterioration, if not the destruction, of America's Judeo-Christian value system. There's not a chance this bill will be stopped because there's a powerful lobby out there in the media and in the homosexual community, and senators are scrambling to put their names on anything that has to do with AIDS."

Weapon, community, homosexual, America, values, Judeo-Christian, AIDS: Was my community "the homosexual community" that Jesse Helms seemed so adept at identifying and annihilating, while I, one of its own members, had struggled so long to find it? Did my assent to this question therefore mean that I was not American? Or not Christian? Or not Latino?

These questions about labels began to swirl in my head as I made my rounds in the hospital each morning, and though their answers might seem obvious, my education and my pride in my accomplishments rose to a painful hard knot in my throat as I stared into the eyes of those who were actually dying, those gaunt men and women who were neither senators nor doctors, those who were not necessarily gay or Latino, or heterosexual or African-American or female or white; their most conspicuous defining characteristic was that they were suffering.

Because my training is both in medicine and in poetry, because my languages are both English and Spanish, because my love is at once conventional and not and because I was born in only one place and at one time, I once had this fantasy: the invention of a single blood test capable of proving beyond all doubt that we are all fundamentally the same creature. I have seen our naked bodies; I know I am just as human as Tom Cruise, whose beautiful image is worth millions of dollars, just as human as my IV-drug-using AIDS patient in the emergency room whose name I forgot within minutes of her death in my arms. I freely admit I am still naïve, believing at times that a touch can heal even in an intensive-care unit or that a prayer can be heard outside the confines of a church.

It has been suggested to me that my problem, however it is defined, has resulted from an exaggerated capacity on my part for dwelling on the innumerable wrongs done to me. I have been told that I must always remember how to forget. Enough with the queer thing, they say, warning me that I am beginning to sound like a frustrated mariachi who wants to wear his pink ruffled shirt to sing in a restaurant that serves only tacos. Too serious, too sensitive, too insistent, my parents say. My poems have an unfortunate tendency to wallow in the misery of their own creation, besides being obsessed with my patriarchal past. Perhaps I have driven my community, whatever it might be, away from me with my unending questions and saturnine social skills. Perhaps I have told one too many a story about a patient whose life or death changed my own.

If these criticisms are accurate, then I accept them; but I realize how I 25
have always, even before my awkward conversation with the dean—sometimes in spite of myself and sometimes with the fullest of hearts—felt compelled to search for some way to give.

I used to feel that the most insurmountable of all the obstacles facing me in the care of my patients was my own selfishness. I was too busy to listen to the pathetic story of another person's suffering, too hungry to stay a few minutes longer to comfort another person in need, too important to be burdened with another person's trivial concerns. But I have tried to internalize what I have learned from my patients themselves. I remember how they have endured and how they have taught me what I once thought was impossible, something I thought I might never learn: the limitless ways that I can give back to many communities.

I wonder who you would see if I were to come to you for help. I am not tall, I have an olive complexion, I have dark straight hair, I have green eyes. I am a bit overweight, I have a job, I have enough money for shelter, for food. I look like the hybrid that I am. Like most hybrids, I will never reproduce. I am toxic to my own inspirations and dreams; in my veins run both the promise of a better life and its incessant denial. My physical appearance marks me, though it remains unmarred, unlike the bodies of so many others of my kind. I walk down the street in San Francisco and am mistaken for a Mexican. I could be illegal. Once, an elderly lady driving a white Cadillac asked me whether I was Jewish. I am the Jew of the Caribbean—isn't that what they call Cubans? My mother was born in Dover, N.J. Her parents' relatives still live in Italy. My father is a United States citizen. I memorized an American version of his own history.

Maybe I can give that back. Maybe I can teach you to love something new, like salsa or black beans and white rice or Gloria Estefan or Andy Garcia. I want you to know something about me, about us, after you finish reading this. I am writing a new poem later today. I want you to read it, too. I want to be mistaken for your brother or your son; I want to remind you of your daughter, your mother, your sister; I want to give you something—not a disease but perhaps a cure. I want you to look into the liquid mirror of my eyes and see someone you recognize. Someone you have always known, someone you might even love.

Yourself.

Understanding

1. What is the overriding purpose of Campo's essay?
2. What's the context for the loss Campo is referring to in his first paragraph? Who is "us" in paragraph 2? Can you infer his background from this introduction?
3. What "youthful idealism" did he bring to a career in medicine?
4. What definition of community did Campo describe?
5. How did Campo arrive at his understanding of "giving back"?
6. The subtitle of the article is *But which one [community]? A doctor's struggle with identity politics.* How does Campo illuminate the political issues involved in knowing one's self? What were his political affiliations? Were they of his choosing?
7. Campo weaves a key term, *love,* throughout his essay. Trace the many ways he refers to love and analyze the effect of repeating a particular word throughout an essay. Does it become repetitive? Does it instead enhance the essay?

Responding

1. Memoir allows writers to invent their truths. Whether or not Campo's interpretation as to why he'd been admitted to medical school is true, does it matter in making his point? That he created a "them" lends power to the argument, especially for those readers who have the same view. Does naming this "they" make them real?
2. The writers in "Taking Stands" have traveled different roads toward what is meaningful in their lives, and for most it has been revealed by an unmistakable empathy for their fellow humans. "To understand the human condition has been the work of my life," says Dr. Sherwin Nuland. Would you say that too?
3. How does Campo's essay reveal "an integrated self"? Analyze it by the factors that contribute to describing a self that you feel is right: Campo's gifts, Campo's wounds, Campo's dreams, Campo's decisions, Campo's biological inheritance, and Campo's communities. Once you have analyzed the article in this way, outline what you would include in a similar article on the various aspects of your life that come together to form your integrated self.

Connecting

1. In "The World of the Self" earlier in this chapter, Csikszentmihalyi wrote, "The ideas that become central representations of the self are those in which a person invests the most psychic energy" (paragraph 12). Are there

instances in Campo's writing where he recounts a large investment of psychic energy? If so, relate them to Csikszentmihalyi's claim.

2. Infer Campo's age. Which of Erik Erikson's stages are the backdrop for Campo's writing of this article? What were the developmental tasks of that stage that the young Campo was working through when he was in medical school? Which was he working with when he actually found the way to integrate his life and community affiliations?

Dear Olga

Václav Havel

Few writers have made as successful a transition to political life as Václav Havel, president of the Czech Republic. Born in 1936 in Prague, Czechoslovakia, of a prominent business family, Havel began publishing articles in literary and theater magazines at the age of nineteen. His early plays, "The Garden Party" (1963), "The Memorandum" (1965), and "The Increased Difficulty of Concentration" (1968) all take issue with the effects of three decades of political conflict which saw his country first overtaken by the Nazi government in 1939 and then spun off into the Soviet orbit following World War II.

In 1968 Soviet troops invaded Czechoslovakia in response to the intellectual ferment called the "Prague Spring," in which Havel took part. In 1975 he spoke out against the continuing oppression in an open letter to then-president Gustave Jusak. Publication of his plays was then banned. Havel continued to defy prohibitions against his writing and was imprisoned. One month after he was last arrested on October 17, 1987, he was proposed as a presidential candidate, and in parliamentary elections was elected president. In January 1993, after the peaceful division of Czechoslovakia, Havel was popularly elected the first president of the Czech Republic.

"As soon as my homeland does not need me in this office," he is quoted as saying in a *New York Times* interview, "I will devote myself with great appetite to my original profession." "Dear Olga," one of 144 letters written to his first wife, dates from the period of his four-and-a-half-year imprisonment for subversion.

6 September 1981

Dear Olga, 1

I'm sure you remember the end of Ionesco's *The Chairs,* when the Orator comes on to give the assembled public an extremely important message: it amounts to the sum total of all that the Old Man and Old Woman have learned during their lifetime—knowledge they must pass on to the world before they leave it; knowledge that will reveal some fundamental truth and explain 'how it all is.' The Orator, it is implied, is going to acquaint his audience with the true meaning of life. But the long-awaited speech consists merely of utter gibberish.

Many have interpreted this as expressing the author's conviction that communication is impossible, that two people can never come to an understanding about anything, much less the 'meaning of life,' because life has no meaning: all is vanity and man is hopelessly submerged in total meaninglessness. Hardly unexpected, therefore, that Ionesco is for many the dramatist of absolute scepticism and nihilism.

What Ionesco meant is his own business. I mention the play now not because I want to impose my own explanation on it, but because the motif of the Orator seems to me a useful starting point.

Notice: the Old Man and Old Woman—aware of how significant their 5
message is, and the importance of giving it to the world in a comprehensible form—do not deliver the message themselves, but hire a professional communicator.

If the Orator's purpose was really to inform the public of the meaning of life, then he failed. Why? Because the meaning of life is not a snippet of unfamiliar information conveyed by someone who knows it to someone who doesn't—as an astronomer might tell us the number of planets in the solar system, or a statistician how many alcoholics there are. The mystery of being and the meaning of life are not 'data,' and people cannot be separated into those who know the data and those who don't. None of us becomes 'better' than anyone else simply by learning something others have not learned, or rather by encountering some fundamental 'truth' that others have missed. Safarik correctly distinguishes between truth and information: information is portable and transmissible; truth is less simple. (In any case, history has adequately demonstrated that the more people who succumb to the delusion that truth is a commodity which can readily be passed on, the greater the horrors that follow—because this delusion inevitably leads to the conviction that the world can be improved simply by spreading the truth as quickly as possible. And what quicker way to spread it than by violence?)

As I understand it, 'the meaning of life' is not 'objectively' knowable or graspable as a concept at all.

For me, the notion of some complete and finite knowledge, that explains everything and raises no further questions, relates clearly to the idea of an end—an end to the spirit, to life, to time and to being. However, anything meaningful ever said on the matter (including every religious gospel) is remarkable for its dramatic openness, its incompleteness. It is not a conclusive statement so much as a challenge or an appeal—to something that is, in the highest sense, living; to something that overwhelms us or speaks to us, obliges or excites us; to something that accords with our innermost experience and may even change our entire life, but which never, of course, attempts to settle unequivocally the unanswerable question of meaning. Instead, it tends to suggest how to live with the question.

Is that too little? I don't think so. Living with the question means constantly 'responding' to it, or rather, having some form of living contact with that meaning, always hearing a faint echo of it. It means not an end to the problem, but an ever-closer co-existence with it. Though we cannot 'answer' it in the traditional sense of the word, we, by longing for it and seeking after it, confront it indirectly over and over again. We are a little like the blind man touching the woman he loves, whom he has never seen and never will. The question of the meaning of life is not a full stop at the end of life, but the beginning of a deeper experience of it. It is like a light whose source we cannot see, but in whose illumination we nevertheless live—whether we delight in its incomprehensible abundance or suffer from its incomprehensible paucity.

10 Ultimately, being in constant touch with this mystery is what makes us genuinely human. Man is the only creature who is both a part of being (and thus a bearer of its mystery) and aware of that mystery as a mystery. He is both the question and the questioner, and cannot help being so. It might even be said that, through man, being can inquire after itself.

The first serious confrontation with the question of meaning does not occur only when one feels that life has lost its meaning; it also happens at the moment when, as a result of one's own reflections, one is seriously touched by meaning itself. This moment also constitutes the beginning of man's history as a human being, of the history of culture, of the history of what we might call 'the order of the spirit.'

This is a history not of 'answering,' but of 'questioning'; it does not begin with a life whose meaning is already known, but with a life knowing itself ignorant of its own meaning and prepared to come to terms with this hard fact constantly.

This 'coming to terms with meaning' is the most complex, the most obscure and at the same time the most important metaphysical experience one can go through in life.

I don't know any other way of tackling the question of 'the meaning of life' than undergoing the experience personally and trying to report on it. In one way or another, this is what I've been trying to do from the outset in my letters, and I intend to carry on, in the hope that whatever I manage to squeeze out in these difficult circumstances will be taken neither literally nor too seriously, but as a stream of improvised attempts to articulate my unarticulated 'inner life.' Above all, let me not sound like Ionesco's Orator.

15 I can't wait for the visit!

Kisses,
Vasek

Understanding

1. What is subversion? What about the content of this letter suggests that Havel was imprisoned for this crime?
2. Assuming that we have the complete text of Havel's letter to Olga, the reader notices that the content is relatively impersonal: There are no intimate details, no questions about the family or life on the outside. What effect does this "neutered" style have on the reader? From the text of this letter, what inferences can you make about Havel's and Olga's quest for an "integrated" life? Support your points with portions of the letter that apply.
3. Eugene Ionesco (1912–94), to whom Havel refers in the first paragraph of his letter, was a celebrated Romanian-born French dramatist whose plays depicted life's absurdities. Fascinated by language—he was inspired to write one of his most famous plays, "The Bald Soprano," by his language

learning experiences—Ionesco has written that if he told his private thoughts it was because he knew that they were not his alone, that practically everyone was trying to say the same things, and that the writer is the only one who says out loud what other people think or whisper. What connection does Ionesco's statement have to those aspects of Havel's thinking that he relates in his letter?

Responding

1. " 'Coming to terms with meaning' is the most complex . . . and . . . the most important metaphysical experience one can go through in life" (paragraph 13). We may add that "coming to terms with meaning" is a step toward integrating the multiple roles and demands that we accept. Describe one or two experiences from your life in which you tried to come to terms with the meaning of an event or a situation. Relate how this process clarified your various roles and assess the importance of this experience in your life.
2. If you could convene anyone, including the authors of the readings in this book, to explore the "meaning of life," whom would you invite? Why? What questions would you ask? If you could choose anyone to be your Orator, who would it be?
3. Many of Havel's public speeches and addresses since becoming president of the Czech Republic are on the Internet. Review at least two of them for themes. Does he refer to the meaning of life in the same way now as he did when he was in prison? Thematically, how do his later writings compare with this letter to Olga?
4. Which of your political, social, or moral beliefs are central to your identity? How strongly do they matter to you? For which of them would you be willing to go to prison? Explain your reasoning.
5. Throughout the centuries, governments have imprisoned writers for publishing ideas contrary to the accepted "truth." Why is this a standard punishment for dissident writers? Is writing a dangerous activity? Explain.

Connecting

1. As Havel states, "the meaning of life is not a snippet of unfamiliar information conveyed by someone who knows it to someone who doesn't" (paragraph 6). How does this statement compare with Plato's analogy in "The Ascent to Wisdom" (chapter six) in which those exposed to the "truth" must "descend again among the prisoners in the den, and partake of their labors and honors"?
2. How is Havel's coming to terms with meaning a particular instance of Frankl's notion in "The Push and Pull of Values" that we choose our attitude in a given set of circumstances?
3. How does Havel's assertion about the importance of coming to terms with meaning relate to Raspberry's belated awareness in "A Father, a Daughter,

and a Lesson" that fathers and stepfathers "have special power to life their daughters' sense of self"?

4. Consider this question: What does it mean that life has no meaning? In the front matter of *Signatures,* in "To the Student: Essential Reading Before You Begin," we quoted Friedrich Nietzsche as saying, "There are no facts, only interpretations." Discuss Havel's assertions regarding the meaning of life in relation to Nietzsche's statement. Then relate your analysis to the quotation from Milan Kundera in the same section of the front matter.
5. To which of Erik Erikson's stages of development is Havel attending?

A Jew Discovered

James McBride

As Václav Havel remarks in his letter to Olga, coming to terms with meaning is the most complex experience we can have in our lives. The events that James McBride details in "A Jew Discovered" seem to confirm this observation.

In this excerpt from his memoir, subtitled *A Black Man's Tribute to His White Mother,* McBride weaves interviews with his mother, Ruth, who grew up in a small Virginia town, the daughter of an arranged marriage between a traveling rabbi turned storekeeper and a disabled Polish woman who couldn't speak English, with reflections on his childhood. The eighth of twelve children who grew up in the all-black housing projects of Red Hook in the Bronx, McBride says that his was "a house where there was little money and little food [where] power was derived from who you could order around."

McBride's mixed-race parentage—his father, Dennis, was black, and Ruth was "as white as Elizabeth Taylor"—bewildered him because his mother refused to discuss it. "We were a close family," he reports, "and my mother insulated us from some of the confusion [about race]. She just kept us occupied with music and art and a respect for knowledge . . . but it did crash in on us when we became adolescents and teenagers and created a lot of problems."

In this excerpt from his memoir *The Color of Water,* McBride relates his attempts to learn about his white Virginia family and its effects on his sense of self. A composer and saxophonist as well as a former writer for the *Boston Globe,* the *Washington Post,* and *People* magazine, McBride is married and lives in South Nyack, New York. The "color of water" in the title is his mother's response to his childhood question, "What color is God's spirit?"

It was afternoon, August 1992, and I was standing in front of the only synagogue in downtown Suffolk, a collection of old storefronts, dimly lit buildings, and old railroad tracks that tell of better, more populous times. It's a small, old, white building with four tall columns and a row of stairs leading to a tall doorway. This is the synagogue that young Rachel Shilsky walked to with her family and where Rabbi Shilsky led the congregation during the Jewish holidays Rosh Hashana, the Jewish New Year, and Yom Kippur, the day of atonement and fasting. When I was a boy, Jewish holidays meant a day off from school for me and that was it. I certainly had no idea they had anything to do with me. 1

I felt like an oddball standing in front of the quiet, empty building, and looked up and down the street every couple of minutes lest the cops come by and wonder why a black man was loitering in front of a white man's building in the middle of the day in Suffolk, Virginia. This is, after all, the nineties, and any black man who loiters in front of a building for a long time looking it over is bound to draw suspicion from cops and others who probably think he's looking for an open entrance so he can climb in and steal something. Black males are closely associated with crime in America, not with white Jewish mothers, and I could not imagine a police officer buying my story as I stood in front of the Jewish temple saying, "Uh, yeah, my grandfather was the rabbi here, you know . . ." The sun was baking the sidewalk and it was so hot I sat down on the steps, placing my tape recorder and notebook next to me.

My long search for the Shilsky family ended here. I had spent considerable time looking through school records, court records, and other documents with mixed results. My grandmother Hudis was buried far from here, in a Long Island graveyard amongst hundreds and hundreds of Jews, more than she ever had the pleasure of living around down here. The U.S. Army forked over the death record of Sergeant Sam Shilsky, who died in February 1944, but the details of his service record were gone forever, lost in a fire of army personnel records. I felt like I was stalking ghosts. No sign of Rabbi Shilsky, whom I traced to a Brooklyn address in the 1960s, where he apparently landed after wandering through Norfolk, Virginia; Belleville, New Jersey; and Manhattan. Dee-Dee vanished from Suffolk shortly before her mother died, and never returned. She withdrew from Suffolk High on January 23, 1942, one semester short of graduation. Her mother died five days later, on January 28, 1942, in New York City. I could only imagine how painful that must have been, having to leave the only real home she ever had at age seventeen, her mother gone, her father with a gentile woman, her brother in the war, her sister disappeared; being completely helpless as the pillars of her life fell away like toothpicks. Everything she had known was gone. Whom did she live with? Maybe the father kept her. Who knows? I had a feeling she was still alive. She would have been about sixty-seven then. I could have tracked her down—I was, after all, a reporter—but after a couple of feeble attempts I gave up. I didn't have the heart. I didn't want to introduce any more pain into her life. She'd seen enough. The closest I could come to her was to sit on these synagogue steps, baking in the August heat, and wonder.

I wanted to see the inside of the synagogue. I wanted to see it, then later tell my black wife and my two children about it—because some of my blood runs through there, because my family has a history there, because there's a part of me in there whether I, or those that run the synagogue, like it or not. In truth, I had never been inside an actual synagogue before, the closest being the time I was working as a reporter and did a story about a Jewish school in Queens that had a synagogue attached to it. In the course of interviewing the headmaster, a woman, I mentioned that my mother was Jewish and she exclaimed, "Well, according to Jewish law that means you're Jewish too! We have a black Jew who works in our school!" She hit the intercom button on her desk phone and said, "Sam, can you come up here a minute?" Minutes later the black janitor walked in, holding a mop, smiling. I'd pay good money for a picture of my face at that moment. Ol' Sam smiled and said hello and I gurgled out a polite response, though I wanted to choke myself for opening up my big mouth.

When I called the rabbi of my mother's old synagogue he spoke to me with neither nostalgia nor surprise, only grudging recognition. He had heard I was in town from other Jews whom I had met. He knew I was black and he knew who my mother was. "I remember your mother," he said. I explained to him that I was writing a book about my family and asked if I might see some of the synagogue records. "There's nothing in them that would help you," he said curtly. I asked if I could see the inside of the synagogue itself. He said, "I'll have to check with some other board members to see who would have time to open it up to let you see it," and hung up. I knew the deal. Given the photo of the board members on the synagogue's anniversary pamphlet I'd obtained, I doubted if half the old geezers on the board were still drawing air. I hung up, muttering to myself, "I didn't want to see your silly old synagogue anyway."

By then I had seen enough anyway. The smell of azaleas and the creeping loneliness that climbed over me as I poked around Suffolk had begun to suffocate me. The isolation my family had felt, the heartbreak they had suffered, seemed to ooze out of the trees, curling through the stately old brick buildings and rising like steam off the Civil War statue that seemed to point its cannon directly at me as I wandered through the town graveyard. I wanted to leave right at that moment, but instead sat on the synagogue steps as if glued, as my mind reeled back to a previous trip in 1982, when fate and luck led me deep into the bowels of a state office building where Aubrey Rubenstein was working for the highway department right-of-way office. Rubenstein was in his early sixties then, a heavyset man with dark hair, a deep southern accent, and a very clear and concise manner. His father had taken over my grandfather's store around 1942 after the old man left town. When I walked into his office and explained who I was, he looked at me a long, long time. He didn't smile. He didn't frown. Finally he spoke: "What a surprise," he said softly. He offered me a seat and a cup of coffee. I accepted. "Don't move from there," he said.

He got on the phone. "Jaffe," he said, "I have incredible news. Fishel Shilsky's grandson is here. Sitting in my office. No kidding. . . . Uh-huh. And you won't believe it. He's black. No. I'm not lying. He's a reporter writing a book about his family. . . . Yep." When he hung up the phone, he said, "When we're done, go around to the slaughterhouse on Main and see Gerry Jaffe and his family. They'd like to see you in person." I knew the name Jaffe. Mommy had spoken of them several times. *The Jaffes had a slaughterhouse down the road. Tateh would take us there to slaughter the cows in the kosher faith.* . . . I made it a point to go see them. Like most of the Jews in Suffolk they treated me very kindly, truly warm and welcoming, as if I were one of them, which in an odd way I suppose I was. I found it odd and amazing when white people treated me that way, as if there were no barriers between us. It said a lot about this religion—Judaism—that some of its followers, old southern crackers who talked with southern twangs and wore straw hats, seemed to believe that its covenants went beyond the color of one's skin. The Sheffers, Helen Weintraub, the Jaffes, they talked to me in person and by letter in a manner and tone that, in essence, said "Don't forget us. We have survived here. Your mother was part of this. . . ."

Sitting in his office, Aubrey Rubenstein talked easily, as a black colleague sat nearby eavesdropping with awe at the macabre conversation that unfolded between this elderly white man and myself. "There are not that many of us left," Aubrey said. "We had maybe twenty-five or thirty Jewish families here at one time, back when your grandfather was around. The older ones died, the younger ones left. Some went to California, some to Virginia Beach, or just moved. The only ones who stayed had businesses with their fathers that dropped down to them."

"Why did they all leave?" I asked.

"Why stay?" he said. "It was not that easy a place for a Jew to live. It was a 10
tiny population of Jews. Most were merchants of one type or another. I suppose some found it easier to make a living elsewhere." Wandering Jews, I thought.

We spoke easily for quite a while. "It's an interesting thing that you've come down to check on your granddaddy," he said. "It's quite a story, I must say."

I asked him about my family. "Well, it was kind of a tragedy, really. Shilsky wasn't the man he could have been. He was a good rabbi—by that I mean he knew what he was teaching. In fact, he taught me a little as a boy. But he went into business full-time, which didn't please a lot of Jews here, and he was seeing another woman for years. I'm not sure whether he was divorced when he left here or not, but I ran into him in New York after the war, maybe '46. Me and another fella went to see him about buying the piece of property next door to his store. He was up in Brooklyn."

"What was he doing there?"

"I don't know. But I believe Mrs. Shilsky had died by then. The whole thing was very tragic." Seeing the expression on my face, he added, "Your grandmother was a fine lady. I still remember her coming to temple, lighting the candles, and standing up to say her prayers. I remember her clearly. She was crippled in the leg. She was a very fine lady."

I asked him if anyone knew how Rabbi Shilsky treated his family, and 15
Rubenstein shrugged.

"There are things that you hear, but no one asked. He was tight with his money and they could have been doing better than they looked. The Shilskys kept to themselves. Your Uncle Sam, he joined the air force and got killed in a plane crash in Alaska. They didn't find his body or that of the other pilot for a long time, if they ever did find them. I heard this and don't know it to be true or not. Your Aunt Gladys, you don't know her, do you? She was a very bright girl. Your mother . . . well, she was a fine girl. Of course we had heard rumors, and I'm being frank, that she had run off and married a black man, but I never knew it to be true or not. My daddy at one time said it, but my parents never gave it any further comment. My father and mother were like liberals in their days. I never heard them knock anybody for being white or black or green or Christian or Jew or Catholic."

I said nothing, listening in silence. I imagined that the news of Mommy's marriage crashed through the Jewish community like an earthquake.

"How is your mother?" he asked.

"Fine."

"You know," he said, fingering the papers on his desk, "you look a little bit like your mother. The smile. Do you attend temple, being part Jewish?"

"No. She didn't raise us Jewish."

"Well, maybe that was for the best," he said.

I was surprised by his candidness and said so.

We talked for a while longer before I rose to go. "Next time you come back I'll see if I can dig up a picture of that old store," he said. "Make sure to tell your mother Aubrey Rubenstein said hello."

I pointed to my tape player on his desk. "The tape is running," I said. "You can say it yourself."

He leaned over to the tape and spoke into it softly. When he was done, he leaned back in his chair, and looked at the ceiling thoughtfully. "She picked that life for herself and she lived it, that's all. What her reasons for it were I don't know. But she did a good job. She raised twelve children. She led a good life."

I told him I'd be back in a few months. "I'll have a picture of that store for you," he promised. But I waited ten years to come back, and when I called on him again he had died. I kept the tape with his greeting to Mommy on it for years, and while I never played it for her, thinking it might be too emotional for her to hear it, I played it for myself many times, thinking, wishing, hoping that the world would be this open-minded, knowing that God is: *Ruth, this is Aubrey Rubenstein. I don't know if you remember me or not, but if you do, I'm glad to meet your son and I see you've accomplished a great deal in your life. If you're ever down this way stop on by and say hello to us. We all remember you. We wish you the best.*

As I sat on the steps of the synagogue in the hot August sun, his words sliced through my memory like raindrops. I watched as two little black girls strode by, waved, and walked on. One was eating a bag of potato chips. I said to myself, "Whatever I'm looking for, I've found it." I got in my car and drove back to the McDonald's where the store had been. I walked around the grounds once again, as if the earth would speak to me. But it did not. It was just a cement parking lot. They ought to take the whole kit and caboodle of these cement parking lots and heave them into the sea, I thought. The Shilskys were gone. Long gone.

That night I slept in a motel just down the road from the McDonald's, and at about four in the morning I sat straight up. Something just drew me awake. I tossed and turned for an hour, then got dressed and went outside, walking down the road toward the nearby wharf. As I walked along the wharf and looked over the Nansemond River, which was colored an odd purple by the light of the moon, I said to myself, "What am I doing here? This place is so lonely. I gotta get out of here." It suddenly occurred to me that my grandmother had walked around here and gazed upon this water many times, and the loneliness and agony that Hudis Shilsky felt as a Jew in this lonely southern town—far from her mother and sisters in New York, unable to speak English, a disabled Polish immigrant whose husband had no love for her and whose dreams of seeing her children grow up in America vanished as her life drained out of her at the age of forty-six—suddenly rose up in my blood and washed over me in waves. A penetrating loneliness covered me, lay on me so heavily I had to sit down and cover my face. I had no tears to shed. They were done long ago, but a new pain and a new awareness were born inside me. The uncertainty that lived inside me began to dissipate; the ache that the little boy who stared in the mirror felt was gone. My own humanity was awakened, rising up to greet me with a handshake as I watched the first glimmers of sunlight peek over the horizon. There's such a big difference between being dead and alive, I told myself, and the greatest gift that anyone can give anyone else is life. And the greatest sin a person can do to another is to take away that life. Next to that, all the rules and religions in the world are secondary; mere words and beliefs that people choose to believe and kill and hate by. My life won't be lived that way, and neither, I hope, will my children's. I left for New York happy in the knowledge that my grandmother had not suffered and died for nothing.

Understanding

1. What is it about McBride's visit to Suffolk that caused "a new pain and a new awareness" to be born inside him?
2. All communities are repositories of values which they attempt to pass along to the next generation. What values did McBride's family communicate to him? What values did his mother Ruth's family exemplify? What values did the Jewish community of Suffolk proclaim?

Responding

1. James McBride went to his mother's hometown to seek his roots. Where would you go to do the same? What happened in the place you chose that inform your decision?
2. From time to time in our lives, we are embraced by a moment of connection with our self similar to the one McBride describes in the last part of this selection. These moments of deep personal awareness—epiphanies, or what Glidewell calls choice points, can occur during prayer or meditation, —while driving, listening to music, or, as they did for McBride, while walking along a wharf. Have you ever experienced such a state of awareness? If so, describe it. How has it influenced your life since then?

Connecting

1. McBride's experience of "self" is a combination of his biological inheritance—his genes—and the influences of his culture. Collect examples from McBride's narrative that suggest that he experienced, as Csikszentmihalyi proposed in "The Veils of Maya and the World of the Genes" (chapter five) and "The World of Culture" (chapter six), the distortions associated with these forces.
2. In what ways does McBride's new awareness compare or contrast with Dubner's religious quest in "Choosing My Religion" (chapter six)?
3. Referring to Allport's examination in chapter six of religion as a solitary quest, how might McBride's epiphany be called a religious experience?

On Freedom and Resources

John C. Glidewell

Freedom, and our personal definitions of it, have a great deal to do with how we integrate the parts of our lives to describe ourselves. The concept of freedom that has pervaded the selections in this chapter is often associated with choice, with the ultimate meaning of life, and with happiness and satisfaction. In this selection from *Choice Points: Essays on the Emotional Problems of Living with People,* John C. Glidewell addresses the compelling but problematic attempt to define freedom. In the end he presents us with a deceptively simple definition and links it to resources.

A social scientist who has taught psychology, sociology, and anthropology, Glidewell has had numerous positions as researcher and professor at such universities as Vanderbilt and the University of Chicago. He is a prolific writer and contributor to his fields because, as he says, "ideas interest me profoundly" and he enjoys trying to express them as clearly and precisely as possible.

Some feelings have been worked into me much too well. To be regularly dependent upon others is to be weak and entrapped. To conform regularly to the expectations of others is to be weak and enslaved. That's how I feel. In my head, I know better. I know that to be dependent is sometimes to be altogether sensible, sensible enough to have good use of resources that I couldn't otherwise have. I know that to conform is sometimes to be wonderfully dependable, dependable enough to have the respect of others who are important to me. I know these things, but I don't feel as if I do or act as if I do. 1

In my time, and I think in most times past, people like me have been endlessly preoccupied about the freedom of man. I want to be free to shape my own destiny from my own resources, to fight my fights, to mount my flights, to find my loves, to live my own life. I try hard to shape my own destiny freely and independently from my own resources, but I find again and again that I can't. I find myself in tight conflicts. The conflicts arise with other men. My own freedom conflicts with the freedom of other men.

The freedom of mankind is, to me, a truly wondrous idea. Its accomplishment would be so great, so enabling to so many people. Even its pursuit is so honorable that it can excite me like nothing else—well, almost like nothing else. I have discovered, just the same, that the goal of the freedom of man is so honorable and so exciting and so unassailable that it can be a snare and a delusion.

It seems to me that freedom has been shouted out as the goal of most of the cruel and destructive little fights to which men have tried to recruit me. It has been shouted out as the goal of most of the bloody riots and butchering rebellions of the history I know.

5 In the bright light of morning, I have heard the rebels' call to attention, I have seen the match put to the fuel of the common spirit of enslaved men, I have felt the electric charge of loyalty to the cause of freedom, I have tasted the glory of a fierce commitment unto death. In the dull dark of night, I have heard the screams of men who died to give another man power, I have seen the shock on the faces of men who had just found that they had traded one form of slavery for another, I have felt the pain of the idealist watching a firing squad, I have tasted the bitter despair of a man who followed a fight for freedom into a jungle of beasts.

Freedom from tyranny has too many, far too many, meanings for me. Freedom, I'm sure, doesn't mean just doing what I want to do. I'm sure it doesn't mean just not having anybody telling me what to do. I'm sure it doesn't mean just being able to tell other people what to do.

Perhaps it means some kind of self-sufficient independence. It's hard to see any freedom in abject poverty. Perhaps freedom means having enough resources under my control that others can influence me no more than they should *and* having no more resources under my control than would allow me to influence them any more than I should. But I don't know how much influence there should be—in either direction. Freedom and the availability of resources get confused.

The lone trapper in the mountains is wonderfully free. He is free from dependency on others and from coercion by others. He is also sorely limited. The only resources available to him are those that he can develop himself. If he has the judgment and the skills, he can develop for himself quite enough food, clothing, and shelter, and he can deeply enjoy the rare and unspoiled beauty that nature provides for all of us who will stop to look. His resources are very limited, though. They are limited by his own interests, aptitudes, and sensitivity to beauty. Nature is not only a dramatic artist and a productive farmer, she is also a demanding mother and a tyrannical caretaker. In her domain, only the fittest survive. The lone trapper in the mountains is wonderfully free. He is also narrowly limited and sorely dependent upon the acts of nature.

An inmate in a modern prison has more resources available to him than the lonely trapper. He can enjoy a wider variety of food. He can be better sheltered from a blizzard. He can enjoy all the entertainment and beauty that the varied talents of his fellow inmates can produce. He has available to him—under conditions no more onerous than many—most of the talents, ideas, skills, and feelings of quite a heterogeneous group of people. He has all sorts of resources available, and he is imprisoned and degraded.

10 What is freedom? The rich are not free. I know that. The poor are not free. I know that, too. Yet, I know that resources and freedom are connected. To be free is to have resources available when I need them, more resources than I can supply for myself. Resources from others ought to be paid for; something must be given in exchange. Perhaps to be free is to have resources available when I need them, and at a fair price.

Understanding

1. What connections does Glidewell make between freedom and resources? What types of resources does he indicate?
2. Does Glidewell value freedom? Indicate particular passages in the reading that support your response.
3. Glidewell has said, "I simply enjoy trying to express ideas." Can you tell that from his writing?

Responding

1. *Ultimate freedom is being in control.* How do you interpret this statement?
2. Describe a situation in which you were faced with a problem of freedom. You may find instances in your responses to the selections in chapter three, "Decisions." How did you resolve the conflict? What resources—inner and external—did you draw on to resolve the conflict?
3. What is *your* definition of freedom? Informally interview people you respect about their definitions of freedom; ask them to illustrate their definitions with specific examples, and record what you're told as faithfully as possible. What commonalities, if any, appear? Did you alter your original definition of freedom as a result of your reading and interviews?
4. Name someone who you think enjoys freedom. Explain your choice in one sentence. Does your explanation contain the notion of resources, both material and spiritual?
5. Which institutions and which people limit your freedom? What resources do these same institutions and people provide you? What choices have you made despite the limitations of these institutions or persons?

Connecting

1. Review Csikszentmihalyi's ("The World of the Self") and Frankl's ("The Push and Pull of Values") use of *freedom* and *choice.* What do they have in common with Glidewell's claims? How do they differ?
2. Does Campo ("'Give Back to Your Community,' She Said") subscribe to a definition of freedom that is similar to Glidewell's? Explain your opinion.
3. Apply Glidewell's idea of freedom and resources to Canetti's selection "Storytellers and Scribes" (chapter six). Would Canetti say he was free? Would Glidewell say the clients of the scribe were free? Why or why not?
4. Does Dugard ("Running on Empty") enjoy Glidewell's kind of freedom? In what way?

Spring Storm

Yōko Mori

A popular writer in her native Japan, Yōko Mori (1940–93) wrote stories about women living in the city and the difficulties that men and women experience in their relationships. The urban flavor of her stories is her literary signature.

As a young woman, Mori studied the violin but abandoned music as a career to work in advertising. She began writing after she and her husband, an English copywriter whom she married in 1964, had seen their three daughters out of infancy. In 1970 she was awarded the Subaru-Bungaku prize for her novel *Jogi*. More novels and essays followed. Influenced by life in the West and the French novelist Françoise Sagan, who made her career out of writing about romantic entanglements, Mori once admitted to being "a complete devotee of things Western who, even as a child, never went to see a Japanese movie."

"Spring Storm" is a spare but penetrating piece of fiction that captures the underlying tension between the characters. Her references to film stars underline the distinctly urban quality of this story as well as the powerful influence of cultural artifacts, especially films, on the definition of personal identity.

The small orange light on the lobby wall showed the elevator was still at 1
the seventh floor. Natsuo's eyes were fixed on it.

From time to time her heart pounded furiously, so furiously that it seemed to begin skipping beats. For some time now she had been wild with excitement.

Intense joy is somewhat like pain, she thought. Or like a dizzy spell. Strangely, it was not unlike grief. The suffocating feeling in her chest was almost unbearable.

The elevator still had not moved from the seventh floor.

The emergency stairway was located alongside the outer walls of the build- 5
ing, completely exposed to the elements. Unfortunately for Natsuo, it was raining outside. There was a wind, too.

A spring storm. The words, perhaps romantic, well described the heavy, slanting rain, driven by a wind that had retained the rawness of winter. If Natsuo were to climb the stairs to the sixth floor, she would be soaked to the skin.

She took a cigarette from her handbag and lit it.

This is unusual for me, she thought. She had never smoked while waiting for the elevator. Indeed, she had not smoked anywhere while standing up.

Exhaling the smoke from the depths of her throat, she fell to thinking. I'll be experiencing all kinds of new things from now on. I've just come a big step up the ladder. No, not just one, I've jumped as many as ten steps in one leap. There were thirty-four rivals, and I beat them all.

All thirty-four people were well-experienced performers. There was a dancer with considerably more skill than she. Physically also the odds were against her: there were a sizable number of women with long, stylish legs and tight, shapely waists. One Eurasian woman had such alluring looks that everyone admired her. There were professional actresses currently active on the stage, too.

In spite of everything, Natsuo was the one selected for the role.

When the agency called to tell her the news, she at first thought she was being teased.

"You must be kidding me," she said, a little irritated. She had indeed taken it for a bad joke. "You can't trick me like this. I don't believe you."

"Let me ask you a question, then," responded the man who had been acting as her manager. In a teasing voice, he continued, "Were you just kidding when you auditioned for that musical?"

"Of course not!" she retorted. She had been quite serious and, although she would not admit it, she had wanted the role desperately. At the audition, she had done her very best.

"But I'm sure I didn't make it," she said to her manager. "At the interview, I blushed terribly."

Whenever she tried to express herself in front of other people, blood would rush to her face, turning it scarlet.

"You're a bashful person, aren't you?" one of her examiners had commented to her at the interview. His tone carried an objective observation rather than sympathetic inquiry.

"Do you think you're an introvert?" another examiner asked.

"I'm probably on the shy side," Natsuo answered, painfully aware that her earlobes had turned embarrassingly red and her palms were moist.

"The heroine of this drama," added the third examiner, "is a spirited woman with strong willpower. Do you know that?"

Natsuo had sensed the skepticism that was running through the panel of examiners. Without doubt she was going to fail the test, unless she did something right now. She looked up.

"It's true that I'm not very good at expressing myself, or speaking up for myself, in front of other people. But playing a dramatic role is something different. It's very different." She was getting desperate. "I'm very bashful about myself. But I'm perfectly all right when I play someone else."

If I am to express someone else's emotion, I have no reason to be shy, she confirmed to herself. I can calmly go about doing the job.

"Well, then, would you please play someone else?" the chief examiner said, with a nod toward the stage.

Natsuo retired to the wings of the stage and tried to calm herself. When she trotted out onto the stage and confidently faced them, she was no longer a timid, blushing woman.

It was impossible to guess, though, how the examiners appraised her performance. They showed little, if any, emotion. When the test was over there was a chorus of murmured "Thank yous." That was all.

Her manager was still speaking on the phone. "I don't know about the third-raters. But I can tell you that most good actors and actresses are introverted, naive, and always feeling nervous inside."

He then added, "If you don't believe me, why don't you go to the office of that production company and find out for yourself?"

Natsuo decided to do just that. 30

At the end of a dimly lit hallway, a small group of men and women were looking at a large blackboard. Most of the board was powdered with half-obliterated previous scribblings, but at the top was written the cast of the new musical, with the names of the actors and actresses selected for the roles.

Natsuo's name was second from the top. It was scrawled in a large, carefree hand. The name at the top was her co-star, a well-known actor in musicals.

Natsuo stood immobile for ten seconds or so, staring at her name on the blackboard. It was her own name, but she felt as if it belonged to someone else. Her eyes still fixed on the name, she moved a few steps backwards. Then she turned around and hurried out of the building. It never occurred to her to stop by the office and thank the staff.

Sheer joy hit her a little later.

It was raining, and there was wind, too. She had an umbrella with her, but 35
she walked without opening it. Finally realizing the fact, she stopped to unfold the umbrella.

"I did it!" she cried aloud. That was the moment. An incomparable joy began to rise up inside her, like the bubbles crowding to exit from a champagne bottle; and not just joy, pain as well, accompanied by the flow and ebb of some new irritation. That was how she experienced her moment of victory.

When she came to, she found herself standing in the lobby of her apartment building. The first person she wanted to tell the news to was, naturally, her husband, Yūsuke.

The elevator seemed to be out of order. It was not moving at all. How long had she been waiting there? Ten minutes? A couple of minutes? Natsuo had no idea. Her senses had been numbed. A round clock on the wall showed 9:25. Natsuo gave up and walked away.

The emergency stairway that zigzagged upwards was quite steep and barely wide enough for one person, so Natsuo could not open her umbrella. She climbed up the stairs at a dash.

By the time she reached the sixth floor, her hair was dripping wet and, 40
with no raincoat on, her dress, too, was heavy with rain.

But Natsuo was smiling. Drenched and panting, she was still beaming with an excess of happiness when she pushed the intercom buzzer of their apartment.

"Why are you grinning? You make me nervous," Yūsuke said as he let her in. "You're soaking wet, too."

"The elevator never came."

"Who would have considered using the emergency stairs in this rain!"

"This apartment is no good, with a stairway like that," Natsuo said with a grin. "Let's move to a better place."

"You talk as if that were something very simple." Yūsuke laughed wryly and tossed a terry robe to her.

"But it is simple."

"Where would we find the money?"

"Just be patient. We'll get the money very soon," Natsuo said cheerfully, taking off her wet clothes.

"You passed the audition, didn't you?" Yūsuke asked, staring intently at her face. "Didn't you?"

Natsuo stared back at him. He looked nervous, holding his breath and waiting for her answer.

"Natsuo, did you pass the audition?" As he asked again, his face collapsed, his shoulders fell. He looked utterly forlorn.

"How . . . ," she answered impulsively, "how could I have passed? I was just kidding."

Yūsuke frowned. "You failed?"

"I was competing with professionals, you know—actresses with real stage experience. How could I have beaten them?" Natsuo named several contending actresses.

"You didn't pass?" Yūsuke repeated, his frown deepening. "Answer me clearly, please. You still haven't told me whether you passed."

"What a mean person you are!" Natsuo stuttered. "You must have guessed by now, but you're forcing me to spell it out." Her eyes met his for a moment. "I didn't make it," she said, averting her eyes. "I failed with flying colors."

There was silence. Wiping her wet hair with a towel, Natsuo was aghast and mystified at her lie.

"No kidding?" said Yūsuke, starting to walk toward the kitchen. "I was in a state of shock for a minute, really."

"How come? Were you so sure I wouldn't make it?" Natsuo spoke to him from behind, her tone a test of his sincerity.

"You were competing with professionals." There was not a trace of consolation in his voice. "It couldn't be helped. You'll have another chance."

Although Yūsuke was showing sympathy, happiness hung in the air about him.

"You sound as if you were pleased to see me fail and lose my chance."

Combing her hair, Natsuo inspected her facial expression in the small mirror on the wall. You're a liar, she told her image. How are you going to unravel this mess you've got yourself into?

"How could I be happy to see you fail?" Yūsuke responded, placing a kettle on the gas range. His words carried with them the tarnish of guilt. "But, you know, it's not that great for you to get chosen for a major role all of a sudden."

"Why not?"

"Because you'd be a star. A big new star."

"You are being a bit too dramatic." Natsuo's voice sank low.

"When that happens, your husband would become like a Mr. Judy Garland. Asai Yūsuke would disappear completely, and in his place there would be just the husband of Midori Natsuo. I wouldn't like that."

"You're inventing problems for yourself," she said, "You are what you are. You are a script writer named Asai Yūsuke."

"A script writer who might soon be forced to write a musical."

"But hasn't that been your dream, to write a musical?" Natsuo's voice was tender. "Suppose, just suppose, that I make a successful debut as an actress in a musical. As soon as I become influential enough and people begin to listen to what I say, I'll let you write a script for a musical."

"Let you write, huh?" Yūsuke picked on Natsuo's phrasing. "If you talk like that even when you're making it up, I wonder how it'd be for real."

The kettle began to erupt steam. Yūsuke flicked off the flame, dropped instant coffee into two cups, and splashed in the hot water.

"Did you hear that story about Ingrid Bergman?" Yūsuke asked, his eyes looking into the distance. "Her third husband was a famous theatrical producer. A talented producer, too." Passing one of the cups to Natsuo, he continued. "One day Bergman asked her producer-husband, 'Why don't you ever try to get me a good play to act in?' He answered, 'Because you're a goose that lays golden eggs. Any play that features you is going to be a success. It will be a sellout for sure. For me, that's too easy.'" Yūsuke sipped the coffee slowly. Then, across the rising steam, he added, "I perfectly understand how he felt."

"Does this mean that I'll have to be a minor actress all my life?" Natsuo mused.

"Who knows? I may become famous one of these days," Yūsuke sighed. "Or maybe you first."

"And what would you do in the latter case?"

"Well," Yūsuke stared at the coffee. "If that happens, we'll get a divorce. That will be the best solution. Then, neither of us will be bothered by all the petty problems."

Natsuo walked toward the window. "Are you serious?" she asked.

"Yes." Yūsuke came and stood next to her. "That's the only way to handle the situation. That way, I'll be able to feel happy for you from the bottom of my heart."

"Can't a husband be happy for his wife's success?"

"Ingrid Bergman's second husband was Roberto Rosselini. Do you know the last words he said to her? He said, 'I'm tired of living as Mr. Ingrid Bergman.' Even Rosselini felt that way."

"You are not a Rosselini, nor I a Bergman."

"Our situation would be even worse."

From time to time, gusts of rain slapped at the window.

"When this spring storm is over, I expect the cherry blossoms will suddenly be bursting out." Yūsuke whispered.

"There'll be another storm in no time. The blossoms will be gone, and summer will be here." Brushing back her still-moist hair with her fingers, Natsuo turned and looked over the apartment she knew so well.

"You've been standing all this time. Aren't you getting tired?" her husband asked in a gentle voice. She shook her head.

"You're looking over the apartment as though it were for the first time," Yūsuke said, gazing at his wife's profile. "Or, is it for the last time?"

Startled by his last words, Natsuo impulsively reached into her handbag for a cigarette and put it in her mouth. Yūsuke produced a lighter from his pocket and lit it for her.

"Aren't you going to continue with your work this evening?" she asked.

"No. No more work tonight."

"What's the matter?"

"I can't concentrate when someone else is in the apartment. You know that, don't you?"

Natsuo nodded.

"Won't you sit down?" Yūsuke said.

"Why?"

"I have an uneasy feeling when you stand there and smoke like that."

Natsuo cast her eyes on the cigarette held between her fingers. "This is the second time today I've been smoking without sitting down." The words seemed to flow from her mouth at their own volition. His back towards her, Yūsuke was collecting some sheets of writing paper scattered on his desk.

"You passed the audition. Right?" he said. His voice was so low that the last word was almost inaudible.

"How did you know?"

"I knew it from the beginning."

"From the beginning?"

"From the moment you came in. You were shouting with your whole body—'I've made it. I'm the winner!' You were trembling like a drenched cat, but your face was lit up like a Christmas tree."

Natsuo did not respond.

"The clearest evidence is the way you're smoking right now."

"Did you notice it?"

"Yes."

"Me, too. It first happened when I was waiting for the elevator down in the lobby. I was so impatient, I smoked a cigarette while standing. I've got the strangest feeling about myself."

"You feel like a celebrity?"

"I feel I've outreached myself."

"But the way you look now, it's not you."

"No, it's not me."

"You'd better not smoke standing up."

"Right. I won't do it again."

There was silence.

"You don't at all feel like congratulating me?" Natsuo asked.

Yūsuke did not answer.

"Somehow I knew it might be like this," Yūsuke continued. "I knew this moment was coming."

Now she knew why her joy had felt like pain, a pain almost indistinguishable from grief. Now she knew the source of the suffocating presence in her chest.

"That Rosselini, you know . . ." Yūsuke began again.

"Can't we drop the topic?"

"Please listen to me, dear. Rosselini was a jealous person and didn't want to see his wife working for any director other than himself. He would say to her, 'Don't get yourself involved in that play. It'll be a disaster.' One time, Bergman ignored the warning and took a part in a play. It was a big success. Rosselini was watching the stage from the wings. At the curtain call, Bergman glanced at him while bowing to the audience. Their eyes met. That instant, they both knew their love was over, with the thundering applause of the audience ringing in their ears . . ." Yūsuke paused, and then added, "I'll go and see your musical on the opening day."

Natsuo contemplated her husband's face from the wings of the room. He looked across.

Their eyes met.

Understanding

1. The title of the story and its atmosphere and symbols—the gathering storm, the rain pounding on the window, the steaming tea kettle (a literal tempest in a teapot?)—parallel the action of the story, a literary effect known as *dramatic irony.* What functions does this irony serve? What other symbols or omens signal the probable outcome of Natsuo and Yūsuke's relationship?
2. Language can be used to reveal or conceal. How genuine is the communication between Natsuo and Yūsuke? How much deception is present in this story? In what actions are these qualities—authentic communication and deception—evident?
3. Choices have consequences; some intended, some not. Identify the choices made by the two characters in this story and describe the consequences.
4. Using specific examples from the story, what about the dynamics of the relationship between Natsuo and Yūsuke could be experienced by any married couple regardless of culture? What about the way Mori describes their relationship suggests that the dynamics are influenced by their culture?
5. Married couples who work in the same field often feel the pull of competition and professional jealousy. Even in a marriage characterized by caring, sharing, and intimacy, the less successful spouse may feel insecure. Yūsuke's references to Judy Garland and Ingrid Bergman suggest that this situation is common in the field of entertainment. As a solution to the possible "conflict of interest" that he imagines will occur, Yūsuke suggests divorce. How would divorce move Natsuo and Yūsuke to a new level of "integrating" their selves? Explain.

Responding

1. Have you ever had to communicate a triumph or a personal success to someone you cared about but who you knew would be disturbed by your success? In what ways was the experience similar to the events of this story? Describe this situation in terms of the conflicting emotions that you experienced.
2. Write the next installment of this story to reflect what you imagine will happen to Natsuo and Yūsuke. What does your story reveal about your perspective on their relationship?
3. The real lives and the screen images of American movie stars exercised a potent influence on Natsuo and Yūsuke's sense of self. Relate an experience in which a celebrity or some other pop culture figure had a similar effect on the expression of your identity.
4. On what symbols of worldly success does your notion of self depend?

Connecting

How do you think this story would end if the characters were Jim and Della Young in O. Henry's "The Gift of the Magi" (chapter one)?

Nowhere to Run, Nowhere to Hide

Kweisi Mfume

Plato tells us that the responsibility of those who have a "truth" is to take it to others. In their search for answers, the writers in this chapter converge in one aspect of their lives that fuels them: a commitment to others. A common driving force is their desire to make a difference for others with their ideas, actions, and writing. In their search for self, many have suffered but emerged with manifestos of insight, epiphany, and miracle. "Nowhere to Run, Nowhere to Hide" is such an example.

Born Frizzell Gray in 1948, but known as Pee Wee for the next twenty-three years, Kweisi Mfume (a Ghanaian name for "conquering son of kings") reveals the mystery that turned around his aimless and depressing life after his mother died. Kweisi Mfume is now the president and chief executive officer of the National Association for the Advancement of Colored People (NAACP). Before that he was a five-term U.S. congressman for the 7th District, Maryland, and served on numerous congressional committees. But life for Mfume wasn't all victorious elections to public office. His story here is based on the enduring values of hard work, loyalty, and the steadfast commitment to a vision that can ignite both personal and political change.

One of the most fascinating aspects of human life is its unpredictable nature, the seemingly arbitrary manner in which events unfold. Some people find the volume of life's uncertainties so unsettling that they remain frozen in a state of perpetual indecision. They feel powerless and view themselves as floating aimlessly toward some unknown destiny. But I don't believe that all people spend their lives merely floating. Many walk a spiritual path revealed to them by a force much greater than themselves. These epiphanies, these moments of spiritual transformation, are a gift of the Divine. They bring revelation, clarity, and purpose to lives that had once seemed mired in chaos. 1

I'm not suggesting that we can define, categorize, or explain every single event that occurs during our lifetime. I am saying that from time to time on our life's path we come upon pivotal events that defy description or analysis, events that lead to a greater understanding of ourselves. Sometimes if we are lucky they offer a life-altering message. Some people see these events as gateways, signposts, or moments of revelation. Others describe them as mysteries or blessings, absent of explanation. I choose to call them miracles.

It is easy to believe that these strange and powerful moments, as inexplicable as they are, might be figments of a vivid imagination. Many have listened skeptically to the recovering alcoholic who swears to have heard angel wings at the moment of his lowest depth, or the hapless sinner who comes crying for grace after holding the cold hand of death. While such testimonials might stretch the boundaries of what we know as reality, we must confess that our realities are limited. When we acknowledge that our human understanding is woefully inadequate to explain spiritual epiphanies, we have taken an important first step. I believe, based on my own personal experience, that what may sound like a far-fetched tale or episode often turns out to be a precious glimpse into how God steps in at times to save us from ourselves. Was it not Saul of Tarsus who was struck blind on the road to Damascus before being transformed into Paul, the disciple of Jesus?

Over the years, many people have asked me how I was able to tear myself away from the strong lure of the streets in West Baltimore. And, try as I might, I have never been able to provide the one-size-fits-all answer that many of them are seeking. I do know that my transformation was not by design or deep introspection. I wasn't that conscious at the time. Many people trapped in the declining spiral of a dismal life have been redeemed without the call of the heavenly trumpet. It's precisely because of this that I continue to marvel over the mysterious event that occurred in my life in the summer of 1972—a mystery that ultimately became my miracle. Just as I've never been able to comprehend the strange howling of that dog on the night my mother died, neither will I ever understand my own epiphany. Nor will I ever forget the spiritual emergency that brought it to be.

5 The city had been steaming hot that Friday afternoon. The rows of marble stoops that lined the sidewalks of West Baltimore seemed to be nothing more than a progression of right angles as dusk began to cool the humid air. The July heat was still lingering in the thick evening haze, but with slightly less intensity. Those who had gone inside their homes to escape the sweltering afternoon sun were starting to come back outside. Some sat on their stoops, while others leaned headfirst out their windows, hoping to catch a rare breeze.

From my bedroom window, I could hear the banter of children laughing and talking down on the street, and the firm beckoning of mothers calling them inside. For a moment, the streets grew calm and peaceful and I, in my youth, grew restless.

Before long, though, the air was filled with the deep, raucous voices of the men who'd begun to congregate. The corner of Laurens and Division streets was now converting to its night shift, with boys in the hood wanting to be men, shooting dice and talking trash. This was the sound that beckoned me that evening, a sound that told me night had truly fallen over the city.

Sweating despite the furious whirring of an electric fan, I pulled on a red silk shirt and black gabardine pants and readied myself for the action outdoors. Maybe I'd smoke some weed, drink some brew, and if my hand was hot, make a little money as well. I reached inside my dresser and grabbed some cash from the bottom drawer. I put the tens and twenties in my back pocket, ones and fives in my front, and tucked a pack of Kools in my socks. With a few round strokes, I rubbed some Dixie Peach pomade in my hair, brushed it back, and pulled the collar up on my shirt. After a final check in the mirror, I left and headed down to the street to the corner I loved.

We called it Hankin's Corner, a testament to our affinity with Hankin's liquor store, which straddled the intersection of Laurens and Division just a block down the street from my house. Hankin's was a run-down store in an even more run-down building whose crumbling stone facade seemed on the brink of collapse. This corner that I loved so well existed in a different solar system from the white world that helped create it. If the segregated housing patterns of the '30s and '40s had spawned the ghetto, then surely corners like Hankin's secured it. Even though it was an eyesore to many, we were the loyal patrons who supported the store. Its wide windows were filthy, blackened with dirt. The corners and sills were encrusted with dead flies from summers past. But Hankin's wine and whiskey kept us so high and disconnected that none of it ever mattered.

Several cardboard posters stood faded in the window—pictures of smiling 10
white people hoisting a glass of booze. A cigarette was always dangling carelessly from their other hand, with a pack of Lucky Strikes or Camels lying clearly within reach. Smaller signs taped to the windows pictured bottles of Wild Irish Rose, Jack Daniel's, and Thunderbird wine. Ironically or deliberately, these potions or products seemed to always be on sale. I often wondered why the white people on those posters always seemed to be so happy. It was obvious that they were trapped in a neighborhood they couldn't get out of, held in the grip of Hankin's Corner, just like me.

By now the corner was bustling with the young and brash of the neighborhood—the hoodlums, slickers, and wanna-be's. Their bodies and black skin, backlit by the red and yellow glow of neon lights, glistened in the nighttime heat. But no illumination could soften the haunted expressions of age etched deeply in their young ebony faces. All the better-known members of the group were out that night. As I walked toward the corner I saw Mumbles, his burly arms folded against his barrel chest and a freshly rolled joint clamped between his thick, dark lips. Beside him was Noxie, sitting on the curb. His long twitchy fingers held a bottle of Thunderbird, and the butt of a pearl-handled revolver peeked out from his waistband. Hovering over him, waiting for the action to start, was Slim the taskmaster. His tall, lanky frame and white teeth gave him the look of a crazed predator whenever he laughed heartily. Lawrence, a dark-skinned, broad-shouldered cat who was usually gregarious, looked withdrawn as he stood staring blankly into the night, talking to Gary in his halting stammer.

As I approached, I could hear their laughter starting to erupt as they deadpanned each other and played the dozens.

"You big buffalo head, coyote breath, teeny dick muthafucka. Your mother's eyes are so crooked, when she cries, tears roll down her back," Noxie cracked to Mumbles as he laughed uncontrollably.

"Fuck you!" Mumbles shouted back. "Your mother's so ugly she make blind rats run. She's so old she was bustin' dishes at the Last Supper."

By now, everyone was laughing, their pearly white grins a striking contrast 15
to their ebony skin. This was the best part of the life on Hankin's Corner. It was a chance to laugh squeezed in between too many chances to die.

It was also a chance to be our age again. For just a moment, we could forget the real possibility that many of us would die near this corner, just as so many of us before had done. This was the place where I had watched my friend Chico drown in his own blood after being shot. The corner where I'd seen Marshall Braxton strangle his own brother to death in a fight over five dollars. This was also the corner where Michael Pink Lips taught me to twirl dice, and the corner where I first saw a cop kill somebody in cold blood. Laughing took my mind off all that, and playing the dozens was the way to start the action.

Before I knew it, two hours of hanging out had passed by and the dice game was well under way, but for some reason I wasn't able to focus on it. Even as I talked shit with the gang, my mind just kept drifting off. Then suddenly I felt a sharp nudge that jarred me out of the spell.

"C'mon, muthafucka, throw down," Bibbs yelled at me. "You in the game, nigga, or are you here to watch a muthafuckin' pro in action?"

Each time I tried to focus, something seemed to be pulling me back into a daze. I felt weak, breathless. My arms and legs were going numb. But still I tried to shake off the feeling and get back to laying bets.

"Fuck 'em," barked Mumbles. "I got you covered for twenty dollars, mu- 20
thafucka. Throw the fuckin' dice, and I bet you don't make your point."

Money was being tossed onto the ground at the feet of the bet makers. The crumpled bills lay there in a large circular web, as Slim grabbed the dice, blew on them, and shook them in his fist in an almost religious ritual.

"C'mon, sweet Jesus," he muttered with his eyes closed, "help me make a blind man see and a crippled man walk."

The red dice went spilling onto the concrete, and it was clear that Jesus didn't hear him. The first of the pair stopped with a one showing, and the second finished its spin and rested the same way. "Snake eyes!" screamed Mumbles as he feverishly scooped up a handful of greenbacks. "I swear to God and four other white folks I'm gonna break your black ass tonight."

Despite all the noise around me, I was slowly being engulfed in an eerie, all-enveloping stillness that seemed to be swallowing up Hankin's Corner. It felt like being trapped inside an invisible cocoon, and I couldn't shake it off. Noxie pushed a joint at me and urged, "Go ahead. Take a hit, nigga. You ready to git a piece of this action now?"

We were all huddled together. But Noxie's voice and everyone else's all 25
seemed to be fading in and out. Soon I could hear nothing but the pounding of my own heart thudding in my ears. Everything appeared to be shrinking around me, as if the world were folding in on itself. I was scared. I wanted to scream, but my lips were parched and my tongue was dry. I couldn't yell and I couldn't swallow.

My eyes quickly cut back and forth across the faces of the dark figures around me. Their movements seemed somehow distorted and exaggerated, as if I were looking at them through a fun-house mirror. I could see them talking—their lips moved, and the veins strained in their necks. But the pounding in my ears was so loud I couldn't hear a word they were saying.

There was a slow-motion quality to everything. Whenever I went to move, it was like pushing against some unseen force, like trying to swim underwater against the tide.

I blinked my eyes hard, trying to find something to focus on—anything that would help me snap back. I was filled with a terrible sense of panic. It may have been a hot humid night in the middle of July but that brick wall I leaned on felt like a glacier against my back. A bone-deep chill had come from nowhere and wrapped itself around me like a sheet of ice. The cold kept getting worse, and I felt like I was freezing to death. Suddenly my legs went all rubbery. Unable to support my weight a minute longer, I began a slow slide down the brick wall.

It was at this moment that something came over me that if I live to be a hundred I will never be able to adequately explain. It was an experience that defied logic, but would be stamped indelibly in my mind and soul for the rest of my life. I could only accept the truth of it on the strength of my faith in God.

As I crouched there on Hankin's Corner on that hot, muggy night, all I could feel was the icy chill of the brick and mortar against my back. The stillness that surrounded me now seemed to muffle even the pounding of my heart. The silence seemed to become a living thing, reaching deep into my soul, and calling me to attention in a way I've never felt before or since. My fear began to melt away—all I felt in its wake was a tremendous sense of anticipation. I knew that something was about to happen, but I had no idea what.

Every nerve ending was straining to hear, to see, to sense what was coming. 30
A haze, a halo of golden light was taking shape, getting bigger, coming closer. It was like a cloud, but it was more real than that, more tangible. It had a vibration to it, almost like music, like the air on a stormy night just after lightning strikes and before the rain begins to fall. That cloud of golden light felt soft, like melted honey, yet it was more powerful than anything I'd ever felt before. It kept moving toward me, moving through me. Filling me with something so familiar, something that felt so good, it was like I was six years old again. What was it, that feeling? I could almost remember.

Love! It was love! I'd been shut down for so long, I'd almost forgotten what it felt like. I could feel tears welling up behind my eyes, but I blinked hard to keep them back. I didn't want to miss a moment of what was happening. I kept staring into the center of that golden haze; it kept pulling me back again and again. Then I began to see something else taking shape deep in the heart of the cloud in which I found myself. It got more solid, clearer, until, at last, I saw!

It was my mother's face, bright as a midsummer's day. There she was, looking straight at me, and I was blinking and looking at her. How had she found me six years after her death, and how could this be at all? I was astounded, ashamed, overjoyed—all at the same time. I knew that she, too, recognized me. I could see it in her eyes, all the loving and the caring I hadn't allowed myself to miss. But there was something else in her eyes. It was like a great sadness overtook her as she watched me out here on Hankin's Corner, a parasite now feeding off the streets and consuming my future. Here on the street where she'd grown up and spent her last days, I watched her eyes close slowly now, as though the pain of seeing what I had become was too much for her.

Then she looked at me again and this time smiled her old familiar smile. There was no disappointment, no judgment, just total love and acceptance. I felt safe and protected, as though we were back home in Turners Station. She never said a word, but I felt her presence powerfully. I felt cradled in an unconditional love. In the light of her clarity I felt washed and clean. For the first time, I could see that I had locked myself away in a prison of darkness. I had to let go, once and for all.

Suddenly I was filled with such a sharp, sweet pain that it took my breath away. The golden fire of Mama's love was burning away all the rage and confusion that had filled me, burning away everything I'd done to dull the pain of her loss, the pain of my present life. "Mama, I didn't know," I said silently to her. "I didn't know. I couldn't see."

Another wave of energy flooded through my body, filling me with the most 35
perfect peace I have ever known. I felt newborn, vulnerable—completely open to the possibilities that lay within me. I felt . . . forgiven. In this one powerful moment I knew I had been completely transformed.

Mama's face slowly began receding back into a golden haze, and I leaned toward her, reaching out to her protective spirit. I wanted to keep her with me forever. But somehow I knew this wasn't to be. As mysteriously and swiftly as she had come, she was gone. The bright haze melted away like the mist at sunrise, and I found myself back in the action on Hankin's Corner.

"Muthafucka," I heard Slim call out to me. "I don't know what you been smokin' but give me some of that shit *now!*"

I looked up and saw their faces again coming into focus. As I staggered to my feet, still leaning against the wall for support, I saw them all staring at me as though I'd lost my mind. But any expression of concern dissolved into indifference as the noise of the street quickly filled my ears.

"Kiss my ass," I quietly mumbled at Slim.

I knew that my mother had seen the emptiness in my life, and I vowed 40
that I would make it up to her. I knew I had to prove to myself that her hopes for me had not been in vain. She'd realized that I needed help, and she'd reached out to let me know that help had come. I had cursed God that night at the moment of her death and spit on the crucifix with anger. As I did not understand the will of God, neither did I understand his redemption. Now it was up to me to accept it.

All those late-night talks we'd had, all the life lessons she repeated to me again and again, how many times she told me that I was supposed to make it if anyone did. I had to make it out of here, out of poverty, off the streets, because if I could break free, Mama could break free. And this was as true for her now as it had been in life.

"God will make a way out of no way," she would say. "A way out of no way." And God had, on this very night, on this blood-soaked corner, made a way for me.

I quickly realized that I had to change, and that I had already been profoundly changed. God had given me a second chance that night. He'd ripped my insides out and shaken me to the core. I knew I'd never, ever, go back to the life I'd been leading. I didn't know how I was going to do it, but I knew that I had to start all over again—and I had to do it now!

At that moment I was flooded with new strength, and a new purpose in life. As on the night in Turners Station when I was left at home alone, I knew I had the courage to face the darkness and to conquer it! The first step was walking away from Hankin's Corner. I stood strong and whole and proudly took it.

The crap game raged on behind me as I got up and began to walk to my 45
house. Over my shoulder I caught a glimpse of those familiar white people on the posters in Hankin's dusty glass window. They were still smiling as they had been for years, holding up their glasses of Jack Daniel's and puffing on their Lucky Strikes. But now, for the first time, I could smile back. I knew that, unlike them, I was on my way out of here. I had broken free of the grip of Hankin's Corner.

That night, when I got back to my room, I fell on my knees and prayed like I'd never prayed before. I prayed and cried all night long. But these were tears of joy as I asked for God's forgiveness. And I asked Mama to please forgive me this one last time for letting her down.

I realized now that I wasn't alone, and that I'd never been alone. And as I knelt and cried on the floor of my room that night, I made a very real promise to myself, and to God. I promised that I would never go back to the life I had known. Now that I had one more chance, I would do everything in my power to make a real difference—not only in my own life, but in the lives of my people.

I learned a powerful lesson that night on Hankin's Corner. Sometimes you have to take a fall to ultimately take a stand.

And I had to keep falling for months afterward. I had to fight for my life to get off that corner. The gangs in the hood were not about to just let me walk away. Every time we crossed, they'd call my bluff, pick a fight, or beat me bloody. But even that didn't change my mind. I'd just fight back as hard as I could, pick myself up again, and head back into my new life. At some point they sensed that I was filled with a new energy, a new resolve, and new insights. After a while, they just gave up on me as a lost cause and left me alone.

I may have been a lost cause to them. But I had found myself and I was 50
never going to get lost again. One door had closed and another had opened as the mystery of life worked its will. If I had ever doubted God's presence in my life, I knew I'd never doubt it again.

Perhaps there's a parallel side to our existence on earth—a sort of way station between life and death. Maybe this is the place the Almighty allows us brief passage at moments of great need, a place where God gives us a sign and offers a second chance for salvation.

Or, perhaps, as some would suggest to me later, my memories or perceptions became distorted that night, when I crossed for a moment into another place. Maybe, they would say, things didn't actually happen the way I thought they had at the time. Maybe, and maybe not. But I know what I know. I'm not a clairvoyant nor an accomplished interpreter of visions or dreams. But that amazing experience made me question the whole direction of my life and changed me in a special way.

I was one person when I walked out to the corner that night. And I was a whole other person when I left it. I had learned the lesson of the wise man and the lesson of the fool. I got a piece of my soul back that night and knew what price I had paid for losing it. What I'd won with that final roll of the dice was the knowledge that life could never be a free ride.

Understanding

1. Pinpoint the physical sensations and thoughts during each part of Mfume's "journey" that night on Hankin's Corner. What is the context for what Mfume calls his epiphany? What generates this transforming experience?
2. For what does Mfume feel forgiven? Why was forgiveness so transforming for him?
3. What was the powerful grip of Hankin's Corner?
4. Mfume said, "I had learned the lesson of the wise man and the lesson of the fool" (paragraph 53). Explain his meaning. What values are highlighted in this narrative? What is his point? What truth does he want his readers to see?

Responding

1. What is your definition of *miracle?* Of *epiphany?* Of *transformation?* Describe a life-altering experience such as Kweisi Mfume's that you have experienced or observed. If appropriate, include how your gifts, wounds, decisions, dreams, biological inheritance, or community contributed to that experience.
2. Mfume gives God the credit for his transformation. Are there other sources for this kind of miracle? Whom or what would you attribute as the source of transformative experiences?
3. At the close of his narrative, Mfume implies that perhaps, in the writing, his memory of that night on Hankin's Corner became distorted. He seems to know, as memorist William Zinsser does, that "memory, one of the writer's most powerful tools, is one of the most unreliable." Would Bibbs, Mumbles, Noxie, Slim, Gary, and Lawrence have told this story in the same way? What does it matter if they would have told a different story? If that night survives only in the act of writing, is that not powerful enough?

Connecting

1. Recall at least two other readings in which forgiveness was central to the writers' completing a painful experience. Compare and contrast those selections with Mfume's experience of forgiveness.
2. Does Frankl's ("The Push and Pull of Values") view of meaning and responsibility play a part in Mfume's transformation? Was his choice to leave

the streets freely made? Do people have to suffer in order to have life-altering experiences? Give examples from both Frankl and Mfume to support your point of view.

3. How does Glidewell's notion of freedom and resources illuminate Mfume's story?
4. Which of Erikson's stages (see Elkind's "Erik Erikson's Eight Ages of Man") was Mfume working through in this story?
5. Compare Mfume's epiphany with McBride's in "A Jew Discovered" earlier in "Living Out Loud." How were their circumstances different and similar? What were both men seeking?

We Have No Real Choice about Death

Victoria L. Macki, M.D.

Writing on the lessons he learned in the many years of his medical practice, physician Sherwin B. Nuland has said that, "The greatest dignity to be found in death is the dignity of the life that preceded it . . . Hope resides in the meaning of what our lives have been." On their own these are provocative statements but, when applied to terminally ill patients and their hope that their last days be lived with dignity, they can take on new meaning. Some patients take the assisted-suicide route; others are assured by their doctors that their last days will be spent in tranquil comfort.

Any thoughtful discussion of the meaning of life, or of the search for self, must inevitably cover the thorny questions of life and death. Victoria L. Macki contributes a vigorous argument—her own definition of life and its power to inform the decisions she must make as a doctor regarding life and death. This selection first appeared as a letter to the editor in the *Newberry News,* a weekly in Newberry, Michigan.

To the Editor:

Over the past months and years, I have become increasingly troubled by what I perceive as a cavalier attitude toward life, and by a lack of public discourse on the subject. Recently, the media circus of the Jack Kevorkian trial has, I feel, obscured the central issue.

This issue is not the "right to die." Any sober reflection on the subject would bring everyone to the conclusion that death is not anything we have a real choice about—we all will die. It is a "right" with which we are endowed at our birth, and a necessity, and a certainty.

The issue is whether or not we should, as a society, condone and applaud and legalize the deliberate and knowing taking of a life. How do we decide? The issue is more than legal, it is moral to its core and moral issues must have a referent to authority.

Who says that taking a life is wrong? (Notice that I did not say "illegal," but wrong.) Who makes that determination? How is the determination made? Must we struggle with these decisions on our own, based solely on our own insight and experience? Does anyone have a right to declare a life-and-death decision either wrong or right?

From my perspective, only the Giver of Life has the authority to take it 1
again. I freely admit that my perspective is a Christian one and that my referent is the moral authority of God who gave life and alone has the authority and right to take it in His time.

Perhaps more than most people my age, I have seen death up close and personal. It is a rare month when I do not have to preside over the end of someone's life, often at the end of a long, lingering illness. I have seen individuals choose to end their own lives, also. I have seen struggle, distress, and also peace. Sometimes death seems an intruder, cutting some down in their prime. Sometimes death seems like a welcome friend. But never have I felt that it was my duty or privilege to push death along.

I draw a clear distinction between facing the inevitability of futile treatment and withdrawing the same, and deliberately pushing some along the path. There are times that no amount of "life support" will work, when there is no life left to support. There are times when "letting nature take its course," and keeping one's meddling hands off, rather than continuing treatment that may be painful and useless, is the right choice. I cannot equate the giving of comfort care to a dying person (rather than aggressive, high-tech care in the face of futility) with euthanasia or assisted suicide.

Many centuries ago, a radical physician articulated a set of principles that have come down to the medical profession as "The Hippocratic Oath." When Hippocrates and his followers vowed that "I will keep [the sick] from harm and injustice. I will neither give a deadly drug to anybody if asked for it, nor will I make a suggestion to this effect," they were breaking with the accepted local value system. In ancient Rome and Greece, suicide, and assisted suicide, were seen as virtuous and acceptable. These guys, doctors, said, "No." They also, incidentally, vowed to induce no abortions. Today most medical school graduating classes are no longer required to take the Hippocratic Oath. (I wasn't.) Does anyone wonder why?

The Netherlands, about 20 years ago, removed the penalty for "assisting" 5
suicide. What has happened in that country since then should be instructive, and alarming. According to a 1992 Dutch government survey, in 8,100 cases of doctors' prescribing lethal overdoses of medication, 61% of the patients had not consented to their own death, and in 45% the doctors didn't even consult family members. The Dutch legal system is now at work trying to come up with policies to govern the mercy killing of newborns.

Does this have a familiar ring? It is just the road taken by Germany in the 1930s when, following Nietzschean philosophy (as expressed in National Socialism policy), it was determined that there was such a thing as "a life unworthy to be lived," and that social policy and government agencies should expend effort to "mercifully" liquidate such lives.

Long before the Jews and ethnic minorities were shipped en masse to concentration and death camps, the social experiment had been done on Germany's own mentally retarded and mentally ill—mercifully overdosed in their "state hospitals," without the permission of either the (incompetent) unworthy lives, but also without bothering the families. It was easy. It was a relief to not have to be bothered with the "unproductive" needy. It worked. And came the Holocaust.

Lest people consider me unnecessarily alarmist, I ask them to thoughtfully investigate these matters. Do you want your physician to become your executioner? Do you want legal safeguards in place to protect the helpless, the weak, the distressed, and the ill—even the terminally ill?

I firmly believe that the reason most people rather blithely assent to the notion of the acceptability of "assisted suicide" is that they have a deep fear of pain and abandonment. They project a future, terrible illness that incapacitates, humiliates, and pains them, and they say that they "would rather be dead." Is it not the doctor's duty and privilege to alleviate pain, provide comfort, and "be there" for their dying patients? If people knew that they could trust their caregivers for such loving and tender care, would they wish to hasten their death? On the issue of dependence and humiliation of having bodily functions decrease, where is the line?

If one considers the "quality" rather than the fact of life to be paramount, 10
how would you respond to the decision of who determines quality? I recently learned of a 26-year-old woman who was euthanatized in the Netherlands by her physician, at her request, because she felt her life had no more meaning. She had developed arthritis in her toes and could no longer dance ballet, which she had been doing since childhood. The doctor felt that she was competent and he had no right to deny her request, so she killed herself because she could no longer twirl on her toes. And her doctor gave her the means.

So is life precious in its essence or in its utility? If life is precious in its essence, we should not and must not condone assisted suicide. If it is only precious because of some utilitarian standard, no matter how high or how low the bar is set, who determines the standard? And what protection, then, would there be for the old, the infirm, the helpless?

There is a vast difference between prolonging the dying process and hastening it. People should be clear with their families and doctors about what care they will and will not accept in the treatment of disease. Mental and physical pain should be alleviated out of mercy as much as possible. But please, don't ask me to kill you.

Understanding

1. Underline Macki's thesis. Mark the text for each section that gives various examples that support her thesis. Is Macki's argument supported by her narrative knowledge (knowledge gained through the experience of living) or her academic knowledge (objective, scientifically proven, statistically tested or reported)? If both, identify each type. Do each give equal strength to her argument?
2. According to Macki, what is the difference between giving comfort care and euthanasia or assisted suicide?
3. Why was Hippocrates a radical? Why would graduating medical students today not be asked to take the Hippocratic Oath? Who still takes it? Conduct an informal poll of any doctors, nurses, or medical students you know to find out whether they took the Hippocratic Oath upon graduation from medical or nursing school. If they did, what does it mean to them today?
4. What reasons does Macki give for people's acceptance of assisted suicide? Do you agree with them?

Responding

1. Distinguish between *essence of life* and *utility of life.* What is the value of this distinction?
2. Macki describes her perspective as a Christian one. Summarize the Christian view according to Macki. For those of you who subscribe to faiths other than Christianity, how is your perspective different or similar?
3. If you are from another country, share your culture's attitudes toward assisted or other kinds of suicide. Is it now, or was it in the past, considered virtuous?
4. Write your answers to these questions from Macki's essay: "Do you want your physician to become your executioner? Do you want legal safeguards in place to protect the helpless, the weak, the distressed, and the ill—even the terminally ill?"
5. If the medical profession were committed to making the last hours of life comfortable, articles like Macki's would not be an issue. Do you agree or disagree?
6. Take the challenge inherent in answering these questions: What is life? What is quality of life?

Connecting

1. As with most of the writers in "Taking Stands," Macki is examining possible answers to an inquiry into the meaning of life. She raises a provocative question: "Is life precious in its essence or in its utility?" Explore the distinctions in this question. How would each of the authors in chapter seven answer her question? How would you?
2. How would Glidewell (see "On Freedom and Resources" earlier in this chapter) discuss the issue of assisted suicide with regard to freedom and resources? Would Macki agree with Glidewell?
3. Using the Internet, find a Web site on assisted suicide. Take notes on what you find there. How would Macki react to the opinions of those you found on the Web site? Use a specific example from the site to share your response. How would Macki respond to a forum on the Internet to discuss assisted suicide?
4. How does Macki's inquiry in paragraphs 9–11 relate to the situation described in the two versions of "Richard Cory" in chapter four, regarding both Cory's suicide and the writer's perception of his own quality of life?

The Reality of Selves

Daniel C. Dennett

Up to this point, the readings in this chapter have examined the relatively noncontroversial aspects of the self. This selection moves us to the highly charged (in academic circles) atmosphere of the "mind-brain" debate. A defining question posed in this debate is: Is the brain the sole source of our mental processes, or are there other "engines" that drive their work?

As Csikszentmihalyi tells us in "The World of the Self," "self-reflective consciousness is a recent development in human evolution." Perhaps because we have no evidence of when people first discovered that they could control their mental processes—their thinking—there is so much contemporary argument about how they originated. This argument about consciousness—how the physical brain and the metaphysical mind interact to produce the consciousness of self—has drawn responses from scholars in many academic fields, from biology, law, and cognitive science to computer science and philosophy. Daniel C. Dennett represents the latter field.

Dennett, an American philosopher who has been described as a true-believing Darwinist, has tried to demonstrate in his work that natural selection has enough creative power to explain "design" or what some people call the work of creation. He compares the brain to a vast parallel computer that can be understood in light of evolution over 3 million years of history and needs no other form of explanation or "first cause." According to Dennett, there is no self about which we can answer questions. Instead there are multiple "self-lets"—all very real—about which we weave intriguing stories. "We spin," he says.

Among his major writings, in addition to *Consciousness Explained,* from which this reading is excerpted, Dennett has written *Content and Consciousness* (1969), *The Intentional Stance,* and *Darwin's Dangerous Idea* (1995). He is professor of philosophy and director of the Center for Cognitive Studies at Tufts University.

Suppose that there be a machine, the structure of which produces thinking, feeling, and perceiving; imagine this machine enlarged but preserving the same proportions, so that you could enter it as if it were a mill. This being supposed, you might visit its inside; but what would you observe there? Nothing but parts which push and move each other, and never anything that could explain perception.

—Gottfried Wilhelm Leibniz (1646–1716), *Monadology*
(first published, 1840)

For my part, when I enter most intimately into what I call myself, *I always stumble on some particular perception or other, of heat or cold, light or shade, love or hatred, pain or pleasure. I never can catch* myself *at any time without a*

> *perception, and never can observe anything but the perception. . . . If anyone, upon serious and unprejudiced reflection, thinks he has a different notion of* himself, *I must confess I can reason no longer with him. All I can allow him is, that he may be in the right as well as I, and that we are essentially different in this particular. He may, perhaps, perceive something simple and continued, which he calls* himself; *though I am certain there is no such principle in me.*
>
> —David Hume (1739)

Since the dawn of modern science in the seventeenth century, there has been nearly unanimous agreement that the self, whatever it is, would be invisible under a microscope, and invisible to introspection, too. For some, this has suggested that the self was a nonphysical soul, a ghost in the machine. For others, it has suggested that the self was nothing at all, a figment of metaphysically fevered imaginations. And for still others, it has suggested only that a self was in one way or another a sort of abstraction, something whose existence was not in the slightest impugned by its invisibility. After all, one might say, a center of gravity is just as invisible—and just as real. Is that real enough? 1

The question of whether there really are selves can be made to look ridiculously easy to answer, in either direction: Do *we* exist? Of course! The question presupposes its own answer. (After all, who is this *I* that has looked in vain for a self, according to Hume?) Are there entities, either in our brains, or *over* and *above* our brains, that control our bodies, think our thoughts, make our decisions? Of course not! Such an idea is either empirical idiocy (James's "pontifical neuron") or metaphysical claptrap (Ryle's "ghost in the machine"). When a simple question gets two answers, "Obviously yes!" and "Obviously no!", a middle-ground position is worth considering (Dennett, 1991a), even though it is bound to be initially counterintuitive to all parties—everyone agrees that it denies one obvious fact or another!

HOW HUMAN BEINGS SPIN A SELF

> In addition they seemed to spend a great deal of time eating and drinking and going to parties, and Frensic, whose appearance tended to limit his sensual pleasures to putting things into himself rather than into other people, was something of a gourmet.
>
> Tom Sharpe (1977)

The novelist Tom Sharpe suggests, in this funny but unsettling passage, that when you get right down to it, all sensual pleasure consists in playing around with one's own boundary, or someone else's, and he is on to something—if not the whole truth, then part of the truth.

People have selves. Do dogs? Do lobsters? If selves are anything at all, then they exist. *Now* there are selves. There was a time, thousands (or millions, or billions) of years ago, when there were none—at least none on this planet. So there has to be—as a matter of logic—a true story to be told about *how there came to be* creatures with selves. This story will have to tell—as a matter of logic—about a process (or a series of processes) involving the activities or behaviors of things that do not yet *have* selves—or *are* not yet selves—but which eventually yield, as a new product, beings that are, or have, selves . . .

Within the walls of human bodies are many, many interlopers, ranging 5
from bacteria and viruses through microscopic mites that live like cliff-dwellers in the ecological niche of our skin and scalp, to larger parasites—horrible tapeworms, for instance. These interlopers are all tiny self-protectors in their own rights, but some of them, such as the bacteria that populate our digestive systems and without which we would die, are just as essential team members in our quest for self-preservation as the antibodies in our immune systems. (If the biologist Lynn Margulis's theory (1970) is correct, the mitochondria that do the work in almost all the cells in our body are the descendants of bacteria with whom "we" joined forces about two billion years ago.) Other interlopers are tolerated parasites—not worth the effort to evict, apparently—and still others are indeed the enemy within, deadly if not rooted out.

This fundamental biological principle of distinguishing self from world, inside from outside, produces some remarkable echoes in the highest vaults of our psychology. The psychologists Paul Rozin and April Fallon (1987) have shown in a fascinating series of experiments on the nature of *disgust* that there is a powerful and unacknowledged undercurrent of blind resistance to certain acts that, rationally considered, should not trouble us. For example, would you please swallow the saliva in your mouth right now? This act does not fill you with revulsion. But suppose I had asked you to get a clean drinking glass and spit into the glass and *then* swallow the saliva from the glass. Disgusting! But why? It seems to have to do with our perception that once something is outside of our bodies it is no longer quite part of us anymore—it becomes alien and suspicious—it has renounced its citizenship and becomes something to be rejected.

Border crossings are thus either moments of anxiety, or, as pointed out by Sharpe, something to be especially enjoyed. Many species have developed remarkable constructions for extending their territorial boundaries, either to make the bad kind of crossings more difficult or the good kind easier. Beavers make dams, and spiders spin webs, for instance. When the spider spins its web, it doesn't have to understand what it is doing; Mother Nature has simply provided its tiny brain with the necessary routines for carrying out this biologically essential task of engineering. Experiments with beavers show that even their magnificently efficient engineering practices are at least largely the product of innate drives and proclivities they need not understand to benefit from. Beavers do learn, and may even teach each other, but mainly, they are driven by powerful innate mechanisms controlling what the behaviorist B. F. Skinner called negative reinforcement. A beaver will cast about quite frantically for something—anything—to stop the sound of running water, and in one experiment a beaver found its relief by plastering mud all over the loudspeaker from which the recorded gurgling emerged! (Wilsson, 1974)

The beaver protects its outer boundary with twigs and mud and one of its inner boundaries with fur. The snail gathers calcium in its food and uses it to exude a hard shell; the hermit crab gets its calcium shell ready-made, taking over the discarded shell of another creature, daintily avoiding the ingestion and exudation process. The difference is not fundamental, according to Richard Dawkins, who points out that the result in either case, which he calls *the extended phenotype* (1982), is a part of the fundamental biological equipment of the individuals who are submitted to the selective forces that drive evolution.

The definition of an extended phenotype not only extends beyond the "natural" boundary of individuals to include external equipment such as shells (and internal equipment such as resident bacteria); it often includes other individuals of the same species. Beavers cannot do it alone, but require teamwork to build a single dam. Termites have to band together by the millions to build their castles.

And consider the astonishing architectural constructions of the Australian 10
bowerbird (Borgia, 1986). The males build elaborate bowers, courtship shrines with grand central naves, richly decorated with brightly colored objects—predominantly deep blue, and including bottle caps, bits of colored glass, and other human artifacts—which are gathered from far afield and carefully arranged in the bower the better to impress the female he is courting. The bowerbird, like the spider, does not really have to understand what he is doing; he simply finds himself hard at work, he knows not why, creating an edifice that is crucial to his success as a bowerbird.

But the strangest and most wonderful constructions in the whole animal world are the amazing, intricate constructions made by the primate, *Homo sapiens*. Each normal individual of this species makes a *self*. Out of its brain it spins a web of words and deeds, and, like the other creatures, it doesn't have to know what it's doing; it just does it. This web protects it, just like the snail's shell, and provides it a livelihood, just like the spider's web, and advances its prospects for sex, just like the bowerbird's bower. Unlike a spider, an individual human doesn't just *exude* its web; more like a beaver, it works hard to gather the materials out of which it builds its protective fortress. Like a bowerbird, it appropriates many found objects which happen to delight it—or its mate—including many that have been designed by others for other purposes.

This "web of discourses" . . . is as much a biological product as any of the other constructions to be found in the animal world. Stripped of it, an individual human being is as incomplete as a bird without its feathers, a turtle without its shell. (Clothes, too, are part of the extended phenotype of *Homo sapiens* in almost every niche inhabited by that species. An illustrated encyclopedia of zoology should no more picture *Homo sapiens* naked than it should picture *Ursus arctus*—the black bear—wearing a clown suit and riding a bicycle.)

So wonderful is the organization of a termite colony that it seemed to some observers that each termite colony had to have a soul (Marais, 1937). We now understand that its organization is simply the result of a million semi-independent little agents, each itself an automaton, doing its thing. So wonderful is the organization of a human self that to many observers it has seemed that each human being had a soul, too: a benevolent Dictator ruling from Headquarters.

In every beehive or termite colony there is, to be sure, a queen bee or queen termite, but these individuals are more patient than agent, more like the crown jewels to be protected than the chief of the protective forces—in fact their royal name is more fitting today than in earlier ages, for they are much more like Queen Elizabeth II than Queen Elizabeth I. There is no Margaret Thatcher bee, no George Bush termite, no Oval Office in the anthill.

Do our selves, our nonminimal *selfy* selves, exhibit the same permeability and flexibility of boundaries as the simpler selves of other creatures? Do we expand our personal boundaries—the boundaries of our *selves*—to enclose any of our "stuff"? In general, perhaps, no, but there are certainly times when this seems true, psychologically. For instance, while some people merely own cars and drive them, others are *motorists;* the inveterate motorist prefers *being* a four-wheeled gas-consuming agent to being a two-legged food-consuming agent, and his use of the first-person pronoun betrays this identification:

> I'm not cornering well on rainy days because my tires are getting bald.

So sometimes we enlarge our boundaries; at other times, in response to perceived challenges real or imaginary, we let our boundaries shrink:

> *I* didn't do that! That wasn't the real me talking. Yes, the words came out of my mouth, but I refuse to recognize them as my own.

I have reminded you of these familiar speeches to draw out the similarities between our selves and the selves of ants and hermit crabs, but the speeches also draw attention to the most important difference: Ants and hermit crabs don't talk. The hermit crab is designed in such a way as to see to it that it acquires a shell. Its organization, we might say, *implies* a shell, and hence, in a *very* weak sense, tacitly *represents* the crab as having a shell, but the crab does not in any stronger sense *represent itself* as having a shell. It doesn't go in for self-representation at all. To whom would it so represent itself and why? It doesn't need to remind itself of this aspect of its nature, since its innate design takes care of that problem, and there are no other interested parties in the offing. And the ants and termites, as we have noted, accomplish their communal projects without relying on any explicitly communicated blueprints or edicts.

We, in contrast, are almost constantly engaged in presenting ourselves to others, and to ourselves, and hence *representing* ourselves—in language and gesture, external and internal. The most obvious difference in our environment that would explain this difference in our behavior is the behavior itself. Our human environment contains not just food and shelter, enemies to fight or flee, and conspecifics with whom to mate, but words, words, words. These words are potent elements of our environment that we readily incorporate, ingesting and extruding them, weaving them like spiderwebs into self-protective strings of *narrative.*

Our fundamental tactic of self-protection, self-control, and self-definition is not spinning webs or building dams, but telling stories, and more particularly concocting and controlling the story we tell others—and ourselves—about who we are. And just as spiders don't have to think, consciously and deliberately, about how to spin their webs, and just as beavers, unlike professional human engineers, do not consciously and deliberately plan the structures they build, we (unlike *professional* human storytellers) do not consciously and deliberately figure out what narratives to tell and how to tell them. Our tales are spun, but for the most part we don't spin them; they spin us. Our human consciousness, and our narrative selfhood, is their product, not their source.

These strings or streams of narrative issue forth *as if* from a single source—not just in the obvious physical sense of flowing from just one mouth, or one pencil or pen, but in a more subtle sense: their effect on any audience is to encourage them to (try to) posit a unified agent whose words they are, about whom they are: in short, to posit a *center of narrative gravity*. Physicists appreciate the enormous simplification you get when you posit a center of gravity for an object, a single point relative to which all gravitational forces may be calculated. We hetero phenomenologists appreciate the enormous simplification you get when you posit a center of narrative gravity for a narrative-spinning human body. Like the biological self, this psychological or narrative self is yet another abstraction, not a thing in the brain, but still a remarkably robust and almost tangible attractor of properties, the "owner of record" of whatever items and features are lying about unclaimed. Who owns your car? You do. Who owns your clothes? You do. Then who owns your body? You do! When you say

> This is *my* body.

you certainly aren't taken as saying

> This body owns itself.

But what can you be saying, then? If what you say is neither a bizarre and pointless tautology (this body is its own owner, or something like that) nor the claim that you are an immaterial soul or ghost puppeteer who owns and operates this body the way you own and operate your car, what else could you mean?

References

Borgia, G. 1986. "Sexual Selection in Bowerbirds," *Scientific American*, **254,** pp. 92–100.

Castaneda, H.-N. 1967. "Indicators and Quasi-Indicators," *American Philosophy Quarterly*, **4,** pp. 85–100.

———. 1968. "On the Logic of Attributions of Self-Knowledge to Others," *Journal of Philosophy*, **65,** pp. 439–456.

Dawkins, R. 1982. *The Extended Phenotype*. San Francisco: Freeman.

de Sousa, R. 1976. "Rational Homunculi" in Amelie O. Rorty, ed., *The Identity of Persons*. Berkeley: University of California Press, pp. 217–238.

Dennett, D. C. 1978b. "Skinner Skinned," ch. 4 in Dennett. 1978a. pp. 53–70.

———. 1981a. "Reflections" on "Software" in Hofstadter and Dennett, 1981.

———. 1984a. *Elbow Room: The Varieties of Free Will Worth Wanting*. Cambridge, MA: MIT Press/A Bradford Book.

———. 1985b. "Music of the Hemispheres," a review of M. Gazzaniga, *The Social Brain*, in *New York Times Book Review*, November 17, 1985, p. 53.

———. 1991a. "Real Patterns," *Journal of Philosophy*, **89,** pp. 27–51.

Eldredge, N., and Gould, S. J. 1972. "Punctuated Equilibria: An Alternative to Phyletic Gradualism," in T. J. M. Schopf, ed., *Models in Paleobiology*. San Francisco: Freeman Cooper, pp. 82–115.

Gazzaniga, M. 1985. *The Social Brain: Discovering the Networks of the Mind.* New York: Basic Books.

Gazzaniga, M., and Ledoux, J. 1978. *The Integrated Mind.* New York: Plenum Press.

Hume, D. 1739. *Treatise on Human Nature.* London: John Noon.

Humphrey, N. 1986. *The Inner Eye.* London: Faber & Faber.

Humphrey, N., and Dennett, D. C. 1989. "Speaking for Our Selves: An Assessment of Multiple Personality Disorder," *Raritan,* **9,** pp. 68, 98.

Johnson-Laird, P. 1988. "A Computational Analysis of Consciousness" in A. J. Marcel and E. Risiach, eds., *Consciousness in Contemporary Science,* Oxford: Clarendon Press; New York: Oxford University Press.

Kinsbourne, M. 1974. "Lateral Interactions in the Brain," in M. Kinsbourne and W. L. Smith, eds., *Hemisphere Disconnection and Cerebral Function.* Springfield, IL: Charles C. Thomas, pp. 239–259.

Leibniz, G. W. 1840. *Monadology,* first published posthumously in J. E. Erdmann, ed., Leibniz, *Opera Philosophica.* 2 vols. Berlin.

Levy, J., and Trevarthen, C. 1976. "Metacontrol of Hemispheric Function in Human Split-Brain Patients," *Journal of Experimental Psychology: Human Perception and Performance,* **3,** pp. 299–311.

Lewis, D. 1979. "Attitudes *De Dicto* and *De Se,*" *Philosophical Review,* **78,** pp. 513–543.

Marais, E. N. 1937. *The Soul of the White Ant.* London: Methuen.

Margulis, L. 1970. *The Origin of Eukaryotic Cells.* New Haven: Yale University Press.

Menzel, E. W., Savage-Rumbaugh, E. S., and Lawson, J. 1985. "Chimpanzee (*Pan troglodytes*) Spatial Problem Solving with the Use of Mirrors and Televised Equivalents of Mirrors," *Journal of Comparative Psychology,* **99,** pp. 211–217.

Minsky, M. 1985. *The Society of Mind.* New York: Simon & Schuster.

Nagel, T. 1971. "Brain Bisection and the Unity of Consciousness," *Synthese,* **22,** pp. 396–413 (reprinted in his *Mortal Questions* [1979]. Cambridge: Cambridge University Press.)

Oakley, D. A., ed. 1985. *Brain and Mind.* London and New York: Methuen.

Parfit, D. 1984. *Reasons and Persons.* Oxford: Clarendon Press.

Penrose, R. 1989. *The Emperor's New Mind.* Oxford: Oxford University Press.

Perlis, 1991. "Intentionality and Defaults" in K. M. Ford and P. J. Hayes, eds., *Reasoning Agents in a Dynamic World.* Greenwich, CT: JAI Press.

Perry, J. 1979. "The Problem of the Essential Indexical," *Nous,* **13,** pp. 3–21.

Richards, R. J. 1987. *Darwin and the Emergence of Evolutionary Theories of Mind and Behavior.* Chicago: University of Chicago Press.

Rozin, P., and Fallon, A. E. 1987. "A Perspective on Disgust," *Psychological Review,* **94,** pp. 23–47.

Sanford, D. 1975. "Infinity and Vagueness," *Philosophical Review,* **84,** pp. 520–535.

Walton, K. 1973. "Pictures and Make Believe," *Philosophical Review,* **82,** pp. 283–319.

———. 1978. "Fearing Fiction," *Journal of Philosophy,* **75,** pp. 6–27.

Wilsson, L. 1974. "Observations and Experiments on the Ethology of the European Beaver," *Viltrevy, Swedish Wildlife,* **8,** pp. 115–266.

Understanding

1. Dennett reports in the preface to *Consciousness Explained* that in his first year of college, "I read Descartes' *Meditations* and was hooked on the mind-body problem." Who was Descartes, and what is the mind-body problem?
2. Dennett refers to the boundaries that even the simplest one-celled creature makes between itself and its environment. In what ways do human

beings erect their own boundaries? Do these boundaries have a purpose? What is it?

3. Like rules that are made to be broken, perhaps boundaries are made to be crossed. In what ways do human beings seek to transcend the boundaries that they have erected around their selves? How successful are they?
4. Explain Dennett's notion of the self as the center of narrative gravity.
5. Dennett proposes that we *Homo sapiens* spin a self out of words and deeds and "like the other creatures, it doesn't have to know what it's doing; it just does it" (paragraph 11). What does he mean? How could we engage in such an important activity without knowing what we are doing?

Responding

1. What boundaries have you constructed around *your* self? Consider the most visible boundaries—what Richard Dawkins has called our "extended phenotype," (e.g., clothing)—to the least visible. What purposes do these boundaries serve? How porous or flexible are they?
2. There is no universal agreement about the sources of the self; there are only theories and hypotheses. Dennett's is one of them. Some theorists argue that what you believe others think of you forms the core of your self; children, for example, form their self-concept based on their sense of how others treat them. Other theorists contend that how you feel about yourself, your organismic experience, is the source of your self. Still others suggest that spiritual experiences play a key role in a person's selfhood. Which, if any, of these perspectives represents the "real you"?
3. Is there a single consistent self that transcends all situations and perceptions, the existence of which remains constant? Or are you, as Dennett has suggested in a speech, the product of multiple drafts? What relationship might the reality of this "single consistent self" or the "multiple drafts" notion have to personal identity?
4. What inner strengths or other admirable qualities do you think you possess? How do you know about them? What weaknesses or areas of risk do you recognize in yourself? How were they brought to your awareness?
5. Consider the ways in which you fail to find your center of narrative gravity (e.g., when you find it difficult to communicate your thoughts and feelings to those around you). What kinds of situations are they? What positive steps can you take to find this center?

Connecting

Choose two of the readings from the "Boundaries" section of chapter six that you think extend Dennett's exposition of biological boundaries to the social or cultural realm. Do you think that these social/cultural boundaries have a biological or genetic underpinning? Explain.

Identity Crisis

Sherry Turkle

In *Life on the Screen,* Sherry Turkle, who has been described as "the leading anthropologist of cyberspace," tells the story of the impact of the computer on our psychological lives, our conception of self, and our evolving ideas about how minds, bodies, and machines interact. In this excerpt from the last chapter of *Life on the Screen,* Turkle explores the newborn culture of simulation and guides the reader to the boundary where the human and the technological intersect. More important, she illuminates how through virtual environments we redefine our identity as multiples rather than as unitary selves. "Virtual environments," Turkle discloses, "are valuable as places where we can acknowledge our inner diversity."

Sherry Turkle is professor of the Sociology of Science at the Massachusetts Institute of Technology and a licensed clinical psychologist, holding a joint Ph.D. in personality, psychology and sociology from Harvard University. She is the author of *A Second Self: Computers and the Human Spirit* and *Psychoanalytic Politics: Jacques Lacan and Freud's French Revolution. Life on the Screen,* she reports, "is a very personal book."

Every era constructs its own metaphors for psychological well-being. Not 1
so long ago, stability was socially valued and culturally reinforced. Rigid gender roles, repetitive labor, the expectation of being in one kind of job or remaining in one town over a lifetime, all of these made consistency central to definitions of health. But these stable social worlds have broken down. In our time, health is described in terms of fluidity rather than stability. What matters most now is the ability to adapt and change—to new jobs, new career directions, new gender roles, new technologies.

In *Flexible Bodies,* the anthropologist Emily Martin argues that the language of the immune system provides us with metaphors for the self and its boundaries.[1] In the past, the immune system was described as a private fortress, a firm, stable wall that protected within from without. Now we talk about the immune system as flexible and permeable. It can only be healthy if adaptable.

The new metaphors of health as flexibility apply not only to human mental and physical spheres, but also to the bodies of corporations, governments, and businesses. These institutions function in rapidly changing circumstances; they too are coming to view their fitness in terms of their flexibility. Martin describes the cultural spaces where we learn the new virtues of change over solidity. In addition to advertising, entertainment, and education, her examples include corporate workshops where people learn wilderness camping, high-wire walking, and zip-line jumping. She refers to all of these as flexibility practicums.

In her study of the culture of flexibility, Martin does not discuss virtual communities, but these provide excellent examples of what she is talking about. In these environments, people either explicitly play roles (as in MUDs) or more subtly shape their online selves. Adults learn about being multiple and fluid—and so do children. "I don't play so many different people online—only three," says June, an eleven-year-old who uses her mother's Internet account to play in MUDs. During our conversation, I learn that in the course of a year in RL, she moves among three households—that of her biological mother and stepfather, her biological father and stepmother, and a much-loved "first stepfather," her mother's second husband. She refers to her mother's third and current husband as "second stepfather." June recounts that in each of these three households the rules are somewhat different and so is she. Online switches among personae seem quite natural. Indeed, for her, they are a kind of practice. Martin would call them practicums.

"LOGINS R US"

On a WELL discussion group about online personae (subtitled "boon or 5
bête-noire") participants shared a sense that their virtual identities were evocative objects for thinking about the self. For several, experiences in virtual space compelled them to pay greater attention to what they take for granted in the real. "The persona thing intrigues me," said one. "It's a chance for all of us who aren't actors to play [with] masks. And think about the masks we wear every day."[2]

In this way, online personae have something in common with the self that emerges in a psychoanalytic encounter. It, too, is significantly virtual, constructed within the space of the analysis, where its slightest shifts can come under the most intense scrutiny.[3]

What most characterized the WELL discussion about online personae was the way many of the participants expressed the belief that life on the WELL introduced them to the many within themselves. One person wrote that through participating in an electronic bulletin board and letting the many sides of ourselves show, "We start to resemble little corporations, 'Logins R Us,' and like any company, we each have within us the bean-counter, the visionary, the heart-throb, the fundamentalist, and the wild child. Long may they wave."[4] Other participants responded to this comment with enthusiasm. One, echoing the social psychologist Kenneth Gergen,[5] described identity as a "pastiche of personalities" in which "the test of competence is not so much the integrity of the whole but the apparent correct representation appearing at the right time, in the right context, not to the detriment of the rest of the internal 'collective.'"[6] Another said that he thought of his ego "as a hollow tube, through which, one at a time, the 'many' speak through at the appropriate moment. . . . I'd like to hear more . . . about the possibilities surrounding the notion that what we perceive as 'one' in any context is, perhaps, a conglomerate of 'ones.'" This writer went on:

> Hindu culture is rooted in the "many" as the root of spiritual experience. A person's momentary behavior reflects some influence

> from one of hundreds of gods and/or goddesses. I am interested in . . . how this natural assumption of the "many" creates an alternative psychology.[7]

Another writer concurred:

> Did you ever see that cartoon by R. Crumb about "Which is the real R. Crumb?" He goes through four pages of incarnations, from successful businessman to street beggar, from media celebrity to gut-gnawing recluse, etc. etc. Then at the end he says, "Which is the real one?" . . . "It all depends on what mood I'm in!"
>
> We're all like that on-line.[8]

Howard Rheingold, the member of the WELL who began the discussion topic, also referred to Gergen's notion of a "saturated self," the idea that communication technologies have caused us to "colonize each other's brains." Gergen describes us as saturated with the many "voices of humankind—both harmonious and alien." He believes that as "we absorb their varied rhymes and reasons, they become part of us and we of them. Social saturation furnishes us with a multiplicity of incoherent and unrelated languages of the self." With our relationships spread across the globe and our knowledge of other cultures relativizing our attitudes and depriving us of any norm, we "exist in a state of continuous construction and reconstruction; it is a world where anything goes that can be negotiated. Each reality of self gives way to reflexive questioning, irony, and ultimately the playful probing of yet another reality. The center fails to hold."[9]

Although people may at first feel anguish at what they sense as a breakdown of identity, Gergen believes they may come to embrace the new possibilities. Individual notions of self vanish "into a stage of relatedness. One ceases to believe in a self independent of the relations in which he or she is embedded."[10] "We live in each other's brains, as voices, images, words on screens," said Rheingold in the online discussion. "We are multiple personalities and we include each other."[11]

Rheingold's evocation of what Gergen calls the "raptures of multiplicitous 10
being" met with support on the WELL. One participant insisted that all pejorative associations be removed from the notion of a saturated self. "Howard, I *like* being a saturated self, in a community of similarly saturated selves. I grew up on TV and pop music, but it just ain't enough. Virtual communities are, among other things, the co-saturation of selves who have been, all their lives, saturated in isolation."[12] To which Rheingold could only reply, "I like being a saturated self too."[13] The cybersociety of the WELL is an object-to-think-with for reflecting on the positive aspects of identity as multiplicity.

IDENTITY AND MULTIPLICITY

Without any principle of coherence, the self spins off in all directions. Multiplicity is not viable if it means shifting among personalities that cannot communicate. Multiplicity is not acceptable if it means being confused to a point of immobility.[14] How can we be multiple and coherent at the same time? In *The Protean Self*, Robert Jay Lifton tries to resolve this seeming contradiction. He begins by assuming that a unitary view of self corresponded to a traditional culture with stable symbols, institutions, and relationships. He finds the old unitary notion no longer viable because traditional culture has broken down and identifies a range of responses. One is a dogmatic insistence on unity. Another is to return to systems of belief, such as religious fundamentalism, that enforce conformity. A third is to embrace the idea of a fragmented self.[15] Lifton says this is a dangerous option that may result in a "fluidity lacking in moral content and sustainable inner form." But Lifton sees another possibility, a healthy protean self. It is capable, like Proteus, of fluid transformations but is grounded in coherence and a moral outlook. It is multiple but integrated.[16] You can have a sense of self without being one self.

Lifton's language is theoretical. Experiences in MUDs, on the WELL, on local bulletin boards, on commercial network services, and on the World Wide Web are bringing his theory down to earth. On the Web, the idiom for constructing a "home" identity is to assemble a "home page" of virtual objects that correspond to one's interests. One constructs a home page by composing or "pasting" on it words, images, and sounds, and by making connections between it and other sites on the Internet or the Web. Like the agents in emergent AI, one's identity emerges from whom one knows, one's associations and connections. People link their home page to pages about such things as music, paintings, television shows, cities, books, photographs, comic strips, and fashion models. As I write this book I am in the process of constructing my own home page. It now contains links to the text of my curriculum vitae, to drafts of recent papers (one about MUDs, one about French psychoanalysis), and to the reading lists for the two courses I shall teach next fall. A "visitor" to my home page can also click a highlighted word and watch images of Michel Foucault and Power Rangers "morph," one into the other, a visual play on my contention that children's toys bring postmodernism down to earth. This display, affectionately referred to as "The Mighty Morphin' Michel Foucault," was a present from my assistant at MIT, Cynthia Col. A virtual home, like a real one, is furnished with objects you buy, build, or receive as gifts.

My future plans for my home page include linking to Paris (the city has a home page), the bot Julia, resources on women's studies, Imari china, and recent research on migraines. I am not limited in the number of links I can create. If we take the home page as a real estate metaphor for the self, its decor is postmodern. Its different rooms with different styles are located on computers all over the world. But through one's efforts, they are brought together to be of a piece.

Home pages on the Web are one recent and dramatic illustration of new notions of identity as multiple yet coherent; in this book we have met others. Recall Case, the industrial designer who plays the female lawyer Mairead in MedievalMUSH. He does not experience himself as a unitary self, yet says that he feels in control of "himselves" and "herselves." He says that he feels fulfilled by his real and virtual work, marriage, and friendships. While conventional thinking tends to characterize multiple personae in pathological terms, this does not seem to capture what is most meaningful about Case playing Mairead or Garrett . . . playing Ribbit.

Within the psychoanalytic tradition, there have been schools that departed from the standard unitary view of identity. As we have seen, the object-relations theorists invented a language for talking about the many voices that we bring inside ourselves in the course of development. Jungian psychology encouraged the individual to become acquainted with a whole range of personae and to understand them as manifestations of universal archetypes, such as innocent virgins, mothers and crones, eternal youths and old men.[17] Jung believed that for each of us, it is potentially most liberating to become acquainted with our dark side, as well as the other-gendered self called anima in men and animus in women. Jung was banished from the ranks of orthodox Freudians for such suggestions. The object-relations school, too, was relegated to the margins. As America became the center of psychoanalytic politics in the mid-twentieth century, ideas about a robust executive ego became the psychoanalytic mainstream.

Through the fragmented selves presented by patients and through theories that stress the decentered subject, contemporary psychology confronts what is left out of theories of the unitary self. Now it must ask, What is the self when it functions as a society?[18] What is the self when it divides its labors among its constituent "alters"?[19] Those burdened by post-traumatic dissociative disorders suffer these questions; here I have suggested that inhabitants of virtual communities play with them.

Ideas about mind can become a vital cultural presence when they are carried by evocative objects-to-think-with.[20] I said earlier that these objects need not be material. For example, dreams and slips of the tongue were objects-to-think-with that brought psychoanalytic ideas into everyday life. People could play with their own and others' dreams and slips. Today, people are being helped to develop ideas about identity as multiplicity by a new practice of identity as multiplicity in online life. Virtual personae are objects-to-think-with.

When people adopt an online persona they cross a boundary into highly-charged territory. Some feel an uncomfortable sense of fragmentation, some a sense of relief. Some sense the possibilities for self-discovery, even self-transformation. Serena, a twenty-six-year-old graduate student in history, says, "When I log on to a new MUD and I create a character and know I have to start typing my description, I always feel a sense of panic. Like I could find out something I don't want to know." Arlie, a twenty-year-old undergraduate, says, "I am always very self-conscious when I create a new character. Usually, I end up creating someone I wouldn't want my parents to know about. It takes me, like, three hours. But that someone is part of me." In these ways and others, many more of us are experimenting with multiplicity than ever before.

With this last comment, I am not implying that MUDs or computer bulletin boards are causally implicated in the dramatic increase of people who exhibit symptoms of multiple personality disorder (MPD), or that people on MUDs have MPD, or that MUDding is like having MPD. What I am saying is that the many manifestations of multiplicity in our culture, including the adoption of online personae, are contributing to a general reconsideration of traditional, unitary notions of identity.

20 The history of a psychiatric symptom is inextricably tied up with the history of the culture that surrounds it. When I was in graduate school in psychology in the 1970s, clinical psychology texts regarded multiple personality as so rare (perhaps one in a million) as to be barely worthy of mention. In these rare cases, there was typically one alter personality in addition to the host personality.[21] Today, cases of multiple personality are much more frequent and typically involve up to sixteen alters of different ages, races, genders, and sexual orientations.[22] In multiple personality disorder, it is widely believed that traumatic events have caused various aspects of the self to congeal into virtual personalities, the "ones" often hiding from the "others" and hiding too from that special alter, the host personality. Sometimes, the alters are known to each other and to the host; some alters may see their roles as actively helping others. Such differences led the philosopher Ian Hacking to write about a "continuum of dissociation."[23] These differences also suggest a way of thinking about the self in terms of a continuum of how accessible its parts are to each other.

At one extreme, the unitary self maintains its oneness by repressing all that does not fit. Thus censored, the illegitimate parts of the self are not accessible. This model would of course function best within a fairly rigid social structure with clearly defined rules and roles. At the other extreme is the MPD sufferer whose multiplicity exists in the context of an equally repressive rigidity. The parts of the self are not in easy communication. Communication is highly stylized; one personality must speak to another personality. In fact, the term "multiple personality" is misleading, because the different parts of the self are not full personalities. They are split-off, disconnected fragments. But if the disorder in multiple personality disorder is the need for the rigid walls between the selves (blocking the secrets those selves protect), then the study of MPD may begin to furnish ways of thinking about healthy selves as nonunitary but with fluid access among their many aspects. Thus, in addition to the extremes of unitary self and MPD, we can imagine a flexible self.

The essence of this self is not unitary, nor are its parts stable entities. It is easy to cycle through its aspects and these are themselves changing through constant communication with each other. The philosopher Daniel Dennett speaks to the flexible self in his multiple drafts theory of consciousness.[24] Dennett's notion of multiple drafts is analogous to the experience of having several versions of a document open on a computer screen where the user is able to move between them at will. The presence of the drafts encourages a respect for the many different versions while it imposes a certain distance from them. No one aspect can be claimed as the absolute, true self. When I got to know French Sherry I no longer saw the less confident English-speaking Sherry as my one authentic self. What most characterizes the model of a flexible self is that the lines of communication between its various aspects are open. The open communication encourages an attitude of respect for the many within us and the many within others.

As we sense our inner diversity we come to know our limitations. We understand that we do not and cannot know things completely, not the outside world and not ourselves. Today's heightened consciousness of incompleteness may predispose us to join with others. The historian of science Donna Haraway equates a "split and contradictory self" with a "knowing self." She is optimistic about its possibilities: "The knowing self is partial in all its guises, never finished, whole, simply there and original; it is always constructed and stitched together imperfectly; and *therefore* able to join with another, to see together without claiming to be another."[25]

When identity was defined as unitary and solid it was relatively easy to recognize and censure deviation from a norm. A more fluid sense of self allows a greater capacity for acknowledging diversity. It makes it easier to accept the array of our (and others') inconsistent personae—perhaps with humor, perhaps with irony. We do not feel compelled to rank or judge the elements of our multiplicity. We do not feel compelled to exclude what does not fit. . . .

CYBORG DREAMS

I have argued that Internet experiences help us to develop models of 25
psychological well-being that are in a meaningful sense postmodern: They admit multiplicity and flexibility. They acknowledge the constructed nature of reality, self, and other. The Internet is not alone in encouraging such models. There are many places within our culture that do so. What they have in common is that they all suggest the value of approaching one's "story" in several ways and with fluid access to one's different aspects. We are encouraged to think of ourselves as fluid, emergent, decentralized, multiplicitous, flexible, and ever in process.[26] The metaphors travel freely among computer science, psychology, children's games, cultural studies, artificial intelligence, literary criticism, advertising, molecular biology, self-help, and artificial life. They reach deep into the popular culture. The ability of the Internet to change popular understandings of identity is heightened by the presence of these metaphors.

For example, a recent *Newsweek* article reports on a new narrative movement in psychotherapy, describing the trend as consistent with the "postmodernist idea that we don't so much perceive the world as interpret it." "The psyche," says *Newsweek,* "is not a fixed objective entity, but a fluid, social construct—a story that is subject to revision."[27] The new therapeutic movement described by *Newsweek* draws on deconstructionist literary criticism and on recent currents of psychoanalytic thought that emphasize conflicting narratives as a way of thinking about the analytic experience.[28] But its breezy and accessible newsmagazine coverage makes it clear that psychotherapy, too, can bring postmodernism down to earth. . . .

The final contest concerns the notion of the real. In simulated science experiments, virtual chemicals are poured from virtual beakers, and virtual light bounces off virtual walls. In financial transactions, virtual money changes hands. In film and photography, realistic-looking images depict scenes that never took place between people who never met. And on the networked computers of our everyday lives, people have compelling interactions that are entirely dependent on their online self-representations. In cyberspace, hundreds of thousands, perhaps already millions, of users create online personae who live in a diverse group of virtual communities where the routine formation of multiple identities undermines any notion of a real and unitary self. Yet the notion of the real fights back. People who live parallel lives on the screen are nevertheless bound by the desires, pain, and mortality of their physical selves. Virtual communities offer a dramatic new context in which to think about human identity in the age of the Internet. They are spaces for learning about the lived meaning of a culture of simulation. Will it be a separate world where people get lost in the surfaces or will we learn to see how the real and the virtual can be made permeable, each having the potential for enriching and expanding the other? The citizens of MUDs are our pioneers.

As we stand on the boundary between the real and the virtual, our experience recalls what the anthropologist Victor Turner termed a liminal moment, a moment of passage when new cultural symbols and meanings can emerge.[29] Liminal moments are times of tension, extreme reactions, and great opportunity. In our time, we are simultaneously flooded with predictions of doom and predictions of imminent utopia. We live in a crucible of contradictory experience. When Turner talked about liminality, he understood it as a transitional state—but living with flux may no longer be temporary. Donna Haraway's characterization of irony illuminates our situation: "Irony is about contradictions that do not resolve into larger wholes . . . about the tension of holding incompatible things together because both or all are necessary and true."[30] It is fitting that the story of the technology that is bringing postmodernism down to earth itself refuses modernist resolutions and requires an openness to multiple viewpoints.

Multiple viewpoints call forth a new moral discourse. I have said that the culture of simulation may help us achieve a vision of a multiple but integrated identity whose flexibility, resilience, and capacity for joy comes from having access to our many selves. But if we have lost reality in the process, we shall have struck a poor bargain. In Wim Wenders's film *Until the End of the World,* a scientist develops a device that translates the electrochemical activity of the brain into digital images. He gives this technology to his family and closest friends, who are now able to hold small battery-driven monitors and watch their dreams. At first, they are charmed. They see their treasured fantasies, their secret selves. They see the images they otherwise would forget, the scenes they otherwise would repress. As with the personae one can play in a MUD, watching dreams on a screen opens up new aspects of the self.

However, the story soon turns dark. The images seduce. They are richer 30
and more compelling than the real life around them. Wenders's characters fall in love with their dreams, become addicted to them. People wander about with blankets over their heads the better to see the monitors from which they cannot bear to be parted. They are imprisoned by the screens, imprisoned by the keys to their past that the screens seem to hold.

We, too, are vulnerable to using our screens in these ways. People can get lost in virtual worlds. Some are tempted to think of life in cyberspace as insignificant, as escape or meaningless diversion. It is not. Our experiences there are serious play. We belittle them at our risk. We must understand the dynamics of virtual experience both to foresee who might be in danger and to put these experiences to best use. Without a deep understanding of the many selves that we express in the virtual we cannot use our experiences there to enrich the real. If we cultivate our awareness of what stands behind our screen personae, we are more likely to succeed in using virtual experience for personal transformation.

The imperative to self-knowledge has always been at the heart of philosophical inquiry. In the twentieth century, it found expression in the psychoanalytic culture as well. One might say that it constitutes the ethic of psychoanalysis. From the perspective of this ethic, we work to know ourselves in order to improve not only our own lives, but those of our families and society. I have said that psychoanalysis is a survivor discourse. Born of a modernist worldview, it has evolved into forms relevant to postmodern times. With mechanistic roots in the culture of calculation, psychoanalytic ideas become newly relevant in the culture of simulation. Some believe that we are at the end of the Freudian century. But the reality is more complex. Our need for a practical philosophy of self-knowledge has never been greater as we struggle to make meaning from our lives on the screen.

Notes

1. Emily Martin, *Flexible Bodies* (Boston: Beacon Press, 1994), pp. 161–225.
2. mcdee, The WELL, conference on virtual communities (vc.20.17), 18 April 1992.
3. The sentiment that life online could provide a different experience of self was seconded by a participant who described himself as a man whose conversational abilities as an adult were impaired by having been a stutterer as a child. Online he was able to discover the experience of participating in the flow of a conversation.

   I echo [the previous contributor] in feeling that my online persona differs greatly from my persona offline. And, in many ways, my online persona is more "me." I feel a lot more freedom to speak here. Growing up, I had a severe stuttering problem. I couldn't speak a word without stuttering, so I spoke only when absolutely necessary. I worked through it in my early 20s and you wouldn't even notice it now (except when I'm stressed out), but at 37 I'm still shy to speak. I'm a lot more comfortable with listening than with talking. And when I do speak I usually feel out of sync: I'll inadvertently step on other people's words, or lose people's attention, or talk through instead of to. I didn't learn the dynamic of conversation that most people take for granted, I think. Here, though, it's completely different: I have a feel for the flow of the "conversations," have the time to measure my response, don't have to worry about the balance of conversational space—we all make as much space as we want just by pressing "r" to respond. It's been a wonderfully liberating experience for me. (Anonymous)
4. spoonman, The WELL, conference on virtual communities (vc.20.65), 11 June 1992.
5. Kenneth Gergen, *The Saturated Self: Dilemmas of Identity in Contemporary Life* (New York: Basic Books, 1991).

6. bluefire (Bob Jacobson), The WELL, conference on virtual reality (vr.85.146), 15 August 1993.
7. The WELL, conference on virtual reality (vr.85.148), 17 August 1993.
8. Art Kleiner, The WELL, conference on virtual reality (vr.47.41), 2 October 1990.
9. Gergen, *The Saturated Self,* p. 6.
10. Gergen, *The Saturated Self,* p. 17.
11. hlr (Howard Rheingold), The WELL, conference on virtual reality (vr.47.351), 2 February 1993.
12. McKenzie Wark, The WELL, conference on virtual reality (vr.47.361), 3 February 1993.
13. hlr (Howard Rheingold), The WELL, conference on virtual reality (vr.47.362), 3 February 1993.
14. James M. Glass, *Shattered Selves: Multiple Personality in a Postmodern World* (Ithaca, N.Y.: Cornell University Press, 1993).
15. Robert Jay Lifton, *The Protean Self: Human Resilience in an Age of Fragmentation* (New York: Basic Books, 1993), p. 192.
16. Lifton, *The Protean Self,* pp. 229–32.
17. See, for example, "Aion: Phenomenology of the Self," in *The Portable Jung,* ed. Joseph Campbell, trans. R. F. C. Hull (New York: Penguin, 1971).
18. See, for example, Marvin Minsky, *The Society of Mind* (New York: Simon & Schuster, 1985).
19. See, for example, Colin Ross, *Multiple Personality Disorder: Diagnosis, Clinical Features, and Treatment* (New York: John Wiley & Sons, 1989).
20. Claude Lévi-Strauss, *The Savage Mind* (Chicago: University of Chicago Press, 1960).
21. Ian Hacking, *Rewriting the Soul: Multiple Personality and the Sciences of Memory* (Princeton, N.J.: Princeton University Press, 1995), p. 21.
22. Hacking, *Rewriting the Soul,* p. 29.
23. See Hacking, *Rewriting the Soul,* pp. 96ff.
24. Daniel C. Dennett, *Consciousness Explained* (Boston: Little, Brown and Company, 1991).
25. Donna Haraway, "The Actors Are Cyborg, Nature Is Coyote, and the Geography Is Elsewhere: Postscript to 'Cyborgs at Large' " in *Technoculture,* eds. Constance Penley and Andrew Ross (Minneapolis: University of Minnesota Press, 1991), p. 22.
26. Allucquere Rosanne Stone has referred to our time in history as the close of the mechanical age, underscoring that we no longer look to clockwork or engines to build our images of self and society. See *The War of Desire and Technology at the Close of the Mechanical Age* (Cambridge, Mass.: MIT Press, 1995).
27. *Newsweek,* 17 April 1995: 70.
28. See, for example, Barbara Johnson, *A World of Difference* (Baltimore: Johns Hopkins University Press, 1987); Donald P. Spence, *Narrative Truth and Historical Truth: Meaning and Interpretation in Psychoanalysis* (New York: W. W. Norton & Company, 1982; and Humphrey Morris, ed., *Telling Facts: History and Narration in Psychoanalysis* (Baltimore: Johns Hopkins University Press, 1992).
29. Victor Turner, *The Ritual Process: Structure and Antistructure* (Chicago: Aldine, 1966).
30. Donna Haraway, "A Cyborg Manifesto," p. 148.

Understanding

1. Turkle introduces the notions of the *flexible self,* the *saturated self,* and the *multiple self* as useful descriptions of personal identity in postmodern soci-

ety. What is postmodern society, and how does she see these conceptions of self as appropriate to it?

2. In the section "Identity and Multiplicity," how does Turkle suggest we deal with the aspects of ourselves that "do not fit"? How does she define those aspects?
3. In what ways does the multiple self that Turkle describes differ from multiple personality disorder? How fine is the line between them?
4. Turkle suggests that the culture of simulation "may help us achieve a vision of a multiple but integrated identity whose flexibility, resilience, and capacity for joy comes from having access to our many selves. But if we have lost reality in the process, we shall have struck a poor bargain." What does she mean "if we have lost reality"? In what ways could we lose reality? How would losing reality be a poor bargain?

Responding

1. Are there places other than "on the screen" where we can safely and reliably frame our multiple selves? If so, where are these places and how do we do it? How do you do it?
2. What forces in American culture move us toward integration? What forces push or pull us toward fragmentation? How do these forces connect with Victor Turner's "liminal moment" to which Turkle refers in the concluding paragraphs of this selection? Are we in such a moment? Explain.
3. In the last two paragraphs of this reading, Turkle advances the idea that virtual experience is a means to personal transformation. Define your vision of this personal transformation, how you think it can be accomplished, and how probable you think it is that virtual experience can be a means to accomplish it.
4. Home pages on the Web, Turkle contends elsewhere in *Lives on the Screen,* illustrate new notions of identity as multiple and coherent. "We stipulate several selves but they attach to that immune system called Me." There is, she admits, some "glue" that we all recognize as the "essential us." How would you define the "essential you"? If you were to construct or reconstruct your home page, what integrating principle or "glue" would you use to unite your multiple selves? How does it unify these aspects of your self?

Connecting

1. In referring in paragraph 11 to Robert Jay Lifton's *The Protean Self* (from the Greek sea god Proteus, who assumed different shapes in order to avoid having to foretell the future), Turkle lists the alternative responses that people can make to the question, "How can we be multiple and coherent at the same time?" One possible response is "a dogmatic insistence on unity." In what readings have you encountered this kind of "dogmatic insistence on unity"? What were or are the consequences of maintaining it?
2. The Internet is one domain in which the conspiracy stories that Kakutani investigates in "Bound by Suspicion" (chapter six) spread like viruses. How

does this dimension of online activity relate to Turkle's contention that the Web engenders psychological well-being?

3. Compare Turkle's commentary on aspects of the self to the notion of "selflets" or "multiple drafts" in Dennett's "The Reality of Selves" and Elkind's "Erik Erikson's Eight Ages of Man." In what ways do their ideas about personal identity complement or diverge from each other? How do they conceive of the idea of personal integration?
4. How would Turkle respond to Rheingold, who asks in paragraph 27 of "Cyberhood vs. Neighborhood: Community" in chapter six if the medium of cyberspace will "be a place where people often end up revealing themselves far more intimately than they would be inclined to do without the intermediation of screens and pseudonyms"?

Ultimately

Sarah Cirese

Sarah Cirese was a mother and college psychology professor at College of Marin before she worked on *Quest: A Search for Self,* from which "Ultimately" is excerpted. Her first purpose in writing *Quest* was to increase her readers' "understanding of the human adventure—the searching and growing we experience as we journey between birth and death." Her second purpose was to encourage readers "to become actively involved in their own self-discovery and self-realization."

In this final reading selection in *Signatures,* Cirese presents the result of her quest in the form of a manifesto. We ask you to consider its source. Perhaps it is a life lived of gift, wound, decision, and dream stories examined for their essence and clarified as a set of tenets. For what are we without our stories? And what are we without the possibility of rewriting them, redescribing ourselves, and declaring how we will approach the rest of our lives?

1 I am a member of my species and of my culture. Both have had a part in determining my potentials. I am a unique manifestation of interactions, developing in my own way in my own time. No one else is or ever will be this singular combination: me.

My life, from birth to death, is a search; it is a quest for finding and knowing my potentials, and for making them actual. Only I can discover my self by repeated experiences of myself in living.

The older I get the more discoveries I make; every day provides me with experiences in choosing to develop in one way rather than another. At any point in my life, I am the sum of the choices I have made, the experiences I have had.

My choices are forks in the road; they come one junction at a time. Every time I choose the North fork, I am unable to follow the path to the South or the West or the East.

5 Every choice I make is limited by the perspective I have at the moment I choose. What I believe to be determines what is for me. Many times I cannot change events; I can only change my viewpoint. I can only strive to be aware.

Choice is not easy. The more aware I am, the more difficult it can seem. But the more I know what I want, the less my anxiety. The more aware I am of my real self, the truer to myself I can be, and the more I can grow.

I grow when I connect with others. When I fear closeness or a commitment to intimacy I limit my potentials for humanness. If I live with the intent to be as truly honest and disclosing with another as I can be, and to trust his or her intent to be concerned for me, then I can maximize my chance for intimacy.

I am true to myself when I understand my sexual potentials and when I choose my sexual expression. When I know I am responsible for my sexual feelings and can be responsible for my own sexuality, I am maximizing my humanness.

I am true to myself when I am not playing a stereotyped role. I am true to myself and to others when I perceive all human beings as individuals and do not judge them with narrow and limiting preconceptions of sex roles.

The best times in my life are those in which I know I am playing games 10
worth playing—games worthy of me, of my effort and mastery.

I need not be bound by ordinary consciousness if I seek to actualize my own inner potentials and to utilize my brain's capacity for intuition, dreams, and other altered states. I can best increase my consciousness with intention and self-control.

As long as I am alive I want to choose. I want to live until I die; I want to *grow* older as I live. I want to know and be able to respect myself. I want to see my past as the series of choices which brought me here to my present. I need to see the effects of my choices; I do not need to hold onto the past with regret.

I am not always aware of an experience as a choice. But as I look back I am sure that all experiences, good or bad, were just the right ones to bring me to this moment.

I can and will choose again, not making the same choices as before, but the next choices.

My life is a quest in which I discover my potentials, actualize some, and 15
ignore others. My quests end when I die. I need to remember, every day I live, that death will come—and that life is now. My quests are ultimately fulfilled in the living of my life.

Understanding

1. What is life for Cirese?
2. List the parts of Cirese's life that she finds crucial to her quest.
3. Twenty years later, do you think Cirese is satisfied with what she wrote in "Ultimately"?
4. How does the manifesto quality of this piece work to make it powerful and fast moving?

Responding

1. Take stock of what you have accomplished thus far in your life. Write a manifesto in the style of Cirese.
2. Pick one statement from "Ultimately" that you would like to carve into granite. Explain its meaningfulness to you.

Connecting

1. Using Glidewell's definition of *choice points* from "A Time for Choosing" (chapter three), identify Cirese's choice points in "Ultimately." Compare them with Glidewell's.
2. Identify writers in this collection who are exemplars of at least two memorable aspects of Cirese's essay and write about why they stand out in that way.

PART THREE WRITING OPTION: Your Signature

Having completed the readings in this chapter, review your responses to the Responding questions for each; choose one that you would like to develop as a final writing exercise to demonstrate your integrated self. It should reflect an understanding of how you have integrated your gifts, wounds, decisions, or dreams and your biology, communities, and culture to form your identity. It should focus on major turning points in your life and other defining experiences.

You might ask, as many of the writers in this section seem to have asked: Have any of these situations been springboards for action or for clarifying my positions or my values? The paper should leave the reader feeling taught, perhaps even wanting to read the paper again because of its movement and power.

As a way to think about this paper, consider Campo's " 'Give Back to Your Community,' She Said" to explicate the kind of data you will want to weave together. Here is a thumbnail sketch according to Campo:

- Campo's *gifts:* the love of another man; English language; Spanish language
- His *wounds:* "the dark one in the room must always be guilty of something"; loss of Cuban identity as "refugee"; "downtrodden immigrant family"
- His *decisions:* to become an internist; to share his thoughts so that others might see him as themselves—as someone readers might like, or even love; to "give back"
- His *dreams:* "to wear America like an expensive suit"; to search for some way to give
- His *biology:* olive complexion; dark straight hair; green eyes; a bit overweight; gay
- His *communities:* Cuban expatriate community, gay community, medical community
- His *culture:* American; Cuban; Latin

Campo used all of these "markers" to make the case for his "giving back" in his essay. You could do the same brief analysis for each writer in this collection of readings—and for yourself as well—as these seven influences determine all that we are. They tell our stories. They compose our signatures.

A second way to approach this paper might be to synthesize or analyze the ideas presented as the design for this book. You may strongly agree, for example, that the ideas in parts one, two, and three contribute to the mystery of who we are. If so, write a paper critiquing this method of "writing your life." Present the thinking behind the design of the book and discuss the value in the readings, apparatus, and writing assignments. Document sources in the book to support your ideas. Finally, include an analysis of what you will take from the course into your future studies. This will be a persuasive piece of analytic writing, so you will need to form a worthwhile question based on the instructions in this exercise and construct a strong, debatable answer as your thesis.

Text Credits

Isabel Allende, "The Death of Rosa the Beautiful," from *The House of the Spirits,* by Isabel Allende, trans. Magda Bogin. Translation copyright © 1985 by Alfred A. Knopf Inc. Reprinted by permission of the publisher.

Gordon W. Allport, "A Solitary Quest," reprinted with the permission of Simon & Schuster from *The Individual and His Religion: A Psychological Interpretation* by Gordon W. Allport, pp. 122–123, 135–142. Copyright © 1950 by Macmillan Publishing Company; copyright renewed 1978 by Robert B. Allport.

Julia Alvarez, "The Kiss," from *How the Garcia Girls Lost Their Accents,* pp. 24–39. Copyright © 1991 by Julia Alvarez. Published by Plume, an imprint of Dutton Signet, a division of Penguin USA, and originally in hardcover by Algonquin Books of Chapel Hill. Reprinted by permission of Susan Bergholz Literary Services, New York. All rights reserved.

Gloria Anzaldúa, "To Live in the Borderlands Means You," from *Borderlands/La Frontera: The New Mestiza* by Gloria Anzaldúa, pp. 194–195, published by Aunt Lute Books. Copyright © 1987 by Gloria Anzaldúa.

John Stanley D. Bacon, "Heredity and Evolution," excerpted by permission of Patricia D. Hume from John Stanley D. Bacon, "Introduction," in *The Science of Heredity* (London: C. A. Watts & Company, 1951).

Mary Catherine Bateson, "Opening to the World," excerpted from *Composing a Life* (New York: Atlantic Monthly Press, 1990), pp. 1–6. Copyright © 1989 by Mary Catherine Bateson. Used by permission of Grove/Atlantic, Inc.

Bruno Bettelheim, "Creating a New Way of Life," reprinted with the permission of Simon & Schuster from *Children of the Dream: Communal Child-Rearing and American Education* by Bruno Bettelheim, pp. 14–26 and parts of bibliography. Copyright © 1969 by Macmillan Publishing Company.

Rick Bragg, "Big Holes Where the Dignity Used to Be," third of seven articles on "The Downsizing of America," *New York Times,* March 5, 1996, pp. A1, A16, A18. Copyright © 1996 by The New York Times Company. Reprinted by permission.

Rafael Campo, "Give Back to Your Community," She Said. Copyright © 1996 by Rafael Campo. Reprinted by permission of Georges Borchardt, Inc. First appeared as an essay, " 'Give Back to Your Community,' She Said," in the *New York Times Magazine,* September 1, 1996, pp. 42–45; adapted from *The Poetry of Healing: A Doctor's Education in Empathy, Identity, and Desire* by Rafael Campo (New York: W. W. Norton, 1997).

Elias Canetti, "Storytellers and Scribes," in *The Voices of Marrakesh: A Record of a Visit,* trans. from the German by J. A. Underwood (New York: Farrar, Straus & Giroux, 1978), pp. 23, 77–80. Originally published as *Die Stimmen von Marrakesch* by Carl Hanser Verlag. Copyright © 1994 by Carl Hanser Verlag, München Wien. Reprinted by permission.

Lorenzo Carcaterra, "Loving Your Enemy," *New York Times Magazine,* March 28, 1993, pp. 16, 18. Copyright © 1993 by The New York Times Co. Reprinted by permission.

Rachel Carson, "The Marginal World," from *The Edge of the Sea,* pp. 1–7, by Rachel Carson. Copyright © 1955 by Rachel L. Carson; © renewed 1983 by Roger Christie. Reprinted by permission of Houghton Mifflin Co. All rights reserved.

Susan Cheever, "Eating, Breathing, Drinking." Copyright © 1996 Susan Cheever. First published in the *New York Times Magazine,* May 12, 1996, pp. 46–48. Reprinted with the permission of The Wylie Agency, Inc.

Anton Chekhov, "To Whom Shall I Tell My Grief?" in *The Short Stories of Anton Chekhov* by Anton Chekhov, edited by Robert N. Linscott, pp. 103–109. Copyright © 1932 and renewed 1960 by The Modern Library, Inc. Reprinted by permission of Random House, Inc.

Sarah Cirese, "Ultimately," from *Quest: A Search for Self* by Sarah Cirese, pp. 400–401. Copyright © 1977 by Henry Holt and Company, Inc. Reprinted by permission of Henry Holt and Company, Inc.

Sandra Cisneros, "My Name," from *The House on Mango Street,* pp. 10–11. Copyright © 1984 by Sandra Cisneros. Published by Vintage Books, a division of Random House, Inc., New York, and in hardcover by Alfred A. Knopf in 1994. Reprinted by permission of Susan Bergholz Literary Services, New York. All rights reserved.

Frank Conroy, "Think About It," *Harper's Magazine,* November 1988, pp. 68–70. Copyright © 1988 by *Harper's Magazine.* All rights reserved. Reproduced from the November issue by special permission.

Stanley Crouch, "Race Is Over: Black, White, Red, Yellow—Same Difference," *New York Times Magazine,* September 29, 1996, pp. 170–171. Copyright © 1996 by The New York Times Company. Reprinted by permission.

Mihaly Csikszentmihalyi, "The Veils of Maya," "The World of Culture," and "The World of the Self," from "The Veils of Maya" in *The Evolving Self: A Psychology for the Third Millennium* by Mihaly Csikszentmihalyi, pp. 55–82. Copyright © 1993 by Mihaly Csikszentmihalyi. Reprinted by permission of HarperCollins Publishers, Inc.

Richard Dawkins, "Ancestors and the Digital River," excerpted from *River Out of Eden: A Darwinian View of Life* by Richard Dawkins, pp. 1–8, 27–29. Copyright © 1995 by Richard Dawkins. Reprinted by permission of Basic Books, a division of HarperCollins Publishers, Inc.

Gabriella De Ferrari, "Our Peruvian Friend," from *Gringa Latina: A Woman of Two Worlds,* pp. 7–20. Copyright © 1995 by Gabriella De Ferrari. Reprinted by permission of Houghton Mifflin Company. All rights reserved.

Sarah L. Delany and A. Elizabeth Delany with Amy Hill Hearth, "Bessie," reprinted with permission from *Having Our Say* by Sarah and A. Elizabeth Delany with Amy Hill Hearth, published by Kodansha America Inc., pp. 154–161. Copyright © 1993 by Amy Hill Hearth, Sarah Louise Delany, and Annie Elizabeth Delany.

Daniel C. Dennett, "The Reality of Selves," from *Consciousness Explained* by Daniel C. Dennett, pp. 412–418. Copyright © 1991 by Daniel C. Dennett. By permission of Little, Brown and Company.

Philip K. Dick, "Do Androids Dream of Electric Sheep?" from *Do Androids Dream of Electric Sheep?* by Philip K. Dick, pp. 42–53. Copyright © 1982 by Philip K. Dick. Reprinted by permission of Ballantine Books, a Division of Random House Inc.

Fyodor Dostoyevsky, "The Morning," in *White Nights.* From *Notes from Underground* by Fyodor Dostoyevsky, translated by Andrew R. MacAndrew, pp. 59–61. Translation copyright © 1961, renewed © 1989 by Andrew R. MacAndrew. Used by permission of Dutton Signet, a division of Penguin Books USA Inc.

Stephen J. Dubner, "Choosing My Religion," *New York Times Magazine,* March 31, 1996, pp. 36–40. Copyright © 1996 by The New York Times Company. Reprinted by permission.

Martin Dugard, "Running on Empty," *American Way*, November 15, 1996, pp. 60+. Reprinted with the permission of *American Way* Magazine and Martin Dugard. Martin Dugard lives in southern California. He went back to the Raid in 1997—and finished.

T. S. Eliot, excerpt from "Little Gidding V" in Four Quartets. Copyright © 1943 by T. S. Eliot, renewed 1971 by Esme Valerie Eliot. Reprinted by permission of Harcourt Brace and Company.

David Elkind, "Erik Erikson's Eight Ages of Man," excerpted from *New York Times Magazine*, April 5, 1970, pp. 25–27, 84, 86, 88, 90, 92, 110, 112, 114 (including the box "Freud's 'Ages of Man.'" *New York Times Magazine*, April 5, 1970, p. 88). Copyright © 1970 by The New York Times Co. Reprinted by permission.

Naomi Epel, "Four Writers' Dreams," all but Amy Tan from *Writers Dreaming* by Naomi Epel, pp. 278–279, 29–30, 142–143. Copyright © 1993 by Naomi Epel. Reprinted by permission of Carol Southern Books, an imprint of Clarkson N. Potter, a division of Crown Publishers, Inc. Amy Tan, *Writers Dreaming*, pp. 284–285, 287–288, reprinted by permission of Amy Tan and the Sandra Dijkstra Literary Agency.

M. F. K. Fisher, "The Broken Chain," from *To Begin Again: Stories and Memoirs, 1908–1929*, by M. F. K. Fisher, pp. 114–119. Copyright © 1992 by The M. F. K. Fisher Literary Trust. Reprinted by permission of Pantheon Books, a division of Random House, Inc.

Richard Ford, "Rules of the House," *Esquire*, June 1986, pp. 231, 234. Reprinted by permission of International Creative Management, Inc. Copyright © 1986 by Richard Ford.

Viktor E. Frankl, "The Push and Pull for Values," from *Man's Search for Meaning: An Introduction to Logotherapy*, by Viktor Frankl, trans. Ilse Lasch, pp. 99–102. Copyright © 1959, 1962 by Viktor Frankl. Used by permission of Beacon Press, Boston.

Malcolm Gladwell, "The CoolHunt," *New Yorker*, March 17, 1997, pp. 78–88. Reprinted by permission of the author.

John C. Glidewell, "A Time for Choosing" and "On Freedom and Resources," in *Choice Points: Essays on the Emotional Problems of Living with People* (Cambridge, Mass.: MIT Press, 1970), pp. 2–8, 50–53. Copyright © 1970 John C. Glidewell. Reprinted by permission of the author.

Daniel Goleman, "Temperament Is Not Destiny," from *Emotional Intelligence* by Daniel Goleman, pp. 215–224, 332. Copyright © 1995 by Daniel Goleman. Used by permission of Bantam Books, a division of Bantam Doubleday Dell Publishing Group, Inc.

Nadine Gordimer, "Town and Country Lovers, Two—Country Lovers," copyright © 1975 by Nadine Gordimer, from *Soldier's Embrace* by Nadine Gordimer. Used by permission of Viking Penguin, a division of Penguin Books USA Inc.

Christine Gorman, "Sizing Up the Sexes," *Time*, January 20, 1992, pp. 42, 44–48, 51. Copyright © 1992 Time Inc. Reprinted by permission.

Pete Hamill, "Steel Memories from Father's Toolbox," *New York Times*, October 25, 1995, pp. B1, B5. Copyright © 1995 by The New York Times Company. Reprinted by permission.

Dag Hammarskjöld, "He Was Impossible" and part opening quotation from *Markings*, trans. Leif Sjöberg and W. H. Auden. Translation copyright © 1964 by Alfred A. Knopf Inc. and Faber & Faber Ltd. Reprinted by permission of Alfred A. Knopf Inc.

Václav Havel, "Dear Olga," excerpted from letter to Olga dated 6 September 1981, in "Letters from Prison," *Granta* 21 (Spring 1987): 226–228. Reprinted with permission from *Granta*. Copyright © 1987 Václav Havel.

Langston Hughes, "Harlem (2)," from *Collected Poems*, p. 426, by Langston Hughes, ed. Arnold Rampersad and David Roessel. Copyright © 1994 by the Estate of Langston Hughes. Reprinted by permission of Alfred A. Knopf Inc.

Rebecca Johnson, "The Just-Do-It Shrink," *New York Times Magazine*, November 17, 1996, pp. 41–45. Copyright © 1996 by The New York Times Company. Reprinted by permission.

Michiko Kakutani, "Bound by Suspicion," *New York Times Magazine*, January 19, 1997, p. 16. Copyright © 1997 by The New York Times Company. Reprinted by permission.

Sam Keen, "Reflections on a Peach-Seed Monkey," in *To a Dancing God* (New York: Harper & Row, 1970), pp. 100–101. Copyright © 1970 Sam Keen. Excerpted by permission of the author.

Natalie Kusz, "Attack," excerpted from *Road Song* by Natalie Kusz, pp. 38–49. Copyright © 1990 by Natalie Kusz. Reprinted by permission of Farrar, Straus & Giroux, Inc.

Andrea Lee, "Back to School," *New Yorker*, April 29, 1994, p. 168. Reprinted by permission of International Creative Management, Inc. Copyright © 1994 by Andrea Lee.

Primo Levi, "Shame," reprinted with the permission of Simon & Schuster from *The Drowned and the Saved* by Primo Levi, trans. Raymond Rosenthal, pp. 79–81. Copyright © 1986 by Giulio Einaudi editore s.p.a., Torino. Translation copyright © 1988 by Simon & Schuster, Inc.

Shirley Park Lowry, "Climbing Jacob's Ladder," from *Familiar Mysteries: The Truth in Myth* by Shirley Park Lowry, pp. 286–291. Copyright © 1982 by Shirley Park Lowry. Used by permission of Oxford University Press, Inc.

Barbara Macdonald, "Ageism in the Sisterhood," from "Outside the Sisterhood: Ageism in Women's Studies" by Barbara Macdonald in *Look Me in the Eye: Old Women, Aging, and Ageism*, expanded edition, by Barbara Macdonald with Cynthia Rich. San Francisco: Spinsters Ink, 1983. Available from Spinsters Ink, 32 East First Street #330, Duluth, Minnesota 55802. Reprinted by permission.

Victoria L. Macki, M.D., "We Have No Real Choice about Death," reprinted by permission of the author from Victoria L. Macki, M.D., "To the Editor," *Newberry News* (a weekly newspaper in Newberry, Michigan), June 5, 1996.

Katherine Mansfield, "Miss Brill," in *The Short Stories of Katherine Mansfield* (New York: Knopf, 1922).

James McBride, "A Jew Discovered," reprinted by permission of Riverhead Books, a division of The Putnam Publishing Group, from *The Color of Water* by James McBride, pp. 171–179. Copyright © 1996 by James McBride.

Kweisi Mfume, "Nowhere to Run, Nowhere to Hide," from *No Free Ride: From the Mean Streets to the Mainstream* by Kweisi Mfume and Ron Stodghill II, pp. 168–178. Copyright © 1996 by Kweisi Mfume and Ron Stodghill II. Reprinted by permission of Ballantine Books, a Division of Random House Inc.

Michel de Montaigne, "On the Art of Conversation," excerpted from *Michel de Montaigne: The Complete Essays,* translated by M. A. Screech (Penguin Classics, 1991), pp. 1045–1050. Translation copyright © 1991 M. A. Screech. Reproduced by permission of Penguin Books Ltd.

Yōko Mori, "Spring Storm," translated by Makoto Ueda from *The Mother of Dreams and Other Short Stories: Portrayals of Women in Modern Japanese Fiction,* edited by Makoto Ueda, pp. 125–132. Copyright © 1989 by Kodansha International Ltd. Reprinted by permission. All rights reserved.

Plato, "The Ascent to Wisdom," excerpted and slightly amended by Ronald Gross from Plato, *The Republic,* Book VII, trans. Benjamin Jowett, in Ronald Gross, ed., *The Teacher and the Taught: Education in Theory and Practice from Plato to James B. Conant* (New York: Dell Publishing, 1963), pp. 2–8.

Ted Poston, "The Revolt of the Evil Fairies," *New Republic,* April 1942, pp. 458–459; reprinted by permission of Ersa H. Poston, widow of Ted Poston, and Ruth Banks.

Colin L. Powell, "Announcement Not to Run for President of the United States," *Chicago Tribune,* November 9, 1995. With copyright permission from Colin L. Powell.

William Raspberry, "A Father, His Daughters, and a Lesson," from William Raspberry, "To Spring from the Brow of Zeus," *Washington Post,* September 8, 1995, p. A25. Copyright © 1995 Washington Post Writers Group. Reprinted with permission.

Howard Rheingold, "Cyberhood vs. Neighborhood: Community," excerpted from *The Virtual Community: Homesteading on the Electronic Frontier,* pp. 17–20, 23–26, 63–64. Copyright © 1993 by Howard Rheingold. Reprinted by permission of Addison Wesley Longman Inc.

Edward Arlington Robinson, "Richard Cory," in *Children of the Night* (1897).

Richard Rodriguez, "The New, New World," excerpted with permission from the libertarian magazine *Reason* (Aug./Sept. 1994). Copyright © 1994 by the Reason Foundation, 3415 S. Sepulveda Blvd., Suite 400, Los Angeles, CA 90034. For a sample issue, call 310/391-2245.

Mike Rose, "I Just Wanna Be Average," reprinted with the permission of The Free Press, a Division of Simon & Schuster, from *Lives on the Boundary: The Struggles and Achievements of America's Underprepared,* by Mike Rose, pp. 18, 23–37. Copyright © 1989 by Mike Rose.

Phyllis Rose, "Hating Goldie," originally appeared in the *New York Times Magazine,* May 12, 1996, pp. 43–44; it also is in her new book, *The Year of Reading Proust* (New York: Scribner, 1997). Copyright © 1996 by Phyllis Rose; reprinted with the permission of The Wylie Agency, Inc.

Loyal D. Rue, "A Sociobiological Hunch about Educating Women," *Chronicle of Higher Education,* March 27, 1985, p. 80. Reprinted by permission of the author, who is Professor of Religion and Philosophy at Luther College.

Ina Russell, ed., "Love and Affection, Damn It!" from *Jeb and Dash: A Diary of Gay Life, 1918–1945,* edited by Ina Russell, pp. 8, 17, 21, 27–33. Copyright © 1993 by Ina Russell. Reprinted by permission of Faber and Faber Publishers, Inc.

Carol Saline, "The Luong Sisters," reprinted with permission from the book *Sisters,* pp. 13, 14, 57–59, published by Running Press Book Publishers. Text copyright © 1994 by Carol Saline.

Luc Sante, "Living in Tongues," *New York Times Magazine,* May 12, 1996, pp. 31, 45–48. Copyright © 1996 by Luc Sante. Reprinted by permission of the author.

Maggie Scarf, "The Beavers Scale of Family Health and Competence: Levels 1–5," from *Intimate Worlds: Life inside the Family,* by Maggie Scarf, pp. 23–36. Copyright © 1995 by Maggie Scarf. Reprinted by permission of Random House, Inc.

Leslie Marmon Silko, "Through the Stories We Hear Who We Are," excerpted from *Landscape, History, and the Pueblo Imagination* by Leslie Marmon Silko. Copyright © 1984 by Leslie Marmon Silko; reprinted with the permission of The Wylie Agency, Inc.

Paul Simon, "Richard Cory," on the album *Sounds of Silence.* Copyright © 1966. Used by permission of the publisher, Paul Simon Music.

Floyd Skloot, "The Royal Family," reprinted by permission of the author from *Glimmer Train,* no. 6 (Spring 1993).

Andrew Solomon, "Questions of Genius." Copyright © 1996 Andrew Solomon. Excerpted with the permission of The Wylie Agency, Inc. First printed in the *New Yorker,* August 26 and September 2, 1996, pp. 113–116, 118–120, 122–123.

Art Spiegelman, "Worse Than My Darkest Dreams," from *Maus II: A Survivor's Tale—And Here My Troubles Began* by Art Spiegelman, pp. 29, 31–34. Copyright © 1986, 1989, 1990, 1991 by Art Spiegelman. Reprinted by permission of Pantheon Books, a division of Random House, Inc.

Studs Terkel, "Five Dreams," reprinted by permission of Donadio & Ashworth, Inc., from Studs Terkel, *American Dreams: Lost and Found* (New York: Ballantine Books, Random House, 1980), pp. xxvi, 56–65, 125–126, 141–142, 290–292, 444–449. Copyright © 1980 Studs Terkel. Musing by T. E. Lawrence is excerpted from T. E. Lawrence, Oriental Assembly, ed. A. W. Lawrence (London: Williams & Norgate, 1939), by permission of Seven Pillars of Wisdom Trust.

James W. Tollefson, "Choosing Not to Fight," from *The Strength Not to Fight: An Oral History of Conscientious Objectors of the Vietnam War* by James W. Tollefson, pp. 12–15, 27–29, 31–38. Copyright © 1993 by James W. Tollefson. By permission of Little, Brown and Company.

Sherry Turkle, "Identity Crisis," excerpted with the permission of Simon & Schuster from *Life on the Screen: Identity in the Age of the Internet* by Sherry Turkle, pp. 255–262, 263–264, 267–269, 318–320. Copyright © 1995 by Sherry Turkle.

Gillian Turner, "Intelligence and the X Chromosome," *Lancet,* vol. 347 (June 29, 1996): 1814–1815. Copyright © 1996 by The Lancet Ltd. Reprinted by permission of The Lancet Ltd. Figure 1, "Abridged Pedigree of the Wedgwood, Darwin, Galton Family Tree," from R. Resta, "Genetic Drift Whispered Hints," *American Journal of Medical Genetics,* vol. 59 (1995): 131–133. Copyright © 1995 by Wiley-Liss, Inc. Reprinted by permission of Wiley-Liss, Inc., a subsidiary of John Wiley & Sons, Inc.

Michael Ventura, "Mickey Mantle's Summer," *Austin Chronicle,* May 24, 1997. Copyright © 1995 by Michael Ventura. Reprinted by permission of the author.

Gloria Wade-Gayles, "Brother Pain: How a Black Woman Came to Terms with Interracial Love," adapted from *Rooted against the Wind: Personal Essays* by Gloria Wade-Gayles, pp. 96, 105–106, 111–112, 116, 119–131. Copyright © 1996 by Gloria Wade-Gayles. Reprinted by permission of Beacon Press.

Elie Wiesel, "What Is a Friend?" excerpted from *The Gates of the Forest,* trans. Frances Frenaye (New York: Schocken Books, 1995; originally published by Holt, Rinehart & Winston, 1966).

Virginia Woolf, "Professions for Women" from *The Death of the Moth and Other Essays* by Virginia Woolf, pp. 235–242. Copyright © 1942 by Harcourt Brace & Company and renewed 1970 by Marjorie T. Parsons, Executrix. Reprinted by permission of the publisher.

Lawrence Wright, "The Biology of Twins," excerpted from "Double Mystery," *New Yorker,* August 7, 1995, pp. 45–51, 60–62. Reprinted by permission of John Wiley & Sons, Inc., publishers of the forthcoming book Wright/TWINS, copyright © 1998 by John Wiley & Sons, Inc.

Robert Wright, "The Biology of Violence." Copyright © 1995 Robert Wright. First published in the *New Yorker,* March 13, 1995, pp. 68–77. Reprinted by permission of the author.

Rosa Elena Yzquierdo, "Abuela," is reprinted with permission from the publisher of *The American Review,* vol. 14, nos. 3–4 (Houston: Arte Publico Press—University of Houston, 1986).

Index of Authors and Titles